T0233907

Pro JPA 2

Second Edition

Mike Keith
Merrick Schincariol

Apress·

Pro JPA 2

Copyright © 2013 by Mike Keith and Merrick Schincariol

This work is subject to copyright. All rights are reserved by the Publisher, whether the whole or part of the material is concerned, specifically the rights of translation, reprinting, reuse of illustrations, recitation, broadcasting, reproduction on microfilms or in any other physical way, and transmission or information storage and retrieval, electronic adaptation, computer software, or by similar or dissimilar methodology now known or hereafter developed. Exempted from this legal reservation are brief excerpts in connection with reviews or scholarly analysis or material supplied specifically for the purpose of being entered and executed on a computer system, for exclusive use by the purchaser of the work. Duplication of this publication or parts thereof is permitted only under the provisions of the Copyright Law of the Publisher's location, in its current version, and permission for use must always be obtained from Springer. Permissions for use may be obtained through RightsLink at the Copyright Clearance Center. Violations are liable to prosecution under the respective Copyright Law.

ISBN-13 (pbk): 978-1-4302-4926-9

ISBN-13 (electronic): 978-1-4302-4927-6

Trademarked names, logos, and images may appear in this book. Rather than use a trademark symbol with every occurrence of a trademarked name, logo, or image we use the names, logos, and images only in an editorial fashion and to the benefit of the trademark owner, with no intention of infringement of the trademark.

The use in this publication of trade names, trademarks, service marks, and similar terms, even if they are not identified as such, is not to be taken as an expression of opinion as to whether or not they are subject to proprietary rights.

While the advice and information in this book are believed to be true and accurate at the date of publication, neither the authors nor the editors nor the publisher can accept any legal responsibility for any errors or omissions that may be made. The publisher makes no warranty, express or implied, with respect to the material contained herein.

President and Publisher: Paul Manning
Lead Editor: James Markham
Technical Reviewer: Manuel Jordan
Editorial Board: Steve Anglin, Mark Beckner, Ewan Buckingham, Gary Cornell, Louise Corrigan, Morgan Ertel,
    Jonathan Gennick, Jonathan Hassell, Robert Hutchinson, Michelle Lowman, James Markham,
    Matthew Moodie, Jeff Olson, Jeffrey Pepper, Douglas Pundick, Ben Renow-Clarke, Dominic Shakeshaft,
    Gwenan Spearing, Matt Wade, Tom Welsh
Coordinating Editor: Katie Sullivan
Copy Editor: Mary Behr
Compositor: SPi Global
Indexer: SPi Global
Artist: SPi Global
Cover Designer: Anna Ishchenko

Distributed to the book trade worldwide by Springer Science+Business Media New York, 233 Spring Street, 6th Floor, New York, NY 10013. Phone 1-800-SPRINGER, fax (201) 348-4505, e-mail orders-ny@springer-sbm.com, or visit www.springeronline.com. Apress Media, LLC is a California LLC and the sole member (owner) is Springer Science + Business Media Finance Inc (SSBM Finance Inc). SSBM Finance Inc is a Delaware corporation.

For information on translations, please e-mail rights@apress.com, or visit www.apress.com.

Apress and friends of ED books may be purchased in bulk for academic, corporate, or promotional use. eBook versions and licenses are also available for most titles. For more information, reference our Special Bulk Sales–eBook Licensing web page at www.apress.com/bulk-sales.

Any source code or other supplementary materials referenced by the author in this text is available to readers at www.apress.com. For detailed information about how to locate your book's source code, go to www.apress.com/source-code.

To my wife Darleen, the perfect mother, and to Cierra, Ariana, Jeremy, and Emma, who brighten my life and make me strive to be a better person.

—Mike

To Anthony, whose boundless creativity continues to inspire me. To Evan, whose boisterous enthusiasm motivates me to take on new challenges. To Kate, who proves that size is no object when you have the right attitude. I love you all.

—Merrick

Contents at a Glance

Contents

About the Authors

Mike Keith was the co-specification lead for JPA 1.0 and a member of the JPA 2.0 and JPA 2.1 expert groups. He sits on a number of other Java Community Process expert groups and the Enterprise Expert Group (EEG) in the OSGi Alliance. He holds a Masters degree in Computer Science from Carleton University, and has over 20 years experience in persistence and distributed systems research and practice. He has written papers and articles on JPA and spoken at numerous conferences around the world. He is employed as an architect at Oracle in Ottawa, Canada, and is married with four kids and two dogs.

Merrick Schincariol is a consulting engineer at Oracle, specializing in middleware technologies. He has a Bachelor of Science degree in Computer Science from Lakehead University, and has more than a decade of experience in enterprise software development. He spent some time consulting in the pre-Java enterprise and business intelligence fields before moving on to write Java and J2EE applications. His experience with large-scale systems and data warehouse design gave him a mature and practiced perspective on enterprise software, which later propelled him into doing Java EE container implementation work.

About the Technical Reviewer

Manuel Jordan Elera is an autodidactic developer and researcher who enjoys learning new technologies for his own experiments and creating new integrations.

Manuel won the 2010 Springy Award-Community Champion and Spring Champion 2013. In his little free time, he reads the Bible and composes music on his guitar. Manuel is a Senior Member in the Spring Community Forums known as dr_pompeii.

He has been the Technical Reviewer for the following books (all published by Apress): *Pro SpringSource dm Server* (2009), *Spring Enterprise Recipes* (2009), *Spring Recipes* (Second Edition) (2010), *Pro Spring Integration* (2011), *Pro Spring Batch* (2011), *Pro Spring 3* (2012), *Pro Spring MVC: With Web Flow* (2012), *Pro Spring Security* (2013), *Pro Hibernate and MongoDB* (2013), and *Practical Spring LDAP* (2013).

Read and contact him through his blog at http://manueljordan.wordpress.com/ and follow him on his Twitter account, @dr_pompeii.

Acknowledgments

We are grateful to Jim Markham and Katie Sullivan for all of their help and patience. Thanks also go to Mary Behr for her copyediting and SPi for their production work.

We would also like to thank the technical reviewers of this edition and the many readers of the previous edition who pointed out corrections and errors.

CHAPTER 1

■ ■ ■

Introduction

Enterprise applications are defined by their need to collect, process, transform, and report on vast amounts of information. And, of course, that information has to be kept somewhere. Storing and retrieving data is a multibillion dollar business, evidenced in part by the growth of the database market as well as the emergence of cloud-based storage services. Despite all the available technologies for data management, application designers still spend much of their time trying to efficiently move their data to and from storage.

Despite the success the Java platform has had in working with database systems, for a long time it suffered from the same problem that has plagued other object-oriented programming languages. Moving data back and forth between a database system and the object model of a Java application was a lot harder than it needed to be. Java developers either wrote lots of code to convert row and column data into objects, or found themselves tied to proprietary frameworks that tried to hide the database from them. Fortunately, a standard solution, the Java Persistence API (JPA), was introduced into the platform to bridge the gap between object-oriented domain models and relational database systems.

In this book we will introduce version 2.1 of the Java Persistence API and explore everything that it has to offer developers. One of its strengths is that it can be slotted into whichever layer, tier, or framework an application needs it to be in. Whether you are building client-server applications to collect form data in a Swing application or building a web site using the latest application framework, JPA can help you to provide persistence more effectively.

To set the stage for JPA, this chapter first takes a step back to show where we've been and what problems we are trying to solve. From there we will look at the history of the specification and give you a high-level view of what it has to offer.

Relational Databases

Many ways of persisting data have come and gone over the years, and no concept has had more staying power than the relational database. Even in the age of the cloud, when "Big Data" and "NoSQL" regularly steal the headlines, relational database services are in consistent demand to enable today's enterprise applications running in the cloud. While key-value and document-oriented NoSQL stores have their place, relational stores remain the most popular general purpose databases in existence, and they are where the vast majority of the world's corporate data is stored. They are the starting point for every enterprise application and often have a lifespan that continues long after the application has faded away.

Understanding relational data is key to successful enterprise development. Developing applications to work well with database systems is a commonly acknowledged hurdle of software development. A good deal of Java's success can be attributed to its widespread adoption for building enterprise database systems. From consumer web sites to automated gateways, Java applications are at the heart of enterprise application development.

Object-Relational Mapping

"The domain model has a class. The database has a table. They look pretty similar. It should be simple to convert one to the other automatically." This is a thought we've probably all had at one point or another while writing yet another Data Access Object (DAO) to convert Java Database Connectivity (JDBC) result sets into something object-oriented. The domain model looks similar enough to the relational model of the database that it seems to cry out for a way to make the two models talk to each other.

The technique of bridging the gap between the object model and the relational model is known as object-relational mapping, often referred to as O-R mapping or simply ORM. The term comes from the idea that we are in some way mapping the concepts from one model onto another, with the goal of introducing a mediator to manage the automatic transformation of one to the other.

Before going into the specifics of object-relational mapping, let's define a brief manifesto of what the ideal solution should be.

- *Objects, not tables*: Applications should be written in terms of the domain model, not bound to the relational model. It must be possible to operate on and query against the domain model without having to express it in the relational language of tables, columns, and foreign keys.

- *Convenience, not ignorance*: Mapping tools should be used only by someone familiar with relational technology. O-R mapping is not meant to save developers from understanding mapping problems or to hide them altogether. It is meant for those who have an understanding of the issues and know what they need, but who don't want to have to write thousands of lines of code to deal with a problem that has already been solved.

- *Unobtrusive, not transparent*: It is unreasonable to expect that persistence be transparent because an application always needs to have control of the objects that it is persisting and be aware of the entity life cycle. The persistence solution should not intrude on the domain model, however, and domain classes must not be required to extend classes or implement interfaces in order to be persistable.

- *Legacy data, new objects*: It is far more likely that an application will target an existing relational database schema than create a new one. Support for legacy schemas is one of the most relevant use cases that will arise, and it is quite possible that such databases will outlive every one of us.

- *Enough, but not too much*: Enterprise developers have problems to solve, and they need features sufficient to solve those problems. What they don't like is being forced to eat a heavyweight persistence model that introduces large overhead because it is solving problems that many do not even agree *are* problems.

- *Local, but mobile*: A persistent representation of data does not need to be modeled as a full-fledged remote object. Distribution is something that exists as part of the application, not part of the persistence layer. The entities that contain the persistent state, however, must be able to travel to whichever layer needs them so that if an application is distributed, then the entities will support and not inhibit a particular architecture.

- *Standard API, with pluggable implementations*: Large companies with sizable applications don't want to risk being coupled to product-specific libraries and interfaces. By depending only on defined standard interfaces, the application is decoupled from proprietary APIs and can switch implementations if another becomes more suitable.

This would appear to be a somewhat demanding set of requirements, but it is one born of both practical experience and necessity. Enterprise applications have very specific persistence needs, and this shopping list of items is a fairly specific representation of the experience of the enterprise community.

The Impedance Mismatch

Advocates of object-relational mapping often describe the difference between the object model and the relational model as the impedance mismatch between the two. This is an apt description because the challenge of mapping one to the other lies not in the similarities between the two, but in the concepts in each for which there is no logical equivalent in the other.

In the following sections, we will present some basic object-oriented domain models and a variety of relational models to persist the same set of data. As you will see, the challenge in object-relational mapping is not so much the complexity of a single mapping but that there are so many possible mappings. The goal is not to explain how to get from one point to the other but to understand the roads that may have to be taken to arrive at an intended destination.

Class Representation

Let's begin this discussion with a simple class. Figure 1-1 shows an Employee class with four attributes: employee id, employee name, date they started, and current salary.

Employee
id: int name: String startDate: Date salary: long

Figure 1-1. *The Employee class*

Now consider the relational model shown in Figure 1-2. The ideal representation of this class in the database corresponds to scenario (A). Each field in the class maps directly to a column in the table. The employee id becomes the primary key. With the exception of some slight naming differences, this is a straightforward mapping.

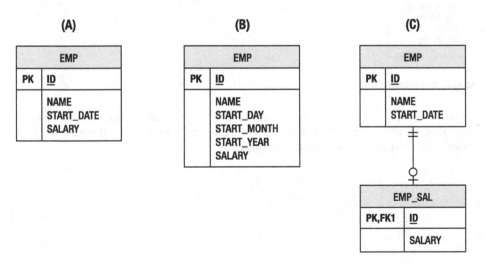

Figure 1-2. *Three scenarios for storing employee data*

In scenario (B), we see that the start date of the employee is actually stored as three separate columns, one each for the day, month, and year. Recall that the class used a Date object to represent this value. Because database schemas are much harder to change, should the class be forced to adopt the same storage strategy in order to remain consistent with the relational model? Also consider the inverse of the problem, in which the class had used three fields, and the table used a single date column. Even a single field becomes complex to map when the database and object model differ in representation.

Salary information is considered commercially sensitive, so it may be unwise to place the salary value directly in the EMP table, which may be used for a number of purposes. In scenario (C), the EMP table has been split so that the salary information is stored in a separate EMP_SAL table. This allows the database administrator to restrict SELECT access on salary information to those users who genuinely require it. With such a mapping, even a single store operation for the Employee class now requires inserts or updates to two different tables.

Clearly, even storing the data from a single class in a database can be a challenging exercise. We concern ourselves with these scenarios because real database schemas in production systems were never designed with object models in mind. The rule of thumb in enterprise applications is that the needs of the database trump the wants of the application. In fact, there are usually many applications, some object-oriented and some based on Structured Query Language (SQL), that retrieve from and store data into a single database. The dependency of multiple applications on the same database means that changing the database would affect every one of the applications, clearly an undesirable and potentially expensive option. It's up to the object model to adapt and find ways to work with the database schema without letting the physical design overpower the logical application model.

Relationships

Objects rarely exist in isolation. Just like relationships in a database, domain classes depend on and associate themselves with other domain classes. Consider the Employee class introduced in Figure 1-1. There are many domain concepts that could be associated with an employee, but for now let's introduce the Address domain class, for which an Employee may have at most one instance. We say in this case that Employee has a one-to-one relationship with Address, represented in the Unified Modeling Language (UML) model by the 0..1 notation. Figure 1-3 demonstrates this relationship.

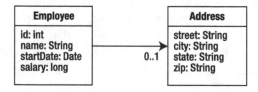

Figure 1-3. *The Employee and Address relationship*

We discussed different scenarios for representing the Employee state in the previous section, and likewise there are several approaches to representing a relationship in a database schema. Figure 1-4 demonstrates three different scenarios for a one-to-one relationship between an employee and an address.

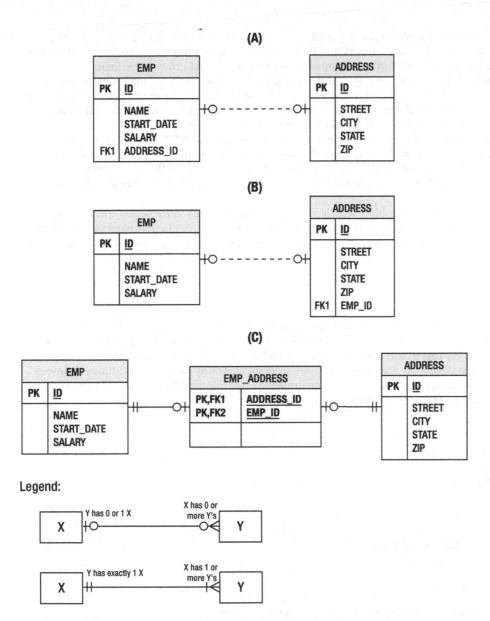

(A)

(B)

(C)

Legend:

Figure 1-4. *Three scenarios for relating employee and address data*

The building block for relationships in the database is the foreign key. Each scenario involves foreign key relationships between the various tables, but in order for there to be a foreign key relationship, the target table must have a primary key. And so before we even get to associate employees and addresses with each other we have a problem. The domain class Address does not have an identifier, yet the table that it would be stored in must have one if it is to be part of any relationships. We could construct a primary key out of all of the columns in the ADDRESS table, but this is considered bad practice. Therefore the ID column is introduced, and the object relational mapping will have to adapt in some way.

Scenario (A) of Figure 1-4 shows the ideal mapping of this relationship. The EMP table has a foreign key to the ADDRESS table stored in the ADDRESS_ID column. If the Employee class holds onto an instance of the Address class, the primary key value for the address can be set during store operations when an EMPLOYEE row gets written.

And yet consider scenario (B), which is only slightly different yet suddenly much more complex. In the domain model, an Address instance did not hold onto the Employee instance that owned it, and yet the employee primary key must be stored in the ADDRESS table. The object-relational mapping must either account for this mismatch between domain class and table or a reference back to the employee will have to be added for every address.

To make matters worse, scenario (C) introduces a join table to relate the EMP and ADDRESS tables. Instead of storing the foreign keys directly in one of the domain tables, the join table holds onto the pair of keys. Every database operation involving the two tables must now traverse the join table and keep it consistent. We could introduce an EmployeeAddress association class into the domain model to compensate, but that defeats the logical representation we are trying to achieve.

Relationships present a challenge in any object-relational mapping solution. This introduction covered only one-to-one relationships, and yet we have been faced with the need for primary keys not in the object model and the possibility of having to introduce extra relationships into the model or even association classes to compensate for the database schema.

Inheritance

A defining element of an object-oriented domain model is the opportunity to introduce generalized relationships between like classes. Inheritance is the natural way to express these relationships and allows for polymorphism in the application. Let's revisit the Employee class shown in Figure 1-1 and imagine a company that needs to distinguish between full-time and part-time employees. Part-time employees work for an hourly rate, while full-time employees are assigned a salary. This is a good opportunity for inheritance, moving wage information to the PartTimeEmployee and FullTimeEmployee subclasses. Figure 1-5 shows this arrangement.

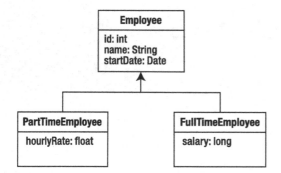

Figure 1-5. *Inheritance relationships between full-time and part-time employees*

Inheritance presents a genuine problem for object-relational mapping. We are no longer dealing with a situation in which there is a natural mapping from a class to a table. Consider the relational models shown in Figure 1-6. Once again, three different strategies for persisting the same set of data are demonstrated.

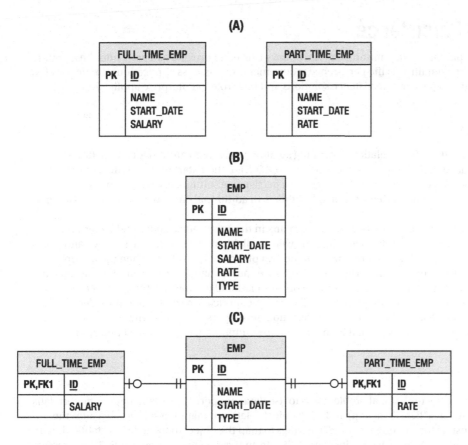

Figure 1-6. Inheritance strategies in a relational model

Arguably the easiest solution for someone mapping an inheritance structure to a database would be to put all of the data necessary for each class (including parent classes) into separate tables. This strategy is demonstrated by scenario (A) in Figure 1-6. Note that there is no relationship between the tables (i.e., each table is independent of the others). This means that queries against these tables are now much more complicated if the user needs to operate on both full-time and part-time employees in a single step.

An efficient but denormalized alternative is to place all the data required for every class in the model in a single table. That makes it very easy to query, but note the structure of the table shown in scenario (B) of Figure 1-6. There is a new column, TYPE, which does not exist in any part of the domain model. The TYPE column indicates whether the employee is part-time or full-time. This information must now be interpreted by an object-relational mapping solution to know what kind of domain class to instantiate for any given row in the table.

Scenario (C) takes this one step further, this time normalizing the data into separate tables for full-time and part-time employees. Unlike scenario (A), however, these tables are related by a common EMP table that stores all of the data common to both employee types. It might seem like overkill for a single column of extra data, but a real schema with many columns specific to each type of employee would likely use this type of table structure. It presents the data in a logical form and also simplifies querying by allowing the tables to be joined together. Unfortunately, what works well for the database does not necessarily work well for an object model mapped to such a schema. Even without associations to other classes, the object-relational mapping of the domain class must now take joins between multiple tables into account.When you start to consider abstract superclasses or parent classes that are not persistent, inheritance rapidly becomes a complex issue in object-relational mapping. Not only is there a challenge with storage of the class data but the complex table relationships are also difficult to query efficiently.

Java Support for Persistence

From the early days of the Java platform, programming interfaces have existed to provide gateways into the database and to abstract away many of the domain-specific persistence requirements of business applications. In the next few sections we will discuss current and past Java persistence solutions and their role in enterprise applications.

Proprietary Solutions

It may come as a surprise to learn that object-relational mapping solutions have been around for a long time; longer even than the Java language itself. Products such as Oracle TopLink got their start in the Smalltalk world before making the switch to Java. A great irony in the history of Java persistence solutions is that one of the first implementations of entity beans was actually demonstrated by adding an additional entity bean layer over TopLink mapped objects.

The two most popular proprietary persistence APIs were TopLink in the commercial space and Hibernate in the open source community. Commercial products like TopLink were available in the earliest days of Java and were successful, but the techniques were just never standardized for the Java platform. It was later, when upstart open source object-relational mapping solutions such as Hibernate became popular, that changes around persistence in the Java platform came about, leading to a convergence toward object-relational mapping as the preferred solution.

These two products and others could be integrated with all the major application servers and provided applications with all the persistence features they needed. Application developers were okay with using a third-party product for their persistence needs, especially given that there were no common and equivalent standards in sight.

Data Mappers

A partial approach to solving the object-relational problem was to use data mappers.[1] The data mapper pattern falls in the space between plain JDBC (see "JDBC" section) and a full object-relational mapping solution because the application developer is responsible for creating the raw SQL strings to map the object to the database tables, but a custom or off-the-shelf framework is typically used to invoke the SQL from the data mapper methods. The framework also helps with other things like result set mapping and SQL statement parameters. The most popular data mapper framework was Apache iBatis (now named MyBatis and hosted at Google Code). It gained a sizable community and is still found in a number of applications.

The biggest advantage of using a data mapping strategy like MyBatis is that the application has complete control over the SQL that is sent to the database. Stored procedures and all of the SQL features available from the driver are all fair game, and the overhead added by the framework is smaller than when using a full-blown ORM framework. However, the major disadvantage of being able to write custom SQL is that it has to be maintained. Any changes made to the object model can have repercussions on the data model and possibly cause significant SQL churn during development. A minimalist framework also opens the door for the developer to create new features as the application requirements grow, eventually leading to a reinvention of the ORM wheel. Data mappers may still have a place in some applications if they are sure that their needs will not grow beyond simple mapping, or if they require very explicit SQL that cannot be generated.

JDBC

The second release of the Java platform, Java Development Kit (JDK) 1.1, released in 1997, ushered in the first major support for database persistence with JDBC. It was created as a Java-specific version of its more generic predecessor, the Object Database Connectivity (ODBC) specification, a standard for accessing any relational database from any

---

[1]Fowler, Martin. *Patterns of Enterprise Application Architecture*, Addison-Wesley, 2003.

language or platform. Offering a simple and portable abstraction of the proprietary client programming interfaces offered by database vendors, JDBC allows Java programs to fully interact with the database. This interaction is heavily reliant on SQL, offering developers the chance to write queries and data manipulation statements in the language of the database, but executed and processed using a simple Java programming model.

The irony of JDBC is that, although the programming interfaces are portable, the SQL language is not. Despite the many attempts to standardize it, it is still rare to write SQL of any complexity that will run unchanged on two major database platforms. Even where the SQL dialects are similar, each database performs differently depending on the structure of the query, necessitating vendor-specific tuning in most cases.

There is also the issue of tight coupling between the Java source and SQL text. Developers are constantly tempted by the lure of ready-to-run SQL queries either dynamically constructed at runtime or simply stored in variables or fields. This is a very attractive programming model until one day you realize that the application has to support a new database vendor that doesn't support the dialect of SQL you have been using.

Even with SQL text relegated to property files or other application metadata, there comes a point when working with JDBC not only feels wrong but also simply becomes a cumbersome exercise in taking tabular row and column data and continuously having to convert it back and forth into objects. The application has an object model—why does it have to be so hard to use with the database?

Enterprise JavaBeans

The first release of the Java 2 Enterprise Edition (J2EE) platform introduced a new solution for Java persistence in the form of the entity bean, part of the Enterprise JavaBean (EJB) family of components. Intended to fully insulate developers from dealing directly with persistence, it introduced an interface-based approach where the concrete bean class was never directly used by client code. Instead, a specialized bean compiler generated an implementation of the bean interface to facilitate such things as persistence, security, and transaction management, delegating the business logic to the entity bean implementation. Entity beans were configured using a combination of standard and vendor-specific XML deployment descriptors, which became notorious for their complexity and verbosity.

It's probably fair to say that entity beans were over-engineered for the problem they were trying to solve, yet ironically the first release of the technology lacked many features necessary to implement realistic business applications. Relationships between entities had to be managed by the application, requiring foreign key fields to be stored and managed on the bean class. The actual mapping of the entity bean to the database was done entirely using vendor-specific configurations, as was the definition of finders (the entity bean term for queries). Finally, entity beans were modeled as remote objects that used RMI and CORBA, introducing network overhead and restrictions that should never have been added to a persistent object to begin with. The entity bean really began by solving the distributed persistent component problem, a cure for which there was no disease, leaving behind the common case of locally accessed lightweight persistent objects.

The EJB 2.0 specification solved many of the problems identified in the early releases. The notion of container-managed entity beans was introduced, where bean classes became abstract and the server was responsible for generating a subclass to manage the persistent data. Local interfaces and container-managed relationships were introduced, allowing associations to be defined between entity beans and automatically kept consistent by the server. This release also saw the introduction of Enterprise JavaBeans Query Language (EJB QL), a query language designed to work with entities that could be portably compiled to any SQL dialect.

Despite the improvements introduced with EJB 2.0, one major problem remained: excessive complexity. The specification assumed that development tools would insulate the developer from the challenge of configuring and managing the many artifacts required for each bean. Unfortunately, these tools took too long to materialize, and so the burden fell squarely on the shoulders of developers, even as the size and scope of EJB applications increased. Developers felt abandoned in a sea of complexity without the promised infrastructure to keep them afloat.

Java Data Objects

Due in part to some of the failures of the EJB persistence model, and some frustration at not having a satisfactory standardized persistence API, another persistence specification was attempted. Java Data Objects (JDO) was inspired and supported primarily by the object-oriented database (OODB) vendors and never really got adopted by the mainstream programming community. It required vendors to enhance the bytecode of domain objects to produce class files that were binary-compatible across all vendors, and every compliant vendor's products had to be capable of producing and consuming them. JDO also had a query language that was decidedly object-oriented in nature, which did not sit well with relational database users, who were in an overwhelming majority.

JDO reached the status of being an extension of the JDK, but never became an integrated part of the enterprise Java platform. It had many good features and was adopted by a small community of devoted users who stuck by it and tried desperately to promote it. Unfortunately, the major commercial vendors did not share the same view of how a persistence framework should be implemented. Few supported the specification, so JDO was talked about, but rarely used.

Some might argue that it was ahead of its time and that its reliance on bytecode enhancement caused it to be unfairly stigmatized. This was probably true, and if it had been introduced three years later, it might have been better accepted by a developer community that now thinks nothing of using frameworks that make extensive use of bytecode enhancement. Once the EJB 3.0 persistence movement was in motion, however, and the major vendors all signed up to be a part of the new enterprise persistence standard, the writing was on the wall for JDO. People soon complained to Sun that they now had two persistence specifications: one that was part of its enterprise platform and also worked in Java SE, and one that was being standardized only for Java SE. Shortly thereafter, Sun announced that JDO would be reduced to specification maintenance mode and that JPA would draw from both JDO and the persistence vendors and become the single supported standard going forward.

Why Another Standard?

Software developers knew what they wanted, but many could not find it in the existing standards, so they decided to look elsewhere. What they found was a range of proprietary persistence frameworks, both commercial and open source. Many of the products that implemented these technologies adopted a persistence model that did not intrude upon the domain objects. For these products, persistence was non-intrusive to the business objects in that, unlike entity beans, they did not have to be aware of the technology that was persisting them. They did not have to implement any type of interface or extend a special class. The developer could simply treat the persistent object like any other Java object, and then map it to a persistent store and use a persistence API to persist it. Because the objects were regular Java objects, this persistence model came to be known as Plain Old Java Object (POJO) persistence.

As Hibernate, TopLink, and other persistence APIs became ensconced in applications and met the needs of the application perfectly well, the question was often asked, "Why bother updating the EJB standard to match what these products already did? Why not just continue to use these products as has already been done for years, or why not even just standardize on an open source product like Hibernate?" There are actually many reasons why this could not be done—and would be a bad idea even if it could.

A standard goes far deeper than a product, and a single product (even a product as successful as Hibernate or TopLink) cannot embody a specification, even though it can implement one. At its very core, the intention of a specification is that it be implemented by different vendors and that it have different products offer standard interfaces and semantics that can be assumed by applications without coupling the application to any one product.

Binding a standard to an open source project like Hibernate would be problematic for the standard and probably even worse for the Hibernate project. Imagine a specification that was based on a specific version or checkpoint of the code base of an open source project, and how confusing that would be. Now imagine an open source software (OSS) project that could not change or could change only in discrete versions controlled by a special committee every two years, as opposed to the changes being decided by the project itself. Hibernate, and indeed any open source project, would likely be suffocated.

Although standardization might not be valued by the consultant or the five-person software shop, to a corporation it is huge. Software technologies are a big investment for most corporate IT departments, and risk must be measured when large sums of money are involved. Using a standard technology reduces that risk substantially and allows the corporation to be able to switch vendors if the initial choice does not end up meeting the need.

Besides portability, the value of standardizing a technology is manifested in all sorts of other areas as well. Education, design patterns, and industry communication are just some of the many benefits that standards bring to the table.

The Java Persistence API

The Java Persistence API is a lightweight, POJO-based framework for Java persistence. Although object-relational mapping is a major component of the API, it also offers solutions to the architectural challenges of integrating persistence into scalable enterprise applications. In the following sections we will look at the evolution of the specification and provide an overview of the major aspects of this technology.

History of the Specification

The Java Persistence API is remarkable not only for what it offers developers but also for the way in which it came to be. The following sections outline the prehistory of object-relational persistence solutions and the genesis of JPA.

EJB 3.0 and JPA 1.0

After years of complaints about the complexity of building enterprise applications with Java, "ease of development" was the theme for the Java EE 5 platform release. EJB 3.0 led the charge and found ways to make Enterprise JavaBeans easier and more productive to use.

In the case of session beans and message-driven beans, solutions to usability issues were reached by simply removing some of the more onerous implementation requirements and letting components look more like plain Java objects.

In the case of entity beans, however, a more serious problem existed. If the definition of "ease of use" is to keep implementation interfaces and descriptors out of application code and to embrace the natural object model of the Java language, how do you make coarse-grained, interface-driven, container-managed entity beans look and feel like a domain model?

The answer was to start over—to leave entity beans alone and introduce a new model for persistence. The Java Persistence API was born out of recognition of the demands of practitioners and the existing proprietary solutions that they were using to solve their problems. To ignore that experience would have been folly.

Thus the leading vendors of object-relational mapping solutions came forward and standardized the best practices represented by their products. Hibernate and TopLink were the first to sign on with the EJB vendors, followed later by the JDO vendors.

Years of industry experience coupled with a mission to simplify development combined to produce the first specification to truly embrace the new programming models offered by the Java SE 5 platform. The use of annotations in particular resulted in a new way of using persistence in applications that had never been seen before.

The resulting EJB 3.0 specification, released in 2006, ended up being divided into three distinct pieces and split across three separate documents. The first document contained all of the legacy EJB component model content, and the second one described the new simplified POJO component model. The third was the Java Persistence API, a stand-alone specification that described the persistence model in both the Java SE and Java EE environments.

JPA 2.0

By the time the first version of JPA was started, ORM persistence had already been evolving for a decade. Unfortunately there was only a relatively short period of time available (approximately two years) in the specification development cycle to create the initial specification, so not every possible feature that had been encountered could be included in the first release. Still, an impressive number of features were specified, with the remainder left for subsequent releases and for the vendors to support in proprietary ways in the meantime.

The next release, JPA 2.0, went final in 2009 and included a number of the features that were not present in the first release, specifically those that had been the most requested by users. These new features included additional mapping capabilities, flexible ways to determine the way the provider accessed the entity state, and extensions to the Java Persistence Query Language (JP QL). Probably the most significant feature was the Java Criteria API, a programmatic way to create dynamic queries. This primarily enabled frameworks to use JPA as a means to programmatically build code to access data.

JPA 2.1

The release of JPA 2.1 in 2013 made it possible for almost all JPA-based applications to be satisfied by the features included in the standard without having to revert to vendor additions. However, no matter how many features are specified, there are always going to be applications that need additional capabilities to work around unusual circumstances. The JPA 2.1 specification added some of the more exotic features, like mapping converters, stored procedure support, and unsynchronized persistence contexts for improved conversational operations. It also added the ability to create entity graphs and pass them to queries, amounting to what are commonly known as fetch group constraints on the returned object set.

Throughout this book we distinguish between the features added in JPA 2.1 from those that were present in JPA 2.0. This will help readers still using an old JPA 2.0 implementation to know what is not available in their provider (and will hopefully encourage them to upgrade to a JPA 2.1 provider).

JPA and You

In the end, there may still be some feature that you, or some other JPA user, might look for in the standard that has not yet been included. If the feature is requested by a sufficient number of users, then it will likely eventually become part of the standard, but that partly depends upon you, the developers. If you think a feature should be standardized, you should speak up and request it from your JPA provider; you should also contact the expert group of the next JPA version. The community helps to shape and drive the standards, and it is you, the community, that must make your needs known.

Note, however, that there will always be a subset of seldom-used features that will probably never make it into the standard simply because they are not mainstream enough to warrant being included. The well-known philosophy of the "needs of the many" outweighing the "needs of the few" (don't even pretend that you don't know the exact episode in which this philosophy was first expressed) must be considered because each new feature adds some non-zero amount of complexity to the specification rendering it that much bigger and that much harder to understand, use, and implement. The lesson is that even though we are asking you for your input, not all of it can possibly be incorporated into the specification.

Overview

The model of JPA is simple and elegant, powerful and flexible. It is natural to use and easy to learn, especially if you have used any of the existing persistence products on the market today on which the API was based. The main operational API that an application will be exposed to is contained within a small number of classes.

POJO Persistence

Perhaps the most important aspect of JPA is the fact that the objects are POJOs, meaning that there is nothing special about any object that is made persistent. In fact, almost any existing non-final application object with a default constructor can be made persistable without so much as changing a single line of code. Object-relational mapping with JPA is entirely metadata-driven. It can be done either by adding annotations to the code or using externally defined XML. The objects that are persisted are only as heavy as the data that is defined or mapped with them.

Non-intrusiveness

The persistence API exists as a separate layer from the persistent objects. The persistence API is called by the application business logic, is passed the persistence objects, and is instructed to operate upon them. So even though the application must be aware of the persistence API because it has to call into it, the persistent objects themselves need not be aware. Because the API does not intrude upon the code in the persistent object classes, it's called non-intrusive persistence.

Some people are under the misconception that non-intrusive persistence means that objects magically get persisted, the way that object databases of yesteryear used to do when a transaction got committed. This is sometimes called transparent persistence and is an incorrect notion that is even more irrational when you think about querying. You need to have some way of retrieving the objects from the data store. This requires a separate API object and, in fact, some object databases required that users invoke special Extent objects to issue queries. Applications absolutely need to manage their persistent objects in very explicit ways, and they require a designated API to do it.

Object Queries

A powerful query framework offers the ability to query across entities and their relationships without having to use concrete foreign keys or database columns. Queries may be expressed in JP QL, a query language that is modeled after SQL for its familiarity but is not tied to the database schema, or defined using the criteria API. Queries use a schema abstraction that is based on the entity model as opposed to the columns in which the entity is stored. Java entities and their attributes are used as the query schema, so knowledge of the database-mapping information is not required. The queries will eventually get translated by the JPA implementation into the SQL appropriate for the target database and executed on the database.

A query may be defined statically in metadata or created dynamically by passing query criteria when constructing it. It is also possible to escape to SQL if a special query requirement exists that cannot be met by the SQL generation from the persistence framework. These queries can return results in the form of entities, projections of specific entity attributes, or even aggregate function values, amongst other options. JPA queries are valuable abstractions that enable querying across the Java domain model instead of across concrete database tables.

Mobile Entities

Client/server and web applications and other distributed architectures are clearly the most popular types of applications in a connected world. To acknowledge this fact means acknowledging that persistent entities must be mobile in the network. Objects must be able to be moved from one Java Virtual Machine (JVM) to another and then back again, and must still be usable by the application.

Objects that leave the persistence layer are called detached. A key feature of the persistence model is the ability to change detached entities and then reattach them upon their return to the originating JVM. The detachment model provides a way of reconciling the state of an entity being reattached with the state that it was in before it became detached. This allows entity changes to be made offline while still maintaining entity consistency in the face of concurrency.

Simple Configuration

There are a great number of persistence features that the specification has to offer and that we will explain in the chapters of this book. All the features are configurable through the use of annotations, XML, or a combination of the two. Annotations offer ease of use that is unparalleled in the history of Java metadata. They are convenient to write and painless to read, and they make it possible for beginners to get an application going quickly and easily. Configuration can also be done in XML for those who like XML or want to externalize the metadata from the code.

Of greater significance than the metadata language is the fact that JPA makes heavy use of defaults. This means that no matter which method is chosen, the amount of metadata that will be required just to get running is the absolute minimum. In some cases, if the defaults are good enough, almost no metadata will be required at all.

Integration and Testability

Multitier applications hosted on an application server have become the de facto standard for application architectures. Testing on an application server is a challenge that few relish. It can bring pain and hardship, and it is often prohibitive to practicing unit testing and white box testing.

This is solved by defining the API to work outside as well as inside the application server. Although it is not as common a use case, applications that do run on two tiers (the application talking directly to the database tier) can use the persistence API without the existence of an application server at all. The more common scenario is for unit tests and automated testing frameworks that can be run easily and conveniently in Java SE environments.

With the Java Persistence API it is now possible to write server-integrated persistence code and be able to reuse it for testing outside the server. When running inside a server container, all the benefits of container support and superior ease of use apply, but with a few changes and a little bit of test framework support the same application can also be configured to run outside the container.

Summary

This chapter presented an introduction to the Java Persistence API. We began with an introduction to the primary problem facing developers trying to use object-oriented domain models in concert with a relational database: the impedance mismatch. To demonstrate the complexity of bridging the gap, we presented three small object models and nine different ways to represent the same information. We explored each a little and discussed how mapping objects to different table configurations can cause differences, not only in the way data evolves in the database but also how expensive the resulting database operations are and how the application performs.

We then presented an overview of some of the proprietary solutions and the current standards for persistence, looking at JDBC, EJB, and JDO. In each case, we looked at the evolution of the standard and where it fell short. You gained some general insights on particular aspects of the persistence problem that were learned along the way.

We concluded the chapter with a brief look at JPA. We looked at the history of the specification and the vendors who came together to create it. We then looked at the role it plays in enterprise application development and gave an introduction to some of the features offered by the specification.

In the next chapter, you will get your feet wet with JPA by taking a whirlwind tour of the basics and building a simple application in the process.

CHAPTER 2

Getting Started

One of the main goals of JPA was that it should be simple to use and easy to understand. Although its problem domain cannot be trivialized or watered down, the technology that enables developers to deal with it can be straightforward and intuitive. In this chapter, we will show how effortless it can be to develop and use entities.

We will start by describing the basic characteristics of entities. We'll define what an entity is and how to create, read, update, and delete it. We'll also introduce entity managers and how they are obtained and used. Then we'll take a quick look at queries and how to specify and execute a query using the EntityManager and Query objects. The chapter will conclude by showing a simple working application that runs in a standard Java SE environment and demonstrates all of the example code in action.

Entity Overview

The entity is not a new thing in data management. In fact, entities have been around longer than many programming languages and certainly longer than Java. They were first introduced by Peter Chen in his seminal paper on entity-relationship modeling.[1] He described entities as things that have attributes and relationships. The expectation was that the attributes and relationships would be persisted in a relational database.

Even now, the definition still holds true. An entity is essentially a noun, or a grouping of state associated together as a single unit. It may participate in relationships to any number of other entities in a number of standard ways. In the object-oriented paradigm, we would add behavior to it and call it an object. In JPA, any application-defined object can be an entity, so the important question might be this: What are the characteristics of an object that has been turned into an entity?

Persistability

The first and most basic characteristic of entities is that they are persistable. This generally just means that they can be made persistent. More specifically, it means that their state can be represented in a data store and can be accessed at a later time, perhaps well after the end of the process that created it.

You could call them persistent objects, and many people do, but it is not technically correct. Strictly speaking, a persistent object becomes persistent the moment it is instantiated in memory. If a persistent object exists, then by definition it is already persistent.

An entity is persistable because it can be saved in a persistent store. The difference is that it is not automatically persisted, and that in order for it to have a durable representation the application must actively invoke an API method to initiate the process. This is an important distinction because it leaves control over persistence firmly in

---

[1]Peter P. Chen, "The entity-relationship model—toward a unified view of data," ACM Transactions on Database Systems 1, no. 1 (1976): 9–36.

the hands of the application. The application has the flexibility to manipulate data and perform business logic on the entity, making it persistent only when the application decides it is the right time. The lesson is that entities may be manipulated without necessarily being persisted, and it is the application that decides whether they are or not.

Identity

Like any other Java object, an entity has an object identity, but when it exists in the database it also has a persistent identity. Object identity is simply the differentiation between objects that occupy memory. Persistent identity, or an identifier, is the key that uniquely identifies an entity instance and distinguishes it from all the other instances of the same entity type. An entity has a persistent identity when there exists a representation of it in the data store; that is, a row in a database table. If it is not in the database, then even though the in-memory entity may have its identity set in a field, it does not have a persistent identity. The entity identifier, then, is equivalent to the primary key in the database table that stores the entity state.

Transactionality

Entities might be called quasi-transactional. Although they can be created, updated, and deleted in any context, these operations are normally done within the context of a transaction[2] because a transaction is required for the changes to be committed in the database. Changes made to the database either succeed or fail atomically, so the persistent view of an entity should indeed be transactional.

In memory, it is a slightly different story in the sense that entities may be changed without the changes ever being persisted. Even when enlisted in a transaction, they may be left in an undefined or inconsistent state in the event of a rollback or transaction failure. The in-memory entities are simple Java objects that obey all of the rules and constraints that are applied by the Java Virtual Machine (JVM) to other Java objects.

Granularity

Finally, a good way to show what entities are is to describe what they are not. They are not primitives, primitive wrappers, or built-in objects with single-dimensional state. These are no more than scalars and do not have any inherent semantic meaning to an application. A string, for example, is too fine-grained an object to be an entity because it does not have any domain-specific connotation. Rather, a string is well-suited and very often used as a type for an entity attribute and given meaning according to the entity attribute that it is typing.

Entities are meant to be fine-grained objects that have a set of aggregated state that is normally stored in a single place, such as a row in a table, and typically have relationships to other entities. In the most general sense, they are business domain objects that have specific meaning to the application that accesses them.

While it is certainly true that entities may be defined in exaggerated ways to be as fine-grained as storing a single string or coarse-grained enough to contain 500 columns' worth of data, JPA entities were definitely intended to be on the smaller end of the granularity spectrum. Ideally, entities should be designed and defined as fairly lightweight objects of a size comparable to that of the average Java object.

Entity Metadata

In addition to its persistent state, every JPA entity has some associated metadata (even if a very small amount) that describes it. This metadata may exist as part of the saved class file or it may be stored external to the class, but it is not persisted in the database. It enables the persistence layer to recognize, interpret, and properly manage the entity from the time it is loaded through to its runtime invocation.

---

[2]In most cases, this is a requirement, but in certain configurations the transaction might not be started until after the operation.

The metadata that is actually required for each entity is minimal, rendering entities easy to define and use. However, like any sophisticated technology with its share of switches, levers, and buttons, there is also the possibility to specify much, much more metadata than is required. It may be extensive amounts, depending upon the application requirements, and may be used to customize every detail of the entity configuration or state mappings.

Entity metadata may be specified in two ways: annotations or XML. Each is equally valid, but the one that you use will depend upon your development preferences or process.

Annotations

Annotation metadata is a language feature introduced in Java SE 5 that allows structured and typed metadata to be attached to the source code. Although annotations are not required by JPA, they are a convenient way to learn and use the API. Because annotations co-locate the metadata with the program artifacts, it is not necessary to escape to an additional file and a special language (XML) just to specify the metadata.

Annotations are used throughout both the examples and the accompanying explanations in this book. All the JPA annotations that are shown and described (except in Chapter 3, which talks about Java EE annotations) are defined in the `javax.persistence` package. Example code snippets can be assumed to have an implicit import of the form `import javax.persistence.*;`.

XML

For those who prefer to use traditional XML, this option is still available. It should be fairly straightforward to switch to using XML descriptors after having learned and understood the annotations because the XML has mostly been patterned after the annotations. Chapter 13 describes how to use XML to specify or override entity mapping metadata.

Configuration by Exception

The notion of configuration by exception means that the persistence engine defines defaults that apply to the majority of applications and that users need to supply values only when they want to override the default value. In other words, having to supply a configuration value is an exception to the rule, not a requirement.

Configuration by exception is ingrained in JPA and contributes strongly to its usability. Most configuration values have defaults, rendering the metadata that does have to be specified more relevant and concise.

The extensive use of defaults and the ease of use that it brings to configuration come at a price, however. When defaults are embedded into the API and do not have to be specified, then they are not visible or obvious to users. This can make it possible for users to be unaware of the complexity of developing persistence applications, making it harder to debug or to change the behavior when it becomes necessary.

Defaults are not meant to shield users from the often complex issues surrounding persistence. They are meant to allow a developer to get started easily and quickly with something that will work and then iteratively improve and implement additional functionality as the complexity of their application increases. Even though the defaults may be what you want to have happen most of the time, it is still important for developers to be familiar with the default values that are being applied. For example, if a table name default is being assumed, it is important to know what table the runtime is expecting, or if schema generation is used, what table will be generated.

For each of the annotations we will also discuss the default value so that it is clear what will be applied if the annotation is not specified. We recommend that you remember these defaults as you learn them. After all, a default value is still part of the configuration of the application; it is just really easy to configure!

Creating an Entity

Regular Java classes are easily transformed into entities simply by annotating them. In fact, by adding a couple of annotations, almost any class with a no-arg constructor can become an entity.

Let's start by creating a regular Java class for an employee. Listing 2-1 shows a simple Employee class.

Listing 2-1. Employee Class

```
public class Employee {
    private int id;
    private String name;
    private long salary;

    public Employee() {}
    public Employee(int id) { this.id = id; }

    public int getId() { return id; }
    public void setId(int id) { this.id = id; }
    public String getName() { return name; }
    public void setName(String name) { this.name = name; }
    public long getSalary() { return salary; }
    public void setSalary (long salary) { this.salary = salary; }
}
```

You may notice that this class resembles a JavaBean-style class with three properties: id, name, and salary. Each of these properties is represented by a pair of accessor methods to get and set the property, and is backed by a member field. Properties or member fields are the units of state within the entity that can be persisted.

To turn Employee into an entity, we first annotate the class with @Entity. This is primarily just a marker annotation to indicate to the persistence engine that the class is an entity.

The second annotation that we need to add is @Id. This annotates the particular field or property that holds the persistent identity of the entity (the primary key) and is needed so the provider knows which field or property to use as the unique identifying key in the table.

Adding these two annotations to the Employee class, we end up with pretty much the same class that we had before, except that now it is an entity. Listing 2-2 shows the entity class.

Listing 2-2. Employee Entity

```
@Entity
public class Employee {
    @Id private int id;
    private String name;
    private long salary;

    public Employee() {}
    public Employee(int id) { this.id = id; }

    public int getId() { return id; }
    public void setId(int id) { this.id = id; }
    public String getName() { return name; }
    public void setName(String name) { this.name = name; }
    public long getSalary() { return salary; }
    public void setSalary (long salary) { this.salary = salary; }
}
```

When we say that the @Id annotation is placed on the field or property, we mean that the user can choose to annotate either the declared field or the getter method[3] of a JavaBean-style property. Either field or property strategy is allowed, depending on the needs and tastes of the entity developer. We have chosen in this example to annotate the field because it is simpler; in general, this will be the easiest and most direct approach. We will discuss the details of annotating persistent state using field or property access in subsequent chapters.

The fields in the entity are automatically made persistable by virtue of their existence in the entity. Default mapping and loading configuration values apply to these fields and enable them to be persisted when the object is persisted. Given the questions that were brought up in the last chapter, one might be led to ask, "How did the fields get mapped, and where do they get persisted to?"

To find the answer, we must first take a quick detour to dig inside the @Entity annotation and look at an element called name that uniquely identifies the entity. The entity name may be explicitly specified for any entity by using this name element in the annotation, as in @Entity(name="Emp"). In practice, this is seldom specified because it gets defaulted to be the unqualified name of the entity class. This is almost always both reasonable and adequate.

Now we can get back to the question about where the data gets stored. It turns out that the default name of the table used to store any given entity of a particular entity type is the name of the entity. If we have specified the name of the entity, it will be the default table name; if not, the default value of the entity name will be used. We just stated that the default entity name was the unqualified name of the entity class, so that is effectively the answer to the question of which table gets used. In the Employee example, the entity name will be defaulted to "Employee" and all entities of type Employee will get stored in a table called EMPLOYEE.

Each of the fields or properties has individual state in it and needs to be directed to a particular column in the table. We know to go to the EMPLOYEE table, but which column should be used for a given field or property? When no columns are explicitly specified, the default column is used for a field or property, which is just the name of the field or property itself. So the employee id will get stored in the ID column, the name in the NAME column, and the salary in the SALARY column of the EMPLOYEE table.

Of course, these values can all be overridden to match an existing schema. We will discuss how to override them when we get to Chapter 4 and discuss mapping in more detail.

Entity Manager

In the "Entity Overview" section, it was stated that a specific API call needs to be invoked before an entity actually gets persisted to the database. In fact, separate API calls are needed to perform many of the operations on entities. This API is implemented by the entity manager and encapsulated almost entirely within a single interface called javax.persistence.EntityManager. When all is said and done, it is to an entity manager that the real work of persistence is delegated. Until an entity manager is used to actually create, read, or write an entity, the entity is nothing more than a regular (nonpersistent) Java object.

When an entity manager obtains a reference to an entity, either by having it explicitly passed in as an argument to a method call or because it was read from the database, that object is said to be managed by the entity manager. The set of managed entity instances within an entity manager at any given time is called its persistence context. Only one Java instance with the same persistent identity may exist in a persistence context at any time. For example, if an Employee with a persistent identity (or id) of 158 exists in the persistence context, then no other Employee object with its id set to 158 may exist within that same persistence context.

Entity managers are configured to be able to persist or manage specific types of objects, read and write to a given database, and be implemented by a particular persistence provider (or provider for short). It is the provider that supplies the backing implementation engine for the entire Java Persistence API, from the EntityManager through to implementation of the query classes and SQL generation.

---

[3] Annotations on setter methods will just be ignored.

All entity managers come from factories of type javax.persistence.EntityManagerFactory. The configuration for an entity manager is templated from the entity manager factory that created it, but it is defined separately as a persistence unit. A persistence unit dictates either implicitly or explicitly the settings and entity classes used by all entity managers obtained from the unique EntityManagerFactory instance bound to that persistence unit. There is, therefore, a one-to-one correspondence between a persistence unit and its concrete EntityManagerFactory instance.

Persistence units are named to allow differentiation of one entity manager factory from another. This gives the application control over which configuration or persistence unit is to be used for operating on a particular entity.

Figure 2-1 shows that for each persistence unit there is an entity manager factory and that many entity managers can be created from a single entity manager factory. The part that may come as a surprise is that many entity managers can point to the same persistence context. We have talked only about an entity manager and its persistence context, but later on you will see that there may in fact be multiple references to different entity managers all pointing to the same group of managed entities. This will enable the control flow to traverse container components but continue to be able access the same persistence context.

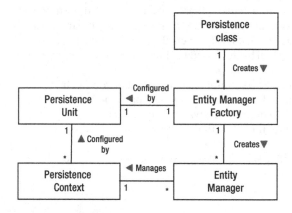

Figure 2-1. *Relationships between JPA concepts*

Table 2-1 summarizes the concepts and API objects previously mentioned or discussed. Note that while some are actual API objects, others are only abstract concepts that help to explain how the API works.

Table 2-1. *Summary of API Objects and Concepts*

Object	API Object	Description
Persistence	Persistence	Bootstrap class used to obtain an entity manager factory
Entity Manager Factory	EntityManagerFactory	Configured factory object used to obtain entity managers
Persistence Unit	--	Named configuration declaring the entity classes and data store info
Entity Manager	EntityManager	Main API object used to perform operations and queries on entities
Persistence Context	--	Set of all entity instances managed by a specific entity manager

Obtaining an Entity Manager

An entity manager is always obtained from an EntityManagerFactory. The factory from which it was obtained determines the configuration parameters that govern its operation. While there are shortcuts that veil the factory from the user view when running in a Java EE application server environment, in the Java SE environment we can use a simple bootstrap class called Persistence. The static createEntityManagerFactory() method in the Persistence class returns the EntityManagerFactory for the specified persistence unit name. The following example demonstrates creating an EntityManagerFactory for the persistence unit named "EmployeeService":

```
EntityManagerFactory emf =
    Persistence.createEntityManagerFactory("EmployeeService");
```

The name of the specified persistence unit "EmployeeService" passed into the createEntityManagerFactory() method identifies the given persistence unit configuration that determines such things as the connection parameters that entity managers generated from this factory will use when connecting to the database.

Now that we have a factory, we can easily obtain an entity manager from it. The following example demonstrates creating an entity manager from the factory acquired in the previous example:

```
EntityManager em = emf.createEntityManager();
```

With this entity manager we are in a position to start working with persistent entities.

Persisting an Entity

Persisting an entity is the operation of taking a transient entity, or one that does not yet have any persistent representation in the database, and storing its state so that it can be retrieved later. This is really the basis of persistence—creating state that may outlive the process that created it. We start by using the entity manager to persist an instance of Employee. Here is a code example that does just that:

```
Employee emp = new Employee(158);
em.persist(emp);
```

The first line in this code segment is simply creating an Employee instance that we want to persist. If we ignore the sad fact of employing a nameless individual and paying him nothing (we are setting only the id, not the name or salary) the instantiated Employee is just a regular Java object.

The next line uses the entity manager to persist the entity. Calling persist() is all that is required to initiate it being persisted in the database. If the entity manager encounters a problem doing this, it will throw an unchecked PersistenceException. When the persist() call completes, emp will have become a managed entity within the entity manager's persistence context.

Listing 2-3 shows how to incorporate this into a simple method that creates a new employee and persists it to the database.

Listing 2-3. Method for Creating an Employee

```
public Employee createEmployee(int id, String name, long salary) {
    Employee emp = new Employee(id);
    emp.setName(name);
    emp.setSalary(salary);
    em.persist(emp);
    return emp;
}
```

This method assumes the existence of an entity manager in the em field of the instance and uses it to persist the Employee. Note that we do not need to worry about the failure case in this example. It will result in a runtime PersistenceException being thrown, which will get propagated up to the caller.

Finding an Entity

Once an entity is in the database, the next thing one typically wants to do is find it again. In this section, you will discover how an entity can be found using the entity manager. There is really only one line that's important:

```
Employee emp = em.find(Employee.class, 158);
```

We are passing in the class of the entity that is being sought (in this example, we are looking for an instance of Employee) and the id or primary key that identifies the particular entity (in this case we want to find the entity that we just created). This is all the information needed by the entity manager to find the instance in the database, and when the call completes, the employee that gets returned will be a managed entity, meaning that it will exist in the current persistence context associated with the entity manager. Passing in the class as a parameter also allows the find method to be parameterized and return an object of the same type that was passed in, saving the caller an extra cast.

What happens if the object has been deleted or if you supply the wrong id by accident? In the event that the object was not found, then the find() call simply returns null. You would need to ensure that a null check is performed before the next time the emp variable is used.

The code for a method that looks up and returns the Employee with a given id is now trivial and is shown in Listing 2-4.

Listing 2-4. Method for Finding an Employee

```
public Employee findEmployee(int id) {
    return em.find(Employee.class, id);
}
```

In the case where no employee exists for the id that is passed in, then the method will return null because that is what find() will return.

Removing an Entity

Removal of an entity from the database is not as common as you might think. Many applications never delete objects, or if they do they just flag the data as being out of date or no longer valid and then just keep it out of sight of clients. We are not talking about that kind of application-level logical removal where the data is not even removed from the database. We are talking about something that results in a DELETE statement being made across one or more tables.

In order to remove an entity, the entity itself must be managed, meaning that it is present in the persistence context. This means that the calling application should have already loaded or accessed the entity and is now issuing a command to remove it. This is not normally a problem given that most often the application will have caused it to become managed as part of the process of determining that this was the object that it wanted to remove.

A simple example of removing an employee is the following:

```
Employee emp = em.find(Employee.class, 158);
em.remove(emp);
```

In this example, we are first finding the entity using the find() call, which returns a managed instance of Employee, and then removing the entity using the remove() call on the entity manager. Of course, you learned in the previous section that if the entity was not found, then the find() method will return null. You would get a `java.lang.IllegalArgumentException` if it turned out that you passed `null` into the `remove()` call because you forgot to include a null check before calling `remove()`.

In the application method for removing an employee, the problem can be fixed by checking for the existence of the employee before issuing the `remove()` call, as shown in Listing 2-5.

Listing 2-5. Method for Removing an Employee

```
public void removeEmployee(int id) {
    Employee emp = em.find(Employee.class, id);
    if (emp != null) {
        em.remove(emp);
    }
}
```

This method will ensure that the employee with the given id, provided the id is not null, is removed from the database. It will return successfully whether the employee exists or not.

Updating an Entity

There are a few different ways of updating an entity, but for now we will illustrate the simplest and most common case. This is where we have a managed entity and want to make changes to it. If we do not have a reference to the managed entity, then we must first get one using `find()` and then perform our modifying operations on the managed entity. The code below adds $1,000 to the salary of the employee with id 158:

```
Employee emp = em.find(Employee.class, 158);
emp.setSalary(emp.getSalary() + 1000);
```

Note the difference between this operation and the others. In this case we are not calling into the entity manager to modify the object, but directly calling the object itself. For this reason it is important that the entity be a managed instance; otherwise, the persistence provider will have no means of detecting the change, and no changes will be made to the persistent representation of the employee.

The method to raise the salary of a given employee will take the id and amount of the raise, find the employee, and change the salary to the adjusted one. Listing 2-6 demonstrates this approach.

Listing 2-6. Method for Updating an Employee

```
public Employee raiseEmployeeSalary(int id, long raise) {
    Employee emp = em.find(Employee.class, id);
    if (emp != null) {
        emp.setSalary(emp.getSalary() + raise);
    }
    return emp;
}
```

If we couldn't find the employee, we return `null` so the caller will know that no change could be made. We indicate success by returning the updated employee.

Transactions

You may feel that the code so far seems inconsistent with what we said earlier about transactionality when working with entities. There were no transactions in any of the preceding examples, even though we said that changes to entities must be made persistent using a transaction.

23

In all the examples except the one that called only find(), we assume that a transaction enclosed each method. The find() call is not a mutating operation, so it may be called any time, with or without a transaction.

Once again, the key is the environment in which the code is being executed. The typical situation when running inside the Java EE container environment is that the standard Java Transaction API (JTA) is used. The transaction model when running in the container is to assume the application will ensure that a transactional context is present when one is required. If a transaction is not present, then either the modifying operation will throw an exception or the change will simply never be persisted to the data store. We will come back to discussing transactions in the Java EE environment in more detail in Chapter 3.

In the example in this chapter, though, we are not running in Java EE. It was in a Java SE environment, and the transaction service that should be used in Java SE is the javax.persistence.EntityTransaction service. When executing in Java SE, we either need to begin and to commit the transaction in the operational methods, or we need to begin and to commit the transaction before and after calling an operational method. In either case, a transaction is started by calling getTransaction() on the entity manager to get the EntityTransaction and then invoking begin() on it. Likewise, to commit the transaction the commit() call is invoked on the EntityTransaction object obtained from the entity manager. For example, starting and committing before and after the method would produce code that creates an employee the way it is done in Listing 2-7.

Listing 2-7. Beginning and Committing an EntityTransaction

```
em.getTransaction().begin();
createEmployee(158, "John Doe", 45000);
em.getTransaction().commit();
```

Further detail about resource-level transactions and the EntityTransaction API are contained in Chapter 6.

Queries

In general, given that most developers have used a relational database at some point or another in their lives, most of us pretty much know what a database query is. In JPA, a query is similar to a database query, except that instead of using Structured Query Language (SQL) to specify the query criteria, we are querying over entities and using a language called Java Persistence Query Language (JP QL).

A query is implemented in code as a Query or TypedQuery<X> object. It is constructed using the EntityManager as a factory. The EntityManager interface includes a variety of API calls that return a new Query or TypedQuery<X> object. As a first-class object, a query can in turn be customized according to the needs of the application.

A query can be defined either statically or dynamically. A static query is typically defined in either annotation or XML metadata, and it must include the query criteria as well as a user-assigned name. This kind of query is also called a named query, and it is later looked up by its name at the time it is executed.

A dynamic query can be issued at runtime by supplying the JP QL query criteria or a criteria object. They may be a little more expensive to execute because the persistence provider cannot do any query preparation beforehand, but JP QL queries are nevertheless very simple to use and can be issued in response to program logic or even user logic.

The following example shows how to create a dynamic query and then execute it to obtain all the employees in the database. Of course, this may not be a very good query to execute if the database is large and contains hundreds of thousands of employees, but it is nevertheless a legitimate example. The simple query is as follows:

```
TypedQuery<Employee> query = em.createQuery("SELECT e FROM Employee e",
                                             Employee.class);
List<Employee> emps = query.getResultList();
```

We create a TypedQuery<Employee> object by issuing the createQuery() call on the EntityManager and passing in the JP QL string that specifies the query criteria, as well as the class that the query should be parameterized on. The JP QL string refers not to an EMPLOYEE database table but to the Employee entity, so this query is selecting all Employee objects without filtering them any further. You will be diving into queries in Chapter 7, JP QL in Chapters 7 and 8, and criteria queries in Chapter 9. You will see that you can be far more discretionary about which objects you want to be returned.

To execute the query we simply invoke getResultList() on it. This returns a List<Employee> containing the Employee objects that matched the query criteria. Notice that the List is parameterized by Employee since the parameterized type is propagated from the initial class argument passed into the createQuery() method. We can easily create a method that returns all of the employees, as shown in Listing 2-8.

Listing 2-8. Method for Issuing a Query

```java
public List<Employee> findAllEmployees() {
    TypedQuery<Employee> query = em.createQuery("SELECT e FROM Employee e",
                                                Employee.class);
    return query.getResultList();
}
```

This example shows how simple queries are to create, execute, and process, but what this example does not show is how powerful they are. In Chapter 7, you will see many other extremely useful and interesting ways of defining and using queries in an application.

Putting It All Together

We can now take all the methods that we have created and combine them into a class. The class acts like a service class, which we call EmployeeService, and allows us to perform operations on employees. The code should be pretty familiar by now. Listing 2-9 shows the complete implementation.

Listing 2-9. Service Class for Operating on Employee Entities

```java
import javax.persistence.*;
import java.util.List;

public class EmployeeService {
    protected EntityManager em;

    public EmployeeService(EntityManager em) {
        this.em = em;
    }

    public Employee createEmployee(int id, String name, long salary) {
        Employee emp = new Employee(id);
        emp.setName(name);
        emp.setSalary(salary);
        em.persist(emp);
        return emp;
    }

    public void removeEmployee(int id) {
        Employee emp = findEmployee(id);
        if (emp != null) {
            em.remove(emp);
        }
    }
```

```
    public Employee raiseEmployeeSalary(int id, long raise) {
        Employee emp = em.find(Employee.class, id);
        if (emp != null) {
            emp.setSalary(emp.getSalary() + raise);
        }
        return emp;
    }

    public Employee findEmployee(int id) {
        return em.find(Employee.class, id);
    }

    public List<Employee> findAllEmployees() {
        TypedQuery<Employee> query = em.createQuery(
                "SELECT e FROM Employee e", Employee.class);
        return query.getResultList();
    }
}
```

This is a simple yet fully functional class that can be used to issue the typical create, read, update, and delete (CRUD) operations on Employee entities. This class requires that an entity manager is created and passed into it by the caller and also that any required transactions are begun and committed by the caller. It may seem strange at first, but decoupling the transaction logic from the operation logic makes this class more portable to the Java EE environment. We will revisit this example in the next chapter, which focuses on Java EE applications.

A simple main program that uses this service and performs all the required entity manager creation and transaction management is shown in Listing 2-10.

Listing 2-10. Using EmployeeService

```
import javax.persistence.*;
import java.util.List;

public class EmployeeTest {

    public static void main(String[] args) {
        EntityManagerFactory emf =
                Persistence.createEntityManagerFactory("EmployeeService");
        EntityManager em = emf.createEntityManager();
        EmployeeService service = new EmployeeService(em);

        // create and persist an employee
        em.getTransaction().begin();
        Employee emp = service.createEmployee(158, "John Doe", 45000);
        em.getTransaction().commit();
        System.out.println("Persisted " + emp);

        // find a specific employee
        emp = service.findEmployee(158);
        System.out.println("Found " + emp);
```

```
        // find all employees
        List<Employee> emps = service.findAllEmployees();
        for (Employee e : emps)
            System.out.println("Found employee: " + e);

        // update the employee
        em.getTransaction().begin();
        emp = service.raiseEmployeeSalary(158, 1000);
        em.getTransaction().commit();
        System.out.println("Updated " + emp);

        // remove an employee
        em.getTransaction().begin();
        service.removeEmployee(158);
        em.getTransaction().commit();
        System.out.println("Removed Employee 158");

        // close the EM and EMF when done
        em.close();
        emf.close();
    }
}
```

Note that at the end of the program we use the `close()` methods to clean up the entity manager and the factory that we used to create it. This ensures that all the resources they might have allocated are properly released.

Packaging It Up

Now that you know the basic building blocks of JPA, you are ready to organize the pieces into an application that runs in Java SE. The only thing left to discuss is how to put it together so that it runs.

Persistence Unit

The configuration that describes the persistence unit is defined in an XML file called `persistence.xml`. Each persistence unit is named, so when a referencing application wants to specify the configuration for an entity, it needs only to reference the name of the persistence unit that defines that configuration. A single `persistence.xml` file can contain one or more named persistence unit configurations, but each persistence unit is separate and distinct from the others, and they can be logically thought of as being in separate `persistence.xml` files.

Many of the persistence unit elements in the `persistence.xml` file apply to persistence units that are deployed within the Java EE container. The only ones that we need to specify for this example are name, `transaction-type`, class, and properties. There are a number of other elements that can be specified in the persistence unit configuration in the `persistence.xml` file, but they will be discussed in more detail in Chapter 14. Listing 2-11 shows the relevant part of the `persistence.xml` file for this example.

Listing 2-11. Elements in the `persistence.xml` File

```
<persistence>
    <persistence-unit name="EmployeeService"
                      transaction-type="RESOURCE_LOCAL">
        <class>examples.model.Employee</class>
        <properties>
```

```
            <property name="javax.persistence.jdbc.driver"
                      value="org.apache.derby.jdbc.ClientDriver"/>
            <property name="javax.persistence.jdbc.url"
                      value="jdbc:derby://localhost:1527/EmpServDB;create=true"/>
            <property name="javax.persistence.jdbc.user" value="APP"/>
            <property name="javax.persistence.jdbc.password" value="APP"/>
        </properties>
    </persistence-unit>
</persistence>
```

The `name` attribute of the `persistence-unit` element indicates the name of the persistence unit and is the string that we specify when we create the `EntityManagerFactory`. We have used "EmployeeService" as the name. The `transaction-type` attribute indicates that the persistence unit uses resource-level `EntityTransaction` instead of JTA transactions. The `class` element lists the entity that is part of the persistence unit. Multiple `class` elements can be specified when there is more than one entity. They would not normally be needed when deploying in a Java EE container because the container will automatically scan for entity classes annotated with `@Entity` as part of the deployment process, but they are needed for portable execution when running in Java SE. We have only a single `Employee` entity.

The last section is just a list of properties that can be standard or vendor-specific. The JDBC database login parameters must be specified when running in a Java SE environment to tell the provider what resource to connect to. Other provider properties, such as logging options, are vendor-specific and might also be useful.

Persistence Archive

The persistence artifacts are packaged in what we will loosely call a persistence archive. This is really just a JAR-formatted file that contains the `persistence.xml` file in the `META-INF` directory and normally the entity class files.

Because the application is running as a simple Java SE application, all we have to do is put the persistence archive, the application classes that use the entities, and the persistence provider JARs on the classpath when the program is executed.

Summary

This chapter discussed just enough of the basics of the Java Persistence API to develop and run a simple application in a Java SE runtime.

We started out discussing the entity, how to define one, and how to turn an existing Java class into one. We discussed entity managers and how they are obtained and constructed in the Java SE environment.

The next step was to instantiate an entity instance and use the entity manager to persist it in the database. After we inserted a new entity, we could retrieve it again and then remove it. We also made some updates and ensured that the changes were written back to the database.

We talked about the resource-local transaction API and how to use it. We then went over some of the different types of queries and how to define and execute them. Finally, we aggregated all these techniques and combined them into a simple application that we can execute in isolation from an enterprise environment.

In the next chapter, we will look at the impact of the Java EE environment when developing enterprise applications using the Java Persistence API.

CHAPTER 3

■ ■ ■

Enterprise Applications

No technology exists in a vacuum, and JPA is no different in this regard. Although the fat-client style of application demonstrated in the previous chapter is a viable use of JPA, the majority of enterprise Java applications are deployed to an application server, typically using Java EE web technologies, and possibly other technologies as well. Therefore it is essential to understand the components that make up a deployed application and the role of JPA in this environment.

We will begin with an overview of the major Java EE technologies relevant to persistence. As part of this overview, we will describe the EJB component model, demonstrating the basic syntax for some of the different types of EJB's.

We will then go on to briefly cover the standard dependency injection (DI) mechanism, mostly using the Java EE Contexts and Dependency Injection (CDI) approach. This chapter is not intended to be a complete or detailed exploration of Java EE or component frameworks, and we can't possibly go into all of the DI frameworks in the DI-sphere, or even the facilities offered by CDI. However, the CDI and EJB examples are fairly typical of DI in general and should give a general idea of how JPA can be used with DI-enabled components, be they of the Java EE variety or some other DI container component, such as Spring or Guice.

We will then look at transactions, another application server technology that has had a major impact on applications using JPA. Transactions are a fundamental element of any enterprise application that needs to ensure data integrity.

Finally, we will demonstrate how to use the technologies described in this chapter within the context of how persistence integrates into each component technology. We will also revisit the Java SE application from the previous chapter and retarget it to the enterprise platform.

Application Component Models

The word "component" has taken on many meanings in software development, so let's begin with a definition. A component is a self-contained, reusable software unit that can be integrated into an application. Clients interact with components via a well-defined contract. In Java, the simplest form of software component is the JavaBean, commonly referred to as just a bean. Beans are components implemented in terms of a single class whose contract is defined by the naming patterns of the methods on the bean. The JavaBean naming patterns are so common now that it is easy to forget that they were originally intended to give user-interface builders a standard way of dealing with third-party components.

In the enterprise space, components focus more on implementing business services, with the contract of the component defined in terms of the business operations that can be carried out by that component. The traditional component model for Java EE has always been the EJB model, which defines ways to package, deploy, and interact with self-contained business services. Then CDI came along and brought a more powerful and flexible model of managed bean component, with CDI beans being either EJB's or non-EJB Java classes.

Choosing whether or not to use a component model in your application is largely a personal preference, but is generally a good design choice. Using components requires organizing the application into layers, with business services living in the component model and presentation services layered on top of it.

Historically, one of the challenges in adopting components in Java EE was the complexity of implementing them. With that problem largely solved, we are left with the following benefits that a well-defined set of business services brings to an application:

- *Loose coupling*: Using components to implement services encourages loose coupling between layers of an application. The implementation of a component can change without any impact to the clients or other components that depend on it.

- *Dependency management*: Dependencies for a component can be declared in metadata and automatically resolved by the container.

- *Lifecycle management*: The lifecycle of components is well defined and managed by the application server. Component implementations can participate in lifecycle operations to acquire and release resources, or perform other initialization and shutdown behavior.

- *Declarative container services*: Business methods for components are intercepted by the application server in order to apply services such as concurrency, transaction management, security, and remoting.

- *Portability*: Components that comply to Java EE standards and that are deployed to standards-based servers can be more easily ported from one compliant server to another.

- *Scalability and reliability*: Application servers are designed to ensure that components are managed efficiently with an eye to scalability. Depending on the component type and server configuration, business operations implemented using components can retry failed method calls or even fail over to another server in a cluster.

As you read this book, you will notice that in some cases an example will make use of a component to house the business logic and invoke the Java Persistence API. In many cases it will be a session bean, in other cases it will be a non-EJB CDI bean, and in still others it will be a CDI managed session bean (session bean with a scope). Session beans will be the preferred component because they are the simplest to write and configure and a natural fit for interacting with JPA. The actual component type we use is less important (the type of component is largely substitutable as long as it is managed by a container that supports JPA and transactions) than illustrating how components fit in with JPA and can invoke JPA.

Session Beans

Session beans are a component technology designed to encapsulate business services. The client accessible operations supported by the service may be defined using a Java interface, or in the absence of an interface, just the set of public methods on the bean implementation class. The bean class is little more than a regular Java class, and yet, by virtue of being part of the EJB component model, the bean has access to a wide array of container services. The significance of the name session bean has to do with the way in which clients access and interact with them. Once a client acquires a reference to a session bean from the server, it starts a session with that bean and can invoke business operations on it.

There are three types of session bean: stateless, stateful, and singleton. Interaction with a stateless session bean begins at the start of a business method call and ends when the method call completes. There is no state that carries over from one business operation to the other. An interaction with stateful session beans becomes more of a conversation that begins from the moment the client acquires a reference to the session bean and ends when the client explicitly releases it back to the server. Business operations on a stateful session bean can maintain state on the bean instance across calls. We will provide more detail on the implementation considerations of this difference in interaction style as we describe each type of session bean.

Singleton session beans can be considered a hybrid of stateless and stateful session beans. All clients share the same singleton bean instance, so it becomes possible to share state across method invocations, but singleton session beans lack the conversational contract and mobility of stateful session beans. State on a singleton session bean also raises issues of concurrency that need to be taken into consideration when deciding whether or not to use this style of session bean.

As with most component containers, clients in an EJB container do not interact directly with a session bean instance. The client references and invokes an implementation of the business interface or bean class provided by the server. This implementation class acts as a proxy to the underlying bean implementation. This decoupling of client from bean allows the server to intercept method calls in order to provide the services required by the bean, such as transaction management. It also allows the server to optimize and reuse instances of the session bean class as necessary.

In the following sections we will discuss session beans using synchronous business method invocations. Asynchronous business methods offer an alternative invocation pattern involving futures, but are beyond the scope of this book.

Stateless Session Beans

As we mentioned, a stateless session bean sets out to complete an operation within the lifetime of a single method. Stateless beans can implement many business operations, but each method cannot assume that any other was invoked before it.

This might sound like a limitation of the stateless bean, but it is by far the most common form of business service implementation. Unlike stateful session beans, which are good for accumulating state during a conversation (such as the shopping cart of a retail application), stateless session beans are designed to carry out independent operations very efficiently. Stateless session beans can scale to large numbers of clients with minimal impact to overall server resources.

Defining a Stateless Session Bean

A session bean is defined in two parts:

- Zero or more business interfaces that define what methods a client can invoke on the bean. When no interface is defined, the set of public methods on the bean implementation class forms a logical client interface.

- A class that implements these interfaces, called the bean class, which is marked with the @Stateless annotation.

Whether you want to front your session bean with an actual interface or not is a matter of preference. We will show examples of both, but will generally not use the interface in subsequent examples.

Let's first look at an interfaced version of a stateless session bean. Listing 3-1 shows the business interface that will be supported by this session bean. In this example, the service consists of a single method, sayHello(), which accepts a String argument corresponding to a person's name and returns a String response. There is no annotation or parent interface to indicate that this is a business interface. When implemented by the session bean, it will be automatically treated as a local business interface, meaning that it is accessible only to clients within the same application server. A second type of business interface for remote clients is also possible but not often used.

Listing 3-1. The Business Interface for a Session Bean

```
public interface HelloService {
    public String sayHello(String name);
}
```

Now let's consider the implementation, which is shown in Listing 3-2. This is a regular Java class that implements the `HelloService` business interface. The only thing unique about this class is the `@Stateless` annotation[1] that marks it as a stateless session bean. The business method is implemented without any special constraints or requirements. This is a regular class that just happens to be an EJB.

Listing 3-2. The Bean Class Implementing the `HelloService` Interface

```
@Stateless
public class HelloServiceBean implements HelloService {
    public String sayHello(String name) {
        return "Hello, " + name;
    }
}
```

In terms of API design, using an interface is probably the best way to expose a session bean's operations, since it separates the interface from the implementation. However, the current norm is to implement components as simple classes containing the business logic without an interface. Using this approach, the session bean would simply be as shown in Listing 3-3.

Listing 3-3. A Session Bean with No Interface

```
@Stateless
public class HelloService {
    public String sayHello(String name) {
        return "Hello, " + name;
    }
}
```

The logical interface of the session bean consists of its public methods; in this case, the `sayHello()` method. Clients use the `HelloServiceBean` class as if it were an interface, and must disregard any nonpublic methods or details of the implementation. Under the covers, the client will be interacting with a proxy that extends the bean class and overrides the business methods to provide the standard container services.

Lifecycle Callbacks

Unlike a regular Java class used in application code, the server manages the lifecycle of a stateless session bean. The server decides when to create and remove bean instances and has to initialize the services for a bean instance after it is constructed, but before the business logic of the bean is invoked. Likewise, the bean might have to acquire a resource, such as a JDBC data source, before business methods can be used. However, in order for the bean to acquire a resource, the server must first have completed initializing its services for the bean. This limits the usefulness of the constructor for the class because the bean won't have access to any resources until server initialization has completed.

To allow both the server and the bean to achieve their initialization requirements, EJBs support lifecycle callback methods that are invoked by the server at various points in the bean's lifecycle. For stateless session beans, there are two lifecycle callbacks: PostConstruct and PreDestroy. The server will invoke the PostConstruct callback as soon as it has completed initializing all the container services for the bean. In effect, this replaces the constructor as the location for initialization logic because it is only here that container services are guaranteed to be available. The server invokes the PreDestroy callback immediately before the server releases the bean instance to be garbage-collected. Any resources acquired during PostConstruct that require explicit shutdown should be released during PreDestroy.

---

[1] All annotations used in this chapter are defined in the `javax.ejb, javax.inject, javax.enterprise.inject` or `javax.annotation` packages.

Listing 3-4 shows a stateless session bean that acquires a reference to a `java.util.logging.Logger` instance during the PostConstruct callback, identified by the `@PostConstruct` marker annotation. Likewise, a PreDestroy callback is identified by the `@PreDestroy` annotation.

Listing 3-4. Using the PostConstruct Callback to Acquire a Logger

```
@Stateless
public class LoggerBean {
    private Logger logger;

    @PostConstruct
    void init() {
        logger = Logger.getLogger("notification");
    }

    public void logMessage(String message) {
        logger.info(message);
    }
}
```

Stateful Session Beans

In our introduction to session beans, we described the difference between stateless and stateful beans as being based on the interaction style between client and server. In the case of stateless session beans, that interaction started and ended with a single method call. Sometimes clients need to issue multiple requests and have each request be able to access or consider the results of previous requests. Stateful session beans are designed to handle this scenario by providing a dedicated service to a client that starts when the client obtains a reference to the bean and ends only when the client chooses to end the conversation.

The quintessential example of the stateful session bean is the shopping cart of an e-commerce application. The client obtains a reference to the shopping cart, starting the conversation. Over the span of the user session, the client adds or removes items from the shopping cart, which maintains state specific to the client. Then, when the session is complete, the client completes the purchase, causing the shopping cart to be removed.

This is not unlike using a nonmanaged Java object in application code. You create an instance, invoke operations on the object that accumulate state, and then dispose of the object when you no longer need it. The only difference with the stateful session bean is that the server manages the actual object instance and the client interacts with that instance indirectly through a proxy object.

Stateful session beans offer a superset of the functionality available in stateless session beans. The features that we covered for stateless session beans apply equally to stateful session beans.

Defining a Stateful Session Bean

Now that we have established the use case for a stateful session bean, let's look at how to define one. Similar to the stateless session bean, a stateful session bean may or may not have an interface implemented by a single bean class. Listing 3-5 shows the bean class for the `ShoppingCart` stateful session bean. The bean class has been marked with the `@Stateful` annotation to indicate to the server that the class is a stateful session bean.

Listing 3-5. Implementing a Shopping Cart Using a Stateful Session Bean

```
@Stateful
public class ShoppingCart {
    private HashMap<String,Integer> items = new HashMap<String,Integer>();
```

```
    public void addItem(String item, int quantity) {
        Integer orderQuantity = items.get(item);
        if (orderQuantity == null) {
            orderQuantity = 0;
        }
        orderQuantity += quantity;
        items.put(item, orderQuantity);
    }

    public void removeItem(String item, int quantity) {
        // ...
    }

    public Map<String,Integer> getItems() {
        // ...
    }

    // ...

    @Remove
    public void checkout(int paymentId) {
        // store items to database
        // ...
    }

    @Remove
    public void cancel() {
    }
}
```

There are two things different in this bean compared with the stateless session beans we have been dealing with so far.

The first difference is that the bean class has state fields that are modified by the business methods of the bean. This is allowed because the client that uses the bean effectively has access to a private instance of the session bean on which to make changes.

The second difference is that there are methods marked with the @Remove annotation. These are the methods that the client will use to end the conversation with the bean. After one of these methods has been called, the server will destroy the bean instance, and the client reference will throw an exception if any further attempt is made to invoke business methods. Every stateful session bean must define at least one method marked with the @Remove annotation, even if the method doesn't do anything other than serve as an end to the conversation. In Listing 3-5, the checkout() method is called if the user completes the shopping transaction, although cancel() is called if the user decides not to proceed. The session bean is removed in either case.

Lifecycle Callbacks

Like the stateless session bean, the stateful session bean also supports lifecycle callbacks in order to facilitate bean initialization and cleanup. It also supports two additional callbacks to allow the bean to gracefully handle passivation and activation of the bean instance. Passivation is the process by which the server serializes the bean instance so that it can either be stored offline to free up resources or replicated to another server in a cluster. Activation is the process of deserializing a passivated session bean instance and making it active in the server once again. Because stateful session beans hold state on behalf of a client and are not removed until the client invokes one of the remove methods on the bean, the server cannot destroy a bean instance to free up resources. Passivation allows the server to temporarily reclaim resources while preserving session state.

Before a bean is passivated, the server will invoke the PrePassivate callback. The bean uses this callback to prepare the bean for serialization, usually by closing any live connections to other server resources. The PrePassivate method is identified by the @PrePassivate marker annotation. After a bean has been activated, the server will invoke the PostActivate callback. With the serialized instance restored, the bean must then reacquire any connections to other resources that the business methods of the bean might be depending on. The PostActivate method is identified by the @PostActivate marker annotation. Listing 3-6 shows a session bean that makes full use of the lifecycle callbacks to maintain a JDBC connection. Note that only the JDBC Connection is explicitly managed. As a resource connection factory, the server automatically saves and restores the data source during passivation and activation.

Listing 3-6. Using Lifecycle Callbacks on a Stateful Session Bean

```
@Stateful
public class OrderBrowser {
    DataSource ds;
    Connection conn;

    @PostConstruct
    void init() {
        // acquire the data source
        // ...

        acquireConnection();
    }

    @PrePassivate
    void passivate() { releaseConnection(); }

    @PostActivate
    void activate() { acquireConnection(); }

    @PreDestroy
    void shutdown() { releaseConnection(); }

    private void acquireConnection() {
        try {
            conn = ds.getConnection();
        } catch (SQLException e) {
            throw new EJBException(e);
        }
    }

    private void releaseConnection() {
        try {
            conn.close();
        } catch (SQLException e) {
        } finally {
            conn = null;
        }
    }
}
```

```
    public Collection<Order> listOrders() {
        // ...
    }

    @Remove
    public void remove() {}
}
```

Singleton Session Beans

Two of the most common criticisms of the stateless session bean have been the perceived overhead of bean pooling and the inability to share state via static fields. The singleton session bean attempts to provide a solution to both concerns by providing a single shared bean instance that can both be accessed concurrently and used as a mechanism for shared state. Singleton session beans share the same lifecycle callbacks as a stateless session bean, and server-managed resources such as persistence contexts behave the same as if they were part of a stateless session bean. But the similarities end there because singleton session beans have a different overall lifecycle than stateless session beans and have the added complexity of developer-controlled locking for synchronization.

Unlike other session beans, the singleton can be declared to be created eagerly during application initialization and exist until the application shuts down. Once created, it will continue to exist until the container removes it, regardless of any exceptions that occur during business method execution. This is a key difference from other session bean types because the bean instance will never be re-created in the event of a system exception.

The long life and shared instance of the singleton session bean make it the ideal place to store common application state, whether read-only or read-write. To safeguard access to this state, the singleton session bean provides a number of concurrency options depending on the needs of the application developer. Methods can be completely unsynchronized for performance, or automatically locked and managed by the container.

Defining a Singleton Session Bean

Following the pattern of stateless and stateful session beans, singleton session beans are defined using the @Singleton annotation. Singleton session beans can include an interface or use a no-interface view. Listing 3-7 shows a simple singleton session bean with a no-interface view to track the number of visits to a web site.

Listing 3-7. Implementing a Singleton Session Bean

```
@Singleton
public class HitCounter {
    int count;

    public void increment() { ++count; }

    public void getCount() { return count; }

    public void reset() { count = 0; }
}
```

If you compare the HitCounter bean in Listing 3-7 with the stateless and stateful session beans defined earlier, you can see two immediate differences. Unlike the stateless session bean, there is state in the form of a count field used to capture the visit count. But unlike the stateful session bean, there is no @Remove annotation to identify the business method that will complete the session.

By default, the container will manage the synchronization of the business methods to ensure that data corruption does not occur. In this example, that means all access to the bean is serialized so that only one client is invoking a business method on the instance at any time.

The lifecycle of the singleton session bean is tied to the lifecycle of the overall application. The container determines the point when the singleton instance gets created unless the bean class is annotated with the @Startup annotation to force eager initialization when the application starts. The container can create singletons that do not specify eager initialization lazily, but this is vendor-specific and cannot be assumed.

Lifecycle Callbacks

The lifecycle callbacks for singleton session beans are the same as for stateless session beans: PostConstruct and PreDestroy. The container will invoke the PostConstruct callback after server initialization of the bean instance and likewise invoke the PreDestroy callback prior to disposing of the bean instance. The key difference is that for singleton session beans PreDestroy is invoked only when the application shuts down as a whole. It will therefore be called only once, whereas the lifecycle callbacks of stateless session beans are called frequently as bean instances are created and destroyed.

Servlets

Servlets are a component technology designed to serve the needs of web developers who need to respond to HTTP requests and generate dynamic content in return. Servlets are the oldest and most popular technology introduced as part of the Java EE platform. They are the foundation for technologies such as JavaServer Pages (JSP) and the backbone of web frameworks such as JavaServer Faces (JSF).

Although you might have some experience with servlets, it is worth describing the impact that web application models have had on enterprise application development. Because of its reliance on the HTTP protocol, the Web is inherently a stateless medium. Much like the stateless session beans described earlier, a client makes a request, the server triggers the appropriate service method in the servlet, and content is generated and returned to the client. Each request is entirely independent from the last.

This presents a challenge because many web applications involve some kind of conversation between the client and the server in which the previous actions of the user influence the results returned on subsequent pages. To maintain that conversational state, many early applications attempted to dynamically embed context information into URLs. Unfortunately, not only does this technique not scale very well but it also requires a dynamic element to all content generation that makes it difficult for nondevelopers to write content for a web application.

Servlets solve the problem of conversational state with the session. Not to be confused with the session bean, the HTTP session is a map of data associated with a session id. When the application requests that a session be created, the server generates a new id and returns an HTTPSession object that the application can use to store key/value pairs of data. It then uses techniques such as browser cookies to link the session id with the client, tying the two together into a conversation. For web applications, the client is largely ignorant of the conversational state that is tracked by the server.

Using the HTTP session effectively is an important element of servlet development. Listing 3-8 demonstrates the steps required to request a session and store conversational data in it. In this example, assuming that the user has logged in, the servlet stores the user id in the session, making it available for use in all subsequent requests by the same client. The getSession() call on the HttpServletRequest object will either return the active session or create a new one if one does not exist. Once obtained, the session acts like a map, with key/value pairs set and retrieved with the setAttribute() and getAttribute() methods, respectively. As you'll see later in this chapter, the servlet session, which stores unstructured data, is sometimes paired with a stateful session bean to manage session information with the benefit of a well-defined business interface.

Listing 3-8. Maintaining Conversational State with a Servlet

```
public class LoginServlet extends HttpServlet {

    protected void doPost(HttpServletRequest request, HttpServletResponse response)
            throws ServletException, IOException {
        String userId = request.getParameter("user");
        HttpSession session = request.getSession();
        session.setAttribute("user", userId);
        // ...
    }
}
```

The rise of application frameworks targeted to the Web has also changed the way in which we develop web applications. Application code written in servlets is rapidly being replaced with application code further abstracted from the base model using frameworks such as JSF. When working in an environment such as this, basic application persistence issues, such as where to acquire and store the entity manager and how to effectively use transactions quickly, become relevant.

Although we will explore some of these issues, persistence in the context of a framework such as JSF is beyond the scope of this book. As a general solution, we recommend adopting a component model in which to focus persistence operations. Session beans, for example, are easily accessible from anywhere within a Java EE application, making them perfect neutral ground for business services. The ability to exchange entities inside and outside of the session bean model means that the results of persistence operations will be directly usable in web frameworks without having to tightly couple your presentation code to the persistence API.

Dependency Management and CDI

The business logic of a Java EE component is typically not completely self-contained. More often than not, the implementation has dependencies on other resources. This might include server resources, such as a JDBC data source, or application-defined resources, such as another component or entity manager for a specific persistence unit. The core Java EE platform contains some fairly limited support for injecting dependencies into a limited number of predefined server resources, such as data sources, managed transactions, and others. However, the CDI standard goes well beyond simple dependency injection (DI) and provides an extensive framework to support a full range of requirements, from the trivial to the exotic. We will begin by describing the basic concepts and support contained within the platform from before CDI and then move on to CDI and its contextual DI model.

Java EE components support the notion of references to resources. A reference is a named link to a resource that can be resolved dynamically at runtime from within application code or resolved automatically by the container when the component instance is created. We'll cover each of these scenarios shortly.

A reference consists of two parts: a name and a target. The name is used by application code to resolve the reference dynamically, whereas the server uses target information to find the resource the application is looking for. The type of resource to be located determines the type of information required to match the target. Each resource reference requires a different set of information specific to the resource type to which it refers.

A reference is declared using one of the resource reference annotations: @Resource, @EJB, @PersistenceContext, or @PersistenceUnit. These annotations can be placed on a class, field, or setter method. The choice of location determines the default name of the reference, and whether or not the server resolves the reference automatically.

Dependency Lookup

The first strategy for resolving dependencies in application code that we will discuss is called dependency lookup. This is the traditional form of dependency management in Java EE, in which the application code is responsible for looking up a named reference using the Java Naming and Directory Interface (JNDI).

All the resource annotations support an attribute called name that defines the JNDI name of the reference. When the resource annotation is placed on the class definition, this attribute is mandatory. If the resource annotation is placed on a field or a setter method, the server will generate a default name. When using dependency lookup, annotations are typically placed at the class level, and the name is explicitly specified. Placing a resource reference on a field or setter method has other effects besides generating a default name that we will discuss in the next section.

The role of the name is to provide a way for the client to resolve the reference dynamically. Every Java EE application server supports JNDI, even though it is less frequently used by applications since the advent of dependency injection, and each Java EE component has its own locally scoped JNDI naming context called the environment naming context. The name of the reference is bound into the environment naming context, and when it is looked up using the JNDI API, the server resolves the reference and returns the target of the reference.

Consider the DeptService session bean shown in Listing 3-9. It has declared a dependency on a session bean using the @EJB annotation and given it the name "deptAudit." The beanInterface element of the @EJB annotation references the session bean class. In the PostConstruct callback, the audit bean is looked up and stored in the audit field. The Context and InitialContext interfaces are both defined by the JNDI API. The lookup() method of the Context interface is the traditional way to retrieve objects from a JNDI context. To find the reference named deptAudit, the application looks up the name "java:comp/env/deptAudit" and casts the result to AuditService. The prefix "java:comp/env/" that was added to the reference name indicates to the server that the environment naming context should be searched to find the reference. If the name is incorrectly specified, the lookup will fail.

Listing 3-9. Looking Up an EJB Dependency

```
@Stateless
@EJB(name="deptAudit", beanInterface=AuditService.class)
public class DeptService {
    private AuditService audit;

    @PostConstruct
    void init() {
        try {
            Context ctx = new InitialContext();
            audit = (AuditService) ctx.lookup("java:comp/env/deptAudit");
        } catch (NamingException e) {
            throw new EJBException(e);
        }
    }

    // ...
}
```

Using the JNDI API to look up resource references from the environment naming context is supported by all Java EE components. It is, however, a somewhat cumbersome method of finding a resource because of the exception-handling requirements of JNDI. EJBs also support an alternative syntax using the lookup() method of the EJBContext interface. The EJBContext interface (and subinterfaces such as SessionContext) is available to any EJB and provides the bean with access to runtime services such as the timer service. Listing 3-10 shows the same example as Listing 3-9 using the lookup() method. The SessionContext instance in this example is provided via a setter method that is called by the container. We will revisit this example later in the section called "Referencing Server Resources" to see how it is invoked.

Listing 3-10. Using the EJBContext lookup() Method

```
@Stateless
@EJB(name="deptAudit", beanInterface=AuditService.class)
public class DeptService {
```

```
    SessionContext context;
    AuditService audit;

    public void setSessionContext(SessionContext context) {
        this.context = context;
    }

    @PostConstruct
    public void init() {
        audit = (AuditService) context.lookup("deptAudit");
    }

    // ...
}
```

The EJBContext lookup() method has two advantages over the JNDI API. The first is that the argument to the method is the name exactly as it was specified in the resource reference. The second is that only runtime exceptions are thrown from the lookup() method so the checked exception handling of the JNDI API can be avoided. Behind the scenes, the exact same sequence of JNDI API calls from Listing 3-9 is being made, but the JNDI exceptions are handled automatically.

Dependency Injection

When a resource annotation is placed on a field or setter method, two things occur. First, a resource reference is declared just as if it had been placed on the bean class (similar to the way the @EJB annotation worked in the example in Listing 3-9), and the name for that resource will be bound into the environment naming context when the component is created. Second, the server does the lookup automatically on your behalf and sets the result into the instantiated class.

The process of automatically looking up a resource and setting it into the class is called dependency injection because the server is said to inject the resolved dependency into the class. This technique, one of several commonly referred to as inversion of control, removes the burden of manually looking up resources from the JNDI environment context.

Dependency injection is considered a best practice for application development, not only because it reduces the need for JNDI lookups but also because it simplifies testing. Without any JNDI API code in the class that has dependencies on the application server runtime environment, the bean class can be instantiated directly in a unit test. The developer can then manually supply the required dependencies and test the functionality of the class in question instead of worrying about how to work around the JNDI lookup.

Field Injection

The first form of dependency injection is called field injection. Injecting a dependency into a field means that after the server looks up the dependency in the environment naming context, it assigns the result directly into the annotated field of the class. Listing 3-11 revisits the example from Listing 3-9 and demonstrates a simpler use of the @EJB annotation, this time by injecting the result into the audit field. The directory interface code used before is gone, and the business methods of the bean can assume that the audit field holds a reference to the AuditService bean.

Listing 3-11. Using Field Injection

```
@Stateless
public class DeptService {
    @EJB AuditService audit;

    // ...
}
```

Field injection is certainly the easiest to implement, and the examples in this book will always opt to use this form rather than the dynamic lookup form. The only thing to consider with field injection is that if you are planning on unit testing, you need either to add a setter method or make the field accessible to your unit tests to manually satisfy the dependency. Private fields, although legal, require unpleasant hacks if there is no accessible way to set their value. Consider package scope for field injection if you want to unit test without having to add a setter.

We mentioned in the previous section that a name is automatically generated for the reference when a resource annotation is placed on a field or setter method. For completeness, we will describe the format of this name, but it is unlikely that you will find many opportunities to use it. The generated name is the fully qualified class name, followed by a forward slash and then the name of the field or property. This means that if the DeptService bean is located in the persistence.session package, the injected EJB referenced in Listing 3-9 would be accessible in the environment naming context under the name "persistence.session.DeptService/audit". Specifying the name element for the resource annotation will override this default value.

Setter Injection

The second form of dependency injection is called setter injection and involves annotating a setter method instead of a class field. When the server resolves the reference, it will invoke the annotated setter method with the result of the lookup. Listing 3-12 revisits Listing 3-9 one more time to demonstrate using setter injection.

Listing 3-12. Using Setter Injection

```
@Stateless
public class DeptService {
    private AuditService audit;

    @EJB
    public void setAuditService(AuditService audit) {
        this.audit = audit;
    }

    // ...
}
```

This style of injection allows for private fields, yet also works well with unit testing. Each test can simply instantiate the bean class and manually perform the dependency injection by invoking the setter method, usually by providing an implementation of the required resource that is tailored to the test.

Declaring Dependencies

The following sections describe some of the resource annotations described in the Java EE specification. Each annotation has a name attribute for optionally specifying the reference name for the dependency. Other attributes on the annotations are specific to the type of resource that needs to be acquired.

Referencing a Persistence Context

In the previous chapter, we demonstrated how to create an entity manager for a persistence context using an EntityManagerFactory returned from the Persistence class. In the Java EE environment, the @PersistenceContext annotation can be used to declare a dependency on a persistence context and have the entity manager for that persistence context acquired automatically.

Listing 3-13 demonstrates using the @PersistenceContext annotation to acquire an entity manager through dependency injection into a stateless session bean. The unitName element specifies the name of the persistence unit on which the persistence context will be based.

■ **Tip**   If the unitName element is omitted, it is vendor-specific how the unit name for the persistence context is determined. Some vendors can provide a default value if there is only one persistence unit for an application, whereas others might require that the unit name be specified in a vendor-specific configuration file.

Listing 3-13. Injecting an EntityManager Instance

```
@Stateless
public class EmployeeService {
    @PersistenceContext(unitName="EmployeeService")
    EntityManager em;

    // ...
}
```

You might be wondering why a state field exists in a stateless session bean; after all, entity managers must maintain their own state to be able to manage a specific persistence context. The good news is that the specification was designed with container integration in mind, so what actually gets injected in Listing 3-13 is not an entity manager instance like the ones we used in the previous chapter. The value injected into the bean is a container-managed proxy that acquires and releases persistence contexts on behalf of the application code. This is a powerful feature of the Java Persistence API in Java EE and is covered extensively in Chapter 6. For now, it is safe to assume that the injected value will "do the right thing." It does not have to be disposed of and works automatically with the transaction management of the application server. Other containers that support JPA, such as Spring, will offer similar functionality but they will generally require some additional configuration for it to work.

Referencing a Persistence Unit

The EntityManagerFactory for a persistence unit can be referenced using the @PersistenceUnit annotation. Like the @PersistenceContext annotation, the unitName element identifies the persistence unit for the EntityManagerFactory instance we want to access. If the persistent unit name is not specified in the annotation, it is vendor-specific how the name is determined.

Listing 3-14 demonstrates injection of an EntityManagerFactory instance into a stateful session bean. The bean then creates an EntityManager instance from the factory during the PostConstruct lifecycle callback. An injected EntityManagerFactory instance can be safely stored on any component instance. It is thread-safe and does not need to be disposed of when the bean instance is removed.

Listing 3-14. Injecting an EntityManagerFactory Instance

```
@Stateful
public class EmployeeService {
    @PersistenceUnit(unitName="EmployeeService")
    private EntityManagerFactory emf;
    private EntityManager em;

    @PostConstruct
```

```
    public void init() {
        em = emf.createEntityManager();
    }

    // ...
}
```

The `EntityManagerFactory` for a persistence unit is not used as often in the Java EE environment because injected entity managers are easier to acquire and use. As you will see in Chapter 6, there are important differences between the entity managers returned from the factory and the ones provided by the server in response to the `@PersistenceContext` annotation.

Referencing Server Resources

The `@Resource` annotation is the catchall reference for Java EE resource types that don't have dedicated annotations. It is used to define references to resource factories, data sources, and other server resources. The `@Resource` annotation is also the simplest to define because the only additional element is `resourceType`, which allows you to specify the type of resource if the server can't figure it out automatically. For example, if the field you are injecting into is of type `Object`, then there is no way for the server to know that you wanted a data source instead. The `resourceType` element can be set to `javax.sql.DataSource` to make the need explicit.

One of the features of the `@Resource` annotation is that it is used to acquire logical resources specific to the component type. This includes `EJBContext` implementations as well as services such as the EJB timer service. Without defining it as such, we used setter injection to acquire the `EJBContext` instance in Listing 3-10. To make that example complete, the `@Resource` annotation could have been placed on the `setSessionContext()` method. Listing 3-15 revisits the example from Listing 3-10, this time demonstrating field injection with `@Resource` to acquire a `SessionContext` instance.

Listing 3-15. Injecting a `SessionContext` Instance

```
@Stateless
@EJB(name="audit", beanInterface=AuditService.class)
public class DeptService {
    @Resource
    SessionContext context;
    AuditService audit;

    @PostConstruct
    public void init() {
        audit = (AuditService) context.lookup("audit");
    }

    // ...
}
```

CDI and Contextual Injection

While the basic platform injection facilities are helpful, they are clearly limited both in terms of what can be injected and how much control can be exerted over the injection process. CDI provides a more powerful injection standard that first extends the notion of a managed bean and platform resource injection and then goes on to define a set of additional injection services available to beans managed by CDI. Of course, the key characteristic of contextual injection is the ability to inject a given object instance according to the currently active context.

43

The capabilities of CDI are broad and extensive, and obviously well beyond the scope of a book on JPA. For the purposes of this book we'll only scratch the surface and show how to create and use simple CDI beans with qualifiers. We suggest that interested readers refer to some of the many books written about CDI to find out more about interceptors, decorators, events, and the many other features available within a CDI container.

CDI Beans

One of the benefits of EJBs is that it provides all of the services that one might need, from security to automatic transaction management and concurrency control. However, the full service model can be seen as a drawback if you don't use or want some of the services, since the perception is that there is at least some cost associated with having them. Managed beans, and the CDI extensions to them, provide more of a pay-as-you-go model. You only get the services that you specify. Don't be fooled, though, into thinking that CDI beans are any less bulky than a modern EJB. When it comes down to implementation, both types of objects are proxied by the container in pretty much the same way and the service hooks will be added in and triggered as necessary.

What are CDI beans, anyway? A CDI bean is any class that qualifies for the CDI injection services, the primary requirement of which is simply that it be a concrete class.[2] Even session beans can be CDI beans and thus qualify for CDI injection services, although there are some caveats about their lifecycle contexts.

Injection and Resolution

A bean may have its fields or properties be the target of injection if they are annotated by @javax.inject.Inject. CDI defines a sophisticated algorithm for resolving the correct type of object to inject, but in the general case, if you have a field declared of type X, then an instance of X will be injected into it. We can rewrite the example in Listing 3-10 to use simple managed CDI beans instead of EJBs. Listing 3-16 shows the use of the injection annotation on a field. The AuditService instance will get injected after the DeptService instance gets instantiated.

Listing 3-16. CDI Bean with Field Injection

```
public class DeptService {
    @Inject AuditService audit;

    // ...
}
```

The annotation could similarly be placed on a property method to employ setter injection. Yet another way to achieve the same result is to use a third kind of injection called constructor injection. As the name suggests, constructor injection involves the container invoking the constructor method and injecting the arguments. Listing 3-17 shows how constructor injection can be configured. Constructor injection is particularly good for testing outside of the container since a test framework can easily do the necessary injection by simply calling the constructor without having to proxy the object.

Listing 3-17. CDI Bean with Constructor Injection

```
public class DeptService {
    private AuditService audit;

    @Inject DeptService(AuditService audit) {
        this.audit = audit;
    }
    // ...
}
```

---

[2]Non-static inner classes excluded.

Scopes and Contexts

A scope defines a pair of temporal demarcation points: a beginning and an end. For example, a request scope would begin when the request starts and end when the reply has been sent back. Similarly, other scopes define durations based upon client actions and conditions. There are five pre-defined scopes, three of which (request, session, and application) are defined by the servlet specification, one more (conversation) that was added by CDI, and another that was added by the JTA spec:

- *Request*: Delineated by a specific client method request.

- *Session*: Starts on initiation from an HTTP client and ends upon the termination of the HTTP session. Shared by all requests in the same HTTP session.

- *Application*: Global to the entire application for as long as it is active.

- *Conversation*: Spans a series of sequential JSF requests.

- *Transaction*: Maps to the lifetime of an active JTA transaction.

A bean type is associated with a scope by annotating the bean class with the intended scope annotation. Managed instances of that bean will have a lifecycle similar to the declared scope.

Each scope that is active will have a current context associated with it. For example, when a request arrives, a request context will be created for that request scope. Each request will have its own current request context, but there will be a single session scoped context for all of the requests coming from the same HTTP session. The context is just the place where the scoped instances reside for the duration of the scope. There can be only one instance of each bean type in each context.

The application scoped AuditService bean that would be injected into the DeptService bean in Listings 3-16 or 3-17 would look like the following:

```
@ApplicationScoped
public class AuditService { ... }
```

Because it is application scoped, only a single instance would be created by CDI and reside in the application scoped context. Note that this is similar to a singleton EJB in that only a single instance would be created and used by the entire application.

An additional scope, dependent, also exists, but is really the absence of scope. If no scope is specified, then the dependent scope is assumed, meaning that no instances of the bean are put into any context and a new instance is created each time an injection of that bean type occurs. The @Dependent annotation can be used to explicitly mark a bean as being dependent. Scope annotations are defined in the javax.enterprise.context package.

■ **Tip** A beans.xml descriptor was required in CDI 1.0. In CDI 1.1, beans may instead be annotated with a bean-defining annotation (i.e., a scope annotation) to preclude the beans.xml descriptor from being required. In the examples that use CDI, we will make use of scope annotations to avoid having to specify a beans.xml file.

Qualified Injection

A qualifier is an annotation that is used to constrain or distinguish a bean type from other bean types that have the same inherited or implemented interface type. A qualifier can help the container resolve which bean type to inject.

The qualifier annotation class is typically defined by the application and then used to annotate one or more bean classes. The qualifier annotation definition should be annotated with the @Qualifier meta-annotation, defined in the javax.inject package. An example of defining a qualifier annotation is in Listing 3-18.

Listing 3-18. Qualifier Annotation Definition

```
@Qualifier
@Target({METHOD, FIELD, PARAMETER, TYPE})
@Retention(RUNTIME)
public @interface Secure { }
```

This annotation can now be used on a bean class, such as the new SecureDeptService bean shown in Listing 3-19. The qualifier indicates that the bean is a secure variety of DeptService, as opposed to a regular (non-secure?) one.

Listing 3-19. Qualified Bean Class

```
@Secure
public class SecureDeptService extends DeptService { ... }
```

When a DeptService is to be injected into another component, the qualifier can be placed at the injection site and CDI will activate its resolution algorithm to determine which instance to create. It will match the qualifiers to use the SecureDeptService instead of DeptService. Listing 3-20 shows how a servlet, for example, might inject a secure DeptService without even having to know the name of the subclass.

Listing 3-20. Qualified Injection

```
public class LoginServlet extends HttpServlet {

    @Inject @Secure DeptService deptService;
    // ...
}
```

Producer Methods and Fields

When the container needs to inject an instance of a bean type, it will first look in the current contexts to see if one already exists. If it does not find one, then it must obtain or create a new instance. CDI provides a way for the application to control the instance that gets "created" for a given type by using a producer method or field.

A producer method is a method that the CDI container will invoke to obtain a new bean instance. The instance may be instantiated by the producer method or the producer may obtain it through some other means; it is entirely up to the implementation of the producer method how it produces the instance. Producer methods may even decide based on runtime conditions to return a different bean subclass.

A producer method can be annotated with a qualifier. Then when an injection site is similarly qualified, the container will call that correspondingly qualified producer method to obtain the instance.

In Listing 3-21, we show a producer method that returns new secure instances of DeptService. This might be useful, for example, if we were not able to modify the SecureDeptService class to annotate it with the @Secure annotation as we did in Listing 3-19. We could instead declare a producer method that returned instances of SecureDeptService and they would be injected into fields qualified with @Secure (such as the one shown in Listing 3-20). Note that a producer method may be on any managed bean. It may be a static or instance method, but it must be annotated with @Produces. We have created a bean class named ProducerMethods to hold the producer method and separate it from the rest of the application logic.

Listing 3-21. Producer Method

```
public class ProducerMethods {

    @Produces @Secure
    DeptService secureDeptServiceProducer() {
        return new SecureDeptService();
    }
}
```

Producer fields work the same way as producer methods except that the container accesses the field to get the instance instead of invoking a method. It is up to the application to ensure that the field contains an instance when the container needs it. You will see an example of using a producer field in the next section.

Using Producer Methods with JPA Resources

Now that you know some of the basics of CDI, it's time to learn how CDI can be used to help manage JPA persistence units and contexts. You can use a combination of Java EE resource injection with CDI producer fields and qualifiers to inject and maintain your persistence contexts.

Let's assume we have two persistence units, one named "Employee" and the other named "Audit". We want to use CDI beans and contextual injection. We will create a class named EmProducers and use producer fields and Java EE resource injection to obtain the entity managers. The producer code and qualifier annotation definitions are in Listing 3-22.

Listing 3-22. Producer Class and Qualifier Annotation Definitions

```
@RequestScoped
public class EmProducers {

    @Produces @EmployeeEM
    @PersistenceContext(unitName="Employee")
    private EntityManager em1;

    @Produces @AuditEM
    @PersistenceContext(unitName="Audit")
    private EntityManager em2;

}

@Qualifier
@Target({METHOD, FIELD, PARAMETER, TYPE})
@Retention(RUNTIME)
public @interface EmployeeEM { }

@Qualifier
@Target({METHOD, FIELD, PARAMETER, TYPE})
@Retention(RUNTIME)
public @interface AuditEM { }
```

The Java EE @PersistenceContext annotation will cause the Java EE container to inject the producer fields with the entity manager for the given persistence unit. The producer fields will then be used by CDI to obtain the entity manager with the matching qualifier of the injection site. Because the producer class is request scoped, new entity managers will be used for each request. The appropriate scope will obviously depend upon the application architecture. The only thing left to do is to have a bean that is injected with these entity managers. A corresponding `DeptService` bean that references the entity managers is shown in Listing 3-23. A same approach could just as easily be used to inject an entity manager factory using the `@PersistenceUnit` resource annotation.

Listing 3-23. DeptService Bean with Injected `EntityManager` Fields

```
public class DeptService {

    @Inject @EmployeeEM
    private EntityManager empEM;

    @Inject @AuditEM
    private EntityManager auditEM;

    // ...
}
```

In the majority of our examples we will simply use the `@PersistenceContext` annotation since it does not involve any additional producer code. It is also supported by Spring and other kinds of JPA containers, so the bean will be more generic.

Transaction Management

More than any other type of enterprise application, applications that use persistence require careful attention to issues of transaction management. When transactions start, when they end, and how the entity manager participates in container-managed transactions are all essential topics for developers using JPA. The following sections will lay out the foundation for transactions in Java EE; we will revisit this topic in detail again in Chapter 6 as we look at the entity manager and how it participates in transactions. Advanced transaction topics are beyond the scope of this book. We recommend *Java Transaction Processing*[3] for an in-depth discussion on using and implementing transactions in Java, and *Principles of Transaction Processing*[4] for a look at transactions and transaction systems in general.

Transaction Review

A transaction is an abstraction that is used to group together a series of operations. Once grouped together, the set of operations is treated as a single unit, and all of the operations must succeed or none of them can succeed. The consequence of only some of the operations being successful is to produce an inconsistent view of the data that will be harmful or undesirable to the application. The term used to describe whether the operations succeed together or not at all is called atomicity, and it is arguably the most important of the four basic properties that are used to characterize how transactions behave. Understanding these four properties is fundamental to understanding transactions. The following list summarizes these properties:

- *Atomicity*: Either all the operations in a transaction are successful or none of them are. The success of every individual operation is tied to the success of the entire group.

- *Consistency*: The resulting state at the end of the transaction adheres to a set of rules that define acceptability of the data. The data in the entire system is legal or valid with respect to the rest of the data in the system.

---

[3]Little, Mark, Jon Maron, and Greg Pavlik. *Java Transaction Processing: Design and Implementation.* Upper Saddle River, N.J.: Prentice Hall PTR, 2004.

[4]Bernstein, Philip A., and Eric Newcomer. *Principles of Transaction Processing.* Burlington, MA: Morgan Kaufmann, 2009.

- *Isolation*: Changes made within a transaction are visible only to the transaction that is making the changes. Once a transaction commits the changes, they are atomically visible to other transactions.

- *Durability*: The changes made within a transaction endure beyond the completion of the transaction.

A transaction that meets all these requirements is said to be an ACID transaction (the familiar ACID term being obtained by combining the first letter of each of the four properties).

Not all transactions are ACID transactions, and those that are often offer some flexibility in the fulfillment of the ACID properties. For example, the isolation level is a common setting that can be configured to provide either looser or tighter degrees of isolation than what was described earlier. They are typically done for reasons of either increased performance or, on the other side of the spectrum, if an application has more stringent data consistency requirements. The transactions that we discuss in the context of Java EE are normally of the ACID variety.

Enterprise Transactions in Java

Transactions actually exist at different levels within the enterprise application server. The lowest and most basic transaction is at the level of the resource, which in our discussion is assumed to be a relational database fronted by a DataSource interface. This is called a resource-local transaction and is equivalent to a database transaction. These types of transactions are manipulated by interacting directly with the JDBC DataSource that is obtained from the application server. Resource-local transactions are used less frequently in servers than container transactions.

The broader container transaction uses the Java Transaction API (JTA) that is available in every compliant Java EE application server and most of the Java-based web servers. This is the typical transaction that is used for enterprise applications and can involve or enlist a number of resources, including data sources as well as other types of transactional resources. Resources defined using Java Connector Architecture (JCA) components can also be enlisted in the container transaction.

Containers typically add their own layer on top of the JDBC DataSource to perform functions such as connection management and pooling that make more efficient use of the resources and provide a seamless integration with the transaction management system. This is also necessary because it is the responsibility of the container to perform the commit or rollback operation on the data source when the container transaction completes.

Because container transactions use JTA and because they can span multiple resources, they are also called JTA transactions or global transactions. The container transaction is a central aspect of programming within Java servers.

Transaction Demarcation

Every transaction has a beginning and an end. Beginning a transaction will allow subsequent operations to become a part of the same transaction until the transaction has completed. Transactions can be completed in one of two ways. They can be committed, causing all of the changes to be persisted to the data store, or rolled back, indicating that the changes should be discarded. The act of causing a transaction to either begin or complete is termed transaction demarcation. This is a critical part of writing enterprise applications, because doing transaction demarcation incorrectly is one of the most common sources of performance degradation.

Resource-local transactions are always demarcated explicitly by the application, whereas container transactions can either be demarcated automatically by the container or by using a JTA interface that supports application-controlled demarcation. The first case, when the container takes over the responsibility of transaction demarcation, is called container-managed transaction (CMT) management, but when the application is responsible for demarcation, it's called bean-managed transaction (BMT) management.

EJBs can use either container-managed transactions or bean-managed transactions. Servlets are limited to the somewhat poorly named bean-managed transaction. The default transaction management style for an EJB component is container-managed. To explicitly configure an EJB to have its transactions demarcated one way or the other, the @TransactionManagement annotation should be specified on the EJB class. The TransactionManagementType enumerated type defines BEAN for bean-managed transactions and CONTAINER for container-managed transactions. Listing 3-24 demonstrates how to enable bean-managed transactions using this approach.

Listing 3-24. Changing the Transaction Management Type of an EJB

```
@Stateless
@TransactionManagement(TransactionManagementType.BEAN)
public class ProjectService {
    // methods in this class manually control transaction demarcation
}
```

■ **Note**   Because the default transaction management for an EJB is container-managed, the @TransactionManagement annotation needs to be specified only if bean-managed transactions are desired.

Container-managed Transactions

The most common way to demarcate transactions is to use CMTs, which spare the application the effort and code to begin and commit transactions explicitly.

Transaction requirements are determined by metadata and are configurable at the granularity of the class or even a method. For example, a session bean can declare that whenever any specific method on that bean gets invoked, the container must ensure that a transaction is started before the method begins. The container is also responsible for committing the transaction after the completion of the method.

It is quite common for one bean to invoke another bean from one or more of its methods. In this case, a transaction started by the calling method will not have been committed because the calling method will not be completed until its call to the second bean has completed. This is why we need settings to define how the container should behave when a method is invoked within a specific transactional context.

For example, if a transaction is already in progress when a method is called, the container might be expected to just make use of that transaction, whereas it might be directed to start a new one if no transaction is active. These settings are called transaction attributes, and they determinethe container-managed transactional behavior.

The defined transaction attribute choices are as follows:

- MANDATORY: If this attribute is specified for a method, a transaction is expected to have already been started and be active when the method is called. If no transaction is active, an exception is thrown. This attribute is seldom used, but can be a development tool to catch transaction demarcation errors when it is expected that a transaction should already have been started.

- REQUIRED: This attribute is the most common case in which a method is expected to be in a transaction. The container provides a guarantee that a transaction is active for the method. If one is already active, it is used; if one does not exist, a new transaction is created for the method execution.

- REQUIRES_NEW: This attribute is used when the method always needs to be in its own transaction; that is, the method should be committed or rolled back independently of methods further up the call stack. It should be used with caution because it can lead to excessive transaction overhead.

- SUPPORTS: Methods marked with supports are not dependent on a transaction, but will tolerate running inside one if it exists. This is an indicator that no transactional resources are accessed in the method.

- NOT_SUPPORTED: A method marked to not support transactions will cause the container to suspend the current transaction if one is active when the method is called. It implies that the method does not perform transactional operations, but might fail in other ways that could undesirably affect the outcome of a transaction. This is not a commonly used attribute.

- NEVER: A method marked to never support transactions will cause the container to throw an exception if a transaction is active when the method is called. This attribute is very seldom used, but can be a development tool to catch transaction demarcation errors when it is expected that transactions should already have been completed.

Any time the container starts a transaction for a method, the container is assumed to also attempt to commit the transaction at the end of the method. Each time the current transaction must be suspended, the container is responsible for resuming the suspended transaction at the conclusion of the method.

There are actually two different ways of specifying container-managed transactions, one for EJBs and one for CDI beans, servlets, JAX-RS resource classes, and all other types of Java EE managed components. EJBs were the first component type to offer a container-managed transaction feature and defined specific metadata for the purpose. CDI beans and other types of Java EE components, such as servlets or JAX-RS resource classes, make use of a transactional interceptor.

EJB Container-managed Transactions

The transaction attribute for an EJB can be indicated by annotating the EJB class, or one of its methods that is part of the optional business interface, with the @TransactionAttribute annotation. This annotation requires a single argument of the enumerated type TransactionAttributeType, the values of which are defined in the preceding list. Annotating the bean class will cause the transaction attribute to apply to all of the business methods in the class, whereas annotating a method applies the attribute only to the method. If both class-level and method-level annotations exist, the method-level annotation takes precedence. In the absence of class-level or method-level @TransactionAttribute annotations, the default attribute of REQUIRED will be applied.

Listing 3-25 shows how the addItem()method from the shopping cart bean in Listing 3-5 might use a transaction attribute. No transaction management setting was supplied, so container-managed transactions will be used. No attribute was specified on the class, so the default behavior of REQUIRED will apply to all the methods of the class. The exception is that the addItem() method has declared a transaction attribute of SUPPORTS, which overrides the REQUIRED setting. Whenever a call to add an item is made, that item will be added to the cart, but if no transaction was active none will need to be started.

Listing 3-25. Specifying an EJB Transaction Attribute

```
@Stateful
public class ShoppingCart {

    @TransactionAttribute(TransactionAttributeType.SUPPORTS)
    public void addItem(String item, Integer quantity) {
        verifyItem(item, quantity);
        // ...
    }

    // ...
}
```

Furthermore, before the addItem() method adds the item to the cart, it does some validation in a private method called verifyItem() that is not shown in the example. When this method is invoked from addItem(), it will run in whatever transactional context addItem() was invoked.

Any bean wanting to cause a container-managed transaction to roll back can do so by invoking the setRollbackOnly() method on the EJBContext object. Although this will not cause the immediate rollback of the transaction, it is an indication to the container that the transaction should be rolled back when the transaction completes. Note that entity managers will also cause the current transaction to be set to roll back when an exception is thrown during an entity manager invocation or when the transaction completes.

Transactional Interceptors

When interceptors were introduced to the Java EE 6 platform, they opened up the future possibility of decoupling the container-managed transaction facility from EJB and offering it to any component that supported interception. In Java EE 7, the @javax.transaction.Transactional annotation was added as a means to specify that a transactional interceptor would be applied to the target component. The mechanism acts similarly to EJB container-managed transactions in that it is declaratively applied on a class or method and a class semantic can be overridden by a method-based one. The main difference is that the @Transactional annotation is used instead of @TransactionAttribute, and the type of the enumerated value is a nested enum called Transactional.TxType instead of the TransactionAttributeType used in EJB. The enum constants in the list above are named exactly the same in Transactional.TxType and have the same semantics.

Perhaps the most relevant difference between transactional interceptor-based components and EJB CMT is the fact that the components that use transactional interceptors do not automatically get CMT but must opt in by using the @Transactional annotation. EJBs get CMT by default and must opt out if they prefer to use BMT.

We can now rewrite Listing 3-25 to use a CDI bean instead of a stateful session bean. The ShoppingCart bean in Listing 3-26 is session scoped so that its state is maintained throughout the session. The empty @Transactional annotation causes the default transactionality to be set to REQUIRED for all of the methods in the class, except for the addItem() method that is explicitly overridden to be SUPPORTS.

Listing 3-26. Transactional Interceptor in a CDI Bean

```
@Transactional
@SessionScoped
public class ShoppingCart {

    @Transactional(TxType.SUPPORTS)
    public void addItem(String item, Integer quantity) {
        verifyItem(item, quantity);
        // ...
    }

    // ...
}
```

■ **Tip** @Transactional can be used on managed beans or CDI beans but may not be used on EJBs. Conversely, @TransactionAttribute can only be used on EJBs.

Bean-managed Transactions

Another way of demarcating transactions is to use BMTs. This just means that the application needs to start and stop transactions explicitly by making API calls. With the exception of EJBs, all managed components default to using bean-managed transactions and are left to do their own transaction demarcation if they don't specify the @Transactional interceptor. Only EJBs are provided container-managed transactions by default.

Declaring that an EJB is using bean-managed transactions means that the bean class is assuming the responsibility to begin and commit the transactions whenever it deems it is necessary. With this responsibility, however, comes the expectation that the bean class will get it right. EJBs that use BMT must ensure that any time a transaction has been started, it must also be completed before returning from the method that started it. Failure to do so will result in the container rolling back the transaction automatically and an exception being thrown.

One penalty of transactions being managed by the EJBs instead of by the container is that they do not get propagated to methods called on another BMT EJB. For example, if EJB A begins a transaction and then calls EJB B, which is using bean-managed transactions, the transaction will not get propagated to the method in EJB B. Any time a transaction is active when a BMT EJB method is invoked, the active transaction will be suspended until control returns to the calling method. This is not true for non-EJB components.

BMT is not generally recommended for use in EJBs because it adds complexity to the application and requires the application to do work that the server can already do for it. While other types of components can use transactional interceptors if they choose, they do not have the same BMT restrictions that EJBs have, so it is more common for them to adopt an application-controlled BMT approach. They have also traditionally used BMT because there was never really a choice in the past. It was only recently, in Java EE 7, that transaction interceptors were introduced.

UserTransaction

For a component to be able to manually begin and commit container transactions, the application must have an interface that supports it. The javax.transaction.UserTransaction interface is the designated object in JTA that application components can hold on to and invoke to manage transaction boundaries. An instance of UserTransaction is not actually the current transaction instance; it is a sort of proxy that provides the transaction API and represents the current transaction. A UserTransaction instance can be injected into components by using either of the Java EE @Resource or CDI @Inject annotations. A UserTransaction is also present in the environment naming context under the reserved name "java:comp/UserTransaction". The UserTransaction interface is shown in Listing 3-27.

Listing 3-27. The UserTransaction Interface

```
public interface UserTransaction {
    public abstract void begin();
    public abstract void commit();
    public abstract int getStatus();
    public abstract void rollback();
    public abstract void setRollbackOnly();
    public abstract void setTransactionTimeout(int seconds);
}
```

Each JTA transaction is associated with an execution thread, so it follows that no more than one transaction can be active at any given time. So if one transaction is active, the user cannot start another one in the same thread until the first one has committed or rolled back. Alternatively, the transaction can time out, causing the transaction to roll back.

We discussed earlier that in certain CMT conditions the container will suspend the current transaction. From the previous API, you can see that there is no UserTransaction method for suspending a transaction. Only the container can do this using an internal transaction management API. In this way, multiple transactions can be associated with a single thread, even though only one can ever be active at a time.

Rollbacks can occur in several different scenarios. The setRollbackOnly() method indicates that the current transaction cannot be committed, leaving rollback as the only possible outcome. The transaction can be rolled back immediately by calling the rollback() method. Alternately, a time limit for the transaction can be set with the setTransactionTimeout() method, causing the transaction to roll back when the limit is reached. The only catch with transaction timeouts is that the time limit must be set before the transaction starts and it cannot be changed once the transaction is in progress.

In JTA, every thread has a transactional status that can be accessed through the getStatus() call. The return value of this method is one of the constants defined on the javax.transaction.Status interface. If no transaction is active, for example, then the value returned by getStatus() will be the STATUS_NO_TRANSACTION. Likewise, if setRollbackOnly() has been called on the current transaction, then the status will be STATUS_MARKED_ROLLBACK until the transaction has begun rolling back.

Listing 3-28 shows a fragment from a servlet using the ProjectService bean to demonstrate using UserTransaction to invoke multiple EJB methods within a single transaction. The doPost() method uses the UserTransaction instance injected with the @Resource annotation to start and commit a transaction. Note the try ... catch block required around the transaction operations to ensure that the transaction is correctly cleaned up in the event of a failure. We catch the exception and then rethrow it within a runtime exception after we perform the rollback.

Listing 3-28. Using the UserTransaction Interface

```
public class ProjectServlet extends HttpServlet {
    @Resource UserTransaction tx;
    @EJB ProjectService bean;

    protected void doPost(HttpServletRequest request, HttpServletResponse response)
        throws ServletException, IOException {
        // ...

        try {
            tx.begin();
            bean.assignEmployeeToProject(projectId, empId);
            bean.updateProjectStatistics();
            tx.commit();
        } catch (Exception e) {
            // Try to roll back (may fail if exception came from begin() or commit(), but that's ok)
            try { tx.rollback(); } catch (Exception e2) {}
            throw new MyRuntimeException(e);
        }

        // ...
    }
}
```

Putting It All Together

Now that we have discussed the application component model and services available as part of a Java EE application server, we can revisit the EmployeeService example from the previous chapter and bring it to the Java EE environment. Along the way, we'll provide example code to show how the components fit together and how they relate back to the Java SE example.

Defining the Component

To begin, let's consider the definition of the EmployeeService class from Listing 2-9 in Chapter 2. The goal of this class is to provide business operations related to the maintenance of employee data. In doing so, it encapsulates all the persistence operations. To introduce this class into the Java EE environment, we must first decide how it should be represented. The service pattern exhibited by the class suggests a session bean or similar component. Because the business methods of the bean have no dependency on each other, we can further decide that any stateless bean, such as a stateless session bean, is suitable. In fact, this bean demonstrates a very typical design pattern called a session façade[5], in which a stateless session bean is used to shield clients from dealing with a particular persistence API. To turn the EmployeeService class into a stateless session bean we need only annotate it with @Stateless.

In the Java SE example, the EmployeeService class must create and maintain its own entity manager instance. We can replace this logic with dependency injection to acquire the entity manager automatically. Having decided on a stateless session bean and dependency injection, the converted stateless session bean is demonstrated in Listing 3-29. With the exception of how the entity manager is acquired, the rest of the class is identical. This is an important feature of the Java Persistence API because the same EntityManager interface can be used both inside and outside of the application server.

Listing 3-29. The EmployeeService Session Bean

```java
@Stateless
public class EmployeeService {
    @PersistenceContext(unitName="EmployeeService")
    protected EntityManager em;

    EntityManager getEntityManager() {
        return em;
    }

    public Employee createEmployee(int id, String name, long salary) {
        Employee emp = new Employee(id);
        emp.setName(name);
        emp.setSalary(salary);
        getEntityManager().persist(emp);
        return emp;
    }

    public void removeEmployee(int id) {
        Employee emp = findEmployee(id);
        if (emp != null) {
            getEntityManager().remove(emp);
        }
    }

    public Employee changeEmployeeSalary(int id, long newSalary) {
        Employee emp = findEmployee(id);
        if (emp != null) {
            emp.setSalary(newSalary);
        }
        return emp;
    }

    public Employee findEmployee(int id) {
        return getEntityManager().find(Employee.class, id);
    }
```

---

[5]Alur et al., *Core J2EE Patterns*.

```
    public List<Employee> findAllEmployees() {
        TypedQuery query = getEntityManager().createQuery("SELECT e FROM Employee e", Employee.class);
        return query.getResultList();
    }
}
```

Defining the User Interface

The next question to consider is how the bean will be accessed. A web interface is a common presentation method for enterprise applications. To demonstrate how this stateless session bean might be used by a servlet, consider Listing 3-30. The request parameters are interpreted to determine the action, which is then carried out by invoking methods on the injected EmployeeService bean. Although only the first action is described, you can see how this could easily be extended to handle each of the operations defined on EmployeeService.

Listing 3-30. Using the EmployeeService Session Bean from a Servlet

```
public class EmployeeServlet extends HttpServlet {
    @EJB EmployeeService bean;

    protected void doPost(HttpServletRequest request,
                          HttpServletResponse response) {
        String action = request.getParameter("action");

        if (action.equals("create")) {
            String id = request.getParameter("id");
            String name = request.getParameter("name");
            String salary = request.getParameter("salary");
            bean.createEmployee(Integer.parseInt(id), name,
                                Long.parseLong(salary));
        }

        // ...
    }
}
```

Packaging It Up

In the Java EE environment, many properties required in the persistence.xml file for Java SE can be omitted. In Listing 3-31, you see the persistence.xml file from Listing 2-11 converted for deployment as part of a Java EE application. Instead of JDBC properties for creating a connection, we now declare that the entity manager should use the data source name "jdbc/EmployeeDS". If the data source was defined to be available in the application namespace instead of the local component naming context, then we might instead use the data source name of "java:app/jdbc/EmployeeDS". The transaction-type attribute has also been removed to allow the persistence unit to default to JTA. The application server will automatically find entity classes, so even the list of classes has been removed. This example represents the ideal minimum Java EE configuration.

Because the business logic that uses this persistence unit is implemented in a stateless session bean, the persistence.xml file would typically be located in the META-INF directory of the corresponding EJB JAR, or the WEB-INF/classes/META-INF directory of the WAR. We will fully describe the persistence.xml file and its placement within a Java EE application in Chapter 14.

Listing 3-31. Defining a Persistence Unit in Java EE

```
<persistence>
    <persistence-unit name="EmployeeService">
        <jta-data-source>jdbc/EmployeeDS</jta-data-source>
    </persistence-unit>
</persistence>
```

Summary

It would be impossible to provide details on all of the features of the Java EE platform in a single chapter. However, we cannot put JPA in context without explaining the application server environment in which it will be used. To this end, we introduced the technologies that are of the most relevance to the developer using persistence in enterprise applications.

We began with an introduction to enterprise software components and introduced the EJB component model. We argued that the use of components is more important than ever before and identified some of the benefits that come from leveraging them. We introduced the fundamentals of stateless, stateful, and singleton session beans and showed the syntax for declaring them as well as the difference in interaction style between them.

We next looked at dependency management in Java EE application servers. We discussed the reference annotation types and how to declare them. We also looked at the difference between dependency lookup and dependency injection. In the case of injection, we looked at the difference between field and setter injection. We then explored each of the resource types, demonstrating how to acquire and inject server and JPA resources.

Building on the foundation of Java EE resource injection, we went on to introduce the CDI model with its generalized notion of a managed bean. We listed the predefined scopes and explained the contexts that CDI uses to cache the contextual instances it injects. We showed how qualifiers can contribute additional constraints to the injection resolution process and how producers can be defined to return the instances the CDI container uses for injection. We then demonstrated a way to use producers to inject qualified persistence resources.

In the section on transaction management, we looked at JTA and its role in building data-centric applications. We then looked at the difference between bean-managed transactions and container-managed transactions for EJBs and non-EJBs. We documented the different types of transaction attributes for CMT beans and showed how to manually control bean-managed transactions.

We concluded the chapter by exploring how to use Java EE components with JPA by converting the example application introduced in the previous chapter from a command-line Java SE application to a web-based application running in an application server.

Now that we have introduced JPA in both the Java SE and Java EE environments, it's time to dive into the specification in detail. In the next chapter we begin this journey with the central focus of JPA: object-relational mapping.

■ ■ ■

CHAPTER 4

Object-Relational Mapping

The largest part of an API that persists objects to a relational database ends up being the object-relational mapping (ORM) component. The topic of ORM usually includes everything from how the object state is mapped to the database columns to how to issue queries across the objects. We are focusing this chapter primarily on how to define and map entity state to the database, emphasizing the simple manner in which it can be done.

This chapter will introduce the basics of mapping fields to database columns and then go on to show how to map and automatically generate entity identifiers. We will go into some detail about different kinds of relationships and illustrate how they are mapped from the domain model to the data model.

Persistence Annotations

We have shown in previous chapters how annotations have been used extensively both in the EJB and JPA specifications. We will discuss persistence and mapping metadata in significant detail, and because we use annotations to explain the concepts, it is worth reviewing a few things about the annotations before we get started.

Persistence annotations can be applied at three different levels: class, method, and field. To annotate any of these levels, the annotation must be placed in front of the code definition of the artifact being annotated. In some cases, we will put them on the same line just before the class, method, or field; in other cases, we will put them on the line above. The choice is based completely on the preferences of the person applying the annotations, and we think it makes sense to do one thing in some cases and the other in other cases. It depends on how long the annotation is and what the most readable format seems to be.

The JPA annotations were designed to be readable, easy to specify, and flexible enough to allow different combinations of metadata. Most annotations are specified as siblings instead of being nested inside each other, meaning that multiple annotations can annotate the same class, field, or property instead of having annotations embedded within other annotations. As with all trade-offs, the piper must be paid, however, and the cost of flexibility is that many possible permutations of top-level metadata will be syntactically correct but semantically invalid. The compiler will be of no use, but the provider runtime will often do some basic checking for improper annotation groupings. The nature of annotations, however, is that when they are unexpected, they will often just not get noticed at all. This is worth remembering when attempting to understand behavior that might not match what you thought you specified in the annotations. It could be that one or more of the annotations are being ignored.

The mapping annotations can be categorized as being in one of two categories: logical annotations and physical annotations. The annotations in the logical group are those that describe the entity model from an object modeling view. They are tightly bound to the domain model and are the sort of metadata that you might want to specify in UML or any other object modeling language or framework. The physical annotations relate to the concrete data model in the database. They deal with tables, columns, constraints, and other database-level artifacts that the object model might never be aware of otherwise.

We will make use of both types of annotations throughout the examples and to demonstrate the mapping metadata. Understanding and being able to distinguish between these two levels of metadata will help you to make decisions about where to declare metadata, and where to use annotations and XML. As you will see in Chapter 13, there are XML equivalents to all the mapping annotations described in this chapter, giving you the freedom to use the approach that best suits your development needs.

Accessing Entity State

The mapped state of an entity must be accessible to the provider at runtime, so that when it comes time to write the data out, it can be obtained from the entity instance and stored in the database. Similarly, when the state is loaded from the database, the provider runtime must be able to insert it into a new entity instance. The way the state is accessed in the entity is called the access mode.

In Chapter 2, you learned that there are two different ways to specify persistent entity state: you can either annotate the fields or annotate the JavaBean-style properties. The mechanism that you use to designate the persistent state is the same as the access mode that the provider uses to access that state. If you annotate fields, the provider will get and set the fields of the entity using reflection. If the annotations are set on the getter methods of properties, those getter and setter methods will be invoked by the provider to access and set the state.

Field Access

Annotating the fields of the entity will cause the provider to use field access to get and set the state of the entity. Getter and setter methods might or might not be present, but if they are present, they are ignored by the provider. All fields must be declared as either protected, package, or private. Public fields are disallowed because it would open up the state fields to access by any unprotected class in the JVM. Doing so is not just an obviously bad practice but could also defeat the provider implementation. Of course, the other qualifiers do not prevent classes within the same package or hierarchy from doing the same thing, but there is an obvious trade-off between what should be constrained and what should be recommended. Other classes must use the methods of an entity in order to access its persistent state, and even the entity class itself should only really manipulate the fields directly during initialization.

The example in Listing 4-1 shows the Employee entity being mapped using field access. The @Id annotation indicates not only that the id field is the persistent identifier or primary key for the entity but also that field access should be assumed. The name and salary fields are then defaulted to being persistent, and they get mapped to columns of the same name.

Listing 4-1. Using Field Access

```
@Entity
public class Employee {
    @Id private long id;
    private String name;
    private long salary;

    public long getId() { return id; }
    public void setId(long id) { this.id = id; }

    public String getName() { return name; }
    public void setName(String name) { this.name = name; }

    public long getSalary() { return salary; }
    public void setSalary(long salary) { this.salary = salary; }
}
```

Property Access

When property access mode is used, the same contract as for JavaBeans applies, and there must be getter and setter methods for the persistent properties. The type of property is determined by the return type of the getter method and must be the same as the type of the single parameter passed into the setter method. Both methods must be either public or protected visibility. The mapping annotations for a property must be on the getter method.

In Listing 4-2, the Employee class has an @Id annotation on the getId() getter method so the provider will use property access to get and set the state of the entity. The name and salary properties will be made persistent by virtue of the getter and setter methods that exist for them, and will be mapped to NAME and SALARY columns, respectively. Note that the salary property is backed by the wage field, which does not share the same name. This goes unnoticed by the provider because by specifying property access, we are telling the provider to ignore the entity fields and use only the getter and setter methods for naming.

Listing 4-2. Using Property Access

```
@Entity
public class Employee {
    private long id;
    private String name;
    private long wage;

    @Id public long getId() { return id; }
    public void setId(long id) { this.id = id; }

    public String getName() { return name; }
    public void setName(String name) { this.name = name; }

    public long getSalary() { return wage; }
    public void setSalary(long salary) { this.wage = salary; }
}
```

Mixed Access

It is also possible to combine field access with property access within the same entity hierarchy, or even within the same entity. This will not be a very common occurrence, but can be useful, for example, when an entity subclass is added to an existing hierarchy that uses a different access type. Adding an @Access annotation with a specified access mode on the subclass entity will cause the default access type to be overridden for that entity subclass.

The @Access annotation is also useful when you need to perform a simple transformation to the data when reading from or writing to the database. Usually you will want to access the data through field access, but in this case you will define a getter/setter method pair to perform the transformation and use property access for that one attribute. In general, there are three essential steps to add a persistent field or property to be accessed differently from the default access mode for that entity.

Consider an Employee entity that has a default access mode of FIELD, but the database column stores the area code as part of the phone number, and we only want to store the area code in the entity phoneNum field if it is not a local number. We can add a persistent property that transforms it accordingly on reads and writes.

The first thing that must be done is to explicitly mark the default access mode for the class by annotating it with the @Access annotation and indicating the access type. Unless this is done, it will be undefined if both fields and properties are annotated. We would tag our Employee entity as having FIELD access:

```
@Entity
@Access(AccessType.FIELD)
public class Employee { ... }
```

The next step is to annotate the additional field or property with the @Access annotation, but this time specifying the opposite access type from what was specified at the class level. It might seem a little redundant, for example, to specify the access type of AccessType.PROPERTY on a persistent property because it is obvious by looking at it that it is a property, but doing so indicates that what you are doing is not an oversight, but a conscious exception to the default case.

```
@Access(AccessType.PROPERTY) @Column(name="PHONE")
protected String getPhoneNumberForDb() { ... }
```

The final thing to remember is that the corresponding field or property to the one being made persistent must be marked as transient so that the default accessing rules do not cause the same state to be persisted twice. For example, because we are adding a persistent property to an entity for which the default access type is through fields, the field in which the persistent property state is being stored in the entity must be annotated with @Transient:

```
@Transient private String phoneNum;
```

Listing 4-3 shows the complete Employee entity class annotated to use property access for only one property.

Listing 4-3. Using Combined Access

```
@Entity
@Access(AccessType.FIELD)
public class Employee {

    public static final String LOCAL_AREA_CODE = "613";

    @Id private long id;
    @Transient private String phoneNum;
    ...
    public long getId() { return id; }
    public void setId(long id) { this.id = id; }

    public String getPhoneNumber() { return phoneNum; }
    public void setPhoneNumber(String num) { this.phoneNum = num; }

    @Access(AccessType.PROPERTY) @Column(name="PHONE")
    protected String getPhoneNumberForDb() {
        if (phoneNum.length() == 10)
            return phoneNum;
        else
            return LOCAL_AREA_CODE + phoneNum;
    }
    protected void setPhoneNumberForDb(String num) {
        if (num.startsWith(LOCAL_AREA_CODE))
            phoneNum = num.substring(3);
        else
            phoneNum = num;
    }
    ...
}
```

Mapping to a Table

You saw in Chapter 2 that in the simplest case, mapping an entity to a table does not need any mapping annotations at all. Only the @Entity and @Id annotations need to be specified to create and map an entity to a database table.

In those cases, the default table name, which was just the unqualified name of the entity class, was perfectly suitable. If it happens that the default table name is not the name that you like, or if a suitable table that contains the state already exists in your database with a different name, you must specify the name of the table. You do this by annotating the entity class with the @Table annotation and including the name of the table using the name element. Many databases have terse names for tables. Listing 4-4 shows an entity that is mapped to a table that has a name different from its class name.

Listing 4-4. Overriding the Default Table Name

```
@Entity
@Table(name="EMP")
public class Employee { ... }
```

■ **Tip** Default names are not specified to be either uppercase or lowercase. Most databases are not case-sensitive, so it won't generally matter whether a vendor uses the case of the entity name or converts it to uppercase. In Chapter 10, we discuss how to delimit database identifiers when the database is set to be case-sensitive.

The @Table annotation provides the ability to not only name the table that the entity state is being stored in but also to name a database schema or catalog. The schema name is commonly used to differentiate one set of tables from another and is indicated by using the schema element. Listing 4-5 shows an Employee entity that is mapped to the EMP table in the HR schema.

Listing 4-5. Setting a Schema

```
@Entity
@Table(name="EMP", schema="HR")
public class Employee { ... }
```

When specified, the schema name will be prepended to the table name when the persistence provider goes to the database to access the table. In this case the HR schema will be prepended to the EMP table each time the table is accessed.

■ **Tip** Some vendors might allow the schema to be included in the name element of the table without having to specify the schema element, such as in @Table(name="HR.EMP"). Support for inlining the name of the schema with the table name is nonstandard.

Some databases support the notion of a catalog. For these databases, the catalog element of the @Table annotation can be specified. Listing 4-6 shows a catalog being explicitly set for the EMP table.

Listing 4-6. Setting a Catalog

```
@Entity
@Table(name="EMP", catalog="HR")
public class Employee { ... }
```

Mapping Simple Types

Simple Java types are mapped as part of the immediate state of an entity in its fields or properties. The list of persistable types is quite lengthy and includes pretty much every built-in type that you would want to persist. They include the following:

- Primitive Java types: `byte, int, short, long, boolean, char, float, double`

- Wrapper classes of primitive Java types: `Byte, Integer, Short, Long, Boolean, Character, Float, Double`

- Byte and character array types: `byte[], Byte[], char[], Character[]`

- Large numeric types: `java.math.BigInteger, java.math.BigDecimal`

- Strings: `java.lang.String`

- Java temporal types: `java.util.Date, java.util.Calendar`

- JDBC temporal types: `java.sql.Date, java.sql.Time, java.sql.Timestamp`

- Enumerated types: Any system or user-defined enumerated type

- Serializable objects: Any system or user-defined serializable type

Sometimes the type of the database column being mapped to is not exactly the same as the Java type. In almost all cases, the provider runtime can convert the type returned by JDBC into the correct Java type of the attribute. If the type from the JDBC layer cannot be converted to the Java type of the field or property, an exception will normally be thrown, although it is not guaranteed.

■ **Tip** When the persistent type does not match the JDBC type, some providers might choose to take proprietary action or make a best guess to convert between the two. In other cases, the JDBC driver might be performing the conversion on its own.

When persisting a field or property, the provider looks at the type and ensures that it is one of the persistable types listed earlier. If it is on the list, the provider will persist it using the appropriate JDBC type and pass it through to the JDBC driver. At that point, if the field or property is not serializable, the result is unspecified. The provider might choose to throw an exception or just try and pass the object through to JDBC. You will see later, in Chapter 10, how converters can be used to extend the list of types that can be persisted in JPA.

An optional `@Basic` annotation can be placed on a field or property to explicitly mark it as being persistent. This annotation is mostly for documentation purposes and is not required for the field or property to be persistent. If it is not there then it is implicitly assumed in the absence of any other mapping annotation. Because of the annotation, mappings of simple types are called basic mappings, whether the `@Basic` annotation is actually present or is just being assumed.

■ **Note** Now that you have seen how you can persist either fields or properties and how they are virtually equivalent in terms of persistence, we will just call them attributes. An attribute is a field or property of a class, and we will use the term attribute from now on to avoid having to continually refer to fields or properties in specific terms.

Column Mappings

The @Basic annotation (or assumed basic mapping in its absence) can be thought of as a logical indication that a given attribute is persistent. The physical annotation that is the companion annotation to the basic mapping is the @Column annotation. Specifying @Column on the attribute indicates specific characteristics of the physical database column that the object model is less concerned about. In fact, the object model might never even need to know to which column it is mapped, and the column name and physical mapping metadata can be located in a separate XML file.

A number of annotation elements can be specified as part of @Column, but most of them apply only to schema generation and will be covered later in the book. The only one that is of consequence is the name element, which is just a string that specifies the name of the column that the attribute has been mapped to. This is used when the default column name is not appropriate or does not apply to the schema being used. You can think of the name element of the @Column annotation as a means of overriding the default column name that would have otherwise been applied. The example in Listing 4-7 shows how to override the default column name for an attribute.

Listing 4-7. Mapping Attributes to Columns

```
@Entity
public class Employee {
    @Id
    @Column(name="EMP_ID")
    private long id;
    private String name;
    @Column(name="SAL")
    private long salary;
    @Column(name="COMM")
    private String comments;
    // ...
}
```

To put these annotations in context, let's look at the full table mapping represented by this entity. The first thing to notice is that no @Table annotation exists on the class, so the default table name of EMPLOYEE will be applied to it.

Next, note that @Column can be used with @Id mappings as well as with basic mappings. The id field is being overridden to map to the EMP_ID column instead of the default ID column. The name field is not annotated with @Column, so the default column name NAME would be used to store and retrieve the employee name. The salary and comments fields, however, are annotated to map to the SAL and COMM columns, respectively. The Employee entity is therefore mapped to the table that is shown in Figure 4-1.

```
┌─────────────────────┐
│      EMPLOYEE        │
├─────┬───────────────┤
│ PK  │ EMP_ID        │
├─────┼───────────────┤
│     │ NAME          │
│     │ SAL           │
│     │ COMM          │
└─────┴───────────────┘
```

Figure 4-1. EMPLOYEE entity table

Lazy Fetching

On occasion, it will be known ahead of time that certain portions of an entity will be seldom accessed. In these situations, you can optimize the performance when retrieving the entity by fetching only the data that you expect to be frequently accessed; the remainder of the data can be fetched only when or if it is required. There are many names for this kind of feature, including lazy loading, deferred loading, lazy fetching, on-demand fetching, just-in-time reading, indirection, and others. They all mean pretty much the same thing, which is just that some data might not be loaded when the object is initially read from the database, but will be fetched only when it is referenced or accessed.

The fetch type of a basic mapping can be configured to be lazily or eagerly loaded by specifying the fetch element in the corresponding @Basic annotation. The FetchType enumerated type defines the values for this element, which can be either EAGER or LAZY. Setting the fetch type of a basic mapping to LAZY means that the provider might defer loading the state for that attribute until it is referenced. The default is to load all basic mappings eagerly. Listing 4-8 shows an example of overriding a basic mapping to be lazily loaded.

Listing 4-8. Lazy Field Loading

```
@Entity
public class Employee {
    // ...
    @Basic(fetch=FetchType.LAZY)
    @Column(name="COMM")
    private String comments;
    // ...
}
```

We are assuming in this example that applications will seldom access the comments in an employee record, so we mark it as being lazily fetched. Note that in this case the @Basic annotation is not only present for documentation purposes but is also required in order to specify the fetch type for the field. Configuring the comments field to be fetched lazily will allow an Employee instance returned from a query to have the comments field empty. The application does not have to do anything special to get it, however. By simply accessing the comments field, it will be transparently read and filled in by the provider if it was not already loaded.

Before you use this feature, you should be aware of a few pertinent points about lazy attribute fetching. First and foremost, the directive to lazily fetch an attribute is meant only to be a hint to the persistence provider to help the application achieve better performance. The provider is not required to respect the request because the behavior of the entity is not compromised if the provider goes ahead and loads the attribute. The converse is not true, though, because specifying that an attribute be eagerly fetched might be critical to being able to access the entity state once the entity is detached from the persistence context. We will discuss detachment more in Chapter 6 and explore the connection between lazy loading and detachment.

Second, on the surface it might appear that this is a good idea for certain attributes of an entity, but in practice it is almost never a good idea to lazily fetch simple types. There is little to be gained in returning only part of a database row unless you are certain that the state will not be accessed in the entity later on. The only times when lazy loading of a basic mapping should be considered are when there are many columns in a table (for example, dozens or hundreds) or when the columns are large (for example, very large character strings or byte strings). It could take significant resources to load the data, and not loading it could save quite a lot of effort, time, and resources. Unless either of these two cases is true, in the majority of cases lazily fetching a subset of object attributes will end up being more expensive than eagerly fetching them.

Lazy fetching is quite relevant when it comes to relationship mappings, though, so we will be discussing this topic later in the chapter.

Large Objects

A common database term for a character or byte-based object that can be very large (up to the gigabyte range) is large object, or LOB for short. Database columns that can store these types of large objects require special JDBC calls to be accessed from Java. To signal to the provider that it should use the LOB methods when passing and retrieving this data to and from the JDBC driver, an additional annotation must be added to the basic mapping. The @Lob annotation acts as the marker annotation to fulfill this purpose and might appear in conjunction with the @Basic annotation, or it might appear when @Basic is absent and implicitly assumed to be on the mapping.

Because the @Lob annotation is really just qualifying the basic mapping, it can also be accompanied by a @Column annotation when the name of the LOB column needs to be overridden from the assumed default name.

LOBs come in two flavors in the database: character large objects, called CLOBs, and binary large objects, or BLOBs. As their names imply, a CLOB column holds a large character sequence, and a BLOB column can store a large byte sequence. The Java types mapped to BLOB columns are byte[], Byte[], and Serializable types, while char[], Character[], and String objects are mapped to CLOB columns. The provider is responsible for making this distinction based on the type of the attribute being mapped.

An example of mapping an image to a BLOB column is shown in Listing 4-9. Here, the PIC column is assumed to be a BLOB column to store the employee picture that is in the picture field. We have also marked this field to be loaded lazily, a common practice applied to LOBs that do not get referenced often.

Listing 4-9. Mapping a BLOB Column

```
@Entity
public class Employee {
    @Id
    private long id;
    @Basic(fetch=FetchType.LAZY)
    @Lob @Column(name="PIC")
    private byte[] picture;
    // ...
}
```

Enumerated Types

Another of the simple types that might be treated specially is the enumerated type. The values of an enumerated type are constants that can be handled differently depending on the application needs.

As with enumerated types in other languages, the values of an enumerated type in Java have an implicit ordinal assignment that is determined by the order in which they were declared. This ordinal cannot be modified at runtime and can be used to represent and store the values of the enumerated type in the database. Interpreting the values as ordinals is the default way that providers will map enumerated types to the database, and the provider will assume that the database column is an integer type.

Consider the following enumerated type:

```
public enum EmployeeType {
    FULL_TIME_EMPLOYEE,
    PART_TIME_EMPLOYEE,
    CONTRACT_EMPLOYEE
}
```

The ordinals assigned to the values of this enumerated type at compile time would be 0 for `FULL_TIME_EMPLOYEE`, 1 for `PART_TIME_EMPLOYEE`, and 2 for `CONTRACT_EMPLOYEE`. In Listing 4-10, we define a persistent field of this type.

Listing 4-10. Mapping an Enumerated Type Using Ordinals

```
@Entity
public class Employee {
    @Id private long id;
    private EmployeeType type;
    // ...
}
```

You can see that mapping `EmployeeType` is trivially easy to the point where you don't actually have to do anything at all. The defaults are applied, and everything will just work. The `type` field will get mapped to an integer `TYPE` column, and all full-time employees will have an ordinal of 0 assigned to them. Similarly the other employees will have their types stored in the `TYPE` column accordingly.

If an enumerated type changes, however, then we have a problem. The persisted ordinal data in the database will no longer apply to the correct value. In this example, if the company benefits policy changed and we started giving additional benefits to part-time employees who worked more than 20 hours per week, we would want to differentiate between the two types of part-time employees. By adding a `PART_TIME_BENEFITS_EMPLOYEE` value after `PART_TIME_EMPLOYEE`, we would be causing a new ordinal assignment to occur, where our new value would get assigned the ordinal of 2 and `CONTRACT_EMPLOYEE` would get 3. This would have the effect of causing all the contract employees on record to suddenly become part-time employees with benefits, clearly not the result that we were hoping for.

We could go through the database and adjust all the `Employee` entities to have their correct type, but if the employee type is used elsewhere, then we would need to make sure that they were all fixed as well. This is not a good maintenance situation to be in.

A better solution would be to store the name of the value as a string instead of storing the ordinal. This would isolate us from any changes in declaration and allow us to add new types without having to worry about the existing data. We can do this by adding an `@Enumerated` annotation on the attribute and specifying a value of `STRING`.

The `@Enumerated` annotation actually allows an `EnumType` to be specified, and the `EnumType` is itself an enumerated type that defines values of `ORDINAL` and `STRING`. While it is somewhat ironic that an enumerated type is being used to indicate how the provider should represent enumerated types, it is wholly appropriate. Because the default value of `@Enumerated` is `ORDINAL`, specifying `@Enumerated(ORDINAL)` is useful only when you want to make this mapping explicit.

In Listing 4-11, we are storing strings for the enumerated values. Now the `TYPE` column must be a string-based type, and all of the full-time employees will have the string `FULL_TIME_EMPLOYEE` stored in their corresponding `TYPE` column.

Listing 4-11. Mapping an Enumerated Type Using Strings

```
@Entity
public class Employee {
    @Id
    private long id;
    @Enumerated(EnumType.STRING)
    private EmployeeType type;
    // ...
}
```

Note that using strings will solve the problem of inserting additional values in the middle of the enumerated type, but it will leave the data vulnerable to changes in the names of the values. For instance, if we wanted to change PART_TIME_EMPLOYEE to PT_EMPLOYEE, then we would be in trouble. This is a less likely problem, though, because changing the names of an enumerated type would cause all the code that uses the enumerated type to have to change also. This would be a bigger bother than reassigning values in a database column.

In general, storing the ordinal is the best and most efficient way to store enumerated types as long as the likelihood of additional values inserted in the middle is not high. New values could still be added on the end of the type without any negative consequences.

One final note about enumerated types is that they are defined quite flexibly in Java. In fact, it is even possible to have values that contain state. There is currently no support in JPA for mapping state contained within enumerated values. Neither is there support for the compromise position between STRING and ORDINAL of explicitly mapping each enumerated value to a dedicated numeric value different from its compiler-assigned ordinal value. More extensive enumerated support is being considered for future releases.

Temporal Types

Temporal types are the set of time-based types that can be used in persistent state mappings. The list of supported temporal types includes the three java.sql types, java.sql.Date, java.sql.Time, and java.sql.Timestamp, and the two java.util types, java.util.Date and java.util.Calendar.

The java.sql types are completely hassle-free. They act just like any other simple mapping type and do not need any special consideration. The two java.util types need additional metadata, however, to indicate which of the JDBC java.sql types to use when communicating with the JDBC driver. This is done by annotating them with the @Temporal annotation and specifying the JDBC type as a value of the TemporalType enumerated type. There are three enumerated values of DATE, TIME, and TIMESTAMP to represent each of the java.sql types.

Listing 4-12 shows how java.util.Date and java.util.Calendar can be mapped to date columns in the database.

Listing 4-12. Mapping Temporal Types

```
@Entity
public class Employee {
    @Id
    private long id;
    @Temporal(TemporalType.DATE)
    private Calendar dob;
    @Temporal(TemporalType.DATE)
    @Column(name="S_DATE")
    private Date startDate;
    // ...
}
```

Like the other varieties of basic mappings, the @Column annotation can be used to override the default column name.

Transient State

Attributes that are part of a persistent entity but not intended to be persistent can either be modified with the `transient` modifier in Java or be annotated with the `@Transient` annotation. If either is specified, the provider runtime will not apply its default mapping rules to the attribute on which it was specified.

Transient fields are used for various reasons. One might be the case earlier on in the chapter when we mixed the access mode and didn't want to persist the same state twice. Another might be when you want to cache some in-memory state that you don't want to have to recompute, rediscover, or reinitialize. For example, in Listing 4-13 we are using a transient field to save the correct locale-specific word for `Employee` so that we print it correctly wherever it is being displayed. We have used the `transient` modifier instead of the `@Transient` annotation so that if the `Employee` gets serialized from one JVM to another, then the translated name will get reinitialized to correspond to the locale of the new JVM. In cases where the non-persistent value should be retained across serialization, the annotation should be used instead of the modifier.

Listing 4-13. Using a Transient Field

```
@Entity
public class Employee {
    @Id private long id;
    private String name;
    private long salary;
    transient private String translatedName;
    // ...

    public String toString() {
        if (translatedName == null) {
            translatedName =
                ResourceBundle.getBundle("EmpResources").getString("Employee");
        }
        return translatedName + ": " + id + " " + name;
    }
}
```

Mapping the Primary Key

Every entity that is mapped to a relational database must have a mapping to a primary key in the table. You have already learned the basics of how the `@Id` annotation indicates the identifier of the entity. In this section, you will explore simple identifiers and primary keys in a little more depth and learn how you can let the persistence provider generate unique identifier values.

■ **Note**   When an entity identifier is composed of only a single attribute, it's called a simple identifier.

Overriding the Primary Key Column

The same defaulting rules apply to id mappings as to basic mappings, which is that the name of the column is assumed to be the same as the name of the attribute. Just as with basic mappings, the `@Column` annotation can be used to override the column name that the id attribute is mapped to.

Primary keys are assumed to be insertable, but not nullable or updatable. When overriding a primary key column the `nullable` and `updatable` elements should not be overridden. Only in the very specific circumstance of mapping the same column to multiple fields/relationships (as described in Chapter 10) should the `insertable` element be set to `false`.

Primary Key Types

Except for its special significance in designating the mapping to the primary key column, an id mapping is almost the same as the basic mapping. The other main difference is that id mappings are generally restricted to the following types:

- Primitive Java types: `byte`, `int`, `short`, `long`, `char`
- Wrapper classes of primitive Java types: `Byte`, `Integer`, `Short`, `Long`, `Character`
- String: `java.lang.String`
- Large numeric type: `java.math.BigInteger`
- Temporal types: `java.util.Date`, `java.sql.Date`

Floating point types such as `float` and `double` are also permitted, as well as the `Float` and `Double` wrapper classes and `java.math.BigDecimal`, but they are discouraged because of the nature of rounding error and the untrustworthiness of the `equals()` operator when applied to them. Using floating types for primary keys is a risky endeavor and is definitely not recommended.

Identifier Generation

Sometimes applications do not want to be bothered with trying to define and ensure uniqueness in some aspect of their domain model and are content to let the identifier values be automatically generated for them. This is called id generation and is specified by the `@GeneratedValue` annotation.

When id generation is enabled, the persistence provider will generate an identifier value for every instance of that entity type. Once the identifier value is obtained, the provider will insert it into the newly persisted entity; however, depending on the way it is generated, it might not actually be present in the object until the entity has been inserted in the database. In other words, the application cannot rely on being able to access the identifier until after either a flush has occurred or the transaction has completed.

Applications can choose one of four different id generation strategies by specifying a strategy in the `strategy` element. The value can be any one of `AUTO`, `TABLE`, `SEQUENCE`, or `IDENTITY` enumerated values of the `GenerationType` enumerated type.

Table and sequence generators can be specifically defined and then reused by multiple entity classes. These generators are named and are globally accessible to all the entities in the persistence unit.

Automatic Id Generation

If an application does not care what kind of generation is used by the provider but wants generation to occur, it can specify a strategy of `AUTO`. This means that the provider will use whatever strategy it wants to generate identifiers. Listing 4-14 shows an example of using automatic id generation. This will cause an identifier value to be created by the provider and inserted into the `id` field of each `Employee` entity that gets persisted.

■ **Tip**   It is not explicitly required that the entity identifier field be an integral type, but it is typically the only type that `AUTO` will create. We recommend that `long` be used to accommodate the full extent of the generated identifier domain.

Listing 4-14. Using Auto Id Generation

```
@Entity
public class Employee {
    @Id @GeneratedValue(strategy=GenerationType.AUTO)
    private long id;
    // ...
}
```

There is a catch to using AUTO, though. The provider gets to pick its own strategy to store the identifiers, but it needs to have some kind of persistent resource in order to do so. For example, if it chooses a table-based strategy, it needs to create a table; if it chooses a sequence-based strategy, it needs to create a sequence. The provider can't always rely on the database connection that it obtains from the server to have permissions to create a table in the database. This is normally a privileged operation that is often restricted to the DBA. There will need to be some kind of creation phase or schema generation to cause the resource to be created before the AUTO strategy is able to function.

The AUTO mode is really a generation strategy for development or prototyping. It works well as a means of getting you up and running more quickly when the database schema is being generated. In any other situation, it would be better to use one of the other generation strategies discussed in the later sections.

Id Generation Using a Table

The most flexible and portable way to generate identifiers is to use a database table. Not only will it port to different databases but it also allows for storing multiple different identifier sequences for different entities within the same table.

An id generation table should have two columns. The first column is a string type used to identify the particular generator sequence. It is the primary key for all the generators in the table. The second column is an integral type that stores the actual id sequence that is being generated. The value stored in this column is the last identifier that was allocated in the sequence. Each defined generator represents a row in the table.

The easiest way to use a table to generate identifiers is to simply specify the generation strategy to be TABLE in the strategy element:

```
@Id @GeneratedValue(strategy=GenerationType.TABLE)
private long id;
```

Because the generation strategy is indicated but no generator has been specified, the provider will assume a table of its own choosing. If schema generation is used, it will be created; if not, the default table assumed by the provider must be known and must exist in the database.

A more explicit approach would be to actually specify the table that is to be used for id storage. This is done by defining a table generator that, contrary to what its name implies, does not actually generate tables. Rather, it is an identifier generator that uses a table to store the identifier values. We can define one by using a @TableGenerator annotation and then refer to it by name in the @GeneratedValue annotation:

```
@TableGenerator(name="Emp_Gen")
@Id @GeneratedValue(generator="Emp_Gen")
private long id;
```

Although we are showing the @TableGenerator annotating the identifier attribute, it can actually be defined on any attribute or class. Regardless of where it is defined, it will be available to the entire persistence unit. A good practice would be to define it locally on the id attribute if only one class is using it but to define it in XML, as described in Chapter 13, if it will be used for multiple classes.

The name element globally names the generator, allowing us to reference it in the generator element of the @GeneratedValue annotation. This is functionally equivalent to the previous example where we simply said that we wanted to use table generation but did not specify the generator. Now we are specifying the name of the generator but not supplying any of the generator details, leaving them to be defaulted by the provider.

A further qualifying approach would be to specify the table details, as in the following:

```
@TableGenerator(name="Emp_Gen",
    table="ID_GEN",
    pkColumnName="GEN_NAME",
    valueColumnName="GEN_VAL")
```

We have included some additional elements after the name of the generator. Following the name are three elements—table, pkColumnName, and valueColumnName—that define the actual table that stores the identifiers for Emp_Gen.

The table element just indicates the name of the table. The pkColumnName element is the name of the primary key column in the table that uniquely identifies the generator, and the valueColumnName element is the name of the column that stores the actual id sequence value being generated. In this case, the table is named ID_GEN, the name of the primary key column (the column that stores the generator names) is named GEN_NAME, and the column that stores the id sequence values is named GEN_VAL.

The name of the generator becomes the value stored in the pkColumnName column for that row and is used by the provider to look up the generator to obtain its last allocated value.

In our example, we named our generator Emp_Gen so our table would look like the one in Figure 4-2.

ID_GEN

GEN_NAME	GEN_VAL
Emp_Gen	0

Figure 4-2. *Table for identifier generation*

Note that the last allocated Employee identifier is 0, which tells us that no identifiers have been generated yet. An initialValue element representing the last allocated identifier can be specified as part of the generator definition, but the default setting of 0 will suffice in almost every case. This setting is used only during schema generation when the table is created. During subsequent executions, the provider will read the contents of the value column to determine the next identifier to give out.

To avoid updating the row for every single identifier that gets requested, an allocation size is used. This will cause the provider to preallocate a block of identifiers and then give out identifiers from memory as requested until the block is used up. Once this block is used up, the next request for an identifier triggers another block of identifiers to be preallocated, and the identifier value is incremented by the allocation size. By default, the allocation size is set to 50. This value can be overridden to be larger or smaller through the use of the allocationSize element when defining the generator.

■ **Tip** The provider might allocate identifiers within the same transaction as the entity being persisted or in a separate transaction. It is not specified, but you should check your provider documentation to see how it can avoid the risk of deadlock when concurrent threads are creating entities and locking resources.

Listing 4-15 shows an example of defining a second generator to be used for Address entities but that uses the same ID_GEN table to store the identifier sequence. In this case, we are actually explicitly dictating the value we are storing in the identifier table's primary key column by specifying the pkColumnvalue element. This element allows the name of the generator to be different from the column value, although doing so is rarely needed. The example shows an Address id generator named Address_Gen but then defines the value stored in the table for Address id generation as Addr_Gen. The generator also sets the initial value to 10000 and the allocation size to 100.

Listing 4-15. Using Table Id Generation

```
@TableGenerator(name="Address_Gen",
    table="ID_GEN",
    pkColumnName="GEN_NAME",
    valueColumnName="GEN_VAL",
    pkColumnValue="Addr_Gen",
    initialValue=10000,
    allocationSize=100)
@Id @GeneratedValue(generator="Address_Gen")
private long id;
```

If both Emp_Gen and Address_Gen generators were defined, then on application startup the ID_GEN table should look like Figure 4-3. As the application allocates identifiers, the values stored in the GEN_VAL column will increase.

ID_GEN

GEN_NAME	GEN_VAL
Emp_Gen	0
Addr_Gen	10000

Figure 4-3. Table for generating Address and Employee identifiers

If you haven't used the automatic schema generation feature (discussed in Chapter 14), the table must already exist or be created in the database through some other means and be configured to be in this state when the application starts up for the first time. The following SQL could be applied to create and initialize this table:

```
CREATE TABLE id_gen (
    gen_name VARCHAR(80),
    gen_val INTEGER,
    CONSTRAINT pk_id_gen
        PRIMARY KEY (gen_name)
);
INSERT INTO id_gen (gen_name, gen_val) VALUES ('Emp_Gen', 0);
INSERT INTO id_gen (gen_name, gen_val) VALUES ('Addr_Gen', 10000);
```

Id Generation Using a Database Sequence

Many databases support an internal mechanism for id generation called sequences. A database sequence can be used to generate identifiers when the underlying database supports them.

As you saw with table generators, if it is known that a database sequence should be used for generating identifiers, and you are not concerned that it be any particular sequence, specifying the generator type alone should be sufficient:

```
@Id @GeneratedValue(strategy=GenerationType.SEQUENCE)
private long id;
```

In this case, no generator is named, so the provider will use a default sequence object of its own choosing. Note that if multiple sequence generators are defined but not named, it is not specified whether they use the same default sequence or different ones. The only difference between using one sequence for multiple entity types and using one for each entity would be the ordering of the sequence numbers and possible contention on the sequence. The safer route would be to define a named sequence generator and refer to it in the @GeneratedValue annotation:

```
@SequenceGenerator(name="Emp_Gen", sequenceName="Emp_Seq")
@Id @GeneratedValue(generator="Emp_Gen")
private long getId;
```

Unless schema generation is enabled, it would require that the sequence be defined and already exist. The SQL to create such a sequence would be as follows:

```
CREATE SEQUENCE Emp_Seq
    MINVALUE 1
    START WITH 1
    INCREMENT BY 50
```

The initial value and allocation size can also be used in sequence generators and would need to be reflected in the SQL to create the sequence. Note that the default allocation size is 50, just as it is with table generators. If schema generation is not being used, and the sequence is being manually created, the INCREMENT BY clause would need to be configured to match the allocationSize element or default allocation size of the corresponding @SequenceGenerator annotation.

Id Generation Using Database Identity

Some databases support a primary key identity column, sometimes referred to as an autonumber column. Whenever a row is inserted into the table, the identity column will get a unique identifier assigned to it. It can be used to generate the identifiers for objects, but once again is available only when the underlying database supports it. Identity is often used when database sequences are not supported by the database or because a legacy schema has already defined the table to use identity columns. They are generally less efficient for object-relational identifier generation because they cannot be allocated in blocks and because the identifier is not available until after commit time.

To indicate that IDENTITY generation should occur, the @GeneratedValue annotation should specify a generation strategy of IDENTITY. This will indicate to the provider that it must reread the inserted row from the table after an insert has occurred. This will allow it to obtain the newly generated identifier from the database and put it into the in-memory entity that was just persisted:

```
@Id @GeneratedValue(strategy=GenerationType.IDENTITY)
private long id;
```

There is no generator annotation for IDENTITY because it must be defined as part of the database schema definition for the primary key column of the entity. Because each entity primary key column defines its own identity characteristic, IDENTITY generation cannot be shared across multiple entity types.

Another difference, hinted at earlier, between using IDENTITY and other id generation strategies is that the identifier will not be accessible until after the insert has occurred. Although no guarantee is made about the accessibility of the identifier before the transaction has completed, it is at least possible for other types of generation to eagerly allocate the identifier. But when using identity, it is the action of inserting that causes the identifier to be generated. It would be impossible for the identifier to be available before the entity is inserted into the database, and because insertion of entities is most often deferred until commit time, the identifier would not be available until after the transaction has been committed.

■ **Tip**　If you use IDENTITY, make sure you are aware of what your persistence provider is doing and that it matches your requirements. Some providers eagerly insert (when the persist method is invoked) entities that are configured to use IDENTITY id generation, instead of waiting until commit time. This will allow the id to be available immediately, at the expense of premature locking and reduced concurrency. Some providers even have an option allowing you to configure which approach gets used.

Relationships

If entities contained only simple persistent state, the business of object-relational mapping would be a trivial one, indeed. Most entities need to be able to reference, or have relationships with, other entities. This is what produces the domain model graphs that are common in business applications.

In the following sections, we will explore the different kinds of relationships that can exist and show how to define and map them using JPA mapping metadata.

Relationship Concepts

Before we go off and start mapping relationships, let's take a quick tour through some of the basic relationship concepts and terminology. Having a firm grasp on these concepts will make it easier to understand the remainder of the relationship mapping sections.

Roles

There is an old adage that says every story has three sides: yours, mine, and the truth. Relationships are kind of the same in that there are three different perspectives. The first is the view from one side of the relationship, the second is from the other side, and the third is from a global perspective that knows about both sides. The "sides" are called roles. In every relationship there are two entities that are related to one another, and each entity is said to play a role in the relationship.

Relationships are everywhere, so examples are not hard to come by. An employee has a relationship to the department that he or she works in. The Employee entity plays the role of working in the department, while the Department entity plays the role of having an employee working in it.

Of course, the role a given entity is playing differs according to the relationship, and an entity might be participating in many different relationships with many different entities. We can conclude, therefore, that any entity might be playing a number of different roles in any given model. If we think of an Employee entity, we realize that it does, in fact, play other roles in other relationships, such as the role of working for a manager in its relationship with another Employee entity, working on a project in its relationship with the Project entity, and so forth. Although there are no metadata requirements to declare the role an entity is playing, roles are nevertheless still helpful as a means of understanding the nature and structure of relationships.

Directionality

In order to have relationships at all, there has to be a way to create, remove, and maintain them. The basic way this is done is by an entity having a relationship attribute that refers to its related entity in a way that identifies it as playing the other role of the relationship. It is often the case that the other entity, in turn, has an attribute that points back to the original entity. When each entity points to the other, the relationship is bidirectional. If only one entity has a pointer to the other, the relationship is said to be unidirectional.

A relationship from an `Employee` to the `Project` that they work on would be bidirectional. The `Employee` should know its `Project`, and the `Project` should point to the `Employee` working on it. A UML model of this relationship is shown in Figure 4-4. The arrows going in both directions indicate the bidirectionality of the relationship.

Figure 4-4. *Employee and Project in a bidirectional relationship*

An `Employee` and its `Address` would likely be modeled as a unidirectional relationship because the `Address` is not expected to ever need to know its resident. If it did, of course, then it would need to become a bidirectional relationship. Figure 4-5 shows this relationship. Because the relationship is unidirectional, the arrow points from the `Employee` to the `Address`.

Figure 4-5. *Employee in a unidirectional relationship with Address*

As you will see later in the chapter, although they both share the same concept of directionality, the object and data models each see it a little differently because of the paradigm difference. In some cases, unidirectional relationships in the object model can pose a problem in the database model.

We can use the directionality of a relationship to help describe and explain a model, but when it comes to actually discussing it in concrete terms, it makes sense to think of every bidirectional relationship as a pair of unidirectional relationships. Instead of having a single bidirectional relationship of an `Employee` working on a `Project`, we would have one unidirectional "project" relationship where the `Employee` points to the `Project` they work on and another unidirectional "worker" relationship where the `Project` points to the `Employee` that works on it. Each of these relationships has an entity that is the source or referring role and the side that is the target or referred-to role. The beauty of this is that we can use the same terms no matter which relationship we are talking about and no matter what roles are in the relationship. Figure 4-6 shows how the two relationships have source and target entities, and how from each relationship perspective the source and target entities are different.

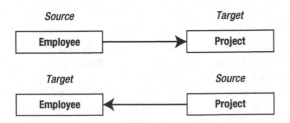

Figure 4-6. *Unidirectional relationships between Employee and Project*

Cardinality

It isn't very often that a project has only a single employee working on it. We would like to be able to capture the aspect of how many entities exist on each side of the same relationship instance. This is called the cardinality of the relationship. Each role in a relationship will have its own cardinality, which indicates whether there can be only one instance of the entity or many instances.

In our Employee and Department example, we might first say that one employee works in one department, so the cardinality of both sides would be one. But chances are that more than one employee works in the department, so we would make the relationship have a many cardinality on the Employee or source side, meaning that many Employee instances could each point to the same Department. The target or Department side would keep its cardinality of one. Figure 4-7 shows this many-to-one relationship. The "many" side is marked with an asterisk (*).

Figure 4-7. *Unidirectional many-to-one relationship*

In our Employee and Project example, we have a bidirectional relationship, or two relationship directions. If an employee can work on multiple projects, and a project can have multiple employees working on it, then we would end up with cardinalities of "many" on the sources and targets of both directions. Figure 4-8 shows the UML diagram of this relationship.

Figure 4-8. *Bidirectional many-to-many relationship*

As the saying goes, a picture is worth a thousand words, and describing these relationships in text is quite a lot harder than showing a picture. In words, though, this picture indicates the following:

- Each employee can work on a number of projects.

- Many employees can work on the same project.

- Each project can have a number of employees working on it.

- Many projects can have the same employee working on them.

Implicit in this model is the fact that there can be sharing of Employee and Project instances across multiple relationship instances.

Ordinality

A role can be further specified by determining whether or not it might be present at all. This is called the ordinality, and it serves to show whether the target entity needs to be specified when the source entity is created. Because the ordinality is really just a Boolean value, it is also referred to as the optionality of the relationship.

In cardinality terms, ordinality would be indicated by the cardinality being a range instead of a simple value, and the range would begin with 0 or 1 depending on the ordinality. It is simpler, though, to merely state that the relationship is either optional or mandatory. If optional, the target might not be present; if mandatory, a source entity without a reference to its associated target entity is in an invalid state.

Mappings Overview

Now that you know enough theory and have the conceptual background to be able to discuss relationships, we can go on to explaining and using relationship mappings.

Each one of the mappings is named for the cardinality of the source and target roles. As shown in the previous sections, a bidirectional relationship can be viewed as a pair of two unidirectional mappings. Each of these mappings is really a unidirectional relationship mapping, and if we take the cardinalities of the source and target of the relationship and combine them together in that order, permuting them with the two possible values of "one" and "many", we end up with the following names given to the mappings:

1. Many-to-one

2. One-to-one

3. One-to-many

4. Many-to-many

These mapping names are also the names of the annotations that are used to indicate the relationship types on the attributes that are being mapped. They are the basis for the logical relationship annotations, and they contribute to the object modeling aspects of the entity. Like basic mappings, relationship mappings can be applied to either fields or properties of the entity.

Single-Valued Associations

An association from an entity instance to another entity instance (where the cardinality of the target is "one") is called a single-valued association. The many-to-one and one-to-one relationship mappings fall into this category because the source entity refers to at most one target entity. We will discuss these relationships and some of their variants first.

Many-to-One Mappings

In our cardinality discussion of the Employee and Department relationship (shown in Figure 4-7), we first thought of an employee working in a department, so we just assumed that it was a one-to-one relationship. However, when we realized that more than one employee works in the same department, we changed it to a many-to-one relationship mapping. It turns out that many-to-one is the most common mapping and is the one that is normally used when creating an association to an entity.

Figure 4-9 shows a many-to-one relationship between Employee and Department. Employee is the "many" side and the source of the relationship, and Department is the "one" side and the target. Once again, because the arrow points in only one direction, from Employee to Department, the relationship is unidirectional. Note that in UML, the source class has an implicit attribute of the target class type if it can be navigated to. For example, Employee has an attribute called department that will contain a reference to a single Department instance. The actual attribute is not shown in the Employee class but is implied by the presence of the relationship arrow.

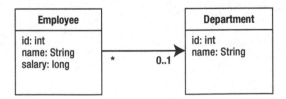

Figure 4-9. Many-to-one relationship from Employee to Department

A many-to-one mapping is defined by annotating the attribute in the source entity (the attribute that refers to the target entity) with the @ManyToOne annotation. Listing 4-16 shows how the @ManyToOne annotation is used to map this relationship. The department field in Employee is the source attribute that is annotated.

Listing 4-16. Many-to-One Relationship from Employee to Department

```
@Entity
public class Employee {
    // ...
    @ManyToOne
    private Department department;
    // ...
}
```

We have included only the bits of the class that are relevant to our discussion, but you can see from the previous example that the code was rather anticlimactic. A single annotation was all that was required to map the relationship, and it turned out to be quite dull, really. Of course, when it comes to configuration, dull is beautiful.

The same kinds of attribute flexibility and modifier requirements that were described for basic mappings also apply to relationship mappings. The annotation can be present on either the field or property, depending on the strategy used for the entity.

Using Join Columns

In the database, a relationship mapping means that one table has a reference to another table. The database term for a column that refers to a key (usually the primary key) in another table is a foreign key column. In JPA, they're called join columns, and the @JoinColumn annotation is the primary annotation used to configure these types of columns.

■ **Note**   Later in the chapter, we will talk about join columns that are present in other tables called join tables. In Chapter 10, we'll cover a more advanced case of using a join table for single-valued associations.

Consider the EMPLOYEE and DEPARTMENT tables shown in Figure 4-10 that correspond to the Employee and Department entities. The EMPLOYEE table has a foreign key column named DEPT_ID that references the DEPARTMENT table. From the perspective of the entity relationship, DEPT_ID is the join column that associates the Employee and Department entities.

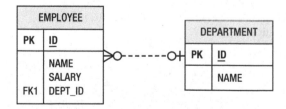

Figure 4-10. EMPLOYEE and DEPARTMENT tables

In almost every relationship, independent of source and target sides, one of the two sides will have the join column in its table. That side is called the owning side or the owner of the relationship. The side that does not have the join column is called the non-owning or inverse side.

Ownership is important for mapping because the physical annotations that define the mappings to the columns in the database (for example, @JoinColumn) are always defined on the owning side of the relationship. If they are not there, the values are defaulted from the perspective of the attribute on the owning side.

▪ **Note** Although we have described the owning side as being determined by the data schema, the object model must indicate the owning side through the use of the relationship mapping annotations. The absence of the mappedBy element in the mapping annotation implies ownership of the relationship, while the presence of the mappedBy element means the entity is on the inverse side of the relationship. The mappedBy element is described in subsequent sections.

Many-to-one mappings are always on the owning side of a relationship, so if there is a @JoinColumn to be found in the relationship that has a many-to-one side, that is where it will be located. To specify the name of the join column, the name element is used. For example, the @JoinColumn(name="DEPT_ID") annotation means that the DEPT_ID column in the source entity table is the foreign key to the target entity table, whatever the target entity of the relationship happens to be.

If no @JoinColumn annotation accompanies the many-to-one mapping, a default column name will be assumed. The name that is used as the default is formed from a combination of both the source and target entities. It is the name of the relationship attribute in the source entity, which is department in our example, plus an underscore character (_), plus the name of the primary key column of the target entity. So if the Department entity were mapped to a table that had a primary key column named ID, the join column in the EMPLOYEE table would be assumed to be named DEPARTMENT_ID. If this is not actually the name of the column, the @JoinColumn annotation must be defined to override the default.

Going back to Figure 4-10, the foreign key column is named DEPT_ID instead of the defaulted DEPARTMENT_ID column name. Listing 4-17 shows the @JoinColumn annotation being used to override the join column name to be DEPT_ID.

Listing 4-17. Many-to-One Relationship Overriding the Join Column

```
@Entity
public class Employee {
    @Id private long id;
    @ManyToOne
    @JoinColumn(name="DEPT_ID")
    private Department department;
    // ...
}
```

Annotations allow us to specify @JoinColumn on either the same line as @ManyToOne or on a separate line, above or below it. By convention, the logical mapping should appear first, followed by the physical mapping. This makes the object model clear because the physical part is less important to the object model.

One-to-One Mappings

If only one employee could work in a department, we would be back to the one-to-one association again. A more realistic example of a one-to-one association, however, would be an employee who has a parking space. Assuming that every employee got assigned his or her own parking space, we would create a one-to-one relationship from Employee to ParkingSpace. Figure 4-11 shows this relationship.

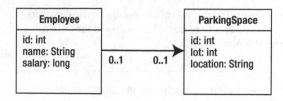

Figure 4-11. *One-to-one relationship from Employee to ParkingSpace*

We define the mapping in a similar way to the way we define a many-to-one mapping, except that we use the @OneToOne annotation instead of a @ManyToOne annotation on the parkingSpace attribute. Just as with a many-to-one mapping, the one-to-one mapping has a join column in the database and needs to override the name of the column in a @JoinColumn annotation when the default name does not apply. The default name is composed the same way as for many-to-one mappings using the name of the source attribute and the target primary key column name.

Figure 4-12 shows the tables mapped by the Employee and ParkingSpace entities. The foreign key column in the EMPLOYEE table is named PSPACE_ID and refers to the PARKING_SPACE table.

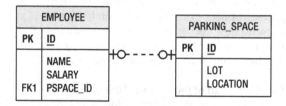

Figure 4-12. *EMPLOYEE and PARKING_SPACE tables*

As it turns out, one-to-one mappings are almost the same as many-to-one mappings except that only one instance of the source entity can refer to the same target entity instance. In other words, the target entity instance is not shared among the source entity instances. In the database, this equates to having a uniqueness constraint on the source foreign key column (that is, the foreign key column in the source entity table). If there were more than one foreign key value that was the same, it would contravene the rule that no more than one source entity instance can refer to the same target entity instance.

Listing 4-18 shows the mapping for this relationship. The @JoinColumn annotation has been used to override the default join column name of PARKINGSPACE_ID to be PSPACE_ID.

Listing 4-18. One-to-One Relationship from Employee to ParkingSpace

```
@Entity
public class Employee {
    @Id private long id;
    private String name;
    @OneToOne
    @JoinColumn(name="PSPACE_ID")
    private ParkingSpace parkingSpace;
    // ...
}
```

Bidirectional One-to-One Mappings

The target entity of the one-to-one often has a relationship back to the source entity; for example, ParkingSpace has a reference back to the Employee that uses it. When this is the case, it is called a bidirectional one-to-one relationship. As you saw previously, we actually have two separate one-to-one mappings, one in each direction, but the combination of the two is called a bidirectional one-to-one relationship. To make our existing one-to-one employee and parking space example bidirectional, we need only change the ParkingSpace to point back to the Employee. Figure 4-13 shows the bidirectional relationship.

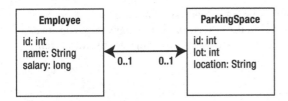

Figure 4-13. *One-to-one relationship between Employee and ParkingSpace*

You already learned that the entity table that contains the join column determines the entity that is the owner of the relationship. In a bidirectional one-to-one relationship, both the mappings are one-to-one mappings, and either side can be the owner, so the join column might end up being on one side or the other. This would normally be a data modeling decision, not a Java programming decision, and it would likely be decided based on the most frequent direction of traversal.

Consider the ParkingSpace entity class shown in Listing 4-19. This example assumes the table mapping shown in Figure 4-12, and it assumes that Employee is the owning side of the relationship. We now have to add a reference from ParkingSpace back to Employee. This is achieved by adding the @OneToOne relationship annotation on the employee field. As part of the annotation, we must add a mappedBy element to indicate that the owning side is the Employee, not the ParkingSpace. Because ParkingSpace is the inverse side of the relationship, it does not have to supply the join column information.

Listing 4-19. Inverse Side of a Bidirectional One-to-One Relationship

```
@Entity
public class ParkingSpace {
    @Id private long id;
    private int lot;
    private String location;
    @OneToOne(mappedBy="parkingSpace")
    private Employee employee;
    // ...
}
```

The mappedBy element in the one-to-one mapping of the employee attribute of ParkingSpace is needed to refer to the parkingSpace attribute in the Employee class. The value of mappedBy is the name of the attribute in the owning entity that points back to the inverse entity.

The two rules, then, for bidirectional one-to-one associations are the following:

- The @JoinColumn annotation goes on the mapping of the entity that is mapped to the table containing the join column, or the owner of the relationship. This might be on either side of the association.

- The mappedBy element should be specified in the @OneToOne annotation in the entity that does not define a join column, or the inverse side of the relationship.

It would not be legal to have a bidirectional association that had mappedBy on both sides, just as it would be incorrect to not have it on either side. The difference is that if it were absent on both sides of the relationship, the provider would treat each side as an independent unidirectional relationship. This would be fine except that it would assume that each side was the owner and that each had a join column.

Bidirectional many-to-one relationships are explained later as part of the discussion of multivalued bidirectional associations.

Collection-Valued Associations

When the source entity references one or more target entity instances, a many-valued association or associated collection is used. Both the one-to-many and many-to-many mappings fit the criteria of having many target entities, and although the one-to-many association is the most frequently used, many-to-many mappings are useful as well when there is sharing in both directions.

One-to-Many Mappings

When an entity is associated with a Collection of other entities, it is most often in the form of a one-to-many mapping. For example, a department would normally have a number of employees. Figure 4-14 shows the Employee and Department relationship that we showed earlier in the section "Many-to-One Mappings," only this time the relationship is bidirectional in nature.

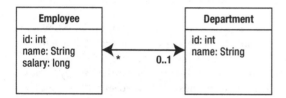

Figure 4-14. *Bidirectional Employee and Department relationship*

As mentioned earlier, when a relationship is bidirectional there are actually two mappings, one for each direction. A bidirectional one-to-many relationship always implies a many-to-one mapping back to the source, so in our Employee and Department example there is a one-to-many mapping from Department to Employee and a many-to-one mapping from Employee back to Department. We could just as easily say that the relationship is bidirectional many-to-one if we were looking at it from the Employee perspective. They are equivalent because bidirectional many-to-one relationships imply a one-to-many mapping back from the target to source, and vice versa.

When a source entity has an arbitrary number of target entities stored in its collection, there is no scalable way to store those references in the database table that it maps to. How would it store an arbitrary number of foreign keys in a single row? Instead, it must let the tables of the entities in the collection have foreign keys back to the source entity table. This is why the one-to-many association is almost always bidirectional and the "one" side is not normally the owning side.

Furthermore, if the target entity tables have foreign keys that point back to the source entity table, the target entities should have many-to-one associations back to the source entity object. Having a foreign key in a table for which there is no association in the corresponding entity object model is not being true to the data model. It is nonetheless still possible to configure, though.

Let's look at a concrete example of a one-to-many mapping based on the Employee and Department example shown in Figure 4-14. The tables for this relationship are exactly the same as those shown in Figure 4-10, which showed a many-to-one relationship. The only difference between the many-to-one example and this one is that we are now implementing the inverse side of the relationship. Because Employee has the join column and is the owner of the relationship, the Employee class is unchanged from Listing 4-16.

On the Department side of the relationship, we need to map the employees collection of Employee entities as a one-to-many association using the @OneToMany annotation. Listing 4-20 shows the Department class that uses this annotation. Note that because this is the inverse side of the relationship, we need to include the mappedBy element, just as we did in the bidirectional one-to-one relationship example.

Listing 4-20. One-to-Many Relationship

```
@Entity
public class Department {
    @Id private long id;
    private String name;
    @OneToMany(mappedBy="department")
    private Collection<Employee> employees;
    // ...
}
```

There are a couple of noteworthy points to mention about this class. The first is that a generic type-parameterized Collection is being used to store the Employee entities. This provides the strict typing that guarantees that only objects of type Employee will exist in the Collection. This is quite useful because it not only provides compile-time checking of our code but also saves us from having to perform cast operations when we retrieve the Employee instances from the collection.

JPA assumes the availability of generics; however, it is still perfectly acceptable to use a Collection that is not type-parameterized. We might just as well have defined the Department class without using generics but defining only a simple Collection type, as we would have done in releases of standard Java previous to Java SE 5 (except for JDK 1.0 or 1.1, when java.util.Collection was not even standardized!). If we did, we would need to specify the type of entity that will be stored in the Collection that is needed by the persistence provider. The code is shown in Listing 4-21 and looks almost identical, except for the targetEntity element that indicates the entity type.

Listing 4-21. Using targetEntity

```
@Entity
public class Department {
    @Id private long id;
    private String name;
    @OneToMany(targetEntity=Employee.class, mappedBy="department")
    private Collection employees;
    // ...
}
```

There are two important points to remember when defining bidirectional one-to-many (or many-to-one) relationships:

- The many-to-one side should be the owning side, so the join column should be defined on that side.

- The one-to-many mapping should be the inverse side, so the mappedBy element should be used.

Failing to specify the mappedBy element in the @OneToMany annotation will cause the provider to treat it as a unidirectional one-to-many relationship that is defined to use a join table (described later). This is an easy mistake to make and should be the first thing you look for if you see a missing table error with a name that has two entity names concatenated together.

Many-to-Many Mappings

When one or more entities are associated with a Collection of other entities, and the entities have overlapping associations with the same target entities, we must model it as a many-to-many relationship. Each of the entities on each side of the relationship will have a collection-valued association that contains entities of the target type. Figure 4-15 shows a many-to-many relationship between Employee and Project. Each employee can work on multiple projects, and each project can be worked on by multiple employees.

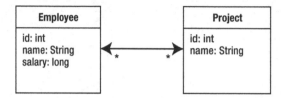

Figure 4-15. *Bidirectional many-to-many relationship*

A many-to-many mapping is expressed on both the source and target entities as a @ManyToMany annotation on the collection attributes. For example, in Listing 4-22 the Employee has a projects attribute that has been annotated with @ManyToMany. Likewise, the Project entity has an employees attribute that has also been annotated with @ManyToMany.

Listing 4-22. Many-to-Many Relationship Between Employee and Project

```
@Entity
public class Employee {
    @Id private long id;
    private String name;
    @ManyToMany
    private Collection<Project> projects;
    // ...
}

@Entity
public class Project {
    @Id private long id;
    private String name;
    @ManyToMany(mappedBy="projects")
    private Collection<Employee> employees;
    // ...
}
```

There are some important differences between this many-to-many relationship and the one-to-many relationship discussed earlier. The first is a mathematical inevitability: when a many-to-many relationship is bidirectional, both sides of the relationship are many-to-many mappings.

The second difference is that there are no join columns on either side of the relationship. You will see in the next section that the only way to implement a many-to-many relationship is with a separate join table. The consequence of not having any join columns in either of the entity tables is that there is no way to determine which side is the owner of the relationship. Because every bidirectional relationship has to have both an owning side and an inverse side, we must pick one of the two entities to be the owner. In this example, we picked `Employee` to be owner of the relationship, but we could have just as easily picked `Project` instead. As in every other bidirectional relationship, the inverse side must use the `mappedBy` element to identify the owning attribute.

Note that no matter which side is designated as the owner, the other side should include the `mappedBy` element; otherwise, the provider will think that both sides are the owner and that the mappings are separate unidirectional relationships.

Using Join Tables

Because the multiplicity of both sides of a many-to-many relationship is plural, neither of the two entity tables can store an unlimited set of foreign key values in a single entity row. We must use a third table to associate the two entity types. This association table is called a join table, and each many-to-many relationship must have one. They might be used for the other relationship types as well, but are not required and are therefore less common.

A join table consists simply of two foreign key or join columns to refer to each of the two entity types in the relationship. A collection of entities is then mapped as multiple rows in the table, each of which associates one entity with another. The set of rows that contain a given entity identifier in the source foreign key column represents the collection of entities related to that given entity.

Figure 4-16 shows the `EMPLOYEE` and `PROJECT` tables for the `Employee` and `Project` entities and the `EMP_PROJ` join table that associates them. The `EMP_PROJ` table contains only foreign key columns that make up its compound primary key. The `EMP_ID` column refers to the `EMPLOYEE` primary key, while the `PROJ_ID` column refers to the `PROJECT` primary key.

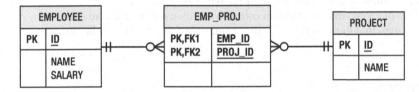

Figure 4-16. *Join table for a many-to-many relationship*

In order to map the tables described in Figure 4-16, we need to add some additional metadata to the `Employee` class that we have designated as the owner of the relationship. Listing 4-23 shows the many-to-many relationship with the accompanying join table annotations.

Listing 4-23. Using a Join Table

```
@Entity
public class Employee {
    @Id private long id;
    private String name;
    @ManyToMany
    @JoinTable(name="EMP_PROJ",
          joinColumns=@JoinColumn(name="EMP_ID"),
          inverseJoinColumns=@JoinColumn(name="PROJ_ID"))
    private Collection<Project> projects;
    // ...
}
```

The @JoinTable annotation is used to configure the join table for the relationship. The two join columns in the join table are distinguished by means of the owning and inverse sides. The join column to the owning side is described in the joinColumns element, while the join column to the inverse side is specified by the inverseJoinColumns element. You can see from Listing 4-23 that the values of these elements are actually @JoinColumn annotations embedded within the @JoinTable annotation. This provides the ability to declare all of the information about the join columns within the table that defines them. The names are plural for times when there might be multiple columns for each foreign key (either the owning entity or the inverse entity has a multipart primary key). This more complicated case will be discussed in Chapter 10.

In our example, we fully specified the names of the join table and its columns because this is the most common case. But if we were generating the database schema from the entities, we would not actually need to specify this information. We could have relied on the default values that would be assumed and used when the persistence provider generates the table for us. When no @JoinTable annotation is present on the owning side, then a default join table named <Owner>_<Inverse> is assumed, where <Owner> is the name of the owning entity, and <Inverse> is the name of the inverse or non-owning entity. Of course, the owner is basically picked at random by the developer, so these defaults will apply according to the way the relationship is mapped and whichever entity is designated as the owning side.

The join columns will be defaulted according to the join column defaulting rules that were previously described in the section "Using Join Columns." The default name of the join column that points to the owning entity is the name of the attribute on the inverse entity that points to the owning entity, appended by an underscore and the name of the primary key column of the owning entity table. So in our example, the Employee is the owning entity, and the Project has an employees attribute that contains the collection of Employee instances. The Employee entity maps to the EMPLOYEE table and has a primary key column of ID, so the defaulted name of the join column to the owning entity would be EMPLOYEES_ID. The inverse join column would be likewise defaulted to be PROJECTS_ID.

It is fairly clear that the defaulted names of a join table and the join columns within it are not likely to match up with an existing table. This is why we mentioned that the defaults are really useful only if the database schema being mapped to was generated by the provider.

Unidirectional Collection Mappings

When an entity has a one-to-many mapping to a target entity, but the @OneToMany annotation does not include the mappedBy element, it is assumed to be in a unidirectional relationship with the target entity. This means that the target entity does not have a many-to-one mapping back to the source entity. Figure 4-17 shows a unidirectional one-to-many association between Employee and Phone.

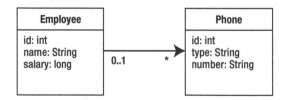

Figure 4-17. *Unidirectional one-to-many relationship*

Consider the data model in Figure 4-18. There is no join column to store the association back from Phone to Employee. Therefore, we have used a join table to associate the Phone entity with the Employee entity.

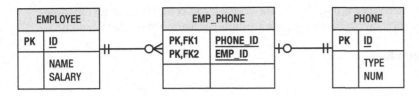

Figure 4-18. *Join table for a unidirectional one-to-many relationship*

Similarly, when one side of a many-to-many relationship does not have a mapping to the other, it is a unidirectional relationship. The join table must still be used; the only difference is that only one of the two entity types actually uses the table to load its related entities or updates it to store additional entity associations.

In both of these two unidirectional collection-valued cases, the source code is similar to the earlier examples, but there is no attribute in the target entity to reference the source entity, and the mappedBy element will not be present in the @OneToMany annotation on the source entity. The join table must now be specified as part of the mapping. Listing 4-24 shows Employee with a one-to-many relationship to Phone using a join table.

Listing 4-24. Unidirectional One-to-Many Relationship

```
@Entity
public class Employee {
    @Id private long id;
    private String name;
    @OneToMany
    @JoinTable(name="EMP_PHONE",
            joinColumns=@JoinColumn(name="EMP_ID"),
            inverseJoinColumns=@JoinColumn(name="PHONE_ID"))
    private Collection<Phone> phones;
    // ...
}
```

Note that when generating the schema, default naming for the join columns is slightly different in the unidirectional case because there is no inverse attribute. The name of the join table would default to EMPLOYEE_PHONE and would have a join column named EMPLOYEE_ID after the name of the Employee entity and its primary key column. The inverse join column would be named PHONES_ID, which is the concatenation of the phones attribute in the Employee entity and the ID primary key column of the PHONE table.

Lazy Relationships

Previous sections showed how to configure an attribute to be loaded when it got accessed and not necessarily before. You learned that lazy loading at the attribute level is not normally very beneficial.

At the relationship level, however, lazy loading can be a big boon to enhancing performance. It can reduce the amount of SQL that gets executed, and speed up queries and object loading considerably.

The fetch mode can be specified on any of the four relationship mapping types. When not specified on a single-valued relationship, the related object is guaranteed to be loaded eagerly. Collection-valued relationships default to be lazily loaded, but because lazy loading is only a hint to the provider, they can be loaded eagerly if the provider decides to do so.

In bidirectional relationship cases, the fetch mode might be lazy on one side but eager on the other. This kind of configuration is actually quite common because relationships are often accessed in different ways depending on the direction from which navigation occurs.

An example of overriding the default fetch mode is if we don't want to load the `ParkingSpace` for an `Employee` every time we load the `Employee`. Listing 4-25 shows the `parkingSpace` attribute configured to use lazy loading.

Listing 4-25. Changing the Fetch Mode on a Relationship

```
@Entity
public class Employee {
    @Id private long id;
    @OneToOne(fetch=FetchType.LAZY)
    private ParkingSpace parkingSpace;
    // ...
}
```

■ **Tip** A relationship that is specified or defaulted to be lazily loaded might or might not cause the related object to be loaded when the getter method is used to access the object. The object might be a proxy, so it might take actually invoking a method on it to cause it to be faulted in.

Embedded Objects

An embedded object is one that is dependent on an entity for its identity. It has no identity of its own, but is merely part of the entity state that has been carved off and stored in a separate Java object hanging off of the entity. In Java, embedded objects appear similar to relationships in that they are referenced by an entity and appear in the Java sense to be the target of an association. In the database, however, the state of the embedded object is stored with the rest of the entity state in the database row, with no distinction between the state in the Java entity and that in its embedded object.

■ **Tip** Although embedded objects are referenced by the entities that own them, they are not said to be in relationships with the entities. The term relationship can only be applied when both sides are entities.

If the database row contains all the data for both the entity and its embedded object, why have such an object anyway? Why not just define the fields of the entity to reference all its persistence state instead of splitting it up into one or more subobjects that are second-class persistent objects dependent on the entity for their existence?

This brings us back to the object-relational impedance mismatch we talked about in Chapter 1. Because the database record contains more than one logical type, it makes sense to make that separation explicit in the object model of the application even though the physical representation is different. You could almost say that the embedded object is a more natural representation of the domain concept than a simple collection of attributes on the entity. Furthermore, once you have identified a grouping of entity state that makes up an embedded object, you can share the same embedded object type with other entities that also have the same internal representation.[1]

An example of such reuse is address information. Figure 4-19 shows an `EMPLOYEE` table that contains a mixture of basic employee information as well as columns that correspond to the home address of the employee.

---

[1] Even though embedded types can be shared or reused, the instances cannot. An embedded object instance belongs to the entity that references it; no other entity instance, of that entity type or any other, can reference the same embedded instance.

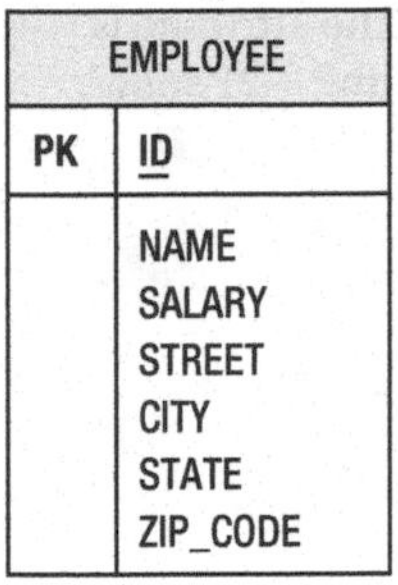

EMPLOYEE	
PK	ID
	NAME
	SALARY
	STREET
	CITY
	STATE
	ZIP_CODE

Figure 4-19. *EMPLOYEE table with embedded address information*

The STREET, CITY, STATE, and ZIP_CODE columns combine logically to form the address. In the object model, this is an excellent candidate to be abstracted into a separate Address embedded type instead of listing each attribute on the entity class. The entity class would then simply have an address attribute pointing to an embedded object of type Address. Figure 4-20 shows how Employee and Address relate to each other. The UML composition association is used to denote that the Employee wholly owns the Address, and that an instance of Address cannot be shared by any other object other than the Employee instance that owns it.

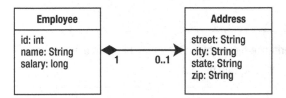

Figure 4-20. *Employee and embedded* Address

With this representation, not only is the address information neatly encapsulated within an object but if another entity such as Company also has address information, it can also have an attribute that points to its own embedded Address object. We will describe this scenario in the next section.

An embedded type is marked as such by adding the @Embeddable annotation to the class definition. This annotation serves to distinguish the class from other regular Java types. Once a class has been designated as embeddable, then its fields and properties will be persistable as part of an entity. We might also want to define the access type of the embeddable object so it is accessed the same way regardless of which entity it is embedded in. Listing 4-26 shows the definition of the Address embedded type.

Listing 4-26. Embeddable Address Type

```
@Embeddable @Access(AccessType.FIELD)
public class Address {
    private String street;
    private String city;
    private String state;
    @Column(name="ZIP_CODE")
    private String zip;
    // ...
}
```

To use this class in an entity, the entity needs to have only an attribute of the embeddable type. The attribute is optionally annotated with the @Embedded annotation to indicate that it is an embedded mapping. Listing 4-27 shows the Employee class using an embedded Address object.

Listing 4-27. Using an Embedded Object

```
@Entity
public class Employee {
    @Id private long id;
    private String name;
    private long salary;
    @Embedded private Address address;
    // ...
}
```

When the provider persists an instance of Employee, it will access the attributes of the Address object just as if they were present on the entity instance itself. Column mappings on the Address type really pertain to columns on the EMPLOYEE table, even though they are listed in a different type.

The decision to use embedded objects or entities depends on whether you think you will ever need to create relationships to them or from them. Embedded objects are not meant to be entities, and as soon as you start to treat them as entities you should probably make them first-class entities instead of embedded objects if the data model permits it.

■ **Tip** It is not portable to define embedded objects as part of inheritance hierarchies. Once they begin to extend one another, the complexity of embedding them increases, and the value for cost ratio decreases.

Before we got to our example, we mentioned that an Address class could be reused in both Employee and Company entities. Ideally we would like the representation shown in Figure 4-21. Even though both the Employee and Company classes comprise the Address class, this is not a problem because each instance of Address will be used by only a single Employee or Company instance.

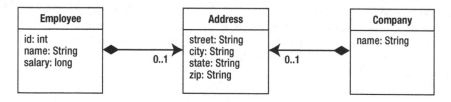

Figure 4-21. Address shared by two entities

Given that the column mappings of the Address embedded type apply to the columns of the containing entity, you might be wondering how sharing could be possible if the two entity tables have different column names for the same fields. Figure 4-22 demonstrates this problem. The COMPANY table matches the default and mapped attributes of the Address type defined earlier, but the EMPLOYEE table in this example has been changed to match the address requirements of a person living in Canada. We need a way for an entity to map the embedded object according to its own entity table needs, and we have one in the @AttributeOverride annotation.

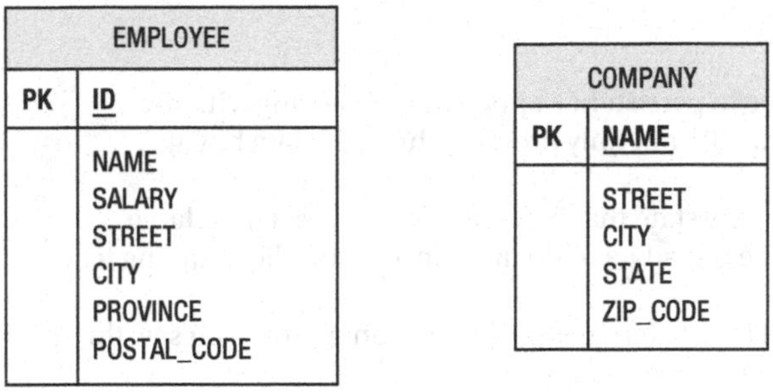

```
  EMPLOYEE
PK  ID
    NAME
    SALARY
    STREET
    CITY
    PROVINCE
    POSTAL_CODE
```

```
  COMPANY
PK  NAME
    STREET
    CITY
    STATE
    ZIP_CODE
```

Figure 4-22. *EMPLOYEE and COMPANY tables*

We use an @AttributeOverride annotation for each attribute of the embedded object that we want to override in the entity. We annotate the embedded field or property in the entity and specify in the name element the field or property in the embedded object that we are overriding. The column element allows us to specify the column that the attribute is being mapped to in the entity table. We indicate this in the form of a nested @Column annotation. If we are overriding multiple fields or properties, we can use the plural @AttributeOverrides annotation and nest multiple @AttributeOverride annotations inside of it.

Listing 4-28 shows an example of using Address in both Employee and Company. The Company entity uses the Address type without change, but the Employee entity specifies two attribute overrides to map the state and zip attributes of the Address to the PROVINCE and POSTAL_CODE columns of the EMPLOYEE table.

Listing 4-28. Reusing an Embedded Object in Multiple Entities

```
@Entity
public class Employee {
    @Id private long id;
    private String name;
    private long salary;
    @Embedded
    @AttributeOverrides({
        @AttributeOverride(name="state", column=@Column(name="PROVINCE")),
        @AttributeOverride(name="zip", column=@Column(name="POSTAL_CODE"))
    })
    private Address address;
    // ...
}
@Entity
public class Company {
    @Id private String name;
    @Embedded
    private Address address;
    // ...
}
```

Summary

Mapping objects to relational databases is of critical importance to persistence applications. Dealing with the impedance mismatch requires a sophisticated suite of metadata. JPA not only provides this metadata but also facilitates easy and convenient development.

In this chapter, we went through the process of mapping entity state that included simple Java types, large objects, enumerated types, and temporal types. We also used the metadata to do meet-in-the-middle mapping to specific table names and columns.

We explained how identifiers are generated and described four different strategies of generation. You saw the different strategies in action and learned how to differentiate them from each other.

We then reviewed some of the relationship concepts and applied them to object-relational mapping metadata. We used join columns and join tables to map single-valued and collection-valued associations and went over some examples. We also discussed special types of objects called embeddables that are mapped but do not have identifiers and can exist only within persistent entities.

The next chapter will discuss more of the intricacies of mapping collection-valued relationships, as well as how to map collections of non-entity objects. We will delve into the different Collection types and the ways that these types can be used and mapped, and see how they affect the database tables that are being mapped to.

■ ■ ■

CHAPTER 5

Collection Mapping

Sometimes a `Collection` is used like a milk crate: it's just a simple container with no apparent order or intended organization. Other cases demand some kind of system of order and arranging so the way objects are retrieved from the collection has meaning. Whether the collection is of the first type or the second, collections of objects require more effort to map than single objects, although in compensation they offer greater flexibility.

In the last chapter, we began the journey of mapping collection-valued relationships, spooning out only the basics of mapping collections of entities to the database. This chapter goes into more detail about how we can map more sophisticated collection types, such as persistently ordered `List`s, and `Map`s with keys and values that are of various object types. We will even explore how to map collections of objects that are not entities.

Relationships and Element Collections

When we speak of mapping collections, there are actually three kinds of objects that we can store in mapped collections. We can map collections of entities, embeddables, or basic types, and each one requires a certain level of understanding to be correctly mapped and efficiently used.

We should clarify one potential point of confusion about these types of objects when they are stored in collections. In the previous chapter, we introduced the concept of relationships from one entity type to another, and you learned that when the source entity has a collection containing instances of the target entity type it is called a multivalued relationship. However, collections of embeddable and basic types are not relationships; they are simply collections of elements that are thus called element collections. Relationships define associations between independent entities, whereas element collections contain objects that are dependent upon the referencing entity, and can be retrieved only through the entity that contains them.

A practical difference between relationships and element collections is the annotation that is used to denote them. A relationship minimally requires the relationship annotation, either @OneToMany or @ManyToMany, whereas an element collection is indicated by the @ElementCollection annotation. Assuming the VacationEntry embeddable class in Listing 5-1, Listing 5-2 shows an example of an element collection of embeddables in the vacationBookings attribute, as well as an element collection of basic types (String) in the nickNames attribute.

Listing 5-1. VacationEntry Embeddable

```
@Embeddable
public class VacationEntry {
    @Temporal(TemporalType.DATE)
    private Calendar startDate;

    @Column(name="DAYS")
    private int daysTaken;
    // ...
}
```

Listing 5-2. *Element Collections of Embeddables and Basic Types*

```
@Entity
public class Employee {
    @Id private int id;
    private String name;
    private long salary;
    // ...

    @ElementCollection(targetClass=VacationEntry.class)
    private Collection vacationBookings;

    @ElementCollection
    private Set<String> nickNames;

    // ...
}
```

You can see from Listing 5-2 that, like the relationship annotations, the @ElementCollection annotation includes a targetClass element that is used to specify the class if the Collection does not define the type of element contained in it. It also includes a fetch element to indicate whether the collection should be lazily loaded.

A more interesting aspect of the mappings in Listing 5-2 is the absence of any additional metadata. Recall that the elements that are being stored in the collections are not entities, so they do not have any mapped table. Embeddables are supposed to be stored in the same table as the entity that refers to them, but if there is a collection of embeddables, how would it be possible to store a multiplicity of like-mapped objects in a single row? Similarly for basic types, we could not map each nickname String to a column in the EMPLOYEE table and expect to store multiple strings in a single row. For this reason, element collections require a separate table called a collection table. Every collection table must have a join column that refers to the containing entity table. Additional columns in the collection table are used to map the attributes of the embeddable element, or the basic element state if the element is of a basic type.

We can specify a collection table using a @CollectionTable annotation, which allows us to designate the name of the table, as well as the join column. Default values will apply if the annotation or specific elements within that annotation are not specified. The table name will default to the name of the referencing entity, appended with an underscore and the name of the entity attribute that contains the element collection. The join column default is similarly the name of the referencing entity, appended with an underscore and the name of the primary key column of the entity table. Because no collection tables were specified in either of the element collections in the vacationBookings and nickNames attributes of the Employee entity defined in Listing 5-2, they are defaulted to use collection tables named EMPLOYEE_VACATIONBOOKINGS and EMPLOYEE_NICKNAMES, respectively. The join column in each of the collection tables will be EMPLOYEE_ID, which is just the name of the entity combined with the mapped Employee primary key column.

We map the fields or properties of the embeddable type to the columns in the collection table instead of to the primary table of the entity, with the usual column name defaulting rules applying. When the element collection contains basic types, the values are also stored in a column in the collection table, with the default column name being the name of the entity attribute. Applying this rule, the nicknames would be stored in the NICKNAMES column. After all the defaults are applied, the mapped tables would look like those in Figure 5-1.

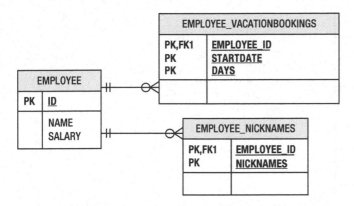

Figure 5-1. *EMPLOYEE entity table and mapped collection tables*

When we first discussed embeddables, you saw how the attributes were mapped within the embeddable object but could be overridden when embedded inside other entities or embeddables. We used the @AttributeOverride annotation to override the column names. The same annotation can also be used to override the embedded attributes in the elements of an element collection. In Listing 5-3, the daysTaken attribute is being remapped, using @AttributeOverride, from being stored in the DAYS column to being stored in the DAYS_ABS column. One important difference between using @AttributeOverride on simple embedded mappings and using it to override the columns of embeddables in an element collection is that in the latter case the column specified by @AttributeOverride actually applies to the collection table, not to the entity table.

Listing 5-3. Overriding Collection Table Columns

```
@Entity
public class Employee {
    @Id private int id;
    private String name;
    private long salary;
    // ...

    @ElementCollection(targetClass=VacationEntry.class)
    @CollectionTable(
        name="VACATION",
        joinColumns=@JoinColumn(name="EMP_ID"))
    @AttributeOverride(name="daysTaken",
                       column=@Column(name="DAYS_ABS"))
    private Collection vacationBookings;

    @ElementCollection
    @Column(name="NICKNAME")
    private Set<String> nickNames;
    // ...
}
```

In order to override the name of the column in which the nicknames are stored, we can use the @Column annotation, remembering again that the name specifies a column in the collection table, not the entity table. Figure 5-2 shows the mapped tables, including the overridden VACATION collection table mapped by the vacationBookings collection.

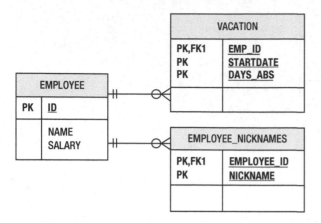

Figure 5-2. *EMPLOYEE entity table and mapped collection tables with overrides*

Using Different Collection Types

We can use different types of collections to store multivalued entity associations and collections of objects. Depending upon the needs of the application, any of Collection, Set, List, and Map might be appropriate. There are rules corresponding to the type of collection, however, that guide its usage, so before using a given collection type, you should be familiar with the rules that govern how that type can be mapped and manipulated.

The first step is to define the collection to be any one of the interface types mentioned previously. You then initialize the attribute with a concrete implementation class. This can be done in a constructor or initialization method of the entity class and allows you to put objects in the implementation collection of a new or unpersisted entity. Once the entity becomes managed or has been persisted by means of an EntityManager.persist() call, the interface must always be used when operating on the collection, whether it has been read in from the database or has been detached from the entity manager. This is because the moment the entity becomes managed, the persistence provider can replace the initial concrete instance with an alternate instance of a Collection implementation class of its own.

Sets or Collections

The most common collection type used in associations is the standard Collection superinterface. This is used when it doesn't matter which implementation is underneath and when the common Collection methods are all that is required to access the entities stored in it.

A Set will prevent duplicate elements from being inserted and might be a simpler and more concise collection model, while a vanilla Collection interface is the most generic. Neither of these interfaces requires additional annotations beyond the original mapping annotation to further specify them. They are used the same way as if they held non-persistent objects. An example of using a Set interface for an element collection and a Collection for another is in Listing 5-3.

Lists

Another common collection type is the List. A List is typically used when the entities or elements are to be retrieved in some user-defined order. Because the notion of row order in the database is not commonly defined, the task of determining the ordering must lie with the application.

There are two ways to determine the order of the List. The first is to map it so that it is ordered according to state that exists in each entity or element in the List. This is the easiest method and is less intrusive on the data model.

The second involves maintaining the order of the List in an additional database column. It is more Java-friendly in that it supports the traditional ordering semantics of a Java List, but can be far less performant, as you will see in the following sections.

Ordering By Entity or Element Attribute

The most prevalent approach to ordering entities or elements in a List is to specify an ordering rule based on the comparison of a particular attribute of the entity or element. If the List is a relationship, the attribute is most often the primary key of the target entity.

We indicate the attribute to order by in the @OrderBy annotation. The value of the annotation is a string that contains one or more comma-separated fields or properties of the object being ordered. Each of the attributes can be optionally followed by an ASC or DESC keyword to define whether the attribute should be ordered in ascending or descending order. If the direction is not specified, the property will be ordered in ascending order.

If the List is a relationship and references entities, specifying @OrderBy with no fields or properties, or not specifying it at all, will cause the List to be ordered by the primary keys of the entities in the List. In the case of an element collection of basic types, then the List will be ordered by the values of the elements. Element collections of embeddable types will result in the List being defaulted to be in some undefined order, typically in the order returned by the database in the absence of any ORDER BY clause.

The example back in Listing 4-20 of the previous chapter had a one-to-many relationship from Department to Employee. If we want the employees to be in a particular order, we can use a List instead of a Collection. By adding an @OrderBy annotation on the mapping, we can indicate that we want the employees to be ordered in ascending alphabetical order by name. Listing 5-4 shows the updated example.

Listing 5-4. One-to-Many Relationship Using a List

```
@Entity
public class Department {
    // ...
    @OneToMany(mappedBy="department")
    @OrderBy("name ASC")
    private List<Employee> employees;
    // ...
}
```

We needn't have included the ASC in the @OrderBy annotations because it would be ascending by default, but it is good style to include it.

We could have just as easily ordered the employee List by an embedded field of Employee. For example, if name had been embedded in an embedded Employee field called info that was of embeddable type EmployeeInfo, we would write the annotation as @OrderBy("info.name ASC").

We might also want to have suborderings using multiple attributes. We can do that by specifying comma-separated <attribute name ASC/DESC> pairs in the annotation. For example, if Employee had a status, we might have ordered by status and then by name by using an @OrderBy annotation of @OrderBy("status DESC, name ASC"). Of course, the prerequisite for using an attribute in an @OrderBy annotation is that the attribute type should be comparable, meaning that it supports comparison operators.

If you were to simply switch the order of two employees in the List, it might appear that they were assuming new positions in the List. However, if in a new persistence context you read the department back in again and accessed its employees the List would come back in the order that it was in before you manipulated it[1]. This is because the List order is based upon the collation order asserted by the @OrderBy annotation. Simply changing the order of the items

---

[1]Assuming that the collection was not returned from a second level shared cache.

in a List in memory will not cause that order to be stored in the database at commit time. In fact, the order specified in @OrderBy will be used only when reading the List back into memory. As a rule of thumb, the List order should always be maintained in memory to be consistent with the @OrderBy ordering rules.

Persistently Ordered Lists

Another example that calls for the order provided by List is a print queue that keeps a list of the print jobs that are queued up at any given time. The PrintQueue is essentially a First In First Out (FIFO) queue that, when the printer is available, takes the next PrintJob from the front of the queue and sends it to the printer for printing. Assuming that PrintQueue and PrintJob are entities, we would have a one-to-many relationship from PrintQueue to PrintJob and a many-to-one relationship back.

Given that you know how to map the relationships, and you just learned above how to map ordered lists using @OrderBy, it would seem pretty straightforward to map this relationship using a List. The PrintJob entity, in Listing 5-5, illustrates its many-to-one side of the bidirectional mapping.

Listing 5-5. PrintJob Entity

```
@Entity
public class PrintJob {
    @Id private int id;
    // ...
    @ManyToOne
    private PrintQueue queue;
    // ...
}
```

The problem arises when we discover that the PrintJob entity does not have an attribute that can be used in @OrderBy. Because the order of the job does not really affect the actual PrintJob that gets serviced, the decision was made to not store the order of a given job within the PrintJob entity. The position of a particular PrintJob in the queue is determined simply by its position in the job List.

The PrintJob entities in the Java List cannot retain their order unless a designated database column has been created to store it. We call this column the order column, and it provides a stronger persistent ordering than @OrderBy. It is in the order column that the object's order is stored and updated when it is moved from one position to another within the same List. It is transparent to the user in that the user does not need to manipulate it, or even necessarily be aware of it, in order to use the List. It does need to be known and considered as part of the mapping process, though, and is declared by means of an @OrderColumn annotation.

Using an @OrderColumn annotation precludes the use of @OrderBy, and vice versa. Listing 5-6 shows how @OrderColumn can be used with our one-to-many relationship mapping in PrintQueue. The table mappings are shown in Figure 5-3.

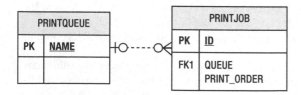

Figure 5-3. *PRINTQUEUE table and target PRINTJOB table with order column*

Listing 5-6. One-To-Many List from PrintQueue to PrintJob

```
@Entity
public class PrintQueue {
    @Id private String name;
    // ...
    @OneToMany(mappedBy="queue")
    @OrderColumn(name="PRINT_ORDER")
    private List<PrintJob> jobs;
    // ...
}
```

You probably noticed something different about the declaration of the order column on the one-to-many side of the relationship. In the last chapter, we explained the practice of mapping the physical columns on the owning side because that is the side that owns the table in which they apply. The order column is an exception to this rule when the relationship is bidirectional because the column is always defined beside the List that it is ordering, even though it is in the table mapped by the owning many-to-one entity side. So in Listing 5-6, the @OrderColumn annotation is on the PrintQueue side of the relationship, but the column named PRINT_ORDER is referring to whatever table the PrintJob entity is mapped to.

Although the @OrderColumn annotation must be present to enable the ordered position of the entity to be stored in a database column, the elements of the annotation are optional. The name just defaults to the name of the entity attribute, appended by the "_ORDER" string. So, if the name had not been overridden in Listing 5-6 to be PRINT_ORDER, it would have defaulted to be JOBS_ORDER.

The table that the order column is stored in depends on the mapping that @OrderColumn is being applied to. It is usually in the table that stores the entity or element being stored. As mentioned, in our bidirectional one-to-many relationship in Listing 5-6, the entity being stored is PrintJob, and the order column would be stored in the PRINTJOB table. If the mapping were an element collection, the order column would be stored in the collection table. In many-to-many relationships, the order column is in the join table.

Some additional comments about using @OrderColumn are necessary because it is a feature that could easily be misused. We said that the order column is transparent to the user of the list, but it turns out that this transparency can have unexpected repercussions for a naïve user.

Consider a busy company with many people and many print jobs being submitted and printed. When a job makes it to the first position, it gets removed from the queue and sent to the printer. Meanwhile, another job inherits the "on deck" position. Every time a job gets serviced, every other PrintJob remaining on the queue moves up by one position and is one step closer to being printed. In other words, with each printed job, the order of each and every other PrintJob changes and must be resaved to the database. In our case, the order column is being stored in the table in which PrintJob entities are stored: the PRINTJOB table.

Needless to say, we are looking at a potentially large cost, further compounded as the queue gets longer. For every job added to a queue of size n, there will be n additional SQL updates sent to the database to change the order of that job before it even makes it to the printer. That could ring alarm bells for a database administrator, especially a vigilant one with a penchant for perusing the SQL audits.

As a final comment on List usage, there is special support in JPA queries that allows ordered subsets or individual items of a List to be accessed and returned. You will see how this can be achieved in Chapter 8.

Maps

The Map is a very common collection that is used in virtually every application and offers the ability to associate a key object with an arbitrary value object. The various underlying implementations are expected to use fast hashing techniques to optimize direct access to the keys.

There is a great deal of flexibility with Map types in JPA, given that the keys and values can be any combination of entities, basic types, and embeddables. Permuting the three types in the two key and value positions renders nine distinct Map types. We will give detailed explanations of the most common combinations in the following sections.

Keys and Values

Although basic types, embeddable types, or entity types can be `Map` keys, remember that if they are playing the role of key, they must follow the basic rules for keys. They must be comparable and respond appropriately to the `hashCode()` method, and `equals()` method when necessary[2]. They should also be unique, at least within the domain of a particular collection instance, so that values are not lost or overwritten in memory. Keys should not be changed, or more specifically, the parts of the key object that are used in the `hashCode()` and `equals()` methods must not be changed while the object is acting as a key in a `Map`.

When keys are basic or embeddable types, they are stored directly in the table being referred to. Depending upon the type of mapping, it can be either the target entity table, join table, or collection table. However, when keys are entities, only the foreign key is stored in the table because entities are stored in their own table, and their identity in the database must be preserved.

It is always the type of the value object in the `Map` that determines what kind of mapping must be used. If the values are entities, the `Map` must be mapped as a one-to-many or many-to-many relationship, whereas if the values of the `Map` are either embeddable or basic types, the `Map` is mapped as an element collection.

Even though the `Map` keys do not affect the type of mapping, they still require annotations, in addition to the relationship or element collection annotations, to indicate the column(s) in which they are stored. These annotations will be covered in the different use cases in the following sections.

Keying By Basic Type

We mentioned in the previous sections that element collections of basic types are stored in collection tables, and basic keys are stored in the tables referred to by the mapping. If the mapping is an element collection keyed by a basic type, the keys will be stored in the same collection table in which the `Map` values are stored. Likewise, if it is a one-to-many relationship, and the foreign key is in the target entity table, the keys will be in the target entity table. If the relationship mapping uses a join table, the keys will be in the join table.

To show the collection table case, let's look at an element collection example that maps the phone numbers of an `Employee`. If we use a `Map`, we can key on the phone number type and store the phone number as the value. So the key of each `Map` entry will be any of "Home", "Work" or "Mobile", as a `String`, and the value will be the associated phone number `String`. Listing 5-7 shows the element collection mapping code.

Listing 5-7. Element Collection of Strings with String Keys

```
@Entity
public class Employee {
    @Id private int id;
    private String name;
    private long salary;

    @ElementCollection
    @CollectionTable(name="EMP_PHONE")
    @MapKeyColumn(name="PHONE_TYPE")
    @Column(name="PHONE_NUM")
    private Map<String, String> phoneNumbers;
    // ...
}
```

---

[2]See the javadoc for java.util.Map for more details.

The @ElementCollection and @CollectionTable annotations are nothing new, and Listing 5-3 showed that we can use the @Column annotation to override the name of the column that stores the values in the Collection. Here we are doing the same thing, except that we are overriding the column in which the Map values would be stored instead of the items in a generic Collection.

The only new annotation is @MapKeyColumn, which is used to indicate the column in the collection table that stores the basic key. When the annotation is not specified, the key is stored in a column named after the mapped collection attribute, appended with the "_KEY" suffix. In Listing 5-7, if we had not specified @MapKeyColumn, the defaulting rule would have caused the key to be mapped to the PHONENUMBERS_KEY column in the EMP_PHONE collection table.

Phone number values can be duplicated in the collection table (for example, multiple employees living at the same home and having the same phone number), so the PHONE_NUM column obviously won't be unique in the table. The types of phone numbers have to be unique only within a given Map or Employee instance, so the PHONE_TYPE column won't be the primary key, either. In fact, because basic types do not have identity, and in some cases the same key-value entries can be duplicated in multiple source entities, the key-value columns can't be the primary key columns on their own. Unique tuples in the collection table must be the combination of the key column and the foreign key column that references the source entity instance. Figure 5-4 shows the resulting collection table, along with the source EMPLOYEE entity table that it references. You can see the primary key constraint on the EMPLOYEE_ID and PHONE_TYPE columns.

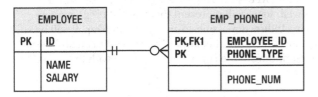

Figure 5-4. *EMPLOYEE entity table and EMP_PHONE collection table*

We should really improve our model, though, because using a String key to store something that is constrained to be one of only three values ("Home", "Mobile", or "Work"), is not great style. An appropriate improvement would be to use an enumerated type instead of String. We can define our enumerated type as follows:

```
public enum PhoneType { Home, Mobile, Work }
```

Now we have the valid options as enumerated constants, and there is no chance of mistyping or having invalid phone types. However, there is one further enhancement to consider. If we want to protect ourselves from future changes to the enumerated type values, either by reordering existing values or inserting additional ones, we should override the way the value is stored in the database. Instead of relying on the default approach of storing the ordinal value of the enumerated element, we want to store the String value, so we get the best of both worlds. The column will contain values that correspond to phone type settings in a human readable way, and the Java Map will have a strongly typed key.

The usual way of overriding the storage strategy for an enumerated type is to use the @Enumerated annotation. However, if we were to put @Enumerated on our Map attribute, it would apply to the values of the element collection, not the keys. That is why there is a special @MapKeyEnumerated annotation (see Listing 5-8). There is also an equivalent @MapKeyTemporal to specify the temporal type when the key is of type java.util.Date. Both @MapKeyEnumerated and @MapKeyTemporal are applicable to keys that are of a basic type, regardless of whether it is an element collection or a relationship.

Listing 5-8. Element Collection of Strings with Enumerated Type Keys

```
@Entity
public class Employee {
    @Id private int id;
    private String name;
    private long salary;

    @ElementCollection
    @CollectionTable(name="EMP_PHONE")
    @MapKeyEnumerated(EnumType.STRING)
    @MapKeyColumn(name="PHONE_TYPE")
    @Column(name="PHONE_NUM")
    private Map<PhoneType, String> phoneNumbers;
    // ...
}
```

Listing 5-4 had a one-to-many relationship that used a List to hold all the employees in a given department. Suppose that we change it to use a Map and keep track of which employee is working in any given office or cubicle. By keying on the cubicle number (which can contain letters as well, so we will represent them as a String), we can easily find which Employee works in that cubicle. Because this is a bidirectional one-to-many relationship, it will be mapped as a foreign key to DEPARTMENT in the EMPLOYEE table. The cubicle number keys will be stored in an additional column in the EMPLOYEE table, each one stored in the row corresponding to the Employee associated with that cubicle. Listing 5-9 shows the one-to-many mapping.

Listing 5-9. One-to-Many Relationship Using a Map with String Key

```
@Entity
public class Department {
    @Id private int id;

    @OneToMany(mappedBy="department")
    @MapKeyColumn(name="CUB_ID")
    private Map<String, Employee> employeesByCubicle;
    // ...
}
```

What if an employee could split his time between multiple departments? We would have to change our model to a many-to-many relationship and use a join table. The @MapKeyColumn will be stored in the join table that references the two entities. The relationship is mapped in Listing 5-10.

Listing 5-10. Many-to-Many Relationship Using a Map with String Keys

```
@Entity
public class Department {
    @Id private int id;
    private String name;

    @ManyToMany
    @JoinTable(name="DEPT_EMP",
        joinColumns=@JoinColumn(name="DEPT_ID"),
        inverseJoinColumns=@JoinColumn(name="EMP_ID"))
```

```
    @MapKeyColumn(name="CUB_ID")
    private Map<String, Employee> employeesByCubicle;
    // ...
}
```

If we did not override the key column with @MapKeyColumn, it would have been defaulted as the name of the collection attribute suffixed by "_KEY". This would have produced a dreadful-looking EMPLOYEESBYCUBICLE_KEY column in the join table, which is not only ugly to read, but does not actually indicate what the key really is. Figure 5-5 shows the resulting tables.

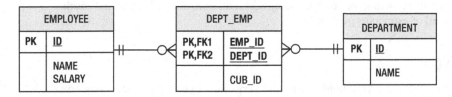

Figure 5-5. *EMPLOYEE and DEPARTMENT entity tables and DEPT_EMP join table*

■ **Note**   You can use a Map on only one side of a many-to-many relationship; it makes no difference which side.

Keying by Entity Attribute

When a one-to-many or many-to-many relationship collection of entities is represented as a Map, it is most often keyed by some attribute of the target entity type. Keying by entity attribute is actually a special case of keying by basic type where the mapping is a relationship, and the basic type of the key is the type of the attribute (that we are keying on) in the target entity. When this common case occurs, the @MapKey annotation can be used to designate the attribute of the target entity that is being keyed on.

If each department keeps track of the employees in it, as in our previous example in Listing 5-4, we could use a Map and key on the Employee id for quick Employee lookup. The updated Department mapping is shown in Listing 5-11.

Listing 5-11. One-to-Many Relationship Keyed by Entity Attribute

```
@Entity
public class Department {
    // ...
    @OneToMany(mappedBy="department")
    @MapKey(name="id")
    private Map<Integer, Employee> employees;
    // ...
}
```

The id attribute of Employee is also the identifier or primary key attribute, and it turns out that keying on the identifier is the most common case of all. It is so common that when no name is specified the entities will by default be keyed by their identifier attribute[3]. When the identifier attribute is defaulted and not explicitly listed, we do need to know the identifier type so we can correctly specify the first type parameter of the Map when using a parameterized Map.

---

[3] The @MapKey annotation is still required, however; otherwise, the @MapKeyColumn defaults would apply.

One of the reasons why the identifier attribute is used for the key is because it fits the key criteria nicely. It responds to the necessary comparison methods, hashCode() and equals(), and it is guaranteed to be unique.

If another attribute is used as the key, it should also be unique, although it is not absolutely required that it be unique across the entire domain of that entity type. It really needs to be unique only within the scope of the relationship. For example, we could key on the employee name as long as we made sure that the name would be unique within any department.

In the previous section, we stated that a basic key is stored in the table referred to by the mapping. The special case of keying by entity attribute is an exception to that rule in that no additional column is needed to store the key. It is already stored as part of the entity. That is why the @MapKeyColumn annotation is never used when keying on an entity attribute. A provider can easily build the contents of a one-to-many relationship Map by loading the entities that are associated with the source entity and extracting the attribute being keyed on from each of the loaded entities. No additional columns need to be read or extra joins performed.

Keying by Embeddable Type

Using embeddables as keys is not something that you should encounter very often. In fact, if you are considering doing it at all, you should probably think twice before proceeding. Just because it's possible does not mean that it is a good idea.

The problem with embeddables is that they are not full-fledged entities. They are not queryable in the sense that they can't be discovered or returned except as an aggregate part of their enclosing entities. Although this might not seem like a very severe limitation at the outset, it often becomes a problem later on in the development cycle.

Identity of embeddables is not defined in general, but when they are used as keys in a Map there must be some notion of uniqueness defined, applicable at least within the given Map. This means that the uniqueness constraint, at least logically, is on the combination of the embedded attributes and the foreign key column to the source entity.

Embeddable key types are similar to basic key types in that they are also stored in the table referred to by the mapping, but with embeddable types there are multiple attributes to store, not just one value. This results in multiple columns contributing to the primary key.

Sharing Embeddable Key Mappings with Values

The code example in Listing 5-11 showed a bidirectional one-to-many relationship from Department to Employee that was keyed by the id attribute of Employee. What if we had wanted to key on multiple attributes of Employee? For example, it might be desirable to look up employees by name in the Map, assuming that the name is unique within a given department. If the name were split into two attributes, one for the first name and one for the last name, as shown in Listing 5-12, then we would need a separate object to combine them and act as the key object in the Map. An embeddable type, such as EmployeeName in Listing 5-13, can be used for this purpose. Having an EmployeeName embeddable type also provides a useful class for passing the encapsulated full name around the system.

Listing 5-12. Employee Entity

```
@Entity
public class Employee {
    @Id private int id;
    @Column(name="F_NAME")
    private String firstName;
    @Column(name="L_NAME")
    private String lastName;
    private long salary;
    // ...
}
```

Listing 5-13. *EmployeeName Embeddable with Read-Only Mappings*

```
@Embeddable
public class EmployeeName {
    @Column(name="F_NAME", insertable=false, updatable=false)
    private String first_Name;
    @Column(name="L_NAME", insertable=false, updatable=false)
    private String last_Name;
    // ...
}
```

Because the bidirectional one-to-many relationship from Department to Employee is stored in the target entity table, the embeddable object key must also be stored there. However, it would be redundant for the two name components to be stored twice in each row, once for the firstName and lastName attributes of Employee and once for the first_Name and last_Name attributes of the EmployeeName key object. With a bit of clever mapping we can just reuse the two columns mapped to the Employee attributes and map them as read-only in the key (setting insertable and updatable to false). That is why in Listing 5-13 we map the first_Name and last_Name attributes to the same columns as the firstName and lastName attributes of Employee. From the Department perspective, the relationship in Listing 5-14 does not change much from Listing 5-11, except that the Map is keyed by EmployeeName instead of by Integer, and @MapKey is not used because the key is an embeddable and not an attribute of Employee.

Listing 5-14. *One-to-Many Relationship Keyed by Embeddable*

```
@Entity
public class Department {
    // ...
    @OneToMany(mappedBy="department")
    private Map<EmployeeName, Employee> employees;
    // ...
}
```

Overriding Embeddable Attributes

Another modeling option is to combine the two name columns within the Employee entity and define an embedded attribute of type EmployeeName, as shown in Listing 5-15.

Listing 5-15. *Employee Entity with Embedded Attribute*

```
@Entity
public class Employee {
    @Id private int id;

    @Embedded
    private EmployeeName name;
    private long salary;
    // ...
}
```

This time we are not sharing columns, so we must ensure that the mappings in EmployeeName are no longer read-only, or else the name will never get written to the database. The updated EmployeeName embeddable is in Listing 5-16.

Listing 5-16. *EmployeeName Embeddable*

```
@Embeddable
public class EmployeeName {
    @Column(name="F_NAME")
    private String first_Name;
    @Column(name="L_NAME")
    private String last_Name;
    // ...
}
```

For the purpose of illustration, let's go back to the many-to-many model described in Listing 5-10, except that we will key on the EmployeeName embeddable instead of the cubicle id. Even though the EmployeeName attributes are stored in the EMPLOYEE table for every Employee, the keys of the Map must still be stored in the DEPT_EMP join table. This is a result of the key being an embeddable type. Keying by either a single attribute of the entity or by a basic type would alleviate this denormalized data scenario.

By default, the key attributes would be mapped to the column names from the mappings defined within EmployeeName, but if the join table already exists and the columns in the join table do not have those names, the names must be overridden. Listing 5-17 shows how the embeddable attribute mappings of the Map key can be overridden from what they are defined to be in the embeddable class.

Listing 5-17. *Many-to-Many Map Keyed by Embeddable Type with Overriding*

```
@Entity
public class Department {
    @Id private int id;

    @ManyToMany
    @JoinTable(name="DEPT_EMP",
        joinColumns=@JoinColumn(name="DEPT_ID"),
        inverseJoinColumns=@JoinColumn(name="EMP_ID"))
    @AttributeOverrides({
        @AttributeOverride(
            name="first_Name",
            column=@Column(name="EMP_FNAME")),
        @AttributeOverride(
            name="last_Name",
            column=@Column(name="EMP_LNAME"))
    })
    private Map<EmployeeName, Employee> employees;
    // ...
}
```

The tables for the mapping are shown in Figure 5-6, with the embeddable attributes mapped to the join table for the key state and in the EMPLOYEE table for the Employee state. If the mapping had been an element collection, the embeddable attributes would be stored in a collection table instead of a join table.

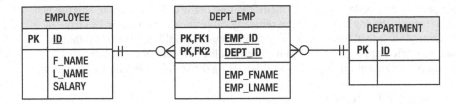

Figure 5-6. *DEPARTMENT and EMPLOYEE entity tables and DEPT_EMP join table*

As you can see from Listing 5-17, the mapping defaults for the key are being overridden through the use of `@AttributeOverride`. If instead of a many-to-many relationship we had an `@ElementCollection` of some embeddable type in a `Map`, we would have to differentiate between the key and the value. We would do this by prefixing the attribute name with "key." or "value.", depending upon which of the embeddable types we were overriding. An element collection of embedded `EmployeeInfo` types, with the same key overrides as those in the relationship in Listing 5-17, would use the following key prefixes:

```
@ElementCollection
@AttributeOverrides({
    @AttributeOverride(name="key.first_Name",
                       column=@Column(name="EMP_FNAME")),
    @AttributeOverride(name="key.last_Name",
                       column=@Column(name="EMP_LNAME"))
})
private Map<EmployeeName, EmployeeInfo> empInfos;
```

Keying by Entity

You might be reluctant to use entities as keys because intuition might lead you to think of this as a more resource-intensive option, with higher load and management costs. While that might be true in some cases, it is not necessarily always so. Quite often the entity you are considering keying on will already be in memory, or needed anyway, and keying on it either just accesses a cached instance or causes the instance to be loaded for later use.

One advantage of keying by entity type is that entity instances are globally unique (within the persistence unit) so there will not be any identity problems to deal with across different relationships or collections. A corollary of the basic identity property of entities is that only a foreign key needs to be stored in the mapped table, leading to a more normalized design and data storage schema.

As with the other types of `Map` keys, the key (in this case, a foreign key to the entity being keyed on) will be stored in the table referred to by the mapping.

Recall that the term used by JPA to represent a foreign key column is join column, and we use join columns in many-to-one and one-to-one relationships, as well as in join tables of collection-valued relationships. We now have a similar situation, except that instead of referring to the target of a relationship, our join column is referring to the entity key in a `Map` entry. To differentiate join columns that point to map keys from the ones used in relationships, a separate `@MapKeyJoinColumn` annotation was created. This annotation is used to override the join column defaults for an entity key. When it is not specified, the join column will have the same default column name as basic keys (the name of the relationship or element collection attribute, appended with the string "_KEY").

To illustrate the case of an entity being used as a key, we can add the notion of the seniority an `Employee` has within a given `Department`. We want to have a loose association between an `Employee` and his seniority, and the seniority has to be local to a `Department`. By defining an element collection `Map` in `Department`, with the seniority as the values and `Employee` entities as the keys, the seniority any `Employee` has in a given `Department` can be looked up by using the `Employee` instance as a key. The seniority is stored in a collection table, and if an `Employee` changes departments none of the other Employee objects needs to change. The indirection of the collection table, and the fact that the connections between the Department, the Employee, and the seniority value are all maintained by virtue of the Map, provide just the right level of coupling. Only the entries in the collection table would need to be updated.

Listing 5-18 shows the element collection mapping, with the join column being overridden using the @MapKeyJoinColumn annotation and the Map value column being overridden using the standard @Column annotation.

Listing 5-18. *Element Collection Map Keyed by EntityType*

```
@Entity
public class Department {
    @Id private int id;
    private String name;
    // ...
    @ElementCollection
    @CollectionTable(name="EMP_SENIORITY")
    @MapKeyJoinColumn(name="EMP_ID")
    @Column(name="SENIORITY")
    private Map<Employee, Integer> seniorities;
    // ...
}
```

Figure 5-7 shows that the collection table is nothing more than the values of the Map (the seniority) with a foreign key to the Department source entity table and another foreign key to the Employee entity key table.

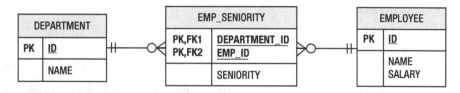

Figure 5-7. *DEPARTMENT and EMPLOYEE entity tables with EMP_SENIORITY collection table*

Untyped Maps

If we did not want to (or were not able to) use the typed parameter version of Map<KeyType, ValueType>, we would define it using the non-parameterized style of Map shown in Listing 5-19.

Listing 5-19. *One-to-Many Relationship Using a Non-parameterized Map*

```
@Entity
public class Department {
    // ...
    @OneToMany(targetEntity=Employee.class, mappedBy="department")
    @MapKey
    private Map employees;
    // ...
}
```

The targetEntity element only ever indicates the type of the Map value. Of course, if the Map holds an element collection and not a relationship, the targetClass element of @ElementCollection is used to indicate the value type of the Map.

In Listing 5-19, the type of the Map key can be easily deduced because the mapping is an entity relationship. The @MapKey default is to use the identifier attribute, id, of type int or Integer. If @MapKey had been specified and dictated that the key be an attribute that was not an identifier attribute, the type would still have been deducible because the entity attributes are all mapped with known types. However, if the key isn't an attribute of the target entity, @MapKeyClass might be used instead of @MapKey. It indicates the type of the key class when the Map is not defined in a typed way using generics. It is also used when the Map references an element collection instead of a relationship because basic or embeddable types do not have identifier attributes, and basic types do not even have attributes.

To illustrate how @MapKeyClass is used, let's take the element collection in Listing 5-7 and assume that it does not define the type parameters on the Map. The typing is filled in through the use of the @MapKeyClass annotation and the targetClass element in @ElementCollection, as shown in Listing 5-20.

Listing 5-20. *Untyped Element Collection of Strings with String Keys*

```
@Entity
public class Employee {
    @Id private int id;
    private String name;
    private long salary;

    @ElementCollection(targetClass=String.class)
    @CollectionTable(name="EMP_PHONE")
    @MapKeyColumn(name="PHONE_TYPE")
    @MapKeyClass(String.class)
    @Column(name="PHONE_NUM")
    private Map phoneNumbers;
    // ...
}
```

The @MapKeyClass annotation should be used whenever the key class cannot be deduced from the attribute definition or the other mapping metadata.

Rules for Maps

Learning about the various Map variants can get kind of confusing given that you can choose any one of three different kinds of key types and three different kinds of value types. Below are some of the basic rules of using a Map.

- Use the @MapKeyClass and targetEntity/targetClass elements of the relationship and element collection mappings to specify the classes when an untyped Map is used.

- Use @MapKey with one-to-many or many-to-many relationship Map that is keyed on an attribute of the target entity.

- Use @MapKeyJoinColumn to override the join column of the entity key.

- Use @Column to override the column storing the values of an element collection of basic types.

- Use @MapKeyColumn to override the column storing the keys when keyed by a basic type.

- Use @MapKeyTemporal and @MapKeyEnumerated if you need to further qualify a basic key that is a temporal or enumerated type.

- Use @AttributeOverride with a "key." or "value." prefix to override the column of an embeddable attribute type that is a Map key or a value, respectively.

Table 5-1 summarizes some of the different aspects of using a Map.

Table 5-1. *Summary of Mapping a Map*

Map	Mapping	Key Annotation	Value Annotation
Map<Basic,Basic>	@ElementCollection	@MapKeyColumn, @MayKeyEnumerated, @MapKeyTemporal	@Column
Map<Basic,Embeddable>	@ElementCollection	@MapKeyColumn, @MayKeyEnumerated, @MapKeyTemporal	Mapped by embeddable, @AttributeOverride, @AssociationOverride
Map<Basic,Entity>	@OneToMany, @ManyToMany	@MapKey, @MapKeyColumn, @MayKeyEnumerated, @MapKeyTemporal	Mapped by entity
Map<Embeddable,Basic>	@ElementCollection	Mapped by embeddable, @AttributeOverride	@Column
Map<Embeddable,Embeddable>	@ElementCollection	Mapped by embeddable, @AttributeOverride	Mapped by embeddable, @AttributeOverride, @AssociationOverride
Map<Embeddable,Entity>	@OneToMany, @ManyToMany	Mapped by embeddable @AttributeOverride	Mapped by entity
Map<Entity,Basic>	@ElementCollection	@MapKeyJoinColumn	@Column
Map<Entity,Embeddable>	@ElementCollection	@MapKeyJoinColumn	Mapped by embeddable, @AttributeOverride, @AssociationOverride
Map<Entity,Entity>	@OneToMany, @ManyToMany	@MapKeyJoinColumn	Mapped by entity

Duplicates

When we were discussing the Set interface we mentioned that it was ideal for preventing duplicates. What we meant was that the Set datatype in Java does not allow them. We didn't really say anything about duplicates in the database. In fact, the JPA specification does not say anything about whether duplicates are allowed in collections, either in the database or in memory, and in most cases they will not be supported. To get a feeling for why supporting duplicates is difficult, let's go to the data model and uncover some of the gory details. You might prefer to skip this section if duplicates are not interesting to you. Read on, however, if you are in a situation where an external application can come in behind your back and insert a duplicate record, for example.

The Collection interface is very general and allows for a multitude of Collection subinterfaces and implementation classes. So it is very soft in its specification of whether duplicates are allowed, instead allowing the subinterface or implementation class to decide what behavior best fits that Collection type.

For a `Collection` that does happen to allow duplicates, collection-valued relationship mappings use either a foreign key in the target entity table or a join table. The first case will always be a one-to-many mapping, and in that case there will be only one row for the target entity, and only one column in that row to contain the foreign key to the source entity. That leaves no way to capture the fact that the target entity is in the collection more than once.

In the join table case, each row stores a join column to the source entity and a join column to the target entity, and the primary key of the join table is composed of the combination of the two. Only duplicate rows in that model could link multiple instances of the target to the same source, and duplicate rows in a relational database are highly frowned upon.

An element collection is in a similar situation, except that instead of a foreign key to the target entity there are one or more columns in the collection table storing the basic or embeddable values. These columns just combine with the foreign key to the source entity to make up the primary key, and once again duplicate rows would be required to have duplicate values in a collection.

The persistently ordered `List` is a little different, however, because it adds an order column to the mix. If the order column were to be included as part of the primary key, multiple relationship entries could exist in the `List`—each of their respective rows potentially having the same element value data and foreign key reference, but differing only by the value of the order column. Thus, the uniqueness of a row is identified not only by the source and target objects but also by its position in the `List`.

In the case of the foreign key in the target table, it would be bad practice indeed to include the order column in the primary key of an entity table, so we won't even explore that as an option. However, when a join table or collection table is used, it is a perfectly reasonable thing to do, allowing duplicate values to be inserted in a persistently ordered `List`. This is possible, though, only if the provider includes the order column in the primary key of the table or gives you the option of configuring it in that way.

Before you rejoice that your provider might allow you to store duplicates, be aware that there is a price to pay. This can be seen in the example of exchanging the order of two elements in the `List`. If the order column were just a regular column, it wouldn't be too much of a stretch for the provider to optimize the database operations by simply updating the order columns of the two records with the correct values. However, if the order column is part of the primary key, what you are really saying is that the ordering of the contained object in the `List` is an integral part of the relationship between the containing and contained objects. Assigning a new order to the contained object is not modifying an aspect of the relationship, but effectively destroying the relationship and creating a new one with a different ordering. That means deleting the two old rows and creating two new ones.

A `Map` has keys that must be unique, so duplicate keys clearly don't make sense. It is similar to a `List` when it comes to its values, however, because it has a key column that can be part of the primary key. Once again, the case of the foreign key in the target table does not allow for multiple keys to point to the same entity, so one-to-many relationships that are mapped that way simply do not permit the same entity to be mapped to multiple keys in the same `Map`.

For join tables and collection tables, duplicates will be possible in the `Map` only if it is keyed by something other than an attribute of the entity, or embeddable, and the key column is included in the primary key. The trade-off in the case of the `Map` is similar to the one that we discussed with `List`, except that the price of allowing duplicates in a `Map` is paid when you want to reassign an existing key to a different value.

Null Values

It is probably even less common to insert null values in a collection than it is to have duplicates. This is one reason why the JPA specification is not particularly clear on what happens when you insert null into a collection. As with duplicates, the cases are a little complex and require individual consideration.

The `Set`, `List`, and `Map` interfaces join the `Collection` interface in being general enough to be wishy-washy when it comes to specifying what happens when null is inserted. They simply delegate the decision to the implementation, so an implementation class might choose to support inserting null values or throw an exception. JPA does no better; it ends up falling to the particular vendor's proxy implementation to allow null or throw a `NullPointerException` when null is added. Note that you cannot make your collection interface allow null simply by initializing it with an implementation instance, such as `HashSet`, that allows null. The provider will replace the instance with one of its own implementation classes the next time the object becomes managed, and the new implementation class might or might not allow null values.

In order for a null value to exist in the database the value column or columns must be nullable. This is the obvious part, but the corollary might be less evident, if a little repetitive. It claims once again that only relationships and element collections that use a join table or collection table can have null values in the collection. The proof is left for you to figure out, but (as a hint) try creating an entity that has all null values, including the identifier, with no identifier generation.

There is a further limitation on null values when it comes to element collections of embeddable objects. Entity references in a join table or element collections of basic types in a collection table are single-column values or references. The problem in the embeddable case is that if a combination of columns mapped to an embeddable are all null, there is no way for the provider to know whether it signifies a null value or an empty embeddable object full of null values. Providers might assume that it is an empty embedded object or they might have a controllable option to dictate whether the nulls get treated one way or the other.

Maps are equally non-committal about allowing null keys, but it really doesn't fit very well with the model of key columns being primary key fields. Most databases do not allow one of the primary key fields to be nullable, and we would not recommend it even for the odd one that does.

Best Practices

With all the options and possibilities that have emerged, we would be cruel indeed if we did not offer at least some measure of guidance to the lonely collections traveler. Of course, the reason why there are so many options is because there are so many different cases to solve, so it is not really appropriate to come up with hard and fast rules. However, some general guidelines will hopefully assist you in picking the right mapping strategy for your specific application use case.

- When using a List, do not assume that it is ordered automatically if you have not actually specified any ordering. The List order might be affected by the database results, which are only partially deterministic with respect to how they are ordered. There are no guarantees that such an ordering will be the same across multiple executions.

- It will generally be possible to order the objects by one of their own attributes. Using the @OrderBy annotation will always be the best approach when compared to a persistent List that must maintain the order of the items within it by updating a specific order column. Use the order column only when it is impossible to do otherwise.

- Map types are very helpful, but they can be relatively complicated to properly configure. Once you reach that stage, however, the modeling capabilities that they offer and the loose association support that can be leveraged makes them ideal candidates for various kinds of relationships and element collections.

- As with the List, the preferred and most efficient use of a Map is to use an attribute of the target object as a key, making a Map of entities keyed by a basic attribute type the most common and useful. It will often solve most of the problems you encounter. A Map of basic keys and values can be a useful configuration for associating one basic object with another.

- Avoid using embedded objects in a Map, particularly as keys, because their identity is typically not defined. Embeddables in general should be treated with care and used only when absolutely necessary.

- Support for duplicate or null values in collections is not guaranteed, and is not recommended even when possible. They will cause certain types of operations on the collection type to be slower and more database-intensive, sometimes amounting to a combination of record deletion and insertion instead of simple updates.

Summary

In this chapter, we took a more in-depth look at various ways of mapping collections to the database. We looked at how the contents of the collection determine how it is mapped, and noted that there are many flexible options for storing different kinds of objects in various types of collections.

We showed that the difference between relationships and element collections was whether entities or basic/embeddable types were being stored in them. We went on to examine the different types of collections, and how `Collection` and `Set` can be used for simple container purposes, while `List` can be used to maintain ordered collections. We showed that there are two different approaches to using a `List` and that maintaining a persistent `List` is possible, but not usually the best strategy.

We then elaborated on all the `Map` types, explaining how combinations of basic, embeddable, and entity types can be used as keys and values. We experimented with and showed examples of using many of the different combinations of key and value types, illustrating how each changed the way the collection was mapped. We then outlined, in list form, the basic rules of using a `Map` type.

We finished off collections by looking at the corner cases of adding duplicates and null values to collections and outlined the cases when support might be reasonable. Some best practices and practical guidance to using collections followed.

The next chapter will discuss using entity managers and persistence contexts in more advanced ways than we did previously, delving into the practices and nuances of injecting and using them in Java EE and Java SE environments.

CHAPTER 6

■ ■ ■

Entity Manager

Entities do not persist themselves when they are created. Nor do they remove themselves from the database when they are garbage-collected. It is the logic of the application that must manipulate entities to manage their persistent lifecycle. JPA provides the `EntityManager` interface for this purpose in order to let applications manage and search for entities in the relational database.

At first, this might seem like a limitation of JPA. If the persistence runtime knows which objects are persistent, why should the application have to be involved in the process? Rest assured that this design is both deliberate and far more beneficial to the application than any transparent persistence solution. Persistence is a partnership between the application and persistence provider. JPA brings a level of control and flexibility that could not be achieved without the active participation of the application.

In Chapter 2 we introduced the `EntityManager` interface and described some of the basic operations that it provides for operating on entities. We extended that discussion in Chapter 3 to include an overview of the Java EE environment and the types of services that impact persistence applications. Finally, in Chapters 4 and 5 we described object-relational mapping, the key to building entities out of objects. With that groundwork in place we are ready to revisit entity managers, persistence contexts, and persistence units, and to begin a more in-depth discussion of these concepts.

Persistence Contexts

Let's begin by reintroducing the core terms of JPA. A persistence unit is a named configuration of entity classes. A persistence context is a managed set of entity instances. Every persistence context is associated with a persistence unit, restricting the classes of the managed instances to the set defined by the persistence unit. Saying that an entity instance is *managed* means that it is contained within a persistence context and it can be acted upon by an entity manager. It is for this reason that we say that an entity manager manages a persistence context.

Understanding the persistence context is the key to understanding the entity manager. An entity's inclusion or exclusion from a persistence context will determine the outcome of any persistent operations on it. If the persistence context participates in a transaction, the in-memory state of the managed entities will get synchronized to the database. Yet despite the important role that it plays, the persistence context is never actually visible to the application. It is always accessed indirectly through the entity manager and assumed to be there when we need it.

So far so good, but how does the persistence context get created and when does this occur? How does the entity manager figure in the equation? This is where it starts to get interesting.

Entity Managers

Up to this point, we have demonstrated only basic entity manager operations in both the Java SE and Java EE environments. We have reached a point, however, where we can finally reveal the full range of entity manager configurations. JPA defines no fewer than *three* different types of entity managers, each of which has a different approach to persistence context management that is tailored to a different application need. As we will see, the persistence context is just one part of the puzzle.

Container-Managed Entity Managers

In the Java EE environment, the most common way to acquire an entity manager is by using the `@PersistenceContext` annotation to inject one. An entity manager obtained in this way is called *container-managed* because the container manages the lifecycle of the entity manager, typically by proxying the one that it gets from the persistence provider. The application does not have to create it or close it. This is the style of entity manager we demonstrated in Chapter 3.

Container-managed entity managers come in two varieties. The style of a container-managed entity manager determines how it works with persistence contexts. The first and most common style is called *transaction-scoped*. This means that the persistence contexts managed by the entity manager are scoped by the active JTA transaction, ending when the transaction is complete. The second style is called *extended*. Extended entity managers work with a single persistence context that is tied to the lifecycle of a stateful session bean and are scoped to the life of that stateful session bean, potentially spanning multiple transactions.

Transaction-Scoped

All the entity manager examples that we have shown so far for the Java EE environment have been transaction-scoped entity managers. A transaction-scoped entity manager is returned whenever the reference created by the `@PersistenceContext` annotation is resolved. As we mentioned in Chapter 3, a transaction-scoped entity manager is stateless, meaning that it can be safely stored on any Java EE component. Because the container manages it for us, it is also basically maintenance-free.

Once again, let's introduce a stateless session bean that uses a transaction-scoped entity manager. Listing 6-1 shows the bean class for a session bean that manages project information. The entity manager is injected into the em field using the `@PersistenceContext` annotation and is then used in the business methods of the bean.

Listing 6-1. *The ProjectService Session Bean*

```
@Stateless
public class ProjectService {
    @PersistenceContext(unitName="EmployeeService")
    EntityManager em;

    public void assignEmployeeToProject(int empId, int projectId) {
        Project project = em.find(Project.class, projectId);
        Employee employee = em.find(Employee.class, empId);
        project.getEmployees().add(employee);
        employee.getProjects().add(project);
    }

    // ...
}
```

We described the transaction-scoped entity manager as stateless. If that is the case, how can it work with a persistence context? The answer lies with the JTA transaction. All container-managed entity managers depend on JTA transactions because they can use the transaction as a way to track persistence contexts. Every time an operation is invoked on the entity manager, the container proxy for that entity manager checks to see whether a persistence context is associated with the container JTA transaction. If it finds one, the entity manager will use this persistence context. If it doesn't find one, it creates a new persistence context and associates it with the transaction. When the transaction ends, the persistence context goes away.

Let's walk through an example. Consider the `assignEmployeeToProject()` method from Listing 6-1. The first thing the method does is search for the Employee and Project instances using the `find()` operation. When the first `find()` method is invoked, the container checks for a transaction. By default, the container will ensure that a transaction is active whenever a session bean method starts, so the entity manager in this example will find one ready. It then checks for a persistence context. This is the first time any entity manager call has occurred, so there isn't a persistence context yet. The entity manager creates a new one and uses it to find the project.

When the entity manager is used to search for the employee, it checks the transaction again and this time finds the one it created when searching for the project. It then reuses this persistence context to search for the employee. At this point, employee and project are both managed entity instances. The employee is then added to the project, updating both the employee and project entities. When the method call ends, the transaction is committed. Because the employee and project instances were managed, the persistence context can detect any state changes in them, and it updates the database during the commit. When the transaction is over, the persistence context goes away.

This process is repeated every time one or more entity manager operations are invoked within a transaction.

Extended

In order to describe the extended entity manager, we must first talk a little about stateful session beans. As you learned in Chapter 3, stateful session beans are designed to hold conversational state. Once acquired by a client, the same bean instance is used for the life of the conversation until the client invokes one of the methods marked @Remove on the bean. While the conversation is active, the business methods of the client can store and access information using the fields of the bean.

Let's try using a stateful session bean to help manage a department. Our goal is to create a business object for a Department entity that provides business operations relating to that entity. Listing 6-2 shows our first attempt. The business method init() is called by the client to initialize the department id. We then store this department id on the bean instance, and the addEmployee() method uses it to find the department and make the necessary changes. From the perspective of the client, they only have to set the department id once, and then subsequent operations always refer to the same department.

Listing 6-2. First Attempt at Department Manager Bean

```
@Stateful
public class DepartmentManager {
    @PersistenceContext(unitName="EmployeeService")
    EntityManager em;
    int deptId;

    public void init(int deptId) {
        this.deptId = deptId;
    }

    public void setName(String name) {
        Department dept = em.find(Department.class, deptId);
        dept.setName(name);
    }

    public void addEmployee(int empId) {
        Department dept = em.find(Department.class, deptId);
        Employee emp = em.find(Employee.class, empId);
        dept.getEmployees().add(emp);
        emp.setDepartment(dept);
    }

    // ...

    @Remove
    public void finished() {
    }
}
```

The first thing that should stand out when looking at this bean is that it seems unnecessary to have to search for the department every time. After all, we have the department id, so why not just store the Department entity instance as well? Listing 6-3 revises our first attempt by searching for the department once during the init() method and then reusing the entity instance for each business method.

Listing 6-3. Second Attempt at Department Manager Bean

```
@Stateful
public class DepartmentManager {
    @PersistenceContext(unitName="EmployeeService")
    EntityManager em;
    Department dept;

    public void init(int deptId) {
        dept = em.find(Department.class, deptId);
    }

    public void setName(String name) {
        dept.setName(name);
    }

    public void addEmployee(int empId) {
        Employee emp = em.find(Employee.class, empId);
        dept.getEmployees().add(emp);
        emp.setDepartment(dept);
    }

    // ...

    @Remove
    public void finished() {
    }
}
```

This version looks better suited to the capabilities of a stateful session bean. It is certainly more natural to reuse the Department entity instance instead of searching for it each time. But there is a problem. The entity manager in Listing 6-3 is transaction-scoped. Assuming there is no active transaction from the client, every method on the bean will start and commit a new transaction because the default transaction attribute for each method is REQUIRED. Because there is a new transaction for each method, the entity manager will use a different persistence context each time.

Even though the Department instance still exists, the persistence context that used to manage it went away when the transaction associated with the init() call ended. We refer to the Department entity in this case as being *detached* from a persistence context. The instance is still around and can be used, but any changes to its state will be ignored. For example, invoking setName() will change the name in the entity instance, but the changes will never be reflected in the database.

This is the situation that the extended entity manager is designed to solve. Designed specifically for stateful session beans, it prevents entities from becoming detached when transactions end. Before we go too much further, let's introduce our third and final attempt at a department manager bean. Listing 6-4 shows our previous example updated to use an extended persistence context.

Listing 6-4. Using an Extended Entity Manager

```
@Stateful
public class DepartmentManager {
    @PersistenceContext(unitName="EmployeeService",
                        type=PersistenceContextType.EXTENDED)
    EntityManager em;
    Department dept;

    public void init(int deptId) {
        dept = em.find(Department.class, deptId);
    }

    public void setName(String name) {
        dept.setName(name);
    }

    public void addEmployee(int empId) {
        Employee emp = em.find(Employee.class, empId);
        dept.getEmployees().add(emp);
        emp.setDepartment(dept);
    }

    // ...

    @Remove
    public void finished() {
    }
}
```

As you can see, we changed only one line. The @PersistenceContext annotation that we introduced in Chapter 3 has a special type attribute that can be set to either TRANSACTION or EXTENDED. These constants are defined by the PersistenceContextType enumerated type. TRANSACTION is the default and corresponds to the transaction-scoped entity managers we have been using up to now. EXTENDED means that an extended entity manager should be used.

With this change made, the department manager bean now works as expected. Extended entity managers create a persistence context when a stateful session bean instance is created that lasts until the bean is removed. Unlike the persistence context of a transaction-scoped entity manager, which begins when the transaction begins and lasts until the end of a transaction, the persistence context of an extended entity manager will last for the entire length of the conversation. Because the Department entity is still managed by the same persistence context, whenever it is used in a transaction any changes will be automatically written to the database.

The extended persistence context allows stateful session beans to be written in a way that is more suited to their capabilities. Later we will discuss special limitations on the transaction management of extended entity managers, but by and large they are well suited to the type of example we have shown here.

Application-Managed Entity Managers

In Chapter 2 we introduced JPA with an example written using Java SE. The entity manager in that example, and any entity manager that is created from the createEntityManager() call of an EntityManagerFactory instance, is what we call an *application-managed* entity manager. This name comes from the fact that the application, rather than the container, manages the lifecycle of the entity manager. Note that all open entity managers, whether container-managed or application-managed, are associated with an EntityManagerFactory instance. The factory used to create the entity manager can be accessed from the getEntityManagerFactory() call on the EntityManager interface.

Although we expect the majority of applications to be written using container-managed entity managers, application-managed entity managers still have a role to play. They are the only entity manager type available in Java SE, and as we will see, they can be used in Java EE as well.

Creating an application-managed entity manager is simple enough. All you need is an `EntityManagerFactory` to create the instance. What separates Java SE and Java EE for application-managed entity managers is not how you create the entity manager but how you get the factory. Listing 6-5 demonstrates use of the `Persistence` class to bootstrap an `EntityManagerFactory` instance that is then used to create an entity manager.

Listing 6-5. *Application-Managed Entity Managers in Java SE*

```java
public class EmployeeClient {
    public static void main(String[] args) {
        EntityManagerFactory emf =
            Persistence.createEntityManagerFactory("EmployeeService");
        EntityManager em = emf.createEntityManager();

        List<Employee> emps = em.createQuery("SELECT e FROM Employee e")
                                                        .getResultList();
        for (Employee e : emps) {
            System.out.println(e.getId() + ", " + e.getName());
        }

        em.close();
        emf.close();
    }
}
```

The `Persistence` class offers two variations of the same `createEntityManager()` method that can be used to create an `EntityManagerFactory` instance for a given persistence unit name. The first, specifying only the persistence unit name, returns the factory created with the default properties defined in the `persistence.xml` file. The second form of the method call allows a map of properties to be passed in, adding to, or overriding the properties specified in `persistence.xml`. This form is useful when required JDBC properties might not be known until the application is started, perhaps with information provided as command-line parameters. The set of active properties for an entity manager can be determined via the `getProperties()` method on the `EntityManager` interface. We will discuss persistence unit properties in Chapter 14.

The best way to create an application-managed entity manager in Java EE is to use the `@PersistenceUnit` annotation to declare a reference to the `EntityManagerFactory` for a persistence unit. Once acquired, the factory can be used to create an entity manager, which can be used just as it would in Java SE. Listing 6-6 demonstrates injection of an `EntityManagerFactory` into a servlet and its use to create a short-lived entity manager in order to verify a user id.

Listing 6-6. *Application-Managed Entity Managers in Java EE*

```java
public class LoginServlet extends HttpServlet {
    @PersistenceUnit(unitName="EmployeeService")
    EntityManagerFactory emf;

    protected void doPost(HttpServletRequest request,
                                        HttpServletResponse response) {
        String userId = request.getParameter("user");
```

```
        // check valid user
        EntityManager em = emf.createEntityManager();
        try {
            User user = em.find(User.class, userId);
            if (user == null) {
                // return error page
                // ...
            }
        } finally {
            em.close();
        }

        // ...
    }
}
```

One thing common to both of these examples is that the entity manager is explicitly closed with the close() call when it is no longer needed. This is one of the lifecycle requirements of an entity manager that must be performed manually in the case of application-managed entity managers; it is normally taken care of automatically by container-managed entity managers. Likewise, the EntityManagerFactory instance must also be closed, but only in the Java SE application. In Java EE, the container closes the factory automatically, so no extra steps are required.

In terms of the persistence context, the application-managed entity manager is similar to an extended container-managed entity manager. When an application-managed entity manager is created, it creates its own private persistence context that lasts until the entity manager is closed. This means that any entities managed by the entity manager will remain that way, independent of any transactions.

The role of the application-managed entity manager in Java EE is somewhat specialized. If resource-local transactions are required for an operation, an application-managed entity manager is the only type of entity manager that can be configured with that transaction type within the server. As we will describe in the next section, the transaction requirements of an extended entity manager can make them difficult to deal with in some situations. Application-managed entity managers can be safely used on stateful session beans to accomplish similar goals.

Transaction Management

Developing a persistence application is as much about transaction management as it is about object-relational mapping. Transactions define when new, changed, or removed entities are synchronized to the database. Understanding how persistence contexts interact with transactions is a fundamental part of working with JPA.

Note that we said persistence contexts, not entity managers. There are several different entity manager types, but all use a persistence context internally. The entity manager type determines the lifetime of a persistence context, but all persistence contexts behave the same way when they are associated with a transaction.

There are two transaction management types supported by JPA. The first is resource-local transactions, which are the native transactions of the JDBC drivers that are referenced by a persistence unit. The second transaction management type is JTA transactions, which are the transactions of the Java EE server, supporting multiple participating resources, transaction lifecycle management, and distributed XA transactions.

Container-managed entity managers always use JTA transactions, while application-managed entity managers can use either type. Because JTA is typically not available in Java SE applications, the provider needs to support only resource-local transactions in that environment. The default and preferred transaction type for Java EE applications is JTA. As we will describe in the next section, propagating persistence contexts with JTA transactions is a major benefit to enterprise persistence applications.

The transaction type is defined for a persistence unit and is configured using the persistence.xml file. We will discuss this setting and how to apply it in Chapter 14.

JTA Transaction Management

In order to talk about JTA transactions, we must first discuss the difference between transaction synchronization, transaction association, and transaction propagation. *Transaction synchronization* is the process by which a persistence context is registered with a transaction so that the persistence context can be notified when a transaction commits. The provider uses this notification to ensure that a given persistence context is correctly flushed to the database. *Transaction association* is the act of binding a persistence context to a transaction. You can also think of this as the *active* persistence context within the scope of that transaction. *Transaction propagation* is the process of sharing a persistence context between multiple container-managed entity managers in a single transaction.

There can be only one persistence context associated with and propagated across a JTA transaction. All container-managed entity managers in the same transaction must share the same propagated persistence context.

Transaction-Scoped Persistence Contexts

As the name suggests, a transaction-scoped persistence context is tied to the lifecycle of the transaction. It is created by the container during a transaction and will be closed when the transaction completes. Transaction-scoped entity managers are responsible for creating transaction-scoped persistence contexts automatically when needed. We say only when needed because transaction-scoped persistence context creation is *lazy*. An entity manager will create a persistence context only when a method is invoked on the entity manager and when there is no persistence context available.

When a method is invoked on the transaction-scoped entity manager, it must first see whether there is a propagated persistence context. If one exists, the entity manager uses this persistence context to carry out the operation. If one does not exist, the entity manager requests a new persistence context from the persistence provider and then marks this new persistence context as the propagated persistence context for the transaction before carrying out the method call. All subsequent transaction-scoped entity manager operations, in this component or any other, will thereafter use this newly created persistence context. This behavior works independently of whether container-managed or bean-managed transaction demarcation has been used.

Propagation of the persistence context simplifies the building of enterprise applications. When an entity is updated by a component inside of a transaction, any subsequent references to the same entity will always correspond to the correct instance, no matter what component obtains the entity reference. Propagating the persistence context gives developers the freedom to build loosely coupled applications, knowing that they will always get the right data even though they are not sharing the same entity manager instance.

To demonstrate propagation of a transaction-scoped persistence context, we introduce an audit service bean that stores information about a successfully completed transaction. Listing 6-7 shows the complete bean implementation. The logTransaction() method ensures that an employee id is valid by attempting to find the employee using the entity manager.

Listing 6-7. *AuditService Session Bean*

```
@Stateless
public class AuditService {
    @PersistenceContext(unitName="EmployeeService")
    EntityManager em;

    public void logTransaction(int empId, String action) {
        // verify employee number is valid
        if (em.find(Employee.class, empId) == null) {
            throw new IllegalArgumentException("Unknown employee id");
        }
        LogRecord lr = new LogRecord(empId, action);
        em.persist(lr);
    }
}
```

Now consider the fragment from the EmployeeService session bean example shown in Listing 6-8. After an employee is created, the logTransaction() method of the AuditService session bean is invoked to record the "created employee" event.

Listing 6-8. Logging EmployeeService Transactions

```
@Stateless
public class EmployeeService {
    @PersistenceContext(unitName="EmployeeService")
    EntityManager em;

    @EJB AuditService audit;

    public void createEmployee(Employee emp) {
        em.persist(emp);
        audit.logTransaction(emp.getId(), "created employee");
    }

    // ...
}
```

Even though the newly created Employee is not yet in the database, the audit bean can find the entity and verify that it exists. This works because the two beans are actually sharing the same persistence context. The transaction attribute of the createEmployee() method is REQUIRED by default because no attribute has been explicitly set. The container will guarantee that a transaction is started before the method is invoked. When persist() is called on the entity manager, the container checks to see whether a persistence context is already associated with the transaction. Let's assume in this case that this was the first entity manager operation in the transaction, so the container creates a new persistence context and marks it as the propagated one.

When the logTransaction() method starts, it issues a find() call on the entity manager from the AuditService. We are guaranteed to be in a transaction because the transaction attribute is also REQUIRED, and the container-managed transaction from createEmployee() has been extended to this method by the container. When the find() method is invoked, the container again checks for an active persistence context. It finds the one created in the createEmployee() method and uses that persistence context to search for the entity. Because the newly created Employee instance is managed by this persistence context, it is returned successfully.

Now consider the case where logTransaction() has been declared with the REQUIRES_NEW transaction attribute instead of the default REQUIRED. Before the logTransaction() method call starts, the container will suspend the transaction inherited from createEmployee() and start a new transaction. When the find() method is invoked on the entity manager, it will check the current transaction for an active persistence context only to determine that one does not exist. A new persistence context will be created starting with the find() call, and this persistence context will be the active persistence context for the remainder of the logTransaction() call. Because the transaction started in createEmployee() has not yet committed, the newly created Employee instance is not in the database and therefore is not visible to this new persistence context. The find() method will return null, and the logTransaction() method will throw an exception as a result.

The rule of thumb for persistence context propagation is that the persistence context propagates as the JTA transaction propagates. Therefore, it is important to understand not only when transactions begin and end, but also when a business method expects to inherit the transaction context from another method and when doing so would be incorrect. Having a clear plan for transaction management in your application is key to getting the most out of persistence context propagation.

Extended Persistence Contexts

The lifecycle of an extended persistence context is tied to the stateful session bean to which it is bound. Unlike a transaction-scoped entity manager that creates a new persistence context for each transaction, the extended entity manager of a stateful session bean always uses the same persistence context. The stateful session bean is associated with a single extended persistence context that is created when the bean instance is created and closed when the bean instance is removed. This has implications for both the association and propagation characteristics of the extended persistence context.

Transaction association for extended persistence contexts is *eager*. In the case of container-managed transactions, as soon as a method call starts on the bean, the container automatically associates the persistence context with the transaction. Likewise in the case of bean-managed transactions, as soon as UserTransaction.begin() is invoked within a bean method, the container intercepts the call and performs the same association.

Because a transaction-scoped entity manager will use an existing persistence context associated with the transaction before it will create a new persistence context, it is possible to share an extended persistence context with other transaction-scoped entity managers. As long as the extended persistence context is propagated before any transaction-scoped entity managers are accessed, the same extended persistence context will be shared by all components.

Similar to the auditing EmployeeService bean demonstrated in Listing 6-8, consider the same change made to a DepartmentManager stateful session bean to audit when an employee is added to a department. Listing 6-9 shows this example.

Listing 6-9. Logging Department Changes

```
@Stateful
public class DepartmentManager {
    @PersistenceContext(unitName="EmployeeService",
                        type=PersistenceContextType.EXTENDED)
    EntityManager em;
    Department dept;
    @EJB AuditService audit;

    public void init(int deptId) {
        dept = em.find(Department.class, deptId);
    }

    public void addEmployee(int empId) {
        Employee emp = em.find(Employee.class, empId);
        dept.getEmployees().add(emp);
        emp.setDepartment(dept);
        audit.logTransaction(emp.getId(),
                        "added to department " + dept.getName());
    }

    // ...
}
```

The addEmployee() method has a default transaction attribute of REQUIRED. Because the container eagerly associates extended persistence contexts, the extended persistence context stored on the session bean will be immediately associated with the transaction when the method call starts. This will cause the relationship between the managed Department and Employee entities to be persisted to the database when the transaction commits. It also means that the extended persistence context will now be shared by other transaction-scoped persistence contexts used in methods called from addEmployee().

The logTransaction() method in this example will inherit the transaction context from addEmployee() because its transaction attribute is the default REQUIRED, and a transaction is active during the call to addEmployee(). When the find() method is invoked, the transaction-scoped entity manager checks for an active persistence context and will find the extended persistence context from the DepartmentManager. It will then use this persistence context to execute the operation. All the managed entities from the extended persistence context become visible to the transaction-scoped entity manager.

Persistence Context Collision

We said earlier that only one persistence context could be propagated with a JTA transaction. We also said that the extended persistence context would always try to make itself the active persistence context. This can lead to situations in which the two persistence contexts collide with each other. Consider, for example, that a stateless session bean with a transaction-scoped entity manager creates a new persistence context and then invokes a method on a stateful session bean with an extended persistence context. During the eager association of the extended persistence context, the container will check to see whether there is already an active persistence context. If there is, it must be the same as the extended persistence context that it is trying to associate, or an exception will be thrown. In this example, the stateful session bean will find the transaction-scoped persistence context created by the stateless session bean, and the call into the stateful session bean method will fail. There can be only one active persistence context for a transaction. Figure 6-1 illustrates this case.

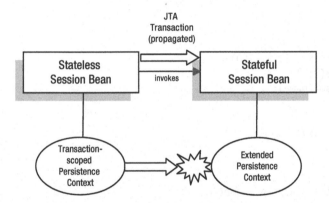

Figure 6-1. *Persistence Context Collision*

While extended persistence context propagation is useful if a stateful session bean with an extended persistence context is the first EJB to be invoked in a call chain, it limits the situations in which other components can call into the stateful session bean if they are also using entity managers. This might or might not be common depending on your application architecture, but it is something to keep in mind when planning dependencies between components.

One way to work around this problem is to change the default transaction attribute for the stateful session bean that uses the extended persistence context. If the default transaction attribute is REQUIRES_NEW, any active transaction will be suspended before the stateful session bean method starts, allowing it to associate its extended persistence context with the new transaction. This is a good strategy if the stateful session bean calls in to other stateless session beans and needs to propagate the persistence context. Note that excessive use of the REQUIRES_NEW transaction attribute can lead to application performance problems because many more transactions than normal will be created, and active transactions will be suspended and resumed.

If the stateful session bean is largely self-contained; that is, it does not call other session beans and does not need its persistence context propagated, a default transaction attribute type of NOT_SUPPORTED can be worth considering. In this case, any active transaction will be suspended before the stateful session bean method starts, but no new transaction will be started. If there are some methods that need to write data to the database, those methods can be overridden to use the REQUIRES_NEW transaction attribute.

Listing 6-10 repeats the DepartmentManager bean, this time with some additional getter methods and customized transaction attributes. We have set the default transaction attribute to REQUIRES_NEW to force a new transaction by default when a business method is invoked. For the getName() method, we don't need a new transaction because no changes are being made, so it has been set to NOT_SUPPORTED. This will suspend the current transaction, but won't result in a new transaction being created. With these changes, the DepartmentManager bean can be accessed in any situation, even if there is already an active persistence context.

Listing 6-10. *Customizing Transaction Attributes to Avoid Collision*

```
@Stateful
@TransactionAttribute(TransactionAttributeType.REQUIRES_NEW)
public class DepartmentManager {
    @PersistenceContext(unitName="EmployeeService",
                        type=PersistenceContextType.EXTENDED)
    EntityManager em;
    Department dept;
    @EJB AuditService audit;

    public void init(int deptId) {
        dept = em.find(Department.class, deptId);
    }

    @TransactionAttribute(TransactionAttributeType.NOT_SUPPORTED)
    public String getName() { return dept.getName(); }
    public void setName(String name) { dept.setName(name); }

    public void addEmployee(int empId) {
        Employee emp = em.find(empId, Employee.class);
        dept.getEmployees().add(emp);
        emp.setDepartment(dept);
        audit.logTransaction(emp.getId(),
                            "added to department " + dept.getName());
    }

    // ...
}
```

Finally, one last option to consider is using an application-managed entity manager instead of an extended entity manager. If there is no need to propagate the persistence context, the extended entity manager is not adding a lot of value over an application-managed entity manager. The stateful session bean can safely create an application-managed entity manager, store it on the bean instance, and use it for persistence operations without having to worry about whether an active transaction already has a propagated persistence context. An example of this technique is demonstrated later in the "Application-Managed Persistence Contexts" section.

Persistence Context Inheritance

The restriction of only one stateful session bean with an extended persistence context being able to participate in a JTA transaction can cause difficulties in some situations. For example, the pattern we followed earlier in this chapter for the extended persistence context was to encapsulate the behavior of an entity behind a stateful session façade.

In our example, clients worked with a DepartmentManager session bean instead of the actual Department entity instance. Because a department has a manager, it makes sense to extend this façade to the Employee entity as well.

Listing 6-11 shows changes to the DepartmentManager bean so that it returns an EmployeeManager bean from the getManager() method in order to represent the manager of the department. The EmployeeManager bean is injected and then initialized during the invocation of the init() method.

Listing 6-11. Creating and Returning a Stateful Session Bean

```
@Stateful
public class DepartmentManager {
    @PersistenceContext(unitName="EmployeeService",
                        type=PersistenceContextType.EXTENDED)
    EntityManager em;
    Department dept;
    @EJB EmployeeManager manager;

    public void init(int deptId) {
        dept = em.find(Department.class, deptId);
        manager.init();
    }

    public EmployeeManager getManager() {
        return manager;
    }

    // ...
}
```

Should the init() method succeed or fail? So far based on what we have described, it looks like it should fail. When init() is invoked on the DepartmentManager bean, its extended persistence context will be propagated with the transaction. In the subsequent call to init() on the EmployeeManager bean, it will attempt to associate its own extended persistence context with the transaction, causing a collision between the two.

Perhaps surprisingly, this example actually works. When a stateful session bean with an extended persistence context creates another stateful session bean that also uses an extended persistence context, the child will inherit the parent's persistence context. The EmployeeManager bean inherits the persistence context from the DepartmentManager bean when it is injected into the DepartmentManager instance. The two beans can now be used together within the same transaction.

Application-Managed Persistence Contexts

Like container-managed persistence contexts, application-managed persistence contexts can be synchronized with JTA transactions. Synchronizing the persistence context with the transaction means that a flush will occur if the transaction commits, but the persistence context will not be considered associated by any container-managed entity managers. There is no limit to the number of application-managed persistence contexts that can be synchronized with a transaction, but only one container-managed persistence context will ever be associated. This is one of the most important differences between application-managed and container-managed entity managers.

An application-managed entity manager participates in a JTA transaction in one of two ways. If the persistence context is created inside the transaction, the persistence provider will automatically synchronize the persistence context with the transaction. If the persistence context was created earlier (outside of a transaction or in a transaction that has since ended), the persistence context can be manually synchronized with the transaction by calling joinTransaction() on the EntityManager interface. Once synchronized, the persistence context will automatically be flushed when the transaction commits.

Listing 6-12 shows a variation of the `DepartmentManager` from Listing 6-11 that uses an application-managed entity manager instead of an extended entity manager.

Listing 6-12. Using Application-Managed Entity Managers with JTA

```
@Stateful
public class DepartmentManager {
    @PersistenceUnit(unitName="EmployeeService")
    EntityManagerFactory emf;
    EntityManager em;
    Department dept;

    public void init(int deptId) {
        em = emf.createEntityManager();
        dept = em.find(Department.class, deptId);
    }

    public String getName() {
        return dept.getName();
    }

    public void addEmployee(int empId) {
        em.joinTransaction();
        Employee emp = em.find(Employee.class, empId);
        dept.getEmployees().add(emp);
        emp.setDepartment(dept);
    }

    // ...

    @Remove
    public void finished() {
        em.close();
    }
}
```

Instead of injecting an entity manager, we are injecting an entity manager factory. Prior to searching for the entity, we manually create a new application-managed entity manager using the factory. Because the container does not manage its lifecycle, we have to close it later when the bean is removed during the call to `finished()`. Like the container-managed extended persistence context, the `Department` entity remains managed after the call to `init()`. When `addEmployee()` is called, there is the extra step of calling `joinTransaction()` to notify the persistence context that it should synchronize itself with the current JTA transaction. Without this call, the changes to the department would not be flushed to the database when the transaction commits.

Because application-managed entity managers do not propagate, the only way to share managed entities with other components is to share the `EntityManager` instance. This can be achieved by passing the entity manager around as an argument to local methods or by storing the entity manager in a common place such as an HTTP session or singleton bean. Listing 6-13 demonstrates a servlet creating an application-managed entity manager and using it to instantiate the `EmployeeService` class we defined in Chapter 2. In these cases, care must be taken to ensure that access to the entity manager is done in a thread-safe manner. While `EntityManagerFactory` instances are thread-safe, `EntityManager` instances are not. Also, application code must not call `joinTransaction()` on the same entity manager in multiple concurrent transactions.

Listing 6-13. Sharing an Application-Managed Entity Manager

```
public class EmployeeServlet extends HttpServlet {
    @PersistenceUnit(unitName="EmployeeService")
    EntityManagerFactory emf;
    @Resource UserTransaction tx;

    protected void doPost(HttpServletRequest request,
                          HttpServletResponse response)
        throws ServletException, IOException {
        // ...
        int id = Integer.parseInt(request.getParameter("id"));
        String name = request.getParameter("name");
        long salary = Long.parseLong(request.getParameter("salary"));
        tx.begin();
        EntityManager em = emf.createEntityManager();
        try {
            EmployeeService service = new EmployeeService(em);
            service.createEmployee(id, name, salary);
        } finally {
            em.close();
        }
        tx.commit();
        // ...
    }
}
```

Listing 6-13 demonstrates an additional characteristic of the application-managed entity manager in the presence of transactions. If the persistence context becomes synchronized with a transaction, changes will still be written to the database when the transaction commits, even if the entity manager is closed. This allows entity managers to be closed at the point where they are created, removing the need to worry about closing them after the transaction ends. Note that closing an application-managed entity manager still prevents any further use of the entity manager. It is only the persistence context that continues until the transaction has completed.

There is a danger in mixing multiple persistence contexts in the same JTA transaction. This occurs when multiple application-managed persistence contexts become synchronized with the transaction or when application-managed persistence contexts become mixed with container-managed persistence contexts. When the transaction commits, each persistence context will receive notification from the transaction manager that changes should be written to the database. This will cause each persistence context to be flushed.

What happens if an entity with the same primary key is used in more than one persistence context? Which version of the entity gets stored? The unfortunate answer is that there is no way to know for sure. The container does not guarantee any ordering when notifying persistence contexts of transaction completion. As a result, it is critical for data integrity that entities never be used by more than one persistence context in the same transaction. When designing your application, we recommend picking a single persistence context strategy (container-managed or application-managed) and sticking to that strategy consistently.

Unsynchronized Persistence Contexts

Under normal circumstances a JTA entity manager is synchronized with the JTA transaction and its managed entity changes will be saved when the transaction commits. However, an exception to this rule was illustrated in Listing 6-12 when an application-managed entity manager that was created in a previous transaction needed to be explicitly joined to a subsequent transaction using the joinTransaction() call in order to cause its managed entity changes to be transactionally committed. It turns out that there is another persistence context option that exhibits a similar behavior. An entity manager can be explicitly specified to have an unsynchronized persistence context, requiring it to manually join any JTA transaction it wants to participate in.

Before we describe how to configure and use such a beast, we should first provide some motivation for its existence in the first place. Why, amongst all the varieties of entity managers and accompanying persistence contexts, is there yet another degree of parameterization? The answer lies in the proverbial "conversational" use case, characterized by the following scenario.

An application wants to perform a number of persistence operations over what is possibly an extended period of time, but does not want to maintain a single transaction for the duration. This group of operations can be called a conversation since it involves multiple interactions between the client and the server. Due to container-managed transaction demarcation, multiple transactions may have been started and completed over the course of the conversation, but the persistence operations should not be enlisted in the transactions since they should not be persisted until the conversation status has been determined. At some point the conversation comes to an end and the application wants to either commit or roll back all of the operations as a group. At this point all of the changes contained in the persistence context need to be transactionally written out to the data store, or discarded.

This scenario could almost be satisfied by an application-managed JTA entity manager except for two things. The first is that application-managed entity managers are automatically synchronized with the transaction if they are created when a transaction is active. While this could be worked around simply by ensuring that the entity manager is always created outside the scope of a transaction, the appearance of an ostensibly synchronized JTA entity manager, that because of a technicality does not happen to be synchronized, is not a very clean solution to the conversation use case. Add to that the second point, that it would be really nice for the programming model if the entity manager could be injected into components, or in other words be a container-managed entity manager. The most appropriate solution was just to allow entity managers the option of having a persistence context that is only synchronized with the transaction if it is explicitly joined.

To obtain a container-managed entity manager with an unsynchronized persistence context, a value of `UNSYNCHRONIZED`, a `SynchronizationType` enum constant, can be supplied in the `synchronization` element of the `@PersistenceContext` annotation.

```
@PersistenceContext(unitName="EmployeeService",
                    synchronization=UNSYNCHRONIZED)
EntityManager em;
```

An application-managed entity manager can be programmatically created with an unsynchronized persistence context by passing the same `UNSYNCHRONIZED` value to the overloaded `EntityManagerFactory` `createEntityManager()` method.

```
@PersistenceUnit(unitName="EmployeeService")
EntityManagerFactory emf;
...
EntityManager em = emf.createEntityManager(UNSYNCHRONIZED);
```

Neither of these persistence contexts will be synchronized with the JTA transaction unless they are explicitly joined using `joinTransaction()`. Once joined to the transaction, they will remain joined until that transaction completes, but being joined to one transaction will not imply being joined to subsequent transactions. An unsynchronized persistence context must be explicitly joined to each and any transaction it wants to be enlisted in.

Given the conversation use case, and the possibility of multiple transactions occurring along the way, it clearly makes the most sense for unsynchronized persistence contexts to be used with extended entity managers. The persist, remove, and refresh operations can then be executed either inside or outside transactional contexts, making it easier to queue up the persistence context changes before finally joining a transaction to cause them to be written out.

■ **Note** When an unsynchronized persistence context has not been joined to a transaction, no writes to the database, such as those resulting from a user-initiated flush() call, may occur. Attempts to do so will cause an exception to be thrown.

For a simple example of an unsynchronized persistence context, look back at the shopping cart example (see Listing 3-25 and Listing 3-26 in Chapter 3.) We set the transaction attribute to be optional for the addItems() method of the ShoppingCart bean because a transaction was not required to add the items. That was fine for a fairly simplistic example. We didn't need to actually persist anything or save any managed entities to a persistence context as part of the user interactions. Extending that example to make use of persistence to create/modify/delete independent entities, we could make use of an unsynchronized extended persistence context. The updated code with some additional methods is in Listing 6-14.

Listing 6-14. Using an Unsynchronized Persistence Context

```
@Stateful
public class ShoppingCart {
    @PersistenceContext(unitName="productInventory",
                        type=EXTENDED,
                        synchronization=UNSYNCHRONIZED)
    EntityManager em;
    CustomerOrder order;

    public void addItem(String itemName, Integer quantity) {
        if (order == null) {
            order = new CustomerOrder();
            em.persist(order);
        }
        OrderItem item = order.getItem(itemName);
        if (item == null) {
            item = new OrderItem(itemName);
            item.setOrder(order);
            order.addItem(item);
            em.persist(item);
        }
        item.setQuantity(item.getQuantity() + quantity);;
    }

    @Remove
    public void process() {
        // Process the order. Join the tx and we are done.
        em.joinTransaction();
    }

    @Remove
    public void cancel() {
        em.clear();
    }

    // ...
}
```

There are a few interesting bits in Listing 6-14 worth highlighting. The first is that the process() operation is trivial. All it does is call joinTransaction() so that the active container-managed transaction will cause the changes in the persistence context to be written out when the method ends. The second is that the cancel() method clears the persistence context. Though unnecessary in this case, since the bean will be removed at that point anyway, we are covered in case we decide to use the bean for a longer period of time and take off the @Remove annotation.

Earlier in the chapter we discussed propagation of persistence contexts and how they get propagated with the JTA transaction. The same rule holds true with unsynchronized persistence contexts. Regardless of whether the persistence context has been joined to the transaction or not, the unsynchronized persistence context will be propagated when the JTA transaction is propagated. There is, however, one exception to this rule for unsynchronized persistence contexts. An unsynchronized persistence context, regardless of whether it is joined or not, is never propagated into a synchronized one.

■ **Note**   The unsynchronized persistence context option was introduced in JPA 2.1.

Resource-Local Transactions

Resource-local transactions are controlled explicitly by the application. The application server, if there is one, has no part in the management of the transaction. Applications interact with resource-local transactions by acquiring an implementation of the javax.persistence.EntityTransaction interface from the entity manager. The getTransaction() method of the EntityManager interface is used for this purpose.

The EntityTransaction interface is designed to imitate the UserTransaction interface defined by JTA, and the two behave very similarly. The main difference is that EntityTransaction operations are implemented in terms of the transaction methods on the JDBC Connection interface. Listing 6-15 shows the complete EntityTransaction interface.

Listing 6-15. The EntityTransaction Interface

```
public interface EntityTransaction {
    public void begin();
    public void commit();
    public void rollback();
    public void setRollbackOnly();
    public boolean getRollbackOnly();
    public boolean isActive();
}
```

There are only six methods on the EntityTransaction interface. The begin()method starts a new resource transaction. If a transaction is active, isActive()will return true. Attempting to start a new transaction while a transaction is active will result in an IllegalStateException being thrown. Once active, the transaction can be committed by invoking commit() or rolled back by invoking rollback(). Both operations will fail with an IllegalStateException if there is no active transaction. A PersistenceException will be thrown if an error occurs during rollback, while a RollbackException, a PersistenceException subclass, will be thrown to indicate the transaction has rolled back because of a commit failure.

If a persistence operation fails while an EntityTransaction is active, the provider will mark it for rollback. It is the application's responsibility to ensure that the rollback actually occurs by calling rollback(). If the transaction is marked for rollback, and a commit is attempted, a RollbackException will be thrown. To avoid this exception, the getRollbackOnly() method can be called to determine whether the transaction is in a failed state. Until the transaction is rolled back, it is still active and will cause any subsequent commit or begin operation to fail.

Listing 6-16 shows a Java SE application that uses the EntityTransaction API to perform a password change for users who failed to update their passwords before they expired.

Listing 6-16. Using the EntityTransaction Interface

```java
public class ExpirePasswords {
    public static void main(String[] args) {
        int maxAge = Integer.parseInt(args[0]);
        String defaultPassword = args[1];

        EntityManagerFactory emf =
            Persistence.createEntityManagerFactory("admin");
        try {
            EntityManager em = emf.createEntityManager();

            Calendar cal = Calendar.getInstance();
            cal.add(Calendar.DAY_OF_YEAR, -maxAge);

            em.getTransaction().begin();
            List<User> expired =
                em.createQuery("SELECT u FROM User u WHERE u.lastChange <= ?1", User.class)
                    .setParameter(1, cal, TemporalType.DATE)
                    .getResultList();
            for (User u : expired) {
                System.out.println("Expiring password for " + u.getName());
                u.setPassword(defaultPassword);
            }
            em.getTransaction().commit();
            em.close();
        } finally {
            emf.close();
        }
    }
}
```

Within the application server, JTA transaction management is the default and should be used by most applications. One example use of resource-local transactions in the Java EE environment might be for logging. If your application requires an audit log stored in the database that must be written regardless of the outcome of any JTA transactions, a resource-local entity manager can be used to persist data outside of the current transaction. Resource transactions can be freely started and committed any number of times within a JTA transaction without impacting the state of the JTA transactions.

Listing 6-17 shows an example of a stateless session bean that provides audit logging that will succeed even if the active JTA transaction fails.

Listing 6-17. Using Resource-Local Transactions in the Java EE Environment

```java
@Stateless
public class LogService {
    @PersistenceUnit(unitName="logging")
    EntityManagerFactory emf;
```

```java
    public void logAccess(int userId, String action) {
        EntityManager em = emf.createEntityManager();
        try {
            LogRecord lr = new LogRecord(userId, action);
            em.getTransaction().begin();
            em.persist(lr);
            em.getTransaction().commit();
        } finally {
            em.close();
        }
    }
}
```

Of course, you could make the argument that this is overkill for a simple logging bean. Direct JDBC would probably work just as easily, but these same log records can have uses elsewhere in the application. It is a trade-off in configuration (defining a completely separate persistence unit in order to enable the resource-local transactions) versus the convenience of having an object-oriented representation of a log record.

Transaction Rollback and Entity State

When a database transaction is rolled back, all the changes made during the transaction are abandoned. The database reverts to whatever state it was in before the transaction began. But as mentioned in Chapter 2, the Java memory model is not transactional. There is no way to take a snapshot of object state and revert to it later if something goes wrong. One of the harder parts of using an object-relational mapping solution is that while you can use transactional semantics in your application to control whether data is committed to the database, you can't truly apply the same techniques to the in-memory persistence context that manages your entity instances.

Any time you are working with changes that must be persisted to the database at a specific point in time, you are working with a persistence context synchronized with a transaction. At some point during the life of the transaction, usually just before it commits, the changes you require will be translated into the appropriate SQL statements and sent to the database. Whether you are using JTA transactions or resource-local transactions is irrelevant. You have a persistence context participating in a transaction with changes that need to be made.

If that transaction rolls back, two things happen. The first is that the database transaction will be rolled back. The next thing that happens is that the persistence context is cleared, detaching all our managed entity instances. If the persistence context was transaction-scoped, it is removed.

Because the Java memory model is not transactional, you are basically left with a bunch of detached entity instances. More importantly, these detached instances reflect the entity state exactly as it was at the point when the rollback occurred. Faced with a rolled-back transaction and detached entities, you might be tempted to start a new transaction, merge the entities into the new persistence context, and start over. The following issues need to be considered in this case:

- If there is a new entity that uses automatic primary key generation, there can be a primary key value assigned to the detached entity. If this primary key was generated from a database sequence or table, the operation to generate the number might have been rolled back with the transaction. This means that the same sequence number could be given out again to a different object. Clear the primary key before attempting to persist the entity again, and do not rely on the primary key value in the detached entity.

- If your entity uses a version field for locking purposes that is automatically maintained by the persistence provider, it might be set to an incorrect value. The value in the entity will not match the correct value stored in the database. We will cover locking and versioning in Chapter 12.

If you need to reapply some of the changes that failed and are currently sitting in the detached entities, consider selectively copying the changed data into new managed entities. This guarantees that the merge operation will not be compromised by stale data left in the detached entity. To merge failed entities into a new persistence context, some providers might offer additional options that avoid some or all these issues. The safe and sure approach is to ensure the transaction boundaries are well enough defined so in the event of a failure the transaction can be retried, including retrieving all managed state and reapplying the transactional operations.

One last point worth mentioning is that rollbacks have no direct effect on persistence contexts that are not synchronized with the rolled-back transaction. The changes made to unsynchronized persistence contexts are not transactional and are therefore mostly immune to transaction failures. We say mostly immune because there is a case, described in the next paragraph, when it can be effected.

If a persistence unit is configured to access a transactional data source (e.g. by setting the `jta-data-source` element in `persistence.xml`) then that data source will be used to read entities from the database, even by entity managers with unsynchronized persistence contexts. If a transaction is active and changes to an entity were written out by another independent entity manager with a synchronized persistence context, then those entity changes will be visible to, and possibly read into, the unsynchronized persistence context through a connection from the transactional data source. If the transaction then rolls back, the uncommitted entity changes will be left sitting in the unsynchronized persistence context.

The situation we just described is a fairly unlikely corner case. However, if you think this corner case could apply to you, there is a remedy. You can define a non-transactional data source in the server and reference it in the persistence unit (by setting the `non-jta-data-source` element in `persistence.xml` to the non-transactional data source) in addition to the transactional one, as shown here:

```
<persistence>
    <persistence-unit name="EmployeeService">
        <jta-data-source>jdbc/EmployeeJtaDS</jta-data-source>
        <non-jta-data-source>jdbc/EmployeeNonJtaDS</non-jta-data-source>
    </persistence-unit>
</persistence>
```

The unsynchronized persistence context would then issue queries through connections from the non-transactional data source, thereby being isolated from any concurrent transactional changes made by others. Only when the persistence context became synchronized with a transaction would it go on to use the transactional data source.

Choosing an Entity Manager

With all the different entity manager types, each with a different lifecycle and different rules about transaction association and propagation, it can all be a little overwhelming. What style is right for your application? Application-managed or container-managed? Transaction-scoped or extended? Synchronized or unsynchronized?

Generally speaking, we believe that container-managed, transaction-scoped entity managers are going to be a very convenient and appropriate model for many applications. This is the design that originally inspired JPA and is the model that commercial persistence providers have been using for years. The selection of this style to be the default for Java EE applications was no accident. It offers the best combination of flexible transaction propagation with easy-to-understand semantics.

Container-managed, extended persistence contexts offer a different programming model, with entities remaining managed after commit, but they are tied to the lifecycle of a Java EE component—in this case, the stateful session bean. There are some interesting new techniques possible with the extended persistence context (some of which we will describe later in this chapter), but they might not apply to all applications.

In some enterprise applications, application-managed entity managers may be of use if they need to be accessed by unmanaged classes. The lack of propagation means that they must be passed around as method arguments or stored in a shared object in order to share the persistence context. Evaluate application-managed entity managers based on your expected transactional needs, and the size and complexity of your application.

More than anything, we recommend that you try to be consistent in how entity managers are selected and applied. Mixing different types of entity managers in an application is going to be hard for an application maintainer to understand and follow, and will likely be frustrating to debug because the different entity manager types can intersect in unexpected ways.

Entity Manager Operations

Armed with information about the different entity manager types and how they work with persistence contexts, we can now revisit the basic entity manager operations we introduced in Chapter 2 and reveal more of the details. The following sections describe the entity manager operations with respect to the different entity manager and persistence context types. Locking modes and the locking variants of the following operations will be discussed in Chapter 12.

Persisting an Entity

The persist() method of the EntityManager interface accepts a new entity instance and causes it to become managed. If the entity to be persisted is already managed by the persistence context, it is ignored. The contains() operation can be used to check whether an entity is already managed, but it is very rare that this should be required. It should not come as a surprise to the application to find out which entities are managed and which are not. The design of the application dictates when entities become managed.

For an entity to be managed does not mean that it is persisted to the database right away. The actual SQL to create the necessary relational data will not be generated until the persistence context is synchronized with the database, typically only when the transaction commits. However, once a new entity is managed, any changes to that entity can be tracked by the persistence context. Whatever state exists on the entity when the transaction commits is what will be written to the database.

When persist() is invoked outside of a transaction, the behavior depends on the type of entity manager. A transaction-scoped entity manager will throw a TransactionRequiredException because there is no persistence context available in which to make the entity managed. Application-managed and extended entity managers will accept the persist request, causing the entity to become managed, but no immediate action will be taken until a new transaction begins and the persistence context becomes synchronized with the transaction. In effect, this queues up the change to happen at a later time. It is only when the transaction commits that changes will be written out to the database.

The persist() operation is intended for new entities that do not already exist in the database. If the provider immediately determines that it is not true, an EntityExistsException will be thrown. If the provider does not make this determination (because it has deferred the existence check and the insert until flush or commit time), and the primary key is in fact a duplicate, an exception will be thrown when the persistence context is synchronized to the database.

Up to this point we have been discussing the persistence of entities only without relationships. But, as we learned in Chapter 4, JPA supports a wide variety of relationship types. In practice, most entities are in a relationship with at least one other entity. Consider the following sequence of operations:

```
Department dept = em.find(Department.class, 30);
Employee emp = new Employee();
emp.setId(53);
emp.setName("Peter");
emp.setDepartment(dept);
dept.getEmployees().add(emp);
em.persist(emp);
```

Despite the brevity of this example, we have covered a lot of points relating to persisting a relationship. We begin by retrieving a pre-existing Department instance. A new Employee instance is then created, supplying the primary key and basic information about the Employee. We then assign the employee to the department, by setting the department attribute of the Employee to point to the Department instance we retrieved earlier. Because the relationship is bidirectional, we then add the new Employee instance to the employees collection in the Department instance. Finally the new Employee instance is persisted with the call to persist(). Assuming a transaction then commits, and the persistence context is synchronized to it, the new entity will be stored in the database.

An interesting thing about this example is that the Department is a passive participant despite the Employee instance being added to its collection. The Employee entity is the owner of the relationship because it is in a many-to-one relationship with the Department. As we mentioned in Chapter 4, the source side of the relationship is the owner, while the target is the inverse in this type of relationship. When the Employee is persisted, the foreign key to the Department is written out to the table mapped by the Employee, and no actual change is made to the Department entity's physical representation. Had we only added the employee to the collection and not updated the other side of the relationship, nothing would have been persisted to the database.

Finding an Entity

The ever-present find() method is the workhorse of the entity manager. Whenever an entity needs to be located by its primary key, find() is usually the best way to go. Not only does it have simple semantics, but most persistence providers will also optimize this operation to use an in-memory cache that minimizes trips to the database.

The find() operation returns a managed entity instance in all cases except when invoked outside of a transaction on a transaction-scoped entity manager. In this case, the entity instance is returned in a detached state. It is not associated with any persistence context.

There exists a special version of find() that can be used in one particular situation. That situation is when a relationship is being created between two entities in a one-to-one or many-to-one relationship in which the target entity already exists and its primary key is well known. Because we are only creating a relationship, it might not be necessary to fully load the target entity to create the foreign key reference to it. Only its primary key is required. The getReference() operation can be used for this purpose. Consider the following example:

```
Department dept = em.getReference(Department.class, 30);
Employee emp = new Employee();
emp.setId(53);
emp.setName("Peter");
emp.setDepartment(dept);
dept.getEmployees().add(emp);
em.persist(emp);
```

The only difference between this sequence of operations and the ones we demonstrated earlier is that the find() call has been replaced with a call to getReference(). When the getReference() call is invoked, the provider can return a proxy to the Department entity without actually retrieving it from the database. As long as only its primary key is accessed, Department data does not need to be fetched. Instead, when the Employee is persisted, the primary key value will be used to create the foreign key to the corresponding Department entry. The getReference() call is effectively a performance optimization that removes the need to retrieve the target entity instance.

There are some drawbacks to using getReference() that must be understood. The first is that if a proxy is used, it might throw an EntityNotFoundException exception if it is unable to locate the real entity instance when an attribute other than the primary key is accessed. The assumption with getReference() is that you are sure the entity with the correct primary key exists. If, for some reason, an attribute other than the primary key is accessed, and the entity does not exist, an exception will be thrown. A corollary to this is that the object returned from getReference() might not be safe to use if it is no longer managed. If the provider returns a proxy, it will be dependent on there being an active persistence context to load entity state.

Given the very specific situation in which getReference() can be used, find() should be used in virtually all cases. The in-memory cache of a good persistence provider is effective enough that the performance cost of accessing an entity via its primary key will not usually be noticed. In the case of EclipseLink, it has a fully integrated shared object cache, so not only is local persistence context management efficient but also all threads on the same server can benefit from the shared contents of the cache. The getReference() call is a performance optimization that should be used only when there is evidence to suggest that it will actually benefit the application.

Removing an Entity

Removing an entity is not a complex task, but it can require several steps depending on the number of relationships in the entity to be removed. At its most basic, removing an entity is simply a case of passing a managed entity instance to the remove() method of an entity manager. As soon as the associated persistence context becomes synchronized with a transaction and commits, the entity is removed. At least that is what we would like to happen. As we will soon show, removing an entity requires some attention to its relationships, or else the integrity of the database can be compromised in the process.

Let's walk through a simple example. Consider the Employee and ParkingSpace relationship that we demonstrated in Chapter 4. The Employee has a unidirectional one-to-one relationship with the ParkingSpace entity. Now imagine that we execute the following code inside a transaction, where empId corresponds to an Employee primary key:

```
Employee emp = em.find(Employee.class, empId);
em.remove(emp.getParkingSpace());
```

When the transaction commits, we see the DELETE statement for the PARKING_SPACE table get generated, but then we get an exception containing a database error that shows that we have violated a foreign key constraint. It turns out that a referential integrity constraint exists between the EMPLOYEE table and the PARKING_SPACE table. The row was deleted from the PARKING_SPACE table, but the corresponding foreign key in the EMPLOYEE table was not set to NULL. To correct the problem we have to explicitly set the parkingSpace attribute of the Employee entity to null before the transaction commits.

```
Employee emp = em.find(Employee.class, empId);
ParkingSpace ps = emp.getParkingSpace();
emp.setParkingSpace(null);
em.remove(ps);
```

Relationship maintenance is the responsibility of the application. We will repeat this statement over the course of this book, but it cannot be emphasized enough. Almost every problem related to removing an entity always comes back to this issue. If the entity to be removed is the target of foreign keys in other tables, those foreign keys must be cleared for the remove to succeed. The remove operation will either fail as it did here or it will result in stale data being left in the foreign key columns referring to the removed entity in the event that there is no referential integrity.

An entity can be removed only if it is managed by a persistence context. This means that a transaction-scoped entity manager can be used to remove an entity only if there is an active transaction. Attempting to invoke remove() when there is no transaction will result in a TransactionRequiredException exception. Like the persist() operation described earlier, application-managed and extended entity managers can remove an entity outside of a transaction, but the change will not take place in the database until a transaction, with which the persistence context is synchronized, is committed.

After the transaction has committed, all entities that were removed in that transaction are left in the state that they were in before they were removed. A removed entity instance can be persisted again with the persist() operation, but the same issues with generated state that we discussed in the "Transaction Rollback and Entity State" section apply here as well.

Cascading Operations

By default, every entity manager operation applies only to the entity supplied as an argument to the operation. The operation will not cascade to other entities that have a relationship with the entity that is being operated on. For some operations, such as remove(), this is usually the desired behavior. We wouldn't want the entity manager to make incorrect assumptions about which entity instances should be removed as a side effect from some other operation. But the same does not hold true for operations such as persist(). Chances are that if we have a new entity and it has a relationship to another new entity, the two must be persisted together.

Consider the sequence of operations in Listing 6-18 that are required to create a new Employee entity with an associated Address entity and make the two persistent. The second call to persist() that makes the Address entity managed is bothersome. An Address entity is coupled to the Employee entity that holds on to it. Whenever a new Employee is created, it makes sense to cascade the persist() operation to the Address entity if it is present. In Listing 6-18 we are manually cascading by means of an explicit persist() call on the associated Address.

Listing 6-18. Persisting Employee and Address Entities

```
Employee emp = new Employee();
emp.setId(2);
emp.setName("Rob");
Address addr = new Address();
addr.setStreet("645 Stanton Way");
addr.setCity("Manhattan");
addr.setState("NY");
emp.setAddress(addr);
em.persist(addr);
em.persist(emp);
```

Fortunately, JPA provides a mechanism to define when operations such as persist() should be automatically cascaded across relationships. The cascade attribute, in all the logical relationship annotations (@OneToOne, @OneToMany, @ManyToOne, and @ManyToMany), defines the list of entity manager operations to be cascaded.

Entity manager operations are identified using the CascadeType enumerated type when listed as part of the cascade attribute. The PERSIST, REFRESH, REMOVE, MERGE, and DETACH constants pertain to the entity manager operation of the same name. The constant ALL is shorthand for declaring that all five operations should be cascaded. By default, relationships have an empty cascade set.

The following sections will define the cascading behavior of the persist() and remove() operations. We will introduce the detach() and merge() operations and their cascading behavior later in this chapter in the "Merging Detached Entities" section. Likewise, we will introduce the refresh() operation and its cascading behavior in Chapter 12.

Cascade Persist

To begin, let's consider the changes required to make the persist() operation cascade from Employee to Address. In the definition of the Employee class, there is a @ManyToOne annotation defined for the address relationship. To enable the cascade, we must add the PERSIST operation to the list of cascading operations for this relationship. Listing 6-19 shows a fragment of the Employee entity that demonstrates this change.

Listing 6-19. Enabling Cascade Persist

```
@Entity
public class Employee {
    // ...
    @ManyToOne(cascade=CascadeType.PERSIST)
    Address address;
    // ...
}
```

To leverage this change, we need only ensure that the Address entity has been set on the Employee instance before invoking persist() on it. As the entity manager encounters the Employee instance and adds it to the persistence context, it will navigate across the address relationship looking for a new Address entity to manage as well. In comparison with the approach in Listing 6-18, this change frees us from having to persist the Address separately.

Cascade settings are unidirectional. This means that they must be explicitly set on both sides of a relationship if the same behavior is intended for both situations. For example, in Listing 6-19, we only added the cascade setting to the address relationship in the Employee entity. If Listing 6-18 were changed to persist only the Address entity, not the Employee entity, the Employee entity would not become managed because the entity manager has not been instructed to navigate out from any relationships defined on the Address entity.

Even though it is legal to do so, it is still unlikely that we would add cascading operations from the Address entity to the Employee entity, because it is a child of the Employee entity. While causing the Employee instance to become managed as a side effect of persisting the Address instance is harmless, application code would not expect the same from the remove() operation, for example. Therefore we must be judicious in applying cascades because there is an expectation of ownership in relationships that influences what developers expect when interacting with these entities.

In the "Persisting an Entity" section, we mentioned that the entity instance is ignored if it is already persisted. This is true, but the entity manager will still honor the PERSIST cascade in this situation. For example, consider our Employee entity again. If the Employee instance is already managed, and a new Address instance is set in it, invoking persist() again on the Employee instance will cause the Address instance to become managed. No changes will be made to the Employee instance because it is already managed.

Because adding the PERSIST cascade is a very common and desirable behavior for relationships, it is possible to make this the default cascade setting for all relationships in the persistence unit. We will discuss this technique in Chapter 10.

Cascade Remove

At first glance, having the entity manager automatically cascade remove() operations might sound attractive. Depending on the cardinality of the relationship, it could eliminate the need to explicitly remove multiple entity instances. And yet, while we could cascade this operation in a number of situations, this should be applied only in certain cases. There are really only two cases in which cascading the remove() operation makes sense: one-to-one and one-to-many relationships, in which there is a clear parent-child relationship. It can't be blindly applied to all one-to-one and one-to-many relationships because the target entities might also be participating in other relationships or might make sense as stand-alone entities. Care must be taken when using the REMOVE cascade option.

With that warning given, let's look at a situation in which cascading the remove() operation makes sense. If an Employee entity is removed (hopefully an uncommon occurrence!), it might make sense to cascade the remove() operation to both the ParkingSpace and Phone entities related to the Employee. These are both cases in which the Employee is the parent of the target entities, meaning they are not referenced by other entities in the system. Listing 6-20 demonstrates the changes to the Employee entity class that enables this behavior. Note that we have added the REMOVE cascade in addition to the existing PERSIST option. Chances are, if an owning relationship is safe to use REMOVE, it is also safe to use PERSIST.

Listing 6-20. Enabling Cascade Remove

```
@Entity
public class Employee {
    // ...
    @OneToOne(cascade={CascadeType.PERSIST, CascadeType.REMOVE})
    ParkingSpace parkingSpace;
    @OneToMany(mappedBy="employee",
                cascade={CascadeType.PERSIST, CascadeType.REMOVE})
    Collection<Phone> phones;
    // ...
}
```

Now let's take a step back and look at what it means to cascade the remove() operation. As it processes the Employee instance, the entity manager will navigate across the parkingSpace and phones relationships and invoke remove() on those entity instances as well. Like the remove() operation on a single entity, this is a database operation and has no effect at all on the in-memory links between the object instances. When the Employee instance becomes detached, its phones collection will still contain all the Phone instances that were there before the remove() operation took place. The Phone instances are detached because they were removed as well, but the link between the two instances remains.

Because the remove() operation can be safely cascaded only from parent to child, it can't help the situation encountered earlier in the "Removing an Entity" section. There is no setting that can be applied to a relationship from one entity to another that will cause it to be removed from a parent without also removing the parent in the process. For example, when trying to remove the ParkingSpace entity, we hit an integrity constraint violation from the database unless the parkingSpace field in the Employee entity is set to null. Setting the REMOVE cascade option on the @OneToOne annotation in the ParkingSpace entity would not cause it to be removed from the Employee; instead, it would cause the Employee instance itself to become removed. Clearly this is not the behavior we desire. There are no shortcuts to relationship maintenance.

Clearing the Persistence Context

Occasionally, it might be necessary to clear a persistence context of its managed entities. This is usually required only for application-managed and extended persistence contexts that are long-lived and have grown too large. For example, consider an application-managed entity manager that issues a query returning several hundred entity instances. After changes are made to a handful of these instances and the transaction is committed, you have left in memory hundreds of objects that you have no intention of changing any further. If you don't want to close the persistence context, you need to be able to clear out the managed entities, or else the persistence context will continue to grow over time.

The clear() method of the EntityManager interface can be used to clear the persistence context. In many respects, this is semantically equivalent to a transaction rollback. All entity instances managed by the persistence context become detached with their state left exactly as it was when the clear() operation was invoked. If a transaction was started at this point and then committed, nothing would be written out to the database because the persistence context is empty. The clear() operation is all or nothing. Selectively cancelling the management of any particular entity instance while the persistence context is still open is achieved via the detach() operation. We discuss this later in the "Detachment and Merging" section.

Although technically possible, clearing the persistence context when there are uncommitted changes is a dangerous operation. The persistence context is an in-memory structure, and clearing it simply detaches the managed entities. If you are in a transaction and changes have already been written to the database, they will not be rolled back when the persistence context is cleared. The detached entities that result from clearing the persistence context also suffer from all the negative effects caused by a transaction rollback even though the transaction is still active. For example, identifier generation and versioning should be considered suspect for any entities detached as a result of using the clear() operation.

Synchronization with the Database

Any time the persistence provider generates SQL and writes it out to the database over a JDBC connection, we say that the persistence context has been flushed. All pending changes that require a SQL statement to become part of the transactional changes in the database have been written out and will be made permanent when the database transaction commits. It also means that any subsequent SQL operation that takes place after the flush will incorporate these changes. This is particularly important for SQL queries that are executed in a transaction that is also changing entity data.

If there are managed entities with changes pending in a synchronized persistence context, a flush is guaranteed to occur in two situations. The first is when the transaction commits. A flush of any required changes will occur before the database transaction has completed. The only other time a flush is guaranteed to occur is when the entity manager flush() operation is invoked. This method allows developers to manually trigger the same process that the entity manager internally uses to flush the persistence context.

That said, a flush of the persistence context could occur at any time if the persistence provider deems it necessary. An example of this is when a query is about to be executed and it depends on new or changed entities in the persistence context. Some providers will flush the persistence context to ensure that the query incorporates all pending changes. A provider might also flush the persistence context often if it uses an eager-write approach to entity updates. Most persistence providers defer SQL generation to the last possible moment for performance reasons, but this is not guaranteed.

Now that we have covered the circumstances in which a flush can occur, let's look at exactly what it means to flush the persistence context. A flush basically consists of three components: new entities that need to be persisted, changed entities that need to be updated, and removed entities that need to be deleted from the database. All this information is managed by the persistence context. It maintains links to all the managed entities that will be created or changed as well as the list of entities that need to be removed.

When a flush occurs, the entity manager first iterates over the managed entities and looks for new entities that have been added to relationships with cascade persist enabled. This is logically equivalent to invoking persist() again on each managed entity just before the flush occurs. The entity manager also checks to ensure the integrity of all the relationships. If an entity points to another entity that is not managed or has been removed, an exception can be thrown.

The rules for determining whether the flush fails in the presence of an unmanaged entity can be complicated. Let's walk through an example that demonstrates the most common issues. Figure 6-2 shows an object diagram for an Employee instance and some of the objects that it is related to. The emp and ps entity objects are managed by the persistence context. The addr object is a detached entity from a previous transaction, and the Phone objects are new objects that have not been part of any persistence operation so far.

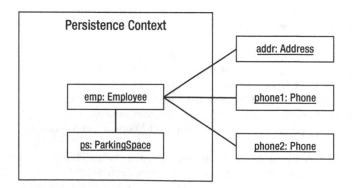

Figure 6-2. *Links to unmanaged entities from a persistence context*

To determine the outcome of flushing the persistence context given the arrangement shown in Figure 6-2, we must first look at the cascade settings of the Employee entity. Listing 6-21 shows the relationships as implemented in the Employee entity. Only the phones relationship has the PERSIST cascade option set. The other relationships are all defaulted so they will not cascade.

Listing 6-21. Relationship Cascade Settings for Employee

```
@Entity
public class Employee {
    // ...
    @OneToOne
    ParkingSpace parkingSpace;
    @OneToMany(mappedBy="employee", cascade=CascadeType.PERSIST)
    Collection<Phone> phones;
    @ManyToOne
    Address address;
    // ...
}
```

Starting with the emp object, let's walk through the flush process as if we are the persistence provider. The emp object is managed and has links to four other objects. The first step in the process is to navigate the relationships from this entity as if we are invoking persist() on it. The first object we encounter in this process is the ps object across the parkingSpace relationship. Because ps is also managed, we don't have to do anything further.

Next we navigate the phones relationship to the two Phone objects. These entities are new, and this would normally cause an exception, but because the PERSIST cascade option has been set, we perform the equivalent of invoking persist() on each Phone object. This makes the objects managed, making them part of the persistence context. The Phone objects do not have any further relationships to cascade the persist operation, so we are done here as well.

Next we reach the addr object across the address relationship. Because this object is detached, we would normally throw an exception, but this particular relationship is a special case in the flush algorithm. Any time a detached object that is the target of the one-to-one or many-to-one relationship is encountered where the source entity is the owner, the flush will still proceed because the act of persisting the owning entity does not depend on the target. The owning entity has the foreign key column and needs to store only the primary key value of the target entity.

This completes the flush of the emp object. The algorithm then moves to the ps object and starts the process again. Because there are no relationships from the ps object to any other, the flush process completes. So in this example even though three of the objects pointed to from the emp object are not managed, the overall flush completes successfully because of the cascade settings and rules of the flush algorithm.

Ideally, during a flush all the objects pointed to by a managed entity will also be managed entities themselves. If this is not the case, the next thing we need to be aware of is the PERSIST cascade setting. If the relationship has this setting, target objects in the relationship will also be persisted, making them managed before the flush completes. If the PERSIST cascade option is not set, an IllegalStateException exception will be thrown whenever the target of the relationship is not managed, except in the special case related to one-to-one and many-to-one relationships that we described previously.

In light of how the flush operation works, it is always safer to update relationships pointing to entities that will be removed before carrying out the remove() operation. A flush can occur at any time, so invoking remove() on an entity without clearing any relationships that point to the removed entity could result in an unexpected IllegalStateException exception if the provider decides to flush the persistence context before you get around to updating the relationships.

In Chapter 7, we will also discuss techniques to configure the data integrity requirements of queries so that the persistence provider is better able to determine when a flush of the persistence context is really necessary.

Detachment and Merging

Simply put, a *detached entity* is one that is no longer associated with a persistence context. It was managed at one point, but the persistence context might have ended or the entity might have been transformed so that it has lost its association with the persistence context that used to manage it. The persistence context, if there still is one, is no longer tracking the entity. Any changes made to the entity won't be persisted to the database, but all the state that was there on the entity when it was detached can still be used by the application. A detached entity cannot be used with any entity manager operation that requires a managed instance.

The opposite of detachment is merging. Merging is the process by which an entity manager integrates detached entity state into a persistence context. Any changes to entity state that were made on the detached entity overwrite the current values in the persistence context. When the transaction commits, those changes will be persisted. Merging allows entities to be changed "offline" and then have those changes incorporated later on.

The following sections will describe detachment and how detached entities can be merged back into a persistence context.

Detachment

There are two views of detachment. On one hand, it is a powerful tool that can be leveraged by applications in order to work with remote applications or to support access to entity data long after a transaction has ended. On the other hand, it can be a frustrating problem when the domain model contains lots of lazy-loading attributes and clients using the detached entities need to access this information.

There are many ways in which an entity can become detached. Each of the following situations will lead to detached entities:

- When the transaction that a transaction-scoped persistence context is associated with commits, all the entities managed by the persistence context become detached.

- If an application-managed persistence context is closed, all its managed entities become detached.

- If a stateful session bean with an extended persistence context is removed, all its managed entities become detached.

- If the clear() method of an entity manager is used, it detaches all the entities in the persistence context managed by that entity manager.

- If the detach() method of an entity manager is used, it detaches a single entity instance from the persistence context managed by that entity manager.

- When transaction rollback occurs, it causes all entities in all persistence contexts associated with the transaction to become detached.

- When an entity is serialized, the serialized form of the entity is detached from its persistence context.

Some of these situations might be intentional and planned for, such as detachment after the end of the transaction or serialization. Others might be unexpected, such as detachment because of rollback.

Explicit detachment of an entity is achieved through the detach() operation. Unlike the clear() operation discussed earlier, if passed an entity instance as a parameter, the detach() operation will be restricted to a single entity and its relationships. Like other cascading operations, the detach() operation will also navigate across relationships that have the DETACH or ALL cascade options set, detaching additional entities as appropriate. Note that passing a new or removed entity to detach() has different behavior than a normal managed entity. The operation does not detach either new or removed entities, but it will still attempt, when configured to cascade, to cascade across relationships on removed entities and detach any managed entities that are the target of those relationships.

In Chapter 4, we introduced the LAZY fetch type that can be applied to any basic mapping or relationship. This has the effect of hinting to the provider that the loading of a basic or relationship attribute should be deferred until it is accessed for the first time. Although not commonly used on basic mappings, marking relationship mappings to be lazy loaded is an important part of performance tuning.

We need to consider, however, the impact of detachment on lazy loading. Consider the Employee entity shown in Listing 6-22. The address relationship will eagerly load because many-to-one relationships eagerly load by default. In the case of the parkingSpace attribute, which would also normally eagerly load, we have explicitly marked the relationship as being lazily loaded. The phones relationship, as a one-to-many relationship, will also lazy load by default.

Listing 6-22. Employee with Lazy-Loading Mappings

```
@Entity
public class Employee {
    // ...
    @ManyToOne
    private Address address;
    @OneToOne(fetch=FetchType.LAZY)
    private ParkingSpace parkingSpace;
    @OneToMany(mappedBy="employee")
    private Collection<Phone> phones;
    // ...
}
```

As long as the Employee entity is managed, everything works as we expect. When the entity is retrieved from the database, only the associated Address entity will be eagerly loaded. The provider will fetch the necessary entities the first time the parkingSpace and phones relationships are accessed.

If this entity becomes detached, the outcome of accessing the parkingSpace and phones relationships is suddenly a more complex issue. If the relationships were accessed while the entity was still managed, the target entities can also be safely accessed while the Employee entity is detached. If the relationships were not accessed while the entity was managed, we have a problem.

The behavior of accessing an unloaded attribute when the entity is detached is not defined. Some vendors might attempt to resolve the relationship, while others might simply throw an exception or leave the attribute uninitialized. If the entity was detached because of serialization, there is virtually no hope of resolving the relationship. The only portable thing to do with attributes that are unloaded is leave them alone. Of course, this implies that you know which attributes have been loaded, and that is not always easy or practical depending upon where the entity is (see the isLoaded() method in the "Utility Classes" section in Chapter 12.)

In the case where entities have no lazy-loading attributes, detachment is not a big deal. All the entity state that was there in the managed version is still available and ready to use in the detached version of the entity. In the presence of lazy-loading attributes, care must be taken to ensure that all the information you need to access offline is available. When possible, try to define the set of detached entity attributes that can be accessed by the offline component. The supplier of the entities should treat that set as a contract and honor it by triggering those attributes while the entity is still managed. Later in the chapter we will demonstrate a number of strategies for planning for, and working with, detached entities, including how to cause unloaded attributes to be loaded.

Merging Detached Entities

The merge() operation is used to merge the state of a detached entity into a persistence context. The method is straightforward to use, requiring only the detached entity instance as an argument. There are some subtleties to using merge() that make it different to use from other entity manager methods. Consider the following example, which shows a session bean method that accepts a detached Employee parameter and merges it into the current persistence context:

```
public void updateEmployee(Employee emp) {
    em.merge(emp);
    emp.setLastAccessTime(new Date());
}
```

Assuming that a transaction begins and ends with this method call, any changes made to the Employee instance while it was detached will be written to the database. What will not be written, however, is the change to the last access time. The argument to merge() does not become managed as a result of the merge. A different managed entity (either a new instance or an existing managed version already in the persistence context) is updated to match the argument, and then this instance is returned from the merge() method. Therefore to capture this change, we need to use the return value from merge() because it is the managed entity. The following example shows the correct implementation:

```
public void updateEmployee(Employee emp) {
    Employee managedEmp = em.merge(emp);
    managedEmp.setLastAccessTime(new Date());
}
```

Returning a managed instance other than the original entity is a critical part of the merge process. If an entity instance with the same identifier already exists in the persistence context, the provider will overwrite its state with the state of the entity that is being merged, but the managed version that existed already must be returned to the client so that it can be used. If the provider did not update the Employee instance in the persistence context, any references to that instance will become inconsistent with the new state being merged in.

When merge() is invoked on a new entity, it behaves similarly to the persist() operation. It adds the entity to the persistence context, but instead of adding the original entity instance, it creates a new copy and manages that instance instead. The copy that is created by the merge() operation is persisted as if the persist() method were invoked on it.

In the presence of relationships, the merge() operation will attempt to update the managed entity to point to managed versions of the entities referenced by the detached entity. If the entity has a relationship to an object that has no persistent identity, the outcome of the merge operation is undefined. Some providers might allow the managed copy to point to the non-persistent object, whereas others might throw an exception immediately. The merge() operation can be optionally cascaded in these cases to prevent an exception from occurring. We will cover cascading of the merge() operation later in this section. If an entity being merged points to a removed entity, an IllegalArgumentException exception will be thrown.

Lazy-loading relationships are a special case in the merge operation. If a lazy-loading relationship was not triggered on an entity before it became detached, that relationship will be ignored when the entity is merged. If the relationship was triggered while managed and then set to null while the entity was detached, the managed version of the entity will likewise have the relationship cleared during the merge.

To illustrate the behavior of merge() with relationships, consider the object diagram shown in Figure 6-3. The detached emp object has relationships to three other objects. The addr and dept objects are detached entities from a previous transaction, whereas the phone1 entity was recently created and persisted using the persist() operation and is now managed as a result. Inside the persistence context there is currently an Employee instance with a relationship to another managed Address. The existing managed Employee instance does not have a relationship to the newly managed Phone instance.

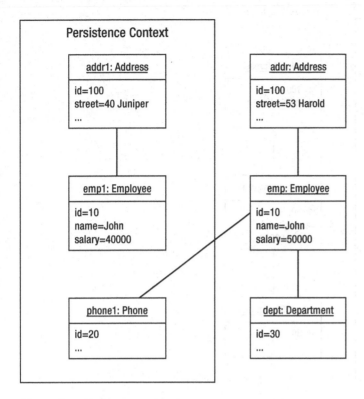

Figure 6-3. *Entity state prior to merge*

Let's consider the effect of invoking merge() on the emp object. The first thing that happens is that the provider checks the persistence context for a pre-existing entity instance with the same identifier. In this example, the emp1 object from the persistence context matches the identifier from the emp object we are trying to merge. Therefore, the basic state of the emp object overwrites the state of the emp1 object in the persistence context, and the emp1 object will be returned from the merge() operation.

The provider next considers the Phone and Department entities pointed to from emp. The phone1 object is already managed, so the provider can safely update emp1 to point to this instance. In the case of the dept object, the provider checks to see whether there is already a persistent Department entity with the same identifier. In this case, it finds one in the database and loads it into the persistence context. The emp1 object is then updated to point to this version of the Department entity. The detached dept object does not become managed again.

Finally, the provider checks the addr object referenced from emp. In this case, it finds a pre-existing managed object addr1 with the same identifier. Because the emp1 object already points to the addr1 object, no further changes are made. At this point let's look at the state of the object model after the merge. Figure 6-4 shows these changes.

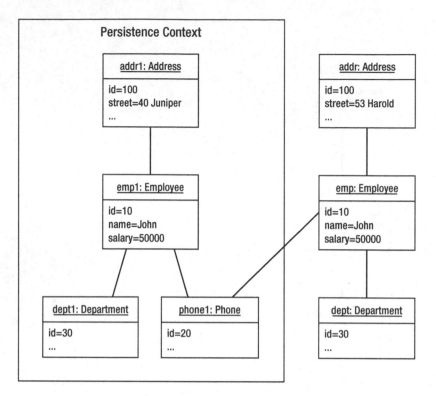

Figure 6-4. *Entity state after merge*

In Figure 6-4 we see that the emp1 object has been updated to reflect the state changes from emp. The dept1 object is new to the persistence context after being loaded from the database. The emp1 object now points to both the phone1 object and the dept1 object in order to match the relationships of the emp object. The addr1 object has not changed at all. The fact that the addr1 object has not changed might come as a surprise. After all, the addr object had pending changes and it was pointed to by the emp object that was merged.

To understand why, we must return to the issue of cascading operations with the entity manager. By default, no operations are cascaded when an entity manager operation is applied to an entity instance. The merge() operation is no different in this regard. In order for the merge to be cascaded across relationships from an Employee, the MERGE cascade setting must be set on the relationship mappings. Otherwise, we would have to invoke merge() on each related object.

Looking back at our example, the problem with the updated Address entity was that the Employee entity did not cascade the merge() operation to it. This had the unfortunate side effect of effectively discarding the changes we had made to the Address entity in favor of the version already in the persistence context. To obtain the behavior that we intended, we must either invoke merge() explicitly on the addr object or change the relationship mappings of the Employee entity to include the MERGE cascade option. Listing 6-23 shows the changed Employee class.

Listing 6-23. Employee Entity with Merge Cascade Setting

```
@Entity
public class Employee {
    @Id private int id;
    private String name;
    private long salary;
    @ManyToOne(cascade=CascadeType.MERGE)
    private Address address;
```

```
@ManyToOne
private Department department;
@OneToMany(mappedBy="employee", cascade=CascadeType.MERGE)
private Collection<Phone> phones;
// ...
}
```

With the Employee entity changed in this way, the merge operation will be cascaded to the Address and Phone entities pointed to by any Employee instances. This is equivalent to invoking merge() on each instance individually. Note that we did not cascade the merge operation to the Department entity. We generally cascade operations only down from parent to child, not upward from child to parent. Doing so is not harmful, but it requires more effort from the persistence provider to search out changes. If the Department entity changes as well, it is better to cascade the merge from the Department to its associated Employee instances and then merge only a single Department instance instead of multiple Employee instances.

Merging detached entities with relationships can be a tricky operation. Ideally, we want to merge the root of an object graph and have all related entities get merged in the process. This can work, but only if the MERGE cascade setting has been applied to all relationships in the graph. If it hasn't, you must merge each instance that is the target of a non-cascaded relationship one at a time.

Before we leave the topic of merging, we must mention that locking and versioning plays a vital role in ensuring data integrity in these situations. We will explore this topic in Chapter 12.

Working with Detached Entities

Let's begin with a scenario that is very common with modern web applications. A servlet calls out to a session bean to execute a query and receives a collection of entities in return. The servlet then places these entities into the request map and forwards the request to a JSP for presentation. This pattern is called Page Controller,[1] a variation of the Front Controller[2] pattern in which there is a single controller for each view instead of one central controller for all views. In the context of the familiar Model-View-Controller (MVC) architecture, the session bean provides the model, the JSP page is the view, and the servlet is the controller.

First consider the managed CDI bean that will produce the results that will be rendered by the JSP page. Listing 6-24 shows the bean implementation. In this example, we are looking at only the findAll() method, which returns all the Employee instances stored in the database.

Listing 6-24. The EmployeeService Bean

```
@Dependent
public class EmployeeService {
    @PersistenceContext(unitName="EmployeeService")
    private EntityManager em;

    public List<Employee> findAll() {
        return em.createQuery("SELECT e FROM Employee e", Employee.class)
                .getResultList();
    }

    // ...
}
```

---

[1]Martin Fowler, *Patterns of Enterprise Application Architecture*. Boston: Addison-Wesley, 2002.
[2]Deepak Alur, John Crupi, and Dan Malks, *Core J2EE Patterns: Best Practices and Design Strategies, Second Edition*. Upper Saddle River, N.J.: Prentice Hall PTR, 2003.

Listing 6-25 shows the source code for a simple servlet that invokes the findAll() method of the EmployeeService bean to fetch all the Employee entities in the database. It then places the results in the request map and delegates to the "listEmployees.jsp" JSP page to render the result.

Listing 6-25. The View Employees Servlet

```java
public class EmployeeServlet extends HttpServlet {
    @Inject EmployeeService bean;

    protected void doGet(HttpServletRequest request, HttpServletResponse response)
            throws ServletException, IOException {
        List emps = bean.findAll();
        request.setAttribute("employees", emps);
        getServletContext().getRequestDispatcher("/listEmployees.jsp")
                        .forward(request, response);
    }
}
```

Finally, Listing 6-26 shows the last part of our MVC architecture, the JSP page to render the results. It uses the JavaServer Pages Standard Tag Library (JSTL) to iterate over the collection of Employee instances and display the name of each employee as well as the name of the department to which that employee is assigned. The employees variable accessed by the <c:forEach/> tag is the List of Employee instances that was placed in the request map by the servlet.

Listing 6-26. JSP Page to Display Employee Information

```jsp
<!DOCTYPE HTML PUBLIC "-//W3C//DTD HTML 4.01 Transitional//EN">
<%@ taglib uri="http://java.sun.com/jsp/jstl/core" prefix="c"%>
<html>
  <head>
    <title>All Employees</title>
  </head>
  <body>
    <table>
      <thead>
        <tr>
          <th>Name</th>
          <th>Department</th>
        </tr>
      </thead>
      <tbody>
        <c:forEach items="${employees}" var="emp">
          <tr>
            <td><c:out value="${emp.name}"/></td>
            <td><c:out value="${emp.department.name}"/></td>
          </tr>
        </c:forEach>
      </tbody>
    </table>
  </body>
</html>
```

The `findAll()` method of the `EmployeeService` bean has no transaction. Because the servlet invoking the method has not started a transaction, `findAll()` is invoked in no transaction context; thus, the results of the query become detached before they are returned to the servlet.

This causes a problem. In this example, the department relationship of the `Employee` class has been configured to use lazy fetching. As you learned previously in the section on detachment, the only portable thing to do is leave them alone. In this example, however, we don't want to leave them alone. In order to display the department name for the employee, the JSP expression navigates to the `Department` entity from the `Employee` entity. Because this is a lazy-loading relationship, the results are unpredictable. It might work, but then again it might not.

This scenario forms the basis of our challenge. In the following sections we will look at a number of strategies to either prepare the entities needed by the JSP page for detachment or avoid detachment altogether.

Planning for Detachment

Knowing that the results of the `findAll()` method will be used to display employee information and that the department name will be required as part of this process, we need to ensure that the `department` relationship of the `Employee` entity has been resolved before the entities become detached. There are several strategies that can be used to resolve lazy-loaded associations in preparation for detachment. We will discuss two of them here, focusing on how to structure application code to plan for detachment. A third strategy, for JP QL queries called fetch joins, will be discussed in Chapter 8, and a fourth, using entity graphs will be explained in Chapter 11.

Triggering Lazy Loading

The first strategy to consider in resolving lazy-loading associations is to simply trigger the lazy loading behavior by accessing the field or relationship. It looks slightly odd in code because the return values of the getter methods are discarded, but nevertheless it has the desired effect. Listing 6-27 shows an alternate implementation of the `findAll()` method of the `EmployeeService` session bean. In this case, we iterate over the `Employee` entities, triggering the department relationship before returning the original list from the method. Because `findAll()` is executed inside of a transaction, the `getDepartment()` call completes successfully, and the `Department` entity instance is guaranteed to be available when the `Employee` instance is detached.

Listing 6-27. Triggering a Lazy-Loading Relationship

```
@Stateless
public class EmployeeService {
    @PersistenceContext(unitName="EmployeeService")
    private EntityManager em;

    public List<Employee> findAll() {
        List<Employee> emps =
            em.createQuery("SELECT e FROM Employee e", Employee.class)
                .getResultList();
        for (Employee emp : emps) {
            Department dept = emp.getDepartment();
            if (dept != null) {
                dept.getName();
            }
        }
        return emps;
    }

    // ...
}
```

One thing that might look odd from Listing 6-27 is that we not only invoked getDepartment() on the Employee instance but we also invoked getName() on the Department instance. If you recall from Chapter 4, the entity returned from a lazy-loading relationship can actually be a proxy that waits until a method is invoked on the proxy before the entity is faulted in. We have to invoke a method on the entity to guarantee that it is actually retrieved from the database. If this were a collection-valued relationship, the size() method of the Collection would be commonly used to force eager loading.

If lazy-loading basic mappings were used on either the Employee or Department entities, those attributes would not be guaranteed to be present after detachment as well. This is another reason why configuring basic mappings to use lazy loading is not recommended. Developers often expect that a relationship is not eagerly loaded but can be caught off guard if a basic state field such as the name attribute of the Employee instance is missing.

Configuring Eager Loading

When an association is continuously being triggered for detachment scenarios, at some point it is worth revisiting whether the association should be lazy loaded in the first place. Carefully switching some relationships to eager loading can avoid a lot of special cases in code that attempt to trigger the lazy loading.

In this example, Employee has a many-to-one relationship with Department. The default fetch type for a many-to-one relationship is eager loading, but the class was modeled by explicitly using lazy loading. By removing the LAZY fetch type from the department relationship or by specifying the EAGER fetch type explicitly, we ensure that the Department instance is always available to the Employee instance.

Collection-valued relationships lazy load by default, so the EAGER fetch type must be explicitly applied to those mappings if eager loading is desired. Be judicious in configuring collection-valued relationships to be eagerly loaded, however, because it might cause excessive database access in cases where detachment is not a requirement.

Avoiding Detachment

The only complete solution to any detachment scenario is not to detach at all. If your code methodically triggers every lazy-loaded relationship or has marked every association on an entity to be eagerly loaded in anticipation of detachment, this is probably a sign that an alternative approach is required.

Avoiding detachment boils down to just two approaches. Either you don't work with entities in your JSP page, or you must keep a persistence context open for the duration of the JSP rendering process so that lazy-loading relationships can be resolved.

Not using entities means copying entity data into a different data structure that does not have the same lazy-loading behavior. One approach would be to use the Transfer Object[3] pattern, but that seems highly redundant given the POJO nature of entities. A better approach, which we will discuss in Chapters 7 and 8, is to use projection queries to retrieve only the entity state that will be displayed on the JSP page instead of retrieving full entity instances.

Keeping a persistence context open requires additional planning but allows the JSP page to work with entity data using the JavaBean properties of the entity class. In practical terms, keeping a persistence context open means that there is either an active transaction for entities fetched from transaction-scoped persistence contexts or that an application-managed or extended persistence context is in use. This obviously isn't an option when entities must be serialized to a separate tier or remote client, but it suits the web application scenario described earlier. We'll cover each of these strategies here.

---

[3] Ibid.

Transaction View

The persistence context created by a transaction-scoped entity manager remains open only as long as the transaction in which it was created has not ended. Therefore, in order to use a transaction-scoped entity manager to execute a query and be able to render the query results while resolving lazy-loading relationships, both operations must be part of the same transaction. When a transaction is started in the web tier and includes both session bean invocation and JSP page rendering before it is committed, we call this pattern a Transaction View.

The benefit of this approach is that any lazy-loading relationships encountered during the rendering of the view will be resolved because the entities are still managed by a persistence context. To implement this pattern in our example scenario, we start a bean-managed transaction before the findAll() method is invoked and commit the transaction after the JSP page has rendered the results. Listing 6-28 demonstrates this approach. Note that to save space we have omitted the handling of the checked exceptions thrown by the UserTransaction operations. The commit() method alone throws no fewer than six checked exceptions.

Listing 6-28. Combining a Session Bean Method and JSP in a Single Transaction

```
public class EmployeeServlet extends HttpServlet {
    @Resource UserTransaction tx;
    @EJB EmployeeService bean;

    protected void doGet(HttpServletRequest request, HttpServletResponse response)
            throws ServletException, IOException {
        // ...
        try {
            tx.begin();
            List emps = bean.findAll();
            request.setAttribute("employees", emps);
            getServletContext().getRequestDispatcher("/listEmployees.jsp")
                            .forward(request, response);
        } finally {
            tx.commit
        }
        // ...
    }
}
```

With this solution in place, the lazy-loading relationships of the Employee entity do not have to be eagerly resolved before the JSP page renders the results. The only downside to this approach is that the servlet must now manage transactions and recover from transaction failures. A lot of logic also has to be duplicated between all the servlet controllers that need this behavior.

One way to work around this duplication is to introduce a common superclass for servlets that use the Transaction View pattern that encapsulates the transaction behavior. If, however, you are using the Front Controller pattern and controller actions are implemented using the Command[4] pattern, this might become more difficult to manage, particularly if the page flow is complex and multiple controllers collaborate to build a composite view. Then not only does each controller need to start transactions but it also needs to be aware of any transactions that were started earlier in the rendering sequence.

---

[4]Erich Gamma, Richard Helm, Ralph Johnson, and John Vlissides, *Design Patterns: Elements of Reusable Object-Oriented Software*. Boston: Addison-Wesley, 1995.

Another possible, though non-portable, solution is to move the transaction logic into a servlet filter. It allows us to intercept the HTTP request before the first controller servlet is accessed and wrap the entire request in a transaction. Such coarse-grained use of transactions is something that needs to be managed carefully, however. If applied to all HTTP requests equally, it might also cause trouble for requests that involve updates to the database. Assuming that these operations are implemented as session beans, the REQUIRES_NEW transaction attribute might be required in order to isolate entity updates and handle transaction failure without impacting the overriding global transaction.

Entity Manager per Request

For applications that do not encapsulate their query operations behind session bean façades, an alternative to the Transaction View pattern is to create a new application-managed entity manager to execute reporting queries, closing it only after the JSP page has been rendered. Because the entities returned from the query on the application-managed entity manager will remain managed until the entity manager is closed, it offers the same benefits as the Transaction View pattern without requiring an active transaction.

Listing 6-29 revisits our EmployeeServlet servlet again, this time creating an application-managed entity manager to execute the query. The results are placed in the map as before, and the entity manager is closed after the JSP page has finished rendering.

Listing 6-29. Using an Application-managed Entity Manager for Reporting

```
public class EmployeeServlet extends HttpServlet {
    @PersistenceUnit(unitName="EmployeeService")
    EntityManagerFactory emf;

    protected void doGet(HttpServletRequest request,
                         HttpServletResponse response)
            throws ServletException, IOException {
        EntityManager em = emf.createEntityManager();
        try {
            List emps = em.createQuery("SELECT e FROM Employee e")
                        .getResultList();
            request.setAttribute("employees", emps);
            getServletContext().getRequestDispatcher("/listEmployees.jsp")
                            .forward(request, response);
        } finally {
            em.close();
        }
    }
}
```

Unfortunately, we now have query logic embedded in our servlet implementation. The query is also no longer reusable the way it was when it was part of a stateless session bean. There are a couple of other options we can explore as a solution to this problem. Instead of executing the query directly, we could create a POJO service class that uses the application-managed entity manager created by the servlet to execute queries. This is similar to the first example we created in Chapter 2. We gain the benefit of encapsulating the query behavior inside business methods while being decoupled from a particular style of entity manager.

Alternatively we can place our query methods on a stateful session bean that uses an extended entity manager. When a stateful session bean uses an extended entity manager, its persistence context lasts for the lifetime of the session bean, which ends only when the user invokes a remove method on the bean. If a query is executed against the extended persistence context of a stateful session bean, the results of that query can continue to resolve lazy-loading relationships as long as the bean is still available.

Let's explore this option and see how it would look instead of the application-managed entity manager we showed in Listing 6-29. Listing 6-30 introduces a stateful session bean equivalent to the `EmployeeService` stateless session bean that we have been using so far. In addition to using the extended entity manager, we have also set the default transaction type to be `NOT_SUPPORTED`. There is no need for transactions because the results of the query will never be modified, only displayed.

Listing 6-30. *Stateful Session Bean with Query Methods*

```
@Stateful
@TransactionAttribute(TransactionAttributeType.NOT_SUPPORTED)
public class EmployeeQuery {
    @PersistenceContext(type=PersistenceContextType.EXTENDED,
                        unitName="EmployeeService")
    EntityManager em;

    public List<Employee> findAll() {
        return em.createQuery("SELECT e FROM Employee e", Employee.class)
                .getResultList();
    }

    // ...

    @Remove
    public void finished() {
    }
}
```

Using this bean is very similar to using the application-managed entity manager. We create an instance of the bean, execute the query, and then remove the bean when the JSP page has finished rendering. Listing 6-31 shows this approach.

Listing 6-31. *Using an Extended Entity Manager for Reporting*

```
@EJB(name="queryBean", beanInterface=EmployeeQuery.class)
public class EmployeeServlet extends HttpServlet

    protected void doGet(HttpServletRequest request, HttpServletResponse response)
            throws ServletException, IOException {
        EmployeeQuery bean = createQueryBean();
        try {
            List emps = bean.findAll();
            request.setAttribute("employees", emps);
            getServletContext().getRequestDispatcher("/listEmployees.jsp")
                            .forward(request, response);
        } finally {
            bean.finished();
        }
    }

    private EmployeeQuery createQueryBean() throws ServletException {
        // look up queryBean
        // ...
    }
}
```

157

At first glance this might seem like an overengineered solution. We gain the benefit of decoupling queries from the servlet, but we have introduced a new session bean just to accomplish this goal. Furthermore, we are using stateful session beans with very short lifetimes. Doesn't that go against the accepted practice of how to use a stateful session bean?

To a certain extent this is true, but the extended persistence context invites us to experiment with new approaches. In practice, stateful session beans do not add a significant amount of overhead to an operation, even when used for short durations. As we will see later in the "Edit Session" section, moving the stateful session bean to the HTTP session instead of limiting it to a single request also opens up new possibilities for web application design.

Merge Strategies

Creating or updating information is a regular part of most enterprise applications. Users typically interact with an application via the Web, using forms to create or change data as required. The most common strategy to handle these changes in a Java EE application that uses JPA is to place the results of the changes into detached entity instances and merge the pending changes into a persistence context so that they can be written to the database.

Let's revisit our simple web application scenario again. This time, instead of simply viewing Employee information, the user can select an Employee and update basic information about that employee. The entities are queried for presentation in a form in one request and then updated in a second request when the user submits the form with changes entered.

Using a Session Façade pattern, this operation is straightforward. The changed entity is updated and handed off to a stateless session bean to be merged. The only complexity involved is making sure that relationships properly merge by identifying cases where the MERGE cascade setting is required.

Similar to the question of whether we can avoid detaching entities to compensate for lazy loading concerns, the long-lived nature of application-managed and extended persistence contexts suggests that there might also be a way to apply a similar technique to this situation. Instead of querying entities in one HTTP request and throwing the entity instances away after the view has been rendered, we want to keep these entities around in a managed state so that they can be updated in a subsequent HTTP request and persisted merely by starting and committing a new transaction.

In the following sections, we will revisit the traditional Session Façade approach to merging and then look at new techniques possible with the extended entity manager that will keep entities managed for the life of a user's editing session.

Session Façade

To use a Session Façade pattern to capture changes to entities, we provide a business method that will merge changes made to a detached entity instance. In our example scenario, this means accepting an Employee instance and merging it into a transaction-scoped persistence context. Listing 6-32 shows an implementation of this technique in our EmployeeService session bean.

Listing 6-32. Business Method to Update Employee Information

```
@Stateless
public class EmployeeService {
    @PersistenceContext(unitName="EmployeeService")
    private EntityManager em;

    public void updateEmployee(Employee emp) {
        if (em.find(Employee.class, emp.getId()) == null) {
            throw new IllegalArgumentException("Unknown employee id: " +
                                                        emp.getId());
        }
        em.merge(emp);
    }

    // ...
}
```

The updateEmployee() method in Listing 6-32 is straightforward. Given the detached Employee instance, it first attempts to check whether a matching identifier already exists. If no matching Employee is found, an exception is thrown because we don't want to allow new Employee records to be created. Then we use the merge() operation to copy the changes into the persistence context, which are then saved when the transaction commits.

Using the façade from a servlet is a two-step approach. During the initial HTTP request to begin an editing session, the Employee instance is queried (typically using a separate method on the same façade) and used to create a web form on which the user can make desired changes. The detached instance is then stored in the HTTP session so it can be updated when the user submits the form from the browser. We need to keep the detached instance around in order to preserve any relationships or other state that will remain unchanged by the edit. Creating a new Employee instance and supplying only partial values could have many negative side effects when the instance is merged.

Listing 6-33 shows an EmployeeUpdateServlet servlet that collects the id, name, and salary information from the request parameters and invokes the session bean method to perform the update. The previously detached Employee instance is retrieved from the HTTP session and then the changes indicated by the request parameters are set into it. We have omitted validation of the request parameters to conserve space, but ideally this should happen before the business method on the session bean is invoked.

Listing 6-33. Using a Session Bean to Perform Entity Updates

```java
public class EmployeeUpdateServlet extends HttpServlet {
    @EJB EmployeeService bean;

    protected void doPost(HttpServletRequest request,
                          HttpServletResponse response)
            throws ServletException, IOException {
        int id = Integer.parseInt(request.getParameter("id"));
        String name = request.getParameter("name");
        long salary = Long.parseLong(request.getParameter("salary"));
        HttpSession session = request.getSession();
        Employee emp = (Employee) session.getAttribute("employee.edit");
        emp.setId(id);
        emp.setName(name);
        emp.setSalary(salary);
        bean.updateEmployee(emp);
        // ...
    }
}
```

If the amount of information being updated is very small, we can avoid the detached object and merge() operation entirely by locating the managed version and manually copying the changes into it. Consider the following example:

```java
public void updateEmployee(int id, String name, long salary) {
    Employee emp = em.find(Employee.class, id);
    if (emp == null) {
        throw new IllegalArgumentException("Unknown employee id: " + id);
    }
    emp.setEmpName(name);
    emp.setSalary(salary);
}
```

The beauty of this approach is its simplicity, but that is also its primary limitation. Typical web applications today offer the ability to update large amounts of information in a single operation. To accommodate these situations with this pattern, there would either have to be business methods taking large numbers of parameters or many business methods that would have to be invoked in sequence to completely update all the necessary information. And, of course, once you have more than one method involved, it may be necessary to maintain a transaction across all the update methods so that the changes are committed as a single unit.

As a result, despite the availability of this approach, the web tier still commonly collects changes into detached entities or transfer objects and passes the changed state back to session beans to be merged and written to the database.

Edit Session

With the introduction of the extended entity manager, we can take a different approach to building web applications that update entities. As we have discussed in this chapter, entities associated with an extended entity manager remain managed as long as the stateful session bean holding the extended entity manager is not removed. By placing a stateful session bean in a central location such as the HTTP session, we can operate on entities managed by the extended entity manager without having to merge in order to persist changes. We will refer to this as the Edit Session pattern to reflect the fact that the primary goal of this pattern is to encapsulate editing use cases using stateful session beans.

Listing 6-34 introduces a stateful session bean that represents an employee editing session. Unlike the EmployeeService session bean that contains a number of reusable business methods, this style of stateful session bean is targeted to a single application use case. In addition to using the extended entity manager, we have also set the default transaction type to be NOT_SUPPORTED with the exception of the save() method. There is no need for transactions for methods that simply access the Employee instance because those methods only operate in memory. It is only when we want to persist the changes to the database that we need a transaction, and that only happens in the save() method.

Listing 6-34. *Stateful Session Bean to Manage an Employee Editing Session*

```
@Stateful
@TransactionAttribute(TransactionAttributeType.NOT_SUPPORTED)
public class EmployeeEdit {
    @PersistenceContext(type=PersistenceContextType.EXTENDED,
                        unitName="EmployeeService")
    EntityManager em;
    Employee emp;

    public void begin(int id) {
        emp = em.find(Employee.class, id);
        if (emp == null) {
            throw new IllegalArgumentException("Unknown employee id: " + id);
        }
    }

    public Employee getEmployee() {
        return emp;
    }

    @Remove
    @TransactionAttribute(TransactionAttributeType.REQUIRES_NEW)
    public void save() {}

    @Remove
    public void cancel() {}
}
```

Let's start putting the operations of the EmployeeEdit bean in context. When the HTTP request arrives and starts the editing session, we will create a new EmployeeEdit stateful session bean and invoke begin() using the id of the Employee instance that will be edited. The session bean then loads the Employee instance and caches it on the bean. The bean is then bound to the HTTP session so that it can be accessed again in a subsequent request once the user has changed the Employee information. Listing 6-35 shows the EmployeeEditServlet servlet that handles the HTTP request to begin a new editing session.

Listing 6-35. Beginning an Employee Editing Session

```java
@EJB(name="EmployeeEdit", beanInterface=EmployeeEdit.class)
public class EmployeeEditServlet extends HttpServlet {

    protected void doPost(HttpServletRequest request, HttpServletResponse response)
            throws ServletException, IOException {
        int id = Integer.parseInt(request.getParameter("id"));
        EmployeeEdit bean = getBean();
        bean.begin(id);
        HttpSession session = request.getSession();
        session.setAttribute("employee.edit", bean);
        request.setAttribute("employee", bean.getEmployee());
        getServletContext().getRequestDispatcher("/editEmployee.jsp")
                        .forward(request, response);
    }

    public EmployeeEdit getBean() throws ServletException {
        // lookup EmployeeEdit bean
        // ...
    }
}
```

Now let's look at the other half of the editing session, in which we wish to commit the changes. When the user submits the form that contains the necessary Employee changes, the EmployeeUpdateServlet is invoked. It begins by retrieving the EmployeeEdit bean from the HTTP session. The request parameters with the changed values are then copied into the Employee instance obtained from calling getEmployee() on the EmployeeEdit bean. If everything is in order, the save() method is invoked to write the changes to the database. Listing 6-36 shows the EmployeeUpdateServlet implementation. Note that we need to remove the bean from the HTTP session once the editing session has completed.

Listing 6-36. Completing an Employee Editing Session

```java
public class EmployeeUpdateServlet extends HttpServlet {

    protected void doPost(HttpServletRequest request, HttpServletResponse response)
            throws ServletException, IOException {
        String name = request.getParameter("name");
        long salary = Long.parseLong(request.getParameter("salary"));
        HttpSession session = request.getSession();
        EmployeeEdit bean = (EmployeeEdit) session.getAttribute("employee.edit");
        session.removeAttribute("employee.edit");
        Employee emp = bean.getEmployee();
```

```
        emp.setName(name);
        emp.setSalary(salary);
        bean.save();
        // ...
    }
}
```

The pattern for using stateful session beans and extended entity managers in the web tier is as follows:

1. For each application use case that modifies entity data, we create a stateful session bean with an extended persistence context. This bean will hold onto all entity instances necessary to make the desired changes.

2. The HTTP request that initiates the editing use case creates an instance of the stateful session bean and binds it to the HTTP session. The entities are retrieved at this point and used to populate the web form for editing.

3. The HTTP request that completes the editing use case obtains the previously bound stateful session bean instance and writes the changed data from the web form into the entities stored on the bean. A method is then invoked on the bean to commit the changes to the database.

In our simple editing scenario, this might seem somewhat excessive, but it can scale to accommodate editing sessions of any complexity. Department, Project, and other information can all be edited in one or even multiple sessions with the results accumulated on the stateful session bean until the application is ready to persist the results.

Another benefit is that web application frameworks such as JSF can directly access the bean bound in the HTTP session from within JSP pages. The entity can be accessed both to display the form for editing and as the target of the form when the user submits the results. In this scenario, the developer only has to ensure that the necessary save and cancel methods are invoked at the correct point in the application page flow.

There are a couple of other points that we need to mention about this approach. Once bound to the HTTP session, the session bean will remain there until it is explicitly removed or until the HTTP session expires. It is therefore important to ensure that the bean is removed once the editing session is complete, regardless of whether the changes will be saved or abandoned. The HttpSessionBindingListener callback interface can be used by applications to track when the HTTP session is destroyed and clean up corresponding session beans appropriately.

The HTTP session is not thread-safe, and neither are stateful session bean references. In some circumstances, it might be possible for multiple HTTP requests from the same user to access the HTTP session concurrently. This is mostly an issue when requests take a long time to process and an impatient user refreshes the page or abandons her editing session for another part of the web application. In these circumstances, the web application will either have to deal with possible exceptions occurring if the stateful session bean is accessed by more than one thread or proxy the stateful session bean with a synchronized wrapper.

Conversation

The last strategy is a kind of extension/improvement to the edit session approach, but that engages the unsynchronized persistence context described earlier in the chapter. CDI can also be used to manage the bean instance within our session scope.

■ **Note**   CDI and JSF provide support for a dedicated conversation scope which allows navigating across multiple views and client pages. We refer readers to books dedicated to CDI and JSF to find out more about the conversation scope and how JSF and CDI interact with each other when using this scope.

The conversation pattern is going to be useful not only when you want to edit multiple objects, or even multiple object types, but when you don't necessarily want the session bean to have to cache or keep track of all of the things that have been edited throughout the conversation. Any entities that have been edited by the client are managed by the JPA persistence context directly.

In Listing 6-37, the stateful session bean provides a load method for the servlet to load an employee and give the user an opportunity to make changes to that employee. The user can then save the changes or cancel out of those individual employee changes. This process can be repeated an arbitrary number of times until the user decides to either accept the changes to all of the employees or abandon them. If accepted, the changes are joined to the transaction that is started as part of the processAllChanges() method and committed when the method and the transaction complete.

Listing 6-37. Stateful Session Bean With Unsynchronized Persistence Context

```
@Stateful
@SessionScoped
public class EmployeeService {
    @PersistenceContext(type=PersistenceContextType.EXTENDED,
                        synchronization=SynchronizationType.UNSYNCHRONIZED,
                        unitName="EmployeeService")
    EntityManager em;

    Employee currentEmployee;

    public Employee getCurrentEmployee() { return currentEmployee; }

    public Employee loadEmployee(int id) {
        Employee emp = em.find(Employee.class, id);
        currentEmployee = emp;
        return emp;
    }

    public void saveChangesToEmployee() {}

    public void cancel() {
        em.detach(currentEmployee);
    }

    public void processAllChanges() {
        em.joinTransaction();
    }

    public void abandonAllChanges() {
        em.clear();
    }
}
```

Looking at the saveChangesToEmployee() method, you may think that some code is missing since the method appears to do nothing. The reason there is no code in the method is because it does not actually need to do anything. The loadEmployee() method returns the managed employee from the persistence context so the employee being modified at the presentation layer is already being tracked by the persistence provider. By contrast, if the user were to cancel the changes we merely detach the object from the persistence context to ensure that those changes will not be committed.

When the user decides to end the conversation by accepting all of the changes, the `processAllChanges()` method does the transaction joining. If the user decides to end it by discarding all of the changes, the `abandonAllChanges()` method clears all of the objects from the persistence context and the conversation can start again.

Before we leave this example we will make one last comment about the session scope that we used. We used CDI and scoped the EmployeeService bean to the session so it will be available to the requesting session-scoped thread. As a result we will have leftover entities in the persistence context when a conversation gets committed, since the context is only cleared when the changes are abandoned. This is okay as long as the session does not carry on excessively. If the session is very long-running, or the entities in different conversations never overlap, the persistence context should probably be cleared. However, if you are tempted to simply add a call to `em.clear()` in the `processAllChanges()` method after the `joinTransaction()` call, you would be in for an unpleasant surprise. If the changes were cleared out before the `processAllChanges()` method has completed, then when the container-managed transaction commits, at the end of that method, there will be no changes in the persistence context to commit! A correct solution would be to clear the persistence context at the beginning of the next conversation instead.

Summary

In this chapter, we have presented a thorough treatment of the entity manager and its interactions with entities, persistence contexts, and transactions. As you have seen, the entity manager can be used in many different ways to accommodate a wide variety of application requirements.

We began by reintroducing the core terminology of JPA and explored the persistence context. We then covered the different types of entity manager: transaction-scoped, extended, and application-managed. We looked at how to acquire and use each type and the types of problems they are designed to solve.

In the transaction management section, we looked at each of the entity manager types and how they relate to container-managed JTA transactions and the resource-local transactions of the JDBC driver. We illustrated why transactions play an important role in all aspects of enterprise application development with JPA. We showed a special kind of persistence context that remains unsynchronized with the JTA transaction until it is programmatically joined, and how it can bring flexibility for longer-running interaction sequences.

Next we revisited the basic operations of the entity manager, this time armed with the full understanding of the different entity manager types and transaction-management strategies. We introduced the notion of cascading and looked at the impact of relationships on persistence.

In our discussion of detachment, we introduced the problem and looked at it both from the perspective of mobile entities to remote tiers and the challenge of merging offline entity changes back into a persistence context. We presented several strategies to minimize the impact of detachment and merging on application design by adopting design patterns specific to JPA.

In the next chapter, we will turn our attention to the query facilities of JPA, showing how to create, execute, and work with the results of query operations.

CHAPTER 7

■ ■ ■

Using Queries

For most enterprise applications, getting data out of the database is at least as important as the ability to put new data in. From searching to sorting, analytics, and business intelligence, efficiently moving data from the database to the application and presenting it to the user is a regular part of enterprise development. Doing so requires the ability to issue bulk queries against the database and interpret the results for the application. Although high-level languages and expression frameworks have in many cases attempted to insulate developers from the task of dealing with database queries at the level of SQL, it's probably fair to say that most enterprise developers have worked with at least one SQL dialect at some point in their career.

Object-relational mapping adds another level of complexity to this task. Most of the time, the developer will want the results converted to entities so that the query results may be used directly by application logic. Similarly, if the domain model has been abstracted from the physical model via object-relational mapping, it makes sense to also abstract queries away from SQL, which is not only tied to the physical model but also difficult to port between vendors. Fortunately, as you will see, JPA can handle a diverse set of query requirements.

JPA supports two methods for expressing queries to retrieve entities and other persistent data from the database: query languages and the Criteria API. The primary query language is Java Persistence Query Language (JP QL), a database-independent query language that operates on the logical entity model as opposed to the physical data model. Queries may also be expressed in SQL to take advantage of the underlying database. We will explore using SQL queries with JPA in Chapter 11. The Criteria API provides an alternative method for constructing queries based on Java objects instead of query strings. Chapter 9 covers the Criteria API in detail.

We will begin our discussion of queries with an introduction to JP QL, followed by an exploration of the query facilities provided by the `EntityManager` and `Query` interfaces.

Java Persistence Query Language

Before discussing JP QL, we should first look to its roots. The Enterprise JavaBeans Query Language (EJB QL) was first introduced in the EJB 2.0 specification to allow developers to write portable finder and select methods for container-managed entity beans. Based on a small subset of SQL, it introduced a way to navigate across entity relationships both to select data and to filter the results. Unfortunately, it placed strict limitations on the structure of the query, limiting results to either a single entity or a persistent field from an entity. Inner joins between entities were possible, but used an odd notation. The initial release didn't even support sorting.

The EJB 2.1 specification tweaked EJB QL a little bit, adding support for sorting, and introduced basic aggregate functions; but again the limitation of a single result type hampered the use of aggregates. You could filter the data, but there was no equivalent to SQL GROUP BY and HAVING expressions.

JP QL significantly extends EJB QL, eliminating many weaknesses of the previous versions while preserving backward compatibility. The following list describes some of the features available above and beyond EJB QL:

- Single and multiple value result types
- Aggregate functions, with sorting and grouping clauses

- A more natural join syntax, including support for both inner and outer joins

- Conditional expressions involving subqueries

- Update and delete queries for bulk data changes

- Result projection into non-persistent classes

The next few sections provide a quick introduction to JP QL intended for readers familiar with SQL or EJB QL. A complete tutorial and reference for JP QL can be found in Chapter 8.

Getting Started

The simplest JP QL query selects all the instances of a single entity type. Consider the following query:

```
SELECT e
FROM Employee e
```

If this looks similar to SQL, it should. JP QL uses SQL syntax where possible in order to give developers experienced with SQL a head start in writing queries. The key difference between SQL and JP QL for this query is that instead of selecting from a table, an entity from the application domain model has been specified instead. The SELECT clause of the query is also slightly different, listing only the Employee alias e. This indicates that the result type of the query is the Employee entity, so executing this statement will result in a list of zero or more Employee instances.

Starting with an alias, we can navigate across entity relationships using the dot (.) operator. For example, if we want just the names of the employees, the following query will suffice:

```
SELECT e.name
FROM Employee e
```

Each part of the expression corresponds to a persistent field of the entity that is a simple or embeddable type, or an association leading to another entity or collection of entities. Because the Employee entity has a persistent field named name of type String, this query will result in a list of zero or more String objects.

We can also select an entity we didn't even list in the FROM clause. Consider the following example:

```
SELECT e.department
FROM Employee e
```

An employee has a many-to-one relationship with her department named department, so the result type of the query is the Department entity.

Filtering Results

Just like SQL, JP QL supports the WHERE clause to set conditions on the data being returned. The majority of operators commonly available in SQL are available in JP QL, including basic comparison operators; IN, LIKE, and BETWEEN expressions; numerous function expressions (such as SUBSTRING and LENGTH); and subqueries. The key difference for JP QL is that entity expressions and not column references are used. The following is an example of filtering using entity expressions in the WHERE clause:

```
SELECT e
FROM Employee e
WHERE e.department.name = 'NA42' AND
      e.address.state IN ('NY','CA')
```

Projecting Results

For applications that need to produce reports, a common scenario is selecting large numbers of entity instances, but using only a portion of that data. Depending on how an entity is mapped to the database, this can be an expensive operation if much of the entity data is discarded. It would be useful to return only a subset of the properties from an entity. The following query demonstrates selecting only the name and salary of each Employee instance:

```
SELECT e.name, e.salary
FROM Employee e
```

Joins Between Entities

The result type of a select query cannot be a collection; it must be a single valued object such as an entity instance or persistent field type. Expressions such as e.phones are illegal in the SELECT clause because they would result in Collection instances (each occurrence of e.phones is a collection, not an instance). Therefore, just as with SQL and tables, if we want to navigate along a collection association and return elements of that collection, we must join the two entities together. In the following code, a join between Employee and Phone entities is implicitly applied in order to retrieve all the cell phone numbers for a specific department:

```
SELECT p.number
FROM Employee e, Phone p
WHERE e = p.employee AND
      e.department.name = 'NA42' AND
      p.type = 'Cell'
```

In JP QL, joins may also be expressed in the FROM clause using the JOIN operator. The advantage of this operator is that the join can be expressed in terms of the association itself, and the query engine will automatically supply the necessary join criteria when it generates the SQL. The previous query can be rewritten to use the JOIN operator. Just as before, the alias p is of type Phone, only this time it refers to each of the phones in the e.phones collection:

```
SELECT p.number
FROM Employee e JOIN e.phones p
WHERE e.department.name = 'NA42' AND
      p.type = 'Cell'
```

JP QL supports multiple join types, including inner and outer joins, as well as a technique called fetch joins for eagerly loading data associated to the result type of a query but not directly returned. See the "Joins" section in Chapter 8 for more information.

Aggregate Queries

The syntax for aggregate queries in JP QL is very similar to that of SQL. There are five supported aggregate functions (AVG, COUNT, MIN, MAX, and SUM), and results may be grouped in the GROUP BY clause and filtered using the HAVING clause. Once again, the difference is the use of entity expressions when specifying the data to be aggregated. An aggregate JP QL query can use many of the aggregate functions within the same query:

```
SELECT d, COUNT(e), MAX(e.salary), AVG(e.salary)
FROM Department d JOIN d.employees e
GROUP BY d
HAVING COUNT(e) >= 5
```

Query Parameters

JP QL supports two types of parameter binding syntax. The first is positional binding, where parameters are indicated in the query string by a question mark followed by the parameter number. When the query is executed, the developer specifies the parameter number that should be replaced. Positional parameter syntax is similar to what JDBC currently supports.

```
SELECT e
FROM Employee e
WHERE e.department = ?1 AND
      e.salary > ?2
```

Named parameters may also be used and are indicated in the query string by a colon followed by the parameter name. When the query is executed, the developer specifies the parameter name that should be replaced. This type of parameter allows for more descriptive parameter specifiers, like so:

```
SELECT e
FROM Employee e
WHERE e.department = :dept AND
      e.salary > :base
```

Defining Queries

JPA provides the Query and TypedQuery interfaces to configure and execute queries. The Query interface is used in cases when the result type is Object or in dynamic queries when the result type may not be known ahead of time. The TypedQuery interface is the preferred one and can be used whenever the result type is known. As TypedQuery extends Query, a strongly typed query can always be treated as an untyped version, though not vice versa. An implementation of the appropriate interface for a given query is obtained through one of the factory methods in the EntityManager interface. The choice of factory method depends on the type of query (JP QL, SQL, or criteria object), whether the query has been predefined, and whether strongly typed results are desired. For now, we will restrict our discussion to JP QL queries. SQL query definition is discussed in Chapter 11, and criteria queries are discussed in Chapter 9.

There are three approaches to defining a JP QL query. A query may either be dynamically specified at runtime, configured in persistence unit metadata (annotation or XML) and referenced by name, or dynamically specified and saved to be later referenced by name. Dynamic JP QL queries are nothing more than strings, and therefore may be defined on the fly as the need arises. Named queries, on the other hand, are static and unchangeable, but are more efficient to execute because the persistence provider can translate the JP QL string to SQL once when the application starts as opposed to every time the query is executed. Dynamically defining a query and then naming it allows a dynamic query to be reused multiple times throughout the life of the application but incur the dynamic processing cost only once.

The following sections compare the approaches and discuss when one should be used instead of the others.

Dynamic Query Definition

A query may be defined dynamically by passing the JP QL query string and expected result type to the createQuery() method of the EntityManager interface. The result type may be omitted to create an untyped query. We will discuss this approach in the "Working with Query Results" section. There are no restrictions on the query definition. All JP QL query types are supported, as well as the use of parameters. The ability to build up a string at runtime and use it for a query definition is useful, particularly for applications where the user may specify complex criteria and the exact shape of the query cannot be known ahead of time. As noted earlier, in addition to dynamic string queries, JPA also supports a Criteria API to create dynamic queries using Java objects. We will discuss this approach in Chapter 9.

An issue to consider with string dynamic queries, however, is the cost of translating the JP QL string to SQL for execution. A typical query engine will have to parse the JP QL string into a syntax tree, get the object-relational mapping metadata for each entity in each expression, and then generate the equivalent SQL. For applications that issue many queries, the performance cost of dynamic query processing can become an issue.

Many query engines will cache the translated SQL for later use, but this can easily be defeated if the application does not use parameter binding and concatenates parameter values directly into query strings. This has the effect of generating a new and unique query every time a query that requires parameters is constructed.

Consider the bean[1] method shown in Listing 7-1 that searches for salary information given the name of a department and the name of an employee. There are two problems with this example, one related to performance and one related to security. Because the names are concatenated into the string instead of using parameter binding, it is effectively creating a new and unique query each time. One hundred calls to this method could potentially generate one hundred different query strings. This not only requires excessive parsing of JP QL but also almost certainly makes it difficult for the persistence provider if it attempts to build a cache of converted queries.

Listing 7-1. Defining a Query Dynamically

```
public class QueryService {
    @PersistenceContext(unitName="DynamicQueries")
    EntityManager em;

    public long queryEmpSalary(String deptName, String empName) {
        String query = "SELECT e.salary " +
                       "FROM Employee e " +
                       "WHERE e.department.name = '" + deptName +
                       "' AND " +
                       "      e.name = '" + empName + "'";
        return em.createQuery(query, Long.class).getSingleResult();
    }
}
```

The second problem with this example is that it is vulnerable to injection attacks, where a malicious user could pass in a value that alters the query to his advantage. Consider a case where the department argument was fixed by the application but the user was able to specify the employee name (the manager of the department is querying the salaries of his or her employees, for example). If the name argument were actually the text `'_UNKNOWN' OR e.name = 'Roberts'`, the actual query parsed by the query engine would be as follows:

```
SELECT e.salary
FROM Employee e
WHERE e.department.name = 'NA65' AND
      e.name = '_UNKNOWN' OR
      e.name = 'Roberts'
```

---

[1] As in most examples in the book, the bean could be a session bean, a CDI bean, or any other kind of container bean that supports entity manager injection.

By introducing the OR condition, the user has effectively given himself access to the salary value for any employee in the company because the original AND condition has a higher precedence than OR, and the fake employee name is unlikely to belong to a real employee in that department.

This type of problem may sound unlikely, but in practice many web applications take text submitted over a GET or POST request and blindly construct queries of this sort without considering side effects. One or two attempts that result in a parser stack trace displayed to the web page, and the attacker will learn everything he needs to know about how to alter the query to his advantage.

Listing 7-2 shows the same method as in Listing 7-1, except that it uses named parameters instead. This not only reduces the number of unique queries parsed by the query engine, but it also eliminates the chance of the query being altered.

Listing 7-2. Using Parameters with a Dynamic Query

```java
public class QueryService {
    private static final String QUERY =
        "SELECT e.salary " +
        "FROM Employee e " +
        "WHERE e.department.name = :deptName AND " +
        "       e.name = :empName ";

    @PersistenceContext(unitName="QueriesUnit")
    EntityManager em;

    public long queryEmpSalary(String deptName, String empName) {
        return em.createQuery(QUERY, Long.class)
                .setParameter("deptName", deptName)
                .setParameter("empName", empName)
                .getSingleResult();
    }
}
```

The parameter binding approach shown in Listing 7-2 defeats the security threat described previously because the original query string is never altered. The parameters are marshaled using the JDBC API and handled directly by the database. The text of a parameter string is effectively quoted by the database, so the malicious attack would actually end up producing the following query:

```
SELECT e.salary
FROM Employee e
WHERE e.department.name = 'NA65' AND
      e.name = '_UNKNOWN'' OR e.name = ''Roberts'
```

The single quotes used in the query parameter here have been escaped by prefixing them with an additional single quote. This removes any special meaning from them, and the entire sequence is treated as a single string value.

We recommend statically defined named queries in general, particularly for queries that are executed frequently. If dynamic queries are a necessity, take care to use parameter binding instead of concatenating parameter values into query strings in order to minimize the number of distinct query strings parsed by the query engine.

Named Query Definition

Named queries are a powerful tool for organizing query definitions and improving application performance. A named query is defined using the @NamedQuery annotation, which may be placed on the class definition for any entity. The annotation defines the name of the query, as well as the query text. Listing 7-3 shows how the query string used in Listing 7-2 would be declared as a named query.

Listing 7-3. Defining a Named Query

```
@NamedQuery(name="findSalaryForNameAndDepartment",
            query="SELECT e.salary " +
                  "FROM Employee e " +
                  "WHERE e.department.name = :deptName AND " +
                  "      e.name = :empName")
```

Named queries are typically placed on the entity class that most directly corresponds to the query result, so the Employee entity would be a good location for this named query. Note the use of string concatenation in the annotation definition. Formatting your queries visually aids in the readability of the query definition. The garbage normally associated with repeated string concatenation will not apply here because the annotation will be processed only once at startup time and will be executed at runtime in query form.

The name of the query is scoped to the entire persistence unit and must be unique within that scope. This is an important restriction to keep in mind, as commonly used query names such as "findAll" will have to be qualified for each entity. A common practice is to prefix the query name with the entity name. For example, the "findAll" query for the Employee entity would be named "Employee.findAll". It is undefined what should happen if two queries in the same persistence unit have the same name, but it is likely that either deployment of the application will fail or one will overwrite the other, leading to unpredictable results at runtime.

If more than one named query is to be defined on a class, they must be placed inside of a @NamedQueries annotation, which accepts an array of one or more @NamedQuery annotations. Listing 7-4 shows the definition of several queries related to the Employee entity. Queries may also be defined (or redefined) using XML. This technique is discussed in Chapter 13.

Listing 7-4. Multiple Named Queries for an Entity

```
@NamedQueries({
    @NamedQuery(name="Employee.findAll",
                query="SELECT e FROM Employee e"),
    @NamedQuery(name="Employee.findByPrimaryKey",
                query="SELECT e FROM Employee e WHERE e.id = :id"),
    @NamedQuery(name="Employee.findByName",
                query="SELECT e FROM Employee e WHERE e.name = :name")
})
```

Because the query string is defined in the annotation, it cannot be altered by the application at runtime. This contributes to the performance of the application and helps to prevent the kind of security issues discussed in the previous section. Due to the static nature of the query string, any additional criteria required for the query must be specified using query parameters. Listing 7-5 demonstrates using the createNamedQuery() call on the EntityManager interface to create and execute a named query that requires a query parameter.

Listing 7-5. Executing a Named Query

```java
public class EmployeeService {
    @PersistenceContext(unitName="EmployeeService")
    EntityManager em;

    public Employee findEmployeeByName(String name) {
        return em.createNamedQuery("Employee.findByName",
                                    Employee.class)
                 .setParameter("name", name)
                 .getSingleResult();
    }

    // ...
}
```

Named parameters are the most practical choice for named queries because they effectively self-document the application code that invokes the queries. Positional parameters are still supported, however, and may be used instead.

Dynamic Named Queries

A hybrid approach is to dynamically create a query and then save it as a named query in the entity manager factory. At that point it becomes just like any other named query that may have been declared statically in metadata. While this may seem like a good compromise, it turns out to be useful in only a few specific cases. The main advantage it offers is if there are queries that are not known until runtime, but then reissued repeatedly. Once the dynamic query becomes a named query it will only bear the cost of processing once. It is implementation-specific whether that cost is paid when the query is registered as a named query, or deferred until the first time it is executed.

A dynamic query can be turned into a named query by using the `EntityManagerFactory addNamedQuery()` method. Listing 7-6 shows how this is done.

Listing 7-6. Dynamically Adding a Named Query

```java
public class QueryService {
    private static final String QUERY =
        "SELECT e.salary " +
        "FROM Employee e " +
        "WHERE e.department.name = :deptName AND " +
        "     e.name = :empName ";

    @PersistenceContext(unitName="QueriesUnit")
    EntityManager em;

    @PersistenceUnit(unitName="QueriesUnit")
    EntityManagerFactory emf;

    @PostConstruct
    public void init() {
        TypedQuery<Long> q = em.createQuery(QUERY, Long.class);
        emf.addNamedQuery("findSalaryForNameAndDepartment", q);
    }
```

```
public long queryEmpSalary(String deptName, String empName) {
    return em.createNamedQuery("findSalaryForNameAndDepartment", Long.class)
            .setParameter("deptName", deptName)
            .setParameter("empName", empName)
            .getSingleResult();
}

// ...
}
```

The bean initialization method, annotated with @PostConstruct, creates the dynamic query and adds it to the set of named queries. As mentioned earlier, named queries are scoped to the entire persistence unit so it makes sense that they be added at the level of the entity manager factory. It also requires some caution in the choosing of names since adding a query with the same name as an existing one would simply cause the existing one to be overwritten. Because we needed the entity manager factory in both of the methods we just injected it into the bean instance using @PersistenceUnit. We could just as easily have accessed it from the entity manager using getEntityManagerFactory().

■ **Note** The addNamedQuery() method was added in JPA 2.1. If it occurred to you that the example is a little less than useful, you are beginning to get the reason why using this mixed approach is less commonly needed. If you can put the query description in a static string at development time, it's more appropriate to just use an annotation to define a static named query. The cases where it might be advantageous to make a named query out of a dynamic query are the following:

- The application gets access to some criteria at runtime that contributes to a query that is predetermined to be commonly executed.

- A named query is already defined but because of some aspect of the runtime environment you want to override the named query with a different one without using an additional XML descriptor.

- There is a preference to define all of the queries in code at startup time.

■ **Tip** When a dynamic query is added as a named query then all of the settings[2] on the query at the time it was added will be saved along with it. Each time the named query is executed, the saved settings will apply, unless they are overridden at execution time. However, as with all other named queries, any setting made to the named query (i.e. the query returned from createNamedQuery()) at execution time will be temporary and apply only to that individual execution.

---

[2]Parameter values that may have already been bound using setParameter() are not saved as part of the named query.

Parameter Types

As mentioned earlier, JPA supports both named and positional parameters for JP QL queries. The query factory methods of the entity manager return an implementation of the Query interface. Parameter values are then set on this object using the setParameter() methods of the Query interface.

There are three variations of this method for both named parameters and positional parameters. The first argument is always the parameter name or number. The second argument is the object to be bound to the named parameter. Date and Calendar parameters also require a third argument that specifies whether the type passed to JDBC is a java.sql.Date, java.sql.Time, or java.sql.TimeStamp value.

Consider the following named query definition, which requires two named parameters:

```
@NamedQuery(name="findEmployeesAboveSal",
            query="SELECT e " +
                "FROM Employee e " +
                "WHERE e.department = :dept AND " +
                "       e.salary > :sal")
```

This query highlights one of the nice features of JP QL in that entity types may be used as parameters. When the query is translated to SQL, the necessary primary key columns will be inserted into the conditional expression and paired with the primary key values from the parameter. It is not necessary to know how the primary key is mapped in order to write the query. Binding the parameters for this query is a simple case of passing in the required Department entity instance as well as a long representing the minimum salary value for the query. Listing 7-7 demonstrates how to bind the entity and primitive parameters required by this query.

Listing 7-7. Binding Named Parameters

```
public List<Employee> findEmployeesAboveSal(Department dept, long minSal) {
    return em.createNamedQuery("findEmployeesAboveSal", Employee.class)
                    .setParameter("dept", dept)
                    .setParameter("sal", minSal)
                    .getResultList();
}
```

Date and Calendar parameters are a special case because they represent both dates and times. In Chapter 4, we discussed mapping temporal types by using the @Temporal annotation and the TemporalType enumeration. This enumeration indicates whether the persistent field is a date, time, or timestamp. When a query uses a Date or Calendar parameter, it must select the appropriate temporal type for the parameter. Listing 7-8 demonstrates binding parameters where the value should be treated as a date.

Listing 7-8. Binding Date Parameters

```
public List<Employee> findEmployeesHiredDuringPeriod(Date start, Date end) {
    return em.createQuery("SELECT e " +
                            "FROM Employee e " +
                            "WHERE e.startDate BETWEEN ?1 AND ?2",
                            Employee.class)
                .setParameter(1, start, TemporalType.DATE)
                .setParameter(2, end, TemporalType.DATE)
                .getResultList();
}
```

One thing to keep in mind with query parameters is that the same parameter can be used multiple times in the query string yet only needs to be bound once using the setParameter() method. For example, consider the following named query definition, where the "dept" parameter is used twice in the WHERE clause:

```
@NamedQuery(name="findHighestPaidByDepartment",
            query="SELECT e " +
                  "FROM Employee e " +
                  "WHERE e.department = :dept AND " +
                  "      e.salary = (SELECT MAX(e.salary) " +
                  "                  FROM Employee e " +
                  "                  WHERE e.department = :dept)")
```

To execute this query, the "dept" parameter needs to be set only once with setParameter(), as in the following example:

```
public Employee findHighestPaidByDepartment(Department dept) {
    return em.createNamedQuery("findHighestPaidByDepartment",
                               Employee.class)
                .setParameter("dept", dept)
                .getSingleResult();
}
```

Executing Queries

The Query and TypedQuery interfaces each provide three different ways to execute a query, depending on whether or not the query returns results and how many results should be expected. For queries that return values, the developer may choose to call either getSingleResult() if the query is expected to return a single result or getResultList() if more than one result may be returned. The executeUpdate() method is used to invoke bulk update and delete queries. We will discuss this method later in the "Bulk Update and Delete" section. Note that both of the query interfaces define the same set of methods and differ only in their return types. We will cover this issue in the next section.

The simplest form of query execution is via the getResultList() method. It returns a collection containing the query results. If the query did not return any data, the collection is empty. The return type is specified as a List instead of a Collection in order to support queries that specify a sort order. If the query uses the ORDER BY clause to specify a sort order, the results will be put into the result list in the same order. Listing 7-9 demonstrates how a query might be used to generate a menu for a command-line application that displays the name of each employee working on a project as well as the name of the department that the employee is assigned to. The results are sorted by the name of the employee. Queries are unordered by default.

Listing 7-9. Iterating over Sorted Results

```
public void displayProjectEmployees(String projectName) {
    List<Employee> result = em.createQuery(
                    "SELECT e " +
                    "FROM Project p JOIN p.employees e "+
                    "WHERE p.name = ?1 " +
                    "ORDER BY e.name",
                    Employee.class)
                .setParameter(1, projectName)
                .getResultList();
```

```
    int count = 0;
    for (Employee e : result) {
        System.out.println(++count + ": " + e.getName() + ", " +
                            e.getDepartment().getName());
    }
}
```

The getSingleResult() method is provided as a convenience for queries that return only a single value. Instead of iterating to the first result in a collection, the object is directly returned. It is important to note, however, that getSingleResult() behaves differently from getResultList() in how it handles unexpected results. Whereas getResultList() returns an empty collection when no results are available, getSingleResult() throws a NoResultException exception. Therefore if there is a chance that the desired result may not be found, then this exception needs to be handled.

If multiple results are available after executing the query instead of the single expected result, getSingleResult() will throw a NonUniqueResultException exception. Again, this can be problematic for application code if the query criteria may result in more than one row being returned in certain circumstances. Although getSingleResult() is convenient to use, be sure that the query and its possible results are well understood; otherwise application code may have to deal with an unexpected runtime exception. Unlike other exceptions thrown by entity manager operations, these exceptions will not cause the provider to roll back the current transaction, if there is one.

Any SELECT query that returns data via the getResultList() and getSingleResult() methods may also specify locking constraints for the database rows impacted by the query. This facility is exposed through the query interfaces via the setLockMode() method. We will defer discussion of the locking semantics for queries until the full discussion of locking in Chapter 12.

Query and TypedQuery objects may be reused as often as needed so long as the same persistence context that was used to create the query is still active. For transaction-scoped entity managers, this limits the lifetime of the Query or TypedQuery object to the life of the transaction. Other entity manager types may reuse them until the entity manager is closed or removed.

Listing 7-10 demonstrates caching a TypedQuery object instance on the bean class of a stateful session bean that uses an extended persistence context. Whenever the bean needs to find the list of employees who are currently not assigned to any project, it reuses the same unassignedQuery object that was initialized during PostConstruct.

Listing 7-10. Reusing a Query Object

```
@Stateful
public class ProjectManager {
    @PersistenceContext(unitName="EmployeeService",
                        type=PersistenceContextType.EXTENDED)
    EntityManager em;

    TypedQuery<Employee> unassignedQuery;

    @PostConstruct
    public void init() {
        unassignedQuery =
            em.createQuery("SELECT e " +
                           "FROM Employee e " +
                           "WHERE e.projects IS EMPTY",
                           Employee.class);
    }
```

```
public List<Employee> findEmployeesWithoutProjects() {
    return unassignedQuery.getResultList();
}

// ...
}
```

Working with Query Results

The result type of a query is determined by the expressions listed in the SELECT clause of the query. If the result type of a query is the Employee entity, then executing getResultList() will result in a collection of zero or more Employee entity instances. There is a wide variety of results possible, depending on the makeup of the query. The following are just some of the types that may result from JP QL queries:

- Basic types, such as String, the primitive types, and JDBC types

- Entity types

- An array of Object

- User-defined types created from a constructor expression

For developers used to JDBC, the most important thing to remember when using the Query and TypedQuery interfaces is that the results are not encapsulated in a JDBC ResultSet. The collection or single result corresponds directly to the result type of the query.

Whenever an entity instance is returned, it becomes managed by the active persistence context. If that entity instance is modified and the persistence context is part of a transaction, the changes will be persisted to the database. The only exception to this rule is the use of transaction-scoped entity managers outside of a transaction. Any query executed in this situation returns detached entity instances instead of managed entity instances. To make changes on these detached entities, they must first be merged into a persistence context before they can be synchronized with the database.

A consequence of the long-term management of entities with application-managed and extended persistence contexts is that executing large queries will cause the persistence context to grow as it stores all the managed entity instances that are returned. If many of these persistence contexts are holding onto large numbers of managed entities for long periods of time, then memory use may become a concern. The clear() method of the EntityManager interface may be used to clear application-managed and extended persistence contexts, removing unnecessary managed entities.

Untyped Results

So far in this chapter we have been demonstrating the strongly typed versions of the query creation methods. We have provided the expected result type and therefore received an instance of TypedQuery that is bound to the expected type. By qualifying the result type in this way, the getResultList() and getSingleResult() methods return the correct types without the need for casting.

In the event that the result type is Object, or the JP QL query selects multiple objects, you may use the untyped versions of the query creation methods. Omitting the result type produces a Query instance instead of a TypedQuery instance, which defines getResultList() to return an unbound List and getSingleResult() to return Object. For an example of using untyped results see the code listings in the "Special Result Types" section.

Optimizing Read-Only Queries

When the query results will not be modified, queries using transaction-scoped entity managers outside of a transaction can be more efficient than queries executed within a transaction when the result type is an entity. When query results are prepared within a transaction, the persistence provider has to take steps to convert the results into managed entities. This usually entails taking a snapshot of the data for each entity in order to have a baseline to compare against when the transaction is committed. If the managed entities are never modified, the effort of converting the results into managed entities is wasted.

Outside of a transaction, in some circumstances the persistence provider may be able to optimize the case where the results will be detached immediately. Therefore it can avoid the overhead of creating the managed versions. Note that this technique does not work on application-managed or extended entity managers because their persistence context outlives the transaction. Any query result from this type of persistence context may be modified for later synchronization to the database even if there is no transaction.

When encapsulating query operations behind a bean with container-managed transactions, the easiest way to execute nontransactional queries is to use the NOT_SUPPORTED transaction attribute for the session bean method. This will cause any active transaction to be suspended, forcing the query results to be detached and enabling this optimization. Listing 7-11 shows an example of this technique using a stateless session bean.

Listing 7-11. Executing a Query Outside of a Transaction

```
@Stateless
public class QueryService {
    @PersistenceContext(unitName="EmployeeService")
    EntityManager em;

    @TransactionAttribute(TransactionAttributeType.NOT_SUPPORTED)
    public List<Department> findAllDepartmentsDetached() {
        return em.createQuery("SELECT d FROM Department d",
                              Department.class)
                .getResultList();
    }

    // ...
}
```

■ **Note** This optimization is completely provider-specific. Some providers may instead opt to create a temporary persistence context for the query and just throw it away after extracting the results from it, making this suggested optimization rather extraneous. Check your provider before making a coding decision.

Special Result Types

Whenever a query involves more than one expression in the SELECT clause, the result of the query will be a List of Object arrays. Common examples include projection of entity fields and aggregate queries where grouping expressions or multiple functions are used. Listing 7-12 revisits the menu generator from Listing 7-9 using a projection query instead of returning full Employee entity instances. Each element of the List is cast to an array of Object that is then used to extract the employee and department name information. We use an untyped query because the result has multiple elements in it.

Listing 7-12. Handling Multiple Result Types

```java
public void displayProjectEmployees(String projectName) {
    List result = em.createQuery(
                        "SELECT e.name, e.department.name " +
                        "FROM Project p JOIN p.employees e " +
                        "WHERE p.name = ?1 " +
                        "ORDER BY e.name")
                    .setParameter(1, projectName)
                    .getResultList();
    int count = 0;
    for (Iterator i = result.iterator(); i.hasNext();) {
        Object[] values = (Object[]) i.next();
        System.out.println(++count + ": " +
                        values[0] + ", " + values[1]);
    }
}
```

Constructor expressions provide developers with a way to map an array of Object result types to custom objects. Typically this is used to convert the results into JavaBean-style classes that provide getters for the different returned values. This makes the results easier to work with and makes it possible to use the results directly in an environment such as JavaServer Faces without additional translation.

A constructor expression is defined in JP QL using the NEW operator in the SELECT clause. The argument to the NEW operator is the fully qualified name of the class that will be instantiated to hold the results for each row of data returned. The only requirement for this class is that it has a constructor with arguments matching the exact type and order that will be specified in the query. Listing 7-13 shows an EmpMenu class defined in the package example that could be used to hold the results of the query that was executed in Listing 7-12.

Listing 7-13. Defining a Class for Use in a Constructor Expression

```java
package example;

public class EmpMenu {
    private String employeeName;
    private String departmentName;

    public EmpMenu(String employeeName, String departmentName) {
        this.employeeName = employeeName;
        this.departmentName = departmentName;
    }

    public String getEmployeeName() { return employeeName; }
    public String getDepartmentName() { return departmentName; }
}
```

Listing 7-14 shows the same example as Listing 7-12 using the fully qualified EmpMenu class name in a constructor expression. Instead of working with array indexes, each result is an instance of the EmpMenu class and is used like a regular Java object. We can also use typed queries again because there is only one expression in the SELECT clause.

Listing 7-14. Using Constructor Expressions

```
public void displayProjectEmployees(String projectName) {
    List<EmpMenu> result =
        em.createQuery("SELECT NEW example.EmpMenu(" +
                                    "e.name, e.department.name) " +
                        "FROM Project p JOIN p.employees e " +
                        "WHERE p.name = ?1 " +
                        "ORDER BY e.name",
                        EmpMenu.class)
            .setParameter(1, projectName)
            .getResultList();
    int count = 0;
    for (EmpMenu menu : result) {
        System.out.println(++count + ": " +
                            menu.getEmployeeName() + ", " +
                            menu.getDepartmentName());
    }
}
```

Query Paging

Large result sets from queries are often a problem for many applications. In cases where it would be overwhelming to display the entire result set, or if the application medium makes displaying many rows inefficient (web applications, in particular), applications must be able to display ranges of a result set and provide users with the ability to control the range of data that they are viewing. The most common form of this technique is to present the user with a fixed-size table that acts as a sliding window over the result set. Each increment of results displayed is called a page, and the process of navigating through the results is called pagination.

Efficiently paging through result sets has long been a challenge for both application developers and database vendors. Before support existed at the database level, a common technique was to first retrieve all the primary keys for the result set and then issue separate queries for the full results using ranges of primary key values. Later, database vendors added the concept of logical row number to query results, guaranteeing that as long as the result was ordered, the row number could be relied on to retrieve portions of the result set. More recently, the JDBC specification has taken this even further with the concept of scrollable result sets, which can be navigated forward and backward as required.

The Query and TypedQuery interfaces provide support for pagination via the setFirstResult() and setMaxResults() methods. These methods specify the first result to be received (numbered from zero) and the maximum number of results to return relative to that point. Values set for these methods may be likewise retrieved via the getFirstResult() and getMaxResults() methods. A persistence provider may choose to implement support for this feature in a number of different ways because not all databases benefit from the same approach. It's a good idea to become familiar with the way your vendor approaches pagination and what level of support exists in the target database platform for your application.

■ **Caution** The setFirstResult() and setMaxResults() methods should not be used with queries that join across collection relationships (one-to-many and many-to-many) because these queries may return duplicate values. The duplicate values in the result set make it impossible to use a logical result position.

To better illustrate pagination support, consider the stateful bean shown in Listing 7-15. Once created, it is initialized with the name of a query to count the total results and the name of a query to generate the report. When results are requested, it uses the page size and current page number to calculate the correct parameters for the setFirstResult() and setMaxResults() methods. The total number of results possible is calculated by executing the count query. By using the next(), previous(), and getCurrentResults() methods, presentation code can page through the results as required. If this bean were bound into an HTTP session, it could be directly used by a JSP or JavaServer Faces page presenting the results in a data table. The class in Listing 7-15 is a general template for a bean that holds intermediate state for an application query from which the results are processed in segments. A stateful session bean is used.

Listing 7-15. Stateful Report Pager

```
@Stateful
public class ResultPager {
    @PersistenceContext(unitName="QueryPaging")
    private EntityManager em;

    private String reportQueryName;
    private long currentPage;
    private long maxResults;
    private long pageSize;

    public long getPageSize() {
        return pageSize;
    }

    public long getMaxPages() {
        return maxResults / pageSize;
    }

    public void init(long pageSize, String countQueryName,
                     String reportQueryName) {
        this.pageSize = pageSize;
        this.reportQueryName = reportQueryName;
        maxResults = em.createNamedQuery(countQueryName, Long.class)
                        .getSingleResult();
        currentPage = 0;
    }

    public List getCurrentResults() {
        return em.createNamedQuery(reportQueryName)
                .setFirstResult(currentPage * pageSize)
                .setMaxResults(pageSize)
                .getResultList();
    }

    public void next() {
        currentPage++;
    }
```

```
public void previous() {
    currentPage--;
    if (currentPage < 0) {
        currentPage = 0;
    }
}

public long getCurrentPage() {
    return currentPage;
}

public void setCurrentPage(long currentPage) {
    this.currentPage = currentPage;
}

@Remove
public void finished() {}
}
```

Queries and Uncommitted Changes

Executing queries against entities that have been created or changed in a transaction is a topic that requires special consideration. As we discussed in Chapter 6, the persistence provider will attempt to minimize the number of times the persistence context must be flushed within a transaction. Optimally this will occur only once, when the transaction commits. While the transaction is open and changes are being made, the provider relies on its own internal cache synchronization to ensure that the right version of each entity is used in entity manager operations. At most the provider may have to read new data from the database in order to fulfill a request. All entity operations other than queries can be satisfied without flushing the persistence context to the database.

Queries are a special case because they are executed directly as SQL against the database. Because the database executes the query and not the persistence provider, the active persistence context cannot usually be consulted by the query. As a result, if the persistence context has not been flushed and the database query would be impacted by the changes pending in the persistence context, incorrect data is likely to be retrieved from the query. The entity manager find() operation, on the other hand, queries for a single entity with a given primary key. It can always check the persistence context before going to the database, so incorrect data is not a concern.

The good news is that by default, the persistence provider will ensure that queries are able to incorporate pending transactional changes in the query result. It might accomplish this by flushing the persistence context to the database, or it might leverage its own runtime information to ensure the results are correct.

And yet, there are times when having the persistence provider ensure query integrity is not necessarily the behavior you need. The problem is that it is not always easy for the provider to determine the best strategy to accommodate the integrity needs of a query. There is no practical way the provider can logically determine at a fine-grained level which objects have changed and therefore need to be incorporated into the query results. If the provider solution to ensuring query integrity is to flush the persistence context to the database, then you might have a performance problem if this is a frequent occurrence.

To put this issue in context, consider a message board application, which has modeled conversation topics as Conversation entities. Each Conversation entity refers to one or more messages represented by a Message entity. Periodically, conversations are archived when the last message added to the conversation is more than 30 days old. This is accomplished by changing the status of the Conversation entity from ACTIVE to INACTIVE. The two queries to obtain the list of active conversations and the last message date for a given conversation are shown in Listing 7-16.

Listing 7-16. Conversation Queries

```
@NamedQueries({
    @NamedQuery(name="findActiveConversations",
                query="SELECT c " +
                      "FROM Conversation c " +
                      "WHERE c.status = 'ACTIVE'"),
    @NamedQuery(name="findLastMessageDate",
                query="SELECT MAX(m.postingDate) " +
                      "FROM Conversation c JOIN c.messages m " +
                      "WHERE c = :conversation")
})
```

Listing 7-17 shows the method used to perform this maintenance, accepting a Date argument that specifies the minimum age for messages in order to still be considered an active conversation. In this example, two queries are being executed. The "findActiveConversations" query collects all the active conversations, while the "findLastMessageDate" returns the last date that a message was added to a Conversation entity. As the code iterates over the Conversation entities, it invokes the "findLastMessageDate" query for each one. As these two queries are related, it is reasonable for a persistence provider to assume that the results of the "findLastMessageDate" query will depend on the changes being made to the Conversation entities. If the provider ensures the integrity of the "findLastMessageDate" query by flushing the persistence context, this could become a very expensive operation if hundreds of active conversations are being checked.

Listing 7-17. Archiving Conversation Entities

```
public void archiveConversations(Date minAge) {
    List<Conversation> active =
        em.createNamedQuery("findActiveConversations",
                            Conversation.class)
            .getResultList();
    TypedQuery<Date> maxAge =
        em.createNamedQuery("findLastMessageDate", Date.class);
    for (Conversation c : active) {
        maxAge.setParameter("conversation", c);
        Date lastMessageDate = maxAge.getSingleResult();
        if (lastMessageDate.before(minAge)) {
            c.setStatus("INACTIVE");
        }
    }
}
```

To offer more control over the integrity requirements of queries, the EntityManager and Query interfaces support a setFlushMode() method to set the flush mode, an indicator to the provider how it should handle pending changes and queries. There are two possible flush mode settings, AUTO and COMMIT, which are defined by the FlushModeType enumerated type. The default setting is AUTO, which means that the provider should ensure that pending transactional changes are included in query results. If a query might overlap with changed data in the persistence context, this setting will ensure that the results are correct. The current flush mode setting may be retrieved via the getFlushMode() method.

The COMMIT flush mode tells the provider that queries don't overlap with changed data in the persistence context, so it does not need to do anything in order to get correct results. Depending on how the provider implements its query integrity support, this might mean that it does not have to flush the persistence context before executing a query because you have indicated that there is no changed data in memory that would affect the results of the database query.

Although the flush mode is set on the entity manager, the flush mode is really a property of the persistence context. For transaction-scoped entity managers, that means the flush mode has to be changed in every transaction. Extended and application-managed entity managers will preserve their flush mode setting across transactions. Flush mode will not apply at all to persistence contexts that are not synchronized with the transaction.

Setting the flush mode on the entity manager applies to all queries, while setting the flush mode for a query limits the setting to that scope. Setting the flush mode on the query overrides the entity manager setting, as you would expect. If the entity manager setting is AUTO and one query has the COMMIT setting, the provider will guarantee query integrity for all the queries other than the one with the COMMIT setting. Likewise, if the entity manager setting is COMMIT and one query has an AUTO setting, only the query with the AUTO setting is guaranteed to incorporate pending changes from the persistence context.

Generally speaking, if you are going to execute queries in transactions where data is being changed, AUTO is the right answer. If you are concerned about the performance implications of ensuring query integrity, consider changing the flush mode to COMMIT on a per-query basis. Changing the value on the entity manager, while convenient, can lead to problems if more queries are added to the application later and they require AUTO semantics.

Coming back to the example at the start of this section, we can set the flush mode on the TypedQuery object for the "findLastMessageDate" query to COMMIT because it does not need to see the changes being made to the Conversation entities. The following fragment shows how this would be accomplished for the archiveConversations() method shown in Listing 7-17:

```java
public void archiveConversations(Date minAge) {
    // ...
    TypedQuery<Date> maxAge = em.createNamedQuery(
                                "findLastMessageDate", Date.class);
    maxAge.setFlushMode(FlushModeType.COMMIT);
    // ...
}
```

Query Timeouts

Generally speaking, when a query executes it will block until the database query returns. In addition to the obvious concern about runaway queries and application responsiveness, it may also be a problem if the query is participating in a transaction and a timeout has been set on the JTA transaction or on the database. The timeout on the transaction or database may cause the query to abort early, but it will also cause the transaction to roll back, preventing any further work in the same transaction.

If an application needs to set a limit on query response time without using a transaction or causing a transaction rollback, the javax.persistence.query.timeout property may be set on the query or as part of the persistence unit. This property defines the number of milliseconds that the query should be allowed to run before it is aborted. Listing 7-18 demonstrates how to set a timeout value for a given query. This example uses the query hint mechanism, which we will discuss in more detail later in the "Query Hints" section. Setting properties on the persistence unit is covered in Chapter 14.

Listing 7-18. Setting a Query Timeout

```java
public Date getLastUserActivity() {
    TypedQuery<Date> lastActive =
        em.createNamedQuery("findLastUserActivity", Date.class);
    lastActive.setHint("javax.persistence.query.timeout", 5000);
    try {
        return lastActive.getSingleResult();
    } catch (QueryTimeoutException e) {
        return null;
    }
}
```

Unfortunately, setting a query timeout is not portable behavior. It may not be supported by all database platforms nor is it a requirement to be supported by all persistence providers. Therefore, applications that want to enable query timeouts must be prepared for three scenarios. The first is that the property is silently ignored and has no effect. The second is that the property is enabled and any select, update, or delete operation that runs longer than the specified timeout value is aborted, and a QueryTimeoutException is thrown. This exception may be handled and will not cause any active transaction to be marked for rollback. Listing 7-18 demonstrates one approach to handling this exception. The third scenario is that the property is enabled, but in doing so the database forces a transaction rollback when the timeout is exceeded. In this case, a PersistenceException will be thrown and the transaction marked for rollback. In general, if enabled the application should be written to handle the QueryTimeoutException, but should not fail if the timeout is exceeded and the exception is not thrown.

Bulk Update and Delete

Like their SQL counterparts, JP QL bulk UPDATE and DELETE statements are designed to make changes to large numbers of entities in a single operation without requiring the individual entities to be retrieved and modified using the entity manager. Unlike SQL, which operates on tables, JP QL UPDATE and DELETE statements must take the full range of mappings for the entity into account. These operations are challenging for vendors to implement correctly, and as a result, there are restrictions on the use of these operations that must be well understood by developers.

The full syntax for UPDATE and DELETE statements is described in Chapter 8. The following sections will describe how to use these operations effectively and the issues that may result when used incorrectly.

Using Bulk Update and Delete

Bulk update of entities is accomplished with the UPDATE statement. This statement operates on a single entity type and sets one or more single-valued properties of the entity (either a state field or a single-valued association) subject to the conditions in the WHERE clause. It can also be used on embedded state in one or more embeddable objects referenced by the entity. In terms of syntax, it is nearly identical to the SQL version with the exception of using entity expressions instead of tables and columns. Listing 7-19 demonstrates using a bulk UPDATE statement. Note that the use of the REQUIRES_NEW transaction attribute type is significant and will be discussed following the examples.

Listing 7-19. Bulk Update of Entities

```
@Stateless
public class EmployeeService {
    @PersistenceContext(unitName="BulkQueries")
    EntityManager em;

    @TransactionAttribute(TransactionAttributeType.REQUIRES_NEW)
    public void assignManager(Department dept, Employee manager) {
        em.createQuery("UPDATE Employee e " +
                        "SET e.manager = ?1 " +
                        "WHERE e.department = ?2")
            .setParameter(1, manager)
            .setParameter(2, dept)
            .executeUpdate();
    }
}
```

Bulk removal of entities is accomplished with the DELETE statement. Again, the syntax is the same as the SQL version, except that the target in the FROM clause is an entity instead of a table, and the WHERE clause is composed of entity expressions instead of column expressions. Listing 7-20 demonstrates bulk removal of entities.

Listing 7-20. Bulk Removal of Entities

```
@Stateless
public class ProjectService {
    @PersistenceContext(unitName="BulkQueries")
    EntityManager em;

    @TransactionAttribute(TransactionAttributeType.REQUIRES_NEW)
    public void removeEmptyProjects() {
        em.createQuery("DELETE FROM Project p " +
                        "WHERE p.employees IS EMPTY")
            .executeUpdate();
    }
}
```

The first issue to consider when using these statements is that the persistence context is not updated to reflect the results of the operation. Bulk operations are issued as SQL against the database, bypassing the in-memory structures of the persistence context. Therefore, updating the salary of all the employees will not change the current values for any entities managed in memory as part of a persistence context. The developer can rely only on entities retrieved after the bulk operation completes.

When using transaction-scoped persistence contexts the bulk operation should either execute in a transaction all by itself or be the first operation in the transaction. Running the bulk operation in its own transaction is the preferred approach because it minimizes the chance of accidentally fetching data before the bulk change occurs. Executing the bulk operation and then working with entities after it completes is also safe because then any find() operation or query will go to the database to get current results. The examples in Listing 7-19 and Listing 7-20 used the REQUIRES_NEW transaction attribute to ensure that the bulk operations occurred within their own transactions.

A typical strategy for persistence providers dealing with bulk operations is to invalidate any in-memory cache of data related to the target entity. This forces data to be fetched from the database the next time it is required. How much cached data gets invalidated depends on the sophistication of the persistence provider. If the provider can detect that the update impacts only a small range of entities, those specific entities may be invalidated, leaving other cached data in place. Such optimizations are limited, however, and if the provider cannot be sure of the scope of the change, the entire cache must be invalidated. This can have an impact on the performance of the application if bulk changes are a frequent occurrence.

■ **Caution**   Native SQL update and delete operations should not be executed on tables mapped by an entity. The JP QL operations tell the provider what cached entity state must be invalidated in order to remain consistent with the database. Native SQL operations bypass such checks and can quickly lead to situations where the in-memory cache is out of date with respect to the database.

The danger present in bulk operations and the reason they must occur first in a transaction is that any entity actively managed by a persistence context will remain that way, oblivious to the actual changes occurring at the database level. The active persistence context is separate and distinct from any data cache that the provider may use for optimizations. Consider the following sequence of operations:

1. A new transaction starts.

2. Entity A is created by calling `persist()` to make the entity managed.

3. Entity B is retrieved from a `find()` operation and modified.

4. A bulk remove deletes entity A.

5. A bulk update changes the same properties on entity B that were modified in step 3.

6. The transaction commits.

What should happen to entities A and B in this sequence? (Before you answer, recall that bulk operations translate directly to SQL and bypass the persistence context!) In the case of entity A, the provider has to assume that the persistence context is correct and so will still attempt to insert the new entity even though it should have been removed. In the case of entity B, again the provider has to assume that the managed version is the correct version and will attempt to update the version in the database, undoing the bulk update change.

This brings us to the issue of extended persistence contexts. Bulk operations and extended persistence contexts are a particularly dangerous combination because the persistence context survives across transaction boundaries, but the provider will never refresh the persistence context to reflect the changed state of the database after a bulk operation has completed. When the extended persistence context is next associated with a transaction, it will attempt to synchronize its current state with the database. Because the managed entities in the persistence context are now out of date with respect to the database, any changes made since the bulk operation could result in incorrect results being stored. In this situation, the only option is to refresh the entity state or ensure that the data is versioned in such a way that the incorrect change can be detected. Locking strategies and refreshing of entity state are discussed in Chapter 12.

Bulk Delete and Relationships

In our discussion of the `remove()` operation in the previous chapter, we emphasized that relationship maintenance is always the responsibility of the developer. The only time a cascading remove occurs is when the REMOVE cascade option is set for a relationship. Even then, the persistence provider won't automatically update the state of any managed entities that refer to the removed entity. As you are about to see, the same requirement holds true when using DELETE statements as well.

A DELETE statement in JP QL corresponds more or less to a DELETE statement in SQL. Writing the statement in JP QL gives you the benefit of working with entities instead of tables, but the semantics are exactly the same. This has implications for how applications must write DELETE statements in order to ensure that they execute correctly and leave the database in a consistent state.

DELETE statements are applied to a set of entities in the database, unlike `remove()`, which applies to a single entity in the persistence context. A consequence of this is that DELETE statements do not cascade to related entities. Even if the REMOVE cascade option is set on a relationship, it will not be followed. It is your responsibility to ensure that relationships are correctly updated with respect to the entities that have been removed. The persistence provider also has no control over constraints in the database. If you attempt to remove data that is the target of a foreign key relationship in another table, you may get a referential integrity constraint violation in return.

Let's look at an example that puts these issues in context. Suppose, for example, that a company wishes to reorganize its department structure. It wants to delete a number of departments and then assign the employees to new departments. The first step is to delete the old departments, so the following statement is to be executed:

```
DELETE FROM Department d
WHERE d.name IN ('CA13', 'CA19', 'NY30')
```

This is a straightforward operation. We want to remove the department entities that match the given list of names using a DELETE statement instead of querying for the entities and using the remove() operation to dispose of them. But when this query is executed, a PersistenceException exception is thrown, reporting that a foreign key integrity constraint has been violated. Another table has a foreign key reference to one of the rows we are trying to delete. Checking the database, we see that the table mapped by the Employee entity has a foreign key constraint against the table mapped by the Department entity. Because the foreign key value in the Employee table is not NULL, the parent key from the Department table can't be removed.

We first need to update the Employee entities in question to make sure they do not point to the department we are trying to delete:

```
UPDATE Employee e
SET e.department = null
WHERE e.department.name IN ('CA13', 'CA19', 'NY30')
```

With this change the original DELETE statement will work as expected. Now consider what would have happened if the integrity constraint had not been in the database. The DELETE operation would have completed successfully, but the foreign key values would still be sitting in the Employee table. The next time the persistence provider tried to load the Employee entities with dangling foreign keys, it would be unable to resolve the target entity. The outcome of this operation is vendor-specific, but it may lead to a PersistenceException exception being thrown, complaining of the invalid relationship.

Query Hints

Query hints are the JPA extension point for query features. A hint is simply a string name and object value. Hints allow features to be added to JPA without introducing a new API. This includes standard features such as the query timeouts demonstrated earlier, as well as vendor-specific features. Note that when not explicitly covered by the JPA specification, no assumptions can be made about the portability of hints between vendors, even if the names are the same. Every query may be associated with any number of hints, set either in persistence unit metadata as part of the @NamedQuery annotation, or on the Query or TypedQuery interfaces using the setHint() method. The current set of hints enabled for a query may be retrieved with the getHints() method, which returns a map of name and value pairs.

In order to simplify portability between vendors, persistence providers are required to ignore hints that they do not understand. Listing 7-21 demonstrates the "eclipselink.cache-usage" hint supported by the JPA Reference Implementation to indicate that the cache should not be checked when reading an Employee from the database. Unlike the refresh() method of the EntityManager interface, this hint will not cause the query result to overwrite the current cached value.

Listing 7-21. Using Query Hints

```
public Employee findEmployeeNoCache(int empId) {
    TypedQuery<Employee> q = em.createQuery(
        "SELECT e FROM Employee e WHERE e.id = :empId", Employee.class);
    // force read from database
    q.setHint("eclipselink.cache-usage", "DoNotCheckCache");
    q.setParameter("empId", empId);
    try {
        return q.getSingleResult();
    } catch (NoResultException e) {
        return null;
    }
}
```

If this query were to be executed frequently, a named query would be more efficient. The following named query definition incorporates the cache hint used earlier:

```
@NamedQuery(name="findEmployeeNoCache",
            query="SELECT e FROM Employee e WHERE e.id = :empId",
            hints={@QueryHint(name="eclipselink.cache-usage",
                              value="DoNotCheckCache")})
```

The `hints` element accepts an array of `@QueryHint` annotations, allowing any number of hints to be set for a query. However, a limitation of using annotations for the named query is that hints are restricted to having values that are strings, whereas when using the `Query.setHint()` method any kind of object can be passed in as a hint value. This may be particularly relevant when using proprietary vendor hints. This also represents another use case that could be added to the list in the "Dynamic Named Queries" section.

Query Best Practices

The typical application using JPA will have many queries defined. It is the nature of enterprise applications that information is constantly being queried from the database for everything from complex reports to drop-down lists in the user interface. Therefore, efficiently using queries can have a major impact on your application's overall performance and responsiveness. As you carry out the performance testing of your queries, we recommend you consider some of the discussion points in the following sections.

Named Queries

First and foremost, we recommend named queries whenever possible. Persistence providers will often take steps to precompile JP QL named queries to SQL as part of the deployment or initialization phase of an application. This avoids the overhead of continuously parsing JP QL and generating SQL. Even with a cache for converted queries, dynamic query definition will always be less efficient than using named queries.

Named queries also enforce the best practice of using query parameters. Query parameters help to keep the number of distinct SQL strings parsed by the database to a minimum. Because databases typically keep a cache of SQL statements on hand for frequently accessed queries, this is an essential part of ensuring peak database performance.

As we discussed in the "Dynamic Query Definition" section, query parameters also help to avoid security issues caused by concatenating values into query strings. For applications exposed to the Web, security has to be a concern at every level of an application. You can either spend a lot of effort trying to validate input parameters, or you can use query parameters and let the database do the work for you.

When naming queries, decide on a naming strategy early in the application development cycle, with the understanding that the query namespace is global for each persistence unit. Collisions between query names are likely to be a common source of frustration if there is no established naming pattern. We recommend prefixing the name of the query with the name of the entity that is being returned, separated by a dot.

Using named queries allows for JP QL queries to be overridden with SQL queries or even with vendor-specific languages and expression frameworks. For applications migrating from an existing object-relational mapping solution, it is quite likely that the vendor will provide some support for invoking their existing query solution using the named query facility in JPA. We will discuss SQL named queries in Chapter 11.

The ability to dynamically create named queries in code may be useful if any of the cases we described earlier applies to you, or if you happen to have some other use case that makes dynamic creation relevant. In general, though, it is preferable and safer if you can declare all of your named queries statically.

Report Queries

If you are executing queries that return entities for reporting purposes and have no intention of modifying the results, consider executing queries using a transaction-scoped entity manager but outside of a transaction. The persistence provider may be able to detect the lack of a transaction and optimize the results for detachment, often by skipping some of the steps required to create an interim managed version of the entity results.

Likewise, if an entity is expensive to construct due to eager relationships or a complex table mapping, consider selecting individual entity properties using a projection query instead of retrieving the full entity result. If all you need is the name and office phone number for 500 employees, selecting only those 2 fields is likely to be far more efficient than fully constructing 1,000 entity instances.

Vendor Hints

It is likely that vendors will entice you with a variety of hints to enable different performance optimizations for queries. Query hints may well be an essential tool in meeting your performance expectations. If source code portability to multiple vendors is important, you should resist the urge to embed vendor query hints in your application code. The ideal location for query hints is in an XML mapping file (which we will be describing in Chapter 13) or at the very least as part of a named query definition. Hints are often highly dependent on the target platform and may well have to be changed over time as different aspects of the application impact the overall balance of performance. Keep hints decoupled from your code if at all possible.

Stateless Beans

We have tried to demonstrate many of the examples in the context of a stateless bean because we believe that to be the best way to organize queries in a Java EE application. Using any kind of stateless bean, be it a stateless session bean, a dependent scoped CDI bean, or a prototype scoped Spring bean, has a number of benefits over simply embedding queries all over the place in application code.

- Clients can execute queries by invoking an appropriately named business method instead of relying on a cryptic query name or multiple copies of the same query string.

- Bean methods can optimize their transaction usage depending on whether or not the results need to be managed or detached.

- Using a transaction-scoped persistence context ensures that large numbers of entity instances don't remain managed long after they are needed.

This is not to say that other components are unsuitable locations for issuing queries, but stateless beans are a well-established best practice for hosting queries in the Java EE environment.

Bulk Update and Delete

If bulk update and delete operations must be used, ensure that they are executed only in an isolated transaction where no other changes are being made. There are many ways in which these queries can negatively impact an active persistence context. Interweaving these queries with other non-bulk operations requires careful management by the application.

Entity versioning and locking requires special consideration when bulk update operations are used. Bulk delete operations can have wide ranging ramifications depending on how well the persistence provider can react and adjust entity caching in response. Therefore, we view bulk update and delete operations as being highly specialized, to be used with care.

Provider Differences

Take time to become familiar with the SQL that your persistence provider generates for different JP QL queries. Although understanding SQL is not necessary for writing JP QL queries, knowing what happens in response to the various JP QL operations is an essential part of performance tuning. Joins in JP QL are not always explicit, and you may find yourself surprised at the complex SQL generated for a seemingly simple JP QL query.

The benefits of features such as query paging are also dependent on the approach used by your persistence provider. There are a number of different techniques that can be used to accomplish pagination, many of which suffer from performance and scalability issues. Because JPA can't dictate a particular approach that will work well in all cases, become familiar with the approach used by your provider and whether or not it is configurable.

Finally, understanding the provider strategy for when and how often it flushes the persistence context is necessary before looking at optimizations such as changing the flush mode. Depending on the caching architecture and query optimizations used by a provider, changing the flush mode may or may not make a difference to your application.

Summary

We began this chapter with an introduction to JP QL, the query language defined by JPA. We briefly discussed the origins of JP QL and its role in writing queries that interact with entities. We also provided an overview of major JP QL features for developers already experienced with SQL.

In the discussion on executing queries, we introduced the methods for defining queries both dynamically at runtime and statically as part of persistence unit metadata. We looked at the Query and TypedQuery interfaces and the types of query results possible using JP QL. We also looked at parameter binding, strategies for handling large result sets, and how to ensure that queries in transactions with modified data complete successfully.

In the section on bulk update and delete we explained how to execute these types of queries and how to ensure that they are used safely by the application. We provided details on how persistence providers deal with bulk operations and the impact that they have on the active persistence context.

We ended our discussion of query features with a look at query hints. We showed how to specify hints and provided an example using hints supported by the JPA Reference Implementation.

Finally, we summarized our view of best practices relating to queries, looking at named queries, different strategies for the various query types, as well as the implementation details that need to be understood for different persistence providers.

In the next chapter, we will continue to focus on queries by examining JP QL in detail.

CHAPTER 8

Query Language

The Java Persistence Query Language (JP QL) is the standard query language of JPA. It is a portable query language designed to combine the syntax and simple query semantics of SQL with the expressiveness of an object-oriented expression language. Queries written using this language can be portably compiled to SQL on all major database servers.

In the last chapter, we looked at programming using the query interfaces and presented a brief introduction to JP QL for users already experienced with SQL. This chapter will explore the query language in detail, breaking the language down piece by piece with examples to demonstrate its features.

Introducing JP QL

In order to describe what JP QL is, it is important to make clear what it is not. JP QL is not SQL. Despite the similarities between the two languages in terms of keywords and overall structure, there are very important differences. Attempting to write JP QL as if it were SQL is the easiest way to get frustrated with the language. The similarities between the two languages are intentional (giving developers a feel for what JP QL can accomplish), but the object-oriented nature of JP QL requires a different kind of thinking.

If JP QL is not SQL, what is it? Put simply, JP QL is a language for querying entities. Instead of tables and rows, the currency of the language is entities and objects. It provides us with a way to express queries in terms of entities and their relationships, operating on the persistent state of the entity as defined in the object model, not in the physical database model.

If JPA supports SQL queries, why introduce a new query language? There are a couple of important reasons to consider JP QL over SQL. The first is portability. JP QL can be translated into the SQL dialects of all major database vendors. The second is that queries are written against the domain model of persistent entities, without any need to know exactly how those entities are mapped to the database. We hope that the examples in this chapter will demonstrate the power present in even the simplest JP QL expressions.

Adopting JP QL does not mean losing all the SQL features you have grown accustomed to using. A broad selection of SQL features are directly supported, including subqueries, aggregate queries, update and delete statements, numerous SQL functions, and more.

Terminology

Queries fall into one of four categories: select, aggregate, update, and delete. Select queries retrieve persistent state from one or more entities, filtering results as required. Aggregate queries are variations of select queries that group the results and produce summary data. Together, select and aggregate queries are sometimes called report queries, since they are primarily focused on generating data for reporting. Update and delete queries are used to conditionally modify or remove entire sets of entities. You will find each query type described in detail in its own section of this chapter.

Queries operate on the set of entities and embeddables defined by a persistence unit. This set of entities and embeddables is known as the abstract persistence schema, the collection of which defines the overall domain from which results can be retrieved.

■ **Note**   To allow this chapter to be used as a companion to the Query Language chapter of the Java Persistence API specification, the same terminology is used where possible.

In query expressions, entities are referred to by name. If an entity has not been explicitly named (using the name attribute of the @Entity annotation, for example), the unqualified class name is used by default. This name is the abstract schema name of the entity in the context of a query.

Entities are composed of one or more persistence properties implemented as fields or JavaBean properties. The abstract schema type of a persistent property on an entity refers to the class or primitive type used to implement that property. For example, if the Employee entity has a property name of type String, the abstract schema type of that property in query expressions is String as well. Simple persistent properties with no relationship mapping comprise the persistent state of the entity and are referred to as state fields. Persistent properties that are also relationships are called association fields.

As you saw in the last chapter, queries can be defined dynamically or statically. The examples in this chapter will consist of queries that can be used either dynamically or statically, depending on the needs of the application.

Finally, it is important to note that queries are not case-sensitive except in two cases: entity names and property names must be specified exactly as they are named.

Example Data Model

Figure 8-1 shows the domain model for the queries in this chapter. Continuing the examples we have been using throughout the book, it demonstrates many different relationship types, including unidirectional, bidirectional, and self-referencing relationships. We have added the role names to this diagram to make the relationship property names explicit.

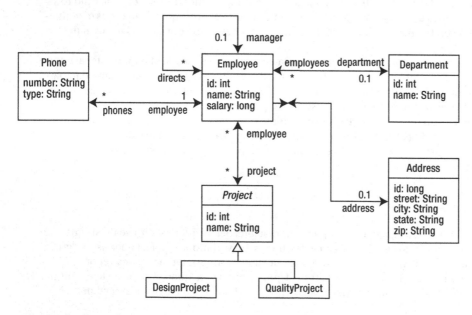

Figure 8-1. *Example application domain model*

The object relational mappings for this model are not included in this chapter except where we describe the SQL equivalent of a particular query. It is not necessary to know how an object is mapped in order to write queries because the query language is based entirely on the object model and the logical relationships between entities. It is the job of the query translator to take the object-oriented query expressions and interpret the mapping metadata in order to produce the SQL required to execute the query on the database.

Example Application

Learning a new language can be a challenging experience. It's one thing to read through page after page of text describing the features of the language, but it's another thing completely to put these features into practice. To get used to writing queries, consider using an application like the one shown in Listing 8-1. This simple application reads queries from the console and executes them against the entities from a particular persistence unit.

Listing 8-1. Application for Testing Queries

```
package persistence;

import java.io.*;
import java.util.*;
import javax.persistence.*;
import org.apache.commons.lang.builder.*;

public class QueryTester {

    public static void main(String[] args) throws Exception {
        String unitName = args[0];

        EntityManagerFactory emf =
            Persistence.createEntityManagerFactory(unitName);
        EntityManager em = emf.createEntityManager();
        BufferedReader reader =
            new BufferedReader(new InputStreamReader(System.in));

        for (;;) {
            System.out.print("JP QL> ");
            String query = reader.readLine();
            if (query.equals("quit")) {
                break;
            }
            if (query.length() == 0) {
                continue;
            }

            try {
                List result = em.createQuery(query).getResultList();
                if (result.size() > 0) {
                    int count = 0;
                    for (Object o : result) {
                        System.out.print(++count + " ");
                        printResult(o);
                    }
```

```
                } else {
                    System.out.println("0 results returned");
                }
            } catch (Exception e) {
                e.printStackTrace();
            }
        }
    }

    private static void printResult(Object result) throws Exception {
        if (result == null) {
            System.out.print("NULL");
        } else if (result instanceof Object[]) {
            Object[] row = (Object[]) result;
            System.out.print("[");
            for (int i = 0; i < row.length; i++) {
                printResult(row[i]);
            }
            System.out.print("]");
        } else if (result instanceof Long ||
                    result instanceof Double ||
                    result instanceof String) {
            System.out.print(result.getClass().getName() + ": " + result);
        } else {
            System.out.print(ReflectionToStringBuilder.toString(result,
                                        ToStringStyle.SHORT_PREFIX_STYLE));
        }
        System.out.println();
    }
}
```

The only requirement for using this application is the name of a persistence unit containing the entities you want to query against. The application will read the persistence unit name from the command line and attempt to create an EntityManagerFactory for that name. If initialization is successful, queries can be typed at the JP QL> prompt. The query will be executed and the results printed out. The format of each result is the class name followed by each of the properties for that class. This example uses the Apache Jakarta Commons-Lang library to generate the object summary. Listing 8-2 demonstrates a sample session with the application.

Listing 8-2. *Example Session with QueryTester*

```
JP QL> SELECT p FROM Phone p WHERE p.type NOT IN ('office', 'home')
1 Phone[id=5,number=516-555-1234,type=cell,employee=Employee@13c0b53]
2 Phone[id=9,number=650-555-1234,type=cell,employee=Employee@193f6e2]
3 Phone[id=12,number=650-555-1234,type=cell,employee=Employee@36527f]
4 Phone[id=18,number=585-555-1234,type=cell,employee=Employee@bd6a5f]
5 Phone[id=21,number=650-555-1234,type=cell,employee=Employee@979e8b]
JP QL> SELECT d.name, AVG(e.salary) FROM Department d JOIN d.employees e ↪
GROUP BY d.name
1 [java.lang.String: QA
java.lang.Double: 52500.0
]
```

```
2 [java.lang.String: Engineering
java.lang.Double: 56833.333333333336
]
JP QL> quit
```

Select Queries

Select queries are the most significant type of query and facilitate the bulk retrieval of data from the database. Not surprisingly, select queries are also the most common form of query used in applications. The overall form of a select query is as follows:

```
SELECT <select_expression>
FROM <from_clause>
[WHERE <conditional_expression>]
[ORDER BY <order_by_clause>]
```

The simplest form of a select query consists of two mandatory parts: the SELECT clause and the FROM clause. The SELECT clause defines the format of the query results, while the FROM clause defines the entity or entities from which the results will be obtained. Consider the following complete query that retrieves all the employees in the company:

```
SELECT e
FROM Employee e
```

The structure of this query is very similar to a SQL query, but with a couple of important differences. The first difference is that the domain of the query defined in the FROM clause is not a table but an entity; in this case, the Employee entity. As in SQL, it has been aliased to the identifier e. This aliased value is known as an identification variable and is the key by which the entity will be referred to in the rest of the select statement. Unlike queries in SQL, where a table alias is optional, the use of identification variables is mandatory in JP QL.

The second difference is that the SELECT clause in this example does not enumerate the fields of the table or use a wildcard to select all the fields. Instead, only the identification variable is listed in order to indicate that the result type of the query is the Employee entity, not a tabular set of rows.

As the query processor iterates over the result set returned from the database, it converts the tabular row and column data into a set of entity instances. The getResultList() method of the Query interface will return a collection of zero or more Employee objects after evaluating the query.

Despite the differences in structure and syntax, every query is translatable to SQL. In order to execute a query, the query engine first builds an optimal SQL representation of the JP QL query. The resulting SQL query is what actually gets executed on the database. In this simple example, the SQL might look something like this, depending upon the mapping metadata for the Employee entity:

```
SELECT id, name, salary, manager_id, dept_id, address_id
FROM emp
```

The SQL statement must read in all the mapped columns required to create the entity instance, including foreign key columns. Even if the entity is cached in memory, the query engine will still typically read all required data to ensure that the cached version is up to date. Note that if the relationships between the Employee and the Department or Address entities had required eager loading, the SQL statement would either be extended to retrieve the extra data or multiple statements would have been batched together in order to completely construct the Employee entity. Every vendor will provide some method for displaying the SQL it generates from translating JP QL. For performance tuning in particular, understanding how your vendor approaches SQL generation can help you write more efficient queries.

Now that we have looked at a simple query and covered the basic terminology, the following sections will move through each of the clauses of the select query, explaining the syntax and features available.

SELECT Clause

The SELECT clause of a query can take several forms, including simple and complex path expressions, scalar expressions, constructor expressions, aggregate functions, and sequences of these expression types. The following sections introduce path expressions and discuss the different styles of SELECT clauses and how they determine the result type of the query. We will defer discussion of scalar expressions until exploring conditional expressions in the WHERE clause. They are fully described in the section called "Scalar Expressions." Aggregate functions are detailed later in the chapter in the section called "Aggregate Queries."

Path Expressions

Path expressions are the building blocks of queries. They are used to navigate out from an entity, either across a relationship to another entity (or collection of entities) or to one of the persistent properties of an entity. Navigation that results in one of the persistent state fields (either field or property) of an entity is referred to as a state field path. Navigation that leads to a single entity is referred to as a single-valued association path, whereas navigation to a collection of entities is referred to as a collection-valued association path.

The dot operator (.) signifies path navigation in an expression. For example, if the Employee entity has been mapped to the identification variable e, e.name is a state field path expression resolving to the employee name. Likewise, the path expression e.department is a single-valued association from the employee to the department to which he or she is assigned. Finally, e.directs is a collection-valued association that resolves to the collection of employees reporting to an employee who is also a manager.

What makes path expressions so powerful is that they are not limited to a single navigation. Instead, navigation expressions can be chained together to traverse complex entity graphs as long as the path moves from left to right across single-valued associations. A path cannot continue from a state field or collection-valued association. Using this technique, we can construct path expressions such as e.department.name, which is the name of the department to which the employee belongs. Note that path expressions can navigate into and across embedded objects as well as normal entities. The only restriction on embedded objects in a path expression is that the root of the path expression must begin with an entity.

Path expressions are used in every clause of a select query, determining everything from the result type of the query to the conditions under which the results should be filtered. Experience with path expressions is the key to writing effective queries.

Entities and Objects

The first and simplest form of the SELECT clause is a single identification variable. The result type for a query of this style is the entity to which the identification variable is associated. For example, the following query returns all the departments in the company:

```
SELECT d
FROM Department d
```

The keyword OBJECT can be used to indicate that the result type of the query is the entity bound to the identification variable. It has no impact on the query, but it can be used as a visual clue.

```
SELECT OBJECT(d)
FROM Department d
```

The only problem with using OBJECT is that even though path expressions can resolve to an entity type, the syntax of the OBJECT keyword is limited to identification variables. The expression OBJECT(e.department) is illegal even though Department is an entity type. For that reason, we do not recommend the OBJECT syntax.

It exists primarily for compatibility with previous versions of the language that required the OBJECT keyword on the assumption that a future revision to SQL would include the same terminology.

A path expression resolving to a state field or single-valued association can also be used in the SELECT clause. The result type of the query in this case becomes the type of the path expression, either the state field type or the entity type of a single-valued association. The following query returns the names for all employees:

```
SELECT e.name
FROM Employee e
```

The result type of the path expression in the SELECT clause is String, so executing this query using getResultList() will produce a collection of zero or more String objects. Path expressions resolving to state fields can also be used as part of scalar expressions, allowing the state field to be transformed in the query results. We will discuss this technique later in the section called "Scalar Expressions."

Entities reached from a path expression can also be returned. The following query demonstrates returning a different entity as a result of path navigation:

```
SELECT e.department
FROM Employee e
```

The result type of this query is the Department entity because that is the result of traversing the department relationship from Employee to Department. Executing the query will therefore result in a collection of zero or more Department objects, including duplicates.

To remove the duplicates, the DISTINCT operator must be used:

```
SELECT DISTINCT e.department
FROM Employee e
```

The DISTINCT operator is functionally equivalent to the SQL operator of the same name. Once the result set is collected, duplicate values (using entity identity if the query result type is an entity) are removed so that only unique results are returned.

The result type of a select query is the type corresponding to each row in the result set produced by executing the query. This can include entities, primitive types, and other persistent attribute types, but never a collection type. The following query is illegal:

```
SELECT d.employees
FROM Department d
```

The path expression d.employees is a collection-valued path that produces a collection type. Restricting queries in this way prevents the provider from having to combine successive rows from the database into a single result object.

It is possible to select embeddable objects navigated to in a path expression. The following query returns only the ContactInfo embeddable objects for all the employees:

```
SELECT e.contactInfo
FROM Employee e
```

The thing to remember about selecting embeddables is that the returned objects will not be managed. If you issue a query to return employees (select e FROM Employee e) and then from the results navigate to their ContactInfo embedded objects, you would be obtaining embeddables that were managed. Changes to any one of those objects would be saved when the transaction committed. Changing any of the ContactInfo object results returned from a query that selected the ContactInfo directly, however, would have no persistent effect.

Combining Expressions

Multiple expressions can be specified in the same SELECT clause by separating them with commas. The result type of the query in this case is an array of type `Object`, where the elements of the array are the results of resolving the expressions in the order in which they appeared in the query.

Consider the following query that returns only the name and salary of an employee:

```
SELECT e.name, e.salary
FROM Employee e
```

When this is executed, a collection of zero or more instances of arrays of type `Object` will be returned. Each array in this example has two elements, the first being a `String` containing the employee name and the second being a `Double` containing the employee salary. The practice of reporting only a subset of the state fields from an entity is called projection because the entity data is projected out from the entity into tabular form.

Projection is a useful technique for web applications in which only a few pieces of information are displayed from a large set of entity instances. Depending on how the entity has been mapped, it might require a complex SQL query to fully retrieve the entity state. If only two fields are required, the extra effort spent constructing the entity instance might have been wasted. A projection query that returns only the minimum amount of data is more useful in these cases.

Constructor Expressions

A more powerful form of the SELECT clause involving multiple expressions is the constructor expression, which specifies that the results of the query are to be stored using a user-specified object type. Consider the following query:

```
SELECT NEW example.EmployeeDetails(e.name, e.salary, e.department.name)
FROM Employee e
```

The result type of this query is the `example.EmployeeDetails` Java class. As the query processor iterates over the results of the query, it instantiates new instances of `EmployeeDetails` using the constructor that matches the expression types listed in the query. In this case, the expression types are `String`, `Double`, and `String`, so the query engine will search for a constructor with those class types for arguments. Each row in the resulting query collection is therefore an instance of `EmployeeDetails` containing the employee name, salary, and department name.

The result object type must be referred to by using the fully qualified name of the object. The class does not have to be mapped to the database in any way, however. Any class with a constructor compatible with the expressions listed in the SELECT clause can be used in a constructor expression.

Constructor expressions are powerful tools for constructing coarse-grained data transfer objects or view objects for use in other application tiers. Instead of manually constructing these objects, a single query can be used to gather together view objects ready for presentation on a web page.

FROM Clause

The FROM clause is used to declare one or more identification variables, optionally derived from joined relationships, that form the domain over which the query should draw its results. The syntax of the FROM clause consists of one or more identification variables and join clause declarations.

Identification Variables

The identification variable is the starting point for all query expressions. Every query must have at least one identification variable defined in the FROM clause, and that variable must correspond to an entity type. When an identification variable declaration does not use a path expression (that is, when it is a single entity name), it is referred to as a range variable declaration. This terminology comes from set theory as the variable is said to range over the entity.

Range variable declarations use the syntax `<entity_name>` [AS] `<identifier>`. We have been using this syntax in all our earlier examples, but without the optional AS keyword. The identifier must follow the standard Java naming rules and can be referenced throughout the query in a case-insensitive manner. Multiple declarations can be specified by separating them with commas.

Path expressions can also be aliased to identification variables in the case of joins and subqueries. The syntax for identification variable declarations in these cases will be covered in the next two sections.

Joins

A join is a query that combines results from multiple entities. Joins in JP QL queries are logically equivalent to SQL joins. Ultimately, once the query is translated to SQL, it is quite likely that the joins between entities will produce similar joins among the tables to which the entities are mapped. Understanding when joins occur is therefore important to writing efficient queries.

Joins occur whenever any of the following conditions are met in a select query.

1. Two or more range variable declarations are listed in the FROM clause and appear in the select clause.

2. The JOIN operator is used to extend an identification variable using a path expression.

3. A path expression anywhere in the query navigates across an association field, to the same or a different entity.

4. One or more WHERE conditions compare attributes of different identification variables.

The semantics of a join between entities are the same as SQL joins between tables. Most queries contain a series of join conditions, which are expressions that define the rules for matching one entity to another. Join conditions can be specified explicitly, such as using the JOIN operator in the FROM clause of a query, or implicitly as a result of path navigation.

An inner join between two entities returns the objects from both entity types that satisfy all the join conditions. Path navigation from one entity to another is a form of inner join. The outer join of two entities is the set of objects from both entity types that satisfy the join conditions plus the set of objects from one entity type (designated as the left entity) that have no matching join condition in the other.

In the absence of join conditions between two entities, queries will produce a Cartesian product. Each object of the first entity type is paired with each object of the second entity type, squaring the number of results[1]. Cartesian products are rare with JP QL queries given the navigation capabilities of the language, but they are possible if two range variable declarations in the FROM clause are specified without additional conditions specified in the WHERE clause.

Further discussion and examples of each join style are provided in the following sections.

---

[1]The exact number of results will be M * N, where M is the number of entity instances of the first type and N is the number of entity instances of the second type.

Inner Joins

All the example queries so far have been using the simplest form of FROM clause, a single entity type aliased to an identification variable. However, as a relational language, JP QL supports queries that draw on multiple entities and the relationships between them.

Inner joins between two entities can be specified in one of the ways that were listed previously. The first and preferred form, because it is explicit and obvious that a join is occurring, is the JOIN operator in the FROM clause. Another form requires multiple range variable declarations in the FROM clause and WHERE clause conditions to provide the join conditions.

JOIN Operator and Collection Association Fields

The syntax of an inner join using the JOIN operator is [INNER] JOIN <path_expression> [AS] <identifier>. Consider the following query:

```
SELECT p
FROM Employee e JOIN e.phones p
```

This query uses the JOIN operator to join the Employee entity to the Phone entity across the phones relationship. The join condition in this query is defined by the object-relational mapping of the phones relationship. No additional criteria need to be specified in order to link the two entities. By joining the two entities together, this query returns all the Phone entity instances associated with employees in the company.

The syntax for joins is similar to the JOIN expressions supported by ANSI SQL. For readers who might not be familiar with this syntax, consider the equivalent SQL form of the previous query written using the traditional join form:

```
SELECT p.id, p.phone_num, p.type, p.emp_id
FROM emp e, phone p
WHERE e.id = p.emp_id
```

The table mapping for the Phone entity replaces the expression e.phones. The WHERE clause also includes the criteria necessary to join the two tables together across the join columns defined by the phones mapping.

Note that the phones relationship has been mapped to the identification variable p. Even though the Phone entity does not directly appear in the query, the target of the phones relationship is the Phone entity, and this determines the identification variable type. This implicit determination of the identification variable type can take some getting used to. Familiarity with how relationships are defined in the object model is necessary to navigate through a written query.

Each occurrence of p outside of the FROM clause now refers to a single phone owned by an employee. Even though a collection association field was specified in the JOIN clause, the identification variable is really referring to entities reached by that association, not the collection itself. The variable can now be used as if the Phone entity were listed directly in the FROM clause. For example, instead of returning Phone entity instances, phone numbers can be returned instead.

```
SELECT p.number
FROM Employee e JOIN e.phones p
```

In the definition of path expressions earlier, it was noted that a path couldn't continue from a state field or collection association field. To work around this situation, the collection association field must be joined in the FROM clause so that a new identification variable is created for the path, allowing it to be the root for new path expressions.

```
                              IN VERSUS JOIN
```

EJBQL as defined by the EJB 2.0 and EJB 2.1 specifications used a special operator IN in the FROM clause to map collection associations to identification variables. Support for this operator was carried over to JP QL. The equivalent form of the query used earlier in this section might be specified as:

```
SELECT DISTINCT p
FROM Employee e, IN(e.phones) p
```

The IN operator is intended to indicate that the variable p is an enumeration of the phones collection. The JOIN operator is a more powerful and expressive way to declare relationships and is the recommended operator for queries.

JOIN Operator and Single-Valued Association Fields

The JOIN operator works with both collection-valued association path expressions and single-valued association path expressions. Consider the following example:

```
SELECT d
FROM Employee e JOIN e.department d
```

This query defines a join from Employee to Department across the department relationship. This is semantically equivalent to using a path expression in the SELECT clause to obtain the department for the employee. For example, the following query should result in similar if not identical SQL representations involving a join between the Employee and Department entities:

```
SELECT e.department
FROM Employee e
```

The primary use case for using a single-valued association path expression in the FROM clause (rather than just using a path expression in the SELECT clause) is for outer joins. Path navigation is equivalent to the inner join of all associated entities traversed in the path expression.

The possibility of implicit inner joins resulting from path expressions is something to be aware of. Consider the following example that returns the distinct departments based in California that are participating in the "Release1" project:

```
SELECT DISTINCT e.department
FROM Project p JOIN p.employees e
WHERE p.name = 'Release1' AND
      e.address.state = 'CA'
```

There are actually four logical joins here, not two. The translator will treat the query as if it had been written with explicit joins between the various entities. We will cover the syntax for multiple joins later in the "Multiple Joins" section, but for now consider the following query that is equivalent to the previous query, reading the join conditions from left to right:

```
SELECT DISTINCT d
FROM Project p JOIN p.employees e JOIN e.department d JOIN e.address a
WHERE p.name = 'Release1' AND
      a.state = 'CA'
```

We say four logical joins because the actual physical mapping might involve more tables. In this case, the Employee and Project entities are related via a many-to-many association using a join table. Therefore, the actual SQL for such a query uses five tables, not four.

```
SELECT DISTINCT d.id, d.name
FROM project p, emp_projects ep, emp e, dept d, address a
WHERE p.id = ep.project_id AND
      ep.emp_id = e.id AND
      e.dept_id = d.id AND
      e.address_id = a.id AND
      p.name = 'Release1' AND
      a.state = 'CA'
```

The first form of the query is certainly easier to read and understand. However, during performance tuning, it might be helpful to understand how many joins can occur as the result of seemingly trivial path expressions.

Join Conditions in the WHERE Clause

SQL queries have traditionally joined tables together by listing the tables to be joined in the FROM clause and supplying criteria in the WHERE clause of the query to determine the join conditions. To join two entities without using a relationship, use a range variable declaration for each entity in the FROM clause.

The previous join example between the Employee and Department entities could also have been written like this:

```
SELECT DISTINCT d
FROM Department d, Employee e
WHERE d = e.department
```

This style of query is usually used to compensate for the lack of an explicit relationship between two entities in the domain model. For example, there is no association between the Department entity and the Employee who is the manager of the department.

We can use a join condition in the WHERE clause to make this possible.

```
SELECT d, m
FROM Department d, Employee m
WHERE d = m.department AND
      m.directs IS NOT EMPTY
```

In this example, we are using one of the special collection expressions, IS NOT EMPTY, to check that the collection of direct reports to the employee is not empty. Any employee with a non-empty collection of directs is by definition a manager.

Multiple Joins

More than one join can be cascaded if necessary. For example, the following query returns the distinct set of projects belonging to employees who belong to a department:

```
SELECT DISTINCT p
FROM Department d JOIN d.employees e JOIN e.projects p
```

The query processor interprets the FROM clause from left to right. Once a variable has been declared, it can be subsequently referenced by other JOIN expressions. In this case, the projects relationship of the Employee entity is navigated once the employee variable has been declared.

Map Joins

A path expression that navigates across a collection-valued association implemented as a `Map` is a special case. Unlike a normal collection, each item in a map corresponds to two pieces of information: the key and the value. When working with JP QL, it is important to note that identification variables based on maps refer to the value by default. For example, consider the case where the phones relationship of the `Employee` entity is modeled as a map, where the key is the number type (work, cell, home, etc.) and the value is the phone number. The following query enumerates the phone numbers for all employees:

```
SELECT e.name, p
FROM Employee e JOIN e.phones p
```

This behavior can be highlighted explicitly through the use of the VALUE keyword. For example, the preceding query is functionally identical to the following:

```
SELECT e.name, VALUE(p)
FROM Employee e JOIN e.phones p
```

To access the key instead of the value for a given map item, we can use the KEY keyword to override the default behavior and return the key value for a given map item. The following example demonstrates adding the phone type to the previous query:

```
SELECT e.name, KEY(p), VALUE(p)
FROM Employee e JOIN e.phones p
WHERE KEY(p) IN ('Work', 'Cell')
```

Finally, in the event that we want both the key and the value returned together in the form of a `java.util.Map.Entry` object, we can specify the ENTRY keyword in the same fashion. Note that the ENTRY keyword can only be used in the SELECT clause. The KEY and VALUE keywords can also be used as part of conditional expressions in the WHERE and HAVING clauses of the query.

Note that in each of the map join examples we joined an entity against one of its Map attributes and came out with a key, value, or key-value pair (entry). However, when viewed from the perspective of the tables, the join is only ever done at the level of the source entity primary key and the values in the Map. No facility is currently available in JPA to join the source entity against the keys of the Map.

Outer Joins

An outer join between two entities produces a domain in which only one side of the relationship is required to be complete. In other words, the outer join of `Employee` to `Department` across the employee `department` relationship returns all employees and the department to which the employee has been assigned, but the department is returned only if it is available. This is in contrast with an inner join that would return only those employees assigned to a department.

An outer join is specified using the following syntax: `LEFT [OUTER] JOIN <path_expression> [AS] <identifier>`. The following query demonstrates an outer join between two entities:

```
SELECT e, d
FROM Employee e LEFT JOIN e.department d
```

If the employee has not been assigned to a department, the department object (the second element of the `Object` array) will be null.

In a typical provider SQL generation, you will see that the previous query would be equivalent to the following:

```
SELECT e.id, e.name, e.salary, e.manager_id, e.dept_id, e.address_id,
       d.id, d.name
FROM employee e LEFT OUTER JOIN department d
ON (d.id = e.department_id)
```

The resulting SQL shows that when an outer join gets generated from JP QL it always specifies an ON condition of equality between the join column that maps the relationship being joined across, and the primary key it is referencing.

An additional ON expression can be supplied to add constraints to the objects that get returned from the right hand side of the join. For example, we can modify the previous JP QL query to have an additional ON condition to limit the departments returned to only those that have a 'QA' prefix:

```
SELECT e, d
FROM Employee e LEFT JOIN e.department d
   ON d.name LIKE 'QA%'
```

This query still returns all of the employees, but the results will not include any departments not matching the added ON condition. The generated SQL would look like:

```
SELECT e.id, e.name, e.salary, e.department_id, e.manager_id, e.address_id,
            d.id, d.name
FROM employee e left outer join department d
   ON ((d.id = e.department_id) and (d.name like 'QA%'))
```

Note that this query is very different from using a WHERE expression:

```
SELECT e, d
FROM Employee e LEFT JOIN e.department d
WHERE d.name LIKE 'QA%'
```

The WHERE clause results in inner join semantics between Employee and Department, so this query would only return the employees who were in a department with a 'QA' prefixed name.

■ **Tip** The ability to add outer join conditions with ON was added in JPA 2.1

Fetch Joins

Fetch joins are intended to help application designers optimize their database access and prepare query results for detachment. They allow queries to specify one or more relationships that should be navigated and prefetched by the query engine so that they are not lazy loaded later at runtime.

For example, if we have an Employee entity with a lazy loading relationship to its address, the following query can be used to indicate that the relationship should be resolved eagerly during query execution:

```
SELECT e
FROM Employee e JOIN FETCH e.address
```

Note that no identification variable is set for the e.address path expression. This is because even though the Address entity is being joined in order to resolve the relationship, it is not part of the result type of the query.

The result of executing the query is still a collection of Employee entity instances, except that the address relationship on each entity will not cause a secondary trip to the database when it is accessed. This also allows the address relationship to be accessed safely if the Employee entity becomes detached. A fetch join is distinguished from a regular join by adding the FETCH keyword to the JOIN operator.

In order to implement fetch joins, the provider needs to turn the fetched association into a regular join of the appropriate type: inner by default or outer if the LEFT keyword was specified. The SELECT expression of the query also needs to be expanded to include the joined relationship. Expressed in JP QL, an equivalent provider interpretation of the previous fetch join example would look like:

```
SELECT e, a
FROM Employee e JOIN e.address a
```

The only difference is that the provider does not actually return the Address entities to the caller. Because the results are processed from this query, the query engine creates the Address entity in memory and assigns it to the Employee entity, but then drops it from the result collection that it builds for the client. This eagerly loads the address relationship, which can then get accessed by navigation from the Employee entity.

A consequence of implementing fetch joins in this way is that fetching a collection association results in duplicate results. For example, consider a department query where the employees relationship of the Department entity is eagerly fetched. The fetch join query, this time using an outer join to ensure that departments without employees are retrieved, would be written as follows:

```
SELECT d
FROM Department d LEFT JOIN FETCH d.employees
```

Expressed in JP QL, the provider interpretation would replace the fetch with an outer join across the employees relationship:

```
SELECT d, e
FROM Department d LEFT JOIN d.employees e
```

Once again, as the results are processed, the Employee entity is constructed in memory but dropped from the result collection. Each Department entity now has a fully resolved employees collection, but the client receives one reference to each department per employee. For example, if four departments with five employees each were retrieved, the result would be a collection of 20 Department instances, with each department duplicated 5 times. The actual entity instances all point back to the same managed versions, but the results are somewhat odd at the very least.

To eliminate the duplicate values, either the DISTINCT operator must be used or the results must be placed into a data structure such as a Set. Because it is not possible to write a SQL query that uses the DISTINCT operator while preserving the semantics of the fetch join, the provider will have to eliminate duplicates in memory after the results have been fetched. This could have performance implications for large result sets.

Given the somewhat peculiar results generated from a fetch join to a collection, it might not be the most appropriate way to eagerly load related entities in all cases. If a collection requires eager fetching on a regular basis, consider making the relationship eager by default. Some persistence providers also offer batch reads as an alternative to fetch joins that issue multiple queries in a single batch and then correlate the results to eagerly load relationships. Another alternative is to use an entity graph to dynamically determine the relationship attributes to be loaded by a query. Entity graphs are described in detail in Chapter 11.

WHERE Clause

The WHERE clause of a query is used to specify filtering conditions to reduce the result set. In this section, we will explore the features of the WHERE clause and the types of expressions that can be formed to filter query results.

The definition of the WHERE clause is deceptively simple. It is simply the keyword WHERE, followed by a conditional expression. However, as the following sections demonstrate, JP QL supports a powerful set of conditional expressions to filter the most sophisticated of queries.

Input Parameters

Input parameters for queries can be specified using either positional or named notation. Positional notation is defined by prefixing the variable number with a question mark. Consider the following query:

```
SELECT e
FROM Employee e
WHERE e.salary > ?1
```

Using the Query interface, any double value, or value that is type-compatible with the salary attribute, can be bound into the first parameter in order to indicate the lower limit for employee salaries in this query. The same positional parameter can occur more than once in the query. The value bound into the parameter will be substituted for each of its occurrences.

Named parameters are specified using a colon followed by an identifier. Here is the same query, this time using a named parameter:

```
SELECT e
FROM Employee e
WHERE e.salary > :sal
```

Input parameters were covered in detail in Chapter 7.

Basic Expression Form

Much of the conditional expression support in JP QL is borrowed directly from SQL. This is intentional and helps to ease the transition for developers already familiar with SQL. The key difference between conditional expressions in JP QL and SQL is that JP QL expressions can leverage identification variables and path expressions to navigate relationships during expression evaluation.

Conditional expressions are constructed in the same style as SQL conditional expressions, using a combination of logical operators, comparison expressions, primitive and function operations on fields, and so on. Although a summary of the operators is provided later, the grammar for conditional expressions is not repeated here. The JPA specification contains the grammar in Backus-Naur form (BNF) and is the place to look for the exact rules about using basic expressions. The following sections do, however, explain the higher-level operators and expressions, particularly those unique to JP QL, and they provide examples for each.

Literal syntax is also similar to SQL (see the "Literals" section).

Operator precedence is as follows.

1. Navigation operator (.)

2. Unary +/–

3. Multiplication (*) and division (/)

4. Addition (+) and subtraction (–)

5. Comparison operators =, >, >=, <, <=, <>, [NOT] BETWEEN, [NOT] LIKE, [NOT] IN, IS [NOT] NULL, IS [NOT] EMPTY, [NOT] MEMBER [OF]

6. Logical operators (AND, OR, NOT)

BETWEEN Expressions

The BETWEEN operator can be used in conditional expressions to determine whether the result of an expression falls within an inclusive range of values. Numeric, string, and date expressions can be evaluated in this way. Consider the following example:

```
SELECT e
FROM Employee e
WHERE e.salary BETWEEN 40000 AND 45000
```

Any employee making $40,000 to $45,000 inclusively is included in the results. This is identical to the following query using basic comparison operators:

```
SELECT e
FROM Employee e
WHERE e.salary >= 40000 AND e.salary <= 45000
```

The BETWEEN operator can also be negated with the NOT operator.

LIKE Expressions

JP QL supports the SQL LIKE condition to provide for a limited form of string pattern matching. Each LIKE expression consists of a string expression to be searched, and a pattern string and optional escape sequence that defines the match conditions. The wildcard characters used by the pattern string are the underscore (_) for single character wildcards and the percent sign (%) for multicharacter wildcards.

```
SELECT d
FROM Department d
WHERE d.name LIKE '__Eng%'
```

We are using a prefix of two underscore characters to wildcard the first two characters of the string candidates, so example department names to match this query would be "CAEngOtt" or "USEngCal", but not "CADocOtt". Note that pattern matches are case-sensitive.

If the pattern string contains an underscore or percent sign that should be literally matched, the ESCAPE clause can be used to specify a character that, when prefixing a wildcard character, indicates that it should be treated literally:

```
SELECT d
FROM Department d
WHERE d.name LIKE 'QA\_%' ESCAPE '\'
```

Escaping the underscore makes it a mandatory part of the expression. For example, "QA_East" would match, but "QANorth" would not.

Subqueries

Subqueries can be used in the WHERE and HAVING clauses of a query. A subquery is a complete select query inside a pair of parentheses that is embedded within a conditional expression. The results of executing the subquery (which will be either a scalar result or a collection of values) are then evaluated in the context of the conditional expression. Subqueries are a powerful technique for solving the most complex query scenarios.

Consider the following query:

```
SELECT e
FROM Employee e
WHERE e.salary = (SELECT MAX(emp.salary)
                  FROM Employee emp)
```

This query returns the employee with the highest salary from among all employees. A subquery consisting of an aggregate query (described later in this chapter) is used to return the maximum salary value, and then this result is used as the key to filter the employee list by salary. A subquery can be used in most conditional expressions and can appear on either the left or right side of an expression.

The scope of an identifier variable name begins in the query where it is defined and extends down into any subqueries. Identifiers in the main query can be referenced by a subquery, and identifiers introduced by a subquery can be referenced by any subquery that it creates. If a subquery declares an identifier variable of the same name, it overrides the parent declaration and prevents the subquery from referring to the parent variable.

■ **Note**   Overriding an identification variable name in a subquery is not guaranteed to be supported by all providers. Unique names should be used to ensure portability.

The ability to refer to a variable from the main query in the subquery allows the two queries to be correlated. Consider the following example:

```
SELECT e
FROM Employee e
WHERE EXISTS (SELECT 1
              FROM Phone p
              WHERE p.employee = e AND p.type = 'Cell')
```

This query returns all the employees who have a cell phone number. This is also an example of a subquery that returns a collection of values. The EXISTS expression in this example returns true if any results are returned by the subquery. Returning the literal 1 from the subquery is a standard practice with EXISTS expressions because the actual results selected by the subquery do not matter; only the number of results is relevant. Note that the WHERE clause of the subquery references the identifier variable e from the main query and uses it to filter the subquery results. Conceptually, the subquery can be thought of as executing once for each employee. In practice, many database servers will optimize these types of queries into joins or inline views in order to maximize performance.

This query could also have been written using a join between the Employee and Phone entities with the DISTINCT operator used to filter the results. The advantage in using the correlated subquery is that the main query remains unburdened by joins to other entities. Quite often if a join is used only to filter the results, there is an equivalent subquery condition that can alternately be used in order to remove constraints on the join clause of the main query or even to improve query performance.

The FROM clause of a subquery can also create new identification variables out of path expressions using an identification variable from the main query. For example, the previous query could also have been written as follows:

```
SELECT e
FROM Employee e
WHERE EXISTS (SELECT 1
              FROM e.phones p
              WHERE p.type = 'Cell')
```

In this version of the query, the subquery uses the collection association path phones from the Employee identification variable e in the subquery. This is then mapped to a local identification variable p that is used to filter the results by phone type. Each occurrence of p refers to a single phone associated with the employee.

To better illustrate how the translator handles this query, consider the equivalent query written in SQL:

```
SELECT e.id, e.name, e.salary, e.manager_id, e.dept_id, e.address_id
FROM emp e
WHERE EXISTS (SELECT 1
              FROM phone p
              WHERE p.emp_id = e.id AND
                    p.type = 'Cell')
```

The expression e.phones is converted to the table mapped by the Phone entity. The WHERE clause for the subquery then adds the necessary join condition to correlate the subquery to the primary query, in this case the expression p.emp_id = e.id. The join criteria applied to the PHONE table results in all the phones owned by the related employee.

IN Expressions

The IN expression can be used to check whether a single-valued path expression is a member of a collection. The collection can be defined inline as a set of literal values or can be derived from a subquery. The following query demonstrates the literal notation by selecting all the employees who live in New York or California:

```
SELECT e
FROM Employee e
WHERE e.address.state IN ('NY', 'CA')
```

The subquery form of the expression is similar, replacing the literal list with a nested query. The following query returns employees who work in departments that are contributing to projects beginning with the prefix "QA":

```
SELECT e
FROM Employee e
WHERE e.department IN (SELECT DISTINCT d
                       FROM Department d JOIN d.employees de JOIN de.projects p
                       WHERE p.name LIKE 'QA%')
```

The IN expression can also be negated using the NOT operator. For example, the following query returns all the Phone entities representing phone numbers other than for the office or home:

```
SELECT p
FROM Phone p
WHERE p.type NOT IN ('Office', 'Home')
```

Collection Expressions

The IS EMPTY operator is the logical equivalent of IS NULL, but for collections. Queries can use the IS EMPTY operator or its negated form IS NOT EMPTY to check whether a collection association path resolves to an empty collection or has at least one value. For example, the following query returns all employees who are managers by virtue of having at least one direct report:

```
SELECT e
FROM Employee e
WHERE e.directs IS NOT EMPTY
```

Note that IS EMPTY expressions are translated to SQL as subquery expressions. The query translator can make use of an aggregate subquery or use the SQL EXISTS expression. Therefore, the following query is equivalent to the previous one:

```
SELECT m
FROM Employee m
WHERE (SELECT COUNT(e)
       FROM Employee e
       WHERE e.manager = m) > 0
```

The MEMBER OF operator and its negated form NOT MEMBER OF are a shorthand way of checking whether an entity is a member of a collection association path. The following query returns all managers who are incorrectly entered as reporting to themselves:

```
SELECT e
FROM Employee e
WHERE e MEMBER OF e.directs
```

A more typical use of the MEMBER OF operator is in conjunction with an input parameter. For example, the following query selects all employees who are assigned to a specified project:

```
SELECT e
FROM Employee e
WHERE :project MEMBER OF e.projects
```

Like the IS EMPTY expression, the MEMBER OF expression will be translated to SQL using either an EXISTS expression or the subquery form of the IN expression. The previous example is equivalent to the following query:

```
SELECT e
FROM Employee e
WHERE :project IN (SELECT p
                   FROM e.projects p)
```

EXISTS Expressions

The EXISTS condition returns true if a subquery returns any rows. Examples of EXISTS were demonstrated earlier in the introduction to subqueries. The EXISTS operator can also be negated with the NOT operator. The following query selects all employees who do not have a cell phone:

```
SELECT e
FROM Employee e
WHERE NOT EXISTS (SELECT p
                  FROM e.phones p
                  WHERE p.type = 'Cell')
```

ANY, ALL, and SOME Expressions

The ANY, ALL, and SOME operators can be used to compare an expression to the results of a subquery. Consider the following example:

```
SELECT e
FROM Employee e
WHERE e.directs IS NOT EMPTY AND
      e.salary < ALL (SELECT d.salary
                      FROM e.directs d)
```

This query returns the managers who are paid less than all the employees who work for them. The subquery is evaluated, and then each value of the subquery is compared to the left-hand expression, in this case the manager salary. When the ALL operator is used, the comparison between the left side of the equation and all subquery results must be true for the overall condition to be true.

The ANY operator behaves similarly, but the overall condition is true as long as at least one of the comparisons between the expression and the subquery result is true. For example, if ANY were specified instead of ALL in the previous example, the result of the query would be all the managers who were paid less than at least one of their employees. The SOME operator is an alias for the ANY operator.

There is symmetry between IN expressions and the ANY operator. Consider the following variation of the project department example used previously, modified only slightly to use ANY instead of IN:

```
SELECT e
FROM Employee e
WHERE e.department = ANY (SELECT DISTINCT d
                          FROM Department d JOIN d.employees de JOIN de.projects p
                          WHERE p.name LIKE 'QA%')
```

Inheritance and Polymorphism

JPA supports inheritance between entities. As a result, the query language supports polymorphic results where multiple subclasses of an entity can be returned by the same query.

In the example model, `Project` is a base class for `QualityProject` and `DesignProject`. If an identification variable is formed from the `Project` entity, the query results will include a mixture of `Project`, `QualityProject`, and `DesignProject` objects and the results can be cast to the subclasses by the caller as necessary. The following query retrieves all projects with at least one employee:

```
SELECT p
FROM Project p
WHERE p.employees IS NOT EMPTY
```

Subclass Discrimination

If we want to restrict the result of the query to a particular subclass, we can use that particular subclass in the FROM clause instead of the root. However, if we want to restrict the results to more than one subclass in the query but not all of the subclasses, we can instead use a type expression in the WHERE clause to filter the results. A type expression consists of the keyword TYPE followed by an expression in parentheses that resolves to an entity. The result of a type expression is the entity name, which can then be used for type comparison purposes. The advantage of a type expression is that we can distinguish between types without relying on a discrimination mechanism in the domain model itself.

The following example demonstrates using a type expression to return only design and quality projects:

```
SELECT p
FROM Project p
WHERE TYPE(p) = DesignProject OR TYPE(p) = QualityProject
```

Note that there are no quotes around the DesignProject and QualityProject identifiers. These are treated as entity names in JP QL, not as strings. Despite this distinction, input parameters can be used in place of hard-coded names in query strings. Creating a parameterized query that returns instances of a given subclass type is straightforward, as illustrated by the following query:

```
SELECT p
FROM Project p
WHERE TYPE(p) = :projectType
```

Downcasting

In most cases at least one of the subclasses contains some additional state, such as the `qaRating` attribute in the `QualityProject`. A subclass attribute could be accessed directly if the query ranged over only the subclass entities, but when the query ranges over a superclass, downcasting must be used. Downcasting is the technique of making an expression that refers to a superclass be applied to a specific subclass. It is achieved through the use of the TREAT operator.

TREAT can be used in the WHERE clause to filter the results based on subtype state of the instances. The following query returns all of the design projects plus all of the quality projects that have a quality rating greater than 4:

```
SELECT p
FROM Project p
WHERE TREAT(p AS QualityProject).qaRating > 4
      OR  TYPE(p) = DesignProject
```

The syntax of the expression begins with the TREAT keyword, followed by its parenthesized argument. The argument is a path expression, followed by the AS keyword and then the entity name of the target subtype.

The path expression must resolve to a superclass of the target type. The resulting downcasted expression resolves to the target subtype, so any of the subtype-specific attributes can be added to the resulting path expression, just as qaRating was in the example.

Multiple TREAT expressions can be included in the WHERE clause, each downcasting to the same or a different entity type.

Normally when a join is performed it includes all of the subclasses of the target entity type in the relationship being joined across. To limit the join to consider only a specific subclass hierarchy, a TREAT expression can be used in the FROM clause. Assigning it an identifier provides the added bonus that the identifier can be referenced both in the WHERE clause as well as in the SELECT clause. The following query returns all of the employees who work on quality projects with quality rating greater than 4, plus the name of the project they work on and its quality rating:

```
SELECT e, q.name, q.qaRating
FROM Employee e JOIN TREAT(e.projects AS QualityProject) q
WHERE q.qaRating > 4
```

The TREAT expression can be used in a similar way for other kinds of joins, too, such as outer joins and fetch joins.

■ **Tip**   Downcasting with the TREAT expression was added in JPA 2.1.

The impact that inheritance between entities has on the generated SQL is important to understand for performance reasons and will be described in Chapter 10.

Scalar Expressions

A scalar expression is a literal value, arithmetic sequence, function expression, type expression, or case expression that resolves to a single scalar value. It can be used in the SELECT clause to format projected fields in report queries or as part of conditional expressions in the WHERE or HAVING clause of a query. Subqueries that resolve to scalar values are also considered scalar expressions, but can be used only when composing criteria in the WHERE clause of a query. Subqueries can never be used in the SELECT clause.

Literals

There are a number of different literal types that can be used in JP QL, including strings, numerics, booleans, enums, entity types, and temporal types.

Throughout this chapter, we have shown many examples of string, integer, and boolean literals. Single quotes are used to demarcate string literals and escaped within a string by prefixing the quote with another single quote. Exact and approximate numerics can be defined according to the conventions of the Java programming language or by using the standard SQL-92 syntax. Boolean values are represented by the literals TRUE and FALSE.

Queries can reference Java enum types by specifying the fully qualified name of the enum class. The following example demonstrates using an enum in a conditional expression, using the PhoneType enum demonstrated in Listing 5-8 from Chapter 5:

```
SELECT e
FROM Employee e JOIN e.phoneNumbers p
WHERE KEY(p) = com.acme.PhoneType.Home
```

An entity type is just the entity name of some defined entity, and is valid only when used with the TYPE operator. Quotes are not used. See the "Inheritance and Polymorphism" section for examples of when to use an entity type literal.

Temporal literals are specified using the JDBC escape syntax, which defines that curly braces enclose the literal. The first character in the sequence is either a "d" or a "t" to indicate that the literal is a date or time, respectively. If the literal represents a timestamp, "ts" is used instead. Following the type indicator is a space separator, and then the actual date, time, or timestamp information wrapped in single quotes. The general forms of the three temporal literal types, with accompanying examples are as follows:

```
{d 'yyyy-mm-dd'}              e.g. {d '2009-11-05'}
{t 'hh-mm-ss'}               e.g. {t '12-45-52'}
{ts 'yyyy-mm-dd hh-mm-ss.f'}  e.g. {ts '2009-11-05 12-45-52.325'}
```

All the temporal information within single quotes is expressed as digits. The fractional part of the timestamp (the ".f" part) can be multiple digits long and is optional.

When using any of these temporal literals remember that they are interpreted only by drivers that support the JDBC escape syntax. The provider will not normally try to translate or preprocess temporal literals.

Function Expressions

Scalar expressions can leverage functions that can be used to transform query results. Table 8-1 summarizes the syntax for each of the supported function expressions.

Table 8-1. *Supported Function Expressions*

Function	Description
ABS(number)	The ABS function returns the unsigned version of the number argument. The result type is the same as the argument type (integer, float, or double).
CONCAT(string1, string2)	The CONCAT function returns a new string that is the concatenation of its arguments, string1 and string2.
CURRENT_DATE	The CURRENT_DATE function returns the current date as defined by the database server.
CURRENT_TIME	The CURRENT_TIME function returns the current time as defined by the database server.
CURRENT_TIMESTAMP	The CURRENT_TIMESTAMP function returns the current timestamp as defined by the database server.
INDEX(identification variable)	The INDEX function returns the position of an entity within an ordered list.
LENGTH(string)	The LENGTH function returns the number of characters in the string argument.
LOCATE(string1, string2 [, start])	The LOCATE function returns the position of string1 in string2, optionally starting at the position indicated by start. The result is zero if the string cannot be found.
LOWER(string)	The LOWER function returns the lowercase form of the string argument.
MOD(number1, number2)	The MOD function returns the modulus of numeric arguments number1 and number2 as an integer.

(continued)

Table 8-1. (*continued*)

Function	Description
SIZE(collection)	The SIZE function returns the number of elements in the collection, or zero if the collection is empty.
SQRT(number)	The SQRT function returns the square root of the number argument as a double.
SUBSTRING(string, start, end)	The SUBSTRING function returns a portion of the input string, starting at the index indicated by start up to length characters. String indexes are measured starting from one.
UPPER(string)	The UPPER function returns the uppercase form of the string argument.
TRIM([[LEADING|TRAILING|BOTH] [char] FROM] string)	The TRIM function removes leading and/or trailing characters from a string. If the optional LEADING, TRAILING, or BOTH keyword is not used, both leading and trailing characters are removed. The default trim character is the space character.

The SIZE function requires special attention because it is shorthand notation for an aggregate subquery. For example, consider the following query that returns all departments with only two employees:

```
SELECT d
FROM Department d
WHERE SIZE(d.employees) = 2
```

Like the collection expressions IS EMPTY and MEMBER OF, the SIZE function will be translated to SQL using a subquery. The equivalent form of the previous example using a subquery is as follows:

```
SELECT d
FROM Department d
WHERE (SELECT COUNT(e)
      FROM d.employees e) = 2
```

The use case for the INDEX function might not be obvious at first. When using ordered collections, each element of the collection actually contains two pieces of information: the value stored in the collection and its numeric position within the collection. Queries can use the INDEX function to determine the numeric position of an element in a collection and then use that number for reporting or filtering purposes. For example, if the phone numbers for an employee are stored in priority order, the following query would return the first (and most important) number for each employee:

```
SELECT e.name, p.number
FROM Employee e JOIN e.phones p
WHERE INDEX(p) = 0
```

Native Database Functions

One of the benefits of JP QL is that it decouples the application from the underlying database. However, occasionally it is necessary to use native functions that are either indigenous to the database or defined by the system administrator. While the use of these functions may bind the query to the target database, there is still an argument for using the entity mapping independence of JP QL.

Database functions may be accessed in JP QL queries through the use of the FUNCTION expression. The FUNCTION keyword, followed by the name of the function and the function arguments, must resolve to a scalar value that is arithmetic, boolean, string, or a temporal type, such as date, time, or timestamp. FUNCTION expressions may be used wherever scalar types fit in an expression, and the result type must match what the rest of the expression expects. The arguments must be either literals, expressions that resolve to scalars, or input parameters.

The following query invokes a database function named "shouldGetBonus." The id of the employee's department and the projects he works on are passed as parameters and the function return type is a boolean. The result creates a condition that makes the query return the set of all employees who get a bonus.

```
SELECT DISTINCT e
FROM Employee e JOIN e.projects p
WHERE FUNCTION('shouldGetBonus', e.department.id, p.id)
```

■ **Tip** The FUNCTION keyword was introduced in JPA 2.1

CASE Expressions

The JP QL case expression is an adaptation of the ANSI SQL-92 CASE expression, taking into account the capabilities of the JP QL language. Case expressions are powerful tools for introducing conditional logic into a query, with the benefit that the result of a case expression can be used anywhere a scalar expression is valid.

Case expressions are available in four forms, depending on the flexibility required by the query. The first and most flexible form is the general case expression. All other case expression types can be composed in terms of the general case expression. It has the following form:

```
CASE {WHEN <cond_expr> THEN <scalar_expr>}+ ELSE <scalar_expr> END
```

The heart of the case expression is the WHEN clause, of which there must be at least one. The query processor resolves the conditional expression of each WHEN clause in order until it finds one that is successful. It then evaluates the scalar expression for that WHEN clause and returns it as the result of the case expression. If none of the WHEN clause conditional expressions yields a true result, the scalar expression of the ELSE clause is evaluated and returned instead. The following example demonstrates the general case expression, enumerating the name and type of each project that has employees assigned to it:

```
SELECT p.name,
       CASE WHEN TYPE(p) = DesignProject THEN 'Development'
            WHEN TYPE(p) = QualityProject THEN 'QA'
            ELSE 'Non-Development'
       END
FROM Project p
WHERE p.employees IS NOT EMPTY
```

Note the use of the case expression as part of the select clause. Case expressions are a powerful tool for transforming entity data in report queries.

A slight variation on the general case expression is the simple case expression. Instead of checking a conditional expression in each WHEN clause, it identifies a value and resolves a scalar expression in each WHEN clause. The first to match the value triggers a second scalar expression that becomes the value of the case expression. It has the following form:

```
CASE <value> {WHEN <scalar_expr1> THEN <scalar_expr2>}+ ELSE <scalar_expr> END
```

The <value> in this form of the expression is either a path expression leading to a state field or a type expression for polymorphic comparison. We can simplify the last example by converting it to a simple case expression.

```
SELECT p.name,
    CASE TYPE(p)
        WHEN DesignProject THEN 'Development'
        WHEN QualityProject THEN 'QA'
        ELSE 'Non-Development'
    END
FROM Project p
WHERE p.employees IS NOT EMPTY
```

The third form of the case expression is the coalesce expression. This form of the case expression accepts a sequence of one or more scalar expressions. It has the following form:

```
COALESCE(<scalar_expr> {,<scalar_expr>}+)
```

The scalar expressions in the COALESCE expression are resolved in order. The first one to return a non-null value becomes the result of the expression. The following example demonstrates this usage, returning either the descriptive name of each department or the department identifier if no name has been defined:

```
SELECT COALESCE(d.name, d.id)
FROM Department d
```

The fourth and final form of the case expression is somewhat unusual. It accepts two scalar expressions and resolves both of them. If the results of the two expressions are equal, the result of the expression is null. Otherwise it returns the result of the first scalar expression. This form of the case expression is identified by the NULLIF keyword.

```
NULLIF(<scalar_expr1>, <scalar_expr2>)
```

One useful trick with NULLIF is to exclude results from an aggregate function. For example, the following query returns a count of all departments and a count of all departments not named 'QA':

```
SELECT COUNT(*), COUNT(NULLIF(d.name, 'QA'))
FROM Department d
```

If the department name is 'QA', NULLIF will return NULL, which will then be ignored by the COUNT function. Aggregate functions ignore NULL values, and are described later in the "Aggregate Queries" section.

ORDER BY Clause

Queries can optionally be sorted using ORDER BY and one or more expressions consisting of identification variables, result variables, a path expression resolving to a single entity, or a path expression resolving to a persistent state field. The optional keywords ASC or DESC after the expression can be used to indicate ascending or descending sorts, respectively. The default sort order is ascending.

The following example demonstrates sorting by a single field:

```
SELECT e
FROM Employee e
ORDER BY e.name DESC
```

Multiple expressions can also be used to refine the sort order:

```
SELECT e, d
FROM Employee e JOIN e.department d
ORDER BY d.name, e.name DESC
```

A result variable can be declared in the SELECT clause for the purpose of specifying an item to be ordered. A result variable is effectively an alias for its assigned selection item. It saves the ORDER BY clause from having to duplicate path expressions from the SELECT clause and permits referencing computed selection items and items that use aggregate functions. The following query defines two result variables in the SELECT clause and then uses them to order the results in the ORDER BY clause:

```
SELECT e.name, e.salary * 0.05 AS bonus, d.name AS deptName
FROM Employee e JOIN e.department d
ORDER BY deptName, bonus DESC
```

If the SELECT clause of the query uses state field path expressions, the ORDER BY clause is limited to the same path expressions used in the SELECT clause. For example, the following query is not legal:

```
SELECT e.name
FROM Employee e
ORDER BY e.salary DESC
```

Because the result type of the query is the employee name, which is of type `String`, the remainder of the `Employee` state fields are no longer available for ordering.

Aggregate Queries

An aggregate query is a variation of a normal select query. An aggregate query groups results and applies aggregate functions to obtain summary information about query results. A query is considered an aggregate query if it uses an aggregate function or possesses a GROUP BY clause and/or a HAVING clause. The most typical form of aggregate query involves the use of one or more grouping expressions and aggregate functions in the SELECT clause paired with grouping expressions in the GROUP BY clause. The syntax of an aggregate query is as follows:

```
SELECT <select_expression>
FROM <from_clause>
[WHERE <conditional_expression>]
[GROUP BY <group_by_clause>]
[HAVING <conditional_expression>]
[ORDER BY <order_by_clause>]
```

The SELECT, FROM, and WHERE clauses behave much the same as previously described under select queries, with the exception of some restrictions on how the SELECT clause is formulated.

The power of an aggregate query comes from the use of aggregate functions over grouped data. Consider the following simple aggregate example:

```
SELECT AVG(e.salary)
FROM Employee e
```

This query returns the average salary of all employees in the company. AVG is an aggregate function that takes a numeric state field path expression as an argument and calculates the average over the group. Because there was no GROUP BY clause specified, the group here is the entire set of employees.

Now consider this variation, where the result has been grouped by the department name:

```
SELECT d.name, AVG(e.salary)
FROM Department d JOIN d.employees e
GROUP BY d.name
```

This query returns the name of each department and the average salary of the employees in that department. The Department entity is joined to the Employee entity across the employees relationship and then formed into a group defined by the department name. The AVG function then calculates its result based on the employee data in this group.

This can be extended further to filter the data so that manager salaries are not included:

```
SELECT d.name, AVG(e.salary)
FROM Department d JOIN d.employees e
WHERE e.directs IS EMPTY
GROUP BY d.name
```

Finally, we can extend this one last time to return only the departments where the average salary is greater than $50,000. Consider the following version of the previous query:

```
SELECT d.name, AVG(e.salary)
FROM Department d JOIN d.employees e
WHERE e.directs IS EMPTY
GROUP BY d.name
HAVING AVG(e.salary) > 50000
```

To understand this query better, let's go through the logical steps that took place to execute it. Databases use many techniques to optimize these types of queries, but conceptually the same process is being followed.

First, the following nongrouping query is executed:

```
SELECT d.name, e.salary
FROM Department d JOIN d.employees e
WHERE e.directs IS EMPTY
```

This will produce a result set consisting of all department name and salary value pairs. The query engine then starts a new result set and makes a second pass over the data, collecting all the salary values for each department name and handing them off to the AVG function. This function returns the group average, which is then checked against the criteria from the HAVING clause. If the average value is greater than $50,000, the query engine generates a result row consisting of the department name and average salary value.

The following sections describe the aggregate functions available for use in aggregate queries and the use of the GROUP BY and HAVING clauses.

Aggregate Functions

Five aggregate functions can be placed in the select clause of a query: AVG, COUNT, MAX, MIN, and SUM.

AVG

The AVG function takes a state field path expression as an argument and calculates the average value of that state field over the group. The state field type must be numeric, and the result is returned as a `Double`.

COUNT

The COUNT function takes either an identification variable or a path expression as its argument. This path expression can resolve to a state field or a single-valued association field. The result of the function is a `Long` value representing the number of values in the group. The argument to the COUNT function can optionally be preceded by the keyword `DISTINCT`, in which case duplicate values are eliminated before counting.

The following query counts the number of phones associated with each employee as well as the number of distinct number types (cell, office, home, and so on):

```
SELECT e, COUNT(p), COUNT(DISTINCT p.type)
FROM Employee e JOIN e.phones p
GROUP BY e
```

MAX

The MAX function takes a state field expression as an argument and returns the maximum value in the group for that state field.

MIN

The MIN function takes a state field expression as an argument and returns the minimum value in the group for that state field.

SUM

The SUM function takes a state field expression as an argument and calculates the sum of the values in that state field over the group. The state field type must be numeric, and the result type must correspond to the field type. For example, if a `Double` field is summed, the result will be returned as a `Double`. If a `Long` field is summed, the response will be returned as a `Long`.

GROUP BY Clause

The GROUP BY clause defines the grouping expressions over which the results will be aggregated. A grouping expression must either be a single-valued path expression (state field, embeddable leading to a state field, or single-valued association field) or an identification variable. If an identification variable is used, the entity must not have any serialized state or large object fields.

The following query counts the number of employees in each department:

```
SELECT d.name, COUNT(e)
FROM Department d JOIN d.employees e
GROUP BY d.name
```

Note that the same field expression used in the SELECT clause is repeated in the GROUP BY clause. All non-aggregate expressions must be listed this way.

More than one aggregate function can be applied:

```
SELECT d.name, COUNT(e), AVG(e.salary)
FROM Department d JOIN d.employees e
GROUP BY d.name
```

This variation of the query calculates the average salary of all employees in each department in addition to counting the number of employees in the department.

Multiple grouping expressions can also be used to further break down the results:

```
SELECT d.name, e.salary, COUNT(p)
FROM Department d JOIN d.employees e JOIN e.projects p
GROUP BY d.name, e.salary
```

Both of the grouping expressions, the department name and employee salary, must be listed in both the SELECT clause and GROUP BY clause. For each department, this query counts the number of projects assigned to employees based on their salary.

In the absence of a GROUP BY clause, aggregate functions will be applied to the entire result set as a single group. For example, the following query returns the number of employees and their average salary across the entire company:

```
SELECT COUNT(e), AVG(e.salary)
FROM Employee e
```

HAVING Clause

The HAVING clause defines a filter to be applied after the query results have been grouped. It is effectively a secondary WHERE clause, and its definition is the same: the keyword HAVING followed by a conditional expression. The key difference with the HAVING clause is that its conditional expressions are mostly limited to state fields or single-valued association fields included in the group.

Conditional expressions in the HAVING clause can also make use of aggregate functions over the elements used for grouping, or aggregate functions that appear in the SELECT clause. In many respects, the primary use of the HAVING clause is to restrict the results based on the aggregate result values. The following query uses this technique to retrieve all employees assigned to two or more projects:

```
SELECT e, COUNT(p)
FROM Employee e JOIN e.projects p
GROUP BY e
HAVING COUNT(p) >= 2
```

Update Queries

Update queries provide an equivalent to the SQL UPDATE statement but with JP QL conditional expressions. The form of an update query is the following:

```
UPDATE <entity name> [[AS] <identification variable>]
SET <update_statement> {, <update_statement>}*
[WHERE <conditional_expression>]
```

Each UPDATE statement consists of a single-valued path expression, the assignment operator (=), and an expression. Expression choices for the assignment statement are slightly restricted compared to regular conditional expressions. The right side of the assignment must resolve to a literal, simple expression resolving to a basic type, function expression, identification variable, or input parameter. The result type of that expression must be compatible with the simple association path or persistent state field on the left side of the assignment.

The following simple example demonstrates the update query by giving employees who make $55,000 a year a raise to $60,000:

```
UPDATE Employee e
SET e.salary = 60000
WHERE e.salary = 55000
```

The WHERE clause of an UPDATE statement functions the same as a SELECT statement and can use the identification variable defined in the UPDATE clause in expressions. A slightly more complex but more realistic update query would be to award a $5,000 raise to employees who worked on a particular project:

```
UPDATE Employee e
SET e.salary = e.salary + 5000
WHERE EXISTS (SELECT p
              FROM e.projects p
              WHERE p.name = 'Release2')
```

More than one property of the target entity can be modified with a single UPDATE statement. For example, the following query updates the phone exchange for employees in the city of Ottawa and changes the terminology of the phone type from "Office" to "Business":

```
UPDATE Phone p
SET p.number = CONCAT('288', SUBSTRING(p.number, LOCATE(p.number, '-'), 4)),
    p.type = 'Business'
WHERE p.employee.address.city = 'Ottawa' AND
      p.type = 'Office'
```

Delete Queries

The delete query provides the same capability as the SQL DELETE statement, but with JP QL conditional expressions. The form of a delete query is the following:

```
DELETE FROM <entity name> [[AS] <identification variable>]
[WHERE <condition>]
```

The following example removes all employees who are not assigned to a department:

```
DELETE FROM Employee e
WHERE e.department IS NULL
```

The WHERE clause for a DELETE statement functions the same as it would for a SELECT statement. All conditional expressions are available to filter the set of entities to be removed. If the WHERE clause is not provided, all entities of the given type are removed.

Delete queries are polymorphic. Any entity subclass instances that meet the criteria of the delete query will also be deleted. Delete queries do not honor cascade rules, however. No entities other than the type referenced in the query and its subclasses will be removed, even if the entity has relationships to other entities with cascade removes enabled.

Summary

In this chapter, we have given you a complete tour of the Java Persistence Query Language, looking at the numerous query types and their syntax. We covered the history of the language, from its roots in the EJB specification to the major enhancements introduced by JPA.

In the section on select queries, we explored each query clause and incrementally built up more complex queries as the full syntax was described. We discussed identification variables and path expressions, which are used to navigate through the domain model in query expressions. We talked about joins and the different ways of triggering inner and outer joining. We delved into subqueries and how they fit into the query language, as well as how to query across inheritance trees of entities. We also looked at the various conditional and scalar expressions supported by the language.

In our discussion of aggregate queries we introduced the additional grouping and filtering clauses that extend select queries. We also demonstrated the various aggregate functions.

In the sections on update and delete queries, we described the full syntax for bulk update and delete statements, whose runtime behavior was described in the previous chapter.

In the next chapter we will continue our exploration of JPA query facilities with an in-depth look at the criteria API, a runtime API for constructing queries.

CHAPTER 9

Criteria API

In the last chapter, we looked in detail at the JP QL query language and the concepts that underlie the JPA query model. In this chapter, we will look at an alternate method for constructing queries that uses a Java programming language API instead of JP QL or native SQL.

We will begin with an overview of the JPA Criteria API and look at a common use case involving constructing dynamic queries in an enterprise application. This will be followed by an in-depth exploration of the Criteria API and how it relates to JP QL.

A related feature of the Criteria API is the JPA metamodel API. We will conclude this chapter with an overview of the metamodel API and look at how it can be used to create strongly typed queries using the Criteria API.

Note that this chapter assumes that you have read Chapter 8 and are familiar with all the concepts and terminology that it introduces. Wherever possible, we will use the upper-case JP QL keywords to highlight different elements of the JPA query model and demonstrate their equivalent behavior with the Criteria API.

Overview

Before languages like JP QL became standardized, the most common method for constructing queries in many persistence providers was through a programming API. The query framework in EclipseLink, for example, was the most effective way to truly unlock the full power of its query engine. And, even with the advent of JP QL, programming APIs have still remained in use to give access to features not yet supported by the standard query language.

JPA 2.0 introduced a Criteria API for constructing queries that standardizes many of the programming features that exist in proprietary persistence products. More than just a literal translation of JP QL to programming interface, it also adopts programming best practices of the proprietary models, such as method chaining, and makes full use of the Java programming language features.

The following sections provide a high-level view of the Criteria API, discussing how and when it is appropriate to use. We also look at a more significant example with a use case that is common in many enterprise settings.

The Criteria API

Let's begin with a simple example to demonstrate the syntax and usage of the Criteria API. The following JP QL query returns all the employees in the company with the name of "John Smith:"

```
SELECT e
FROM Employee e
WHERE e.name = 'John Smith'
```

And here is the equivalent query constructed using the Criteria API:

```
CriteriaBuilder cb = em.getCriteriaBuilder();
CriteriaQuery<Employee> c = cb.createQuery(Employee.class);
Root<Employee> emp = c.from(Employee.class);
c.select(emp)
 .where(cb.equal(emp.get("name"), "John Smith"));
```

There is a lot going on in just a few lines of code in this example, but right away you should see parallels between the JP QL version and the criteria-based version. The JP QL keywords SELECT, FROM, WHERE and LIKE have matching methods in the form of select(), from(), where(), and like(). The Employee entity class takes the place of the entity name in the invocation of from(), and the name attribute of Employee is still being accessed, but instead of the JP QL dot operator here we have the get() method.

As we progress through this chapter, we will explore each of these methods in detail, but for now we will look at the bigger picture. First, there's the CriteriaBuilder interface, obtained here from the EntityManager interface through the getCriteriaBuilder() method. The CriteriaBuilder interface is the main gateway into the Criteria API, acting as a factory for the various objects that link together to form a query definition. The variable cb will be used in the examples in this chapter to represent the CriteriaBuilder object.

The first use of the CriteriaBuilder interface in this example is to create an instance of CriteriaQuery. The CriteriaQuery object forms the shell of the query definition and generally contains the methods that match up with the JP QL query clauses. The second use of the CriteriaBuilder interface in this example is to construct the conditional expressions in the WHERE clause. All of the conditional expression keywords, operators, and functions from JP QL are represented in some manner on the CriteriaBuilder interface.

Given that background, it is easy to see how the query comes together. The first step is to establish the root of the query by invoking from() to get back a Root object. This is equivalent to declaring the identification variable e in the JP QL example and the Root object will form the basis for path expressions in the rest of the query. The next step establishes the SELECT clause of the query by passing the root into the select() method. The last step is to construct the WHERE clause, by passing an expression composed from CriteriaBuilder methods that represent JP QL condition expressions into the where() method. When path expressions are needed, such as accessing the name attribute in this example, the get() method on the Root object is used to create the path.

Parameterized Types

The preceding example demonstrated the use of Java generics in the Criteria API. The API uses parameterized types extensively: almost every interface and method declaration uses Java generics in one form or another. Generics allow the compiler to detect many cases of incompatible type usage and, like the Java collection API, removes the need for casting in most cases.

Any API that uses Java generics can also be used without type parameters, but when compiled the code will emit compiler warnings. For example, code that uses a simple untyped ("raw") List type will generate a warning to the effect that a reference to a generic type should be parameterized. The following line of code will generate two such warnings, one for using List and one for using ArrayList:

```
List list = new ArrayList();
```

The Criteria API can similarly be used without binding the criteria objects to specific types, although this clearly discards the typing benefits. The preceding example could be rewritten as:

```
CriteriaBuilder cb = em.getCriteriaBuilder();
CriteriaQuery c = cb.createQuery(Employee.class);
Root emp = c.from(Employee.class);
c.select(emp)
 .where(cb.equal(emp.get("name"), "John Smith"));
```

This code is functionally identical to the original example, but just happens to be more prone to errors during development. Nevertheless, some people may be willing to have less development-time type safety but more code readability in the absence of "type clutter." This is particularly understandable considering that most people run at least minimal tests on a query before shipping the query code, and once you get to the point of knowing that the query works, then you are already as far ahead as you would be with compile-time type checking.

If you are in the category of people who would rather the code were simpler to read and develop at the cost of somewhat less compile-time safety, then depending upon your tolerance for compiler warnings you may want to disable them. This can be achieved by adding a @SuppressWarnings("unchecked") annotation on your class. However, be warned (no pun intended!) that this will cause all type checking warnings to be suppressed, not just the ones relating to the use of the Criteria API.

Dynamic Queries

To demonstrate a good potential use of the Criteria API, we will look at a common use case in many enterprise applications: crafting dynamic queries where the structure of the criteria is not known until runtime.

In Chapter 7, we discussed how to create dynamic JP QL queries. You build up the query string at runtime and then pass it to the createQuery() method of the EntityManager interface. The query engine parses the query string and returns a Query object that you can use to get results. Creating dynamic queries is required in situations where the output or criteria of a query varies depending on end-user choices.

Consider a web application used to search for employee contact information. This is a common feature in many large organizations that allows users to search by name, department, phone number, or even location, either separately or using a combination of query terms. Listing 9-1 shows an example implementation of a session bean that accepts a set of criteria and then builds up and executes a JP QL query depending on which criteria parameters have been set. It does not use the Criteria API. This example and others in this chapter use the data model described in Figure 8-1 in Chapter 8.

Listing 9-1. Employee Search Using Dynamic JP QL Query

```
@Stateless
public class SearchService {
    @PersistenceContext(unitName="EmployeeHR")
    EntityManager em;

    public List<Employee> findEmployees(String name, String deptName,
                                        String projectName, String city) {
        StringBuffer query = new StringBuffer();
        query.append("SELECT DISTINCT e ");
        query.append("FROM Employee e LEFT JOIN e.projects p ");

        query.append("WHERE ");
        List<String> criteria = new ArrayList<String>();
        if (name != null) { criteria.add("e.name = :name"); }
        if (deptName != null) { criteria.add("e.dept.name = :dept"); }
        if (projectName != null) { criteria.add("p.name = :project"); }
        if (city != null) { criteria.add("e.address.city = :city"); }
        if (criteria.size() == 0) {
            throw new RuntimeException("no criteria");
        }
        for (int i = 0; i < criteria.size(); i++) {
            if (i > 0) { query.append(" AND "); }
            query.append(criteria.get(i));
        }
```

```
            Query q = em.createQuery(query.toString());
            if (name != null) { q.setParameter("name", name); }
            if (deptName != null) { q.setParameter("dept", deptName); }
            if (projectName != null) { q.setParameter("project", projectName); }
            if (city != null) { q.setParameter("city", city); }
            return (List<Employee>)q.getResultList();
    }
}
```

The findEmployees() method in Listing 9-1 has to perform a number of tasks every time it is invoked. It has to build up a query string with a variable set of criteria, create the query, bind parameters, and then execute the query. It's a fairly straightforward implementation, and will do the job, but every time the query string is created the provider has to parse the JP QL and build up an internal representation of the query before parameters can be bound and SQL generated. It would be nice if we could avoid the parsing overhead and construct the various criteria options using Java API instead of strings. Consider Listing 9-2.

Listing 9-2. Employee Search Using Criteria API

```
@Stateless
public class SearchService {
    @PersistenceContext(unitName="EmployeeHR")
    EntityManager em;

    public List<Employee> findEmployees(String name, String deptName,
                                        String projectName, String city) {

        CriteriaBuilder cb = em.getCriteriaBuilder();
        CriteriaQuery<Employee> c = cb.createQuery(Employee.class);
        Root<Employee> emp = c.from(Employee.class);
        c.select(emp);
        c.distinct(true);
        Join<Employee,Project> project =
            emp.join("projects", JoinType.LEFT);

        List<Predicate> criteria = new ArrayList<Predicate>();
        if (name != null) {
            ParameterExpression<String> p =
                cb.parameter(String.class, "name");
            criteria.add(cb.equal(emp.get("name"), p));
        }
        if (deptName != null) {
            ParameterExpression<String> p =
                cb.parameter(String.class, "dept");
            criteria.add(cb.equal(emp.get("dept").get("name"), p));
        }
        if (projectName != null) {
            ParameterExpression<String> p =
                cb.parameter(String.class, "project");
            criteria.add(cb.equal(project.get("name"), p));
        }
```

```
        if (city != null) {
            ParameterExpression<String> p =
                cb.parameter(String.class, "city");
            criteria.add(cb.equal(emp.get("address").get("city"), p));
        }

        if (criteria.size() == 0) {
            throw new RuntimeException("no criteria");
        } else if (criteria.size() == 1) {
          c.where(criteria.get(0));
        } else {
            c.where(cb.and(criteria.toArray(new Predicate[0])));
        }

        TypedQuery<Employee> q = em.createQuery(c);
        if (name != null) { q.setParameter("name", name); }
        if (deptName != null) { q.setParameter("dept", deptName); }
        if (project != null) { q.setParameter("project", projectName); }
        if (city != null) { q.setParameter("city", city); }
        return q.getResultList();
    }
}
```

Listing 9-2 shows the same EmployeeSearch service from Listing 9-1 redone using the Criteria API. This is a much larger example than our initial look at the Criteria API, but once again you can see the general pattern of how it is constructed. The basic query construction and clause methods of the CriteriaBuilder and CriteriaQuery interfaces are present as before, but there are a few new elements in this query we can explore. The first is the join between Employee and Project, here constructed using the join() method on the Root object. The Join object that is returned can also be used to construct path expressions such as the Root object. In this example, we can also see a path expression involving more than one relationship, from Employee to Address to the city attribute.

The second new element in this query is the use of parameters. Unlike JP QL where parameters are just an alias, in the Criteria API parameters are strongly typed and created from the parameter() call. The ParameterExpression object that is returned can then be used in other parts of the query such as the WHERE or SELECT clauses. In terms of expressions, this example also includes the CriteriaBuilder methods equal() and and(), equivalent to the JP QL predicates = and AND. Note the somewhat odd invocation of the and() method. Like many other Criteria API methods, and() accepts a varying number of arguments, which in turn can be represented as an array of the appropriate argument type. Unfortunately, the designers of the Collection.toArray() method decided that, in order to avoid casting the return type, an array to be populated should also be passed in as an argument or an empty array in the case where we want the collection to create the array for us. The syntax in the example is shorthand for the following code:

```
Predicate[] p = new Predicate[criteria.size()];
p = criteria.toArray(p);
c.where(cb.and(p));
```

The last feature in this query that we did not demonstrate previously is the execution of the query itself. As we demonstrated in Chapter 7, the TypedQuery interface is used to obtain strongly typed query results. Query definitions created with the Criteria API have their result type bound using Java generics and therefore always yield a TypedQuery object from the createQuery() method of the EntityManager interface.

Building Criteria API Queries

Our high-level look at Criteria API examples concluded, the following sections will look at each aspect of creating a query definition in detail. Wherever possible, we try to highlight the similarity between JP QL and Criteria API concepts and terminology.

Creating a Query Definition

As we demonstrated in the previous sections, the heart of the Criteria API is the `CriteriaBuilder` interface, obtained from the `EntityManager` interface by calling the `getCriteriaBuilder()` method. The `CriteriaBuilder` interface is large and serves several purposes within the Criteria API. It is a factory with which we create the query definition itself, an instance of the `CriteriaQuery` interface, as well as many of various components of the query definition such as conditional expressions.

The `CriteriaBuilder` interface provides three methods for creating a new select query definition, depending on the desired result type of the query. The first and most common method is the `createQuery(Class<T>)` method, passing in the class corresponding to the result of the query. This is the approach we used in Listing 9-2. The second method is `createQuery()`, without any parameters, and corresponds to a query with a result type of `Object`. The third method, `createTupleQuery()`, is used for projection or report queries where the SELECT clause of the query contains more than one expression and you wish to work with the result in a more strongly typed manner. It is really just a convenience method that is equivalent to invoking `createQuery(Tuple.class)`. Note that `Tuple` is an interface that contains an assortment of objects or data and applies typing to the aggregate parts. It can be used whenever multiple items are returned and you want to combine them into a single typed object.

It is worth noting that, despite the name, a `CriteriaQuery` instance is not a `Query` object that may be invoked to get results from the database. It is a query definition that may be passed to the `createQuery()` method of the `EntityManager` interface in place of a JP QL string. The only real difference between a criteria query definition and a JP QL string is the method of building the query definition (programming API versus text) and that criteria queries are typically typed, so the result type does not have to be specified when invoking `createQuery()` on `EntityManager` in order to obtain a `TypedQuery` instance. You may also find it useful to think of a fully defined `CriteriaQuery` instance as being similar to the internal representation of a JP QL query that a persistence provider might use after parsing the JP QL string.

The Criteria API is comprised of a number of interfaces that work together to model the structure of a JPA query. As you progress through this chapter, you may find it useful to refer to the interface relationships shown in Figure 9-1.

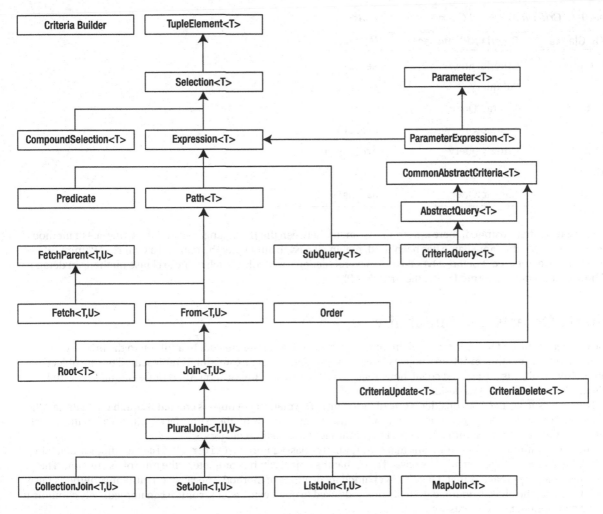

Figure 9-1. *Criteria API Interfaces*

Basic Structure

In the discussion of JP QL in Chapter 8, you learned that there are six possible clauses to be used in a select query: SELECT, FROM, WHERE, ORDER BY, GROUP BY and HAVING. Each of these JP QL clauses has an equivalent method on one of the Criteria API query definition interfaces. Table 9-1 summarizes these methods.

Table 9-1. *Criteria API Select Query Clause Methods*

JP QL Clause	Criteria API Interface	Method
SELECT	CriteriaQuery	`select()`
	Subquery	`select()`
FROM	AbstractQuery	`from()`
WHERE	AbstractQuery	`where()`
ORDER BY	CriteriaQuery	`orderBy()`
GROUP BY	AbstractQuery	`groupBy()`
HAVING	AbstractQuery	`having()`

As we have demonstrated, there is a strong symmetry between the JP QL language and the Criteria API methods. Wherever possible, the same name has been used, making it easy to anticipate the name of a Criteria API method, even if you have not used it before. Over the next several sections, we look at each of these clause methods in detail and how expressions are formed using the Criteria API.

Criteria Objects and Mutability

Typical usage of the Criteria API will result in many different objects being created. In addition to the primary `CriteriaBuilder` and `CriteriaQuery` objects, every component of every expression is represented by one object or another. Not all objects are created equal, however, and effective use of the Criteria API requires familiarity with the coding patterns assumed in its design.

The first issue we need to consider is one of mutability. The majority of objects created through the Criteria API are in fact immutable. There are no setter methods or mutating methods on these interfaces. Almost all of the objects created from the methods on the `CriteriaBuilder` interface fall into this category.

The use of immutable objects means that the arguments passed into the `CriteriaBuilder` methods are rich in detail. All relevant information must be passed in so that the object can be complete at the time of its creation. The advantage of this approach is that it facilitates chained invocations of methods. Because no mutating methods have to be invoked on the objects returned from the methods used to build expressions, control can immediately continue to the next component in the expression.

Only the `CriteriaBuilder` methods that create query definition objects produce truly mutable results. The `CriteriaQuery` and `Subquery` objects are intended to be modified many times by invoking methods such as `select()`, `from()`, and `where()`. But even here care must be taken as invoking methods twice can have one of two different effects. In most cases, invoking a method twice replaces the contents within the object with the argument being supplied. For example, invoking `select()` twice with two different arguments results in only the argument from the second invocation actually remaining as part of the query definition.

In some cases, however, invoking a method twice is in fact addition. Invoking `from()` twice with different arguments results in multiple query roots being added to the query definition. While we refer to these cases in the sections where they are described, you should be familiar with the Javadoc comments on the Criteria API as they also call out this behavior.

The second issue is the presence of getter methods on Criteria API objects. These behave as expected, returning information about the component of the query that each object represents. But it is worth noting that such methods are primarily of interest to tool developers who wish to work with query definitions in a truly generic way. In the vast majority of cases, and those that we demonstrate in this chapter, you will not have to make use of the getter methods in the construction of your criteria queries.

Query Roots and Path Expressions

A newly created `CriteriaQuery` object is basically an empty shell. With the exception of defining the result type of the query, no additional content has yet been added to fill out the query. As with JP QL queries, the developer is responsible for defining the various clauses of the query necessary to fetch the desired data from the database. Semantically speaking, there is no difference between JP QL and Criteria API query definitions. Both have SELECT, FROM, WHERE, GROUP BY, HAVING and ORDER clauses; only the manner of defining them is different. Before we can fill in the various clauses of the query definition, let's first revisit two key concepts defined in Chapter 8 and look at the equivalent Criteria API syntax for those concepts.

Query Roots

The first fundamental concept to revisit is the identification variable used in the FROM clause of JP QL queries to alias declarations that cover entity, embeddable, and other abstract schema types. In JP QL, the identification variable takes on a central importance, as it is the key to tying the different clauses of the query together. But with the Criteria API we represent query components with objects and therefore rarely have aliases with which to concern ourselves. Still, in order to define a FROM clause we need a way to express which abstract schema types we are interested in querying against.

The `AbstractQuery` interface (parent of `CriteriaQuery`) provides the `from()` method to define the abstract schema type that will form the basis for the query. This method accepts an entity type as a parameter and adds a new *root* to the query. A root in a criteria query corresponds to an identification variable in JP QL, which in turn corresponds to a range variable declaration or join expression. In Listing 9-2, we used the following code to obtain our query root:

```
CriteriaQuery<Employee> c = cb.createQuery(Employee.class);
Root<Employee> emp = c.from(Employee.class);
```

The `from()` method returns an instance of Root corresponding to the entity type. The `Root` interface is itself extended from the `From` interface, which exposes functionality for joins. The `From` interface extends `Path`, which further extends `Expression` and then `Selection`, allowing the root to be used in other parts of the query definition. The role of each of these interfaces will be described in later sections. Calls to the `from()` method are additive. Each call adds another root to the query, resulting in a Cartesian product when more than one root is defined if no further constraints are applied in the WHERE clause. The following example from Chapter 8 demonstrates multiple query roots, replacing a conventional join with the more traditional SQL approach:

```
SELECT DISTINCT d
FROM Department d, Employee e
WHERE d = e.department
```

To convert this query to the Criteria API we need to invoke `from()` twice, adding both the Department and Employee entities as query roots. The following example demonstrates this approach:

```
CriteriaQuery<Department> c = cb.createQuery(Department.class);
Root<Department> dept = c.from(Department.class);
Root<Employee> emp = c.from(Employee.class);
c.select(dept)
 .distinct(true)
 .where(cb.equal(dept, emp.get("department")));
```

Path Expressions

The second fundamental concept to revisit is the path expression. The path expression is the key to the power and flexibility of the JP QL language, and it is likewise a central piece of the Criteria API. We discussed path expressions in detail in Chapter 8 so if you feel you need a refresher we recommend going back to review that section.

We went over query roots in the previous section, and roots are actually just a special type of path expression. Query roots in hand, we can now look at how to obtain and extend path expressions. Consider the following basic JP QL query, which returns all the employees living in New York City:

```
SELECT e
FROM Employee e
WHERE e.address.city = 'New York'
```

Thinking in terms of the Criteria API, the query root for this expression is the Employee entity. This query also contains a path expression in the WHERE clause. To represent this path expression using the Criteria API, we would use the following expression:

```
emp.get("address").get("city")
```

The emp object in this example corresponds to the query root for Employee. The get() method is derived from the Path interface extended by the Root interface and is equivalent to the dot operator used in JP QL path expressions to navigate along a path. Because the get() method returns a Path object, the method calls can be chained together, avoiding the unnecessary declaration of intermediate local variables. The argument to get() is the name of the attribute we are interested in. Because the result of constructing a path expression is an Expression object that we can use to build conditional expressions, we can then express the complete query as follows:

```
CriteriaQuery<Employee> c = cb.createQuery(Employee.class);
Root<Employee> emp = c.from(Employee.class);
c.select(emp)
 .where(cb.equal(emp.get("address").get("city"), "New York"));
```

Much like JP QL, path expressions may be used throughout the different clauses of the query definition. With the Criteria API it is necessary to hold onto the root object in a local variable and use it to form path expressions where required. Once again it is worth emphasizing that the from() method of AbstractQuery should never be invoked more than once for each desired root. Invoking it multiple times will result in additional roots being created and a Cartesian product if not careful. Always store the root objects locally and refer to them when necessary.

The SELECT Clause

There are several forms that the SELECT clause of a query may take. The simplest form involves a single expression, while others involve multiple expressions or the use of a constructor expression to create new object instances. Each form is expressed differently in the Criteria API.

Selecting Single Expressions

The select() method of the CriteriaQuery interface is used to form the SELECT clause in a Criteria API query definition. All forms of the SELECT clause may be represented via the select() method, although convenience methods also exist to simplify coding. The select() method requires an argument of type Selection, an interface extended by Expression as well as CompoundSelection to handle the case where the result type of a query is a Tuple or array of results.

■ Note Some vendors may allow the call to `select()` to be omitted in the case where there is a single query root and it matches the declared result type for the query. This is non-portable behavior.

Thus far, we have been passing in a query root to the `select()` method, therefore indicating that we want the entity to be the result of the query. We could also supply a single-valued expression such as selecting an attribute from an entity or any compatible scalar expression. The following example demonstrates this approach by selecting the name attribute of the `Employee` entity:

```
CriteriaQuery<String> c = cb.createQuery(String.class);
Root<Employee> emp = c.from(Employee.class);
c.select(emp.<String>get("name"));
```

This query will return all employee names, including any duplicates. Duplicate results from a query may be removed by invoking `distinct(true)` from the `AbstractQuery` interface. This is identical in behavior to the DISTINCT keyword in a JP QL query.

Also note the unusual syntax we used to declare that the "name" attribute was of type String. The type of the expression provided to the `select()` method must be compatible with the result type used to create the `CriteriaQuery` object. For example, if the `CriteriaQuery` object was created by invoking `createQuery(Project.class)` on the `CriteriaBuilder` interface, then it will be an error to attempt to set an expression resolving to the `Employee` entity using the `select()` method. When a method call such as `select()` uses generic typing in order to enforce a compatibility constraint, the type may be prefixed to the method name in order to qualify it in cases where the type could not otherwise be automatically determined. We need to use that approach in this case because the `select()` method has been declared as follows:

```
CriteriaQuery<T> select(Selection<? extends T> selection);
```

The argument to `select()` must be a type that is compatible with the result type of the query definition. The `get()` method returns a `Path` object, but that `Path` object is always of type `Path<Object>` because the compiler cannot infer the correct type based on the attribute name. To declare that the attribute is really of type `String`, we need to qualify the method invocation accordingly. This syntax has to be used whenever the `Path` is being passed as an argument for which the parameter has been strongly typed, such as the argument to the `select()` method and certain `CriteriaBuilder` expression methods. We have not had to use them so far in our examples because we have been using them in methods like `equal()`, where the parameter was declared to be of type `Expression<?>`. Because the type is wildcarded, it is valid to pass in an argument of type `Path<Object>`. Later in the chapter, we will look at the strongly typed versions of the Criteria API methods that remove this requirement.

Selecting Multiple Expressions

When defining a SELECT clause that involves more than one expression, the Criteria API approach required depends on how the query definition was created. If the result type is `Tuple`, then a `CompoundSelection<Tuple>` object must be passed to `select()`. If the result type is a non-persistent class that will be created using a constructor expression, then the argument must be a `CompoundSelection<[T]>` object, where `[T]` is the class type of the non-persistent class. Finally, if the result type is an array of objects, then a `CompoundSelection<Object[]>` object must be provided. These objects are created with the `tuple()`, `construct()` and `array()` methods of the `CriteriaBuilder` interface, respectively. The following example demonstrates how to provide multiple expressions to a `Tuple` query:

```
CriteriaQuery<Tuple> c= cb.createTupleQuery();
Root<Employee> emp = c.from(Employee.class);
c.select(cb.tuple(emp.get("id"), emp.get("name")));
```

As a convenience, the multiselect() method of the CriteriaQuery interface may also be used to set the SELECT clause. The multiselect() method will create the appropriate argument type given the result type of the query. This can take three forms depending on how the query definition was created.

The first form is for queries that have Object or Object[] as their result type. The list of expressions that make up each result are simply passed to the multiselect() method.

```
CriteriaQuery<Object[]> c = cb.createQuery(Object[].class);
Root<Employee> emp = c.from(Employee.class);
c.multiselect(emp.get("id"), emp.get("name"));
```

Note that, if the query result type is declared as Object instead of Object[], the behavior of multiselect() in this form changes slightly. The result is always an instance of Object, but if multiple arguments are passed into multiselect() then the result must be cast to Object[] in order to access any particular value. If only a single argument is passed into multiselect(), then no array is created and the result may be cast directly from Object to the desired type. In general, it is more convenient to be explicit about the query result type. If you want to work with an array of results, then declaring the query result type to be Object[] avoids casting later and makes the shape of the result more explicit if the query is invoked separately from the code that creates it.

The second form is a close relative of the first form, but for queries that result in Tuple. Again, the list of expressions is passed into the multiselect() call.

```
CriteriaQuery<Tuple> c = cb.createTupleQuery();
Root<Employee> emp = c.from(Employee.class);
c.multiselect(emp.get("id"), emp.get("name"));
```

The third and final form is for queries with constructor expressions that result in non-persistent types. The multiselect() method is again invoked with a list of expressions, but it uses the type of the query to figure out and automatically create the appropriate constructor expression, in this case a data transfer object of type EmployeeInfo.

```
CriteriaQuery<EmployeeInfo> c = cb.createQuery(EmployeeInfo.class);
Root<Employee> emp = c.from(Employee.class);
c.multiselect(emp.get("id"), emp.get("name"));
```

This is equivalent to the following:

```
CriteriaQuery<EmployeeInfo> c = cb.createQuery(EmployeeInfo.class);
Root<Employee> emp = c.from(Employee.class);
c.select(cb.construct(EmployeeInfo.class,
                      emp.get("id"),
                      emp.get("name")));
```

As convenient as the multiselect() method is for constructor expressions, there are still cases where you will need to use the construct() method from the CriteriaBuilder interface. For example, if the result type of the query is Object[] and it also includes a constructor expression for only part of the results, the following would be required:

```
CriteriaQuery<Object[]> c = cb.createQuery(Object[].class);
Root<Employee> emp = c.from(Employee.class);
c.multiselect(emp.get("id"),
            cb.construct(EmployeeInfo.class,
                      emp.get("id"),
                      emp.get("name")));
```

Using Aliases

Like JP QL, aliases may also be set on expressions in the SELECT clause, which will then be included in the resulting SQL statement. They are of little use from a programming perspective as we construct the ORDER BY clause through the use of the Selection objects used to construct the SELECT clause.

Aliases are useful when the query has a result type of Tuple. The aliases will be available through the resulting Tuple objects. To set an alias, the alias() method of the Selection interface (parent to Expression) must be invoked. The following example demonstrates this approach:

```
CriteriaQuery<Tuple> c= cb.createTupleQuery();
Root<Employee> emp = c.from(Employee.class);
c.multiselect(emp.get("id").alias("id"), emp.get("name").alias("fullName"));
```

This example actually demonstrates two facets of the alias() method. The first is that it returns itself, so it can be invoked as part of the call to select() or multiselect(). The second is, once again, that it returns itself, and is therefore mutating what should be an otherwise immutable object. The alias() method is an exception to the rule that only the query definition interfaces, CriteriaQuery and Subquery, contain mutating operations. Invoking alias() changes the original Selection object and returns it from the method invocation. It is invalid to set the alias of a Selection object more than once.

Making use of the alias when iterating over the query results is as simple as requesting the expression by name. Executing the previous query would allow it to be processed as follows:

```
TypedQuery<Tuple> q = em.createQuery(c);
for (Tuple t : q.getResultList()) {
    String id = t.get("id", String.class);
    String fullName = t.get("fullName", String.class);
    // ...
}
```

The FROM Clause

In the "Query Roots" section, we covered the from() method of the AbstractQuery interface and the role of query roots in forming the query definition. We will now elaborate on that discussion and look at how joins are expressed using the Criteria API.

Inner and Outer Joins

Join expressions are created using the join() method of the From interface, which is extended both by Root, which we covered earlier, and Join, which is the object type returned by creating join expressions. This means that any query root may join, and that joins may chain with one another. The join() method requires a path expression argument and optionally an argument to specify the type of join, JoinType.INNER or JoinType.LEFT, for inner and outer joins respectively.

■ **Tip** The JoinType.RIGHT enumerated value specifies that a right outer join should be applied. Support for this option is not required by the specification so applications that make use of it will not be portable.

When joining across a collection type (except for Map, which we will discuss later in this chapter), the join will have two parameterized types: the type of the source and the type of the target. This maintains the type safety on both sides of the join, and makes it clear what types are being joined.

The join() method is additive, so each call results in a new join being created; therefore, the Join instance returned from invoking the method should be retained in a local variable for forming path expressions later. Because Join also extends Path, it behaves like Root objects when defining paths.

In Listing 9-2, we demonstrated an outer join from Employee to Project.

```
Join<Employee,Project> project = emp.join("projects", JoinType.LEFT);
```

Had the JoinType.LEFT argument been omitted, the join type would have defaulted to be an inner join. Just as in JP QL, multiple joins may be associated with the same From instance. For example, to navigate across the directs relationship of Employee and then to both the Department and Project entities would require the following, which assumes inner joining:

```
Join<Employee,Employee> directs = emp.join("directs");
Join<Employee,Project> projects = directs.join("projects");
Join<Employee,Department> dept = directs.join("dept");
```

Joins may also be cascaded in a single statement. The resulting join will be typed by the source and target of the last join in the statement:

```
Join<Employee,Project> project = dept.join("employees").join("projects");
```

Joins across collection relationships that use Map are a special case. JP QL uses the KEY and VALUE keywords to extract the key or value of a Map element for use in other parts of the query. In the Criteria API, these operators are handled by the key() and value() methods of the MapJoin interface. Consider the following example assuming a Map join across the phones relationship of the Employee entity:

```
SELECT e.name, KEY(p), VALUE(p)
FROM Employee e JOIN e.phones p
```

To create this query using the Criteria API, we need to capture the result of the join as a MapJoin, in this case using the joinMap() method. The MapJoin object has three type parameters: the source type, key type, and value type. It can look a little more daunting, but makes it explicit what types are involved.

```
CriteriaQuery<Object> c = cb.createQuery();
Root<Employee> emp = c.from(Employee.class);
MapJoin<Employee,String,Phone> phone = emp.joinMap("phones");
c.multiselect(emp.get("name"), phone.key(), phone.value());
```

We need to use the joinMap() method in this case because there is no way to overload the join() method to return a Join object or MapJoin object when all we are passing in is the name of the attribute. Collection, Set, and List relationships are likewise handled with the joinCollection(), joinSet(), and joinList() methods for those cases where a specific join interface must be used. The strongly typed version of the join() method, which we will demonstrate later, is able to handle all join types though the single join() call.

Fetch Joins

As with JP QL, the Criteria API supports the fetch join, a query construct that allows data to be prefetched into the persistence context as a side effect of a query that returns a different, but related, entity. The Criteria API builds fetch joins through the use of the `fetch()` method on the `FetchParent` interface. It is used instead of `join()` in cases where fetch semantics are required and accepts the same argument types.

Consider the following example we used in the previous chapter to demonstrate fetch joins of single-valued relationships:

```
SELECT e
FROM Employee e JOIN FETCH e.address
```

To re-create this query with the Criteria API, we use the `fetch()` method.

```
CriteriaQuery<Employee> c = cb.createQuery(Employee.class);
Root<Employee> emp = c.from(Employee.class);
emp.fetch("address");
c.select(emp);
```

Note that when using the `fetch()` method the return type is `Fetch`, not `Join`. `Fetch` objects are not paths and may not be extended or referenced anywhere else in the query.

Collection-valued fetch joins are also supported and use similar syntax. In the following example, we demonstrate how to fetch the Phone entities associated with each Employee, using an outer join to prevent Employee entities from being skipped if they don't have any associated Phone entities. We use the `distinct()` setting to remove any duplicates.

```
CriteriaQuery<Employee> c = cb.createQuery(Employee.class);
Root<Employee> emp = c.from(Employee.class);
emp.fetch("phones", JoinType.LEFT);
c.select(emp)
  .distinct(true);
```

The WHERE Clause

As you saw in Table 9-1 and in several examples, the WHERE clause of a query in the Criteria API is set through the `where()` method of the `AbstractQuery` interface. The `where()` method accepts either zero or more `Predicate` objects, or a single `Expression<Boolean>` argument. Each call to `where()` will render any previously set WHERE expressions to be discarded and replaced with the newly passed-in ones.

Building Expressions

The key to building up expressions with the Criteria API is the `CriteriaBuilder` interface. This interface contains methods for all of the predicates, expressions, and functions supported by the JP QL language as well as other features specific to the Criteria API. Table 9-2, Table 9-3, Table 9-4, and Table 9-5 summarize the mapping between JP QL operators, expressions, and functions to their equivalent methods on the `CriteriaBuilder` interface. Note that in some cases there is no direct equal to a method and a combination of `CriteriaBuilder` methods is required to get the same result. In other cases, the equivalent criteria method is actually on a class other than `CriteriaBuilder`.

Table 9-2. *JP QL to CriteriaBuilder Predicate Mapping*

JP QL Operator	CriteriaBuilder Method
AND	and()
OR	or()
NOT	not()
=	equal()
<>	notEqual()
>	greaterThan(), gt()
>=	greaterThanOrEqualTo(), ge()
<	lessThan(), lt()
<=	lessThanOrEqualTo(), le()
BETWEEN	between()
IS NULL	isNull()
IS NOT NULL	isNotNull()
EXISTS	exists()
NOT EXISTS	not(exists())
IS EMPTY	isEmpty()
IS NOT EMPTY	isNotEmpty()
MEMBER OF	isMember()
NOT MEMBER OF	isNotMember()
LIKE	like()
NOT LIKE	notLike()
IN	in()
NOT IN	not(in())

Table 9-3. *JP QL to CriteriaBuilder Scalar Expression Mapping*

JP QL Expression	CriteriaBuilder Method
ALL	all()
ANY	any()
SOME	some()
-	neg(), diff()
+	sum()
*	prod()
/	quot()
COALESCE	coalesce()
NULLIF	nullif()
CASE	selectCase()

Table 9-4. *JP QL to CriteriaBuilder Function Mapping*

JP QL Function	CriteriaBuilder Method
ABS	abs()
CONCAT	concat()
CURRENT_DATE	currentDate()
CURRENT_TIME	currentTime()
CURRENT_TIMESTAMP	currentTimestamp()
LENGTH	length()
LOCATE	locate()
LOWER	lower()
MOD	mod()
SIZE	size()
SQRT	sqrt()
SUBSTRING	substring()
UPPER	upper()
TRIM	trim()

Table 9-5. *JP QL to CriteriaBuilder Aggregate Function Mapping*

JP QL Aggregate Function	CriteriaBuilder Method
AVG	avg()
SUM	sum(), sumAsLong(), sumAsDouble()
MIN	min(), least()
MAX	max(), greatest()
COUNT	count()
COUNT DISTINCT	countDistinct()

In addition to the straight translation of JP QL operators, expressions, and functions, there are some techniques specific to the Criteria API that need to be considered when developing expressions. The following sections will look at these techniques in detail and explore those parts of the Criteria API that have no equivalent in JP QL.

Predicates

In Listing 9-2, we passed an array of Predicate objects to the and() method. This has the behavior of combining all of the expressions with the AND operator. Equivalent behavior for the OR operator exists via the or() method. One shortcut that works for AND operators is to pass all of the expressions as arguments to the where() method. Passing multiple arguments to where() implicitly combines the expressions using AND operator semantics.

The Criteria API also offers a different style of building AND and OR expressions for those who wish to build things incrementally rather than as a list. The conjunction() and disjunction() methods of the CriteriaBuilder interface create Predicate objects that always resolve to true and false respectively. Once obtained, these primitive predicates can then be combined with other predicates to build up nested conditional expressions in a tree-like fashion. Listing 9-3 rewrites the predication construction portion of the example from Listing 9-2 using the conjunction() method. Note how each conditional statement is combined with its predecessor using an and() call.

Listing 9-3. Predicate Construction Using Conjunction

```
Predicate criteria = cb.conjunction();
if (name != null) {
    ParameterExpression<String> p =
        cb.parameter(String.class, "name");
    criteria = cb.and(criteria, cb.equal(emp.get("name"), p));
}
if (deptName != null) {
    ParameterExpression<String> p =
        cb.parameter(String.class, "dept");
    criteria = cb.and(criteria,
                    cb.equal(emp.get("dept").get("name"), p));
}
if (projectName != null) {
    ParameterExpression<String> p =
        cb.parameter(String.class, "project");
    criteria = cb.and(criteria, cb.equal(project.get("name"), p));
}
```

```
if (city != null) {
    ParameterExpression<String> p =
        cb.parameter(String.class, "city");
    criteria = cb.and(criteria,
                    cb.equal(emp.get("address").get("city"), p));
}

if (criteria.getExpressions().size() == 0) {
    throw new RuntimeException("no criteria");
}
```

With respect to other predicate concerns, in Table 9-2 it should be noted that there are two sets of methods available for relative comparisons. For example, there is greaterThan() and gt(). The two-letter forms are specific to numeric values and are strongly typed to work with number types. The long forms must be used for all other cases.

Literals

Literal values may require special handling when expressed with the Criteria API. In all the cases encountered so far, methods are overloaded to work with both Expression objects and Java literals. However, there may be some cases where only an Expression object is accepted (in cases where it is assumed you would never pass in a literal value or when any of a number of types would be acceptable). If you encounter this situation then, to use these expressions with Java literals, the literals must be wrapped using the literal() method. NULL literals are created from the nullLiteral() method, which accepts a class parameter and produces a typed version of NULL to match the passed-in class. This is necessary to extend the strong typing of the API to NULL values.

Parameters

Parameter handling for Criteria API queries is different from JP QL. Whereas JP QL strings simply prefix string names with a colon to denote a parameter alias, this technique will not work in the Criteria API. Instead, we must explicitly create a ParameterExpression of the correct type that can be used in conditional expressions. This is achieved through the parameter() method of the CriteriaBuilder interface. This method requires a class type (to set the type of the ParameterExpression object) and an optional name for use with named parameters. Listing 9-4 demonstrates this method.

Listing 9-4. Creating Parameter Expressions

```
CriteriaQuery<Employee> c = cb.createQuery(Employee.class);
Root<Employee> emp = c.from(Employee.class);
c.select(emp);
ParameterExpression<String> deptName =
    cb.parameter(String.class, "deptName");
c.where(cb.equal(emp.get("dept").get("name"), deptName));
```

If the parameter will not be reused in other parts of the query, it can be embedded directly in the predicate expression to make the overall query definition more concise. The following code revises the Listing 9-4 to use this technique:

```
CriteriaQuery<Employee> c = cb.createQuery(Employee.class);
Root<Employee> emp = c.from(Employee.class);
c.select(emp)
  .where(cb.equal(emp.get("dept").get("name"),
                cb.parameter(String.class, "deptName")));
```

Subqueries

The AbstractQuery interface provides the subquery() method for creation of subqueries. Subqueries may be correlated (meaning that they reference a root, path, or join from the parent query) or non-correlated. The Criteria API supports both correlated and non-correlated subqueries, again using query roots to tie the various clauses and expressions together. The argument to subquery() is a class instance representing the result type of the subquery. The return value is an instance of Subquery, which is itself an extension of AbstractQuery. With the exception of restricted methods for constructing clauses, the Subquery instance is a complete query definition like CriteriaQuery that may be used to create both simple and complex queries.

To demonstrate subquery usage, let's look at a more significant example, modifying Listing 9-2 to use subqueries instead of the distinct() method to eliminate duplicates. According to the data model shown in Figure 8-1, the Employee entity has relationships with four other entities: single-valued relationships with Department and Address, and collection-valued relationships with Phone and Project. Whenever we join across a collection-valued relationship, we have the potential to return duplicate rows; therefore, we need to change the criteria expression for Project to use a subquery. Listing 9-5 shows the code fragment required to make this change.

Listing 9-5. Modified Employee Search With Subqueries

```
@Stateless
public class SearchService {
    @PersistenceContext(unitName="EmployeeHR")
    EntityManager em;

    public List<Employee> findEmployees(String name, String deptName,
                                        String projectName, String city) {
        CriteriaBuilder cb = em.getCriteriaBuilder();
        CriteriaQuery<Employee> c = cb.createQuery(Employee.class);
        Root<Employee> emp = c.from(Employee.class);
        c.select(emp);

        // ...

        if (projectName != null) {
            Subquery<Employee> sq = c.subquery(Employee.class);
            Root<Project> project = sq.from(Project.class);
            Join<Project,Employee> sqEmp = project.join("employees");
            sq.select(sqEmp)
              .where(cb.equal(project.get("name"),
                              cb.parameter(String.class, "project")));
            criteria.add(cb.in(emp).value(sq));
        }

        // ...
    }
}
```

Listing 9-5 contains a couple of significant changes to the example first presented in Listing 9-2. First, the `distinct()` method call has been removed as well as the join to the `Project` entity. We have also introduced a new non-correlated subquery against `Project`. Because the subquery from Listing 9-5 declares its own root and does not reference anything from the parent query, it runs independently and is therefore non-correlated. The equivalent JP QL query with only `Project` criteria would be:

```
SELECT e
FROM Employee e
WHERE e IN (SELECT emp
            FROM Project p JOIN p.employees emp
            WHERE p.name = :project)
```

Whenever we write queries that use subqueries, there is often more than one way to achieve a particular result. For example, we could rewrite the previous example to use EXISTS instead of IN and shift the conditional expression into the WHERE clause of the subquery.

```
if (projectName != null) {
    Subquery<Project> sq = c.subquery(Project.class);
    Root<Project> project = sq.from(Project.class);
    Join<Project,Employee> sqEmp = project.join("employees");
    sq.select(project)
      .where(cb.equal(sqEmp, emp),
             cb.equal(project.get("name"),
                      cb.parameter(String.class,"project")));
    criteria.add(cb.exists(sq));
}
```

By referencing the `Employee` root from the parent query in the WHERE clause of the subquery, we now have a correlated subquery. This time the query takes the following form in JP QL:

```
SELECT e
FROM Employee e
WHERE EXISTS (SELECT p
             FROM Project p JOIN p.employees emp
             WHERE emp = e AND
                   p.name = :name)
```

We can still take this example further and reduce the search space for the subquery by moving the reference to the `Employee` root to the FROM clause of the subquery and joining directly to the list of projects specific to that employee. In JP QL, we would write this as follows:

```
SELECT e
FROM Employee e
WHERE EXISTS (SELECT p
             FROM e.projects p
             WHERE p.name = :name)
```

In order to re-create this query using the Criteria API, we are confronted with a dilemma. We need to base the query on the Root object from the parent query but the from() method only accepts a persistent class type. The solution is the correlate() method from the Subquery interface. It performs a similar function to the from() method of the AbstractQuery interface, but does so with Root and Join objects from the parent query. The following example demonstrates how to use correlate() in this case:

```
if (projectName != null) {
    Subquery<Project> sq = c.subquery(Project.class);
    Root<Employee> sqEmp = sq.correlate(emp);
    Join<Employee,Project> project = sqEmp.join("projects");
    sq.select(project)
      .where(cb.equal(project.get("name"),
                      cb.parameter(String.class,"project")));
    criteria.add(cb.exists(sq));
}
```

Before we leave subqueries in the Criteria API, there is one more corner case with correlated subqueries to explore: referencing a join expression from the parent query in the FROM clause of a subquery. Consider the following example that returns projects containing managers with direct reports earning an average salary higher than a user-defined threshold:

```
SELECT p
FROM Project p JOIN p.employees e
WHERE TYPE(p) = DesignProject AND
      e.directs IS NOT EMPTY AND
      (SELECT AVG(d.salary)
        FROM e.directs d) >= :value
```

When creating the Criteria API query definition for this query, we must correlate the employees attribute of Project and then join it to the direct reports in order to calculate the average salary. This example also demonstrates the use of the type() method of the Path interface in order to do a polymorphic comparison of types:

```
CriteriaQuery<Project> c = cb.createQuery(Project.class);
Root<Project> project = c.from(Project.class);
Join<Project,Employee> emp = project.join("employees");
Subquery<Number> sq = c.subquery(Number.class);
Join<Project,Employee> sqEmp = sq.correlate(emp);
Join<Employee,Employee> directs = sqEmp.join("directs");
c.select(project)
  .where(cb.equal(project.type(), DesignProject.class),
         cb.isNotEmpty(emp.<Collection>get("directs")),
         cb.ge(sq.select(cb.avg(directs.get("salary"))),
                   cb.parameter(Number.class, "value")));
```

In Expressions

Unlike other operators, the IN operator requires some special handling in the Criteria API. The `in()` method of the `CriteriaBuilder` interface only accepts a single argument, the single-valued expression that will be tested against the values of the IN expression. In order to set the values of the IN expression, we must use the `CriteriaBuilder.In` object returned from the `in()` method. Consider the following JP QL query:

```
SELECT e
FROM Employee e
WHERE e.address.state IN ('NY', 'CA')
```

To convert this query to the Criteria API, we must invoke the `value()` method of the `CriteriaBuilder.In` interface to set the state identifiers we are interested in querying, like so:

```
CriteriaQuery<Employee> c = cb.createQuery(Employee.class);
Root<Employee> emp = c.from(Employee.class);
c.select(emp)
 .where(cb.in(emp.get("address")
                .get("state")).value("NY").value("CA"));
```

Note the chained invocation of the `value()` method in order to set multiple values into the IN expression. The argument to `in()` is the expression to search for against the list of values provided via the `value()` method.

In cases where there are a large number of `value()` calls to chain together that are all of the same type, the `Expression` interface offers a shortcut for creating IN expressions. The `in()` methods of this interface allow one or more values to be set in a single call.

```
CriteriaQuery<Employee> c = cb.createQuery(Employee.class);
Root<Employee> emp = c.from(Employee.class);
c.select(emp)
 .where(emp.get("address")
            .get("state").in("NY","CA"));
```

In this case, the call to `in()` is suffixed to the expression rather than prefixed as was the case in the previous example. Note the difference in argument type between the `CriteriaBuilder` and `Expression` interface versions of `in()`. The `Expression` version of `in()` accepts the values to be searched, not the expression to search for. The `in()` method of the `CriteriaBuilder` interface allows more typing options, but for the most part it is largely a case of personal preference when deciding which approach to use.

IN expressions that use subqueries are written using a similar approach. For a more complex example, in the previous chapter, we demonstrated a JP QL query using an IN expression in which the department of an employee is tested against a list generated from a subquery. The example is reproduced here.

```
SELECT e
FROM Employee e
WHERE e.department IN
  (SELECT DISTINCT d
   FROM Department d JOIN d.employees de JOIN de.project p
   WHERE p.name LIKE 'QA%')
```

We can convert this example to the Criteria API as shown in Listing 9-6.

Listing 9-6. IN Expression Using a Subquery

```
CriteriaQuery<Employee> c = cb.createQuery(Employee.class);
Root<Employee> emp = c.from(Employee.class);
Subquery<Department> sq = c.subquery(Department.class);
Root<Department> dept = sq.from(Department.class);
Join<Employee,Project> project =
    dept.join("employees").join("projects");
sq.select(dept.<Integer>get("id"))
  .distinct(true)
  .where(cb.like(project.<String>get("name"), "QA%"));
c.select(emp)
 .where(cb.in(emp.get("dept").get("id")).value(sq));
```

The subquery is created separately and then passed into the value() method as the expression to search for the Department entity. This example also demonstrates using an attribute expression as a value in the search list.

Case Expressions

Like the IN expression, building CASE expressions with the Criteria API requires the use of a helper interface. In this example we will convert the examples used in Chapter 8 to the Criteria API, demonstrating general and simple case expressions, as well as COALESCE.

■ **Tip** Although case statements are required by JPA providers, they may not be supported by all databases. The use of a case statement on a database platform that does not support case expressions is undefined.

We will begin with the general form of the CASE expression, the most powerful but also the most complex.

```
SELECT p.name,
       CASE WHEN TYPE(p) = DesignProject THEN 'Development'
            WHEN TYPE(p) = QualityProject THEN 'QA'
            ELSE 'Non-Development'
       END
FROM Project p
WHERE p.employees IS NOT EMPTY
```

The selectCase() method of the CriteriaBuilder interface is used to create the CASE expression. For the general form it takes no arguments and returns a CriteriaBuilder.Case object that we may use to add the conditional expressions to the CASE statement. The following example demonstrates this approach:

```
CriteriaQuery<Object[]> c = cb.createQuery(Object[].class);
Root<Project> project = c.from(Project.class);
c.multiselect(project.get("name"),
        cb.selectCase()
          .when(cb.equal(project.type(), DesignProject.class),
                "Development")
          .when(cb.equal(project.type(), QualityProject.class),
                "QA")
```

```
        .otherwise("Non-Development"))
  .where(cb.isNotEmpty(project.<List<Employee>>get("employees"))));
```

The when() and otherwise() methods correspond to the WHEN and ELSE keywords from JP QL. Unfortunately, "else" is already a keyword in Java so "otherwise" must be used as a substitute.

The next example simplifies the previous example down to the simple form of the case statement.

```
SELECT p.name,
       CASE TYPE(p)
            WHEN DesignProject THEN 'Development'
            WHEN QualityProject THEN 'QA'
            ELSE 'Non-Development'
       END
FROM Project p
WHERE p.employees IS NOT EMPTY
```

In this case, we pass the primary expression to be tested to the selectCase() method and use the when() and otherwise() methods of the CriteriaBuilder.SimpleCase interface. Rather than a predicate or boolean expression, these methods now accept single-valued expressions that are compared to the base expression of the CASE statement.

```
CriteriaQuery<Object[]> c = cb.createQuery(Object[].class);
Root<Project> project = c.from(Project.class);
c.multiselect(project.get("name"),
         cb.selectCase(project.type())
            .when(DesignProject.class, "Development")
            .when(QualityProject.class, "QA")
            .otherwise("Non-Development"))
  .where(cb.isNotEmpty(project.<List<Employee>>("employees"))));
```

The last example we will cover in this section concerns the JP QL COALESCE expression.

```
SELECT COALESCE(d.name, d.id)
FROM Department d
```

Building a COALESCE expression with the Criteria API requires a helper interface like the other examples we have looked at in this section, but it is closer in form to the IN expression than the CASE expressions. Here we invoke the coalesce() method without arguments to get back a CriteriaBuilder.Coalesce object that we then use the value() method of to add values to the COALESCE expression. The following example demonstrates this approach:

```
CriteriaQuery<Object> c = cb.createQuery();
Root<Department> dept = c.from(Department.class);
c.select(cb.coalesce()
            .value(dept.get("name"))
            .value(dept.get("id")));
```

Convenience versions of the coalesce() method also exist for the case where only two expressions are being compared.

```
CriteriaQuery<Object> c = cb.createQuery();
Root<Department> dept = c.from(Department.class);
c.select(cb.coalesce(dept.get("name"),
                     dept.get("id")));
```

A final note about case expressions is that they are another exception to the rule that the `CriteriaBuilder` methods are non-mutating. Each `when()` method causes another conditional expression to be added incrementally to the case expression, and each `value()` method adds an additional value to the coalesce list.

Function Expressions

Not to be confused with the built-in functions of JP QL, criteria function expressions are the Criteria API equivalent of the FUNCTION keyword in JP QL. They allow native SQL stored functions to be mixed with other Criteria API expressions. They are intended for cases where a limited amount of native SQL is required to satisfy some requirement but you don't want to convert the entire query to SQL.

Function expressions are created with the `function()` method of the `CriteriaBuilder` interface. It requires as arguments the database function name, the expected return type, and a variable list of arguments, if any, that should be passed to the function. The return type is an `Expression`, so it can be used in many other places within the query. The following example invokes a database function to capitalize the first letter of each word in a department name:

```
CriteriaQuery<String> c = cb.createQuery(String.class);
Root<Department> dept = c.from(Department.class);
c.select(cb.function("initcap", String.class, dept.get("name")));
```

As always, developers interested in maximizing the portability of their applications should be careful in using function expressions. Unlike native SQL queries, which are clearly marked, function expressions are a small part of what otherwise looks like a normal portable JPA query that is actually tied to database-specific behavior.

Downcasting

JPA 2.1 introduced support for type downcasting when querying over an entity inheritance hierarchy via the TREAT operation in JP QL. In the Criteria API, this operation is exposed via the `treat()` method of the `CriteriaBuilder` interface. It may be used when constructing joins to limit results to a specific subclass or as part of general criteria expressions in order to access state fields from specific subclasses.

The `treat()` method has been overloaded to return either `Join` or `Path` objects depending on the type of arguments. Recall the example in Chapter 8 that demonstrated using `treat()` to limit an `Employee` query to only those employees who are working on a `QualityProject` for which the quality rating is greater than five:

```
SELECT e FROM Employee e JOIN TREAT(e.projects AS QualityProject) qp
WHERE qp.qualityRating > 5
```

The criteria equivalent of this query is as follows:

```
CriteriaQuery<Employee> q = cb.createQuery(Employee.class);
Root<Employee> emp = q.from(Employee.class);
Join<Employee,QualityProject> project = cb.treat(emp.join(emp.get("projects"), QualityProject.class);
q.select(emp)
  .where(cb.gt(project.<Integer>get("qualityRating"), 5));
```

In this example, `treat()` accepts a `Join` object and returns a `Join` object and can be referenced in the WHERE clause because it is saved in a variable. When used directly in a criteria expression, such as in a WHERE clause, it accepts a `Path` or a `Root` object and returns a `Path` that corresponds to the subclass requested. For example, we could use the `treat()` method to access the quality rating or the design phase in a query across projects.

```
CriteriaQuery<Project> q = cb.createQuery(Project.class);
Root<Project> project = q.from(Project.class);
q.select(project)
```

```
.where(cb.or(
            cb.gt(cb.treat(project, QualityProject.class). <Integer>get("qualityRating"), 5),
            cb.gt(cb.treat(project, DesignProject.class). <Integer>get("designPhase"), 3)));
```

■ **Tip** Support for downcasting to a subtype was added in JPA 2.1.

Outer Join Criteria

Earlier in the chapter we demonstrated how to use the Criteria API to construct joins between entities. We have also demonstrated how to use the where() method of the AbstractQuery interface and the expression framework of the Criteria API to construct the filtering conditions that will limit the result set. This works fine for inner joins, but as we discussed in the last chapter, outer joins require additional support to establish filtering criteria that still preserves the optionality of the joined entities. Like the where() method of the AbstractQuery interface, the Join interface supports the on() method for specifying outer join criteria that must be evaluated as the result set is being created. This is equivalent to the ON condition of the JP QL JOIN expression. The following is a simple example of using the ON keyword in JP QL:

```
SELECT e FROM Employee e JOIN e.projects p ON p.name = 'Zooby'
```

The on() method takes a single predicate object to represent the join condition. The criteria equivalent of the JP QL query above would be expressed as:

```
CriteriaQuery<Employee> q = cb.createQuery(Employee.class);
Root<Employee> emp = q.from(Employee.class);
Join<Employee,Project> project = emp.join("projects", JoinType.LEFT)
            .on(cb.equal(project.get("name"), "Zooby"));
q.select(emp);
```

■ **Tip** Support for the ON condition of outer join queries was added in JPA 2.1.

The ORDER BY Clause

The orderBy() method of the CriteriaQuery interface sets the ordering for a query definition. This method accepts one or more Order objects, which are created by the asc() and desc() methods of the CriteriaBuilder interface, for ascending and descending ordering respectively. The following example demonstrates the orderBy() method:

```
CriteriaQuery<Tuple> c = cb.createQuery(Tuple.class);
Root<Employee> emp = c.from(Employee.class);
Join<Employee,Department> dept = emp.join("dept");
c.multiselect(dept.get("name"), emp.get("name"));
c.orderBy(cb.desc(dept.get("name")),
          cb.asc(emp.get("name")));
```

Query ordering through the Criteria API is still subject to the same constraints as JP QL. The arguments to asc() and desc() must be single-valued expressions, typically formed from the state field of an entity. The order in which the arguments are passed to the orderBy() method determines the generation of SQL. The equivalent JP QL for the query shown in the previous example is as follows:

```
SELECT d.name, e.name
FROM Employee e JOIN e.dept d
ORDER BY d.name DESC, e.name
```

The GROUP BY and HAVING Clauses

The groupBy() and having() methods of the AbstractQuery interface are the Criteria API equivalent of the GROUP BY and HAVING clauses from JP QL, respectively. Both arguments accept one or more expressions that are used to group and filter the data. By this point in the chapter, the usage pattern for these methods should be more intuitive to you. Consider the following example from the previous chapter:

```
SELECT e, COUNT(p)
FROM Employee e JOIN e.projects p
GROUP BY e
HAVING COUNT(p) >= 2
```

To re-create this example with the Criteria API, we will need to make use of both aggregate functions and the grouping methods. The following example demonstrates this conversion:

```
CriteriaQuery<Object[]> c = cb.createQuery(Object[].class);
Root<Employee> emp = c.from(Employee.class);
Join<Employee,Project> project = emp.join("projects");
c.multiselect(emp, cb.count(project))
 .groupBy(emp)
 .having(cb.ge(cb.count(project),2));
```

Bulk Update and Delete

The CriteriaBuilder interface is not limited to report queries. Bulk update and delete queries may also be created using the createCriteriaUpdate() and createCriteriaDelete() methods, respectively. Like their report query counterparts, the CriteriaBuilder versions of bulk update and delete queries use the same methods for generating the FROM and WHERE clauses of the query. Methods specific to bulk update and delete operations are encapsulated in the CriteraUpdate and CriteriaDelete interfaces.

■ **Tip** Although bulk updates and deletes have existed in JP QL since JPA 1.0, support for performing bulk updates and deletes using the Criteria API was not added until JPA 2.1.

Bulk update queries in JP QL use the SET expression to change the state of entities. Mirroring this functionality, the set() method of the CriteriaUpdate query allows the developer to assign expressions constructed from the Criteria API to modify designated entity state fields. In Chapter 8, we demonstrated the following query to allocate a raise to employees associated with a specific project:

```
UPDATE Employee e
SET e.salary = e.salary + 5000
```

```
WHERE EXISTS (SELECT p
              FROM e.projects p
              WHERE p.name = 'Release2')
```

Using the Criteria API, the same query would be constructed as follows:

```
CriteriaUpdate<Employee> q = cb.createCriteriaUpdate(Employee.class);
Root<Employee> e = q.from(Employee.class);
Subquery<Project> sq = c.subquery(Project.class);
Root<Employee> sqEmp = sq.correlate(emp);
Join<Employee,Project> project = sqEmp.join("projects");
sq.select(project)
  .where(cb.equal(project.get("name"),"Release2"));
q.set(emp.get("salary"), cb.sum(emp.get("salary"), 5000))
  .where(cb.exists(sq));
```

The set() method may be invoked multiple times for the same query. It also supports the same invocation chaining capability that is used by other query methods in the Criteria API.

Bulk delete operations are very straightforward with the Criteria API. The following example converts the JP QL DELETE query example from Chapter 8 to use the Criteria API:

```
DELETE FROM Employee e
WHERE e.department IS NULL

CriteriaDelete<Employee> q = cb.createCriteriaDelete(Employee.class);
Root<Employee> emp = c.from(Employee.class);
q.where(cb.isNull(emp.get("dept")));
```

If executed, this example will remove all employees that are not assigned to any department.

Strongly Typed Query Definitions

Throughout this chapter, we have been demonstrating Criteria API query definitions constructed using string names to refer to attributes in path expressions. This subset of the Criteria API is referred to as the string-based API. We have mentioned a few times, however, that an alternative approach for constructing path expressions also existed that offered a more strongly typed approach. In the following sections, we will establish some theory around the metamodel that underlies the strongly typed approach and then demonstrate its usage with the Criteria API.

The Metamodel API

Before we look at strongly typed query definitions, we must first set the stage for our discussion with a short digression into the metamodel for persistence units in a JPA application. The *metamodel* of a persistence unit is a description of the persistent type, state, and relationships of entities, embeddables, and managed classes. With it, we can interrogate the persistence provider runtime to find out information about the classes in a persistence unit. A wide variety of information, from names to types to relationships, is stored by the persistence provider and made accessible through the metamodel API.

The metamodel API is exposed through the getMetamodel() method of the EntityManager interface. This method returns an object implementing the Metamodel interface which we can then use to begin navigating the metamodel. The Metamodel interface can be used to list the persistent classes in a persistence unit or to retrieve information about a specific persistent type.

For example, to obtain information about the `Employee` class we have been demonstrating in this chapter, we would use the `entity()` method.

```
Metamodel mm = em.getMetamodel();
EntityType<Employee> emp_ = mm.entity(Employee.class);
```

The equivalent methods for embeddables and managed classes are `embeddable()` and `managedType()`, respectively. It is important to note that the call to `entity()` in this example is not creating an instance of the `EntityType` interface. Rather it is retrieving a metamodel object that the persistence provider would have initialized when the `EntityManagerFactory` for the persistence unit was created. Had the class argument to `entity()` not been a pre-existing persistent type, an `IllegalArgumentException` would have been thrown.

The `EntityType` interface is one of many interfaces in the metamodel API that contain information about persistent types and attributes. Figure 9-2 shows the relationships between the interfaces that make up the metamodel API.

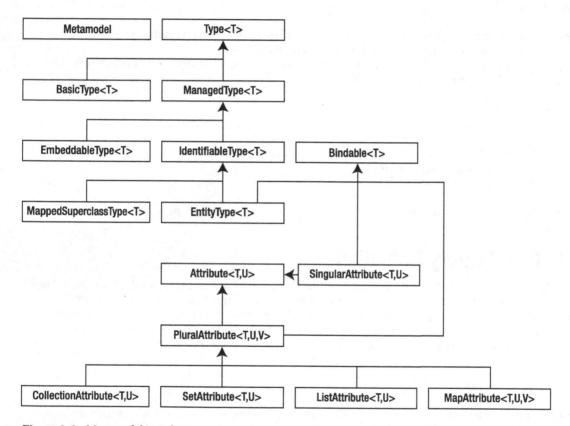

Figure 9-2. *Metamodel interfaces*

To further expand on this example, consider a tool that inspects a persistent unit and prints out summary information to the console. To enumerate all of the attributes and their types, we could use the following code:

```
public <T> void listAttributes(EntityType<T> type) {
    for (Attribute<? super T, ?> attr : type.getAttributes()) {
        System.out.println(attr.getName() + " " +
```

```
                          attr.getJavaType().getName() + " " +
                          attr.getPersistentAttributeType());
       }
}
```

For the `Employee` entity, this would result in the following:

```
id int BASIC
name java.lang.String BASIC
salary float BASIC
dept com.acme.Department MANY_TO_ONE
address com.acme.Address MANY_TO_ONE
directs com.acme.Employee ONE_TO_MANY
phones com.acme.Phone ONE_TO_MANY
projects com.acme.Project ONE_TO_MANY
```

In just a few method calls, we have uncovered a lot of information about the `Employee` entity. We have listed all of the attributes and for each one we now know the attribute name, class type, and persistent type. Collections have been unwrapped to reveal the underlying attribute type, and the various relationship types are clearly marked.

From the perspective of the Criteria API and providing strongly typed queries, we are mostly interested in the type information exposed by the metamodel API interfaces. In the next section, we will demonstrate how it can be used in that context.

The metamodel of a persistence unit is not a new concept. Previous versions of JPA have always maintained similar structures internally for use at runtime, but only with JPA 2.0 was this kind of metamodel exposed directly to developers. Direct usage of the metamodel classes is somewhat specialized, but, for tool developers or applications that need to work with a persistence unit in a completely generic way, the metamodel is a useful source of information about persistent types.

Strongly Typed API Overview

The string-based API within the Criteria API centers around constructing path expressions: `join()`, `fetch()`, and `get()` all accept string arguments. The strongly typed API within the Criteria API also supports path expressions by extending the same methods, but is also present in all aspects of the `CriteriaBuilder` interface, simplifying typing and enforcing type safety where possible.

The strongly typed API draws its type information from the metamodel API classes we introduced in the previous section. For example, the `join()` method is overloaded to accept arguments of type `SingularAttribute`, `CollectionAttribute`, `SetAttribute`, `ListAttribute`, and `MapAttribute`. Each overloaded version uses the type information associated with the attribute interface to create the appropriate return type such as `MapJoin` for arguments of type `MapAttribute`.

To demonstrate this behavior, we will revisit an example from earlier in the chapter where we were forced to use `joinMap()` with the string-based API in order to access the `MapJoin` object. This time we will use the metamodel API to obtain entity and attribute type information and pass it to the Criteria API methods.

```
CriteriaQuery<Object> c = cb.createQuery();
Root<Employee> emp = c.from(Employee.class);
EntityType<Employee> emp_ = emp.getModel();
MapJoin<Employee,String,Phone> phone =
    emp.join(emp_.getMap("phones", String.class, Phone.class));
c.multiselect(emp.get(emp_.getSingularAttribute("name", String.class)),
              phone.key(), phone.value());
```

There are several things to note about this example. First is the use of getModel(). This method exists on many of the Criteria API interfaces as a shortcut to the underlying metamodel object. We assign it to a variable, emp_, and add an underscore by convention to help denote it as a metamodel type. Second are the two calls to methods from the EntityType interface. The getMap() invocation returns the MapAttribute object for the phones attribute while the getSingularAttribute() invocation returns the SingularAttribute object for the name attribute. Again, we have to supply the type information for the attribute, partly to satisfy the generic type requirements of the method invocation but also as a type checking mechanism. Had any of the arguments been incorrect, an exception would have been thrown. Also note that the join() method no longer qualifies the collection type yet returns the correct MapJoin instance. The join() method is overloaded to behave correctly in the presence of the different collection attribute interfaces from the metamodel API.

The potential for error in using the metamodel objects is actually the heart of what makes it strongly typed. By enforcing that the type information is available, the Criteria API is able to ensure that not only are the appropriate objects being passed around as method arguments but also that compatible types are used in various expression building methods.

There is no question, however, that this is a much more verbose way of constructing a query. Fortunately, the JPA 2.0 specification also defines an alternate presentation of the persistence unit metamodel that is designed to make strongly typed programming easier. We will discuss this model in the next section.

The Canonical Metamodel

Our usage of the metamodel API so far has opened the doors to strong type checking but at the expense of readability and increased complexity. The metamodel APIs are not complex, but they are verbose. To simplify their usage, JPA also provides a *canonical metamodel* for a persistence unit.

The canonical metamodel consists of dedicated classes, typically generated, one per persistent class, that contain static declarations of the metamodel objects associated with that persistent class. This allows you to access the same information exposed through the metamodel API, but in a form that applies directly to your persistent classes. Listing 9-7 shows an example of a canonical metamodel class.

Listing 9-7. The Canonical Metamodel Class for Employee

```
@StaticMetamodel(Employee.class)
public class Employee_ {
    public static volatile SingularAttribute<Employee, Integer> id;
    public static volatile SingularAttribute<Employee, String> name;
    public static volatile SingularAttribute<Employee, String> salary;
    public static volatile SingularAttribute<Employee, Department> dept;
    public static volatile SingularAttribute<Employee, Address> address;
    public static volatile CollectionAttribute<Employee, Project> project;
    public static volatile MapAttribute<Employee, String, Phone> phones;
}
```

Each canonical metamodel class contains a series of static fields, one for each attribute in the persistent class. Each field in the canonical metamodel class is of the metamodel type that corresponds to the type of the like-named field or property in the persistent class. If a persistent field or property in an entity is of a primitive type or a single-valued relationship, then the like-named field in the canonical metamodel class will be of type SingularAttribute. Similarly, if a persistent field or property is collection-valued, then the field in the canonical metamodel class will be of type ListAttribute, SetAttribute, MapAttribute, or CollectionAttribute, depending upon the type of collection. Additionally, each canonical metamodel class is annotated with @StaticMetamodel, which identifies the persistent class it is modeling.

A canonical metamodel class is generated in the same package as its associated persistent class and has the same name, but with an additional underscore suffix. Non-canonical metamodel classes may be generated in other packages and with different names if there is a need to do so. Some generation tools may provide these kinds of options. The @StaticMetamodel annotation provides the binding between the metamodel class and the entity, not the name or package, so there is no standard way of reading in such metamodels. If a provider tool can generate the concrete metamodel classes in some non-canonical form, then that runtime might be needed to recognize or detect them as well.

Using the Canonical Metamodel

We are now in the position of being able to leverage the metamodel without actually using the metamodel API. As an example, we can convert the example from the previous section to use the statically generated canonical classes.

```
CriteriaQuery<Object> c = cb.createQuery();
Root<Employee> emp = c.from(Employee.class);
MapJoin<Employee,String,Phone> phone = emp.join(Employee_.phones);
c.multiselect(emp.get(Employee_.name), phone.key(), phone.value());
```

This is a much more concise approach to using the metamodel objects than the interfaces we discussed earlier while offering the exact same benefits. Coupled with a development environment that has good code completion features, you may find it more convenient to develop using the canonical metamodel than with the string-based API.

We can convert a more complex example to illustrate using the canonical metamodel. Listing 9-8 converts the example in Listing 9-6, showing an IN expression that uses a subquery, from using the string-based attribute names to using the strongly typed approach.

Listing 9-8. Strongly Typed Query

```
CriteriaQuery<Employee> c = cb.createQuery(Employee.class);
Root<Employee> emp = c.from(Employee.class);
Subquery<Department> sq = c.subquery(Department.class);
Root<Department> dept = sq.from(Department.class);
Join<Employee,Project> project =
    dept.join(Department_.employees).join(Employee_.projects);
sq.select(dept.get(Department_.id))
  .distinct(true)
  .where(cb.like(project.get(Project_.name), "QA%"));
c.select(emp)
  .where(cb.in(emp.get(Employee_.dept).get(Department_.id)).value(sq));
```

Note that there are two main differences between this example and Listing 9-6. First, the use of typed metamodel static fields to indicate entity attributes helps avert typing errors in attribute strings. Second, there is no longer the need to do inlined typing to convert the Path<Object>, returned from the get() method, to a narrower type. The stronger typing solves that problem for us.

All the examples in this chapter can be easily converted to use the canonical metamodel classes by simply changing the string-based attributes to the corresponding static fields of the generated metamodel classes. For example, emp.get("name") can be replaced with emp.get(Employee_.name), and so on.

Generating the Canonical Metamodel

If you choose to use the generated metamodel in your queries, you should be aware of some of the details of the development process in case inconsistency or configuration issues crop up. The canonical metamodel classes will need to be updated or regenerated when certain changes to entities have occurred during development. For example, changing the name of a field or property, or changing its shape, would require an updated canonical metamodel class for that entity.

The generation tools offered by providers may vary widely in function or in operation. Generation may involve reading the persistence.xml file, as well as accessing annotations on entities and XML mapping files to determine what the metamodel classes should look like. Since the specification does not require such tools to even exist, a provider may choose to not support it at all, expecting that if developers want to use the canonical metamodel classes they will handcode them. Most providers do offer some kind of generation tool, though; it's just a matter of understanding how that vendor-specific tool works. It might run statically as a separate command line tool, or it might use the compiler hook offered in the JDK (starting in Java SE 6) to look at the entities and generate the classes at compile-time. For example, to run the command line mode of the tool shipped with the EclipseLink Reference Implementation, you could set the javac -processor and -proc:only options. These two options indicate the EclipseLink code/annotation processor[1] for the compiler to invoke, and instruct the compiler to call only the processor but not do any actual compilation.

```
javac -processor org.eclipse.persistence.internal.jpa.modelgen.CanonicalModelProcessor
      -proc:only
      -classpath lib/*.jar;punit
      *.java
```

The options are on separate lines to make them easier to see. It is assumed that the lib directory contains the necessary EclipseLink JAR and JPA interface JAR, and that the META-INF/persistence.xml is in the punit directory.

Metamodel generation tools will also typically run in an IDE, and there will likely be IDE-specific configuration necessary to direct the incremental compiler to use the tool's annotation processor. In some IDEs, there must be an additional code/annotation processor JAR to configure. The generated metamodel classes will need to go in a specific directory and be on the build classpath so the criteria queries that reference them can compile. Consult the IDE help files on how annotation processors or APT is supported, as well as the provider documentation on what to configure in order to enable generation in a given IDE.

Choosing the Right Type of Query

Now that you are familiar with criteria queries, you are well armed with two of the three distinct languages in which to create queries: JP QL, native SQL, and the Criteria API. We have demonstrated that the Criteria API is relatively easy to understand and use, but when should it be used? The answer is a combination of your own preferences as a developer and the capabilities of the different query approaches.

Native SQL queries are an easy choice to make: either you need to access a vendor-specific feature or you don't. If you do, there is only one option available if you can't work around the dependency. You discovered in this chapter that JP QL and the Criteria API are almost completely equivalent in functionality. When should you use a text-based query definition over one created from programming APIs?

The programming API flows smoothly from the application. It can be strongly typed to reduce the chance of errors, and with the code completion features of most modern development environments it can be relatively quick to put together. It is also ideal for cases where the query definition can't be fully constructed with the input of a user.

---

[1]This is often referred to as an annotation processing tool, or APT, because it used to be a standalone tool shipped with the JDK and used only for processing annotations. Since Java SE 6, it is actually a generalized compile-time hook to perform any kind of pre-processing or code generation.

JP QL, on the other hand, is more concise and familiar to anyone experienced with SQL. It can also be embedded with the application annotations or XML descriptors and maintained independently of the regular programming process. Some development environments also offer visual builders for JP QL queries, making it a seamless part of the development process.

There is no right answer when it comes to choosing between JP QL and the Criteria API. They can be mixed and matched within an application as you see fit. In general, however, we still encourage developers to use named queries as much as possible, and, for this, JP QL is the ideal choice.

Summary

In this chapter we have taken a tour of the Criteria API. We started with an overview and example focused on dynamic query creation.

In investigating the Criteria API, we started with JP QL concepts and sought to draw parallels between the query language and the Criteria API. We looked at how to formulate each clause of a query with the Criteria API and addressed some of the more complex issues that developers encounter.

We introduced the metamodel API and showed how it can be used to create strongly typed queries with the Criteria API. We looked at programming with the metamodel API using both runtime interfaces and through the generated classes of a canonical metamodel implementation.

Finally we discussed the advantages of the different approaches to building queries using JP QL, native SQL, and the Criteria API. We highlighted some of the strengths of the query languages and presented some advice on when one might be more beneficial. We reiterated that the right query language for you will mostly come down to style and personal preference.

Over the course of the chapter, we have tried to demonstrate that although the form of the Criteria API is very different from the JP QL query language, the underlying semantics are almost identical and switching between the two is relatively easy once you get the hang of the API coding patterns.

In the next chapter we switch back to object-relational mapping and cover advanced concepts such as inheritance, composite primary keys and associations, and multiple table mappings.

■ ■ ■

CHAPTER 10

Advanced Object-Relational Mapping

Every application is different, and, while most have some elements of complexity in them, the difficult parts in one application will tend to be different than those in other types of applications. Chances are that whichever application you are working on at any given time will need to make use of at least one advanced feature of the API. This chapter will introduce and explain some of these more advanced ORM features.

Many of the features in this chapter are targeted at applications that need to reconcile the differences between an existing data model and an object model. For example, when the data in an entity table would be better decomposed in the object model as an entity and a dependent object that is referenced by the entity, then the mapping infrastructure should be able to support that. Likewise, when the entity data is spread across multiple tables, the mapping layer should allow for this kind of configuration to be specified.

There has been no shortage of discussion in this book about how entities in JPA are just regular Java classes and not special objects that are required to extend a specific subclass or implement special methods. One of the benefits of entities being regular Java classes is that they can adhere to already established concepts and practices that exist in object-oriented systems. One of the traditional object-oriented innovations is the use of inheritance and creating objects in a hierarchy in order to inherit state and behavior.

This chapter will discuss some of the more advanced mapping features and delve into the diverse possibilities offered by the API and the mapping layer. We will also see how inheritance works within the framework of the Java Persistence API and how it affects the model.

Table and Column Names

In previous sections, we have shown the names of tables and columns as uppercase identifiers. We did this, first, because it helps differentiate them from Java identifiers and, second, because the SQL standard defines that undelimited database identifiers do not respect case, and most tend to display them in uppercase.

Anywhere a table or column name is specified, or is defaulted, the identifier string is passed through to the JDBC driver exactly as it is specified, or defaulted. For example, when no table name is specified for the Employee entity, then the name of the table assumed and used by the provider will be Employee, which by SQL definition is no different from EMPLOYEE. The provider is neither required nor expected to do anything to try to adjust the identifiers before passing them to the database driver.

The following annotations should, therefore, be equivalent in that they refer to the same table in a SQL standard compliant database:

```
@Table(name="employee")
@Table(name="Employee")
@Table(name="EMPLOYEE")
```

Some database names are intended to be case-specific and must be explicitly delimited. For example, a table might be called EmployeeSales, but without case distinction would become EMPLOYEESALES, clearly less readable and harder to ascertain its meaning. While it is by no means common, or good practice, a database in theory could have an EMPLOYEE table as well as an Employee table. These would need to be delimited in order to distinguish between the two. The method of delimiting is the use of a second set of double quotes, which must be escaped, around the identifier. The escaping mechanism is the backslash (the \ character), which would cause the following annotations to refer to different tables:

```
@Table(name="\"Employee\"")
@Table(name="\"EMPLOYEE\"")
```

Notice that the outer set of double quotes is just the usual delimiter of strings in annotation elements, but the inner double quotes are preceded by the backslash to cause them to be escaped, indicating that they are part of the string, not string terminators.

When using an XML mapping file, the identifier is also delimited by including quotes in the identifier name. For example, the following two elements represent different columns:

```
<column name="&quot;ID&quot;"/>
<column name="&quot;Id&quot;"/>
```

The method of XML escaping is different than the one used in Java. Instead of using the backslash, XML escapes with an ampersand (&) character followed by a word describing the specific thing being escaped (in this case, "quot") and finally a trailing semicolon (;) character.

■ **Tip**   Some vendors support features to normalize the case of the identifiers that are stored and passed back and forth between the provider and the JDBC driver. This works around certain JDBC drivers that, for example, accept uppercase identifiers in the native SQL query select statement, but pass them back mapped to lowercase identifiers.

Sometimes the database is set to use case-specific identifiers, and it would become rather tedious (and look exceedingly ugly) to have to put the extra quotes on every single table and column name. If you find yourself in that situation, there is a convenience setting in the XML mapping file that will be of value to you.

By including the empty delimited-identifiers element in the XML mapping file, all identifiers in the persistence unit will be treated as delimited, and quotes will be added to them when they are passed to the driver. The only catch is that there is no way to override this setting. Once the delimited-identifiers flag is turned on, all identifiers must be specified exactly as they exist in the database. Furthermore, if you decide to turn on the delimited-identifiers option, make sure you remove any escaped quotes in your identifier names or you will find that they will be included in the name. Using escaping in addition to the delimited identifiers option will take the escaped quotes and wrap them with further quotes, making the escaped ones become part of the identifier.

Converting Entity State

Back in Chapter 4 we showed some of the ways that specific kinds of data, such as enumerated types, temporal types, and large objects, can be stored in the database. However, it would be impractical to define targeted support for each and every kind of data that is not a primitive, particularly because there will always be some application that wants to store the data in a new and different way, or is forced to do so because of a legacy database. Furthermore, an application might define its own set of types that the specification could clearly never predict. A more flexible and scalable solution, therefore, is to devise a way that enables the application to define its own conversion strategy for whatever type it deems necessary to convert. This is made possible through the use of converters.

■ **Note**   Converters were added to the JPA 2.1 specification.

Creating a Converter

A converter is a application-specified class that implements the `AttributeConverter<X,Y>` interface. It can be declaratively applied to persistent attributes in any entity, mapped superclass, or embeddable class to control how the state of the attribute is stored in the database. It similarly defines how the state is converted from the database back into the object. These two conversion operations comprise the two methods of the `AttributeConverter<X,Y>` interface, shown in Listing 10-1.

Listing 10-1. AttributeConverter Interface

```
public interface AttributeConverter<X,Y> {

    public Y convertToDatabaseColumn (X attribute);

    public X convertToEntityAttribute (Y dbData);
}
```

Note that the interface should be defined with two type parameters. The first type parameter represents the type of the entity attribute while the second represents the JDBC type to be used when storing the data in the database column. A sample converter implementation class is shown in Listing 10-2. It illustrates a simple converter needed to store a boolean entity attribute as an integer in the database.

Listing 10-2. Boolean-to-Integer Converter

```
@Converter
public class BooleanToIntegerConverter  implements AttributeConverter<Boolean,Integer> {

    public Integer convertToDatabaseColumn (Boolean attrib) {
        return (attrib ? 1 : 0);
    }

    public Boolean convertToEntityAttribute (Integer dbData) {
        return (dbData > 0)
    }
}
```

■ **Note**   There is currently only support to convert an entity attribute to a single column in the database. The ability to store it across multiple columns may be standardized in a future release.

The converter class is annotated so that the container can detect and validate it. The conversion methods are trivial in this case because the conversion process is such a simple one, but the conversion logic could be more extensive if more was needed.

Converters can be used for explicit or automatic conversion of basic state, as the following sections describe.

■ **Note**   Converters are *managed classes*, hence when running in Java SE each converter class should be included in a `class` element in the `persistence.xml` descriptor.

Declarative Attribute Conversion

A converter can be used explicitly to convert an entity attribute by annotating the attribute with `@Convert` and setting the converter element to the converter class. For example, if we had a `Boolean` attribute named "bonded" in our `Employee` entity, it could be converted to an `Integer` in the mapped database column if we annotated the attribute with `@Convert` and specified the converter class declared in the previous section:

```
@Convert(converter=BooleanToIntegerConverter.class)
private Boolean bonded;
```

The attribute being converted should be of the correct type. Since the first parameterized type of the converter is `Boolean`, the attribute we are converting should be of type `Boolean`. However, wrapper and primitive types are autoboxed during conversion, so the attribute could also have been of type `boolean`.

Converting Embedded Attributes

If the attribute to be converted is part of an embeddable type and we are converting it from within a referencing entity, then we use the `attributeName` element to specify the attribute to convert. For example, if the bonded attribute from above was contained within a `SecurityInfo` embeddable object and the `Employee` entity had a `securityInfo` attribute, then we could convert it as in Listing 10-3:

Listing 10-3. Converting an Embedded Attribute

```
@Entity
public class Employee {
    // ...
    @Convert(converter=BooleanToIntegerConverter.class, attributeName="bonded")
    private SecurityInfo securityInfo;
    // ...
}

@Embeddable
public class SecurityInfo {
    private Boolean bonded;
    // ...
}
```

In the "Complex Embedded Objects" section later in this chapter we will describe more advanced usages of embeddables; in particular, the dot notation will be shown as a means to override nested embeddables. This same notation may also be used in the `attributeName` of the `@Convert` annotation to reference a nested embedded attribute.

Converting Collections

In Chapter 5 we showed that collections may be mapped as element collections if the values are a basic or embeddable type, or mapped as one-to-many or many-to-many relationships if the values are an entity type. Converters may be applied to element collections but since converters do not convert entity instances they may not, in general, be applied to relationship mappings.[1]

Element collections of basic types are simple to convert. They are annotated the same way as basic attributes that are not collections. Thus, if we had an attribute that was of type List<Boolean>, we would annotate it just as we did our bonded attribute above, and all of the boolean values in the collection would be converted:

```
@ElementCollection
@Convert(converter=BooleanToIntegerConverter.class)
private List<Boolean> securityClearances;
```

If an element collection is a Map with values that are of a basic type, then the values of the Map will be converted. To perform conversion on the keys, the attributeName element should be used with a special value of "key" to indicate that the keys of the Map are to be converted instead of the values.

Recall from the "Overriding Embeddable Attributes" section in Chapter 5 that if we had an element collection that was a Map, and it contained embeddables, then we prefixed the name element of @AttributeOverride with "key." or "value". This was to distinguish whether we were overriding the column for an embeddable key or value of the Map. Similarly, if we want to convert an embeddable attribute in a Map, then we would prefix the attributeName element with "key." or "value." followed by the name of the embeddable attribute to be converted. As a special case, we can use the "key" or "key." prefix on either of the one-to-many or many-to-many collection relationships to map the keys if they are basic or embeddable types, respectively. Using the domain model in Listing 5-17, if we wanted to convert the employee last name to be stored as uppercase characters (assuming we have defined the corresponding converter class), we would annotate the attribute as shown in Listing 10-4:

Listing 10-4. Converting an Embeddable Attribute Key in a Relationship Map

```
@Entity
public class Department {
    // ...
    @ManyToMany
    @Convert(converter=UpperCaseConverter.class, attributeName="key.lastName")
    private Map<EmployeeName, Employee> employees;
    // ...
}
```

Limitations

There are a few restrictions placed on converters, mostly to prevent users from doing things that would get them into trouble. For instance, converters cannot be used on identifier attributes, version attributes, or relationship attributes (unless you are converting the key part of a relationship Map, as in Listing 10-4). Hopefully this will not come as a surprise to you, since in most cases converting these types of attributes would arguably be a pretty bad idea. These attributes are heavily used by the provider as it manages the entities; changing their shape or even their value could cause inconsistencies or incorrect results.

Converters also cannot be used on attributes annotated with @Enumerated or @Temporal, but that doesn't mean you can't convert enumerated types or temporal types. It just means that if you use the standard @Enumerated or @Temporal annotations to map those types, then you also cannot use custom converters. If you are using a custom

---

[1]Except in the case described later in this section.

converter class, then you are taking over control of the value that gets stored and there is no need for you to use any of those annotations to get the JPA provider to do the conversion for you. Put simply, if you are doing custom conversion using converters on enumerated or temporal types, just leave the @Enumerated or @Temporal annotations off.

Automatic Conversion

When we defined a converter to convert a boolean to an integer, we likely had in mind that it would be used in very specific places, on one or possibly a few attributes. You generally don't want to convert every boolean attribute in your domain to an integer. However, if you frequently use a more semantically rich data type, such as the URL class, then you might want every attribute of that type to be converted. You can do this by setting the autoApply option on the @Converter annotation. In Listing 10-5, a URL converter is declared with the autoApply option enabled. This will cause every persistent attribute of type URL in the persistence unit to be converted to a string when the entity that contains it is written to the database.

Listing 10-5. URL-to-String Converter

```
@Converter(autoApply=true)
public class URLConverter implements AttributeConverter<URL,String> {

    public String convertToDatabaseColumn (URL attrib) {
        return attrib.toString();
    }

    public URL convertToEntityAttribute (String dbData) {
        return new URL(dbData);
    }
}
```

■ **Note**   It is undefined if two converters are declared to be auto-applied to the same attribute type.

We can override the conversion on a per-attribute basis. If, instead of the auto-applied converter, we want to use a different converter for a given attribute, then we can annotate the attribute with the @Convert annotation and specify the converter class we want to use. Alternatively, if we want to disable the conversion altogether and let the provider revert to serialization of the URL, then we can use the disableConversion attribute:

```
@Convert(disableConversion=true)
URL homePage;
```

Converters and Queries

Defining the converters and configuring which attributes to convert is pretty much all you need to do to get conversion to work. But there are a couple of additional points related to conversion that you should be aware of when querying.

The first is that the query processor will apply the converter to both the attributes targeted for conversion as well as the literals they are being compared against in a query. However, the operators are not modified. This means that only certain comparison operators will work once the query is converted. To illustrate this point, consider the following query:

```
SELECT e FROM Employee e WHERE e.bonded = true
```

This query will work fine if bonded is set to be converted from boolean to integer. The generated SQL will have converted both the bonded attribute and the literal "true" to the corresponding integer by invoking the convertToDatabaseColumn() method on it and the equals operator will work just as well on integers as it does on booleans.

However, we may want to query for all of the employees who are not bonded:

```
SELECT e FROM Employee e WHERE NOT e.bonded
```

If we try to execute this query the parser will have no problem with it, but when it comes time to execute it the resulting SQL will contain a NOT and the value of e.bonded will have been converted to be an integer. This will generally cause a database exception since the NOT operation cannot be applied to an integer.

It is possible that you will bump into an issue or two if you do any significant querying across converted attributes. While you can usually rely on conversion of literals and input parameters used in comparison, if they are contained within a function, such as UPPER() or MOD(), they probably will not be converted. Even some of the more advanced comparison operations, such as LIKE, may not apply conversion to the literal operand. The moral is to try not to use converted attributes in queries, and if you do, play around and do some experimenting to make sure your queries work as expected.

Complex Embedded Objects

In Chapter 4, we looked at embedding objects within entities, and how an embedded object becomes part of, and dependent upon, the entity that embeds it. We will now explain how more can be done with embedded objects, and how they can contain more than just basic mappings.

Advanced Embedded Mappings

Embedded objects can embed other objects, have element collections of basic or embeddable types, and have relationships to entities. This is all possible under the assumption that objects embedded within other embedded objects are still dependent upon the embedding entity. Similarly, when bidirectional relationships exist within an embedded object, they are treated as though they exist in the owning entity, and the target entity points back to the owning entity, not to the embedded object.

As an example, let's bring back our Employee and embedded Address objects from Chapter 4 and update the model just a little bit. Insert a ContactInfo object, containing the address plus the phone information, into each employee. Instead of having an address attribute, our Employee entity would now have an attribute named contactInfo, of type ContactInfo, annotated with @Embedded. The model is shown in Figure 10-1.

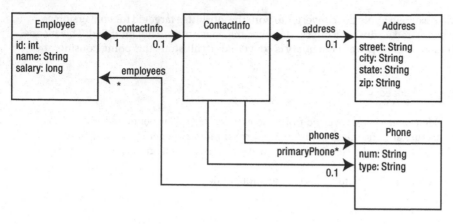

Figure 10-1. *Nested embeddables with relationships*

The ContactInfo class contains an embedded object, as well as some relationships, and would be annotated as shown in Listing 10-6.

Listing 10-6. Embeddable ContactInfo Class

```
@Embeddable @Access(AccessType.FIELD)
public class ContactInfo {
    @Embedded
    private Address residence;

    @ManyToOne
    @JoinColumn(name="PRI_NUM")
    private Phone primaryPhone;

    @ManyToMany @MapKey(name="type")
    @JoinTable(name="EMP_PHONES")
    private Map<String, Phone> phones;
    // ...
}
```

The Address class remains the same as in Listing 4-26, but we have added more depth to our contact information. Within the ContactInfo embeddable, we have the address as a nested embedded object, but we also have an additional unidirectional relationship to the phone number serving as the primary contact number. A bidirectional many-to-many relationship to the employee's phone numbers would have a default join table named EMPLOYEE_PHONE, and on the Phone side the relationship attribute would refer to a list of Employee instances, with the mappedBy element being the qualified name of the embedded relationship attribute. By qualified, we mean that it must first contain the attribute within Employee that contains the embeddable, as well as a dot separator character (.) and the relationship attribute within the embeddable. Listing 10-7 shows the Phone class and its mapping back to the Employee entity.

Listing 10-7. Phone Class Referring To Embedded Attribute

```
@Entity
public class Phone {
    @Id private String num;
```

```
@ManyToMany(mappedBy="contactInfo.phones")
private List<Employee> employees;

private String type;
// ...
}
```

A proviso about embeddable types is that if an embedded object is a part of an element collection, then the embedded object in the collection can only include mappings where the foreign key is stored in the source table. It can contain owned relationships, such as one-to-one and many-to-one, but it cannot contain one-to-many or many-to-many relationships where the foreign key is in either the target table or a join table. Similarly, it can't contain other collection table-based mappings like element collections.

Overriding Embedded Relationships

When we first introduced embeddables back in Chapter 4, we showed how embeddable types could be reused by being embedded within multiple entity classes. Even though the state is mapped within the embeddable, the embedding entity can override those mappings by using @AttributeOverride to redefine how the embedded state is mapped within that particular entity table. Now that we are using relationships within embeddables, @AttributeOverride does not suffice. To override how a relationship is mapped, we need to use @AssociationOverride, which provides us with the ability to override relationship join columns and join tables.

Before we look at an example of overriding an embeddable with a relationship in it, let's first think about the reusability of such an object. If a relationship from entity A to entity B is defined within the embeddable of type E, then either the relationship is owned by A and the foreign key is in the table corresponding to A (or in a join table owned by A), or it is owned by B and the foreign key is going to be in B's table (or a join table owned by B). If it is owned by B, then the foreign key will be to A's table, and there would be no way to use E in any other entity because the foreign key would be to the wrong table. Similarly, if the relationship was bidirectional, then the attribute in B would be of type A (or a collection of A) and could not refer to an object of some other type. It can be understood, therefore, that only embeddables with relationships that are owned by the source entity, A, and that are unidirectional, can be reused in other entities.

Suppose the many-to-many relationship in ContactInfo was unidirectional and Phone didn't have a reference back to the Employee that embedded the ContactInfo. We might want to embed instances of ContactInfo within a Customer entity as well. The CUSTOMER table, however, might have a PRI_CONTACT foreign key column instead of PRI_NUM, and of course we would not be able to share the same join table for both Employee and Customer relationships to the Phone. The resulting Customer class is shown in Listing 10-8.

Listing 10-8. Customer Class Embedding ContactInfo

```
@Entity
public class Customer {
    @Id int id;

    @Embedded
    @AttributeOverride(name="address.zip", column=@Column(name="ZIP"))
    @AssociationOverrides({
        @AssociationOverride(name="primaryPhone",
                             joinColumns=@JoinColumn(name="EMERG_PHONE")),
```

```
        @AssociationOverride(name="phones",
                             joinTable=@JoinTable(name="CUST_PHONE"))})
    private ContactInfo contactInfo;

    // ...
}
```

We can override the `zip` attribute in the address that is embedded within `contactInfo` by using `@AttributeOverride` and navigating to the attribute in the nested embedded `Address` object.

Because we are overriding two associations we need to use the plural variant of `@AssociationOverrides`. Note that if there had not been a join table explicitly specified for the phones attribute, then the default join table name would have been different depending upon which entity was embedding the `ContactInfo`. Since the default name is composed partly of the name of the owning entity, the table joining the `Employee` entity to the `Phone` entity would have defaulted to `EMPLOYEE_PHONE`, whereas in `Customer` the join table would have defaulted to `CUSTOMER_PHONE`.

■ **Tip**   There is currently no way to override the collection table for an element collection in an embeddable.

Compound Primary Keys

In some cases, an entity needs to have a primary key or identifier that is composed of multiple fields, or from the database perspective the primary key in its table is made up of multiple columns. This is more common for legacy databases and also occurs when a primary key is composed of a relationship, a topic that we will discuss later in this chapter.

There are two options available for having compound primary keys in an entity, depending on how the entity class is structured. Both of them require the use of a separate class containing the primary key fields called a primary key class; the difference between the two options is determined by what the entity class contains.

Primary key classes must include method definitions for `equals()` and `hashCode()` in order to be able to be stored and keyed on by the persistence provider, and their fields or properties must be in the set of valid identifier types listed in the previous chapter. They must also be public, implement `Serializable`, and have a no-arg constructor.

As an example of a compound primary key, we will look at the `Employee` entity again, only this time the employee number is specific to the country where he works. Two employees in different countries can have the same employee number, but only one can be used within any given country. Figure 10-2 shows the `EMPLOYEE` table structured with a compound primary key to capture this requirement. Given this table definition, we will now look at how to map the `Employee` entity using the two different styles of primary key class.

EMPLOYEE	
PK PK	COUNTRY EMP_ID
	NAME SALARY

Figure 10-2. EMPLOYEE table with a compound primary key

Id Class

The first and most basic type of primary key class is an id class. Each field of the entity that makes up the primary key is marked with the @Id annotation. The primary key class is defined separately and associated with the entity by using the @IdClass annotation on the entity class definition. Listing 10-9 demonstrates an entity with a compound primary key that uses an id class. The accompanying id class is shown in Listing 10-10.

Listing 10-9. Using an Id Class

```
@Entity
@IdClass(EmployeeId.class)
public class Employee {
    @Id private String country;
    @Id
    @Column(name="EMP_ID")
    private int id;
    private String name;
    private long salary;
    // ...
}
```

The primary key class must contain fields or properties that match the primary key attributes in the entity in both name and type. Listing 10-10 shows the EmployeeId primary key class. It has two fields, one to represent the country and one to represent the employee number. We have also supplied equals() and hashCode() methods to allow the class to be used in sorting and hashing operations.

Listing 10-10. The EmployeeId Id Class

```
public class EmployeeId implements Serializable {
    private String country;
    private int id;

    public EmployeeId() {}
    public EmployeeId(String country, int id) {
      this.country = country;
      this.id = id;
    }

    public String getCountry() { return country; }
    public int getId() { return id; }

    public boolean equals(Object o) {
        return ((o instanceof EmployeeId) &&
                country.equals(((EmployeeId)o).getCountry()) &&
                id == ((EmployeeId)o).getId());
    }

    public int hashCode() {
        return country.hashCode() + id;
    }
}
```

Note that there are no setter methods on the EmployeeId class. Once it has been constructed using the primary key values, it can't be changed. We do this to enforce the notion that a primary key value cannot be changed, even when it is made up of multiple fields. Because the @Id annotation was placed on the fields of the entity, the provider will also use field access when it needs to work with the primary key class.

The id class is useful as a structured object that encapsulates all of the primary key information. For example, when doing a query based upon the primary key, such as the find() method of the EntityManager interface, an instance of the id class can be used as an argument instead of some unstructured and unordered collection of primary key data. Listing 10-11 shows a code snippet that searches for an Employee with a given country name and employee number. A new instance of the EmployeeId class is constructed using the method arguments and then used as the argument to the find() method.

Listing 10-11. Invoking a Primary Key Query on an Entity with an Id Class

```
EmployeeId id = new EmployeeId(country, id);
Employee emp = em.find(Employee.class, id);
```

■ **Tip** Because the argument to find() is of type Object, vendors can support passing in simple arrays or collections of primary key information. Passing arguments that are not primary key classes is not portable.

Embedded Id Class

An entity that contains a single field of the same type as the primary key class is said to use an embedded id class. The embedded id class is just an embedded object that happens to be composed of the primary key components. We use an @EmbeddedId annotation to indicate that it is not just a regular embedded object but also a primary key class. When we use this approach, there are no @Id annotations on the class, nor is the @IdClass annotation used. You can think of @EmbeddedId as the logical equivalent to putting both @Id and @Embedded on the field.

Like other embedded objects, the embedded id class must be annotated with @Embeddable, but the access type might differ from that of the entity that uses it. Listing 10-12 shows the EmployeeId class again, this time as an embeddable primary key class. The getter methods, equals() and hashCode() implementations are the same as the previous version from Listing 10-10.

Listing 10-12. Embeddable Primary Key Class

```
@Embeddable
public class EmployeeId {
    private String country;
    @Column(name="EMP_ID")
    private int id;

    public EmployeeId() {}
    public EmployeeId(String country, int id) {
        this.country = country;
        this.id = id;
    }

    // ...
}
```

Using the embedded primary key class is no different than using a regular embedded type, except that the annotation used on the attribute is @EmbeddedId instead of @Embedded. Listing 10-13 shows the Employee entity adjusted to use the embedded version of the EmployeeId class. Note that since the column mappings are present on the embedded type, we do not specify the mapping for EMP_ID as was done in the case of the id class. If the embedded primary key class is used by more than one entity, then the @AttributeOverride annotation can be used to customize mappings just as you would for a regular embedded type. To return the country and id attributes of the primary key from getter methods, we must delegate to the embedded id object to obtain the values.

Listing 10-13. Using an Embedded Id Class

```
@Entity
public class Employee {
    @EmbeddedId private EmployeeId id;
    private String name;
    private long salary;

    public Employee() {}
    public Employee(String country, int id) {
        this.id = new EmployeeId(country, id);
    }

    public String getCountry() { return id.getCountry(); }
    public int getId() { return id.getId(); }
    // ...
}
```

We can create an instance of EmployeeId and pass it to the find() method just as we did for the id class example, but, if we want to create the same query using JP QL and reference the primary key, we have to traverse the embedded id class explicitly. Listing 10-14 shows this technique. Even though id is not a relationship, we still traverse it using the dot notation in order to access the members of the embedded class.

Listing 10-14. Referencing an Embedded Id Class in a Query

```
public Employee findEmployee(String country, int id) {
    return (Employee)
        em.createQuery("SELECT e " +
                       "FROM Employee e " +
                       "WHERE e.id.country = ?1 AND e.id.id = ?2")
          .setParameter(1, country)
          .setParameter(2, id)
          .getSingleResult();
}
```

The decision to use a single embedded identifier attribute or a group of identifier attributes, each mapped separately in the entity class, mostly comes down to personal preference. Some people like to encapsulate the identifier components into a single entity attribute of the embedded identifier class type. The trade-off is that it makes dereferencing a part of the identifier a little bit longer in code or in JP QL, although having helper methods, like those in Listing 10-13, can help.

If you access or set parts of the identifier individually, then it might make more sense to create a separate entity attribute for each of the constituent identifier parts. This presents a more representative model and interface for the separate identifier components. However, if most of the time you reference and pass around the entire identifier as an object, then you might be better off with an embedded identifier that creates and stores a single instance of the composite identifier.

Derived Identifiers

When an identifier in one entity includes a foreign key to another entity, it's called a derived identifier. Because the entity containing the derived identifier depends upon another entity for its identity, the first is called the dependent entity. The entity that it depends upon is the target of a many-to-one or one-to-one relationship from the dependent entity, and is called the parent entity. Figure 10-3 shows an example of a data model for the two kinds of entities, with DEPARTMENT table representing the parent entity and PROJECT table representing the dependent entity. Note that in this example there is an additional name primary key column in PROJECT, meaning that the corresponding Project entity has an identifier attribute that is not part of its relationship to Department.

The dependent object cannot exist without a primary key, and since that primary key consists of the foreign key to the parent entity it should be clear that a new dependent entity cannot be persisted without the relationship to the parent entity being established. It is undefined to modify the primary key of an existing entity, thus the one-to-one

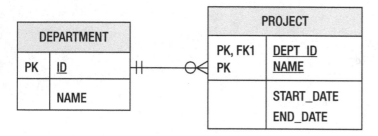

Figure 10-3. *Dependent and parent entity tables*

or many-to-one relationship that is part of a derived identifier is likewise immutable and must not be reassigned to a new entity once the dependent entity has been persisted or already exists.

We spent the last few sections discussing different kinds of identifiers, and you might think back to what you learned and realize that there are a number of different parameters that might affect how a derived identifier can be configured. For example, the identifier in either of the entities might be composed of one or a plurality of attributes. The relationship from the dependent entity to the parent entity might make up the entire derived identifier, or, as in Figure 10-3, there might be additional state in the dependent entity that contributes to it. One of the entities might have a simple or compound primary key, and in the compound case might have an id class or an embedded id class. All of these factors combine to produce a multitude of scenarios, each of which requires slightly different configurations. The basic rules for derived identifiers are outlined first, with some more detailed descriptions in the following sections.

Basic Rules for Derived Identifiers

Most of the rules for derived identifiers can be summarized in a few general statements, although applying the rules together might not be quite as easy. We will go through some of the cases later to explain them, and even show an exception case or two to keep it interesting, but to lay the groundwork for those use cases the rules can be laid out as follows:

- A dependent entity might have multiple parent entities (i.e., a derived identifier might include multiple foreign keys).

- A dependent entity must have all its relationships to parent entities set before it can be persisted.

- If an entity class has multiple id attributes, then not only must it use an id class, but there must also be a corresponding attribute of the same name in the id class as each of the id attributes in the entity.

- Id attributes in an entity might be of a simple type, or of an entity type that is the target of a many-to-one or one-to-one relationship.

- If an id attribute in an entity is of a simple type, then the type of the matching attribute in the id class must be of the same simple type.

- If an id attribute in an entity is a relationship, then the type of the matching attribute in the id class is of the same type as the primary key type of the target entity in the relationship (whether the primary key type is a simple type, an id class, or an embedded id class).

- If the derived identifier of a dependent entity is in the form of an embedded id class, then each attribute of that id class that represents a relationship should be referred to by a @MapsId annotation on the corresponding relationship attribute.

The following sections describe how these rules may be applied.

Shared Primary Key

A simple, if somewhat less common case, is when the derived identifier is composed of a single attribute that is the relationship foreign key. As an example, suppose there was a bidirectional one-to-one relationship between Employee and EmployeeHistory entities. Because there is only ever one EmployeeHistory per Employee, we might decide to share the primary key. In Listing 10-15, if the EmployeeHistory is the dependent entity, then we indicate that the relationship foreign key is the identifier by annotating the relationship with @Id.

Listing 10-15. Derived Identifier with Single Attribute

```
@Entity
public class EmployeeHistory {
    // ...
    @Id
    @OneToOne
    @JoinColumn(name="EMP_ID")
    private Employee employee;
    // ...
}
```

The primary key type of EmployeeHistory is going to be of the same type as Employee, so if Employee has a simple integer identifier then the identifier of EmployeeHistory is also going to be an integer. If Employee has a compound primary key, either with an id class or an embedded id class, then EmployeeHistory is going to share the same id class (and should also be annotated with the @IdClass annotation). The problem is that this trips over the id class rule that there should be a matching attribute in the entity for each attribute in its id class. This is the exception to the rule, because of the very fact that the id class is shared between both parent and dependent entities.

Occasionally, somebody might want the entity to contain a primary key attribute as well as the relationship attribute, with both attributes mapped to the same foreign key column in the table. Even though the primary key attribute is unnecessary in the entity, some people might want to define it separately for easier access. Despite the fact that the two attributes map to the same foreign key column (which is also the primary key column), the mapping does not have to be duplicated in both places. The @Id annotation is placed on the identifier attribute and @MapsId annotates the relationship attribute to indicate that it is mapping the id attribute as well. This is shown in Listing 10-16. Note that physical mapping annotations (e.g. @Column) should not be specified on the empId attribute since @MapsId is indicating that the relationship attribute is where the mapping occurs.

Listing 10-16. Derived Identifier with Shared Mappings

```
@Entity
public class EmployeeHistory {
    // ...
    @Id
    int empId;

    @MapsId
    @OneToOne
    @JoinColumn(name="EMP_ID")
    private Employee employee;
    // ...
}
```

There are a couple of additional points worth mentioning about @MapsId, before we move on to derived identifiers with multiple mapped attributes.

The first point is really a logical follow-on to the fact that the relationship annotated with @MapsId defines the mapping for the identifier attribute as well. If there is no overriding @JoinColumn annotation on the relationship attribute, then the join column will be defaulted according to the usual defaulting rules. If this is the case, then the identifier attribute will also be mapped to that same default. For example, if the @JoinColumn annotation was removed from Listing 10-16 then both the employee and the empId attributes would be mapped to the default EMPLOYEE_ID foreign key column (assuming the primary key column in the EMPLOYEE table was ID).

Secondly, even though the identifier attribute shares the database mapping defined on the relationship attribute, from the perspective of the identifier attribute it is really a read-only mapping. Updates or inserts to the database foreign key column will only ever occur through the relationship attribute. This is one of the reasons why you must always remember to set the parent relationships before trying to persist a dependent entity.

■ **Note** Do not attempt to set only the identifier attribute (and not the relationship attribute) as a means to shortcut persisting a dependent entity. Some providers may have special support for doing this, but it will not portably cause the foreign key to be written to the database.

The identifier attribute will get filled in automatically by the provider when an entity instance is read from the database, or flushed/committed. However, it cannot be assumed to be there when first calling persist() on an instance unless the user sets it explicitly.

Multiple Mapped Attributes

A more common case is probably the one in which the dependent entity has an identifier that includes not only a relationship, but also some state of its own. We will use the example shown in Figure 10-3, where a Project has a compound identifier composed of a name and a foreign key to the department that manages it. With the unique identifier being the combination of its name and department, no department would be permitted to create more than one project with the same name. However, two different departments may choose the same name for their own projects. Listing 10-17 illustrates the trivial mapping of the Project identifier using @Id on both the name and dept attributes.

Listing 10-17. Project with Dependent Identifier

```java
@Entity
@IdClass(ProjectId.class)
public class Project {

    @Id private String name;

    @Id
    @ManyToOne
    @JoinColumns({
        @JoinColumn(name="DEPT_NUM",
                        referencedColumnName="NUM"),
        @JoinColumn(name="DEPT_CTY",
                        referencedColumnName="COUNTRY")})
    private Department dept;
    // ...
}
```

The compound identifier means that we must also specify the primary key class using the @IdClass annotation. Recall our rule that primary key classes must have a matching named attribute for each of the id attributes on the entity, and usually the attributes must also be of the same type. However, this rule only applies when the attributes are of simple types, not entity types. If @Id is annotating a relationship, then that relationship attribute is going to be of some target entity type, and the rule extension is that the primary key class attribute must be of the same type as the primary key of the target entity. This means that the ProjectId class specified as the id class for Project in Listing 10-17 must have an attribute named name, of type String, and another named dept that will be the same type as the primary key of Department. If Department has a simple integer primary key, then the dept attribute in ProjectId will be of type int, but if Department has a compound primary key, with its own primary key class, say DeptId, then the dept attribute in ProjectId would be of type DeptId, as shown in Listing 10-18.

Listing 10-18. ProjectId and DeptId Id Classes

```java
public class ProjectId implements Serializable {
    private String name;
    private DeptId dept;

    public ProjectId() {}
    public ProjectId(DeptId deptId, String name) {
        this.dept = deptId;
        this.name = name;
    }
    // ...
}

public class DeptId implements Serializable {
    private int number;
    private String country;

    public DeptId() {}
    public DeptId (int number, String country) {
```

```
            this.number = number;
            this.country = country;
        }
        // ...
    }
}
```

Using EmbeddedId

It is also possible to have a derived identifier when one or the other (or both) of the entities uses @EmbeddedId. When the id class is embedded, the non-relationship identifier attributes are mapped within the embeddable id class, as usual, but the attributes in the embedded id class that correspond to relationships are mapped by the relationship attributes in the entity. Listing 10-19 shows how the derived identifier is mapped in the Project class when an embedded id class is used. We annotate the relationship attribute with @MapsId("dept"), indicating that it is also specifying the mapping for the dept attribute of the embedded id class. The dept attribute of ProjectId is of the same primary key type as Department in Listing 10-20.

Listing 10-19. Project and Embedded ProjectId Class

```
@Entity
public class Project {

    @EmbeddedId private ProjectId id;

    @MapsId("dept")
    @ManyToOne
    @JoinColumns({
        @JoinColumn(name="DEPT_NUM", referencedColumnName="NUM"),
        @JoinColumn(name="DEPT_CTRY", referencedColumnName="CTRY")})
    private Department department;
    // ...
}

@Embeddable
public class ProjectId implements Serializable {
    @Column(name="P_NAME")
    private String name;
    @Embedded
    private DeptId dept;

    // ...
}
```

Listing 10-20. Department and Embedded DeptId Class

```
@Entity
public class Department {
    @EmbeddedId private DeptId id;

    @OneToMany(mappedBy="department")
    private List<Project> projects;

    // ...
}
```

```
@Embeddable
public class DeptId implements Serializable {
    @Column(name="NUM")
    private int number;
    @Column(name="CTRY")
    private String country;
    // ...
}
```

Note that we have used multiple join columns on the department relationship because Department has a compound primary key. Mapping multipart identifiers is explained in more detail in the "Compound Join Columns" section later in the chapter.

The Department entity has an embedded identifier, but it is not a derived identifier because the DeptId id class does not have any attributes that correspond to relationship attributes in Department. The @Column annotations in the DeptId class map the identifier fields in the Department entity, but when DeptId is embedded in ProjectId, those column mappings do not apply. Once the dept attribute is mapped by the department relationship in Project, the @JoinColumn annotations on that relationship are used as the column mappings for the PROJECT table.

If the Department class had a simple primary key, for example a long instead of an id class, then the dept attribute in ProjectId would just be the simple primary key type of Department (the long type), and there would only be one join column on the many-to-one department attribute in Project.

ALTERNATIVE TO DERIVED IDENTIFIERS

The @MapsId annotation and the ability to apply @Id to relationship attributes was introduced in JPA 2.0 to improve the situation that existed in JPA 1.0. At that time, only the one-to-one shared primary key scenario was specified using the @PrimaryKeyJoinColumn annotation (using the @Id annotation is the preferred and recommended method going forward).

Although there was no specified way to solve the general case of including a foreign key in an identifier, it was generally supported through the practice of adding one or more additional (redundant) fields to the dependent entity. Each added field would hold a foreign key to the related entity, and, because both the added field and the relationship would be mapped to the same join column(s), one or the other of the two would need to be marked as read-only (see "Read-Only Mappings" section), or not updatable or insertable. The following example shows how Listing 10-17 would be done using JPA 1.0. The id class would be the same. Since the deptNumber and deptCountry attributes are identifier attributes, and can't be changed in the database, there is no need to set their updatability to false.

```
@Entity
@IdClass(ProjectId.class)
public class Project {
    @Id private String name;

    @Id
    @Column(name="DEPT_NUM", insertable=false)
    private int deptNumber;

    @Id
    @Column(name="DEPT_CTRY", insertable=false)
    private String deptCountry;
```

```
    @ManyToOne
    @JoinColumns({
        @JoinColumn(name="DEPT_NUM", referencedColumnName="NUM"),
        @JoinColumn(name="DEPT_CTRY", referencedColumnName="CTRY")})
    private Department department;

// ...

}
```

Advanced Mapping Elements

Additional elements may be specified on the @Column and @JoinColumn annotations (and their @MapKeyColumn, @MapKeyJoinColumn, and @OrderColumn relatives), some of which apply to schema generation that will be discussed in Chapter 14. Other parts we can describe separately as applying to columns and join columns in the following sections.

Read-Only Mappings

JPA does not really define any kind of read-only entity, although it will likely show up in a future release. The API does, however, define options to set individual mappings to be read-only using the insertable and updatable elements of the @Column and @JoinColumn annotations. These two settings default to true but can be set to false if we want to ensure that the provider will not insert or update information in the table in response to changes in the entity instance. If the data in the mapped table already exists and we want to ensure that it will not be modified at runtime, then the insertable and updatable elements can be set to false, effectively preventing the provider from doing anything other than reading the entity from the database. Listing 10-21 demonstrates the Employee entity with read-only mappings.

Listing 10-21. Making An Entity Read-only

```
@Entity
public class Employee {
    @Id
    @Column(insertable=false)
    private int id;
    @Column(insertable=false, updatable=false)
    private String name;
    @Column(insertable=false, updatable=false)
    private long salary;

    @ManyToOne
    @JoinColumn(name="DEPT_ID", insertable=false, updatable=false)
    private Department department;
    // ...
}
```

We don't need to worry about the identifier mapping being modified, because it is illegal to modify identifiers. The other mappings, though, are marked as not being able to be inserted or updated, so we are assuming that there are already entities in the database to be read in and used. No new entities will be persisted, and existing entities will never be updated.

Note that this does not guarantee that the entity state will not change in memory. Employee instances could still get changed either inside or outside a transaction, but at transaction commit time or whenever the entities get flushed to the database, this state will not be saved and the provider will likely not throw an exception to indicate it. Be careful modifying read-only mappings in memory, however, as changing the entities can cause them to become inconsistent with the state in the database and could wreak havoc on a vendor-specific cache.

Even though all of these mappings are not updatable, the entity as a whole could still be deleted. A proper read-only feature will solve this problem once and for all in a future release, but in the meantime some vendors support the notion of read-only entities, and can optimize the treatment of them in their caches and persistence context implementations.

Optionality

As we will see in Chapter 14, when we talk about schema generation, there exists metadata that either permits the database columns to be null or requires them to have values. While this setting will affect the physical database schema, there are also settings on some of the logical mappings that allow a basic mapping or a single-valued association mapping to be left empty or required to be specified in the object model. The element that requires or permits such behavior is the optional element in the @Basic, @ManyToOne, and @OneToOne annotations.

When the optional element is specified as false, it indicates to the provider that the field or property mapping may not be null. The API does not actually define what the behavior is in the case when the value is null, but the provider may choose to throw an exception or simply do something else. For basic mappings, it is only a hint and can be completely ignored. The optional element may also be used by the provider when doing schema generation, because, if optional is set to true, then the column in the database must also be nullable.

Because the API does not go into any detail about ordinality of the object model, there is a certain amount of non-portability associated with using it. An example of setting the manager to be a required attribute is shown in Listing 10-22. The default value for optional is true, making it necessary to be specified only if a false value is needed.

Listing 10-22. Using Optional Mappings

```
@Entity
public class Employee {
    // ...
    @ManyToOne(optional=false)
    @JoinColumn(name="DEPT_ID", insertable=false, updatable=false)
    private Department department;
    // ...
}
```

Advanced Relationships

If you are in the opportune position of starting from a Java application and creating a database schema, then you have complete control over what the schema looks like and how you map the classes to the database. In this case, it is likely that you will not need to use very many of the advanced relationship features that are offered by the API. The flexibility of being able to define a data model usually makes for a less demanding mapping configuration. However, if you are in the unfortunate situation of mapping a Java model to an existing database, then in order to work around the data schema you might need access to more mappings than those we have discussed so far. The mappings described in the following sections are primarily for mapping to legacy databases, and will most often be used because they are the only option. A notable exception is the orphan removal feature, used to model a parent–child relationship.

Using Join Tables

We have already seen mappings such as the many-to-many and unidirectional one-to-many mappings that use join tables. Sometimes a database schema uses a join table to relate two entity types, even though the cardinality of the target entity in the relationship is one. A one-to-one or many-to-one relationship does not normally need a join table because the target will only ever be a single entity and the foreign key can be stored in the source entity table. But if the join table already exists for a many-to-one relationship, then of course we must map the relationship using that join table. To do so, we need only add the @JoinTable annotation to the relationship mapping.

Whether the relationship is unidirectional or bidirectional, the @JoinTable annotation is a physical annotation and must be defined on the owning side of the relationship, just as with all other mappings. However, because a join table is not the default configuration for mappings that are not many-to-many or unidirectional one-to-many, we do need to specify the annotation when we want a join table to be used. The elements of the @JoinTable annotation can still be used to override the various schema names.

In Listing 10-23, we see a join table being used for a many-to-one relationship from Employee to Department. The relationship may be unidirectional or it may be bidirectional, with a one-to-many relationship from Department back to Employee, but in either case the "many" side must always be the owner. The reason is because even if it were bidirectional, the @ManyToOne side could not be the owner because there would be no way for the @ManyToOne attribute to refer to the owning @OneToMany attribute side. There is no mappedBy element in the @ManyToOne annotation definition.

Listing 10-23. Many-to-One Mapping Using a Join Table

```
@Entity
public class Employee {
    @Id private int id;
    private String name;
    private long salary;

    @ManyToOne
    @JoinTable(name="EMP_DEPT")
    private Department department;
    // ...
}
```

As with most other mappings, the non-owning side of a bidirectional relationship does not change based upon whether the relationship is mapped using a join table or not. It simply refers to the owning relationship and lets it map to the physical tables/columns accordingly.

Avoiding Join Tables

Up to this point, we have discussed a unidirectional one-to-many mapping in the context of using a join table, but it is also possible to map a unidirectional mapping without using a join table. It requires the foreign key to be in the target table, or "many" side of the relationship, even though the target object does not have any reference to the "one" side. This is called a unidirectional one-to-many target foreign key mapping, because the foreign key is in the target table instead of a join table.

To use this mapping, we first indicate that the one-to-many relationship is unidirectional by not specifying any mappedBy element in the annotation. Then we specify a @JoinColumn annotation on the one-to-many attribute to indicate the foreign key column. The catch is that the join column that we are specifying applies to the table of the target object, not the source object in which the annotation appears.

The example in Listing 10-24 shows how simple it is to map a unidirectional one-to-many mapping using a target foreign key. The DEPT_ID column refers to the table mapped by Employee, and is a foreign key to the DEPARTMENT table, even though the Employee entity does not have any relationship attribute back to Department.

Listing 10-24. Unidirectional One-to-Many Mapping Using a Target Foreign Key

```
@Entity
public class Department {
    @Id private int id;

    @OneToMany
    @JoinColumn(name="DEPT_ID")
    private Collection<Employee> employees;
    // ...
}
```

Before you use this mapping, you should understand the implications of doing so, as they can be quite negative, both from a modeling perspective and a performance perspective. Each row in the EMPLOYEE table corresponds to an Employee instance, with each column corresponding to some state or relationship in the instance. When there is a change in the row, there is the assumption that some kind of change occurred to the corresponding Employee, but in this case that does not necessarily follow. The Employee might have just been changed to a different Department, and because there was no reference to the Department from the Employee there was no change to the Employee.

From a performance standpoint, think of the case when both the state of an Employee is changed and the Department that it belongs to is changed. When writing out the Employee state, the foreign key to the Department is not known because the Employee entity does not have any reference to it. In this case, the Employee might have to be written out twice, once for the changed state of the Employee, and a second time when the Department entity changes are written out, and the foreign key from Employee to Department must be updated to point to the Department that is referring to it.

Compound Join Columns

Now that we have discussed how to create entities with compound primary keys, it is not a far stretch to figure out that, as soon as we have a relationship to an entity with a compound identifier, we will need some way to extend the way we currently reference it.

Up to this point, we have dealt with the physical relationship mapping only as a join column, but, if the primary key that we are referencing is composed of multiple fields, then we will need multiple join columns. This is why we have the plural @JoinColumns annotation that can hold as many join columns as we need to put into it.

There are no default values for join column names when we have multiple join columns. The simplest answer is to require the user to assign them, so, when multiple join columns are used, both the name element and the referencedColumnName element, which indicates the name of the primary key column in the target table, must be specified.

Now that we are getting into more complex scenarios, let's add a more interesting relationship to the mix. Let's say that employees have managers and that each manager has a number of employees that work for him. You may not find that very interesting until you realize that managers are themselves employees, so the join columns are actually self-referential, that is, referring to the same table they are stored in. Figure 10-4 shows the EMPLOYEE table with this relationship.

EMPLOYEE	
PK	COUNTRY
PK	EMP_ID
	NAME
	SALARY
FK1	MGR_COUNTRY
FK1	MGR_ID

Figure 10-4. EMPLOYEE table with self-referencing compound foreign key

Listing 10-25 shows a version of the Employee entity that has a manager relationship, which is many-to-one from each of the managed employees to the manager, and a one-to-many directs relationship from the manager to its managed employees.

Listing 10-25. Self-referencing Compound Relationships

```
@Entity
@IdClass(EmployeeId.class)
public class Employee {
    @Id private String country;
    @Id
    @Column(name="EMP_ID")
    private int id;

    @ManyToOne
    @JoinColumns({
        @JoinColumn(name="MGR_COUNTRY", referencedColumnName="COUNTRY"),
        @JoinColumn(name="MGR_ID", referencedColumnName="EMP_ID")
    })
    private Employee manager;

    @OneToMany(mappedBy="manager")
    private Collection<Employee> directs;
    // ...
}
```

Any number of join columns can be specified, although in practice very seldom are there more than two. The plural form of @JoinColumns may be used on many-to-one or one-to-one relationships or more generally whenever the single @JoinColumn annotation is valid.

Another example to consider is in the join table of a many-to-many relationship. We can revisit the Employee and Project relationship described in Chapter 4 to take into account our compound primary key in Employee. The new table structure for this relationship is shown in Figure 10-5.

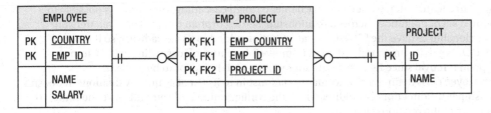

Figure 10-5. Join table with a compound primary key

If we keep the Employee entity as the owner, where the join table is defined, then the mapping for this relationship will be as shown in Listing 10-26.

Listing 10-26. Join Table with Compound Join Columns

```
@Entity
@IdClass(EmployeeId.class)
public class Employee {
    @Id private String country;
    @Id
    @Column(name="EMP_ID")
    private int id;

    @ManyToMany
    @JoinTable(
        name="EMP_PROJECT",
        joinColumns={
            @JoinColumn(name="EMP_COUNTRY", referencedColumnName="COUNTRY"),
            @JoinColumn(name="EMP_ID", referencedColumnName="EMP_ID")},
        inverseJoinColumns=@JoinColumn(name="PROJECT_ID"))
    private Collection<Project> projects;
    // ...
}
```

Orphan Removal

The orphanRemoval element provides a convenient way of modeling parent-child relationships, or more specifically privately owned relationships. We differentiate these two because privately owned is a particular variety of parent-child in which the child entity may only be a child of one parent entity, and may not ever belong to a different parent. While some parent-child relationships allow the child to migrate from one parent to another, in a privately owned mapping the owned entity was created to belong to the parent and cannot ever be migrated. Once it is removed from the parent, it is considered orphaned and is deleted by the provider.

Only relationships with single cardinality on the source side can enable orphan removal, which is why the orphanRemoval option is defined on the @OneToOne and @OneToMany relationship annotations, but on neither of the @ManyToOne or @ManyToMany annotations.

When specified, the orphanRemoval element causes the child entity to be removed when the relationship between the parent and the child is broken. This can be done either by setting to null the attribute that holds the related entity, or additionally in the one-to-many case by removing the child entity from the collection. The provider is then responsible, at flush or commit time (whichever comes first), for removing the orphaned child entity.

In a parent-child relationship, the child is dependent upon the existence of the parent. If the parent is removed, then by definition the child becomes an orphan and must also be removed. This second feature of orphan removal behavior is exactly equivalent to a feature that we covered in Chapter 6 called cascading, in which it is possible to cascade any subset of a defined set of operations across a relationship. Setting orphan removal on a relationship automatically causes the relationship to have the REMOVE operation option added to its cascade list, so it is not necessary to explicitly add it. Doing so is simply redundant. It is impossible to turn off cascading REMOVE from a relationship marked for orphan removal since its very definition requires such behavior to be present.

In Listing 10-27, the Employee class defines a one-to-many relationship to its list of annual evaluations. It doesn't matter whether the relationship is unidirectional or bidirectional, the configuration and semantics are the same, so we need not show the other side of the relationship.

Listing 10-27. Employee Class with Orphan Removal of Evaluation Entities

```
@Entity
public class Employee {
    @Id private int id;
    @OneToMany(orphanRemoval=true)
    private List<Evaluation> evals;
    // ...
}
```

Suppose an employee receives an unfair evaluation from a manager. The employee might go to the manager to correct the information and the evaluation might be modified, or the employee might have to appeal the evaluation, and if successful the evaluation might simply be removed from the employee record. This would cause it to be deleted from the database as well. If the employee decided to leave the company, then when the employee is removed from the system his evaluations will be automatically removed along with him.

If the collection in the relationship was a Map, keyed by a different entity type, then orphan removal would only apply to the entity values in the Map, not to the keys. This means that entity keys are never privately owned.

Finally, if the orphaned object is not currently managed in the persistence context, either because it has been created in memory and not yet persisted or because it is simply detached from the persistence context, orphan removal will not be applied. Similarly, if it has already been removed in the current persistence context orphan removal will not be applied.

Mapping Relationship State

There are times when a relationship actually has state associated with it. For example, let's say that we want to maintain the date an employee was assigned to work on a project. Storing the state on the employee is possible but less helpful, since the date is really coupled to the employee's relationship to a particular project (a single entry in the many-to-many association). Taking an employee off a project should really just cause the assignment date to go away, so storing it as part of the employee means that we have to ensure that the two are consistent with each other, which can be bothersome. In UML, we would show this kind of relationship using an association class. Figure 10-6 shows an example of this technique.

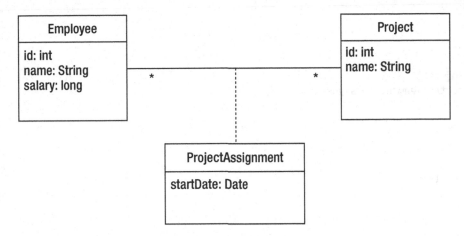

Figure 10-6. *Modeling state on a relationship using an association class*

In the database, everything is rosy because we can simply add a column to the join table. The data model provides natural support for relationship state. Figure 10-7 shows the many-to-many relationship between EMPLOYEE and PROJECT with an expanded join table.

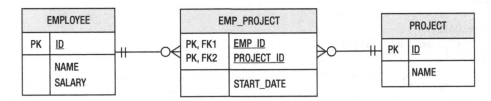

Figure 10-7. *Join table with additional state*

When we get to the object model, however, it becomes much more problematic. The issue is that Java has no inherent support for relationship state. Relationships are just object references or pointers, hence no state can ever exist on them. State exists on objects only, and relationships are not first-class objects.

The Java solution is to turn the relationship into an entity that contains the desired state and map the new entity to what was previously the join table. The new entity will have a many-to-one relationship to each of the existing entity types, and each of the entity types will have a one-to-many relationship back to the new entity representing the relationship. The primary key of the new entity will be the combination of the two relationships to the two entity types. Listing 10-28 shows all of the participants in the Employee and Project relationship.

Listing 10-28. *Mapping Relationship State with an Intermediate Entity*

```
@Entity
public class Employee {
    @Id private int id;
    // ...
    @OneToMany(mappedBy="employee")
    private Collection<ProjectAssignment> assignments;
    // ...
}
```

```
@Entity
public class Project {
    @Id private int id;
    // ...
    @OneToMany(mappedBy="project")
    private Collection<ProjectAssignment> assignments;
    // ...
}

@Entity
@Table(name="EMP_PROJECT")
@IdClass(ProjectAssignmentId.class)
public class ProjectAssignment {
    @Id
    @ManyToOne
    @JoinColumn(name="EMP_ID")
    private Employee employee;

    @Id
    @ManyToOne
    @JoinColumn(name="PROJECT_ID")
    private Project project;

    @Temporal(TemporalType.DATE)
    @Column(name="START_DATE", updatable=false)
    private Date startDate;
    // ...
}

public class ProjectAssignmentId implements Serializable {
    private int employee;
    private int project;
    // ...
}
```

Here we have the primary key entirely composed of relationships, with the two foreign key columns making up the primary key in the EMP_PROJECT join table. The date at which the assignment was made could be manually set when the assignment is created, or it could be associated with a trigger that causes it to be set when the assignment is created in the database. Note that, if a trigger were used, then the entity would need to be refreshed from the database in order to populate the assignment date field in the Java object.

Multiple Tables

The most common mapping scenarios are of the so-called meet-in-the-middle variety. This means that the data model and the object model already exist, or, if one does not exist, then it is created independently of the other model. This is relevant because there are a number of features in the Java Persistence API that attempt to address concerns that arise in this case.

Up to this point, we have assumed that an entity gets mapped to a single table and that a single row in that table represents an entity. In an existing or legacy data model, it was actually quite common to spread data, even data that was tightly coupled, across multiple tables. This was done for different administrative as well as performance reasons, one of which was to decrease table contention when specific subsets of the data were accessed or modified.

To account for this, entities may be mapped across multiple tables by making use of the @SecondaryTable annotation and its plural @SecondaryTables form. The default table or the table defined by the @Table annotation is called the primary table, and any additional ones are called secondary tables. We can then distribute the data in an entity across rows in both the primary table and the secondary tables simply by defining the secondary tables as annotations on the entity and then specifying when we map each field or property which table the column is in. We do this by specifying the name of the table in the table element in @Column or @JoinColumn. We did not need to use this element earlier, because the default value of table is the name of the primary table.

The only bit that is left is to specify how to join the secondary table or tables to the primary table. We saw in Chapter 4 how the primary key join column is a special case of a join column where the join column is just the primary key column (or columns in the case of composite primary keys). Support for joining secondary tables to the primary table is limited to primary key join columns and is specified as a @PrimaryKeyJoinColumn annotation as part of the @SecondaryTable annotation.

To demonstrate the use of a secondary table, consider the data model shown in Figure 10-8. There is a primary key relationship between the EMP and EMP_ADDRESS tables. The EMP table stores the primary employee information, while the address information has been moved to the EMP_ADDRESS table.

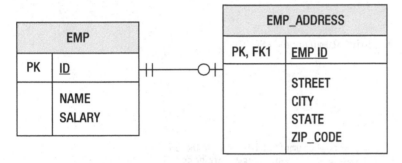

Figure 10-8. *EMP and EMP_ADDRESS tables*

To map this table structure to the Employee entity, we must declare EMP_ADDRESS as a secondary table and use the table element of the @Column annotation for every attribute stored in that table. Listing 10-29 shows the mapped entity. The primary key of the EMP_ADDRESS table is in the EMP_ID column. If it had been named ID, then we would not have needed to use the name element in the @PrimaryKeyJoinColumn annotation. It defaults to the name of the primary key column in the primary table.

Listing 10-29. Mapping an Entity Across Two Tables

```
@Entity
@Table(name="EMP")
@SecondaryTable(name="EMP_ADDRESS",
    pkJoinColumns=@PrimaryKeyJoinColumn(name="EMP_ID"))
public class Employee {
    @Id private int id;
    private String name;
    private long salary;
    @Column(table="EMP_ADDRESS")
    private String street;
    @Column(table="EMP_ADDRESS")
    private String city;
    @Column(table="EMP_ADDRESS")
```

```
    private String state;
    @Column(name="ZIP_CODE", table="EMP_ADDRESS")
    private String zip;
    // ...
}
```

In Chapter 4, we learned how to use the schema or catalog elements in @Table to qualify the primary table to be in a particular database schema or catalog. This is also valid in the @SecondaryTable annotation.

Previously, when discussing embedded objects, we mapped the address fields of the Employee entity into an Address embedded type. With the address data in a secondary table, it is still possible to do this by specifying the mapped table name as part of the column information in the @AttributeOverride annotation. Listing 10-30 demonstrates this approach. Note that we have to enumerate all of the fields in the embedded type even though the column names may match the correct default values.

Listing 10-30. Mapping an Embedded Type to a Secondary Table

```
@Entity
@Table(name="EMP")
@SecondaryTable(name="EMP_ADDRESS",
                pkJoinColumns=@PrimaryKeyJoinColumn(name="EMP_ID"))
public class Employee {
    @Id private int id;
    private String name;
    private long salary;
    @Embedded
    @AttributeOverrides({
        @AttributeOverride(name="street", column=@Column(table="EMP_ADDRESS")),
        @AttributeOverride(name="city", column=@Column(table="EMP_ADDRESS")),
        @AttributeOverride(name="state", column=@Column(table="EMP_ADDRESS")),
        @AttributeOverride(name="zip",
                        column=@Column(name="ZIP_CODE", table="EMP_ADDRESS"))
    })
    private Address address;
    // ...
}
```

Let's consider a more complex example involving multiple tables and compound primary keys. Figure 10-9 shows the table structure we wish to map. In addition to the EMPLOYEE table, there are two secondary tables, ORG_STRUCTURE and EMP_LOB. The ORG_STRUCTURE table stores employee and manager reporting information. The EMP_LOB table stores large objects that are infrequently fetched during normal query options. Moving large objects to a secondary table is a common design technique in many database schemas.

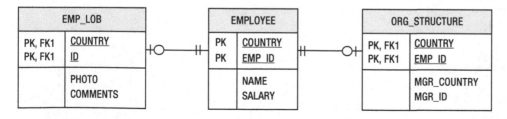

Figure 10-9. Secondary tables with compound primary key relationships

Listing 10-31 shows the `Employee` entity mapped to this table structure. The `EmployeeId` id class from Listing 10-10 has been reused in this example.

Listing 10-31. Mapping an Entity with Multiple Secondary Tables

```
@Entity
@IdClass(EmployeeId.class)
@SecondaryTables({
    @SecondaryTable(name="ORG_STRUCTURE", pkJoinColumns={
        @PrimaryKeyJoinColumn(name="COUNTRY", referencedColumnName="COUNTRY"),
        @PrimaryKeyJoinColumn(name="EMP_ID", referencedColumnName="EMP_ID")}),
    @SecondaryTable(name="EMP_LOB", pkJoinColumns={
        @PrimaryKeyJoinColumn(name="COUNTRY", referencedColumnName="COUNTRY"),
        @PrimaryKeyJoinColumn(name="ID", referencedColumnName="EMP_ID")})
})
public class Employee {
    @Id private String country;
    @Id
    @Column(name="EMP_ID")
    private int id;

    @Basic(fetch=FetchType.LAZY)
    @Lob
    @Column(table="EMP_LOB")
    private byte[] photo;

    @Basic(fetch=FetchType.LAZY)
    @Lob
    @Column(table="EMP_LOB")
    private char[] comments;

    @ManyToOne
    @JoinColumns({
        @JoinColumn(name="MGR_COUNTRY", referencedColumnName="COUNTRY",
                    table="ORG_STRUCTURE"),
        @JoinColumn(name="MGR_ID", referencedColumnName="EMP_ID",
                    table="ORG_STRUCTURE")
    })
    private Employee manager;
    // ...
}
```

We have thrown a few curves into this example to make it more interesting. The first is that we have defined `Employee` to have a composite primary key. This requires additional information to be provided for the `EMP_LOB` table, because its primary key is not named the same as the primary table. The next difference is that we are storing a relationship in the `ORG_STRUCTURE` secondary table. The `MGR_COUNTRY` and `MGR_ID` columns combine to reference the id of the manager for this employee. Since the employee has a composite primary key, the manager relationship must also specify a set of join columns instead of only one, and the `referencedColumnName` elements in those join columns refer to the primary key columns `COUNTRY` and `EMP_ID` in the entity's own primary table `EMPLOYEE`.

Inheritance

One of the common mistakes made by novice object-oriented developers is that they get converted to the principle of reuse, but carry it too far. It is too easy to get caught up in the quest for reuse and create complex inheritance hierarchies all for the sake of sharing a few methods. These kinds of multi-level hierarchies will often lead to pain and hardship down the road as the application becomes difficult to debug and a challenge to maintain.

Most applications do enjoy the benefits of at least some inheritance in the object model. As with most things, though, moderation should be applied, especially when it comes to mapping the classes to relational databases. Large hierarchies can often lead to significant performance reduction, and it may be that the cost of code reuse is higher than you might want to pay.

In the following sections, we will explain the support that exists in the API to map inheritance hierarchies and outline some of the repercussions.

Class Hierarchies

Because this is a book about the Java Persistence API, the first and most obvious place to start talking about inheritance is in the Java object model. Entities are objects, after all, and should be able to inherit state and behavior from other entities. This is not only expected but also essential for the development of object-oriented applications.

What does it mean when one entity inherits state from its entity superclass? It can imply different things in the data model, but in the Java model it simply means that when a subclass entity is instantiated, it has its own version or copy of both its locally defined state and its inherited state, all of which is persistent. While this basic premise is not at all surprising, it opens up the less obvious question of what happens when an entity inherits from something other than another entity. Which classes is an entity allowed to extend, and what happens when it does?

Consider the class hierarchy shown in Figure 10-10. As we saw in Chapter 1, there are a number of ways that class inheritance can be represented in the database. In the object model, there may even be a number of different ways to implement a hierarchy, some of which may include non-entity classes. We will use this example as we explore ways to persist inheritance hierarchies in the following sections.

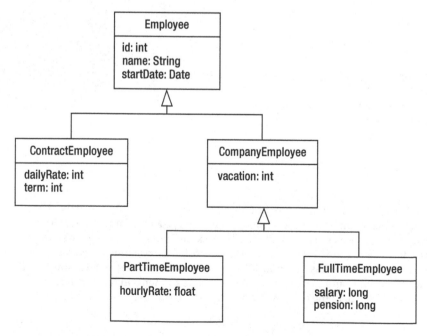

Figure 10-10. Inheritance class hierarchy

We differentiate between a general class hierarchy, which is a set of various types of Java classes that extend each other in a tree, and an entity hierarchy, which is a tree consisting of persistent entity classes interspersed with non-entity classes. An entity hierarchy is rooted at the first entity class in the hierarchy.

Mapped Superclasses

The Java Persistence API defines a special kind of class called a mapped superclass that is quite useful as a superclass for entities. A mapped superclass provides a convenient class in which to store shared state and behavior that entities can inherit from, but it is itself not a persistent class and cannot act in the capacity of an entity. It cannot be queried over and cannot be the target of a relationship. Annotations such as @Table are not permitted on mapped superclasses because the state defined in them applies only to its entity subclasses.

Mapped superclasses can be compared to entities in somewhat the same way that an abstract class is compared to a concrete class; they can contain state and behavior but just can't be instantiated as persistent entities. An abstract class is of use only in relation to its concrete subclasses, and a mapped superclass is useful only as state and behavior that is inherited by the entity subclasses that extend it. They do not play a role in an entity inheritance hierarchy other than contributing that state and behavior to the entities that inherit from them.

Mapped superclasses may or may not be defined as abstract in their class definitions, but it is good practice to make them actual abstract Java classes. We don't know of any good use cases for creating concrete Java instances of them without ever being able to persist them, and chances are that, if you happen to find one, you probably want the mapped superclass to be an entity.

All of the default mapping rules that apply to entities also apply to the basic and relationship state in mapped superclasses. The biggest advantage of using mapped superclasses is being able to define partial shared state that should not be accessed on its own without the additional state that its entity subclasses add to it. If you are not sure whether to make a class an entity or a mapped superclass, then you need only ask yourself if you will ever need to query across or access an instance that is only exposed as an instance of that mapped class. This also includes relationships, since a mapped superclass can't be used as the target of a relationship. If you answer yes to any variant of that question, then you should probably make it a first-class entity.

Looking back at Figure 10-10, we could conceivably treat the CompanyEmployee class as a mapped superclass instead of an entity. It defines shared state, but perhaps we have no reason to query over it.

A class is indicated as being a mapped superclass by annotating it with the @MappedSuperclass annotation. The class fragments from Listing 10-32 show how the hierarchy would be mapped with CompanyEmployee as a mapped superclass.

Listing 10-32. Entities Inheriting from a Mapped Superclass

```
@Entity
public class Employee {
    @Id private int id;
    private String name;
    @Temporal(TemporalType.DATE)
    @Column(name="S_DATE")
    private Date startDate;
    // ...
}

@Entity
public class ContractEmployee extends Employee {
    @Column(name="D_RATE")
    private int dailyRate;
    private int term;
    // ...
}
```

```java
@MappedSuperclass
public abstract class CompanyEmployee extends Employee {
    private int vacation;
    // ...
}

@Entity
public class FullTimeEmployee extends CompanyEmployee {
    private long salary;
    private long pension;
    // ...
}

@Entity
public class PartTimeEmployee extends CompanyEmployee {
    @Column(name="H_RATE")
    private float hourlyRate;
    // ...
}
```

Transient Classes in the Hierarchy

Classes in an entity hierarchy, that are not entities or mapped superclasses, are called transient classes. Entities may extend transient classes either directly or indirectly through a mapped superclass. When an entity inherits from a transient class, the state defined in the transient class is still inherited in the entity, but it is not persistent. In other words, the entity will have space allocated for the inherited state, according to the usual Java rules, but that state will not be managed by the persistence provider. It will be effectively ignored during the lifecycle of the entity. The entity might manage that state manually through the use of lifecycle callback methods that we describe in Chapter 12, or other approaches, but the state will not be persisted as part of the provider-managed entity lifecycle.

One could conceive of having a hierarchy that is composed of an entity that has a transient subclass, which in turn has one or more entity subclasses. While this case is not really a common one, it is nonetheless possible and can be achieved in the rare circumstances when having shared transient state or common behavior is desired. It would normally be more convenient, though, to declare the transient state or behavior in the entity superclass than to create an intermediate transient class. Listing 10-33 shows an entity that inherits from a superclass that defines transient state that is the time an entity was created in memory.

Listing 10-33. Entity Inheriting from a Transient Superclass

```java
public abstract class CachedEntity {
    private long createTime;

    public CachedEntity() { createTime = System.currentTimeMillis(); }

    public long getCacheAge() { return System.currentTimeMillis() - createTime; }
}

@Entity
public class Employee extends CachedEntity {
    public Employee() { super(); }
    // ...
}
```

In this example, we moved the transient state from the entity class into a transient superclass, but the end result is really quite the same. The previous example might have been a little neater without the extra class, but this example allows us to share the transient state and behavior across any number of entities that need only extend CachedEntity.

Abstract and Concrete Classes

We have mentioned the notion of abstract versus concrete classes in the context of mapped superclasses, but we didn't go into any more detail about entity and transient classes. Most people, depending upon their philosophy, might expect that all non-leaf classes in an object hierarchy should be abstract, or at the very least that some of them would be. A restriction that entities must always be concrete classes would mess this up quite handily, and fortunately this is not the case. It is perfectly acceptable for entities, mapped superclasses, or transient classes to be either abstract or concrete at any level of the inheritance tree. As with mapped superclasses, making transient classes concrete in the hierarchy doesn't really serve any purpose, and as a general rule should be avoided to prevent accidental development errors and misuse.

The case that we have not talked about is the one where an entity is an abstract class. The only difference between an entity that is an abstract class and one that is a concrete class is the Java rule that prohibits abstract classes from being instantiated. They can still define persistent state and behavior that will be inherited by the concrete entity subclasses below them. They can be queried, the result of which will be composed of concrete entity subclass instances. They can also bear the inheritance mapping metadata for the hierarchy.

Our hierarchy in Figure 10-10 had an Employee class that was a concrete class. We would not want users to accidentally instantiate this class and then try to persist a partially defined employee. We could protect against this by defining it to be abstract. We would then end up with all of our non-leaf classes being abstract and the leaf classes being persistent.

Inheritance Models

JPA provides support for three different data representations. The use of two of them is fairly widespread, while the third is less common and not required to be supported, though it is still fully defined with the intention that providers might be required to support it in the future.

When an entity hierarchy exists, it is always rooted at an entity class. Recall that mapped superclasses do not count as levels in the hierarchy because they contribute only to the entities beneath them. The root entity class must signify the inheritance hierarchy by being annotated with the @Inheritance annotation. This annotation indicates the strategy that should be used for mapping and must be one of the three strategies described in the following sections.

Every entity in the hierarchy must either define or inherit its identifier, which means that the identifier must be defined either in the root entity or in a mapped superclass above it. A mapped superclass may be higher up in the class hierarchy than where the identifier is defined.

Single-Table Strategy

The most common and performant way of storing the state of multiple classes is to define a single table to contain a superset of all the possible state in any of the entity classes. This approach is called, not surprisingly, a single-table strategy. It has the consequence that, for any given table row representing an instance of a concrete class, there may be columns that do not have values because they apply only to a sibling class in the hierarchy.

From Figure 10-10 we see that the id is located in the root Employee entity class and is shared by the rest of the persistence classes. All the persistent entities in an inheritance tree must use the same type of identifier. We don't need to think about it very long before we see why this makes sense at both levels. In the object layer, it wouldn't be possible to issue a polymorphic find() operation on a superclass if there were not a common identifier type that we could pass in. Similarly, at the table level, we would need multiple primary key columns but without being able to fill them all in on any given insertion of an instance that only made use of one of them.

The table must contain enough columns to store all the state in all the classes. An individual row stores the state of an entity instance of a concrete entity type, which would normally imply that there would be some columns left unfilled in every row. Of course, this leads to the conclusion that the columns mapped to concrete subclass state should be nullable, which is normally not a big issue but could be a problem for some database administrators.

In general, the single-table approach tends to be more wasteful of database tablespace, but it does offer peak performance for both polymorphic queries and write operations. The SQL that is needed to issue these operations is simple, optimized, and does not require joining.

To specify the single-table strategy for the inheritance hierarchy, the root entity class is annotated with the @Inheritance annotation with its strategy set to SINGLE_TABLE. In our previous model, this would mean annotating the Employee class as follows:

```
@Entity
@Inheritance(strategy=InheritanceType.SINGLE_TABLE)
public abstract class Employee { ... }
```

As it turns out, though, the single-table strategy is the default one, so we wouldn't strictly even need to include the strategy element at all. An empty @Inheritance annotation would do the trick just as well.

In Figure 10-11, we see the single-table representation of our Employee hierarchy model. In terms of the table structure and schema architecture for the single-table strategy, it makes no difference whether CompanyEmployee is a mapped superclass or an entity.

EMPLOYEE	
PK	ID
	NAME
	S_DATE
	D_DATE
	TERM
	VACATION
	H_RATE
	SALARY
	PENSION
	EMO_TYPE

Figure 10-11. *A single-table inheritance data model*

Discriminator Column

You may have noticed an extra column named EMP_TYPE in Figure 10-11 that was not mapped to any field in any of the classes in Figure 10-10. This field has a special purpose and is required when using a single table to model inheritance. It is called a discriminator column and is mapped using the @DiscriminatorColumn annotation in conjunction with the @Inheritance annotation we have already learned about. The name element of this annotation specifies the name of the column that should be used as the discriminator column, and if not specified will be defaulted to a column named "DTYPE".

A discriminatorType element dictates the type of the discriminator column. Some applications prefer to use strings to discriminate between the entity types, while others like using integer values to indicate the class. The type of the discriminator column may be one of three predefined discriminator column types: INTEGER, STRING, or CHAR. If the discriminatorType element is not specified, then the default type of STRING will be assumed.

Discriminator Value

Every row in the table will have a value in the discriminator column called a discriminator value, or a class indicator, to indicate the type of entity that is stored in that row. Every concrete entity in the inheritance hierarchy, therefore, needs a discriminator value specific to that entity type so that the provider can process or assign the correct entity type when it loads and stores the row. The way this is done is to use a @DiscriminatorValue annotation on each concrete entity class. The string value in the annotation specifies the discriminator value that instances of the class will get assigned when they are inserted into the database. This will allow the provider to recognize instances of the class when it issues queries. This value should be of the same type as was specified or defaulted as the discriminatorType element in the @DiscriminatorColumn annotation.

If no @DiscriminatorValue annotation is specified, then the provider will use a provider-specific way of obtaining the value. If the discriminatorType is STRING, then the provider will just use the entity name as the class indicator string. If the discriminatorType is INTEGER, then we would either have to specify the discriminator values for every entity class or none of them. If we were to specify some but not others, then we could not guarantee that a provider-generated value would not overlap with one that we specified.

Listing 10-34 shows how our Employee hierarchy is mapped to a single-table strategy.

Listing 10-34. Entity Hierarchy Mapped Using Single-Table Strategy

```java
@Entity
@Table(name="EMP")
@Inheritance
@DiscriminatorColumn(name="EMP_TYPE")
public abstract class Employee { ... }

@Entity
public class ContractEmployee extends Employee { ... }

@MappedSuperclass
public abstract class CompanyEmployee extends Employee { ... }

@Entity
@DiscriminatorValue("FTEmp")
public class FullTimeEmployee extends CompanyEmployee { ... }

@Entity(name="PTEmp")
public class PartTimeEmployee extends CompanyEmployee { ... }
```

The Employee class is the root class, so it establishes the inheritance strategy and discriminator column. We have assumed the default strategy of SINGLE_TABLE and discriminator type of STRING.

Neither the Employee nor the CompanyEmployee classes have discriminator values, because discriminator values should not be specified for abstract entity classes, mapped superclasses, transient classes, or any abstract classes for that matter. Only concrete entity classes use discriminator values since they are the only ones that actually get stored and retrieved from the database.

The ContractEmployee entity does not use a @DiscriminatorValue annotation, because the default string "ContractEmployee", which is the default entity name that is given to the class, is just what we want. The FullTimeEmployee class explicitly lists its discriminator value to be "FTEmp", so that is what is stored in each row for instances of

FullTimeEmployee. Meanwhile, the PartTimeEmployee class will get "PTEmp" as its discriminator value because it set its entity name to be "PTEmp", and the entity name gets used as the discriminator value when none is specified.

In Figure 10-12, we can see a sample of some of the data that we might find given the earlier model and settings. We can see from the EMP_TYPE discriminator column that there are three different types of concrete entities. We also see null values in the columns that do not apply to an entity instance.

EMPLOYEE

ID	NAME	S_DATE	D_RATE	TERM	VACATION	H_RATE	SALARY	PENSION	EMP_TYPE
1	John	020101	500	12					ContractEmployee
2	Paul	020408	600	24					ContractEmployee
3	Sarah	030610	700	18					ContractEmployee
4	Patrick	040701			15		55000	100000	FTEmp
5	Joan	030909			15		59000	200000	FTEmp
6	Sam	000312			20		60000	450000	FTEmp
7	Mark	041101			15	17.00			PTEmp
8	Ryan	051205			15	16.00			PTEmp
9	Jackie	080103			10	15.00			PTEmp

Figure 10-12. *Sample of single-table inheritance data*

Joined Strategy

From the perspective of a Java developer, a data model that maps each entity to its own table makes a lot of sense. Every entity, whether it is abstract or concrete, will have its state mapped to a different table. Consistent with our earlier description, mapped superclasses do not get mapped to their own tables but are mapped as part of their entity subclasses.

Mapping a table per entity provides the data reuse that a normalized[2] data schema offers and is the most efficient way to store data that is shared by multiple subclasses in a hierarchy. The problem is that, when it comes time to reassemble an instance of any of the subclasses, the tables of the subclasses must be joined together with the superclass tables. It makes it fairly obvious why this strategy is called the joined strategy. It is also somewhat more expensive to insert an entity instance, because a row must be inserted in each of its superclass tables along the way.

Recall from the single-table strategy that the identifier must be of the same type for every class in the hierarchy. In a joined approach, we will have the same type of primary key in each of the tables, and the primary key of a subclass table also acts as a foreign key that joins to its superclass table. This should ring a bell because of its similarity to the multiple-table case earlier in the chapter where we joined the tables together using the primary keys of the tables and used the @PrimaryKeyJoinColumn annotation to indicate it. We use this same annotation in the joined inheritance case since we have multiple tables that each contain the same primary key type and each potentially has a row that contributes to the final combined entity state.

While joined inheritance is both intuitive and efficient in terms of data storage, the joining that it requires makes it somewhat expensive to use when hierarchies are deep or wide. The deeper the hierarchy, the more joins it will take to assemble instances of the concrete entity at the bottom. The broader the hierarchy the more joins it will take to query across an entity superclass.

In Figure 10-13, we see our Employee example mapped to a joined table architecture. The data for an entity subclass is spread across the tables in the same way that it is spread across the class hierarchy. When using a joined architecture, the decision as to whether CompanyEmployee is a mapped superclass or an entity makes a difference,

---

[2]Normalization of data is a database practice that attempts to remove redundantly stored data. For the seminal paper on data normalization, see "A Relational Model of Data for Large Shared Databanks" by E. F. Codd (Communications of the ACM, 13(6) June 1970). Also, any database design book or paper should have an overview.

since mapped superclasses do not get mapped to tables. An entity, even if it is an abstract class, always does. Figure 8-13 shows it as a mapped superclass, but if it were an entity, then an additional COMPANY_EMP table would exist with ID and VACATION columns in it, and the VACATION column in the FT_EMP and PT_EMP tables would not be present.

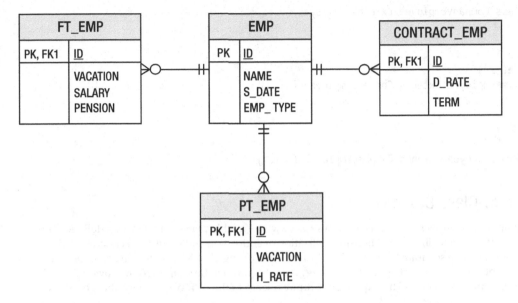

Figure 10-13. *Joined inheritance data model*

To map an entity hierarchy to a joined model, the @Inheritance annotation need only specify JOINED as the strategy. Like the single-table example, the subclasses will adopt the same strategy that is specified in the root entity superclass.

Even though there are multiple tables to model the hierarchy, the discriminator column is only defined on the root table, so the @DiscriminatorColumn annotation is placed on the same class as the @Inheritance annotation.

■ **Tip** Some vendors offer implementations of joined inheritance without the use of a discriminator column. Discriminator columns should be used if provider portability is required.

Our Employee hierarchy example can be mapped using the joined approach shown in Listing 10-35. In this example, we have used integer discriminator columns instead of the default string type.

Listing 10-35. Entity Hierarchy Mapped Using the Joined Strategy

```
@Entity
@Table(name="EMP")
@Inheritance(strategy=InheritanceType.JOINED)
@DiscriminatorColumn(name="EMP_TYPE", discriminatorType=DiscriminatorType.INTEGER)
public abstract class Employee { ... }

@Entity
@Table(name="CONTRACT_EMP")
```

```
@DiscriminatorValue("1")
public class ContractEmployee extends Employee { ... }

@MappedSuperclass
public abstract class CompanyEmployee extends Employee { ... }

@Entity
@Table(name="FT_EMP")
@DiscriminatorValue("2")
public class FullTimeEmployee extends CompanyEmployee { ... }

@Entity
@Table(name="PT_EMP")
@DiscriminatorValue("3")
public class PartTimeEmployee extends CompanyEmployee { ... }
```

Table-per-Concrete-Class Strategy

A third approach to mapping an entity hierarchy is to use a strategy where a table per concrete class is defined. This data architecture goes in the reverse direction of non-normalization of entity data and maps each concrete entity class and all its inherited state to a separate table. This has the effect of causing all shared state to be redefined in the tables of all the concrete entities that inherit it. This strategy is not required to be supported by providers but is included because it is anticipated that it will be required in a future release of the API. We will describe it briefly for completeness.

The negative side of using this strategy is that it makes polymorphic querying across a class hierarchy more expensive than the other strategies. The problem is that it must either issue multiple separate queries across each of the subclass tables, or query across all of them using a UNION operation, which is generally regarded as being expensive when lots of data is involved. If there are non-leaf concrete classes, then each of them will have its own table. Subclasses of the concrete classes will have to store the inherited fields in their own tables, along with their own defined fields.

The bright side of table-per-concrete-class hierarchies when compared to joined hierarchies is seen in cases of querying over instances of a single concrete entity. In the joined case, every query requires a join, even when querying across a single concrete entity class. In the table-per-concrete-class case, it is akin to the single-table hierarchy because the query is confined to a single table. Another advantage is that the discriminator column goes away. Every concrete entity has its own separate table, and there is no mixing or sharing of schema, so no class indicator is ever needed.

Mapping our example to this type of hierarchy is a matter of specifying the strategy as TABLE_PER_CLASS and making sure there is a table for each of the concrete classes. If a legacy database is being used, then the inherited columns could be named differently in each of the concrete tables and the @AttributeOverride annotation would come in handy. In this case, the CONTRACT_EMP table didn't have the NAME and S_DATE columns but instead had FULLNAME and SDATE for the name and startDate fields defined in Employee.

If the attribute that we wanted to override was an association instead of a simple state mapping, then we could still override the mapping, but we would need to use an @AssociationOverride annotation instead of @AttributeOverride. The @AssociationOverride annotation allows us to override the join columns used to reference the target entity of a many-to-one or one-to-one association defined in a mapped superclass. To show this, we need to add a manager attribute to the CompanyEmployee mapped superclass. The join column is mapped by default in the CompanyEmployee class to the MANAGER column in the two FT_EMP and PT_EMP subclass tables, but in PT_EMP the name of the join column is actually MGR. We override the join column by adding the @AssociationOverride annotation to the PartTimeEmployee entity class and specifying the name of the attribute we are overriding and the join column that we are overriding it to be. Listing 10-36 shows a complete example of the entity mappings, including the overrides.

Listing 10-36. Entity Hierarchy Mapped Using Table-per-Concrete-Class Strategy

```java
@Entity
@Inheritance(strategy=InheritanceType.TABLE_PER_CLASS)
public abstract class Employee {
    @Id private int id;
    private String name;
    @Temporal(TemporalType.DATE)
    @Column(name="S_DATE")
    private Date startDate;
    // ...
}

@Entity
@Table(name="CONTRACT_EMP")
@AttributeOverrides({
    @AttributeOverride(name="name", column=@Column(name="FULLNAME")),
    @AttributeOverride(name="startDate", column=@Column(name="SDATE"))
})
public class ContractEmployee extends Employee {
    @Column(name="D_RATE")
    private int dailyRate;
    private int term;
    // ...
}

@MappedSuperclass
public abstract class CompanyEmployee extends Employee {
    private int vacation;
    @ManyToOne
    private Employee manager;
    // ...
}

@Entity @Table(name="FT_EMP")
public class FullTimeEmployee extends CompanyEmployee {
    private long salary;
    @Column(name="PENSION")
    private long pensionContribution;
    // ...
}

@Entity
@Table(name="PT_EMP")
@AssociationOverride(name="manager",
                    joinColumns=@JoinColumn(name="MGR"))
public class PartTimeEmployee extends CompanyEmployee {
    @Column(name="H_RATE")
    private float hourlyRate;
    // ...
}
```

The table organization shows how these columns are mapped to the concrete tables. See Figure 10-14 for a clear picture of what the tables would look like and how the different types of employee instances would be stored.

CONTRACT_EMP	
PK	ID
	FULLNAME
	S_DATE
	D_RATE
	TERM

FT_EMP	
PK	ID
	NAME
	S_DATE
	VACATION
	SALARY
	FENSION
FK1	MANAGER

PT_EMP	
PK	ID
	NAME
	S_DATE
	VACATION
	H_RATE
FK1	MGR

Figure 10-14. Table-per-concrete-class data model

Mixed Inheritance

We should begin this section by saying that the practice of mixing inheritance types within a single inheritance hierarchy is currently outside the specification. We are including it because it is both useful and interesting, but we are offering a warning that it might not be portable to rely on such behavior, even if your vendor supports it.

Furthermore, it really makes sense to mix only single-table and joined inheritance types. We will show an example of mixing these two, bearing in mind that support for them is vendor-specific. The intent is that, in future releases of the specification, the more useful cases will be standardized and required to be supported by compliant implementations.

The premise for mixing inheritance types is that it is well within the realm of possibilities that a data model includes a combination of single-table and joined-table designs within a single entity hierarchy. This can be illustrated by taking our joined example in Figure 10-13 and storing the FullTimeEmployee and PartTimeEmployee instances in a single table. This would produce a model that looks like the one shown in Figure 10-15.

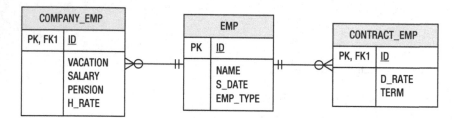

Figure 10-15. Mixed inheritance data model

In this example, the joined strategy is used for the Employee and ContractEmployee classes, while the CompanyEmployee, FullTimeEmployee, and PartTimeEmployee classes revert to a single-table model. To make this inheritance strategy switch at the level of the CompanyEmployee, we need to make a simple change to the hierarchy. We need to turn CompanyEmployee into an abstract entity instead of a mapped superclass so that it can bear the new inheritance metadata. Note that this is simply an annotation change, not making any change to the domain model.

The inheritance strategies can be mapped as shown in Listing 10-37. Notice that we do not need to have a discriminator column for the single-table subhierarchy since we already have one in the superclass EMP table.

Listing 10-37. Entity Hierarchy Mapped Using Mixed Strategies

```
@Entity
@Table(name="EMP")
@Inheritance(strategy=InheritanceType.JOINED)
@DiscriminatorColumn(name="EMP_TYPE")
public abstract class Employee {
    @Id private int id;
    private String name;
    @Temporal(TemporalType.DATE)
    @Column(name="S_DATE")
    private Date startDate;
    // ...
}

@Entity
@Table(name="CONTRACT_EMP")
public class ContractEmployee extends Employee {
    @Column(name="D_RATE") private int dailyRate;
    private int term;
    // ...
}

@Entity
@Table(name="COMPANY_EMP")
@Inheritance(strategy=InheritanceType.SINGLE_TABLE)
public abstract class CompanyEmployee extends Employee {
    private int vacation;
    // ...
}

@Entity
public class FullTimeEmployee extends CompanyEmployee {
    private long salary;
    @Column(name="PENSION")
    private long pensionContribution;
    // ...
}

@Entity
public class PartTimeEmployee extends CompanyEmployee {
    @Column(name="H_RATE")
    private float hourlyRate;
    // ...
}
```

Summary

Entity mapping requirements often go well beyond the simplistic mappings that map a field or a relationship to a named column. In this chapter, we addressed some of the more varied and diverse mapping practices that are supported by the Java Persistence API.

We discussed how to delimit database identifiers on a case-by-case basis, or for all the mappings in a persistence unit. We illustrated how delimiting identifiers allows the inclusion of special characters and provides case-sensitivity when the target database requires it.

A method of doing fine-grained conversion of basic attribute state was shown to be a powerful technique to adapt data. By creating converters we were also able to persist existing and newly defined data types in highly customizable ways. Conversion can be declaratively controlled on a flexible per-attribute or across-the-board basis.

We showed how embeddable objects can have state, element collections, further nested embeddables, and even relationships. We gave examples of reusing an embeddable object with relationships in it by overriding the relationship mappings within the embedding entity.

Identifiers may be composed of multiple columns. We revealed the two approaches for defining and using compound primary keys, and demonstrated when they could be used. We established how other entities can have foreign key references to entities with compound identifiers and explained how multiple join columns can be used in any context when a single join column applies. We also showed some examples of mapping identifiers, called derived identifiers, which included a relationship as part of their identities.

We explained some advanced relationship features, such as read-only mappings and optionality, and showed how they could be of benefit to some models. We then went on to describe some of the more advanced mapping scenarios that included using join tables or sometimes avoiding the use of join tables. The topic of orphan removal was also touched upon and clarified.

We went on to show how to distribute entity state across multiple tables and how to use the secondary tables with relationships. We even saw how an embedded object can map to a secondary table of an entity.

Finally, we went into detail about the three different inheritance strategies that can be used to map inheritance hierarchies to tables. We explained mapped superclasses and how they can be used to define shared state and behavior. We went over the data models that differentiate the various approaches and showed how to map an entity hierarchy to the tables in each case. We finished off by illustrating how to mix inheritance types within a single hierarchy.

In the next chapter, we will continue our discussion of advanced topics but turn our attention to queries and the use of native SQL and stored procedures. We will also exlain how to create entity graphs and use them to create query fetch plans.

■ ■ ■

CHAPTER 11

Advanced Queries

At this point, most of you will know enough about queries from what you have learned so far that you will likely not need any of the material from this chapter. In fact, roughly half of this chapter deals with using queries that will couple your application to a target database, so they should be used with some degree of planning and caution in any case.

We will start by going through the JPA support for native SQL queries and show how the results can be mapped to entities, non-entities, or simple data projection results. We will then move on to stored procedure queries and explain how a stored procedure can be invoked from within a JPA application and how the results may be returned.

The second half of the chapter deals with entity graphs and how they can be used to override the fetch type of a mapping during a query. When passed as fetch graphs or load graphs they provide great flexibility at runtime for controlling what state should get loaded and when.

SQL Queries

With all the effort that has gone into abstracting away the physical data model, both in terms of object-relational mapping and JP QL, it might be surprising to learn that SQL is alive and well in JPA. Although JP QL is the preferred method of querying over entities, SQL cannot be overlooked as a necessary element in many enterprise applications. The sheer size and scope of the SQL features, supported by the major database vendors, means that a portable language such as JP QL will never be able to fully encompass all their features.

■ **Note**   SQL queries are also known as native queries. `EntityManager` methods and query annotations related to SQL queries also use this terminology. While this allows other query languages to be supported in the future, any query string in a native query operation is assumed to be SQL.

Before discussing the mechanics of SQL queries, let's first consider some of the reasons why a developer using JP QL might want to integrate SQL queries into their application.

First, JP QL, despite the enhancements made in JPA 2.0, still contains only a subset of the features supported by many database vendors. Inline views (subqueries in the FROM clause), hierarchical queries, and additional function expressions to manipulate date and time values are just some of the features not supported in JP QL.

Second, although vendors may provide hints to assist with optimizing a JP QL expression, there are cases where the only way to achieve the performance required by an application is to replace the JP QL query with a hand-optimized SQL version. This may be a simple restructuring of the query that the persistence provider was generating, or it may be a vendor-specific version that leverages query hints and features specific to a particular database.

Of course, just because you can use SQL doesn't mean you should. Persistence providers have become very skilled at generating high-performance queries, and many of the limitations of JP QL can often be worked around in application code. We recommend avoiding SQL initially if possible and then introducing it only when necessary. This will enable your queries to be more portable across databases and more maintainable as your mappings change.

The following sections will discuss how SQL queries are defined using JPA and how their result sets can be mapped back to entities. One of the major benefits of SQL query support is that it uses the same Query interface used for JP QL queries. With some small exceptions that will be described later, all the Query interface operations discussed in previous chapters apply equally to both JP QL and SQL queries.

Native Queries vs. JDBC

A perfectly valid question for anyone investigating SQL support in JPA is whether it is needed at all. JDBC has been in use for years, provides a broad feature set, and works well. It's one thing to introduce a persistence API that works on entities, but another thing entirely to introduce a new API for issuing SQL queries.

The main reason to consider using SQL queries in JPA, instead of just issuing JDBC queries, is when the result of the query will be converted back into entities. As an example, let's consider a typical use case for SQL in an application that uses JPA. Given the employee id for a manager, the application needs to determine all the employees who report to that manager either directly or indirectly. For example, if the query were for a senior manager, the results would include all the managers who report to that senior manager as well as the employees who report to those managers. This type of query cannot be implemented by using JP QL, but a database such as Oracle natively supports hierarchical queries for just this purpose. Listing 11-1 demonstrates the typical sequence of JDBC calls to execute this query and transform the results into entities for use by the application.

Listing 11-1. Querying Entities Using SQL and JDBC

```
@Stateless
public class OrgStructureBean implements OrgStructure {
    private static final String ORG_QUERY =
        "SELECT emp_id, name, salary " +
        "FROM emp " +
        "START WITH manager_id = ? " +
        "CONNECT BY PRIOR emp_id = manager_id";

    @Resource
    DataSource hrDs;

    public List findEmployeesReportingTo(int managerId) {
        Connection conn = null;
        PreparedStatement sth = null;
        try {
            conn = hrDs.getConnection();
            sth = conn.prepareStatement(ORG_QUERY);
            sth.setLong(1, managerId);
            ResultSet rs = sth.executeQuery();

            ArrayList<Employee> result = new ArrayList<Employee>();
            while (rs.next()) {
                Employee emp = new Employee();
                emp.setId(rs.getInt(1));
                emp.setName(rs.getString(2));
                emp.setSalary(rs.getLong(3));
                result.add(emp);
            }
```

```
                return result;
            } catch (SQLException e) {
                throw new EJBException(e);
            }
        }
    }
}
```

Now consider the alternative syntax supported by JPA, as shown in Listing 11-2. By simply indicating that the result of the query is the Employee entity, the query engine uses the object-relational mapping of the entity to figure out which result columns map to the entity properties and builds the result set accordingly.

Listing 11-2. Querying Entities Using SQL and the Query Interface

```
@Stateless
public class OrgStructureBean implements OrgStructure {
    private static final String ORG_QUERY =
        "SELECT emp_id, name, salary, manager_id, dept_id, address_id " +
        "FROM emp " +
        "START WITH manager_id = ? " +
        "CONNECT BY PRIOR emp_id = manager_id";

    @PersistenceContext(unitName="EmployeeService")
    EntityManager em;

    public List findEmployeesReportingTo(int managerId) {
        return em.createNativeQuery(ORG_QUERY, Employee.class)
                .setParameter(1, managerId)
                .getResultList();
    }
}
```

Not only is the code much easier to read but it also makes use of the same Query interface that can be used for JP QL queries. This helps to keep application code consistent because it needs to concern itself only with the EntityManager and Query interfaces.

An unfortunate result of adding the TypedQuery interface in JPA 2.0 is that the createNativeQuery() method was already defined in JPA 1.0 to accept a SQL string and a result class and return an untyped Query interface. Now there is no backward compatible way to return a TypedQuery instead of a Query. The regrettable consequence is that when the createNativeQuery() method is called with a result class argument one might mistakenly think it will produce a TypedQuery, like createQuery() and createNamedQuery() do when a result class is passed in.

Defining and Executing SQL Queries

SQL queries may be defined dynamically at runtime or named in persistence unit metadata, similar to the JP QL query definitions discussed in Chapter 7. The key difference between defining JP QL and SQL queries lies in the understanding that the query engine should not parse and interpret vendor-specific SQL. In order to execute a SQL query and get entity instances in return, additional mapping information about the query result is required.

The first and simplest form of dynamically defining a SQL query that returns an entity result is to use the createNativeQuery() method of the EntityManager interface, passing in the query string and the entity type that will be returned. Listing 11-2 in the previous section demonstrated this approach to map the results of an Oracle hierarchical query to the Employee entity. The query engine uses the object-relational mapping of the entity to figure out which result column aliases map to which entity properties. As each row is processed, the query engine instantiates a new entity instance and sets the available data into it.

If the column aliases of the query do not match up exactly with the object-relational mappings for the entity, or if the results contain both entity and non-entity results, SQL result set mapping metadata is required. SQL result set mappings are defined as persistence unit metadata and are referenced by name. When the createNativeQuery() method is invoked with a SQL query string and a result set mapping name, the query engine uses this mapping to build the result set. SQL result set mappings are discussed in the next section.

Named SQL queries are defined using the @NamedNativeQuery annotation. This annotation may be placed on any entity and defines the name of the query as well as the query text. Like JP QL named queries, the name of the query must be unique within the persistence unit. If the result type is an entity, the resultClass element may be used to indicate the entity class. If the result requires a SQL mapping, the resultSetMapping element may be used to specify the mapping name. Listing 11-3 shows how the hierarchical query demonstrated earlier would be defined as a named query.

Listing 11-3. Using an Annotation to Define a Named Native Query

```
@NamedNativeQuery(
    name="orgStructureReportingTo",
    query="SELECT emp_id, name, salary, manager_id, dept_id, address_id " +
        "FROM emp " +
        "START WITH manager_id = ? " +
        "CONNECT BY PRIOR emp_id = manager_id",
    resultClass=Employee.class
)
```

One advantage of using named SQL queries is that the application can use the createNamedQuery() method on the EntityManager interface to create and execute the query. The fact that the named query was defined using SQL instead of JP QL is not important to the caller. A further benefit is that createNamedQuery() can return a TypedQuery whereas the createNativeQuery() method returns an untyped Query.

Listing 11-4 demonstrates the reporting structure bean again, this time using a named query. The other advantage of using named queries instead of dynamic queries is that they can be overridden using XML mapping files. A query originally specified in JP QL can be overridden with a SQL version, and vice versa. This technique is described in Chapter 13.

Listing 11-4. Executing a Named SQL Query

```
@Stateless
public class OrgStructureBean implements OrgStructure {
    @PersistenceContext(unitName="EmployeeService")
    EntityManager em;

    public List<Employee> findEmployeesReportingTo(int managerId) {
        return em.createNamedQuery("orgStructureReportingTo",
                                    Employee.class)
                .setParameter(1, managerId)
                .getResultList();
    }
}
```

One thing to be careful of with SQL queries that return entities is that the resulting entity instances become managed by the persistence context, just like the results of a JP QL query. If you modify one of the returned entities, it will be written to the database when the persistence context becomes associated with a transaction. This is normally what you want, but it requires that any time you select data that corresponds to existing entity instances, it is important to ensure that all the necessary data required to fully construct the entity is part of the query. If you leave out a field from the query, or default it to some value and then modify the resulting entity, there is a possibility that you will overwrite the correct version already stored in the database. This is because the missing state will be null (or some default value according to the type) in the entity. When the transaction commits, the persistence context does not know that the state was not properly read in from the query and might just attempt to write out null or the default value.

There are two benefits to getting managed entities back from a SQL query. The first is that a SQL query can replace an existing JP QL query and that application code should still work without changes. The second benefit is that it allows the developer to use SQL queries as a method of constructing new entity instances from tables that may not have any object-relational mapping. For example, in many database architectures, there is a staging area to hold data that has not yet been verified or requires some kind of transformation before it can be moved to its final location. Using JPA, a developer could start a transaction, query the staged data to construct entities, perform any required changes, and then commit. The newly created entities will get written to the tables mapped by the entity, not the staging tables used in the SQL query. This is more appealing than the alternative of having a second set of mappings that maps the same entities (or even worse, a second parallel set of entities) to the staging tables and then writing some code that reads, copies, and rewrites the entities.

SQL data-manipulation statements (INSERT, UPDATE, and DELETE) are also supported as a convenience so that JDBC calls do not have to be introduced in an application otherwise limited to JPA. To define such a query, use the createNativeQuery() method, but without any mapping information. Listing 11-5 demonstrates these types of queries in the form of a session bean that logs messages to a table. Note that the bean methods run in a REQUIRES_NEW transaction context to ensure that the message is logged even if an active transaction rolls back.

Listing 11-5. Using SQL INSERT and DELETE Statements

```java
@Stateless
@TransactionAttribute(TransactionAttributeType.REQUIRES_NEW)
public class LoggerBean implements Logger {
    private static final String INSERT_SQL =
        "INSERT INTO message_log (id, message, log_dttm) " +
        "        VALUES(id_seq.nextval, ?, SYSDATE)";
    private static final String DELETE_SQL =
        "DELETE FROM message_log";

    @PersistenceContext(unitName="Logger")
    EntityManager em;

    public void logMessage(String message) {
        em.createNativeQuery(INSERT_SQL)
          .setParameter(1, message)
          .executeUpdate();
    }

    public void clearMessageLog() {
        em.createNativeQuery(DELETE_SQL)
          .executeUpdate();
    }
}
```

Executing SQL statements that make changes to data in tables mapped by entities is generally discouraged. Doing so may cause cached entities to be inconsistent with the database because the provider cannot track changes made to entity state that has been modified by data-manipulation statements.

SQL Result Set Mapping

In the SQL query examples shown so far, the result mapping was straightforward. The column aliases in the SQL string matched up directly with the object-relational column mapping for a single entity. It is not always the case that the names match up, nor is it always the case that only a single entity type is returned. JPA provides SQL result set mappings to handle these scenarios.

A SQL result set mapping is defined using the @SqlResultSetMapping annotation. It may be placed on an entity class and consists of a name (unique within the persistence unit) and one or more entity and column mappings. The entity result class argument on the createNativeQuery() method is really a shortcut to specifying a simple SQL result set mapping. The following mapping is equivalent to specifying Employee.class in a call to createNativeQuery():

```
@SqlResultSetMapping(
    name="EmployeeResult",
    entities=@EntityResult(entityClass=Employee.class)
)
```

Here we have defined a SQL result set mapping called "EmployeeResult" that may be referenced by any query returning Employee entity instances. The mapping consists of a single entity result, specified by the @EntityResult annotation, which references the Employee entity class. The query must supply values for all columns mapped by the entity, including foreign keys. It is vendor-specific whether the entity is partially constructed or whether an error occurs if any required entity state is missing.

Mapping Foreign Keys

Foreign keys do not need to be explicitly mapped as part of the SQL result set mapping. When the query engine attempts to map the query results to an entity, it considers foreign key columns for single-valued associations as well. Let's look at the reporting structure SQL query again.

```
SELECT emp_id, name, salary, manager_id, dept_id, address_id
FROM emp
START WITH manager_id IS NULL
CONNECT BY PRIOR emp_id = manager_id
```

The MANAGER_ID, DEPT_ID, and ADDRESS_ID columns all map to the join columns of associations on the Employee entity. An Employee instance returned from this query can use the methods getManager(), getDepartment(), and getAddress(), and the results will be as expected. The persistence provider will retrieve the associated entity based on the foreign key value read in from the query. There is no way to populate collection associations from a SQL query. Entity instances constructed from this example are effectively the same as they would have been had they been returned from a JP QL query.

Multiple Result Mappings

A query may return more than one entity at a time. This is most often useful if there is a one-to-one relationship between two entities; otherwise, the query will result in duplicate entity instances. Consider the following query:

```
SELECT emp_id, name, salary, manager_id, dept_id, address_id,
       id, street, city, state, zip
FROM emp, address
WHERE address_id = id
```

The SQL result set mapping to return both the Employee and Address entities out of this query is defined in Listing 11-6. Each entity is listed in an @EntityResult annotation, an array of which is assigned to the entities element. The order in which the entities are listed is not important. The query engine uses the column names of the query to match against entity mapping data, not column position.

Listing 11-6. *Mapping a SQL Query that Returns Two Entity Types*

```
@SqlResultSetMapping(
    name="EmployeeWithAddress",
    entities={@EntityResult(entityClass=Employee.class),
              @EntityResult(entityClass=Address.class)}
)
```

Mapping Column Aliases

If the column aliases in the SQL statement do not directly match up with the names specified in the column mappings for the entity, field result mappings are required for the query engine to make the correct association. Suppose, for example, that both the EMP and ADDRESS tables listed in the previous example used the column ID for their primary key. The query would have to be altered to alias the ID columns so that they are unique:

```
SELECT emp.id AS emp_id, name, salary, manager_id, dept_id, address_id,
       address.id, street, city, state, zip
FROM emp, address
WHERE address_id = address.id
```

The @FieldResult annotation is used to map column aliases to the entity attributes in situations where the name in the query is not the same as the one used in the column mapping. Listing 11-7 shows the mapping required to convert the EMP_ID alias to the id attribute of the entity. More than one @FieldResult may be specified, but only the mappings that are different need to be specified. This can be a partial list of entity attributes.

Listing 11-7. *Mapping a SQL Query with Unknown Column Aliases*

```
@SqlResultSetMapping(
    name="EmployeeWithAddress",
    entities={@EntityResult(entityClass=Employee.class,
                            fields=@FieldResult(
                                       name="id",
                                       column="EMP_ID")),
              @EntityResult(entityClass=Address.class)}
)
```

Mapping Scalar Result Columns

SQL queries are not limited to returning only entity results, although it is expected that this will be the primary use case. Consider the following query:

```
SELECT e.name AS emp_name, m.name AS manager_name
FROM emp e,
     emp m
WHERE e.manager_id = m.emp_id (+)
START WITH e.manager_id IS NULL
CONNECT BY PRIOR e.emp_id = e.manager_id
```

Non-entity result types, called scalar result types, are mapped using the @ColumnResult annotation. One or more column mappings may be assigned to the columns attribute of the mapping annotation. The only attribute available for a column mapping is the column name. Listing 11-8 shows the SQL mapping for the employee and manager hierarchical query.

Listing 11-8. Scalar Column Mappings

```
@SqlResultSetMapping(
    name="EmployeeAndManager",
    columns={@ColumnResult(name="EMP_NAME"),
             @ColumnResult(name="MANAGER_NAME")}
)
```

Scalar results may also be mixed with entities. In this case, the scalar results are typically providing additional information about the entity.

Let's look at a more complex example in which this would be the case. A report for an application needs to see information about each department, showing the manager, the number of employees, and the average salary. The following JP QL query produces the correct report:

```
SELECT d, m, COUNT(e), AVG(e.salary)
FROM Department d LEFT JOIN d.employees e
                  LEFT JOIN d.employees m
WHERE m IS NULL OR m IN (SELECT de.manager
                         FROM Employee de
                         WHERE de.department = d)
GROUP BY d, m
```

This query is particularly challenging because there is no direct relationship from Department to the Employee who is the manager of the department. Therefore, the employees relationship must be joined twice: once for the employees assigned to the department and once for the employee in that group who is also the manager. This is possible because the subquery reduces the second join of the employees relationship to a single result. We also need to accommodate the fact that there might not be any employees currently assigned to the department, and further that a department might not have a manager assigned. This means that each of the joins must be an outer join and that we further have to use an OR condition to allow for the missing manager in the WHERE clause.

Once in production, it is determined that the SQL query generated by the provider is not performing well, so the DBA proposes an alternate query that takes advantage of the inline views possible with the Oracle database. The query to accomplish this result is shown in Listing 11-9.

Listing 11-9. Department Summary Query

```
SELECT d.id, d.name AS dept_name,
       e.emp_id, e.name, e.salary, e.manager_id, e.dept_id,
       e.address_id,
       s.tot_emp, s.avg_sal
FROM dept d,
    (SELECT *
     FROM emp e
     WHERE EXISTS(SELECT 1 FROM emp WHERE manager_id = e.emp_id)) e,
    (SELECT d.id, COUNT(*) AS tot_emp, AVG(e.salary) AS avg_sal
     FROM dept d, emp e
```

```
      WHERE d.id = e.dept_id (+)
      GROUP BY d.id) s
WHERE d.id = e.dept_id (+) AND
      d.id = s.id
```

Fortunately, mapping this query is a lot easier than reading it. The query results consist of a `Department` entity, an `Employee` entity, and two scalar results, the number of the employees and the average salary. Listing 11-10 shows the mapping for this query.

Listing 11-10. Mapping for the Department Query

```
@SqlResultSetMapping(
    name="DepartmentSummary",
    entities={
        @EntityResult(entityClass=Department.class,
                      fields=@FieldResult(name="name", column="DEPT_NAME")),
        @EntityResult(entityClass=Employee.class)
    },
    columns={@ColumnResult(name="TOT_EMP"),
             @ColumnResult(name="AVG_SAL")}
)
```

Mapping Compound Keys

When a primary or foreign key is composed of multiple columns that have been aliased to unmapped names, a special notation must be used in the `@FieldResult` annotations to identify each part of the key. Consider the query shown in Listing 11-11 that returns both the employee and the manager of the employee. The table in this example is the same one we demonstrated in Figure 10-4 of Chapter 10. Because each column is repeated twice, the columns for the manager state have been aliased to new names.

Listing 11-11. SQL Query Returning Employee and Manager

```
SELECT e.country, e.emp_id, e.name, e.salary,
       e.manager_country, e.manager_id, m.country AS mgr_country,
       m.emp_id AS mgr_id, m.name AS mgr_name, m.salary AS mgr_salary,
       m.manager_country AS mgr_mgr_country, m.manager_id AS mgr_mgr_id
FROM   emp e,
       emp m
WHERE  e.manager_country = m.country AND
       e.manager_id = m.emp_id
```

The result set mapping for this query depends on the type of primary key class used by the target entity. Listing 11-12 shows the mapping in the case where an id class has been used. For the primary key, each attribute is listed as a separate field result. For the foreign key, each primary key attribute of the target entity (the `Employee` entity again in this example) is suffixed to the name of the relationship attribute.

Listing 11-12. Mapping for Employee Query Using id Class

```
@SqlResultSetMapping(
    name="EmployeeAndManager",
    entities={
        @EntityResult(entityClass=Employee.class),
```

```
    @EntityResult(
        entityClass=Employee.class,
        fields={
            @FieldResult(name="country", column="MGR_COUNTRY"),
            @FieldResult(name="id", column="MGR_ID"),
            @FieldResult(name="name", column="MGR_NAME"),
            @FieldResult(name="salary", column="MGR_SALARY"),
            @FieldResult(name="manager.country",
                            column="MGR_MGR_COUNTRY"),
            @FieldResult(name="manager.id", column="MGR_MGR_ID")
        }
    )
    }
)
```

If Employee uses an embedded id class instead of an id class, the notation is slightly different. We have to include the primary key attribute name as well as the individual attributes within the embedded type. Listing 11-13 shows the result set mapping using this notation.

Listing 11-13. Mapping for Employee Query Using Embedded id Class

```
@SqlResultSetMapping(
    name="EmployeeAndManager",
    entities={
        @EntityResult(entityClass=Employee.class),
        @EntityResult(
            entityClass=Employee.class,
            fields={
                @FieldResult(name="id.country", column="MGR_COUNTRY"),
                @FieldResult(name="id.id", column="MGR_ID"),
                @FieldResult(name="name", column="MGR_NAME"),
                @FieldResult(name="salary", column="MGR_SALARY"),
                @FieldResult(name="manager.id.country",
                                column="MGR_MGR_COUNTRY"),
                @FieldResult(name="manager.id.id", column="MGR_MGR_ID")
            }
        )
    }
)
```

Mapping Inheritance

In many respects, polymorphic queries in SQL are no different from regular queries returning a single entity type. All columns must be accounted for, including foreign keys and the discriminator column for single-table and joined inheritance strategies. The key thing to remember is that if the results include more than one entity type, each of the columns for all the possible entity types must be represented in the query. The field result mapping techniques demonstrated earlier may be used to customize columns that use unknown aliases. These columns may be at any level in the inheritance tree. The only special element in the @EntityResult annotation for use with inheritance is the discriminatorColumn element. This element allows the name of the discriminator column to be specified in the unlikely event that it is different from the mapped version.

Assume that the Employee entity had been mapped to the table shown in Figure 10-11 from Chapter 10. To understand aliasing a discriminator column, consider the following query that returns data from another EMPLOYEE_STAGE table structured to use single-table inheritance:

```
SELECT id, name, start_date, daily_rate, term, vacation,
       hourly_rate, salary, pension, type
FROM employee_stage
```

To convert the data returned from this query to Employee entities, the following result set mapping would be used:

```
@SqlResultSetMapping(
    name="EmployeeStageMapping",
    entities=
        @EntityResult(
            entityClass=Employee.class,
            discriminatorColumn="TYPE",
            fields={
                @FieldResult(name="startDate", column="START_DATE"),
                @FieldResult(name="dailyRate", column="DAILY_RATE"),
                @FieldResult(name="hourlyRate", column="HOURLY_RATE")
            }
        )
)
```

Mapping to Non-Entity Types

New with JPA 2.1 is the ability to construct non-entity types from native queries via constructor expressions. Constructor expressions in native queries, much like the constructor expressions from JP QL, result in the instantiation of user-specified types by using the row data of the underlying result set to invoke the constructor. All of the data required to construct the object must be represented as arguments to the constructor.

Consider the constructor expression example that we introduced in Chapter 8 to create instances of the EmployeeDetails data type by selecting specific fields from the Employee entity:

```
SELECT NEW example.EmployeeDetails(e.name, e.salary, e.department.name)
FROM Employee e
```

In order to replace this query with its native equivalent and achieve the same result, we must define both the replacement native query and an SqlResultSetMapping that defines how the query results map to the user-specified type. Let's begin by defining the SQL native query to replace the JP QL.

```
SELECT e.name, e.salary, d.name AS deptName
FROM emp e, dept d
WHERE e.dept_id = d.id
```

The mapping for this query is more verbose than the JP QL equivalent. Unlike JP QL where the columns are implicitly mapped to the constructor based on their position, native queries must fully define the set of data that will be mapped to the constructor in the mapping annotation. The following example demonstrates the mapping for this query:

```
@SqlResultSetMapping(
    name="EmployeeDetailMapping",
```

```
    classes={
        @ConstructorResult(
            targetClass=example.EmployeeDetails.class,
            columns={
                @ColumnResult(name="name"),
                @ColumnResult(name="salary", type=Long.class),
                @ColumnResult(name="deptName")
        })})
```

As with other examples that use `ColumnResult`, the name field refers to the column alias as defined in the SQL statement. The column results are applied to the constructor of the user-specified type in the order in which the column result mappings are defined. In cases where there are multiple constructors that may be ambiguous based on position only, the column result type may also be specified in order to ensure the correct match.

It is worth noting that should an entity type be specified as the target class of a `ConstructorResult` mapping, any resulting entity instances would be considered unmanaged by the current persistence context. Entity mappings on user-specified types are ignored when processed as part of a native query using constructor expressions.

■ **Tip** Mapping SQL queries to non-entity types was only added in JPA 2.1.

Parameter Binding

SQL queries have traditionally supported only positional parameter binding. The JDBC specification itself supports only named parameters on `CallableStatement` objects, not `PreparedStatement`, and not all database vendors even support this syntax. As a result, JPA guarantees only the use of positional parameter binding for SQL queries. Check with your vendor to see whether the named parameter methods of the `Query` interface are supported, but understand that using them may make your application non-portable between persistence providers.

Another limitation of parameter support for SQL queries is that entity parameters cannot be used. The specification does not define how these parameter types should be treated. Be careful when converting or overriding a named JP QL query with a native SQL query that the parameter values are still interpreted correctly.

Stored Procedures

One of the important new features added to JPA 2.1 is the ability to map and invoke stored procedures from a database. While stored procedures could be invoked in some circumstances using the native query support in previous versions of the specification, JPA 2.1 introduces first class support for stored procedure queries on the `EntityManager` and defines a new query type, `StoredProcedureQuery`, which extends `Query` and better handles the range of options open to developers who leverage stored procedures in their applications.

The following sections will describe how to map and invoke stored procedure queries using JPA. Note that the implementation of stored procedures is highly database dependent and is therefore outside the scope of this book. Unlike JP QL and other types of native queries, the body of a stored procedure is never defined in JPA and is instead only ever referenced by name in the application.

Defining and Executing Stored Procedure Queries

Like other types of JPA queries, stored procedure queries may be created programmatically from the `EntityManager` interface or they may be defined using annotation metadata and later referenced by name. In order to define a stored procedure mapping, the name of the stored procedure must be provided as well as the name and type of all parameters to that stored procedure.

JPA stored procedure definitions support the main parameter types defined for JDBC stored procedures: IN, OUT, INOUT, and REF_CURSOR. As their name suggests, IN and OUT parameter types pass data to the stored procedure or return it to the caller, respectively. INOUT parameter types combine IN and OUT behavior into a single type that can both accept and return a value to the caller. REF_CURSOR parameter types are used to return result sets to the caller. Each of these types has a corresponding enum value defined on the ParameterMode type.

Stored procedures are assumed to return all values through parameters except in the case where the database supports returning a result set (or multiple result sets) from a stored procedure. Databases that support this method of returning result sets usually do so as an alternative to the use of REF_CURSOR parameter types. Unfortunately, stored procedure behavior is very vendor specific, and this is an example where writing to a particular feature of a database is unavoidable in application code.

Scalar Parameter Types

To begin, let's consider a simple stored procedure named "hello" that accepts a single string argument named "name" and returns a friendly greeting to the caller via the same parameter. The following example demonstrates how to define and execute such a stored procedure:

```
StoredProcedureQuery q = em.createStoredProcedureQuery("hello");
q.registerStoredProcedureParameter("name", String.class, ParameterMode.INOUT);
q.execute();
String value = q.getOutputParameterValue("name");
```

After the query has been executed via the execute() method, any IN or INOUT parameter values returned to the caller may be accessed using one of the getOutputParameterValue() methods, specifying either the name of the parameter or its position. As with native queries, parameter positions are numbered beginning with one. Therefore, if an OUT parameter is registered in the second position for a query, then the number two would be used to access that value, even if the first parameter is of IN type and does not return any value.

Note that calling the getSingleResult() or getResultList() methods of the inherited Query interface will result in an exception if the stored procedure only returns scalar values through parameters.

Result Set Parameter Types

Now let's move to a more sophisticated example in which we have a stored procedure named "fetch_emp" that retrieves employee data and returns it to the caller via a REF_CURSOR parameter. In this case, we will use the overloaded form of createStoredProcedureQuery() to indicate that the result set consists of Employee entities. The following example demonstrates this approach:

```
StoredProcedureQuery q = em.createStoredProcedureQuery("fetch_emp");
q.registerStoredProcedureParameter("empList", void.class, ParameterMode.REF_CURSOR);
if (q.execute()) {
    List<Employee> emp = (List<Employee>)q.getOutputParameterValue("empList");
    // ...
}
```

The first thing to note about this example is that we are not specifying a parameter class type for the empList parameter. Whenever REF_CURSOR is specified as the parameter type, the class type argument to registerStoredProcedureParameter() is ignored. The second thing to note is that we are checking the return value of execute() to see any result sets were returned during the execution of the query. If no result sets are returned (or the query only returns scalar values), execute() will return false. In the event that no records were returned and we did not check the result of execute(), then the parameter value would be null.

Previously it was noted that some databases allow result sets to be returned from stored procedures without having to specify a REF_CURSOR parameter. In this case, we can simplify the example by using the getResultList() method of the query interface to directly access the results:

```
StoredProcedureQuery q = em.createStoredProcedureQuery("fetch_emp");
List<Employee> emp = (List<Employee>)q.getResultList();
// ...
```

As a shortcut for executing queries, both getResultList() and getSingleResult() implicitly invoke execute(). In the case where the stored procedure returns more than one result set, each call to getResultList() will return the next result set in the sequence.

Stored Procedure Mapping

Stored procedure queries may be declared using the @NamedStoredProcedureQuery annotation and then referred to by name using the createNamedStoredProcedureQuery() method on EntityManager. This simplifies the code required to invoke the query and allows for more complex mappings than are possible using the StoredProcedureQuery interface. Like other JPA query types, names for stored procedure queries must be unique within the scope of a persistence unit.

We'll begin by declaring the simple "hello" example using annotations and then progressively move to more complex examples. The "hello" stored procedure would be mapped as follows:

```
@NamedStoredProcedureQuery(
    name="hello",
    procedureName="hello",
    parameters={
        @StoredProcedureParameter(name="name", type=String.class,
                                        mode=ParameterMode.INOUT)
})
```

Here we can see that the native procedure name must be specified in addition to the name of the stored procedure query. It is not defaulted as it is when using the createStoredProcedureQuery() method. As with the programmatic example, all parameters must be specified using the same arguments as would be used with registerStoredProcedureParameter().

The "fetch_emp" query is mapped similarly, but in this example we must also specify a mapping for the result set type:

```
@NamedStoredProcedureQuery(
    name="fetch_emp",
    procedureName="fetch_emp",
    parameters={
        @StoredProcedureParameter(name="empList", type=void.class,
                                        mode=ParameterMode.REF_CURSOR)
    },
    resultClasses=Employee.class)
```

The list of classes provided to the resultClasses field is a list of entity types. In the version of this example where REF_CURSOR is not used and the results are returned directly from the stored procedure, the empList parameter would simply be omitted. The resultClasses field would be sufficient. It is important to note that the entities referenced in resultClasses must match the order in which result set parameters are declared for the stored procedure. For example, if there are two REF_CURSOR parameters, "empList" and "deptList", then the resultClasses field must contain Employee and Department in that order.

For cases where the result sets returned by the query do not natively map to entity types, SQL result set mappings may also be included in the NamedStoredProcedureQuery annotation using the resultSetMappings field. For example, a stored procedure that performed the employee and manager query defined in Listing 11-11 (and mapped in Listing 11-12) would be mapped as follows:

```
@NameStoredProcedureQuery(
    name="queryEmployeeAndManager",
    procedureName="fetch_emp_and_mgr",
    resultSetMappings = "EmployeeAndManager"
)
```

As with resultClasses, multiple result set mappings may also be specified if the stored procedure returns multiple result sets. It should be noted, however, that combining resultClasses and resultSetMappings is undefined. Support for result set mappings in the NamedStoredProcedureQuery annotation ensures that even the most complex stored procedure definitions can likely be mapped by JPA, simplifying access and centralizing metadata in a manageable way.

■ **Tip**   Stored procedure query support was added in JPA 2.1.

Entity Graphs

Unlike what its name implies, an entity graph is not really a graph of entities, but rather a template for specifying entity and embeddable attributes. It serves as a pattern that can be passed into a find method or query to specify which entity and embeddable attributes should be fetched in the query result. In more concrete terms, entity graphs are used to override at runtime the fetch settings of attribute mappings. For example, if an attribute is mapped to be eagerly fetched (set to FetchType.EAGER) it can set to be lazily fetched for a single execution of a query. This feature is similar to what has been referred to by some as the ability to set a fetch plan, load plan, or fetch group.

■ **Note**   Although entity graphs are currently being used for overriding attribute fetch state in queries, they are just structures that define attribute inclusion. There are no inherent semantics stored in them. They could just as easily be used as an input to any operation that might benefit from an entity attribute template, and in future they might be used with other operations as well. However, we will focus on what exists right now and discuss entity graphs in the context of defining fetch plans.

The structure of an entity graph is fairly simple in that there are really only three types of objects that are contained within it.

- *Entity graph nodes*: There is exactly one entity graph node for every entity graph. It is the root of the entity graph and represents the root entity type. It contains all of the attribute nodes for that type, plus all of the subgraph nodes for types associated with the root entity type.[1]

- *Attribute nodes*: Each attribute node represents an attribute in an entity or embeddable type. If it is for a basic attribute, then there will be no subgraph associated with it, but if it is for a relationship attribute, embeddable attribute, or element collection of embeddables, then it may refer to a named subgraph.

- *Subgraph nodes*: A subgraph node is the equivalent of an entity graph node in that it contains attribute nodes and subgraph nodes, but represents a graph of attributes for an entity or embeddable type that is not the root type.[2]

To help illustrate the structure, let's assume that we have the domain model described in Figure 8-1 and want an entity graph representation that specifies a subset of those attributes and entities, as shown in Figure 11-1.

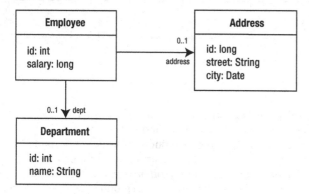

Figure 11-1. Domain model subset

The state in Figure 11-1 is clearly a subset of the state in Figure 8-1, and the entity graph structure to store a representative fetch plan for this state might look like the depiction in Figure 11-2.

---

[1] In a @NamedEntityGraph annotation it will contain the subgraph nodes for the entire entity graph.
[2] A subgraph can be defined for the root type, but in that case it is an additional fetch plan used when the root entity type is being accessed through a relationship.

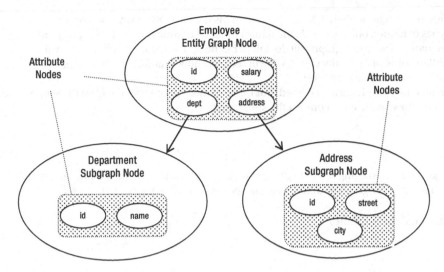

Figure 11-2. *Entity graph state*

Entity graphs can be defined statically in annotation form or dynamically through an API. The composition differs slightly when using the annotation form of creating entity graphs versus creating them with the API; however, Figure 11-2 shows the basic structure.

A key point to mention is that identifier and version attributes (see Chapter 12 for a complete description about version attributes) will always be included in both the entity graph node and each of the subgraph nodes. They do not need to be explicitly included when creating an entity graph, although if either of them is included, it is not an error, just a redundancy.

Every entity and embeddable class has a *default fetch graph* that is composed of the transitive closure of all of the attributes that are either explicitly defined as, or defaulted to be, eagerly fetched. The transitive closure part means that the rule is recursively applied, so the default fetch graph of an entity includes not only all of the eager attributes defined on it, but also all of the eager attributes of the entities that are related to it, and so on until the relationship graph has been exhausted. The default fetch graph will save us a lot of effort when it comes time to define more expansive entity graphs.

■ **Tip** Entity graphs and the ability to dynamically override the fetch type of an entity or embeddable attribute during a query or `find()` method was introduced in JPA 2.1.

Entity Graph Annotations

Defining an entity graph statically in an annotation is useful when you know ahead of time that an attribute access fetch pattern needs to be different than what has been configured in the mappings. You can define any number of entity graphs for the same entity, each depicting a different attribute fetch plan.

The parent annotation to define an entity graph is `@NamedEntityGraph`. It must be defined on the root entity of the entity graph. All of its components are nested within the one annotation, so this means two things. First, if you are defining a large and involved entity graph, then your annotation is going to also be large and involved (and not likely very pretty). Second, if you are defining multiple entity graphs, you cannot share any of the constituent subgraph parts of one with another.[3] They are completely encapsulated within the enclosing named entity graph.

---

[3]You can share subgraphs within the same entity graph, though.

You likely noticed that the annotation begins with the "Named" prefix. This is a clear giveaway that entity graphs are named, and like other types of named objects in JPA, the names must be unique within the scope of the persistence unit. If not specified, the name of an entity graph will default to be the entity name (which, as you will recall from Chapter 2, is the unqualified name of the entity class). We will see later how a name is used to refer to a given entity graph when obtaining it from the entity manager.

Note that the subgraphs within an entity graph are also named, but those names are only valid within the scope of the entity graph and, as you will see below, are used to connect the subgraphs.

Basic Attribute Graphs

Let's use the domain model from Figure 8-1 as a starting point. In that model there is an Address entity with some basic attributes. We could create a simple named entity graph by annotating the Address entity, as shown in Listing 11-14.

Listing 11-14. Named Entity Graph with Basic Attributes

```
@Entity
@NamedEntityGraph(
    attributeNodes={
        @NamedAttributeNode("street"),
        @NamedAttributeNode("city"),
        @NamedAttributeNode("state"),
        @NamedAttributeNode("zip")}
)
public class Address {
    @Id private long id;
    private String street;
    private String city;
    private String state;
    private String zip;
    // ...
}
```

The entity graph is assigned the default name of "Address" and all of the attributes are explicitly included in the attributeNodes element, meaning that they should be fetched. There is actually a shortcut for this case by means of a special includeAllAttributes element in the @NamedEntityGraph annotation:

```
@Entity
@NamedEntityGraph(includeAllAttributes=true)
public class Address { ... }
```

Since the Address entity contains only eager attributes anyway (all basic attributes default to being eager), we can make it even shorter:

```
@Entity
@NamedEntityGraph
public class Address { ... }
```

Annotating the class without listing any attributes is a shorthand for defining a named entity graph that is composed of the default fetch graph for that entity. Putting the annotation on the class causes the named entity graph to be created and referenceable by name in a query.

Using Subgraphs

The Address entity was a rather simple entity, though, and didn't even have any relationships. The Employee entity is more complicated and requires that we add in some subgraphs, as shown in Listing 11-15.

Listing 11-15. Named Entity Graph with Subgraphs

```
@Entity
@NamedEntityGraph(name="Employee.graph1",
    attributeNodes={
        @NamedAttributeNode("name"),
        @NamedAttributeNode("salary"),
        @NamedAttributeNode(value="address"),
        @NamedAttributeNode(value="phones", subgraph="phone"),
        @NamedAttributeNode(value="department" subgraph="dept")},
    subgraphs={
        @NamedSubgraph(name="phone",
            attributeNodes={
                @NamedAttributeNode("number"),
                @NamedAttributeNode("type")}),
        @NamedSubgraph(name="dept",
            attributeNodes={
                @NamedAttributeNode("name")})
    })
public class Employee {
    @Id
    private int id;
    private String name;
    private long salary;
    @Temporal(TemporalType.DATE)
    private Date startDate;

    @OneToOne
    private Address address;

    @OneToMany(mappedBy="employee")
    private Collection<Phone> phones = new ArrayList<Phone>();

    @ManyToOne
    private Department department;

    @ManyToOne
    private Employee manager;

    @OneToMany(mappedBy="manager")
    private Collection<Employee> directs = new ArrayList<Employee>();

    @ManyToMany(mappedBy="employees")
    private Collection<Project> projects = new ArrayList<Project>();
    // ...
}
```

For every `Employee` attribute that we want fetched, there is a `@NamedAttributeNode` listing the name of the attribute. The `address` attribute is a relationship, though, so listing it means that the address will be fetched, but what state will be fetched in the `Address` instance? This is where the default fetch group comes in. When a relationship attribute is listed in the graph but does not have any accompanying subgraph, then the default fetch group of the related class will be assumed. In fact, the general rule is that for any embeddable or entity type that has been specified to be fetched, but for which there is no subgraph, the default fetch graph for that class will be used. This is as you might expect since the default fetch graph specifies the behavior you get when you don't use an entity graph at all, so the absence of specifying one should be equivalent. For our address example from above you saw that the default fetch graph of `Address` is all of its (basic) attributes.

For the other relationship attributes the `@NamedAttributeNode` additionally includes a `subgraph` element, which references the name of a `@NamedSubgraph`. The named subgraph defines the attribute list for that related entity type, so the subgraph we named "dept" defines the attributes of the `Department` entity related via the `department` attribute of `Employee`.

All of the named subgraphs are defined in the `subgraphs` element of `@NamedEntityGraph`, regardless of where they fit in the type graph. This means that if the subgraph type contained a relationship attribute, then its named attribute node would contain a reference to yet another subgraph, which would also be listed in the `subgraphs` element of `@NamedEntityGraph`. We can even define a subgraph that defines an alternative fetch plan for our root entity graph class when it gets loaded through a related entity. As a matter of fact, there are times when we will need to do exactly that. Let's look at an example in Listing 11-16.

Listing 11-16. Named Entity Graph with Multiple Type Definitions

```
@Entity
@NamedEntityGraph(name="Employee.graph2",
    attributeNodes={
        @NamedAttributeNode("name"),
        @NamedAttributeNode("salary"),
        @NamedAttributeNode(value="address"),
        @NamedAttributeNode(value="phones", subgraph="phone"),
        @NamedAttributeNode(value="manager", subgraph="namedEmp"),
        @NamedAttributeNode(value="department", subgraph="dept")},
    subgraphs={
        @NamedSubgraph(name="phone",
            attributeNodes={
                @NamedAttributeNode("number"),
                @NamedAttributeNode("type"),
                @NamedAttributeNode(value="employee", subgraph="namedEmp")}),
        @NamedSubgraph(name="namedEmp",
            attributeNodes={
                @NamedAttributeNode("name")}),
        @NamedSubgraph(name="dept",
            attributeNodes={
                @NamedAttributeNode("name")})
    })
public class Employee { ... }
```

This named entity graph contains two major changes from the previous one. The first change is that we have added the `manager` attribute to be fetched. Since the manager is an `Employee` entity you might be surprised that the "namedEmp" subgraph is specified, thinking that the manager `Employee` would just get loaded according to the fetch plan described by the named entity graph that we are defining (it is an Employee entity graph, after all). This is not what the rule states, however. The rule is that unless a subgraph is specified for a relationship attribute type, the default fetch graph for that type will be used as the fetch plan. For `Employee`, that would mean the manager would have all of its eager relationships loaded, and all of the eager relationships of its related entities, and so on. This could cause much more data to be loaded than we expected. The solution is to do as shown in Listing 11-16 and specify a minimal subgraph for the manager Employee.

The second change to this entity graph is that the "phone" subgraph includes the employee attribute. Once again, we are referencing the "namedEmp" subgraph to specify that the employee not be loaded according to the default fetch graph. The first thing of note is that we can reuse the same named subgraph in multiple places in the entity graph. After that you should notice that the employee attribute is really a back pointer to an employee in the result set of the named entity graph. We just want to make sure that referencing it from the phone does not cause more to be fetched than what is already defined by the employee named entity graph, itself.

Entity Graphs with Inheritance

We have so far steered clear of the inheritance aspect of our entity model, but we will ignore it no longer. A scaled-back entity graph that includes only the employee name and projects is shown in Listing 11-17.

Listing 11-17. Named Entity Graph with Inheritance

```
@Entity
@NamedEntityGraph(name="Employee.graph3",
    attributeNodes={
        @NamedAttributeNode("name"),
        @NamedAttributeNode(value="projects", subgraph="project")},
    subgraphs={
        @NamedSubgraph(name="project", type=Project.class,
            attributeNodes={
                @NamedAttributeNode("name")}),
        @NamedSubgraph(name="project", type=QualityProject.class,
            attributeNodes={
                @NamedAttributeNode("qaRating")})
    })
public class Employee { ... }
```

The attribute fetch state for the projects attribute is defined in a subgraph called "project", but as you can see, there are two subgraphs named "project". Each of the possible classes/subclasses that could be in that relationship has a subgraph named "project" and includes its defined state that should be fetched, plus a type element to identify which subclass it is. However, since DesignProject does not introduce any new state, we don't need to include a subgraph named "project" for that class.

The inheritance case that this doesn't cover is when the root entity class is itself a superclass. For this special case there is a subclassSubgraphs element to list the root entity subclasses. For example, if there was a ContractEmployee subclass of Employee that had an additional hourlyRate attribute that we wanted fetched, then we could use the entity graph shown in Listing 11-18.

Listing 11-18. Named Entity Graph with Root Inheritance

```
@Entity
@NamedEntityGraph(name="Employee.graph4",
    attributeNodes={
        @NamedAttributeNode("name"),
        @NamedAttributeNode("address"),
        @NamedAttributeNode(value="department", subgraph="dept")},
    subgraphs={
        @NamedSubgraph(name="dept",
```

```
                    attributeNodes={
                        @NamedAttributeNode("name")})},
        subclassSubgraphs={
            @NamedSubgraph(name="notUsed", type=ContractEmployee.class,
                attributeNodes={
                    @NamedAttributeNode("hourlyRate")})
        })
public class Employee { ... }
```

■ **Tip**   A minor issue in the annotation definition is that the subclassSubgraphs element is of type NamedSubgraph[ ], meaning that a name is required to be specified even though in this case it is not used anywhere. We have labeled it "notUsed" to show that it is extraneous.

Map Key Subgraphs

The last special case is reserved for our old friend, the Map. When a relationship attribute is of type Map, there is the issue of the additional key part of the Map. If the key is an embeddable or an entity type, then an additional subgraph might need to be specified (or else the default fetch graph rule will apply). To handle these cases there is a keySubgraph element in NamedAttributeNode. To illustrate having a Map with an embeddable key subgraph, we will use an EmployeeName embeddable class similar to Listing 5-13, and modify our Department entity slightly to be similar to Listing 5-14. We list the type definitions in Listing 11-19 and add a named entity graph.

Listing 11-19. Named Entity Graph with Map Key Subgraph

```
@Embeddable
public class EmployeeName {
    private String firstName;
    private String lastName;
    // ...
}

@Entity
@NamedEntityGraph(name="Department.graph1",
    attributeNodes={
        @NamedAttributeNode("name"),
        @NamedAttributeNode(value="employees",
            subgraph="emp",
            keySubgraph="empName")},
    subgraphs={
        @NamedSubgraph(name="emp",
            attributeNodes={
                @NamedAttributeNode(value="name",
                    subgraph="empName"),
                @NamedAttributeNode("salary")}),
        @NamedSubgraph(name="empName",
            attributeNodes={
                @NamedAttributeNode("firstName"),
                @NamedAttributeNode("lastName")})
    })
```

```
public class Department {
    @Id private int id;
    private String name;
    @OneToMany(mappedBy="department")
    @MapKey(name="name")
    private Map<EmployeeName, Employee> employees;
    // ...
}
```

At this point you have just about as much expertise on named entity graphs as almost any developer out there, so after seeing all of the annotation examples you might have noticed that they were more complicated than they needed to be. In many cases they listed attributes that could have been easily defaulted by using the default fetch graph rule. This was to try to keep the model as simple as possible but still be correct and able to demonstrate the concepts. Now that you have the rules straight in your mind, you should go back through each of the named entity graphs and as an exercise see how they could be shortened using the default fetch graph rule.

Entity Graph API

The API is useful for creating, modifying, and adding entity graphs dynamically in code. The entity graphs can be used to generate fetch plans based on program parameters, user input, or in some cases even static data when programmatic creation is preferred. In this section, we will describe the classes and most of the methods of the API. We will apply them in examples showing how to create dynamic equivalents of the named entity graphs in the previous annotation section.

While the entity graphs resulting from annotations are the same as those created using the API, there are some minor differences between the models they each employ. This is primarily because of the inherent differences between annotations and a code API, but is also somewhat by style choice.

The way to get started building a new entity graph is to use the `createEntityGraph()` factory method on `EntityManager`. It takes the root entity class as a parameter and returns a new `EntityGraph` instance typed to the entity class:

```
EntityGraph<Address> graph = em.createEntityGraph(Address.class);
```

The next step is to add attribute nodes to the entity graph. The adding methods are designed to do most of the work of creating the node structures for you. We can use the variable-arg `addAttributeNodes()` method to add the attributes that will not have subgraphs associated with them:

```
graph.addAttributeNodes("street","city", "state", "zip");
```

This will create an `AttributeNode` object for each of the named attribute parameters and add it to the entity graph. There is unfortunately no method equivalent to the `includeAllAttributes` element in the `@NamedEntityGraph` annotation.

There are also strongly typed method equivalents to the ones that take string-based attribute names. The typed versions use the metamodel, so you would need to ensure that the metamodel has been generated for your domain model (see Chapter 9). A sample invocation of the strongly typed `addAttributeNodes()` method would be:

```
graph.addAttributeNodes(Address_.street, Address_.city,
                        Address_.state, Address_.zip);
```

When adding an attribute for which you also intend to add a subgraph, the addAttributeNodes() methods should not be used. Instead, there are a number of addSubgraph() method variants that should be used instead. Each of the addSubgraph() methods will first create an instance of AttributeNode for the passed-in attribute, then create an instance of Subgraph, then link the subgraph to the attribute node, and finally return the Subgraph instance. The string-based version can be used to replicate our named entity graph from Listing 11-15. The resulting entity graph is shown in Listing 11-20.

Listing 11-20. Dynamic Entity Graph with Subgraphs

```
EntityGraph<Employee> graph = em.createEntityGraph(Employee.class);
graph.addAttributeNodes("name","salary", "address");
Subgraph<Phone> phone = graph.addSubgraph("phones");
phone.addAttributeNodes("number", "type");
Subgraph<Department> dept = graph.addSubgraph("department");
dept.addAttributeNodes("name");
```

The API-based entity graph is clearly shorter and neater than the annotation-based one. This is one of those cases when methods are not only more expressive than annotations but also easier to read. Of course, the variable argument methods don't hurt either.

The example in Listing 11-16 illustrated having an entity graph containing a second definition of the root entity class, as well as having one subgraph refer to another. Listing 11-21 shows that the API actually suffers in this case because it doesn't allow sharing of a subgraph within the same entity graph. Since there is no API to pass in an existing Subgraph instance, we need to construct two identical named employee subgraphs.

Listing 11-21. Dynamic Entity Graph with Multiple Type Definitions

```
EntityGraph<Employee> graph = em.createEntityGraph(Employee.class);
graph.addAttributeNodes("name","salary", "address");
Subgraph<Phone> phone = graph.addSubgraph("phones");
phone.addAttributeNodes("number", "type");

Subgraph<Employee> namedEmp = phone.addSubgraph("employee");
namedEmp.addAttributeNodes("name");

Subgraph<Department> dept = graph.addSubgraph("department");
dept.addAttributeNodes("name");

Subgraph<Employee> mgrNamedEmp = graph.addSubgraph("manager");
mgrNamedEmp.addAttributeNodes("name");
```

The inheritance example in Listing 11-17 can be translated into an API-based version. When a related class is actually a class hierarchy, then each call to addSubgraph() can take the class as a parameter to distinguish between the different subclasses, as shown in Listing 11-22.

Listing 11-22. Dynamic Entity Graph with Inheritance

```
EntityGraph<Employee> graph = em.createEntityGraph(Employee.class);
graph.addAttributeNodes("name","salary", "address");
Subgraph<Project> project = graph.addSubgraph("projects", Project.class);
project.addAttributeNodes("name");
Subgraph<QualityProject> qaProject = graph.addSubgraph("projects", QualityProject.class);
qaProject.addAttributeNodes("qaRating");
```

When inheritance exists at the root entity class, the addSubclassSubgraph() method should be used. The class is the only parameter that is required. The API version of the annotation in Listing 11-18 is shown in Listing 11-23.

Listing 11-23. Dynamic Entity Graph with Root Inheritance

```
EntityGraph<Employee> graph = em.createEntityGraph(Employee.class);
graph.addAttributeNodes("name","address");
graph.addSubgraph("department").addAttributeNodes("name");
graph.addSubclassSubgraph(ContractEmployee.class).addAttributeNodes("hourlyRate");
```

Note that in Listing 11-23 we make use of the fact that no further subgraphs are being added to the subgraphs connected to the entity graph node, so neither of the created subgraphs are saved in stack variables. Rather, the addAttributeNodes() method is invoked directly on each of the Subgraph results of the addSubgraph() and addSubclassSubgraph() methods.

Our final example to convert is the Map example from Listing 11-19. The API equivalent is shown in Listing 11-24. The root entity is the Department entity and the Map is keyed by the EmployeeName embeddable.

Listing 11-24. Dynamic Entity Graph with Map Key Subgraph

```
EntityGraph<Department> graph = em.createEntityGraph(Department.class);
graph.addAttributeNodes("name");
graph.addSubgraph("employees").addAttributeNodes("salary");
graph.addKeySubgraph("employees").addAttributeNodes("firstName", "lastName");
```

In the above example, the addKeySubgraph() method was invoked on the root entity graph node but the same method also exists on Subgraph, so a key subgraph can be added at any level where a Map occurs.

Managing Entity Graphs

The previous sections taught you how to create named and dynamic entity graphs, so the next logical step is to see how they can be managed. For the purposes of this section, managing entity graphs means accessing them, saving them, changing them, and creating new ones using an existing one as a starting point.

Accessing Named Entity Graphs

It is easy to access a dynamic entity graph since you have it stored in the same variable that you used during the process of entity graph creation. When you have defined a named entity graph, though, you must access it through the entity manager before it can be used. This is achieved by passing in the name of the entity graph to the getEntityGraph() method. It will be returned as an EntityGraph object. We can access the entity graph that we defined in Listing 11-16 with the following statement:

```
EntityGraph<?> empGraph2 = em.getEntityGraph("Employee.graph2");
```

Note that the type parameter is wildcarded because the type of the entity graph is not known by the entity manager. Later, when we show ways to use an entity graph, you will see that it is not necessary to strongly type it in order to use it.

If there are many entity graphs defined on a single class and we have a reason to sequence through them, we can do so using the class-based accessor method. The following code looks at the attribute names of the root entity classes for each of the Employee entity graphs:

```
List<EntityGraph<? super Employee>> egList =
                               em.getEntityGraphs(Employee.class);
for (EntityGraph<? super Employee> graph : egList) {
    System.out.println("EntityGraph: " + graph.getName());
    List<AttributeNode<?>> attribs = graph.getAttributeNodes();
    for (AttributeNode<?> attr : attribs) {
        System.out.println("  Attribute: " + attr.getAttributeName());
    }
}
```

In this case, the EntityGraph parameter type is lower bounded to be Employee, but may also be some superclass of Employee as well. If, for example, Person was a superclass entity of Employee, then we would also get the Person entity graphs included in the output.

Adding Named Entity Graphs

The Entity Graph API allows dynamic creation of entity graphs, but you can go even further by taking those entity graphs and saving them as named entity graphs. Once they are named they can be used just like a named entity graph that was statically defined in an annotation.

We can add any of the entity graphs that we created in Listings 11-20 to 11-24 as a named entity graph by using the addNamedEntityGraph() method on the entity manager factory:

```
em.getEntityManagerFactory().addNamedEntityGraph("Employee.graphX", graph);
```

Note that the name we choose for the entity graph is up to us, just as it was when we defined it in annotation form, except that in this case there is no default name. We must supply a name as a parameter.

If a named entity graph with the same name already existed in the named entity graph namespace, it will be overridden by the one we are supplying in the addNamedEntityGraph() call, since there can only be one entity graph of a given name in a persistence unit.

Creating New Entity Graphs From Named Ones

In some cases you may find that you have an existing entity graph but want to create a new one that is very similar to the existing one, but differs by some small factor. This may be especially true due to the fact that subgraphs cannot be shared across entity graphs. The best way to do this is to use the createEntityGraph() method. By using an existing graph you can modify just the parts that you want changed and then resave the modified one under a different name.

In Listing 11-16, we defined an entity graph for Employee that included their phones and their department, but not their projects. In Listing 11-25, we access that entity graph and change it to also include their projects. Adding an attribute node that is a relationship, but not adding a subgraph for it, will cause the default fech graph for that entity type to be applied. We can then choose to save the entity graph under the same name, effectively overwriting the previous one, or save it under a different name so that we have both entity graphs to choose from. Listing 11-25 does the latter.

Listing 11-25. Creating an Entity Graph from an Existing Graph

```
EntityGraph<?> graph = em.createEntityGraph("Employee.graph2");
graph.addAttributeNodes("projects");
em.getEntityManagerFactory().addNamedEntityGraph("Employee.newGraph", graph);
```

The change that we made to the entity graph in Listing 11-25 was actually fairly trivial on purpose because it turns out that you may be somewhat limited in what you can do when it comes to making changes to an existing entity graph. The reason is that the javadoc for the Entity Graph API does not specify whether you can mutate the collection accessors. For example, EntityGraph has a getAttributeNodes() method but the method does not specify whether the List<AttributeNode<?>> returned by it is the actual List referred to by the EntityGraph instance. If it is a copy, then if it is modified, it will have no effect on the EntityGraph instance it was obtained from. This would make it impossible to remove an attribute from the graph since there is no alternative API to modify the collections other than to add to them.

Using Entity Graphs

The hardest part of entity graphs is creating them to be correct and to produce the result that you are expecting. Once you have created the right entity graphs, using them is fairly simple. They are passed as the values of one of two standard properties. These properties can either be passed into a find() method or set as a query hint on any named or dynamic query. Depending upon which property is used, the entity graph will take on the role of either a fetch graph or a load graph. The following sections explain the semantics of the two types of graphs and show some examples of how and when they can be used.

Fetch Graphs

When an entity graph is passed into a find() method or a query as the value to the "javax.persistence.fetchgraph" property, the entity graph will be treated as a fetch graph. The semantics of a fetch graph are that all attributes included in the graph are to be treated as having a fetch type of EAGER, as if the mapping had been specified as fetch=FetchType.EAGER, regardless of what the static mapping actually specifies. Attributes that are not included in the graph are to be treated as LAZY. As described earlier, all identifier or version attributes will be treated as EAGER and loaded, regardless of whether they are included in the graph or not. Also, as we explained above, if a relationship or embedded attribute is included in the graph but no subgraph is specified for it, then the default fetch graph for that type will be used.

The usefulness of a fetch graph is primarily to enable attributes to be fetched lazily when they were configured or defaulted to be eagerly fetched in the mapping. The thing to remember is that the same semantics of LAZY apply here as those that were described in Chapter 4. That is, when an attribute is marked as LAZY, there is no guarantee that the attribute will remain unloaded until the first time it is accessed. If an attribute is LAZY, it only means that the provider can optimize by not fetching the state of the attribute until it is accessed. The provider always has a right to load LAZY attributes eagerly if it wants to.

Let's look at an example of using a fetch graph. In Listing 11-16, we defined an entity graph for the Employee entity. Since it was defined as a named entity graph, we can access it using the getEntityGraph() method and use it as the value for our javax.persistence.fetchgraph property.

```
Map<String,Object> props = new HashMap<String,Object>();
props.put("javax.persistence.fetchgraph",
          em.getEntityGraph("Employee.graph2"));
Employee emp = em.find(Employee.class, empId, props);
```

We can just as easily pass in the dynamic version that we created in Listing 11-21. If the dynamic graph was being created in the "graph" variable, then we could simply pass it in to the find() method, or as a query hint:

```
EntityGraph<Employee> graph = em.createEntityGraph(Employee.class);
// ... (compose graph as in Listing 11-21)
TypedQuery<Employee> query = em.createQuery(
      "SELECT e FROM Employee e WHERE e.salary > 50000", Employee.class);
query.setHint("javax.persistence.fetchgraph",graph);
List<Employee> results = query.getResultList();
```

Load Graphs

A load graph is an entity graph that is supplied as the value to the "javax.persistence.loadgraph" property. The main difference between a fetch graph and a load graph is how the missing attributes are treated. While in a fetch graph an excluded attribute is to be treated as LAZY, in a load graph all missing attributes are to be treated as they are defined in the mappings. Expressing it in terms of the default fetch graph that we discussed in the above sections, an empty load graph with no attributes included is the same as the default fetch graph for that type. The value of using a load graph is in the ability to cause one or more attributes to be treated as EAGER even though they were statically defined to be LAZY.

In Chapter 6, we showed some examples of ways to ensure the employee department was loaded, even though it was specified to be LAZY. This is a perfect case for using a load graph. In Listing 11-26, we show an alternative version of Listing 6-27.

Listing 11-26. Triggering a Lazy Relationship

```
@Stateless
public class EmployeeService {
    @PersistenceContext(unitName="EmployeeService")
    private EntityManager em;

    public List findAll() {
        EntityGraph<Employee> graph = em.createEntityGraph(Employee.class);
        graph.addAttributeNodes("department");
        TypedQuery<Employee> query = em.createQuery(
                "SELECT e FROM Employee e", Employee.class);
        query.setHint("javax.persistence.loadgraph", graph);
        return query.getResultList();
    }
    // ...
}
```

As you can see, the graph creation is quite simple since we are only adding one attribute and no subgraphs. The department attribute is a relationship, and we did not include a subgraph for it so the default fetch graph for Department will be used.

THE CASE OF THE MISSING PROPERTY

The difficulty with using a fetch graph is that it is a complete specification for the type. To make a single attribute be lazy, you will need to specify all of the eager attributes. In other words, you cannot just override the fetch mode for a single attribute; when you create a fetch graph for an entity or embeddable type, you are effectively overriding all of the attributes of the type, either by including them or excluding them from the fetch graph. What the spec really needs is an additional property, javax.persistence.lazygraph, that would specify that all of the attributes included in the graph are to be lazy and all of the excluded attributes revert to what they are defined to be in their mappings. This would allow selective inclusion of lazy attributes.

Best Practices for Fetch and Load Graphs

When and how to use a fetch graph or a load graph will become obvious as you try to use one or the other; it won't take long to discover which one fits your attribute loading needs. However, we will offer a few tips to get you going and perhaps save you a little bit of time at the outset.

Learn what your target provider supports in terms of laziness. If your provider loads every lazy attribute eagerly and you are planning to create a series of fetch graphs for your queries to make attributes be lazy, then it might not be worth going through the effort at all. You can test the loading behavior of your provider by using the `PersistenceUnitUtil.isLoaded()` method on a lazy attribute before it is accessed. Try it out on the different types of attributes that you are planning to set to LAZY.

If your entity graphs are not acting the way that you think they should be, then look for attributes that do not have subgraphs. Remember that the default fetch graph will be used when no subgraph is specified. This is relevant for all bidirectional relationships (remember to set a subgraph for the relationship back to the original object type), but especially those that navigate back to the root entity type. Your intuition may tell you that the root entity graph specification will be used, but it is the default fetch graph that will be used instead.

If you end up using a fetch or load graph to change the fetch type of an attribute more times than not, you may want to consider changing how the fetch type is defined in the mapping. The mapping should define the most commonly used fetch mode, with the fetch or load graphs overriding it in the exceptional cases.

Using named entity graphs provides reusability of the entity graph and is a convenient way to create a slightly different graph for one-off modifications. While declaring them in code is a neater and preferred way to define entity graphs, you should go on to register them as named entity graphs to achieve the reusability. You will also want to define them in code that you are sure will be executed before any of the queries that use them get executed.

Summary

We began the chapter with a look at SQL queries. We looked at the role of SQL in applications that also use JP QL and the specialized situations where only SQL can be used. To bridge the gap between native SQL and entities, we described the result set mapping process in detail, showing a wide range of queries and how they translate back into the application domain model.

We then showed how stored procedures can be invoked through a JPA query and how the results can be obtained through output parameters, ref cursors, and result sets. Stored procedures are always going to be somewhat database-specific so care must be taken when using them.

We finished off by talking about entity graphs, what they are, and how they are constructed. We showed how named entity graphs can be defined in annotation form and went on to describe the API for creating dynamic entity graphs in code. The entity manager methods for obtaining named or modifiable entity graphs was discussed, including an example that took an existing named entity graph, made a change to it, then added the changed graph as a separate named entity graph. Lastly, we showed how entity graphs are used. You saw how they take on the semantics of fetch graphs or load graphs when they are passed as property values to `find()` methods or queries.

In the next chapter, we will look at more advanced topics, primarily in the areas of lifecycle callbacks, entitylisteners, validation, concurrency, locking, and caching.

CHAPTER 12

■ ■ ■

Other Advanced Topics

When a chapter title includes the phrase "Advanced Topics" there is always the risk that the content might not line up with what every reader considers advanced. The term "advanced" is subjective at best and depends upon the background and experience of the developer as well as the complexity of application being developed.

What we can say is that, in large part, the topics in this chapter are those that were intended (during development of the specification) to be of a more advanced nature or to be used by more advanced developers. There are a few exceptions to this rule, though. For example, we included optimistic locking in this chapter even though most applications do need to be aware of and make use of optimistic locking. However, the actual locking calls are seldom used, and it just made sense to cover all the lock modes together. In general, we think that most applications will not use more than a few of the features described in this chapter. With this in mind, let's explore some of the other features of the Java Persistence API.

Lifecycle Callbacks

Every entity has the potential to go through one or more of a defined set of lifecycle events. Depending upon the operations invoked upon an entity, these events may or may not occur for that entity, but there is at least the potential for them to occur. In order to respond to any one or more of the events, an entity class or any of its superclasses may declare one or more methods that will be invoked by the provider when the event gets fired. These methods are called callback methods.

Lifecycle Events

The event types that make up the lifecycle fall into four categories: persisting, updating, removing, and loading. These are really data-level events that correspond to the database operations of inserting, updating, deleting, and reading; and except for loading, each has a `Pre` event and a `Post` event. In the load category there is only a `PostLoad` event because it would not make any sense for there to be `PreLoad` on an entity that was not yet built. Thus the full suite of lifecycle events that can occur is composed of `PrePersist`, `PostPersist`, `PreUpdate`, `PostUpdate`, `PreRemove`, `PostRemove`, and `PostLoad`.

PrePersist and PostPersist

The `PrePersist` event notifies an entity when `EntityManager.persist()` has been successfully invoked on it. `PrePersist` events may also occur on a `merge()` call when a new entity has been merged into the persistence context. If the `PERSIST` cascade option is set on a relationship of an object that is being persisted and the target object is also a new object, the `PrePersist` event is triggered on the target object. If multiple entities are cascaded to during the same operation, the order in which the `PrePersist` callbacks occur cannot be relied upon.

PostPersist events occur when an entity is inserted, which normally occurs during the transaction completion phase. Firing of a PostPersist event does not indicate that the entity has committed successfully to the database because the transaction in which it was persisted may be rolled back after the PostPersist event but before the transaction successfully commits.

PreRemove and PostRemove

When an EntityManager.remove() call is invoked on an entity, the PreRemove callback is triggered. This callback implies that an entity is being queued for deletion, and any related entities across relationships that have been configured with the REMOVE cascade option will also get a PreRemove notification. When the SQL for deletion of an entity finally does get sent to the database, the PostRemove event will get fired. As with the PostPersist lifecycle event, the PostRemove event does not guarantee success. The enclosing transaction may still be rolled back.

PreUpdate and PostUpdate

Updates to managed entities may occur at any time, either within a transaction or (in the case of an extended persistence context) outside a transaction. Because there is no explicit method on the EntityManager, the PreUpdate callback is guaranteed to be invoked only at some point before the database update. Some implementations may track changes dynamically and may invoke the callback on each change, while others may wait until the end of the transaction and just invoke the callback once.

Another difference between implementations is whether PreUpdate events get fired on entities that were persisted in a transaction and then modified in the same transaction before being committed. This would be a rather unfortunate choice because unless the writes were done eagerly on each entity call, there would be no symmetric PostUpdate call because in the usual deferred writing case, a single persist to the database would occur when the transaction ends. The PostUpdate callback occurs right after the database update. The same potential for rollback exists after PostUpdate callbacks as with PostPersist and PostRemove.

PostLoad

The PostLoad callback occurs after the data for an entity is read from the database and the entity instance is constructed. This can get triggered by any operation that causes an entity to be loaded, normally by either a query or traversal of a lazy relationship. It can also happen as a result of a refresh() call on the entity manager. When a relationship is set to cascade REFRESH, the entities that get cascaded to will also get loaded. The invocation of entities in a single operation, be it a query or a refresh, is not guaranteed to be in any order, so we should not rely upon any observed order in any implementation.

■ **Tip** Other lifecycle methods may be defined by specific providers, such as when an entity is merged or copied/cloned.

Callback Methods

Callback methods may be defined a few different ways, the most basic of which is to simply define a method on the entity class. Designating the method as a callback method involves two steps: defining the method according to a given signature and annotating the method with the appropriate lifecycle event annotation.

The required signature definition is very simple. The callback method may have any name, but must have a signature that takes no parameters and has a return type of void. A method such as public void foo() {} is an example of a valid method. Final or static methods are not valid callback methods, however.

Checked exceptions may not be thrown from callback methods because the method definition of a callback method is not permitted to include a throws clause. Runtime exceptions may be thrown, though, and if they are thrown while in a transaction, they will cause the provider to not only abandon invocation of subsequent lifecycle event methods in that transaction, but also mark the transaction for rollback.

A method is indicated as being a callback method by being annotated with a lifecycle event annotation. The relevant annotations match the names of the events listed earlier: @PrePersist, @PostPersist, @PreUpdate, @PostUpdate, @PreRemove, @PostRemove, and @PostLoad. A method may be annotated with multiple lifecycle event annotations, but only one lifecycle annotation of a given type may be present in an entity class.

Certain types of operations may not be portably performed inside callback methods. For example, invoking methods on an entity manager or executing queries obtained from an entity manager are not supported, as well as accessing entities other than the one to which the lifecycle event applies. Looking up resources in JNDI or using JDBC and JMS resources are allowed, so looking up and invoking EJB session beans would be allowed.

Now that you know all the different kinds of lifecycle events that can be handled, let's look at an example that uses them. One common usage of lifecycle events is to maintain non-persistent state inside a persistent entity. If we want the entity to record its cached age or the time it was last synchronized with the database, we could easily do this right inside the entity using callback methods. Note that the entity is considered synchronized with the database each time it is read from or written to the database. The entity is shown in Listing 12-1. Users of this Employee entity could check on the cached age of this object to see if it meets their freshness requirements.

Listing 12-1. Using Callback Methods on an Entity

```java
@Entity
public class Employee {
    @Id private int id;
    private String name;
    @Transient private long syncTime;

    // ...

    @PostPersist
    @PostUpdate
    @PostLoad
    private void resetSyncTime() {
        syncTime = System.currentTimeMillis();
    }

    public long getCachedAge() {
        return System.currentTimeMillis() - syncTime;
    }

    // ...
}
```

Enterprise Contexts

When a callback method is invoked, the provider will not take any particular action to suspend or establish any different kind of naming, transaction, or security context in the Java EE environment. Callback methods are executed in whatever contexts are active at the time they are invoked.

Remembering this fact is important because it will often be a bean with a container-managed transaction that invokes calls on the entity manager, and it will be that bean's contexts that will be in effect when the Pre calls are invoked. Depending upon where the transaction started and is committed, the Post calls will likely be invoked at the end of the transaction and could actually be in an entirely different set of contexts than the Pre methods. This is especially true in the case of an extended persistence context where the entities are managed and persisted outside a transaction, yet the next transaction commit will cause the entities that were persisted to be written out.

Entity Listeners

Callback methods in the entity are fine when you don't mind if the event callback logic is included in the entity, but what if you want to pull the event handling behavior out of the entity class into a different class? To do this, you can use an entity listener. An entity listener is not an entity; it is a class on which you can define one or more lifecycle callback methods to be invoked for the lifecycle events of an entity. Similar to the callback methods on the entity, however, only one method in each listener class may be annotated for each event type. Multiple event listeners may be applied to an entity, though.

When the callback is invoked on a listener, the listener typically needs to have access to the entity state. For example, if we were to implement the previous example of the cached age of an entity instance, then we would want to get passed the entity instance. For this reason, the signature required of callback methods on entity listeners is slightly different from the one required on entities. On an entity listener, a callback method must have a similar signature as an entity with the exception that it must also have a single defined parameter of a type that is compatible with the entity type, as the entity class, a superclass (including Object), or an interface implemented by the entity. A method with the signature public void foo(Object o) {} is an example of a valid callback method on an entity listener. The method must then be annotated with the necessary event annotation(s).

Entity listener classes must be stateless,[1] meaning that they should not declare any fields. A single instance may be shared among multiple entity instances and may even be invoked upon concurrently for multiple entity instances. In order for the provider to be able to create instances of the entity listener, every entity listener class must have a public no-argument constructor.

Entity Listeners as CDI Beans

If CDI is enabled in the Container, then entity listeners can also be CDI beans. If an entity listener is a CDI bean, then not only can it be an injection target, but it also has a component lifecycle and can include the PostConstruct and PreDestroy lifecycle methods discussed in Chapter 3. However, unlike most other types of CDI beans, entity listeners are not contextual, so instances are not stored in a specific context for subsequent injection into other objects.

■ Note Entity listeners are the only JPA objects that can be CDI beans.

Clearly, if an entity listener is a CDI bean, then it is not going to be stateless and *can* have state fields. Otherwise there would be no point in making it a CDI bean. But since it is not legal to use the entity manager from a lifecycle callback there would be no point in injecting an entity manager. It would be more useful to inject other kinds of resources used by the entity listener, such as a CDI contextual bean, a message queue, or some other container resource.

■ Tip Only since JPA 2.1 has it been possible to make entity listeners also be CDI beans.

---

[1]Unless the listener is also a CDI bean, as described in the subsequent section.

Attaching Entity Listeners to Entities

An entity designates the entity listeners that should be notified of its lifecycle events through the use of the @EntityListeners annotation. One or more entity listeners may be listed in the annotation. When a lifecycle event occurs, the provider will iterate through each of the entity listeners in the order in which they were listed and instantiate an instance of the entity listener class that has a method annotated with the annotation for the given event. It will invoke the callback method on the listener, passing in the entity to which the event applies. After it has done this for all the listed entity listeners, it will invoke the callback method on the entity if there is one. If any of the listeners throws an exception, it will abort the callback process, causing the remaining listeners and the callback method on the entity to not be invoked.

Now let's look at the cached entity age example and add some entity listeners into the mix. Because we now have the ability to do multiple tasks in multiple listeners, we can add a listener to do some name validation as well as some extra actions on employee record changes. Listing 12-2 shows the entity with its added listeners.

Listing 12-2. Using Multiple Entity Listeners

```
@Entity
@EntityListeners({EmployeeDebugListener.class, NameValidator.class})
public class Employee implements NamedEntity {
    @Id private int id;
    private String name;
    @Transient private long syncTime;

    public String getName() { return name; }

    @PostPersist
    @PostUpdate
    @PostLoad
    private void resetSyncTime() {
        syncTime = System.currentTimeMillis();
    }

    public long getCachedAge() {
        return System.currentTimeMillis() - syncTime;
    }

    // ...
}

public interface NamedEntity {
    public String getName();
}

public class NameValidator {
    static final int MAX_NAME_LEN = 40;

    @PrePersist
    public void validate(NamedEntity obj) {
        if (obj.getName().length()) > MAX_NAME_LEN)
            throw new ValidationException("Identifier out of range");
    }
}
```

341

```java
public class EmployeeDebugListener {
    @PrePersist
    public void prePersist(Employee emp) {
        System.out.println("Persist on employee id: " + emp.getId());
    }

    @PreUpdate
    public void preUpdate(Employee emp) { ... }

    @PreRemove
    public void preRemove(Employee emp) { ... }

    @PostLoad
    public void postLoad(Employee emp) { ... }
}
```

As you can see, different listener callback methods take different types of parameters. The callback methods in the `EmployeeDebugListener` class take `Employee` as a parameter because they are being applied only to `Employee` entities. In the `NameValidator` class, the `validate()` method parameter is of type `NamedEntity`. The `Employee` entity and any number of other entities that have names may implement this interface. The validation logic may be needed because a particular aspect of the system may have a current name-length limitation but may change in the future. It is preferable to centralize this logic in a single class than to duplicate the validation logic in each of the class setter methods if there is any possibility of an inheritance hierarchy.

Even though entity listeners are convenient, we have decided to leave the cache age logic in the entity because it is actually modifying the state of the entity and because putting it in a separate class would have required us to relax the access of the private `resetSyncTime()` method. In general, when a callback method accesses state beyond what should be publicly accessible, it is best suited to being in the entity and not in an entity listener.

Default Entity Listeners

A listener may be attached to more than one type of entity simply by being listed in the `@EntityListeners` annotation of more than one entity. This can be useful in cases where the listener provides a more general facility or wide-ranging runtime logic.

For even broader usage of an entity listener across all the entities in a persistence unit, one or more default entity listeners may be declared. There is currently no standard annotation target for persistence unit scoped metadata, so this kind of metadata can be declared only in an XML mapping file. See Chapter 13 for the specifics of how to declare default entity listeners.

When a list of default entity listeners is declared, it will be traversed in the order they were listed in the declaration, and each one that has a method annotated or declared for the current event will be invoked upon. Default entity listeners will always get invoked before any of the entity listeners listed in the `@EntityListeners` annotation for a given entity.

Any entity may opt out of having the default entity listeners applied to it by using the `@ExcludeDefaultListeners` annotation. When an entity is annotated with this annotation, none of the declared default listeners will get invoked for the lifecycle events for instances of that entity type.

Inheritance and Lifecycle Events

The presence of events with class hierarchies requires that we explore the topic of lifecycle events in a little more depth. What happens when we have multiple entities that each define callback methods or entity listeners or both? Do they all get invoked on a subclass entity or only those that are defined on or in the subclass entity?

These and many other questions arise because of the added complexity of inheritance hierarchies. It follows that there must be rules for defining predictable behavior in the face of potentially complex hierarchies where lifecycle event methods are scattered throughout the hierarchy.

Inheriting Callback Methods

Callback methods may occur on any entity or mapped superclass, be it abstract or concrete. The rule is fairly simple. It is that every callback method for a given event type will be invoked in the order according to its place in the hierarchy, most general classes first. Thus, if in the `Employee` hierarchy that was in Figure 10-10 the `Employee` class contains a `PrePersist` callback method named `checkName()`, and `FullTimeEmployee` also contains a `PrePersist` callback method named `verifyPension()`, when the `PrePersist` event occurs, the `checkName()` method will get invoked, followed by the `verifyPension()` method.

We could also have a method on the `CompanyEmployee` mapped superclass that we want to apply to all the entities that subclassed it. If we add a `PrePersist` method named `checkVacation()` that verifies that the vacation carryover is less than a certain amount, it will be executed after `checkName()` and before `verifyPension()`.

It gets more interesting if we define a `checkVacation()` method on the `PartTimeEmployee` class because part-time employees don't get as much vacation. Annotating the overridden method with `PrePersist` would cause the `PartTimeEmployee.checkVacation()` method to be invoked instead of the one in `CompanyEmployee`.

Inheriting Entity Listeners

Like callback methods in an entity, the `@EntityListeners` annotation is also valid on entities or mapped superclasses in a hierarchy, whether they are concrete or abstract. Also similar to callback methods, the listeners listed in the entity superclass annotation get invoked before the listeners in the subclass entities. In other words, defining an `@EntityListeners` annotation on an entity is additive in that it only adds listeners; it does not redefine them or their order of invocation.

To redefine which entity listeners get invoked and their order of invocation, an entity or mapped superclass should be annotated with `@ExcludeSuperclassListeners`. This will cause the listeners defined in all the superclasses to not be invoked for any of the lifecycle events of the annotated entity subclass. If we want a subset of the listeners to still be invoked, they must be listed in the `@EntityListeners` annotation on the overriding entity and in the order that is appropriate.

Lifecycle Event Invocation Order

The rules for lifecycle event invocation are now a little more complex, so they warrant being laid out more carefully. Perhaps the best way to describe it is to outline the process that the provider must follow to invoke the event methods. If a given lifecycle event X occurs for entity A, the provider will do the following:

1. Check whether any default entity listeners exist (see Chapter 13). If they do, iterate through them in the order they are defined and look for methods that are annotated with the lifecycle event X annotation. Invoke the lifecycle method on the listener if a method was found.

2. Check the highest mapped superclass or entity in the hierarchy for classes that have an `@EntityListeners` annotation. Iterate through the entity listener classes that are listed in the annotation and look for methods that are annotated with the lifecycle event X annotation. Invoke the lifecycle method on the listener if a method was found.

3. Repeat step 2 going down the hierarchy on entities and mapped superclasses until entity A is reached, and then repeat it for entity A.

4. Check the highest mapped superclass or entity in the hierarchy for methods that are annotated with the lifecycle event X annotation. Invoke the callback method on the entity if a method was found and the method is not also defined in entity A with the lifecycle event X annotation on it.

5. Repeat step 2 going down the hierarchy on entities and mapped superclasses until entity A is reached.

6. Invoke any methods that are defined on A and annotated with the lifecycle event X annotation.

This process might be easier to follow if you can see code that includes these cases and we go through the order in which they are executed. Listing 12-3 shows the entity hierarchy with a number of listeners and callback methods on it.

Listing 12-3. Using Entity Listeners and Callback Methods in a Hierarchy

```
@Entity
@Inheritance(strategy=InheritanceType.JOINED)
@EntityListeners(NameValidator.class)
public class Employee implements NamedEntity {
    @Id private int id;
    private String name;
    @Transient private long syncTime;

    public String getName() { return name; }

    @PostPersist
    @PostUpdate
    @PostLoad
    private void resetSyncTime() { syncTime = System.currentTimeMillis(); }
    // ...
}

public interface NamedEntity {
    public String getName();
}

@Entity
@ExcludeSuperclassListeners
@EntityListeners(LongNameValidator.class)
public class ContractEmployee extends Employee {
    private int dailyRate;
    private int term;

    @PrePersist
    public void verifyTerm() { ... }
    // ...
}
```

```java
@MappedSuperclass
@EntityListeners(EmployeeAudit.class)
public abstract class CompanyEmployee extends Employee {
    protected int vacation;
    // ...

    @PrePersist
    @PreUpdate
    public void verifyVacation() { ... }
}

@Entity
public class FullTimeEmployee extends CompanyEmployee {
    private long salary;
    private long pension;
    // ...
}

@Entity
@EntityListeners({})
public class PartTimeEmployee extends CompanyEmployee {
    private float hourlyRate;
    // ...

    @PrePersist
    @PreUpdate
    public void verifyVacation() { ... }
}

public class EmployeeAudit {
    @PostPersist
    public void auditNewHire(CompanyEmployee emp) { ... }
}

public class NameValidator {
    @PrePersist
    public void validateName(NamedEntity obj) { ... }
}

public class LongNameValidator {
    @PrePersist
    public void validateLongName(NamedEntity obj) { ... }
}

public class EmployeeDebugListener {
    @PrePersist
    public void prePersist(Employee emp) {
        System.out.println("Persist called on: " + emp);
    }
```

```
    @PreUpdate
    public void preUpdate(Employee emp) { ... }

    @PreRemove
    public void preRemove(Employee emp) { ... }

    @PostLoad
    public void postLoad(Employee emp) { ... }
}
```

This is a pretty complex example to study, and the easiest way to make use of it is to say what happens when a given event occurs for a specific entity. We will assume that the EmployeeDebugListener class has been set in the XML mapping file as a default entity listener for all entities.

Let's see what happens when we create a new instance of PartTimeEmployee and pass it to em.persist(). Because the first step is always to invoke the default listeners, and our default listener does indeed have a PrePersist method on it, the EmployeeDebugListener.prePersist() method will be invoked first.

The next step is to traverse down the hierarchy looking for entity listeners. The first class we find is the Employee class, which defines a NameValidator entity listener. The NameValidator class does define a PrePersist method, so the next method to get executed is NameValidator.validateName(). The next class we hit moving down the hierarchy is the CompanyEmployee class. This class defines an EmployeeAudit listener that does not happen to have a PrePersist method on it, so we skip past it.

Next, we get to the PartTimeEmployee class that has an @EntityListeners annotation but does not define any listeners. This is essentially a false alarm that does not really override anything, but is simply a no-op in terms of adding listeners (probably a leftover of a listener that was once there but has since been removed).

The next phase in the process is to start looking for callback methods on entities and mapped superclasses. Once again we start at the top of the hierarchy and look at the Employee class to see whether a PrePersist method exists, but none does. We have PostPersist and others, but no PrePersist. We continue on down to CompanyEmployee and see a PrePersist method called verifyVacation(), but looking down on the PartTimeEmployee entity we find that the method has been overridden by a verifyVacation() method that also has an @PrePersist annotation on it. This is a case of overriding the callback method and will result in the PartTimeEmployee.verifyVacation() method being called instead of the CompanyEmployee.verifyVacation() method. We are finally done, and the entity will be persisted.

The next event might then be a PostPersist event on the same entity at commit time. This will bypass the default listener because there is no PostPersist method in EmployeeDebugListener and will also bypass the NameValidator because there is no PostPersist event method there either. The next listener that it tries will be the EmployeeAudit listener class, which does include a PostPersist method called auditNewHire(), which will then get invoked. There are no more listeners to examine, so we move on to the callback methods and find the resetSyncTime() method in Employee. This one gets called, and because we find no more PostPersist callback methods in the hierarchy, we are done.

The next thing we can try is persisting a ContractEmployee. This is a simple persistence structure with only the Employee and ContractEmployee entities in it. When we create a ContractEmployee and the PrePersist event gets triggered, we first get our default EmployeeDebugListener.prePersist() callback and then move on to processing the entity listeners. The curve is that the @ExcludeSuperclassListeners annotation is present on the ContractEmployee, so the NameValidator.validateName() method that would otherwise have been invoked will not be considered. We instead go right to the @EntityListeners annotation on the ContractEmployee class and find that we need to look at LongNameValidator. When we do, we find that it has a validateLongName() method on it that we execute and then go on to executing the callback methods. There are callback methods in both classes in the hierarchy, and the Employee.resetSyncTime() method gets invoked first, followed by the ContractEmployee.verifyTerm() method.

Validation

Listing 12-2 showed an example of an entity listener in which we validated that a name was no longer than we expected it to be before the entity was persisted to the database. The constraint may have been imposed by a database schema definition or a business rule in the application. In Java EE 6, validation was introduced as a separate aspect of the application; a mechanism was developed and standardized (in JSR 303[2]) for the platform. It was also designed to function in a stand-alone Java SE environment. In Java EE 7, some minor editions were added to version 1.1 of the Bean Validation specification as part of JSR 349. We will give an overview of validation and how it can be used, but for more details we refer you to the JSR 349 specification[3] developed within the Java Community Process.

Validation has an annotation model and a dynamic API that can be invoked from any layer, and on almost any bean. Constraint annotations are placed on the field or property of the object to be validated, or even on the object class itself, and later when the validator runs the constraints will be checked. The validation specification provides a few predefined constraint annotations that can be used by any bean developer, but more importantly it includes a model for creating user-defined constraints that are specific to application logic or schemas.

Using Constraints

Adding constraints to an object can be as simple as annotating the class, its fields, or its JavaBean-style properties. For example, using the built-in @Size constraint, we can validate the Employee entity in Listing 12-2 and save ourselves having to code an entity listener. Listing 12-4 shows an Employee object class containing constraints.

Listing 12-4. Using Predefined Constraints

```
public class Employee {
    @NotNull
    private int id;

    @NotNull(message="Employee name must be specified")
    @Size(max=40)
    private String name;

    @Past
    private Date startDate;
    // ...
}
```

The @Size constraint ensures the name is within the 40-character range, just as our entity listener validator did. We also added a @NotNull constraint to validate that a name was always specified. If this constraint was not satisfied in our previous Employee entity, our listener would have exploded with a NullPointerException because it did not check for null before verifying the length. Using validation, these concerns are separated and can be imposed independently. The @Past annotation will validate that the start date is a valid date that occurs in the past. Note that null is a valid value in this case. If we wanted to ensure that a date was present, we would annotate it with @NotNull as well.

In the second @NotNull constraint we have also included a message to be included in the exception if the constraint check fails. Every built-in constraint annotation has a message element that may be specified to override the default message that would be generated.[4]

---

[2]See www.jcp.org/en/jsr/summary?id=303
[3]See www.jcp.org/en/jsr/summary?id=349
[4]Some localization mechanisms are built into the validation message interpolator, but custom message interpolation can also be plugged into the validator to perform localization in custom ways.

The complete set of built-in constraints that can be used with validation is shown in Table 12-1. These are defined in the javax.validation.constraints package.

Table 12-1. *Built-in Validation Constraints*

Constraint	Attributes[5]	Description
@Null		Element must be null.
@NotNull		Element must not be null.
@AssertTrue		Element must be true.
@AssertFalse		Element must be false.
@Min	long value()	Element must have a value greater than or equal to the minimum.
@Max	long value()	Element must have a value less than or equal to the maximum.
@DecimalMin	String value()	Element must have a value greater than or equal to the minimum.
@DecimalMax	String value()	Element must have a value less than or equal to the maximum.
@Size	int min() int max()	Element must be of a length within the specified limits.
@Digits	int integer() int fraction()	Element must be a number within the specified range.
@Past		Element must be a date in the past.
@Future		Element must be a date in the future.
@Pattern	String regexpr() Flag[] flags	Element must match the specified regular expression. (Flags offer regular expression settings.)

Invoking Validation

The main API class for invoking validation on an object is the javax.validation.Validator class. Once a Validator instance is obtained, the validate()[6] method can be invoked on it, passing in the object to be validated.

Validation is designed similarly to JPA in many respects. It is divided into a set of APIs and a validation implementation, or validation provider, and the way that providers advertise themselves is by using the same service provider model. Providers contain META-INF/services files that indicate their SPI classes to be invoked.

Like JPA, validation is used slightly differently depending upon whether it is used in container mode or in Java SE mode. In a container, a Validator instance may be injected into any Java EE component that supports injection. The example definition of a stateless session bean in Listing 12-5 shows that the regular Java EE @Resource injection annotation can be used.

---

[5]Only the non-standard attributes are listed. The standard/required attributes will be discussed in the section on creating new constraints.
[6]validateProperty() and validateValue() methods are also available, but we will discuss only the representative validate() method.

Listing 12-5. Injection of a Validator

```
@Stateless
public class EmployeeOperationsEJB implements EmployeeOperations {

    @Resource
    Validator validator;

    public void newEmployee(Employee emp) {
        validator.validate(emp);
        //...
    }
    //...
}
```

In a non-container environment, a `Validator` instance is obtained from a `javax.validation.ValidatorFactory`, which can in turn be acquired from a bootstrap `javax.validation.Validation` class, as follows:

```
ValidatorFactory factory =
    Validation.buildDefaultValidatorFactory();
Validator validator = factory.getValidator();
```

Once the validator is obtained, we may invoke the `validate()` method on it just as in Listing 12-5.

When the validate method fails and a constraint is not satisfied, a `ValidationException` is thrown with an accompanying message String that is dictated by the definition of the constraint that was not met, specifically by the value of its `message` annotation element that was described in the preceding section.

Validation Groups

It may be that the same object needs to be validated at different times for multiple different constraint sets. To achieve this, we would create separate validation groups and specify which group or groups the constraint belongs to. When a group is passed as an argument during validation, all constraints that are a part of that group are checked for validity. When no group is specified on a constraint or as an argument to the `validate()` method, the `Default` group is assumed.

Groups are defined and referenced as classes, so a couple of examples of defining groups might be the following:

```
public interface FullTime extends Default {}
public interface PartTime extends Default {}
```

There is nothing of value within the group class, apart from the class itself, so they are defined as simple interfaces. Although these two extend the `javax.validation.groups.Default` group interface (an interface defined by the specification) this is certainly not a requirement, but because a subclass group includes any groups it inherits, it is convenient to make these extend the `Default` group.

Listing 12-6 shows an object class that uses these groups to ensure that the correct wage field is set according to whether an employee is being hired to work on a full-time or part-time basis.

Listing 12-6. Using Constraint Groups

```
public class Employee {
    @NotNull
    private int id;
```

```
@NotNull
@Size(max=40)
private String name;

@NotNull(groups=FullTime.class)
@Null(groups=PartTime.class)
private long salary;

@NotNull(groups=PartTime.class)
@Null(groups=FullTime.class)
private double hourlyWage;

// ...
}
```

Because the constraints on the id and name fields do not have a group assigned to them, they are assumed to belong to the Default group and will be checked whenever either the Default group, or no group, is passed to the validate() method. However, because our two new groups extended Default, the two fields will also be validated when either the FullTime or PartTime groups are passed in. If we had not extended Default in our two group definitions, we would have had to include the two groups in the constraints on the id and name fields if we wanted them to be checked when either of the two groups were specified in the validate() method, as shown in Listing 12-7.

Listing 12-7. Specifying Multiple Groups

```
public class Employee {
    @NotNull(groups={FullTime.class,PartTime.class})
    private int id;

    @NotNull(groups={FullTime.class,PartTime.class})
    @Size(groups={FullTime.class,PartTime.class},max=40)
    private String name;
    // ...
}
```

Creating New Constraints

One of the most valuable aspects of validation is the ability to add new constraints for a given application, or even to share across applications. Constraints may be implemented to be application-specific and tied to a particular business logic, or they may be generalized and bundled up in constraint libraries for reuse. We won't go into great detail in this area, but hopefully you will get the idea from a couple of simple examples, and if you want to do more extensive validation programming, you can look into the specification further. Unfortunately, even after the second release there are still no references available as of this writing, save the actual specifications previously referenced.

Each new constraint is composed of two parts: the annotation definition and the implementation or validation classes. We have been showing examples of built-in annotations in our examples so far, so you know how to use them. However, you haven't seen the accompanying implementation classes for those built-in annotations because they are assumed to be implemented by the validation provider. When you write your own constraint, you need to supply an implementation class for each different type of object that may be annotated by your new constraint annotation. Then, during the validation process, the validator will invoke the corresponding implementation class for the type of object that is being validated.

Constraint Annotations

It is not a difficult task to define a new constraint annotation, but there are a few required ingredients to consider when doing so. They are included in the simple constraint annotation definition in Listing 12-8 that marks a number as being even. Note that it is good practice to document in the constraint definition what types it may annotate.

Listing 12-8. Defining a Constraint Annotation

```
/**
 * Indicate that a number should be even.
 * May be applied on fields or properties of type Integer.
 */
@Constraint(validatedBy={EvenNumberValidator.class})
@Target({METHOD, FIELD})
@Retention(RUNTIME)
public @interface Even {
    String message() default "Number must be even";
    Class<?>[] groups() default {};
    Class<? extends Payload>[] payload() default {};
    boolean includeZero() default true;
}
```

As the example shows, the @Retention policy must be set to RUNTIME, and the @Target must include at least one or more of TYPE, FIELD, METHOD, or ANNOTATION_TYPE. Other target types may also be included, but only these are required to be discovered by validation providers. The definition must also be annotated with the @Constraint meta-annotation, which indicates the implementation class to go along with this annotation and contains the validation code. We will discuss how to create implementation classes in the next section.

There are three elements that are mandatory in every constraint annotation. We have already discussed the first one, the message element, and how it can be used to set a default exception message when constraints are not met. We discussed groups in the previous section, so you also know that the groups element is used when the validation of a constraint should occur as part of one or more sets of related other constraint checks. The third element is the payload element, which is just a place to pass context-specific metadata to the validation class. The classes passed to this element are defined by the constraint creator and must extend the specification-defined javax.validation. PayLoad type. Any number of additional constraint-specific elements may also be added. In this example, we have added an option to either include or exclude zero as an even number.

While each of the required elements has its purposes, it is rather unfortunate that they are all required. Requiring them just because they might be useful to some applications is somewhat reminiscent of the days of early EJB, when applications were forced to insert extra code (that they had no desire to either include or use) just because the specification said they had to. This will hopefully be fixed in a future release of the validation specification.

Constraint Implementation Classes

For each constraint annotation, there must be one or more constraint implementation classes. Each class must implement the javax.validation.ConstraintValidator interface and provide the logic to validate the value being checked. Listing 12-9 is the implementation class to accompany our @Even constraint annotation.

Listing 12-9. Defining a Constraint Implementation Class

```
public class EvenNumberValidator
        implements ConstraintValidator<Even,Integer> {

    boolean includesZero;
```

```
public void initialize(Even constraint) {
    includesZero = constraint.includeZero();
}

public boolean isValid(Integer value,
                        ConstraintValidatorContext ctx) {
    if (value == null)
        return true;
    if (value == 0)
        return includesZero;
    return value % 2 == 0;
}
}
```

The validation class implements the javax.validation.ConstraintValidator interface with two type parameters. The first type is the constraint annotation type, and the second is the type of value that the implementation class is expecting to validate. In our case, we are validating integer types, which means that the @Even constraint annotation may be applied to fields or getters of type Integer, or any subtypes (of which there are none in this case). The primitive int type corresponding to the wrapper type is also a candidate type.

The two methods that must be implemented are initialize() and isValid(). The initialize() method is invoked first and passes in the annotation instance that caused the validating class to be invoked in the first place. We take any state from the instance and initialize the validation class with it, so when the isValid() method is called we can validate the value passed to us according to the parameters of the constraint that is annotating it. The additional ConstraintValidatorContext parameter can be used for more advanced error generation, but it is somewhat obtuse and beyond the scope of our validation overview.

Validation in JPA

Now that you have some basic validation knowledge, we are ready to put things in a JPA context. When validating JPA entities there is a specific integration required with the JPA provider. There are a few reasons for this integration.

First and foremost, an entity may have lazily loaded attributes, and because a validator does not have a dependency on, or knowledge of, JPA, it would not know when an attribute has not been loaded. The process of validation could unwittingly cause the entire object graph to be loaded into memory! Another case is if validation is occurring on a JPA entity on the client side and the unloaded attributes are not even loadable. In this case, validation would produce an exception, not quite as bad as loading the entire object graph, but still clearly undesirable.

The most practical reason for a JPA integration is that most often we want validation to be invoked automatically at specific lifecycle phases. Recall that in our example in Listing 12-2 we validated at the PrePersist phase to ensure that we did not persist an entity in an invalid state. It turns out that the most convenient lifecycle events to trigger validation at are PrePersist, PreUpdate, and PreRemove, so if validation is enabled, these events will cause the validator to do its work. Listing 12-10 shows an entity and an embeddable type with validation constraints on them.

Listing 12-10. Validating an Entity

```
@Entity
public class Employee {
    @Id @NotNull
    private int id;
```

```
    @NotNull
    @Size(max=40)
    private String name;

    @Past
    private Date startDate;

    @Embedded
    @Valid
    private EmployeeInfo info;

    @ManyToOne
    private Address address;
    // ...
}

@Embeddable
public class EmployeeInfo {
    @Past
    private Date dob;

    @Embedded
    private PersonInfo spouse;
}
```

When an entity is validated, each of the fields or properties, or even the type itself, is validated according to the regular validation rules. However, the validation specification dictates that when a @Valid annotation is present on a field or property, the validation process proceeds to the object stored in that field or property. Embeddables may optionally be annotated with @Valid in order to be traversed during validation, but relationships may not. In other words, the EmployeeInfo object in the info field will be validated when the Employee is validated, but the spouse will not be, and related entities, such as the Address, will also not be validated unless they themselves have been persisted, updated, or removed.

Enabling Validation

When no overriding settings are present at the JPA configuration level, validation is on by default when a validation provider is on the classpath. To explicitly control whether validation should be enabled or disabled, there are two possible settings.

- validation-mode element in the persistence.xml file. This element may be set to one of three possible values.

- AUTO: Turn on validation when a validation provider is present on the classpath (default).

- CALLBACK: Turn on validation and throw an error if no validation provider is available.

- NONE: Turn off validation.

- javax.persistence.validation.mode persistence property. This property may be specified in the Map passed to the createEntityManagerFactory() method and overrides the validation-mode setting if present. Possible values are the string equivalents of the validation-mode values (AUTO, CALLBACK, and NONE) and have exactly the same meanings as their validation-mode counterparts.

Setting Lifecycle Validation Groups

By default, each of the `PrePersist` and `PreUpdate` lifecycle events will trigger validation on the affected entity, immediately following the event callback, using the `Default` validation group. No group will be validated, by default, during the `PreRemove` phase. To change the groups being validated at the three different lifecycle event types, any of the following properties may be specified, either as properties in the `properties` section of the `persistence.xml` file, or in the `Map` passed into `createEntityManagerFactory()`:

- `javax.persistence.validation.group.pre-persist`: Set the groups to validate at `PrePersist` time.

- `javax.persistence.validation.group.pre-update`: Set the groups to validate at `PreUpdate` time.

- `javax.persistence.validation.group.pre-remove`: Set the groups to validate at `PreRemove` time.

By setting these properties to a particular group or groups, you can isolate the kinds of validation that get performed on entities across different lifecycle events. For example, you may create groups called `Create`, `Update`, and `Remove`, and then when you want some kind of validation to occur on one or more of these events, you need only set the groups on the relevant constraints to be checked. In fact, it is more common for validation to occur at creation and updating, and for the same validation to occur at both stages, so the `Default` group will most often be sufficient for both of these. However, you may want to specify a separate group for `PreRemove`, as shown in Listing 12-11.

Listing 12-11. Varying Validation According to Lifecycle Events

```
@Entity
public class Employee {
    @Id @NotNull
    private int id;

    @NotNull
    @Size(max=40)
    private String name;

    @Past
    private Date startDate;

    @Size(groups=Remove.class,min=0,max=0)
    private long vacationDays;

    // ...
}
```

The validation in Listing 12-11 ensures that no employee is removed from the system either owing or being owed vacation time. The rest of the constraints are validated during the `PrePersist` and `PreUpdate` events. This assumes that the Remove group has been defined, and that the following property is present in the `persistence.xml` file:

```
<property name="javax.persistence.validation.group.pre-remove"
        value="Remove"/>
```

■ **Tip**   It is not currently portable in JPA to set the groups on a per-entity basis, although some providers may provide such capabilities. Providers that do support it would typically allow the entity name to be an additional suffix on the property name (e.g., `javax.persistence.validation.group.pre-remove.Employee`).

Concurrency

The concurrency of entity access and entity operations is not heavily specified, but there are a few rules that dictate what we can and can't expect. We will go over these and leave the rest to the vendors to explain in the documentation for their respective implementations.

Entity Operations

A managed entity belongs to a single persistence context and should not be managed by more than one persistence context at any given time. This is an application responsibility, however, and may not necessarily be enforced by the persistence provider. Merging the same entity into two different open persistence contexts could produce undefined results.

Entity managers and the persistence contexts that they manage are not intended to be accessed by more than one concurrently executing thread. The application cannot expect it to be synchronized and is responsible for ensuring that it stays within the thread that obtained it.

Entity Access

Applications may not access an entity directly from multiple threads while it is managed by a persistence context. An application may choose, however, to allow entities to be accessed concurrently when they are detached. If it chooses to do so, the synchronization must be controlled through the methods coded on the entity. Concurrent entity state access is not recommended, however, because the entity model does not lend itself well to concurrent patterns. It would be preferable to simply copy the entity and pass the copied entity to other threads for access and then merge any changes back into a persistence context when they need to be persisted.

Refreshing Entity State

The `refresh()` method of the `EntityManager` interface can be useful in situations when we know or suspect that there are changes in the database that we do not have in our managed entity. The refresh operation applies only when an entity is managed because when we are detached we typically only need to issue a query to get an updated version of the entity from the database.

Refreshing makes more sense the longer the duration of the persistence context that contains it. Refreshing is especially relevant when using an extended or application-managed persistence context because it prolongs the interval of time that an entity is effectively cached in the persistence context in isolation from the database.

To refresh a managed entity, we simply call `refresh()` on the entity manager. If the entity that we try to refresh is not managed, an `IllegalArgumentException` exception will be thrown. To clarify some of the issues around the refresh operation, we will use the example bean shown in Listing 12-12.

Listing 12-12. Periodic Refresh of a Managed Entity

```
@Stateful
@TransactionAttribute(TransactionAttributeType.NOT_SUPPORTED)
public class EmployeeService {
    public static final long REFRESH_THRESHOLD = 300000;

    @PersistenceContext(unitName="EmployeeService",
                        type=PersistenceContextType.EXTENDED)
    EntityManager em;
    Employee emp;
    long loadTime;

    public void loadEmployee (int id) {
        emp = em.find(Employee.class, id);
        if (emp == null)
            throw new IllegalArgumentException(
                "Unknown employee id: " + id);
        loadTime = System.currentTimeMillis();
    }

    public void deductEmployeeVacation(int days) {
        refreshEmployeeIfNeeded();
        emp.setVacationDays(emp.getVacationDays() - days);
    }

    public void adjustEmployeeSalary(long salary) {
        refreshEmployeeIfNeeded();
        emp.setSalary(salary);
    }

    @Remove
    @TransactionAttribute(TransactionAttributeType.REQUIRED)
    public void finished() {}

    private void refreshEmployeeIfNeeded() {
        if ((System.currentTimeMillis() - loadTime) > REFRESH_THRESHOLD) {
            em.refresh(emp);
            loadTime = System.currentTimeMillis();
        }
    }

    // ...
}
```

The bean in Listing 12-12 uses an extended persistence context in order to keep an Employee instance managed while various operations are applied to it via the business methods of the session bean. It might allow a number of modifying operations on it before it commits the changes, but we need to include only a couple of operations for this example.

Let's look at this bean in detail. The first thing to notice is that the default transaction attribute has been changed from REQUIRED to NOT_SUPPORTED. This means that as the Employee instance is changed by the various business methods of the bean, those changes will not be written to the database. This will occur only when the finished() method is invoked, which has a transaction attribute of REQUIRED. This is the only method on the bean that will associate the extended persistence context with a transaction and cause it to be synchronized with the database.

The second interesting thing about this bean is that it stores the time the Employee instance was last accessed from the database. Because the bean instance may exist for a long time, the business methods use the refreshEmployeeIfNeeded() method to see if it has been too long since the Employee instance was last refreshed. If the refresh threshold has been reached, the refresh() method is used to update the Employee state from the database.

Unfortunately, the refresh operation does not behave as the author of the session bean expected. When refresh is invoked, it will overwrite the managed entity with the state in the database, causing any changes that have been made to the entity to be lost. For example, if the salary is adjusted and five minutes later the vacation is adjusted, the Employee instance will get refreshed, causing the previous change to the salary to be lost. So even though the example in Listing 12-12 does indeed do a periodic refresh of the managed entity, the result is not only an inappropriate use of refresh() but also a detrimental outcome to the application.

So when is refreshing valid for objects that we are modifying? The answer is, not as often as you think. One of the primary use cases is to "undo" or discard changes made in the current transaction, reverting them back to their original value. It may also be used in long-lived persistence contexts where read-only managed entities are being cached. In these scenarios, the refresh() operation can safely restore an entity to its currently recorded state in the database. This would have the effect of picking up changes made in the database since the entity had been last loaded into the persistence context. The stipulation is that the entity should be read-only or not contain any changes.

Recall our editing session in Listing 6-34. Using refresh(), we can add the ability to revert an entity when the user decides to cancel their changes to an Employee editing session. Listing 12-13 shows the bean with its additional revertEmployee() method.

Listing 12-13. Employee Editing Session with Revert

```java
@Stateful
@TransactionAttribute(TransactionAttributeType.NOT_SUPPORTED)
public class EmployeeEdit {
    @PersistenceContext(unitName="EmployeeService",
                        type=PersistenceContextType.EXTENDED)
    EntityManager em;
    Employee emp;

    public void begin(int id) {
        emp = em.find(Employee.class, id);
        if (emp == null) {
            throw new IllegalArgumentException("Unknown employee id: " + id);
        }
    }

    public Employee getEmployee() { return emp; }

    public Employee revertEmployee() {
        em.refresh(emp);
        return emp;
    }
```

```
@Remove
@TransactionAttribute(TransactionAttributeType.REQUIRES_NEW)
public void save() {}

@Remove
public void cancel() {}
}
```

Refresh operations may also be cascaded across relationships. This is done on the relationship annotation by setting the cascade element to include the REFRESH value. If the REFRESH value is not present in the cascade element, the refresh will stop at the source entity. Listing 12-14 demonstrates how to set the REFRESH cascade operation for a many-to-one relationship.

Listing 12-14. Cascading a Refresh Operation

```
@Entity
public class Employee {
    @Id private int id;
    private String name;
    @ManyToOne(cascade={CascadeType.REFRESH})
    private Employee manager;
    // ...
}
```

Locking

Locking surfaces at many different levels and is intrinsic to JPA. It is used and assumed at various points throughout the API and the specification. Whether your application is simple or complex, chances are that you will make use of locking somewhere along the way.

While we will discuss all the locking defined and used in JPA, we will focus primarily on optimistic locking because it is not only the most prevalent but also the most useful way to scale an application.

Optimistic Locking

When we talk about locking, we are often referring to optimistic locking. The optimistic locking model is based on the premise that there is a good chance that the transaction in which changes are made to an entity will be the only one that actually changes the entity during that interval. This translates into the decision to not acquire a lock on the entity until the change is actually made to the database, usually at the end of the transaction.

When the data actually does get sent to the database to get updated at flush time or at the end of the transaction, the entity lock is acquired and a check is made on the data in the database. The flushing transaction must see whether any other transaction has committed a change to the entity in the intervening time since this transaction read it in and changed it. If a change occurred, it means that the flushing transaction has data that does not include those changes and should not write its own changes to the database, lest it overwrite the changes from the intervening transaction. At this stage, it must roll back the transaction and throw a special exception called OptimisticLockException. The example in Listing 12-15 shows how this could happen.

Listing 12-15. Method That Adjusts Vacation Balance

```
@Stateless
public class EmployeeService {
    @PersistenceContext(unitName="EmployeeService")
    EntityManager em;

    public void deductEmployeeVacation(int id, int days) {
        Employee emp = em.find(Employee.class, id);
        int currentDays = emp.getVacationDays();
        // Do some other stuff like notify HR system, etc.
        // ...
        emp.setVacationDays(currentDays - days);
    }
}
```

While this method might seem harmless enough, it is really just an accident waiting to happen. The problem is as follows. Imagine that two HR data-entry operators, Frank and Betty, were charged with entering a backlog of vacation adjustments into the system and they both happened to be entering an adjustment for the employee with id 42 at the same time. Frank is supposed to deduct 1 day from employee 42, while Betty is deducting 12 days. Frank's console calls deductEmployeeVacation() first, which immediately reads employee 42 in from the database, finds that employee 42 has 20 days, and then proceeds into the HR notification step. Meanwhile, Betty starts to enter her data on her console, which also calls deductEmployeeVacation(). It also reads employee 42 in from the database and finds that the employee has 20 vacation days, but Betty happens to have a much faster connection to the HR system. As a result, Betty gets past the HR notification before Frank does and proceeds to set the vacation day count to 8 before committing her transaction and going on to the next item. Frank finally gets past the HR system notification and deducts 1 day from the 20, and then commits his transaction. If Frank commits, he has overwritten Betty's deduction and employee 42 gets an extra 12 days of vacation.

Instead of committing Frank's transaction, though, an optimistic locking strategy would find out when it was time to commit that someone else had changed the vacation count. When Frank attempted to commit his transaction, an OptimisticLockException would have been thrown, and his transaction would have been rolled back instead. The result is that Frank would have to reenter his change and try again, which is far superior to getting an incorrect result for employee 42.

Versioning

The question that you might have been asking is how the provider can know whether somebody made changes in the intervening time since the committing transaction read the entity. The answer is that the provider maintains a versioning system for the entity. In order for it to do this, the entity must have a dedicated persistent field or property declared in it to store the version number of the entity that was obtained in the transaction. The version number must also be stored in the database. When going back to the database to update the entity, the provider can check the version of the entity in the database to see if it matches the version that it obtained previously. If the version in the database is the same, the change can be applied and everything goes ahead without any problems. If the version was greater, somebody else changed the entity since it was obtained in the transaction, and an exception should be thrown. The version field will get updated both in the entity and in the database whenever an update to the entity is sent to the database.

Version fields are not required, but we recommend that version fields be in every entity that has any chance of being concurrently modified by more than one process. A version column is an absolute necessity whenever an entity gets modified as a detached entity and merged back into a persistence context again afterward. The longer an entity stays in memory, the higher the chance that it will be changed in the database by another process, rendering the in-memory copy invalid. Version fields are at the core of optimistic locking and provide the best and most performant protection for infrequent concurrent entity modification.

Version fields are defined simply by annotating the field or property on the entity with a `@Version` annotation. Listing 12-16 shows an `Employee` entity annotated to have a version field.

Listing 12-16. Using a Version Field

```
@Entity
public class Employee {
    @Id private int id;
    @Version private int version;
    // ...
}
```

Version-locking fields defined on the entity can be of type `int`, `short`, `long`, the corresponding wrapper types, and `java.sql.Timestamp`. The most common practice is just to use `int` or one of the numeric types, but some legacy databases use timestamps.

As with the identifier, the application should not set or change the version field once the entity has been created. It might access it, though, for its own purposes if it wants to make use of the version number for some application-dependent reason.

■ **Tip** Some providers do not require that the version field be defined and stored in the entity. Variations of storing it in the entity are storing it in a vendor-specific cache, or not storing anything at all but instead using field comparison. For example, a popular option is to compare some application-specified combination of the entity state in the database with the entity state being written and then use the results as criteria to decide whether state has been changed.

A couple of words of warning about version fields are in order. The first is that they are not guaranteed to be updated, either in the managed entities or the database, as part of a bulk update operation. Some vendors offer support for automatic updating of the version field during bulk updates, but this cannot be portably relied upon. For those vendors that do not support automatic version updates, the entity version can be manually updated as part of the UPDATE statement, as exhibited by the following query:

```
UPDATE Employee e
SET e.salary = e.salary + 1000, e.version = e.version + 1
WHERE EXISTS (SELECT p
                FROM e.projects p
                WHERE p.name = 'Release2')
```

The second point worth remembering is that version fields will be automatically updated only when either the non-relationship fields or the owning foreign key relationship fields (e.g., many-to-one and one-to-one source foreign key relationships) are modified. If you want a non-owned, collection-valued relationship to cause an update to the entity version, you might need to use one of the locking strategies described in the following locking sections.

Advanced Optimistic Locking Modes

By default, JPA assumes what is defined in the ANSI/ISO SQL specification and known in transaction isolation parlance as Read Committed isolation. This standard isolation level simply guarantees that any changes made inside a transaction will not be visible to other transactions until the changing transaction has been committed. Normal execution using version locking works with Read Committed isolation to provide additional data-consistency checks in the face of interleaved writes. Satisfying tighter locking constraints than what this locking offers requires that an additional locking strategy be used. To be portable, these strategies can be used only on entities with version fields.

Locking options can be specified by means of a number of different calls:

- `EntityManager.lock()`: Explicit method for locking objects already in the persistence context.

- `EntityManager.refresh()`: Permits a lock mode to be passed in and applies to the object in the persistence context being refreshed.

- `EntityManager.find()`: Permits a lock mode to be passed in and applies to the object being returned.

- `Query.setLockMode()`: Sets the lock mode to be in effect during execution of the query.

Each of the `EntityManager` methods must be invoked within a transaction. Although the `Query.setLockMode()` method may be invoked at any time, a query that has its lock mode set must be executed within the context of a transaction.

The `lock()` and `refresh()` methods are invoked on objects already in the persistence context, so depending upon the particular implementation there might or might not be any action taken other than simply flagging the objects as being locked.

Optimistic Read Locking

The next level of transaction isolation is termed Repeatable Read and prevents the so-called non-repeatable read anomaly. This anomaly can be described a few different ways, but perhaps the simplest is to say that when a transaction queries for the same data twice in the same transaction, the second query returns a different version of the data than was returned the first time because another transaction modified it in the intervening time. Put another way, the Repeatable Read isolation level means that once a transaction has accessed data and another transaction modifies that data, at least one of the transactions must be prevented from committing. An optimistic read lock in JPA provides this level of isolation.

To optimistically read-lock an entity, a lock mode of `LockModeType.OPTIMISTIC` can be passed to one of the locking methods. The resulting lock will guarantee that both the transaction that obtains the entity read lock and any other that tries to change that entity instance will not both succeed. At least one will fail, but like the database isolation levels, which one fails depends upon the implementation.

■ **Tip**   The `LockModeType.OPTIMISTIC` value was introduced in JPA 2.0 and is really just a rename of the `LockModeType.READ` option that existed in JPA 1.0. Although `READ` is still a valid option, `OPTIMISTIC` should be used in all new applications going forward.

The way read locking is implemented is entirely up to the provider. Even though it is called an optimistic read lock, a provider might choose to be heavy-handed and obtain an eager write lock on the entity, in which case any other transaction that tries to change the entity will fail or block until the locking transaction completes. The provider will, however, most often optimistically read-lock the object, meaning that the provider will not actually go to the database for a lock when the locking method is called. It will instead wait until the end of the transaction, and at commit time it will reread the entity to see if the entity has been changed since it was last read in the transaction. If it has not changed, the read lock was honored, but if the entity has changed, the gamble was lost and the transaction will be rolled back.

A corollary to this optimistic form of read-locking implementation is that it doesn't matter at which point the locking method is actually invoked during the transaction. It can be invoked right up until just before the commit, and the exact same results will be produced. All the method does is flag the entity for being reread at commit time. It doesn't really matter when, during the transaction, the entity gets added to this list because the actual read operation will not occur until the end of the transaction. You can think of the `lock()` or locking `refresh()` calls as being retroactive to the point at which the entity was read into the transaction to begin with because that is the point at which the version is read and recorded in the managed entity.

The quintessential case for using this kind of lock is when an entity has an intrinsic dependency on one or more other entities for consistency. There is often a relationship between the entities, but not always. To demonstrate this, think of a Department that has employees; we want to generate a salary report for a given set of departments and have the report indicate the salary expenditures of each department. We have a method called generateDepartmentsSalaryReport() that will iterate through the set of departments and use an internal method to find the total salary for each one. The method defaults to having a transaction attribute of REQUIRED, so it will be executed entirely within the context of a transaction. The code is in Listing 12-17.

Listing 12-17. Department Salaries Report

```java
@Stateless
public class EmployeeService {
    @PersistenceContext(unitName="EmployeeService")
    EntityManager em;

    // ...

    public SalaryReport generateDepartmentsSalaryReport(
                                        List<Integer> deptIds) {
        SalaryReport report = new SalaryReport();
        long total = 0;
        for (Integer deptId : deptIds) {
            long deptTotal = totalSalaryInDepartment(deptId);
            report.addDeptSalaryLine(deptId, deptTotal);
            total += deptTotal;
        }
        report.addSummarySalaryLine(total);
        return report;
    }

    protected long totalSalaryInDepartment(int deptId) {
        long total = 0;
        Department dept = em.find(Department.class, deptId);
        for (Employee emp : dept.getEmployees())
            total += emp.getSalary();
        return total;
    }

    public void changeEmployeeDepartment(int deptId, int empId) {
        Employee emp = em.find(Employee.class, empId);
        emp.getDepartment().removeEmployee(emp);
        Department dept = em.find(Department.class, deptId);
        dept.addEmployee(emp);
        emp.setDepartment(dept);
    }
    // ...
}
```

The report will get generated easily, but is it correct? What happens if an employee gets moved from one department to another during the time we are computing the total salary? For example, say we make a request for a report on departments 10, 11, and 12. The request starts to generate the report for department 10. It finishes department 10 and moves on to department 11. As it is iterating through all the employees in department 11, the employee with id 50 in department 10 gets changed to be in department 12. Somewhere a manager invokes the changeEmployeeDepartment() method, the transaction commits, and employee 50 is changed to be in department 12. Meanwhile, the report generator has finished department 11 and is now going on to generate a salary total for department 12. When it iterates through the employees, it will find employee 50 even though it already counted that employee in department 10, so employee 50 will be counted twice. We did everything in transactions but we still got an inconsistent view of the employee data. Why?

The problem was in the fact that we did not lock any of the employee objects from being modified during our operation. We issued multiple queries and were vulnerable to viewing the same object with different state in it, which is the non-repeatable read phenomenon. We could fix it in a number of ways, one of which would be to set the database isolation to Repeatable Read. Because we are explaining the lock() method, we will use it to lock each of the employees so that either they could not change while our transaction was active, or if one did, our transaction would fail. Listing 12-18 shows the updated method that does the locking.

Listing 12-18. Using an Optimistic Read Lock

```
protected long totalSalaryInDepartment(int deptId) {
    long total = 0;
    Department dept = em.find(Department.class, deptId);
    for (Employee emp : dept.getEmployees()) {
        em.lock(emp, LockModeType.OPTIMISTIC);
        total += emp.getSalary();
    }
    return total;
}
```

We mentioned that the implementation is permitted to lock eagerly or defer acquisition of the locks until the end of the transaction. Most major implementations defer the locking until commit time and by doing so provide far superior performance and scalability without sacrificing any of the semantics.

Optimistic Write Locking

A second level of advanced optimistic locking is called an optimistic write lock, which by virtue of its name hints correctly that we are actually locking the object for writing. The write lock guarantees all that the optimistic read lock does, but also pledges to increment the version field in the transaction regardless of whether a user updated the entity or not. This provides a promise of an optimistic lock failure if another transaction also tries to modify the same entity before this one commits. This is equivalent to making a forced update to the entity in order to trigger the version number to be augmented, and is why the option is called OPTIMISTIC_FORCE_INCREMENT. The obvious conclusion is that if the entity is being updated or removed by the application, it never needs to be explicitly write-locked, and that write-locking it anyway would be redundant at best and at worst could lead to an additional update, depending upon the implementation.

■ **Tip** The LockModeType.OPTIMISTIC_FORCE_INCREMENT value was introduced in JPA 2.0 and is really just a rename of the LockModeType.WRITE option that existed in JPA 1.0. Although WRITE is still a valid option, OPTIMISTIC_FORCE_INCREMENT should be used in all new applications going forward.

Recall that updates to the version column do not normally occur when changes are made to a non-owned relationship. Due to this, the common case for using OPTIMISTIC_FORCE_INCREMENT is to guarantee consistency across entity relationship changes (often they are one-to-many relationships with target foreign keys) when in the object model the entity relationship pointers change, but in the data model no columns in the entity table change.

For example, let's say an employee has a set of assigned uniforms that were given to him, and his company has a cheap cleaning service that bills him automatically through payroll deduction. So Employee has a one-to-many relationship to Uniform, and Employee has a cleaningCost field that contains the amount that will get deducted from his paycheck at the end of the month. If there are two different stateful session beans that have extended persistence contexts, one for managing employees (EmployeeManagement) and another that manages the cleaning fees (CleaningFeeManagement) for the company, then if the Employee exists in both of the persistence contexts, there is a possibility of inconsistency.

Both copies of the Employee entity start out the same, but let's say that an operator records that the employee has received an additional brand new uniform. This implies creation of a new Uniform entity and adding it to the one-to-many collection of the Employee. The transaction is committed and everything is fine, except that now the EmployeeManagement persistence context has a different version of the Employee than the CleaningFeeManagement persistence context has. The operator has done the first maintenance task and now goes on to computing the cleaning charge for clients. The CleaningFeeManagement session computes the cleaning charges based on the one-to-many relationship that it knows about (without the extra uniform) and writes out a new version of the Employee with the employee's cleaning charge based on one less uniform. The transaction commits successfully even though the first transaction had already committed and though the changes to the uniform relationship had already committed to the database. Now we have an inconsistency between the number of uniforms and the cost of cleaning them, and the CleaningFeeManagement persistence context could go on with its stale copy of the Employee without even knowing about the new uniform and never get a lock conflict.

The reason why the change was not seen and no lock exception occurred for the second operation was because in the first operation no writes to the Employee actually occurred and thus the version column was not updated. The only changes to the Employee were to its relationship, and because it was owned by the Uniform side there was no reason to make any updates to the Employee. Unfortunately for the company (but not for the employee) this means they will be out a cleaning fee for the uniform.

The solution is to use the OPTIMISTIC_FORCE_INCREMENT option, as shown in Listing 12-19, and force an update to the Employee when the relationship changed in the first operation. This will cause any updates in any other persistence contexts to fail if they make changes without knowing about the relationship update.

Listing 12-19. Using an Optimistic Write Lock

```
@Stateful
public class EmployeeManagement {
    @PersistenceContext(unitName="EmployeeService",
                        type=PersistenceContextType.EXTENDED)
    EntityManager em;

    public void addUniform(int id, Uniform uniform) {
        Employee emp = em.find(Employee.class, id);
        em.lock(emp, LockModeType.OPTIMISTIC_FORCE_INCREMENT);
        emp.addUniform(uniform);
        uniform.setEmployee(emp);
    }

    // ...
}

@Stateful
public class CleaningFeeManagement {
    static final Float UNIFORM_COST = 4.7f;

    @PersistenceContext(unitName="EmployeeService",
                        type=PersistenceContextType.EXTENDED)
    EntityManager em;
```

```
    public void calculateCleaningCost(int id) {
        Employee emp = em.find(Employee.class, id);
        Float cost = emp.getUniforms().size() * UNIFORM_COST;
        emp.setCost(emp.getCost() + cost);
    }

    // ...
}
```

Recovering from Optimistic Failures

An optimistic failure means that one or more of the entities that were modified were not fresh enough to be allowed to record their changes. The version of the entity that was modified was stale, and the entity had since been changed in the database, hence an `OptimisticLockException` was thrown. There is not always an easy solution to recovering, and depending upon the application architecture, it may or may not even be possible, but if and when appropriate, one solution might be to get a fresh copy of the entity and then reapply the changes. In other cases, it might only be possible to give the client (such as a web browser) an indication that the changes were in conflict with another transaction and must be reentered. The harsh reality is that in the majority of cases it is neither practical nor feasible to handle optimistic lock problems other than to simply retry the operation at a convenient transactional demarcation point.

The first problem you might encounter when an `OptimisticLockException` is thrown could be the one you never see. Depending on your settings, for example whether the calling bean is container-managed or bean-managed, and whether the interface is remote or local, you might only get a container-initiated `EJBException`. This exception will not necessarily even wrap the `OptimisticLockException` because all that is formally required of the container is to log it before throwing the exception.

Listing 12-20 shows how this could happen when invoking a method on a session bean that initiates a new transaction.

Listing 12-20. BMT Session Bean Client

```
@Stateless
@TransactionManagement(TransactionManagementType.BEAN)
public class EmpServiceClient {
    @EJB EmployeeService empService;

    public void adjustVacation(int id, int days) {
        try {
            empService.deductEmployeeVacation(id, days);
        } catch (EJBException ejbEx) {
            System.out.println(
                "Something went wrong, but I have no idea what!");
        } catch (OptimisticLockException olEx) {
            System.out.println(
                "This exception would be nice, but I will " +
                                    "probably never get it!");
        }
    }
}
```

The problem is that when an optimistic exception occurs down in the bowels of the persistence layer, it will get passed back to the EmployeeService session bean and get handled according to the rules of runtime exception handling by the container. Because the EmpServiceClient uses bean-managed transactions and does not start a transaction, and EmployeeService defaults to container-managed transactions with a REQUIRED attribute, a transaction will be initiated when the call to deductVacationBalance() occurs.

Once the method has completed and the changes have been made, the container will attempt to commit the transaction. In the process of doing this, the persistence provider will get a transaction synchronization notification from the transaction manager to flush its persistence context to the database. As the provider attempts its writes, it finds during its version number check that one of the objects has been modified by another process since being read by this one, so it throws an OptimisticLockException. The problem is that the container treats this exception the same way as any other runtime exception. The exception simply gets logged and the container throws an EJBException.

The solution to this problem is to perform a flush() operation from inside the container-managed transaction at the moment just before we are ready to complete the method. This forces a write to the database and locks the resources only at the end of the method so the effects on concurrency are minimized. It also allows us to handle an optimistic failure while we are in control, without the container interfering and potentially swallowing the exception. If we do get an exception from the flush() call, we can throw an application exception that the caller can recognize. This is shown in Listing 12-21.

Listing 12-21. Catching and Converting OptimisticLockException

```java
@Stateless
public class EmployeeService {
    @PersistenceContext(unitName="EmployeeService")
    EntityManager em;

    public void deductEmployeeVacation(int id, int days) {
        Employee emp = em.find(Employee.class, id);
        emp.setVacationDays(emp.getVacationDays() - days);
        // ...
        flushChanges();
    }

    public void adjustEmployeeSalary(int id, long salary) {
        Employee emp = em.find(Employee.class, id);
        emp.setSalary(salary);
        // ...
        flushChanges();
    }

    protected void flushChanges() {
        try {
            em.flush();
        } catch (OptimisticLockException optLockEx) {
            throw new ChangeCollisionException();
        }
    }
    // ...
}

@ApplicationException
public class ChangeCollisionException extends RuntimeException {
    public ChangeCollisionException() { super(); }
}
```

The `OptimisticLockException` might contain the object that caused the exception, but it is not guaranteed to. In Listing 12-21, there is only one object in the transaction (the `Employee`), so we know that it was the one that caused the failure. If there were multiple objects in the transaction, we could have invoked `getEntity()` on the caught exception to see whether the offending object was included.

We factor out the flushing from the rest of the processing code because every method must flush and catch the exception and then rethrow a domain-specific application exception. The `ChangeCollisionException` class is annotated with `@ApplicationException`, which is an EJB container annotation in the `javax.ejb` package, to indicate to the container that the exception is not really a system-level exception but should be thrown back to the client as-is. Normally, defining an application exception will cause the container to not roll back the transaction, but this is an EJB container notion. The persistence provider that threw the `OptimisticLockException` does not know about the special semantics of designated application exceptions and, seeing a runtime exception, will go ahead and mark the transaction for rollback.

The client code that you saw earlier can now receive and handle the application exception and potentially do something about it. At the very least, it is aware of the fact that the failure was a result of a data collision instead of some other more fatal error. The client bean is shown in Listing 12-22.

Listing 12-22. Handling OptimisticLockException

```
@Stateless
@TransactionManagement(TransactionManagementType.BEAN)
public class EmpServiceClient {
    @EJB EmployeeService empService;

    public void adjustVacation(int id, int days) {
        try {
            empService.deductEmployeeVacation(id, days);
        } catch (ChangeCollisionException ccEx) {
            System.out.println(
                    "Collision with other change - Retrying...");
            empService.deductEmployeeVacation(id, days);
        }
    }
}
```

When an `OptimisticLockException` occurs in this context, the easy answer is to retry. This was really quite a trivial case, so the decision to retry was not hard to make. If we are in an extended persistence context, however, we might have a much harder job of it because all the entities in the extended persistence context become detached when a transaction rolls back. Essentially we would need to reenlist all our objects after having reread them and then replay all the changes that we had applied in the previous failed transaction. Not a very easy thing to do in most cases.

In general, it is quite difficult to code for the optimistic exception case. When running in a server environment, chances are that any `OptimisticLockException` will be wrapped by a component level exception or server exception. The best approach is to simply treat all transaction failures equally and retry the transaction from the beginning or to indicate to the browser client that they must restart and retry.

Pessimistic Locking

Pessimistic locking implies obtaining a lock on one or more objects immediately, instead of optimistically waiting until the commit phase and hoping that the data has not changed in the database since it was last read in. A pessimistic lock is synchronous in that by the time the locking call returns, it is guaranteed that the locked object will not be modified by another transaction until after the current transaction completes and releases its lock. This does not leave the window open for transaction failure due to concurrent changes, a very real possibility when simple optimistic locking is used.

It was probably obvious from the preceding section that handling optimistic lock exceptions is not always a simple matter. This is likely one of the reasons why many developers tend to use pessimistic locking because it is always easier to write your application logic when you know up front whether your update will succeed or not.

In actuality, though, they are often limiting the scalability of their applications because needless locking serializes many operations that could easily occur in parallel. The reality is that very few applications actually need pessimistic locking, and those that do only need it for a limited subset of queries. The rule is that if you think you need pessimistic locking, think again. If you are in a situation where you have a very high degree of write concurrency on the same object(s) and the occurrence of optimistic failures is high, then you might need pessimistic locking because the cost of retries can become so prohibitively expensive that you are better off locking pessimistically. If you absolutely cannot retry your transactions and are willing to sacrifice some amount of scalability for it, this also might lead you to use pessimistic locking.

Pessimistic Locking Modes

Assuming that your application does fall within the small percentage of applications that should acquire pessimistic locks, you can pessimistically lock entities using the same API methods described in the "Advanced Optimistic Locking Modes" section. Like the optimistic modes, the pessimistic locking modes also guarantee Repeatable Read isolation, they just do so pessimistically. Similarly, a transaction must be active in order to acquire a pessimistic lock.

There are three supported pessimistic locking modes, but by far the most common is pessimistic write locking, so we will discuss that one first.

Pessimistic Write Locking

When a developer decides that he wants to use pessimistic locking, he is usually thinking about the kind of locking that is offered by the PESSIMISTIC_WRITE mode. This mode will be translated by most providers into a SQL "SELECT FOR UPDATE" statement in the database, obtaining a write lock on the entity so no other applications can modify it. Listing 12-23 shows an example of using the lock() method with PESSIMISTIC_WRITE mode. It shows a process that runs every day and accrues the vacation amount for each employee.

Listing 12-23. Pessimistic Write Locking

```
@Stateless
public class VacationAccrualService {
    @PersistenceContext(unitName="Employee")
    EntityManager em;

    public void accrueEmployeeVacation(int id) {
        Employee emp = em.find(Employee.class, id);
        // Find amt according to union rules and emp status
        EmployeeStatus status = emp.getStatus();
        double accruedDays = calculateAccrual(status);
        if accruedDays > 0 {
            em.lock(emp, LockModeType.PESSIMISTIC_WRITE);
            emp.setVacationDays(emp.getVacationDays() + accruedDays);
        }
    }
}
```

The session bean uses container-managed transactions, thus a new transaction is started when the `accrueEmployeeVacation()` method is called. The pessimistic lock is within the container transaction and happens only if there is something to add, so we appear to not be acquiring the lock unnecessarily. On the surface it all seems to be clever and correct. It isn't, however, and has some flaws that must be remedied before any process that calls this code should be started.

Ignoring the possibility that the employee may not exist (and the `find()` method might return `null`), the most serious problem is that the code assumes the pessimistic lock is retroactive to the time the employee was read. Locking at the last minute in order to minimize the time the exclusive lock is held is the right idea, but the employee data that is being locked in the database might not actually be the same as the state that we are looking at. The problem is rooted in the fact that we read the employee at the beginning of the method, but locked it much later, leaving the window open for another process to change the employee. Meanwhile, we are using the state of the employee that we initially read, and modifying it. If we don't have a version field on the `Employee` entity, the change that some other process made would be overridden with our stale copy, even though we used a pessimistic lock.

If we do have a version field, the optimistic locking check that always occurs even when pessimistic locking is used would catch the stale version, and we would get an `OptimisticLockException`. This exception would catch the code in Listing 12-23 by surprise because no handling is in place. Also, we might have used pessimistic locking because we didn't want to be surprised at commit time and have to deal with problems so late in the transaction.

The solution is to either acquire the lock on the employee up front in the `find()` method (and risk the scalability implications) or do a locking `refresh()`. Listing 12-24 shows the improved refreshing version of the `accrueEmployeeVacation()` method.

Listing 12-24. *Pessimistic Locking with Refresh*

```
public void accrueEmployeeVacation(int id) {
    Employee emp = em.find(Employee.class, id);
    // Find amt according to union rules and emp status
    EmployeeStatus status = emp.getStatus();
    double accruedDays = calculateAccrual(status);
    if (accruedDays > 0) {
        em.refresh(emp, LockModeType.PESSIMISTIC_WRITE);
        if (status != emp.getStatus())
            accruedDays = calculateAccrual(emp.getStatus());
        if (accruedDays > 0)
            emp.setVacationDays(emp.getVacationDays() + accruedDays);
    }
}
```

When we do a refresh, the possibility arises that the employee state on which our calculations initially depended has since changed. To ensure that we do not end up with an inconsistent employee we do one last check of the employee status. If it has changed, we recalculate using the new status and finally make the update.

Pessimistic Read Locking

Some databases support locking mechanisms to get repeatable read isolation without acquiring a write lock. A `PESSIMISTIC_READ` mode can be used to pessimistically achieve repeatable read semantics when no writes to the entity are expected. The fact that this kind of situation will not be encountered very often, combined with the allowance that providers have of implementing it using a pessimistic write lock, leads us to say that this mode is not one to be easily picked up and commonly used.

When an entity locked with a pessimistic read lock does end up getting modified, the lock will be upgraded to a pessimistic write lock. However, the upgrade might not occur until the entity is flushed, so it is of little efficacy because a failed lock acquisition exception won't be thrown until transaction commit time, rendering the lock equivalent to an optimistic one.

Pessimistic Forced Increment Locking

Another mode that targets the case of acquiring pessimistic locks, even though the entity is only being read, is the PESSIMISTIC_FORCE_INCREMENT mode. Like the OPTIMISTIC_FORCE_INCREMENT, this mode will also increment the version field of the locked entity regardless of whether changes were made to it. It is a somewhat overlapping case with pessimistic read locking and optimistic write locking, for example, when non-owned collection-valued relationships are present in the entity and have been modified. Forcing the version field to be incremented can maintain a certain degree of version consistency across relationships.

Pessimistic Scope

The "Versioning" section mentioned that changes to any owned relationships would cause the version field of the owning entity to be updated. If a unidirectional one-to-many relationship were to change, for example, the version would be updated even though no changes to the entity table would otherwise have been asserted.

When it comes to pessimistic locking, acquiring exclusive locks on entities in other entity tables can increase the likelihood of deadlock occurring. To avoid this, the default behavior of pessimistically locking queries is to not acquire locks on tables that are not mapped to the entity. An extra property exists to enable this behavior in case someone needs to acquire the locks as part of a pessimistic query. The javax.persistence.lock.scope property can be set on the query as a property, with its value set to PessimisticLockScope.EXTENDED. When set, target tables of unidirectional relationships, element collection tables, and owned many-to-many relationship join tables will all have their corresponding rows pessimistically locked.

This property should normally be avoided, except when it is absolutely necessary to lock such tables as join tables that cannot be conveniently locked any other way. Strict ordering and a solid understanding of the mappings and operation ordering should be a prerequisite to enabling this property to ensure that deadlocks do not result.

Pessimistic Timeouts

Until now we have made no mention of timeouts or how to specify how long to wait for locks. Although JPA does not normatively describe how providers must support timeout modes for pessimistic lock acquisition, JPA does define a hint that providers can use. Though not mandatory, the javax.persistence.lock.timeout hint is likely supported by the major JPA providers; however, make sure that your provider supports it before coding to this hint. Its value can be either 0, meaning do not block waiting for the lock, or some integer describing the number of milliseconds to wait for the lock. It can be passed into any of the EntityManager API methods that accept both a lock mode and a Map of properties or hints:

```
Map<String,Object> props = new HashMap<String,Object>();
props.put("javax.persistence.lock.timeout",5000);
em.find(Employee.class, 42, LockModeType.PESSIMISTIC_WRITE, props);
```

It can also be set on a query as a hint:

```
TypedQuery<Employee> q = em.createQuery(
        "SELECT e FROM EMPLOYEE e WHERE e.id = 42",
        Employee.class);
q.setLockMode(LockModeType.PESSIMISTIC_WRITE);
q.setHint("javax.persistence.lock.timeout",5000);
```

Unfortunately there is no default behavior when the timeout hint is not specified. Between the provider and the database it may be blocking, it may be "no wait", or it may have a default timeout.

Recovering From Pessimistic Failures

The last topic to discuss around pessimistic locking is what happens when the lock cannot be acquired. We did not place any exception handling code around our examples, but pessimistic locking calls can obviously fail for numerous reasons.

When a failure occurs as a result of not being able to acquire a lock during a query, or for any reason that is considered by the database as being non-fatal to the transaction, a `LockTimeoutException` will be thrown, and the caller can catch it and simply retry the call if he desires to do so. However, if the failure is severe enough to cause a transaction failure, a `PessimisticLockException` will be thrown and the transaction will be marked for rollback. When this exception occurs, then some of the ideas in the "Recovering from Optimistic Failures" section may help because the transaction is doomed to fail and we would appear to be in the same boat here. The key difference, though, is that a `PessimisticLockException` occurs as a result of method call, not as a deferred failure during the commit phase. We have more control and could catch the exception and convert it to a more meaningful one before throwing it back to the transaction demarcation initiator.

Caching

Caching is a fairly broad term that generally implies saving something in memory for quicker access later on. Even in a JPA context, caching can mean rather different things to different people, depending upon the perspective. In this section, we are talking about caching entities or the state that makes up an entity.

Sorting Through the Layers

If there is one thing that we software types like to do, it is to break things down into layers. We do this because dividing a complex system into multiple cohesive pieces helps us to more easily understand and communicate aspects of the system. Because it works pretty well, and we are not ones to ignore a good thing, we will similarly partition the JPA architecture into layers to illustrate different opportunities to cache. Figure 12-1 gives a pictorial view of the different caching layers that might exist.

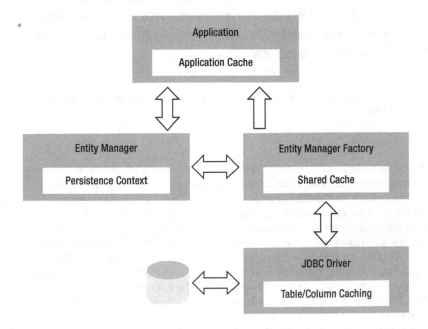

Figure 12-1. *Layers of caching in JPA*

The first layer we encounter is actually at the application tier. Any application might be written to cache as many entities as it likes simply by holding on to references to them. This should be done with the realization that the entities are likely going to become detached at some point, and the longer they sit in application space, the higher the probability they will become stale. Application caches have their place, but are generally discouraged because the cached entity instances will never be included in any future JPA query results or persistence contexts.

Next, the persistence context referenced by an entity manager can be considered a cache because it keeps references to all the managed entities. If, as is done in hardware architectures, we categorize the different layers of caching into levels, we would call the persistence context the first real level of JPA caching because it is the first place that a persistence provider could retrieve an in-memory entity from. When running in a transaction-scoped entity manager that has a persistence context demarcated by the transaction boundaries, the persistence context can be termed a transactional cache because it is around only for the duration of the transaction. When the entity manager is an extended one, its persistence context cache is longer-lived and will go away only when the entity manager is cleared or closed.

Executing a `find()` or a query method can be thought of as loading one or more entities into the cache, while invoking `detach()` on an entity can in some ways be considered a persistence context cache eviction of that entity. The difference is that if there are pending state changes in that entity, they will be lost unless a flush operation occurs before the entity is detached.

Caching in the entity manager factory is referred to by some as the second level cache, but of course this name makes sense only if there are no caching layers between it and the persistence context, which is not the case for all providers. One thing that is fairly prevalent across all providers is that the entity data in this cache is shared across the entity managers from the factory that contains the cache, so a better name for it is a shared cache. This cache has a specific API associated with it and is discussed in its own section.

The last cache that can contribute entity state to JPA is the JDBC driver cache. Most drivers cache connections and statements. Some caches also keep track of table or column state that is essentially transparent to the JPA provider, but that nonetheless can offer some savings in terms of not having to go to the database to get data on every call. This is generally feasible in the driver only if it is known that either the data is read-only or the driver controls database access exclusively.

■ **Note**   Some providers, such as the EclipseLink JPA Reference Implementation, provide much more sophisticated and exotic caching layers and features, such as isolated caching for Virtual Private Database (VPD) support, fine-grained options to determine automatic entity eviction policies, and distributed cache coordination mechanisms. Many also offer integrations with deluxe and highly specialized distributed caching products.

To see how the various levels of caching in the system get accessed during the course of a typical operation, let's trace a `find()` request for the Employee with id 100:

```
Employee emp = em.find(Employee.class, 100);
```

The first thing that happens is that the client looks in its local cache for the employee and finds that it doesn't have that Employee instance with id 100. It then issues the `find()` call on the entity manager. The entity manager will likely have a persistence context associated with it, so it checks in its persistence context for the entity of type Employee with id 100. If the entity exists in the persistence context, the managed instance is returned. If it does not exist or no persistence context had yet been associated with the entity manager, the entity manager goes to the factory to see if the shared cache has the entity instance. If it does, a new Employee instance with id 100 is created from the shared one and inserted into the persistence context, and the new managed instance is returned to the caller. If it is not in the shared cache, an SQL query is generated to select the entity from the database. The JDBC driver may have some data cached, so it could short-circuit the select clause and return at least part of the needed data. The resulting query data is then composed into an object and passed back. That object is inserted into the shared entity manager factory cache, and a new instance copy of it is created and inserted into the persistence context to be managed. That entity instance is finally returned to the client application for the client to cache, if it is so inclined.

Shared Cache

In the early days of JPA 1.0, when people would ask for standardization of shared caching at the entity manager factory layer, we generally figured that it wasn't worth it because every provider seemed to do caching differently. Some providers cache raw JDBC data, others cache entire objects, others prefer the middle ground of caching partial objects without the relationships built, while others don't cache at all. In the end, operating at the entity level is the best way to interface with the cache, and is the most natural and convenient granularity to use for the API.

The shared cache is manipulated in JPA through a slim `javax.persistence.Cache` interface. An object that implements `Cache` can be obtained from the entity manager factory by invoking `EntityManagerFactory.getCache()`. Even if a provider does not support caching, a `Cache` object will be returned, the difference being that the operations will have no effect.

The interface currently supports only a `contains()` method and a few method variants of eviction. While it isn't a very full API, applications should not really be using a caching interface in application code, so not much of an API is necessary. In general, caching operations are useful primarily for testing and debugging, and applications should not need to dynamically modify the cache at runtime. The most convenient way to use the cache is to simply clear it between test cases to ensure proper cleanup and isolate test behavior. Listing 12-25 shows a simple Junit 4 test case template that ensures that the shared cache is cleared after each test is executed.

Listing 12-25. Using the Cache Interface

```
public class SimpleTest {

    static EntityManagerFactory emf;
    EntityManager em;

    @BeforeClass
    public static void classSetUp() {
        emf = Persistence.createEntityManagerFactory("HR");
    }

    @AfterClass
    public static void classCleanUp() {
        emf.close();
    }

    @Before
    public void setUp() {
        em = emf.createEntityManager();
    }

    @After
    public void cleanUp() {
        em.close();
        emf.getCache().evictAll();
    }

    @Test
    public void testMethod() {
        // Test code ...
    }
}
```

If we accessed only a single Employee entity with primary key 42 in the tests and wanted to be more surgical about what we did to the cache, we could evict only that entity by calling evict(Employee.class, 42). Or, we could evict all instances of the Employee class by invoking evict(Employee.class). The problem with removing specific entities or classes of entities is that if the cache is object-based, this could leave it in an inconsistent state with dangling references to uncached objects. For example, if our Employee with id 42 had a bidirectional relationship to an Office entity and we evicted the Employee entity by using the class-based or instance-based eviction method, we would be leaving the cached Office entity pointing to an uncached Employee. The next time the Employee with id 42 is queried for and brought into the cache, its reference to its related Office will be properly set to point to the cached Office entity. The problem is that the pointer back from the Office to the Employee will not be corrected and we would be in a position where the Office entity is not pointing to the same Employee instance that is pointing back to it. The moral is that it is clearly not a good idea to go around evicting classes of objects that have relationships to, or are referenced by, other cached entities. We prefer the big evictAll hammer that sweeps everything out of the cache and ensures that it is entirely clean and consistent.

On the debugging side, we can check to see if the particular entity is cached by calling contains(Employee.class, 42). A provider that does not do any shared caching will simply return false on every invocation.

Static Configuration of the Cache

The greatest value offered by the JPA cache abstraction is the ability to configure it. Caching can be configured at the level of the global persistence unit or on a per-class basis. It is achieved through a combination of a persistence unit setting and class settings.

The persistence unit cache setting is controlled by the shared-cache-mode element in the persistence.xml file or the equivalent javax.persistence.sharedCache.mode property that can be passed in at entity manager factory creation time. It has five options, one of which is the default NOT_SPECIFIED. This means when the shared cache setting is not explicitly specified in the persistence.xml file or by the presence of the javax.persistence. sharedCache.mode property, it is up to the provider to either cache or not cache, depending upon its own defaults and inclinations. While this might seem a little odd to a developer, it truly is the appropriate default because different providers have different implementations that rely more or less heavily on caching.

Two other options, ALL and NONE, are more obvious in their meaning and semantics, and cause the shared cache to be completely enabled or disabled, respectively.

■ **Caution** Developers that maintain volatile entities changed by multiple clients often think that they should be disabling the shared cache for consistency. This is not often the right approach. Setting the cache mode to NONE can not only cause severe slowdown to the application but also potentially defeat provider mechanisms that optimize for caching. Using the locking, concurrency, and refreshing measures described earlier in this chapter is the preferred and recommended path.

When an entity class is highly volatile and highly concurrent, it is occasionally advantageous to disable caching of instances only of that class. This is achieved by setting the shared cache to DISABLE_SELECTIVE and then annotating the specific entity class that is to remain uncached with @Cacheable(false). The DISABLE_SELECTIVE option will cause the default behavior to cache every entity in the persistence unit. Each time an entity class is annotated with @Cacheable(false), you are effectively overriding the default and disabling the cache for instances of that entity type. This can be done to as many entity classes as you want. When applied to an entity class, the cacheability of its subclasses is also affected by the @Cacheable annotation on the entity. It can be overridden, though, at the level of the subclass, if the need arises.

If you get to the point where you have to annotate more classes than not, you can go the opposite route and set the shared cache to ENABLE_SELECTIVE, meaning that the default is to disable caching for all entities except those that have been annotated with @Cacheable(true) (or just @Cacheable because the default value of @Cacheable is true). In a nutshell, the @Cacheable annotation is useful when either of the two *_SELECTIVE options are in effect, and depending upon which is active, the boolean values in all the @Cacheable annotations in the persistence unit should be all true or all false.

Dynamic Cache Management

It is also possible at runtime to override whether entities get read from the cache during query execution or get put into the cache when entities are obtained from the database. In order for these overrides to be in effect, though, caching must already be enabled for the relevant entity class(es). This could be true because the static settings described in the previous section were used because the provider is defaulting caching to be on, or because a provider-specific caching option enabled the cache.

We mentioned the two possibilities of reading from or writing to the cache as separate options because, although related, they are distinct from each other and may be chosen independently. Each has its own property name and can be passed as a property to an entity manager to set a default caching behavior for that entity manager. It can also be passed to a find()method or as a hint to a query. The property names are javax.persistence.cache.retrieveMode and javax.persistence.cache.storeMode, with the values being members of the CacheRetrieveMode and CacheStoreMode enumerated types, respectively.

The retrieve mode has two simple options: CacheRetrieveMode.USE to use the cache when reading entities from the database, and CacheRetrieveMode.BYPASS to bypass the cache. The USE option is the default because caching must be enabled anyway for the property to be used. When BYPASS is active, entities should not be looked for in the shared cache. Note that the only reason USE even exists is to allow resetting the retrieve mode back to using the cache when an entity manager is set to BYPASS.

■ **Note**   Under normal circumstances the retrieve mode will have no practical effect if the entities are already present in the persistence context. Retrieve mode only dictates whether a lookup in the shared cache is performed. If queried entities exist in the active persistence context, those instances will always be returned.

The store mode supports a default CacheStoreMode.USE option, which places objects in the cache when obtained from or committed to the database. The CacheStoreMode.BYPASS option can be used to cause instances not to be inserted into the shared cache. A third store mode option, CacheStoreMode.REFRESH, is useful when objects may change outside the realm of the shared cache. For example, if an entity can be changed by a different application that uses the same database, or even by a different entity manager factory (perhaps in a different JVM in a cluster), the instance in the shared cache might become stale. Setting the store mode to REFRESH will cause the entity instance in the cache to be refreshed the next time it is read from the database.

■ **Caution**   The REFRESH option should always be turned on if there is a chance that application data may be changed from outside of the JPA application.

Consider the example in Listing 12-26 that returns all the stocks that have a price greater than a certain amount. Both the retrieve and store cache mode types are used to ensure that the results are as fresh as possible and that the cache is refreshed with those results.

Listing 12-26. Using the Cache Mode Properties

```
public List<Stock> findExpensiveStocks(double threshold) {
    TypedQuery<Stock> q = em.createQuery(
        "SELECT s FROM Stock s WHERE s.price > :amount",
        Stock.class);
    q.setHint("javax.persistence.cache.retrieveMode",
                CacheRetrieveMode.BYPASS);
    q.setHint("javax.persistence.cache.storeMode",
                CacheStoreMode.REFRESH);
    q.setParameter("amount", threshold);
    return q.getResultList();
}
```

At first it may seem a little odd that the cache is being bypassed in the retrieve mode, yet being refreshed in the store mode. It is assuming that not every query will be bypassing the cache, so refreshing will give subsequent cache hits access to the fresh data.

Note that the REFRESH option is not necessary when entities have simply been updated in a transaction. During commit, the default USE store mode option will cause the shared cache entry to be updated with the changes from the transaction. The added value of REFRESH applies only for database reads. This is why REFRESH is not necessary in the situation when the database is essentially dedicated to the JPA application. If all updates to the database go through the JPA application, its shared entity manager factory cache would always have the most up-to-date data and there would never be any reason to refresh the cache.

A store mode option may be passed into one method to which retrieve mode does not apply. The semantics of the entity manager refresh() method are that the entity instance in the persistence context is refreshed with the state from the database. Passing in a retrieve mode of USE is of debatable value because the point of the refresh was to get the latest data, and you will only find that in the database. However, the refresh() method semantics do not include updating the shared cache with the fresh database state. For that to occur, you need to also include the store mode REFRESH option as a property argument to the method.

```
HashMap props = new HashMap();
props.put("javax.persistence.cache.storeMode",
            CacheStoreMode.REFRESH);
em.refresh(emp, props);
```

■ **Tip** For applications that require REFRESH to be the default, many vendors provide support for setting it at the persistence unit level as a persistence unit property. Because refreshing may be more necessary for specific entity classes than others, the REFRESH options may also be supported at the level of the entity class, meaning that all entities of a given type are automatically refreshed in the cache when read from the database.

Using the dynamic caching options is preferred over simply disabling the cache, either globally or on a per-class basis. It gives you fine-grained control over performance and consistency, and still offers the provider the opportunity to optimize for the cases when optimization is appropriate.

Utility Classes

A handful of methods are available on two utility interfaces, PersistenceUnitUtil and PersistenceUtil in the javax.persistence package. These methods will not be used often by an application at runtime, but can be useful primarily for tool providers or in application frameworks.

PersistenceUtil

An instance of PersistenceUtil is obtained from the Persistence class in both Java SE and Java EE environments. The static getPersistenceUtil() method is the only method on the Persistence class that a managed or container-based application would normally use in a managed environment. It exports only two methods, both variants of determining whether state is loaded or not. The isLoaded(Object) method will return whether the entity passed in has all of its non-lazy state loaded. For example, the following might return false:

```
Persistence.getPersistenceUtil().isLoaded(
        em.getReference(Employee.class, 42));
```

We say "might" because the provider is free to load some or all the fields or properties of the Employee instance that gets returned; it just isn't compelled to do so.

The second variant, isLoaded(Object, String), accepts an extra String parameter describing a named attribute of the entity, and returns whether that attribute has been loaded in the entity instance passed in. It will return false either if isLoaded(Object) is false, or if the attribute is marked as lazy and has not been loaded. Assuming a definition of an Employee entity that has a phoneNumbers relationship attribute marked as lazy, the following will likely return false:

```
Persistence.getPersistenceUtil().isLoaded(
        em.find(Employee.class, 42), "phoneNumbers");
```

The PersistenceUtil class would be used only on the client side, or in a different application layer from persistence, when the entity manager or factory associated with the entity is not known. Each of the methods enters a provider resolution phase before calling the corresponding method on the correct provider. This may add some overhead, depending upon the implementation, caching of providers, and frequency of calling. On the server side, you might know which entity manager or factory to use for the entity, and in that case the more efficient PersistenceUnitUtil class, described in the next section, should be used instead.

PersistenceUnitUtil

A PersistenceUnitUtil instance can be obtained from an entity manager factory through the getPersistenceUnitUtil() method. It serves as a utility class for the persistence unit, and although it does not contain many methods now, in the future more utility functions will be added.

The same two isLoaded() methods are defined on the PersistenceUnitUtil class as were defined on the PersistenceUtil class. The difference is that invoking them on this class does not require provider resolution. The PersistenceUnitUtil interface is implemented by the provider, so the user is already invoking a provider class that is assumed to have intimate knowledge of the domain model mappings and the supporting JPA implementation.

An additional method named getIdentifier() returns the value of the identifier attribute if the entity has a simple or an embedded identifier. If the entity has multiple identifier attributes, an instance of the identifier class will be returned. This method enables a layer to dynamically obtain the identifier of a given entity without having to know anything about the entity mappings, or even its type. This is a fairly typical situation for a framework to be in. The method in Listing 12-27 collects all the identifiers for a given List of entities.

Listing 12-27. Collecting Entity Identifiers

```
public List<Object> getEntityIdentifiers(List<T> entities) {
    PersistenceUnitUtil util = emf.getPersistenceUnitUtil();
    List<Object> result = new ArrayList<Object>();
    for (T entity : entities) {
        result.add(util.getIdentifier(entity));
    }
    return result;
}
```

Summary

This chapter covered a number of diverse topics, from events to caching. Not everything we have described will be immediately usable in a new application, but some features, such as optimistic locking, are likely to play a prominent role in many enterprise applications.

The lifecycle callbacks section introduced the lifecycle of an entity and showed the points at which an application can monitor events that are fired as an entity moves through different stages of its lifecycle. We looked at two different approaches to implementing callback methods: on the entity class and as part of a separate listener class.

We introduced validation and gave an overview of what it was, how it could be used, and how it could be extended to provide application-specific validation constraints. We showed how it can save us having to write explicit code for error conditions and boundary checking. We brought more context to validation by explaining how it is integrated with JPA and how the integration points can be configured to meet the needs of your application.

In our discussion of locking and versioning, we introduced optimistic locking and described the vital role it plays in many applications, particularly those that use detached entities. We also looked at the different kinds of additional locking options and when they may be usefully applied. We explained their correspondence to isolation levels in the database and the extent to which they should be relied upon. We described the difficulties of recovering from lock failures and when it is appropriate to refresh the state of a managed entity. We went on to pessimistic locking and how it affects scalability. We described the primary pessimistic mode and two other less-prevalent ones. We showed how timeouts can be configured and highlighted the conditions under which the two different kinds of pessimistic exceptions are thrown and can be handled.

We looked at caching and spent some time going over how the shared cache can be managed and controlled using global cache settings and local cache mode properties. We discussed how the cache mode properties affect queries and offered advice about which modes to use and when to use them. Finally, we uncovered a couple of the JPA utility classes that provide additional features, such as being able to determine whether a JPA entity has been fully loaded and obtaining the identifier of any entity instance.

In the next chapter, we will look at the XML mapping file, showing how to use XML with or instead of annotations, and how annotation metadata can be overridden.

CHAPTER 13

■ ■ ■

XML Mapping Files

Back in the early days, after the release of Java SE 5, there was a quiet, and sometimes not-so-quiet, debate about whether annotations were better or worse than XML. The defenders of annotations vigorously proclaimed how annotations are so much simpler and provide in-lined metadata that is co-located with the code that it is describing. The claim was that this avoids the need to replicate the information that is inherent in the source code context of where the metadata applies. The XML proponents then retorted that annotations unnecessarily couple the metadata to the code, and that changes to metadata should not require changes to the source code.

The truth is that both sides were right, and there are appropriate times for using annotation metadata and other times for using XML. When the metadata really is coupled to the code, it does make sense to use annotations because the metadata is just another aspect of the program. For example, specification of the identifier field of an entity is not only a relevant piece of information to the provider but also a necessary detail known and assumed by the referencing application code. Other kinds of metadata, such as which column a field is mapped to, can be safely changed without needing to change the code. This metadata is akin to configuration metadata and might be better expressed in XML, where it can be configured according to the usage pattern or execution environment.

The arguments also tended to unfairly compartmentalize the issue because in reality it goes deeper than simply deciding when it might make sense to use one type of metadata or another. In many talks and forums before the release of the JPA 1.0 specification, we asked people whether they planned on using annotations or XML, and we consistently saw that there was a split. The reason was that there were other factors that have nothing to do with which is better, such as existing development processes, source control systems, developer experience, and so forth.

Now that developers have a few years of using annotations under their belts there is not nearly the same hesitation to embed annotations in their code as there once was. In fact, most people are perfectly happy with annotations, making their acceptance pretty much a fait accompli. Nevertheless, there are still use cases for employing XML, so we continue to describe and illustrate how mapping metadata is allowed to be specified in either format. In fact, XML mapping usage is defined to allow annotations to be used and then overridden by XML. This provides the ability to use annotations for some things and XML for others, or to use annotations for an expected configuration but then supply an overriding XML file to suit a particular execution environment. The XML file might be sparse and supply only the information that is being overridden. You will see later on in this chapter that the granularity with which this metadata can be specified offers a good deal of object-relational mapping flexibility.

Over the course of this chapter, we will describe the structure and content of the mapping file and how it relates to the metadata annotations. We will also discuss how XML mapping metadata can combine with and override annotation metadata. We have tried to structure the chapter in a format that will allow it to be used as both a source of information and a reference for the mapping file format.

The Metadata Puzzle

The rules of XML and annotation usage and overriding can be a little confusing to say the least, especially given the permutation space of mixing annotations with XML. The trick to understanding the semantics, and being able to properly specify metadata the way that you would like it to be specified, is to understand the metadata collection process. Once you have a solid understanding of what the metadata processor does, you will be well on your way to understanding what you need to do to achieve a specific result.

The provider can choose to perform the metadata gathering process in any way it chooses, but the result is that it must honor the requirements of the specification. Developers understand algorithms, so we decided that it would be easier to understand if we presented the logical functionality as an algorithm, even though the implementation might not actually implement it this way. The following algorithm can be considered as the simplified logic for obtaining the metadata for the persistence unit:

1. Process the annotations. The set of entities, mapped superclasses, and embedded objects (we'll call this set E) is discovered by looking for the @Entity, @MappedSuperclass, and @Embeddable annotations. The class and method annotations in all the classes in set E are processed, and the resulting metadata is stored in set C. Any missing metadata that was not explicitly specified in the annotations is left empty.

2. Add the classes defined in XML. Look for all the entities, mapped superclasses, and embedded objects that are defined in the mapping files and add them to E. If we find that one of the classes already exists in E, we apply the overriding rules for class-level metadata that we found in the mapping file. Add or adjust the class-level metadata in C according to the overriding rules.

3. Add the attribute mappings defined in XML. For each class in E, look at the fields or properties in the mapping file and try to add the method metadata to C. If the field or property already exists there, apply the overriding rules for attribute-level mapping metadata.

4. Apply defaults. Determine all default values according to the scoping rules and where defaults might have been defined (see the following for description of default rules). The classes, attribute mappings, and other settings that have not yet been filled in are assigned values and put in C.

Some of the following cases might cause this algorithm to be modified slightly, but in general this is what will logically happen when the provider needs to obtain the mapping metadata.

You already learned in the mapping chapters that annotations might be sparse and that not annotating a persistent attribute will usually cause it to default to being mapped as a basic mapping. Other mapping defaults were also explained, and you saw how much easier they made configuring and mapping entities. You will notice in our algorithm that the defaults are applied at the end, so the same defaults that you saw for annotations will be applied when using mapping files as well. It should be of some comfort to XML users that mapping files might be sparsely specified in the same way as annotations. They also have the same requirements for what needs to be specified; for example, an identifier must be specified, a relationship mapping must have at least its cardinality specified, and so forth.

The Mapping File

By this point, you are well aware that if you don't want to use XML for mapping, you don't need to use XML. In fact, as you will see in Chapter 14, any number of mapping files, or none, might be included in a persistence unit. If you do use one, however, each mapping file that is supplied must conform and be valid against the orm_2_1.xsd schema located at http://xmlns.jcp.org /xml/ns/persistence/orm_2_1.xsd.

■ **Note**   When using a JPA 1.0 or JPA 2.0 implementation, the schema will be `orm_1_0.xsd` or `orm_2_0.xsd`, respectively, located at `http://xmlns.jcp.org/xml/ns/persistence/`. These older versions used to be hosted at `http://java.sun.com/xml/ns/persistence/` and as of this writing are still there, but they could disappear from that site at some point in the future.

This schema defines a namespace called `http://xmlns.jcp.org/xml/ns/persistence/orm` that includes all the ORM elements that can be used in a mapping file. A typical XML header for a mapping file is shown in Listing 13-1.

Listing 13-1. XML Header for Mapping File

```
<?xml version="1.0" encoding="UTF-8"?>
<entity-mappings xmlns="http:// xmlns.jcp.org /xml/ns/persistence/orm"
    xmlns:xsi="http://www.w3.org/2001/XMLSchema-instance"
    xsi:schemaLocation="http:// xmlns.jcp.org/xml/ns/persistence/orm
                        http:// xmlns.jcp.org/xml/ns/persistence/orm_2_1.xsd"
    version="2.1">
```

The root element of the mapping file is called `entity-mappings`. All object-relational XML metadata is contained within this element, and as seen in the example, the header information is also specified as attributes in this element. The subelements of `entity-mappings` can be categorized into four main scoping and functional groups: persistence unit defaults, mapping files defaults, queries and generators, and managed classes and mappings. There is also a special setting that determines whether annotations should be considered in the metadata for the persistence unit. These groups are discussed in the following sections. For the sake of brevity, we won't include the header information in the XML examples in these sections.

Disabling Annotations

For those who are perfectly happy with XML and don't feel the need for annotations, there are ways to skip the annotation processing phase (step 1 in the previous algorithm). The `xml-mapping-metadata-complete` element and `metadata-complete` attribute provide a convenient way to reduce the overhead that is required to discover and process all the annotations on the classes in the persistence unit. It is also a way to effectively disable any annotations that do exist. These options will cause the processor to completely ignore them as if they did not exist at all.

xml-mapping-metadata-complete

When the `xml-mapping-metadata-complete` element is specified, all annotations in the entire persistence unit will be ignored, and only the mapping files in the persistence unit will be considered as the total set of provided metadata. Only entities, mapped superclasses, and embedded objects that have entries in a mapping file will be added to the persistence unit.

The `xml-mapping-metadata-complete` element needs to be in only one of the mapping files if there are multiple mapping files in the persistence unit. It is specified as an empty subelement of the `persistence-unit-metadata` element, which is the first[1] subelement of `entity-mappings`. An example of using this setting is in Listing 13-2.

---

[1]Technically, there is a description element in many of the elements, just as there are in most of the standard schemas in Java EE, but they have little functional value and will not be mentioned here. They might be of some use to tools that parse XML schemas and use the descriptions for tooltips and similar actions.

Listing 13-2. *Disabling Annotation Metadata for the Persistence Unit*

```
<entity-mappings>
    <persistence-unit-metadata>
        <xml-mapping-metadata-complete/>
    </persistence-unit-metadata>
    ...
</entity-mappings>
```

If enabled, there is no way to portably override this setting. It will apply globally to the persistence unit, regardless of whether any `metadata-complete` attribute is set to `false` in an entity.

metadata-complete

The `metadata-complete` attribute is an attribute on the `entity`, `mapped-superclass`, and `embeddable` elements. If specified, all annotations on the specified class and on any fields or properties in the class will be ignored, and only the metadata in the mapping file will be considered as the set of metadata for the class.

■ **Caution** Annotations defining queries, generators, or result set mappings are ignored if they are defined on a class that is marked as `metadata-complete` in an XML mapping file.

When `metadata-complete` is enabled, the same rules that we applied to annotated entities will still apply when using XML-mapped entities. For example, the identifier must be mapped, and all relationships must be specified with their corresponding cardinality mappings inside the `entity` element.

An example of using the `metadata-complete` attribute is shown in Listing 13-3. The entity mappings in the annotated class are disabled by the `metadata-complete` attribute, and because the fields are not mapped in the mapping file, the default mapping values will be used. The `name` and `salary` fields will be mapped to the `NAME` and `SALARY` columns, respectively.

Listing 13-3. *Disabling Annotations for a Managed Class*

```
@Entity
public class Employee {
    @Id private int id;
    @Column(name="EMP_NAME")
    private String name;
    @Column(name="SAL")
    private long salary;
    // ...
}
```

orm.xml snippet:

```
<entity-mappings>
    ...
    <entity class="examples.model.Employee"
            metadata-complete="true">
        <attributes>
            <id name="id"/>
```

```
        </attributes>
    </entity>
    ...
</entity-mappings>
```

Persistence Unit Defaults

One of the conditions for using annotation metadata is that we need to have something to annotate. If we want to define metadata for a persistence unit, we are in the unfortunate position of not having anything to annotate because a persistence unit is just a logical grouping of Java classes, basically a configuration. This brings us back to the discussion we had earlier when we decided that if metadata is not coupled to code, maybe it shouldn't really be in the code. These are the reasons why persistence unit metadata can be specified only in an XML mapping file.

In general, a persistence unit default means that whenever a value for that setting is not specified at a more local scope, the persistence unit default value will apply. It is a convenient way to set default values that will apply to all entities, mapped superclasses, and embedded objects in the entire persistence unit, be they in any of the mapping files or annotated classes. The default values will not be applied if a value is present at any level below the persistence unit. This value can be in the form of a mapping file default value, some value in an entity element, or an annotation on one of the managed classes or persistent fields or properties.

The element that encloses all the persistence unit level defaults is the aptly named `persistence-unit-defaults` element. It is the other subelement of the `persistence-unit-metadata` element (after `xml-mapping-metadata-complete`). If more than one mapping file exists in a persistence unit, only one of the files should contain these elements.

There are six settings that can be configured to have default values for the persistence unit. They are specified using the `schema`, `catalog`, `delimited-identifiers`, `access`, `cascade-persist`, and `entity-listeners` elements.

schema

The `schema` element is useful if you don't want to have to specify a schema in every `@Table`, `@SecondaryTable`, `@JoinTable`, `@CollectionTable`, or `@TableGenerator` annotation; or table, secondary-table, join-table, collection-table, or table-generator XML element in the persistence unit. When set here, it will apply to all tables in the persistence unit, whether they were actually defined or defaulted by the provider. The value of this element can be overridden by any of the following:

- schema element defined in the mapping file defaults (see the "Mapping File Defaults" section)

- schema attribute on any `table`, `secondary-table`, `join-table`, `collection-table`, `sequence-generator`, or `table-generator` element in a mapping file

- schema defined within a `@Table`, `@SecondaryTable`, `@JoinTable`, `@CollectionTable`, `@SequenceGenerator`, or `@TableGenerator` annotation; or in a `@TableGenerator` annotation (unless `xml-mapping-metadata-complete` is set)

Listing 13-4 shows an example of how to set the schema for all the tables in the persistence unit that do not already have their schema set.

Listing 13-4. Setting the Default Persistence Unit Schema

```
<entity-mappings>
    <persistence-unit-metadata>
        <persistence-unit-defaults>
            <schema>HR</schema>
```

```
        </persistence-unit-defaults>
    </persistence-unit-metadata>
    ...
</entity-mappings>
```

catalog

The catalog element is exactly analogous to the schema element, but it is for databases that support catalogs. It can be used independently whether schema is specified or not, has the same behavior as schema, and is overridden in exactly the same ways. The exact same rules can be applied to the catalog mapping file default as described in the preceding schema section.

delimited-identifiers

The delimited-identifiers element causes database table, schema, and column identifiers used in the persistence unit, defined in annotation form, XML, or defaulted, to be delimited when sent to the database (refer to Chapter 10 for more on delimited identifiers). It cannot be disabled locally, so it is important to have a full understanding of the consequences before enabling this option. If an annotation or XML element is locally delimited with quotes, they will be treated as part of the identifier name.

No value or text is included in the delimited-identifiers element. Only the empty element should be specified within the persistence-unit-defaults element to enable persistence unit identifier delimiting.

access

The access element that is defined in the persistence-unit-defaults section is used to set the access type for all the managed classes in the persistence unit that have XML entries but are not annotated. Its value can be either "FIELD" or "PROPERTY," indicating how the provider should access the persistent state.

The access setting is a subtly different default that does not affect any of the managed classes that have annotated fields or properties. It is a convenience for when XML is used and obviates having to specify the access for all the entities listed in all the XML mapping files.

This element affects only the managed classes defined in the mapping files because a class with annotated fields or properties is considered to have overridden the access mode by virtue of its having annotations placed on its fields or properties. If the xml-mapping-metadata-complete element is enabled, the persistence unit access default will be applied to these annotated classes that have entries in XML. Put another way, the annotations that would have otherwise overridden the access mode would no longer be considered, and the XML defaults, including the default access mode, would be applied.

The value of this element can be overridden by one or more of the following:

- access element defined in the mapping file defaults (see the "Mapping File Defaults" section)

- access attribute on any entity, mapped-superclass, or embeddable element in a mapping file

- access attribute on any basic, id, embedded-id, embedded, many-to-one, one-to-one, one-to-many, many-to-many, element-collection, or version element in a mapping file

- @Access annotation on any entity, mapped superclass, or embeddable class

- @Access annotation on any field or property in an entity, mapped superclass, or embedded object

- An annotated field or property in an entity, mapped superclass, or embedded object

In Listing 13-5 we show an example of setting the access mode to "PROPERTY" for all the managed classes in the persistence unit that do not have annotated fields.

384

Listing 13-5. Setting the Default Access Mode for the Persistence Unit

```
<entity-mappings>
    <persistence-unit-metadata>
        <persistence-unit-defaults>
            <access>PROPERTY</access>
        </persistence-unit-defaults>
    </persistence-unit-metadata>
    ...
</entity-mappings>
```

cascade-persist

The cascade-persist element is unique in a different way. When the empty cascade-persist element is specified, it is analogous to adding the PERSIST cascade option to all the relationships in the persistence unit. Refer to Chapter 6 for a discussion about the cascade options on relationships.

The term "persistence-by-reachability" is often used to signify that when an object is persisted, all the objects that are reachable from that object are also automatically persisted. The cascade-persist element provides the persistence-by-reachability semantics that some people are used to having. This setting cannot currently be overridden, the assumption being that when somebody is accustomed to persistence-by-reachability semantics they don't normally want to be turning it off. If more fine-grained control over cascading of the persist operation is needed, this element should not be specified, and the relationships should have the PERSIST cascade option specified locally.

An example of using the cascade-persist element is shown in Listing 13-6.

Listing 13-6. Configuring for Persistence-by-Reachability Semantics

```
<entity-mappings>
    <persistence-unit-metadata>
        <persistence-unit-defaults>
            <cascade-persist/>
        </persistence-unit-defaults>
    </persistence-unit-metadata>
    ...
</entity-mappings>
```

entity-listeners

This is the only place where a list of default entity listeners can be specified. A default entity listener is a listener that will be applied to every entity in the persistence unit. They will be invoked in the order that they are listed in this element, before any other listener or callback method is invoked on the entity. It is the logical equivalent of adding the listeners in this list to the front of the @EntityListeners list in the root superclass. We discussed entity listeners in the last chapter, so refer to Chapter 12 to review the order of invocation if you need to. A description of how to specify an entity listener is given in the "Entity Listeners" section of that chapter.

The entity-listeners element is composed of zero or more entity-listener elements that each defines an entity listener. They can be overridden or disabled in either of the following two ways:

- exclude-default-listeners element in an entity or mapped-superclass mapping file element

- @ExcludeDefaultListeners annotation on an entity or mapped superclass (unless xml-mapping-metadata-complete is set)

Mapping File Defaults

The next level of defaults, after the ones defined for the entire persistence unit, are those that pertain only to the entities, mapped superclasses, and embedded objects that are contained in a particular mapping file. In general, if there is a persistence unit default defined for the same setting, this value will override the persistence unit default for the managed classes in the mapping file. Unlike the persistence unit defaults, the mapping file defaults do not affect managed classes that are annotated and not defined in the mapping file. In terms of our algorithm, the defaults in this section apply to all the classes of C that have entries in the mapping file.

The mapping file defaults consist of four optional subelements of the `entity-mappings` element. They are `package`, `schema`, `catalog`, and `access`; and they follow the `persistence-unit-metadata` element.

package

The package element is intended to be used by developers who don't want to have to repeat the fully qualified class name in all the mapping file metadata. It can be overridden in the mapping file by fully qualifying a class name in any element or attribute in which a class name is expected. They are the following:

- `class` attribute of `id-class`, `entity-listener`, `entity`, `mapped-superclass`, or `embeddable` elements

- `target-entity` attribute of `many-to-one`, `one-to-one`, `one-to-many`, and `many-to-many` elements

- `target-class` attribute of `element-collection` element

- `result-class` attribute of `named-native-query` element

- `entity-class` attribute of `entity-result` element

An example of using this element is shown in Listing 13-7. We set the default mapping file package name to `examples.model` for the entire mapping file and can just use the unqualified `Employee` and `EmployeePK` class names throughout the file. The package name will not be applied to `OtherClass`, though, because it is already fully specified.

Listing 13-7. Using the package Element

```
<entity-mappings>
    <package>examples.model</package>
    ...
    <entity class="Employee">
        <id-class class="EmployeePK"/>
        ...
    </entity>
    <entity class="examples.tools.OtherClass">
        ...
    </entity>
    ...
</entity-mappings>
```

schema

The `schema` element will set a default schema to be assumed for every table, secondary table, join table, or table generator defined or defaulted within the mapping file. This element can be overridden by the specification of the `schema` attribute on any `table`, `secondary-table`, `join-table`, `collection-table`, `sequence-generator`, or `table-generator` element in the mapping file.

Listing 13-8 shows the mapping file schema default set to "HR," so the EMP table that Employee is mapped to is assumed to be in the HR schema.

Listing 13-8. Using the schema Element

```
<entity-mappings>
    <package>examples.model</package>
    <schema>HR</schema>
    ...
    <entity class="Employee">
        <table name="EMP"/>
        ...
    </entity>
    ...
</entity-mappings>
```

The mapping file schema default will also affect @Table, @SecondaryTable, @JoinTable, @CollectionTable, @SequenceGenerator, and @TableGenerator annotations on classes that have entries in the mapping file. For example, because Employee is listed in the mapping file, it becomes part of the set of classes to which the default applies. If there was a @TableGenerator(name="EmpGen", table="IDGEN") annotation on Employee, the mapping file default will be applied to it, and the IDGEN table will be assumed to be in the HR schema.

catalog

The catalog element is again exactly analogous to the schema element, but it is for databases that support catalogs. It can be used independently of whether schema is specified or not, has the same behavior as schema at the mapping file default level, and is overridden in exactly the same ways. As we mentioned in the persistence unit section, the exact same rules can be applied to the catalog mapping file default, as described in the schema mapping file default section.

access

Setting a particular access mode as the mapping file default value affects only the managed classes that are defined in the mapping file. The default mapping file access mode can be overridden by one or more of the following:

- access attribute on any entity, mapped-superclass, or embeddable element in a mapping file

- access attribute on any basic, id, embedded-id, embedded, many-to-one, one-to-one, one-to-many, many-to-many, element-collection, or version element in a mapping file

- @Access annotation on any entity, mapped superclass, or embeddable class

- @Access annotation on any field or property in an entity, mapped superclass, or embedded object

- An annotated field or property in an entity, mapped superclass, or embedded object

Queries and Generators

Some persistence artifacts, such as id generators and queries, are defined as annotations on a class even though they are actually global to the persistence unit in scope because they are annotations and there is no other place to put them other than on a class. Earlier, we pointed out the inappropriateness of expressing persistence unit metadata as annotations on a random class, but generators and queries create something concrete, as opposed to being just settings. Nevertheless, it is still not ideal, and in XML this global query-related metadata does not need to be placed arbitrarily within a class but can be defined at the level of subelements of the entity-mappings element.

The global query metadata elements are made up of generator and query elements that include `sequence-generator`, `table-generator`, `named-query`, `named-native-query`, and `sql-result-set-mapping`. For historical reasons, these elements might appear in different contexts, but they are nevertheless still scoped to the persistence unit. There are three different persistence unit namespaces, one for queries, one for generators, and one for result set mappings that are used for native queries. When any of the elements that we just listed are defined in the mapping file, the artifacts they define will be added into the persistence unit namespace to which they apply. The namespaces will already contain all the existing persistence unit artifacts that might have been defined in annotations or in another mapping file. Because these artifacts share the same global persistence unit namespace type, when one of the artifacts defined in XML shares the same name as one that already exists in the namespace of the same type, it is viewed as an override. The artifact that is defined in XML overrides the one that was defined by the annotation. There is no concept of overriding queries, generators, or result set mappings within the same or different mapping files. If one or more mapping files contains one of these objects defined with the same name, it is undefined, which overrides the other because the order that they are processed in is not specified.[2]

sequence-generator

The `sequence-generator` element is used to define a generator that uses a database sequence to generate identifiers. It corresponds to the `@SequenceGenerator` annotation (refer to Chapter 4) and can be used to define a new generator or override a generator of the same name that is defined by a `@SequenceGenerator` annotation in any class in the persistence unit. It can be specified either at the global level as a subelement of `entity-mappings`, at the entity level as a subelement of `entity`, or at the field or property level as a subelement of the `id` mapping element.

The attributes of `sequence-generator` line up exactly with the elements in the `@SequenceGenerator` annotation. Listing 13-9 shows an example of defining a sequence generator.

Listing 13-9. Defining a Sequence Generator

```
<entity-mappings>
    ...
    <sequence-generator name="empGen" sequence-name="empSeq"/>
    ...
</entity-mappings>
```

table-generator

The `table-generator` element defines a generator that uses a table to generate identifiers. Its annotation equivalent is the `@TableGenerator` annotation (refer to Chapter 4). This element might define a new generator or it might be overriding a generator defined by a `@TableGenerator` annotation. Like the `sequence-generator` element, it can be defined within any of `entity-mappings`, `entity`, or `id` elements.

The attributes of `table-generator` also match the `@TableGenerator` annotation elements. Listing 13-10 shows an example of defining a sequence generator in annotation form but overriding it to be a table generator in XML.

Listing 13-10. Overriding a Sequence Generator with a Table Generator

```
@Entity
public class Employee {
    @SequenceGenerator(name="empGen")
    @Id @GeneratedValue(generator="empGen")
```

---

[2]It is possible, and even probable, that vendors will process the mapping files in the order that they are listed, but this is neither required nor standardized.

```
    private int id;
    // ...
}
```

orm.xml snippet:

```
<entity-mappings>
    ...
    <table-generator name="empGen" table="ID_GEN" pk-column-value="EmpId"/>
    ...
</entity-mappings>
```

named-query

Static or named queries can be defined both in annotation form using @NamedQuery (refer to Chapter 7) or in a mapping file using the named-query element. A named-query element in the mapping file can also override an existing query of the same name that was defined as an annotation. It makes sense, of course, when overriding a query to override it only with a query that has the same result type, be it an entity, data, or projection of data. Otherwise, all the code that executes the query and processes the results stands a pretty good chance of breaking.

A named-query element can appear as a subelement of entity-mappings or as a subelement of entity. Regardless of where it is defined, it will be keyed by its name in the persistence unit query namespace.

The name of the query is specified as an attribute of the named-query element, while the query string goes in a query subelement within it. Any one of the enumerated LockModeType constants can be included. Any number of query hints can also be provided as hint subelements.

Listing 13-11 shows an example of two named queries, one of which uses a hint that bypasses the cache.

Listing 13-11. Named Query in a Mapping File

```
<entity-mappings>
    ...
    <named-query name="findEmpsWithName">
        <query>SELECT e FROM Employee e WHERE e.name LIKE :empName</query>
        <hint name="javax.persistence.cacheRetrieveMode"
              value="CacheRetrieveMode.BYPASS"/>
    </named-query>
    <named-query name="findEmpsWithHigherSalary">
        <query><![CDATA[SELECT e FROM Employee e WHERE e.salary > :salary]]></query>
    </named-query>
    ...
</entity-mappings>
```

Query strings can also be expressed as CDATA within the query element. You can see in Listing 13-11 that this is helpful in cases when the query includes XML characters such as > that would otherwise need to be escaped.

named-native-query

Native SQL can also be used for named queries by defining a @NamedNativeQuery annotation (refer to Chapter 11) or by specifying a named-native-query element in a mapping file. Both named queries and native queries share the same query namespace in the persistence unit, so using either the named-query or named-native-query element will cause that query to override any query of the same name defined in annotation form.

Native queries are the same as named queries in that the `native-named-query` element can appear as a subelement of `entity-mappings` or as a subelement of `entity`. The name is specified using the `name` attribute, and the query string uses a `query` subelement. The hints are also specified in the same way. The only difference is that two additional attributes have been added to `named-native-query` to supply the result class or the result set mapping.

One use case for overriding queries is when the DBA comes to you and demands that your query run a certain way on a certain database. You can leave the query as generic JP QL for the other databases, but it turns out that, for example, the Oracle database can do this one particular thing very well using native syntax. By putting this query in a DB-specific XML file, it will be much easier to manage in the future. Listing 13-12 has an example of a vanilla named query in JP QL that is being overridden by a native SQL query.

Listing 13-12. Overriding a JP QL Query with SQL

```
@NamedQuery(name="findAllManagers"
            query="SELECT e FROM Employee e WHERE e.directs IS NOT EMPTY")
@Entity
public class Employee { ... }
```

orm.xml snippet:

```
<entity-mappings>
    ...
    <named-native-query name="findAllManagers"
                        result-class="examples.model.Employee">
        <query>
            SELECT /*+ FULL(m) */ e.id, e.name, e.salary,
                    e.manager_id, e.dept_id, e.address_id
            FROM   emp e,
                    (SELECT DISTINCT manager_id AS id FROM emp) m
            WHERE  e.id = m.id
        </query>
    </named-native-query>
    ...
</entity-mappings>
```

named-stored-procedure-query

A stored procedure can be represented by a named query by defining a @NamedStoredProcedureQuery annotation (refer to Chapter 11) or by specifying a `named-stored-procedure-query` element in a mapping file. Like other named queries, named stored procedure queries can be specified as subelements of `entity-mappings` or `entity`. While they may share the same persistence unit query namespace with all of the other named queries, the API creation method of a named stored procedure query returns an instance of `StoredProcedureQuery`. This means that in practice they are different types of named queries and you will not, for example, be able to override a JP QL named query with a stored procedure query. You could, however, override a stored procedure query defined in annotation form with a stored procedure query defined using the `named-stored-procedure-query` element.

Similar to other named queries, the name of the query is specified using the `name` attribute, and any number of `hint` subelements can be used to supply query hints. However, since multiple result sets can be returned from stored procedure queries, instead of the `result-class` and `result-set-mapping` attributes that existed on `named-native-query`, multiple `result-class` and `result-set-mapping` subelements can be specified under the `named-stored-procedure-query` element. Although the schema does not disallow it, using both `result-class` and `result-set-mapping` subelements for different result sets in the same query is not permitted.

The unique parts of a stored procedure query are the additional procedure-name attribute to specify the name of the stored procedure in the database and the parameter subelements to define the parameter names and types. Each parameter subelement has a name, class, and mode attribute to indicate the parameter name, the JDBC class, and whether the parameter is an IN, OUT, INOUT, or REF_CURSOR parameter. The parameters must be defined in the order they appear in the actual stored procedure definition.

Listing 13-13 shows an example of using a named-stored-procedure-query element to add the stored procedure query from Chapter 11.

Listing 13-13. Defining a Named Stored Procedure Query

```
@NamedStoredProcedureQuery(
    name="fetch_emp",
    procedureName="fetch_emp",
    parameters={
        @StoredProcedureParameter(name="empList", type=void.class,
                                  mode=ParameterMode.REF_CURSOR)
    },
    resultClasses=Employee.class
)
```

orm.xml snippet:

```
<entity-mappings>
    ...
    <named-stored-procedure-query name="fetch_emp" procedure-name="fetch_emp">
        <parameter name="empList" class="void" mode="REF_CURSOR"/>
        <result-class>Employee</result-class>
    </named-stored-procedure-query>
    ...
</entity-mappings>
```

sql-result-set-mapping

A result set mapping is used by native queries or stored procedure queries to instruct the persistence provider how to map the results. The sql-result-set-mapping element corresponds to the @SqlResultSetMapping annotation. The name of the result set mapping is specified in the name attribute of the sql-result-set-mapping element. The result can be mapped as one or more entity types, non-entity Java types, projection data, or a combination of these. Just as @SqlResultSetMapping encloses arrays of @EntityResult, @ConstructorResult, and @ColumnResult, so also can the sql-result-set-mapping element contain multiple entity-result, constructor-result, and column-result elements. Similarly, because each @EntityResult contains an array of @FieldResult, the entity-result element can contain multiple field-result elements. The other entityClass and discriminatorColumn elements of the @EntityResult annotation map directly to the entity-class and discriminator-column attributes of the entity-result element. Likewise, a @ConstructorResult contains an array of @ColumnResult, so the constructor-result subelement contains an arbitrary number of column subelements, along with a target-class attribute to specify the name of the non-entity class to construct.

Each sql-result-set-mapping can define a new mapping or override an existing one of the same name that was defined by an annotation. It is not possible to override only a part of the result set mapping. If you're overriding an annotation, the entire annotation will be overridden, and the components of the result set mapping defined by the sql-result-set-mapping element will apply.

Having said all this about overriding, there is really not that much use in overriding a @SqlResultSetMapping because they are used to structure the result format from a static native or stored procedure query. As we mentioned earlier, queries tend to be executed with a certain expectation of the result that is being returned. Result set mappings are typically defined in a mapping file because that is also generally where the query that is defining the result is defined.

Listing 13-14 shows the "DepartmentSummary" result set mapping that we defined in Chapter 11 and its equivalent XML mapping file form.

Listing 13-14. Specifying a Result Set Mapping

```
@SqlResultSetMapping(
    name="DepartmentSummary",
    entities={
        @EntityResult(entityClass=Department.class,
                      fields=@FieldResult(name="name", column="DEPT_NAME")),
        @EntityResult(entityClass=Employee.class)
    },
    columns={@ColumnResult(name="TOT_EMP"),
             @ColumnResult(name="AVG_SAL")}
)
```

orm.xml snippet:

```
<entity-mappings>
    ...
    <sql-result-set-mapping name="DepartmentSummary">
        <entity-result entity-class="examples.model.Department">
            <field-result name="name" column="DEPT_NAME"/>
        </entity-result>
        <entity-result entity-class="examples.model.Employee"/>
        <column-result name="TOT_EMP"/>
        <column-result name="AVG_SAL"/>
    </sql-result-set-mapping>
    ...
</entity-mappings>
```

Managed Classes and Mappings

The main portion of every mapping file will typically be the managed classes in the persistence unit that are the entity, mapped-superclass, and embeddable elements and their state and relationship mappings. Each of them has its class specified as a class attribute of the element and its access type specified in an access attribute. The access attribute is required only when there are no annotations on the managed class or when metadata-complete (or xml-mapping-metadata-complete) has been specified for the class. If neither of these conditions apply and annotations do exist on the class, the access attribute setting should match the access used by the annotations.

For entities, an optional cacheable attribute can also be set to a boolean value. This attribute corresponds to the @Cacheable annotation and when specified will override the value of the annotation. Like the annotation, it dictates whether the shared cache is used for instances of the entity class, and is applicable only when the shared-cache-mode (see Chapter 14) is set to one of the selective modes. The cacheable attribute is inherited by subclasses and is overridden by either the @Cacheable annotation on the subclass, or the cacheable attribute in the subclass element.

Queries and generators can be specified within an entity element. Generators can also be defined inside an id element in an entity or mapped superclass. They have already been described in the preceding "Queries and Generators" section.

Attributes

Unfortunately, the word "attribute" is grossly overloaded. It can be a general term for a field or property in a class, it can be a specific part of an XML element that can be inlined in the element tag, or it can be a generic term referring to a characteristic. Throughout these sections, we have usually referred to it in the context of the second meaning because we have been talking a lot about XML elements. In this section, however, it refers to the first definition of a state attribute in the form of a field or property.

The attributes element is a subelement of the entity, mapped-superclass, and embeddable elements. It is an enclosing element that groups all the mapping subelements for the fields or properties of the managed class. Because it is only a grouping element, it does not have an analogous annotation. It dictates which mappings are allowed for each type of managed class.

In the entity and mapped-superclass elements, there are a number of mapping subelements that can be specified. For identifiers, either multiple id subelements or a single embedded-id subelement can be included. The simple basic, version, and transient mapping subelements can also be specified, as well as the many-to-one, one-to-one, one-to-many, and many-to-many association subelements. The mapping mix is rounded out with the embedded and element-collection subelements. An embeddable element is not permitted to contain id, embedded-id, or version mapping subelements. These elements will all be discussed separately in their own sections later, but they all have one thing in common. Each one has a name attribute (in the XML attribute sense) that is required to indicate the name of the attribute (in this case, we mean field or property) that it is mapping.

A general comment about overriding attribute mappings is that overriding annotations with XML is done at the level of the attribute (field or property) name. Our algorithm will apply to these mappings as they are keyed by attribute name, and XML overrides will be applied by attribute name alone. All the annotated mapping information for the attribute will be overridden as soon as a mapping element for that attribute name is defined in XML.

There is nothing to stop the type of attribute mapping defined in annotation form from being overridden in XML to be a different mapping type. The provider is responsible only for implementing the overriding rules and likely won't prevent this kind of behavior. This leads us to our second comment about overriding, which is that when overriding annotations, you should use the correct and compatible XML mapping. There are some cases where it might be valid to actually map an attribute differently in XML, but these cases are few and far between and primarily for exceptional types of testing or debugging.

For example, one could imagine overriding a field mapped in annotation form as a basic mapping with a transient mapping in XML. This would be completely legal, but not necessarily a good idea. At some point, a client of the entity might actually be trying to access that state, and if it is not being persisted, the client might get quite confused and fail in curious ways that are difficult to debug. An address association property mapped as a many-to-one mapping could conceivably be overridden to be stored serially as a blob, but this could not only break client access but also spill over to break other areas like JP QL queries that traverse the address.

The rule of thumb is that mappings should be overridden primarily to change the data-level mapping information. This would normally need to be done when, for example, an application is developed on one database but deployed to another or must deploy to multiple different databases in production. In these cases, the XML mappings would likely be xml-mapping-metadata-complete anyway, and the XML metadata would be used in its entirety rather than cobbling together bits of annotations and bits of XML and trying to keep it all straight across multiple database XML mapping configurations.

Tables

Specifying tables in XML works pretty much the same way as it does in annotation form. The same defaults are applied in both cases. There are two elements for specifying table information for a managed class: table and secondary-table.

table

A table element can occur as a subelement of entity and describes the table that the entity is mapped to. It corresponds to the @Table annotation (refer to Chapter 4) and has name, catalog, and schema attributes. One or more unique-constraint subelements might be included if unique column constraints are to be created in the table during schema generation.

If a @Table annotation exists on the entity, the table element will override the table defined by the annotation. Overriding a table is usually accompanied also by the overridden mappings of the persistent state to the overridden table. Listing 13-15 shows how an entity can be mapped to a different table than what it is mapped to by an annotation.

Listing 13-15. Overriding a Table

```
@Entity
@Table(name="EMP", schema="HR")
public class Employee { ... }
```

    orm.xml snippet:

```
<entity class="examples.model.Employee">
    <table name="EMP_REC" schema="HR"/>
    ...
</entity>
```

secondary-table

Any number of secondary tables can be added to the entity by adding one or more secondary-table subelements to the entity element. This element corresponds to the @SecondaryTable annotation (refer to Chapter 10), and if it is present in an entity element, it will override any and all secondary tables that are defined in annotations on the entity class. The name attribute is required, just as the name is required in the annotation. The schema and catalog attributes and the unique-constraint subelements can be included, just as with the table element.

Every secondary table needs to be joined to the primary table through a primary key join column (refer to Chapter 10). The primary-key-join-column element is a subelement of the secondary-table element and corresponds to the @PrimaryKeyJoinColumn annotation. As with the annotation, this is required only if the primary key column of the secondary table is different from that of the primary table. If the primary key happens to be a compound primary key, multiple primary-key-join-column elements can be specified.

Listing 13-16 compares the specification of secondary tables in annotation and XML form.

Listing 13-16. Specifying Secondary Tables

```
@Entity
@Table(name="EMP")
@SecondaryTables({
    @SecondaryTable(name="EMP_INFO"),
    @SecondaryTable(name="EMP_HIST",
                    pkJoinColumns=@PrimaryKeyJoinColumn(name="EMP_ID"))
})
public class Employee {
    @Id private int id;
    // ...
}
```

orm.xml snippet:

```
<entity class="examples.model.Employee">
    <table name="EMP"/>
    <secondary-table name="EMP_INFO"/>
    <secondary-table name="EMP_HIST">
        <primary-key-join-column name="EMP_ID"/>
    </secondary-table>
    ...
</entity>
```

Identifier Mappings

The three different types of identifier mappings can also be specified in XML. Overriding applies to the configuration information within a given identifier type, but the identifier type of a managed class should almost never be changed.

id

The id element is the most common method used to indicate the identifier for an entity. It corresponds to the @Id annotation but also encapsulates metadata that is relevant to identifiers. This includes a number of subelements, the first of which is the column subelement. It corresponds to the @Column annotation that might accompany an @Id annotation on the field or property. When not specified, the default column name will be assumed even if a @Column annotation exists on the field or property. As we discussed in the "Attributes" section, this is because the XML mapping of the attribute overrides the entire group of mapping metadata on the field or property.

A generated-value element corresponding to the @GeneratedValue annotation can also be included in the id element. It is used to indicate that the identifier will have its value automatically generated by the provider (refer to Chapter 4). This generated-value element has strategy and generator attributes that match those on the annotation. The named generator can be defined anywhere in the persistence unit. Sequence and table generators can also be defined within the id element. These were discussed in the "Queries and Generators" section.

An example of overriding an id mapping is to change the generator for a given database (see Listing 13-17).

Listing 13-17. Overriding an Id Generator

```
@Entity
public class Employee {
    @Id @GeneratedValue(strategy=GenerationType.TABLE, generator="empTab")
    @TableGenerator(name="empTab", table="ID_GEN")
    private long id;
    // ...
}
```

orm.xml snippet:

```
<entity class="examples.model.Employee">
    ...
    <attributes>
        <id name="id">
            <generated-value strategy="SEQUENCE" generator="empSeq"/>
            <sequence-generator name="empSeq" sequence-name="mySeq"/>
        </id>
```

```
        ...
    </attributes>
</entity>
```

embedded-id

An embedded-id element is used when a compound primary key class is used as the identifier (refer to Chapter 10). It corresponds to the @EmbeddedId annotation and is really just mapping an embedded class as the identifier. All the state is actually mapped within the embedded object, so there are only attribute overrides available within the embedded-id element. As we will discuss in the "Embedded Object Mappings" section, attribute overrides allow mapping of the same embedded object in multiple entities. The zero or more attribute-override elements in the property or field mapping of the entity provide the local overrides that apply to the entity table. Listing 13-18 shows how to specify an embedded identifier in annotation and XML form.

Listing 13-18. Specifying an Embedded Id

```
@Entity
public class Employee {
    @EmbeddedId private EmployeePK id;
    // ...
}
```

orm.xml snippet:

```
<entity class="examples.model.Employee">
    ...
    <attributes>
        <embedded-id name="id"/>
        ...
    </attributes>
</entity>
```

id-class

An id class is one strategy that can be used for a compound primary key (refer to Chapter 10). The id-class subelement of an entity or mapped-superclass element corresponds to the @IdClass annotation, and when it is specified in XML, it will override any @IdClass annotation on the class. Overriding the id class should not normally be done in practice because code that uses the entities will typically assume a particular identifier class.

The name of the class is indicated as the value of the class attribute of the id-class element, as shown in Listing 13-19.

Listing 13-19. Specifying an Id Class

```
@Entity
@IdClass(EmployeePK.class)
public class Employee { ... }
```

orm.xml snippet:

```
<entity class="examples.model.Employee">
    ...
    <id-class="examples.model.EmployeePK"/>
    ...
</entity>
```

Simple Mappings

A simple mapping takes an attribute and maps it to a single column in a table. The majority of persistent state mapped by an entity will be composed of simple mappings. In this section, we will discuss basic mappings and also cover the metadata for versioning and transient attributes.

basic

Basic mappings were discussed in detail in the early part of the book; they map a simple state field or property to a column in the table. The basic element provides this same ability in XML and corresponds to the @Basic annotation. Unlike the @Basic annotation (described in Chapter 4) that is rarely used, the basic element is required when mapping persistent state to a specific column. Just as with annotations, when a field or property is not mapped, it will be assumed to be a basic mapping and will be defaulted as such. This will occur if the field or property is not annotated or has no named subelement entry in the attributes element.

In addition to a name, the basic element has fetch and optional attributes that can be used for lazy loading and optionality. They are not required and not very useful at the level of a field or property. The only other attribute of the basic element is the access attribute. When specified, it will cause the state to be accessed using the prescribed mode.

The most important and useful subelement of basic is the column element. One of four other subelements can optionally be included inside the basic element. They are primarily for indicating the type to use when communicating with the JDBC driver. The first is an empty lob element that corresponds to the @Lob annotation. This is used when the target column is a large object type. Whether it is a character or binary object depends upon the type of the field or property.

The second one is the temporal element that contains one of DATE, TIME, or TIMESTAMP as its content. It corresponds to the @Temporal annotation and is used for fields of type java.util.Date or java.util.Calendar.

The third is used if the field or property is an enumerated type, and the enumerated values are to be mapped using strings instead of ordinals. In this case, the enumerated element should be used. It corresponds to the @Enumerated annotation and contains either ORDINAL or STRING as its content.

Finally, if the attribute is to be converted using a converter, then the convert annotation can be added. The convert element is discussed later in the "Converters" section.

Listing 13-20 shows some examples of basic mappings. By not specifying the column in the basic element mapping for the name field, the column is overridden from using the annotated EMP_NAME column to being defaulted to NAME. The comments field, however, is overridden from using the default to being mapped to the COMM column. It is also stored in a character large object (CLOB) column due to the lob element being present and the fact that the field is a String. The type field is overridden to be mapped to the STR_TYPE column, and the enumerated type of STRING is specified to indicate that the values should be stored as strings. The salary field does not have any metadata either in annotation or XML form and continues to be mapped to the default column name of SALARY.

Listing 13-20. *Overriding Basic Mappings*

```java
@Entity
public class Employee {
    // ...
    @Column(name="EMP_NAME")
    private String name;
    private String comments;
    private EmployeeType type;
    private long salary;
    // ...
}
```

orm.xml snippet:

```xml
<entity class="examples.model.Employee">
    ...
    <attributes>
        ...
        <basic name="name"/>
        <basic name="comments">
            <column name="COMM"/>
            <lob/>
        </basic>
        <basic name="type">
            <column name="STR_TYPE"/>
            <enumerated>STRING</enumerated>
        </basic>
        ...
    </attributes>
</entity>
```

transient

A transient element marks a field or property as being non-persistent. It is equivalent to the @Transient annotation or having a transient qualifier on the field or property. Listing 13-21 shows an example of how to set a field to be transient.

Listing 13-21. *Setting a Transient Field in a Mapping File*

```xml
<entity-mappings>
    <entity class="examples.model.Employee">
        <attributes>
            <transient name="cacheAge"/>
            ...
        </attributes>
    </entity>
</entity-mappings>
```

version

The version element is used to map the version number field in the entity. It corresponds to the @Version annotation and is normally mapped to an integral field for the provider to increment when it makes persistent changes to the entity (refer to Chapter 12). The column subelement specifies the column that stores the version data. Only one version field should exist for each entity. Listing 13-22 shows how a version field is specified in annotations and XML.

Listing 13-22. Specifying the Version

```
@Entity
public class Employee {
    // ...
    @Version
    private int version;
    // ...
}
```

orm.xml snippet:

```
<entity-mappings>
    <entity class="examples.model.Employee">
        <attributes>
            ...
            <version name="version"/>
            ...
        </attributes>
    </entity>
    ...
</entity-mappings>
```

Relationship and Collection Mappings

Like their annotation counterparts, the XML relationship and collection elements are used to map the associations and element collections.

We are now confronted yet again with the problem of an overloaded term. Throughout this chapter, we have been using the term "element" to signify an XML token (the thing with angled brackets around it). But in Chapter 5 we introduced the notion of an element collection, a mapping that designates a collection of either simple objects or embeddable objects. The following sections discuss each of the relationship and element collection mapping types that exist in XML.

many-to-one

To create a many-to-one mapping for a field or property, the many-to-one element can be specified. This element corresponds to the @ManyToOne annotation and, like the basic mapping, has fetch, optional, and access attributes.

Normally the target entity is known by the provider because the field or property is almost always of the target entity type, but if not, then the target-entity attribute should also be specified. When the many-to-one foreign key contributes to the identifier of the entity and the @MapsId annotation described in Chapter 10 applies, then the maps-id attribute would be used. The value, when required, is the name of the embeddable attribute of the embedded id class that maps the foreign key relationship. If, on the other hand, the relationship is part of the identifier but a simple @Id would be applied to the relationship field or property, the boolean id attribute of the many-to-one element should be specified and set to true.

A join-column element can be specified as a subelement of the many-to-one element when the column name is different from the default. If the association is to an entity with a compound primary key, multiple join-column elements will be required. Mapping an attribute using a many-to-one element causes the mapping annotations that might have been present on that attribute to be ignored. All the mapping information for the relationship, including the join column information, must be specified or defaulted within the many-to-one XML element.

Instead of a join column, it is possible to have a many-to-one or one-to-many relationship that uses a join table. It is for this case that a join-table element can be specified as a subelement of the many-to-one element. The join-table element corresponds to the @JoinTable annotation and contains a collection of join-column elements that join to the owning entity, which is normally the many-to-one side. A second set of join columns joins the join table to the inverse side of the relationship. They are called inverse-join-column elements. In the absence of one or both of these, the default values will be applied.

Unique to relationships is the ability to cascade operations across them. The cascade settings for a relationship dictate which operations are cascaded to the target entity of the many-to-one mapping. To specify how cascading should occur, a cascade element should be included as a subelement of the many-to-one element. Within the cascade element, we can include our choice of empty cascade-all, cascade-persist, cascade-merge, cascade-remove, cascade-refresh, or cascade-detach subelements that dictate that the given operations be cascaded. Of course, specifying cascade elements in addition to the cascade-all element is simply redundant.

Now we come to an exception to the rule that we gave earlier when we said that overriding of mappings will typically be for physical data overrides. When it comes to relationships, there are times where you will want to test the performance of a given operation and would like to be able to set certain relationships to load eagerly or lazily. You will not want to go through the code and have to keep changing these settings back and forth, however. It would be more practical to have the mappings that you are tuning in XML and just change them when required.[3] Listing 13-23 shows overriding two many-to-one relationships to be lazily loaded.

Listing 13-23. Overriding Fetch Mode

```
@Entity
public class Employee {
    // ...
    @ManyToOne
    private Address address;
    @ManyToOne
    @JoinColumn(name="MGR")
    private Employee manager;
    // ...
}
```

orm.xml snippet:

```
<entity class="examples.model.Employee">
    ...
    <attributes>
        ...
        <many-to-one name="address" fetch="LAZY"/>
        <many-to-one name="manager" fetch="LAZY">
            <join-column name="MGR"/>
        </many-to-one>
        ...
    </attributes>
</entity>
```

---

[3]Some have argued that these kinds of tuning exercises are precisely why XML should be used to begin with.

one-to-many

A one-to-many mapping is created by using a one-to-many element. This element corresponds to the @OneToMany annotation and has the same optional target-entity, fetch, and access attributes that were described in the many-to-one mapping. It has an additional attribute called mapped-by, which indicates the field or property of the owning entity (refer to Chapter 4) and an orphan-removal attribute to specify that orphaned entities should be automatically removed (refer to Chapter 10).

A one-to-many mapping is a collection-valued association, and the collection can be a List, Map, Set, or Collection. If it is a List, the elements can be populated in a specific order by specifying an order-by subelement. This element corresponds to the @OrderBy annotation and will cause the contents of the list to be ordered by the specific field or property name that is specified in the element content. Alternatively, a List can have its order persisted using an order-column subelement, which provides all the functionality of its @OrderColumn annotation counterpart.

If the collection is a Map, there are a number of different options, depending upon the key type. If the key type is a field or property of the target entity, an optional map-key subelement can be specified to indicate the name of the field or property to use as the key. This element corresponds to the @MapKey annotation and will default to the primary key field or property when none is specified. If the key type is an entity, a map-key-join-column can be used, whereas if the key is a basic type, a map-key-column subelement indicates the column that stores the key. Furthermore, for basic keys, map-key-enumerated or map-key-temporal can be used if the basic type is an enumerated or temporal type, respectively. If the key type is an embeddable type, map-key-attribute-override can be specified to override where an embedded field or property of the embeddable type is mapped. The map-key-class subelement is included to indicate the type of the key when the Map is not generically typed, and the key is not a field or property of the target entity. The map-key-convert element can be used if the key is a basic type and is to be converted using a converter. The map-key-convert element contains the same attributes as the convert element described in the "Converters" section below.

A join table is used by default to map a unidirectional one-to-many association that does not store a join column in the target entity. To make use of this kind of mapping, the mapped-by attribute is omitted, and the join-table element is included. If the mapping is a unidirectional one-to-many with the foreign key in the target table, one or more join-column subelements are used instead of the join-table. The join-column elements apply to the target entity table, though, not the source entity table (refer to Chapter 10).

Finally, cascading across the relationship is specified through an optional cascade element. Listing 13-24 shows a bidirectional one-to-many mapping, both in annotations and XML.

Listing 13-24. Specifying a One-to-Many Mapping

```
@Entity
public class Employee {
    // ...
    @OneToMany(mappedBy="manager")
    @OrderBy
    private List<Employee> directs;
    @ManyToOne
    private Employee manager;
    // ...
}
```

    orm.xml snippet:

```
<entity class="examples.model.Employee">
    ...
```

```
    <attributes>
        ...
        <one-to-many name="directs" mapped-by="manager">
            <order-by/>
        </one-to-many>
        <many-to-one name="manager"/>
        ...
    </attributes>
</entity>
```

one-to-one

To map a one-to-one association, the one-to-one element must be used. This element corresponds to the @OneToOne annotation described in Chapter 4 and has the same target-entity, fetch, optional, access, maps-id, and id attributes that the many-to-one element has. It also has the mapped-by and orphan-removal attributes that are in the one-to-many mapping to refer to the owning entity and to cause orphaned target entities to be automatically removed.

A one-to-one element might contain a join-column element if it is the owner of the relationship or it might have multiple join-column elements if the association is to an entity with a compound primary key. In some legacy systems, it is mapped using a join table, so a join-table element should be used in this case.

When the one-to-one association is joined using the primary keys of the two entity tables, instead of using either the maps-id or id attributes, the one-to-one element might contain a primary-key-join-column element. When it has a compound primary key, multiple primary-key-join-column elements will be present. Either of primary-key-join-column or join-column elements might be present, but not both.

■ **Note** The use of primary key join columns for one-to-one primary key associations was instituted in JPA 1.0. In JPA 2.0, the option to use id and maps-id was introduced, and it is the preferred method going forward.

The annotated classes and XML mapping file equivalents for a one-to-one mapping using a primary key association are shown in Listing 13-25.

Listing 13-25. One-to-One Primary Key Association

```
@Entity
public class Employee {
    // ...
    @OneToOne(mappedBy="employee")
    private ParkingSpace parkingSpace;
    // ...
}

@Entity
public class ParkingSpace {
    @Id
    private int id;
    // ...
    @OneToOne @MapsId
    private Employee employee;
    // ...
}
```

orm.xml snippet:

```
<entity-mappings>
    <entity class="examples.model.Employee">
        <attributes>
            ...
            <one-to-one name="parkingSpace" mapped-by="employee"/>
            ...
        </attributes>
    </entity>
    <entity class="examples.model.ParkingSpace">
        <attributes>
            ...
            <one-to-one name="employee" maps-id="true"/>
            ...
        </attributes>
    </entity>
</entity-mappings>
```

many-to-many

Creating a many-to-many association is done through the use of a many-to-many element. This element corresponds to the @ManyToMany annotation (refer to Chapter 4) and has the same optional target-entity, fetch, access, and mapped-by attributes that were described in the one-to-many mapping.

Also, being a collection-valued association like the one-to-many mapping, it supports the same order-by, order-column, map-key, map-key-class, map-key-column, map-key-join-column, map-key-enumerated, map-key-temporal, map-key-attribute-override, map-key-convert, join-table, and cascade subelements as the one-to-many mapping. Listing 13-26 shows an entity class example and equivalent XML, with a sample many-to-many relationship.

Listing 13-26. Many-to-Many Mapping Annotations and XML

```
@Entity
public class Employee {
    // ...
    @ManyToMany
    @MapKey(name="name")
    @JoinTable(name="EMP_PROJ",
            joinColumns=@JoinColumn(name="EMP_ID"),
            inverseJoinColumns=@JoinColumn(name="PROJ_ID"))
    private Map<String, Project> projects;
    // ...
}

@Entity
public class Project {
    // ...
    private String name;
    @ManyToMany(mappedBy="projects")
    private Collection<Employee> employees;
    // ...
}
```

orm.xml snippet:

```
<entity-mappings>
    <entity class="examples.model.Employee">
        <attributes>
            ...
            <many-to-many name="projects">
                <map-key name="name"/>
                <join-table name="EMP_PRJ">
                    <join-column name="EMP_ID"/>
                    <inverse-join-column name="PROJ_ID"/>
                </join-table>
            </many-to-many>
            ...
        </attributes>
    </entity>
    <entity class="examples.model.Project">
        <attributes>
            ...
            <many-to-many name="employee" mapped-by="projects"/>
            ...
        </attributes>
    </entity>
</entity-mappings>
```

element-collection

A collection of basic or embeddable objects is mapped using an `element-collection` element, which corresponds to the `@ElementCollection` annotation (refer to Chapter 5) and has the same optional `target-entity`, `fetch`, and `access` attributes that were described in the one-to-many and many-to-many mapping sections.

If the collection is a `List`, one of `order-by` or `order-column` can be specified as a subelement. If the collection is a `Map` and contains embeddables as values, a `map-key` element can be used to indicate that a field or property in the embeddable value is to be used as the map key. Alternatively, the various `map-key-column`, `map-key-join-column`, `map-key-enumerated`, `map-key-temporal`, `map-key-attribute-override`, `map-key-convert`, and `map-key-class` can be used as described in the one-to-many section.

Embeddables can contain basic mappings as well as relationships, so in order to override the columns and join columns that embeddable objects are mapped to, the `attribute-override` and `association-override` subelements are used.

If the value is a basic type, the `column` subelement—with the possibility of one of `temporal`, `lob`, `enumerated` or `convert` subelements—can be included. These all refer to the basic values in the collection, and the `column` element refers to the column in the collection table that stores the values.

Finally, element collections are stored in a collection table, so the `collection-table` subelement will obviously be a common one. It corresponds to the `@CollectionTable` annotation and refers to the table that stores the basic or embeddable objects in the collection as well as the keys that index them if the collection is a `Map`. An example of a `Map` element collection is one that stores the number of hours worked against a particular project name, as shown in Listing 13-27.

Listing 13-27. Element Collection of Integers with String Keys

```
@Entity
public class Employee {
    // ...
    @ElementCollection(targetClass=java.lang.Integer)
    @MapKeyClass(name="java.lang.String")
    @MapKeyColumn(name="PROJ_NAME")
    @Column(name="HOURS_WORKED")
    @CollectionTable(name="PROJ_TIME")
    private Map projectHours;
    // ...
}
```

orm.xml snippet:

```
<entity class="examples.model.Employee">
    <attributes>
        ...
        <element-collection name="projectHours" target-class="java.lang.Integer">
            <map-key-class name="java.lang.String"/>
            <map-key-column name="PROJ_NAME"/>
            <column name="HOURS_WORKED"/>
            <collection-table name="PROJ_TIME"/>
        </element-collection>
    </attributes>
></entity>
```

Embedded Object Mappings

An embedded object is a class that depends on its parent entity for its identity. Embedded objects are specified in XML using the embedded element and are customized using the `attribute-override` element.

embedded

An embedded element is used for mapping an embedded object contained within a field or property (refer to Chapter 4). It corresponds to the @Embedded annotation and permits an access attribute to be specified to dictate whether the state is to be accessed using a field or property. Because the persistent state is mapped within the embedded object, only the `attribute-override`, `association-override`, and `convert` subelements are allowed within the embedded element.

There must be an embeddable class entry in a mapping file for the embedded object, or it must be annotated as @Embeddable. An example of overriding an embedded Address is shown in Listing 13-28.

Listing 13-28. Embedded Mappings in Annotations and XML

```
@Entity
public class Employee {
    // ...
    @Embedded
    private Address address;
    // ...
}
```

```
@Embeddable
public class Address {
    private String street;
    private String city;
    private String state;
    private String zip;
    // ...
}
```

orm.xml snippet:

```
<entity-mappings>
    <entity class="examples.model.Employee">
        <attributes>
            ...
            <embedded name="address"/>
            ...
        </attributes>
    </entity>
    <embeddable class="examples.model.Address"/>
</entity-mappings>
```

The convert subelement is used to apply or override conversion for a particular field or property in the embedded object. See the "Converters" section for details on how the convert element can be used to override conversion.

attribute-override

When an embedded object is used by multiple entity types, it is likely that some of the basic mappings in the embedded object will need to be remapped by one or more of the entities (refer to Chapter 4). The attribute-override element can be specified as a subelement of the embedded, embedded-id, and element-collection elements to accommodate this case.

The annotation that corresponds to the attribute-override element is the @AttributeOverride annotation. This annotation can be on the entity class or on a field or property that stores an embedded object, collection of embedded objects, or embedded id. When an @AttributeOverride annotation is present in the entity, it will be overridden only by an attribute-override element in the entity mapping file entry that specifies the same named field or property. Our earlier algorithm still holds if we think of the attribute overrides as keyed by the name of the field or property that they are overriding. All the annotation overrides for an entity are gathered, and all the XML overrides for the class are applied on top of the annotation overrides. If there is an override in XML for the same named field or property, it will overwrite the annotated one. The remaining non-overlapping overrides from annotations and XML will also be applied.

The attribute-override element stores the name of the field or property in its name attribute and the column that the field or property maps to as a column subelement. Listing 13-29 revisits Listing 13-28 and overrides the state and zip fields of the embedded address.

Listing 13-29. Using Attribute Overrides

```
@Entity
public class Employee {
    // ...
    @Embedded
```

```
    @AttributeOverrides({
        @AttributeOverride(name="state", column=@Column(name="PROV")),
        @AttributeOverride(name="zip", column=@Column(name="PCODE"))})
    private Address address;
    // ...
}
```

orm.xml snippet:

```xml
<entity class="examples.model.Employee">
    <attributes>
        ...
        <embedded name="address">
            <attribute-override name="state">
                <column name="PROV"/>
            </attribute-override>
            <attribute-override name="zip">
                <column name="PCODE"/>
            </attribute-override>
        </embedded>
        ...
    </attributes>
</entity>
```

association-override

Embeddable objects also support relationship mappings, although it is a less common requirement. When a many-to-one or one-to-one relationship is present in an embeddable, a join column is mapped either explicitly or by default by the association in the embedded object. Reusing the embeddable type within another entity class means there is a possibility that the join column will need to be remapped. The association-override element, which corresponds to the @AssociationOverride annotation (refer to Chapter 10), can be included as a subelement of the embedded, embedded-id, and element-collection elements to accommodate this case.

The association-override element maps the name of the field or property in its name attribute and the join columns that the field or property maps to as one or more join-column subelements. If the mapping being overridden uses a join table, the join-table subelement is used instead of join-column.

The same XML overriding annotation rules apply as were described for attribute overrides.

Listing 13-30 revisits our embedded example again, but this time overrides the city association in the embedded address.

Listing 13-30. Using Association Overrides

```java
@Entity
public class Employee {
    // ...
    @Embedded
    @AssociationOverride(name="city", joinColumns=@JoinColumn(name="CITY_ID"))
    private Address address;
    // ...
}
```

```
@Embeddable
public class Address {
    private String street;
    @ManyToOne
    @JoinColumn(name="CITY")
    private City city;
    // ...
}
```

orm.xml snippet:

```xml
<entity class="examples.model.Employee">
    <attributes>
        ...
        <embedded name="address">
            <association-override name="city">
                <join-column name="CITY_ID"/>
            </association-override>
        </embedded>
        ...
    </attributes>
</entity>
```

Inheritance Mappings

An entity inheritance hierarchy is mapped using the inheritance, discriminator-column, and discriminator-value elements. If the inheritance strategy is changed, it must be overridden for the entire entity hierarchy.

inheritance

The inheritance element is specified to indicate the root of an inheritance hierarchy. It corresponds to the @Inheritance annotation and indicates the inheritance-mapping strategy that is to be used. When it is included in the entity element, it will override any inheritance strategy that is defined or defaulted in the @Inheritance annotation on the entity class.

Changing the inheritance strategy can cause repercussions that spill out into other areas. For example, changing a strategy from single table to joined will likely require adding a table to each of the entities below it. The example in Listing 13-31 overrides an entity hierarchy from using a single table to using a joined strategy.

Listing 13-31. Overriding an Inheritance Strategy

```java
@Entity
@Table(name="EMP")
@Inheritance
@DiscriminatorColumn(name="TYPE")
public abstract class Employee { ... }

@Entity
@DiscriminatorValue("FT")
public class FullTimeEmployee { ... }
```

```
@Entity
@DiscriminatorValue("PT")
public class PartTimeEmployee { ... }
```

orm.xml snippet:

```
<entity-mappings>
    <entity class="examples.model.Employee">
        <table name="EMP"/>
        <inheritance strategy="JOINED"/>
        ...
    </entity>
    <entity class="examples.model.FullTimeEmployee">
        <table name="FT_EMP"/>
        ...
    </entity>
    <entity class="examples.model.PartTimeEmployee">
        <table name="PT_EMP"/>
        ...
    </entity>
</entity-mappings>
```

discriminator-column

Discriminator columns store values that differentiate between concrete entity subclasses in an inheritance hierarchy (refer to Chapter 10). The discriminator-column element is a subelement of the entity or entity-result elements and is used to define or override the discriminator column. It corresponds to and overrides the @DiscriminatorColumn annotation and has attributes that include the name, discriminator-type, columnDefinition, and length. It is an empty element that has no subelements.

The discriminator-column element is not typically used to override a column on its own but in conjunction with other inheritance and table overrides. Listing 13-32 demonstrates specifying a discriminator column.

Listing 13-32. Specifying a Discriminator Column

```
@Entity
@Inheritance
@DiscriminatorColumn(name="TYPE")
public abstract class Employee { ... }
```

orm.xml snippet:

```
<entity class="examples.model.Employee">
    <inheritance/>
    <discriminator-column name="TYPE"/>
    ...
</entity >
```

discriminator-value

A discriminator-value element is used to declare the value that identifies the concrete entity subclass that is stored in a database row (refer to Chapter 10). It exists only as a subelement of the entity element. The discriminator value is indicated by the content of the element. It has no attributes or subelements.

The discriminator-value element corresponds to the @DiscriminatorValue annotation and overrides it when it exists on the entity class. As with the other inheritance overrides, it is seldom used as an override. Even when a hierarchy is remapped to a different database or set of tables, it will not normally be necessary to override the value. Listing 13-33 shows how to specify a discriminator value in annotation and XML form.

Listing 13-33. Specifying a Discriminator Column

```
@Entity
@DiscriminatorValue("FT")
public class FullTimeEmployee extends Employee { ... }
```

orm.xml snippet:

```
<entity class="examples.model.FullTimeEmployee">
    <discriminator-value>FT</discriminator-value>
    ...
</entity >
```

attribute-override and association-override

Simple mappings and associations can be overridden through the use of attribute overrides and association overrides, but only in the case of an entity that is the subclass of a mapped superclass. Simple persistent state or association state that is inherited from an entity superclass cannot portably be overridden.

An example of overriding two simple name and salary persistent field mappings, and a manager association with a compound primary key, is shown in Listing 13-34.

Listing 13-34. Using Attribute and Association Overrides with Inheritance

```
@MappedSuperclass
@IdClass(EmployeePK.class)
public abstract class Employee {
    @Id private String name;
    @Id private java.sql.Date dob;
    private long salary;
    @ManyToOne
    private Employee manager;
    // ...
}

@Entity
@Table(name="PT_EMP")
@AttributeOverrides({
    @AttributeOverride(name="name", column=@Column(name="EMP_NAME")),
    @AttributeOverride(name="salary", column=@Column(name="SAL"))})
@AssociationOverride(name="manager",
    joinColumns={
        @JoinColumn(name="MGR_NAME", referencedName="EMP_NAME"),
        @JoinColumn(name="MGR_DOB", referencedName="DOB")})
public class PartTimeEmployee extends Employee { ... }
```

orm.xml snippet:

```
<entity class="examples.model.PartTimeEmployee">
    ...
    <attribute-override name="name">
        <column name="EMP_NAME"/>
    </attribute-override>
    <attribute-override name="salary">
        <column name="SAL"/>
    </attribute-override>
    <association-override name="manager">
        <join-column name="MGR_NAME"  referenced-column-name="EMP_NAME"/>
        <join-column name="MGR_DOB" referenced-column-name="DOB"/>
    </association-override>
    ...
</entity>
```

Lifecycle Events

All the lifecycle events that can be associated with a method in an entity listener can also be associated directly with a method in an entity or mapped superclass (refer to Chapter 12). The pre-persist, post-persist, pre-update, post-update, pre-remove, post-remove, and post-load methods are all valid subelements of the entity or mapped-superclass elements. Each of them can occur only once in each class. Each lifecycle event element will override any entity callback method of the same event type that might be annotated in the entity class.

Before anyone goes out and overrides all their annotated callback methods with XML overrides, we should mention that the use case for doing such a thing borders on, if not completely falls off into, the non-existent. An example of specifying an entity callback method in annotations and in XML is shown in Listing 13-35.

Listing 13-35. Specifying Lifecycle Callback Methods

```
@Entity
public class Employee {
    // ...
    @PrePersist
    @PostLoad
    public void initTransientState() { ... }
    // ...
}
```

orm.xml snippet:

```
<entity class="examples.model.Employee">
    ...
    <pre-persist method-name="initTransientState"/>
    <post-load method-name="initTransientState"/>
    ...
</entity>
```

Entity Listeners

Lifecycle callback methods defined on a class other than the entity class are called entity listeners. The following sections describe how to configure entity listeners in XML using the `entity-listeners` element and how to exclude inherited and default listeners.

entity-listeners

One or more ordered entity listener classes can be defined in an `@EntityListeners` annotation on an entity or mapped superclass (refer to Chapter 12). When a lifecycle event fires, the listeners that have methods for the event will get invoked in the order in which they are listed. The `entity-listeners` element can be specified as a subelement of an `entity` or `mapped-superclass` element to accomplish exactly the same thing. It will also have the effect of overriding the entity listeners defined in an `@EntityListeners` annotation with the ones defined in the `entity-listeners` element.

An `entity-listeners` element includes a list of ordered `entity-listener` subelements, each of which defines an `entity-listener` class in its `class` attribute. For each listener, the methods corresponding to lifecycle events must be indicated as subelement events. The events can be one or more of `pre-persist`, `post-persist`, `pre-update`, `post-update`, `pre-remove`, `post-remove`, and `post-load`, which correspond to the `@PrePersist`, `@PostPersist`, `@PreUpdate`, `@PostUpdate`, `@PreRemove`, `@PostRemove`, and `@PostLoad` annotations, respectively. Each of the event subelements has a `method-name` attribute that names the method to be invoked when its lifecycle event is triggered. The same method can be supplied for multiple events, but no more than one event of the same type can be specified on a single listener class.

The `entity-listeners` element can be used to disable all the entity listeners defined on a class or just add an additional listener. Disabling listeners is not recommended, of course, because listeners defined on a class tend to be fairly coupled to the class itself, and disabling them might introduce bugs into either the class or the system as a whole.

Listing 13-36 shows that the XML mapping file is overriding the entity listeners on the `Employee` class. It is keeping the existing ones, but also adding one more at the end of the order to notify the IT department to remove an employee's user accounts when he or she leaves the company.

Listing 13-36. Overriding Entity Listeners

```
@Entity
@EntityListeners({ EmployeeAuditListener.class, NameValidator.class })
public class Employee { ... }

public class EmployeeAuditListener {
    @PostPersist
    public void employeeCreated(Employee emp) { ... }
    @PostUpdate
    public void employeeUpdated(Employee emp) { ... }
    @PostRemove
    public void employeeRemoved(Employee emp) { ... }
}
public class NameValidator {
    @PrePersist
    public void validateName(Employee emp) { ... }
}
public class EmployeeExitListener {
    public void notifyIT(Employee emp) { ... }
}
```

orm.xml snippet:

```
<entity class="examples.model.Employee">
    ...
    <entity-listeners>
        <entity-listener class="examples.listeners.EmployeeAuditListener">
            <post-persist method-name="employeeCreated"/>
            <post-update method-name="employeeUpdated"/>
            <post-remove method-name="employeeRemoved"/>
        </entity-listener>
        <entity-listener class="examples.listeners.NameValidator">
            <pre-persist method-name="validateName"/>
        </entity-listener>
        <entity-listener class="examples.listeners.EmployeeExitListener">
            <post-remove method-name="notifyIT"/>
        </entity-listener>
    </entity-listeners>
    ...
</entity>
```

Note that we have fully specified each of the entity callback listeners in XML. Some vendors will find the lifecycle event annotations on the `EmployeeAuditListener` and `NameValidator` entity listener classes, but this is not required behavior. To be portable, the lifecycle event methods should be specified in each of the `entity-listener` elements.

exclude-default-listeners

The set of default entity listeners that applies to all entities is defined in the `entity-listeners` subelement of the `persistence-unit-defaults` element (see the `entity-listeners` section). These listeners can be turned off or disabled for a particular entity or hierarchy of entities by specifying an empty `exclude-default-listeners` element within the `entity` or `mapped-superclass` element. This is equivalent to the `@ExcludeDefaultListeners` annotation, and if either one is specified for a class, default listeners are disabled for that class. Note that `exclude-default-listeners` is an empty element, not a `Boolean`. If default entity listeners are disabled for a class by an `@ExcludeDefaultListeners` annotation, there is currently no way to re-enable them through XML.

exclude-superclass-listeners

Entity listeners defined on the superclass of an entity will normally be fired before the entity listeners defined on the entity class itself are fired (refer to Chapter 12). To disable the listeners defined on an entity superclass or mapped superclass, an empty `exclude-superclass-listeners` element can be supplied inside an `entity` or `mapped-superclass` element. This will disable the superclass listeners for the managed class and all its subclasses.

The `exclude-superclass-listeners` element corresponds to the `@ExcludeSuperclassListeners` annotation and, like the `exclude-default-listeners`/`@ExcludeDefaultListeners` pair, either one of the two can be specified in order to disable the superclass listeners for the entity or mapped superclass and its subclasses.

Named Entity Graphs

Named entity graphs act as fetch plans for object queries and can override the fetch mode of field or property mappings for entity and embeddable types (see Chapter 11). The `named-entity-graph` element is equivalent to the `@NamedEntityGraph` annotation (see Chapter 11) and can only occur as a subelement of the `entity` element. Any named entity graphs defined in XML will be added to the named entity graphs defined in annotation form. If an XML named entity graph is named the same as one defined by an annotation, then the XML version will supercede the annotation definition.

A named-entity-graph has two optional attributes: a name attribute to explicitly declare its name and an includeAllAttributes boolean attribute that serves as a short form for including each and every field or property of the entity. Three subelements may multiply occur within named-entity-graph:

- A named-attribute-node subelement is added for each named field or property to be fetched and is similar in structure to the @NamedAttributeNode annotation. It has a mandatory name attribute and optional subgraph and key-subgraph String attributes to refer to a subgraph element (see below).

- The subgraph subelement of named-entity-graph is the analogue to the @NamedSubgraph annotation and is used to specify a type template for an entity or embeddable type. It has a mandatory name attribute and a class attribute that is only used when the subgraph is for a class in an inheritance hierarchy. A named-attribute-node subelement must be specified for each field or property that is to be included in the subgraph.

- The subclass-subgraph subelement of named-entity-graph can be specified the same as a subgraph element, with name and class attributes, and a named-attribute-node subelement for each field or property to be fetched. The subclass-subgraph element is only used to specify subgraphs for the subclasses of the entity that is the root of the named entity graph.

An example will make it much easier to see how the XML compares with the annotation. Listing 13-37 starts by showing an annotation from Chapter 11 that defines a named entity graph with multiple subgraph type definitions. Below it is the XML equivalent that uses multiple named-attribute-node and subgraph subelements.

Listing 13-37. Named Entity Graph with Multiple Subgraphs

```
@NamedEntityGraph(
    attributeNodes={
        @NamedAttributeNode("name"),
        @NamedAttributeNode("salary"),
        @NamedAttributeNode(value="address"),
        @NamedAttributeNode(value="phones", subgraph="phone"),
        @NamedAttributeNode(value="manager", subgraph="namedEmp"),
        @NamedAttributeNode(value="department", subgraph="dept")},
    subgraphs={
        @NamedSubgraph(name="phone",
            attributeNodes={
                @NamedAttributeNode("number"),
                @NamedAttributeNode("type"),
                @NamedAttributeNode(value="employee", subgraph="namedEmp")}),
        @NamedSubgraph(name="namedEmp",
            attributeNodes={
                @NamedAttributeNode("name")}),
        @NamedSubgraph(name="dept",
            attributeNodes={
                @NamedAttributeNode("name")})
})
```

orm.xml snippet:

```
<named-entity-graph>
    <named-attribute-node name="name"/>
    <named-attribute-node name="salary"/>
    <named-attribute-node name="address"/>
    <named-attribute-node name="phones", subgraph="phone"/>
    <named-attribute-node name="manager", subgraph="namedEmp"/>
    <named-attribute-node name="department", subgraph="dept"/>
    <subgraph name="phone">
        <named-attribute-node name="number"/>
        <named-attribute-node name="type"/>
        <named-attribute-node name="employee" subgraph="namedEmp"/>
    </subgraph>
    <subgraph name="namedEmp">
        <named-attribute-node name="name"/>
    </subgraph>
    <subgraph name="dept">
        <named-attribute-node name="name"/>
    </subgraph>
</named-entity-graph>
```

Converters

Converters are a way to programmatically transform the data in a basic mapped field or property into an alternate form before it gets saved to the database, and then reverse the transformation again when the data gets read from the database back into the entity.

There are two parts to conversion: first, defining a converter, and second, applying it to entity fields or properties. This section discusses doing each of these in XML.

converter

A converter is a managed class that can be declared either using the @Converter annotation or in the mapping file using the converter subelement of entity-mappings. The converter element can be specified at the same level as the entity, embeddable, or mapped-superclass elements. It has only two attributes: class and auto-apply. The class attribute refers to the class that implements the javax.persistence.AttributeConverter<X,Y> interface while the auto-apply boolean option dictates whether the converter is to be automatically applied to entity fields or properties of type X throughout the persistence unit. See Chapter 10 for more details on how to use the auto-apply feature.

It is undefined[4] to have more than one converter class declared using the @Converter annotation to be auto-applied to the same target field or property type. However, an annotated converter can be overridden by using the converter element to declare a different (unannotated) converter class auto-applied to the same target type. For example, if we had a SecureURLConverter class that implemented AttributeConverter<URL,String>, then we could override the annotated URLConverter defined in Listing 10-5 with the secure version by declaring it in a converter element, as shown in Listing 13-38.

---

[4] The provider may pick one at random or throw an exception at startup time and disallow it altogether.

Listing 13-38. Declaring an Auto-applied Converter

```
<entity-mappings>
    ...
    <converter class="examples.SecureURLConverter" auto-apply="true"/>
    ...
</entity-mappings>
```

convert

If a converter is not auto-applied, then it must be explicitly applied to a field or property in order for it to take effect. A converter can be applied to a field or property either by annotating it with the @Convert annotation or adding a convert subelement to the basic or element-collection element that maps the field or property.

The convert element contains three attributes. The first attribute, converter, is used to indicate the name of the converter class to apply. It is used whenever conversion is being explicitly applied to a field or property. Listing 13-39 shows how to apply a converter to an entity attribute using the convert element.

Listing 13-39. Applying Conversion to an Entity Attribute

```
<entity-mappings>
    ...
    <entity class="examples.model.Employee">
        <attributes>
            ...
            <basic name="homePage">
                <convert converter="URLConverter"/>
            </basic>
        </attributes>
    </entity>
    ...
</entity-mappings>
```

Two other attributes are used for overriding or adding conversion to an embedded or inherited field or property. One is the attribute-name attribute, which contains the name of the entity field or property to override or apply a converter to. The next attribute is a boolean-valued attribute called disable-conversion and is used to override conversion in order to cause it not to occur.

A field or property can be marked for conversion, or overridden to not be converted, when the convert element is used within an entity or embedded element. Listing 13-40 shows how FTEmployee, an Employee subclass, can override the converter that was applied to homePage in Listing 13-39.

Listing 13-40. Overriding a Converter in an Inherited Entity Attribute

```
<entity-mappings>
    ...
    <entity class="examples.model.FTEmployee">
        ...
        <convert converter="SecureURLConverter" attribute-name="homePage"/>
    </entity>
    ...
</entity-mappings>
```

Summary

With all the XML mapping information under your belt, you should now be able to map entities using annotations, XML, or a combination of the two. In this chapter, we went over all the elements in the mapping file and compared them with their corresponding annotations. We discussed how each of the elements is used, what they override, and how they are overridden. We also used them in some short examples.

Defaults can be specified in the mapping files at different levels, from the global persistence unit level to the mapping file level. We covered what each of the defaulting scopes was and how they were applied.

The next chapter shows how to package and deploy applications that use JPA. We will also look at how XML mapping files are referenced as part of a persistence unit configuration.

CHAPTER 14

■ ■ ■

Packaging and Deployment

Configuring a persistence application involves specifying the bits of information, additional to the code, that the execution environment or persistence platform may require in order for the code to function as a runtime application. Packaging means putting all the pieces together in a way that makes sense and can be correctly interpreted and used by the infrastructure when the application is deployed into an application server or run in a stand-alone JVM. Deployment is the process of getting the application into an execution environment and running it.

One could view the mapping metadata as part of the overall configuration of an application, but we won't cover that in this chapter because it has already been discussed in previous chapters. In this chapter, we will be discussing the primary runtime persistence configuration file, `persistence.xml`, which defines persistence units. We will go into detail about how to specify the different elements of this file, when they are required, and what the values should be.

Once the persistence unit has been configured, we will package a persistence unit with a few of the more common deployment units, such as EJB archives, web archives, and the application archives in a Java EE server. The resulting package will then be deployable into a compliant application server. We will also step through the packaging and deployment rules for Java SE applications.

Schema generation is the process of generating the schema tables to which the entities are mapped. We will list the properties that activate schema generation and describe the different forms it can take, such as creating tables in the database or generating DDL in script files. We will then outline all of the annotations that play a role in what gets generated.

Configuring Persistence Units

The persistence unit is the primary unit of runtime configuration. It defines the various pieces of information that the provider needs to know in order to manage the persistent classes during program execution and is configured within a `persistence.xml` file. There may be one or more `persistence.xml` files in an application, and each `persistence.xml` file may define multiple persistence units. There will most often be only one, though. Since there is one `EntityManagerFactory` for each persistence unit, you can think of the configuration of the persistence unit as the configuration of the factory for that persistence unit.

A common configuration file goes a long way to standardizing the runtime configuration, and the `persistence.xml` file offers exactly that. While some providers might still require an additional provider-specific configuration file, most will also support their properties being specified within the properties section (described in the "Adding Properties" section) of the `persistence.xml` file.

The `persistence.xml` file is the first step to configuring a persistence unit. All the information required for the persistence unit should be specified in the `persistence.xml` file. Once a packaging strategy has been chosen, the `persistence.xml` file should be placed in the `META-INF` directory of the chosen archive.

Each persistence unit is defined by a `persistence-unit` element in the `persistence.xml` file. All the information for that persistence unit is enclosed within that element. The following sections describe the metadata that a persistence unit may define when deploying to a Java EE server.

Persistence Unit Name

Every persistence unit must have a name that uniquely identifies it within the scope of its packaging. We will be discussing the different packaging options later, but in general, if a persistence unit is defined within a Java EE module, there must not be any other persistence unit of the same name in that module. For example, if a persistence unit named "EmployeeService" is defined in an EJB JAR named emp_ejb.jar, there should not be any other persistence units named "EmployeeService" in emp_ejb.jar. There may be persistence units named "EmployeeService" in a web module or even in another EJB module within the application, though.

We have seen in some of the examples in previous chapters that the name of the persistence unit is just an attribute of the persistence-unit element, as in the following:

```
<persistence-unit name="EmployeeService"/>
```

This empty persistence-unit element is the minimal persistence unit definition. It may be all that is needed if the server defaults the remaining information, but not all servers will do this. Some may require other persistence unit metadata to be present, such as the data source to be accessed.

Transaction Type

The factory that is used to create entity managers for a given persistence unit will generate entity managers to be of a specific transactional type. We went into detail in Chapter 6 about the different types of entity managers, and one of the things we saw was that every entity manager must either use JTA or resource-local transactions. Normally, when running in a managed server environment, the JTA transaction mechanism is used. It is the default transaction type that a server will assume when none is specified for a persistence unit and is generally the only one that most applications will ever need, so in practice the transaction type will not need to be specified very often.

If the data source is required by the server, as it often will be, a JTA-enabled data source should be supplied (see the "Data Source" section). Specifying a data source that is not JTA-enabled might actually work in some cases, but the database operations will not be participating in the global JTA transaction or necessarily be atomic with respect to that transaction.

In situations such as those described in Chapter 6, when you want to use resource-local transactions instead of JTA, the transaction-type attribute of the persistence-unit element is used to explicitly declare the transaction type of RESOURCE_LOCAL or JTA, as in the following example:

```
<persistence-unit name="EmployeeService"
                 transaction-type="RESOURCE_LOCAL"/>
```

Here we are overriding the default JTA transaction type to be resource-local, so all the entity managers created in the "EmployeeService" persistence unit must use the EntityTransaction interface to control transactions.

Persistence Provider

The Java Persistence API has a pluggable Service Provider Interface (SPI) that allows any compliant Java EE server to communicate with any compliant JPA persistence provider implementation. Servers normally have a default provider, though, that is native to the server, meaning that it is implemented by the same vendor or is shipped with the server. In most cases, this default provider will be used by the server, and no special metadata will be necessary to explicitly specify it.

In order to switch to a different provider, the provider-supplied class that implements the javax.persistence.spi.PersistenceProvider interface must be listed in the provider element. Listing 14-1 shows a simple persistence unit that explicitly defines the EclipseLink provider class. The only requirement is that the provider JARs be on the server or application classpath and accessible to the running application at deployment time. The complete persistence header element is also included in Listing 14-1, but will not be included in the subsequent XML examples.

Listing 14-1. Specifying a Persistence Provider

```
<persistence xmlns="http://xmlns.jcp.org/xml/ns/persistence"
       xmlns:xsi="http://www.w3.org/2001/XMLSchema-instance"
       xsi:schemaLocation="http://xmlns.jcp.org/xml/ns/persistence
         http://xmlns.jcp.org/xml/ns/persistence/persistence_2_1.xsd"
       version="2.1">
   <persistence-unit name="EmployeeService">
       <provider>org.eclipse.persistence.jpa.PersistenceProvider</provider>
   </persistence-unit>
</persistence>
```

Data Source

A fundamental part of the persistence unit metadata is the description of where the provider should obtain database connections from in order to read and write entity data. The target database is specified in terms of the name of a JDBC data source that is in the server JNDI space. This data source must be globally accessible since the provider accesses it when the persistence application is deployed.

The typical case is that JTA transactions are used, so it is in the `jta-data-source` element that the name of the JTA data source should be specified. Similarly, if the transaction type of the persistence unit is resource-local, the `non-jta-data-source` element should be used.

Although JPA defines the standard elements in which to specify data source names, it does not dictate the format. In the past, a data source was made available in JNDI by being configured in a server-specific configuration file or management console. The name was not officially portable but in practice they were usually of the form "jdbc/SomeDataSource". Listing 14-2 shows how a data source would be specified using an application-scoped JNDI name. This example assumes the provider is being defaulted.

Listing 14-2. Specifying JTA Data Source

```
<persistence-unit name="EmployeeService">
   <jta-data-source>java:app/jdbc/EmployeeDS</jta-data-source>
</persistence-unit>
```

JAVA EE 6 NAMESPACES

Many applications use the old-style naming approach that assumes a component-scoped name (e.g., jdbc/SomeDataSource), but as of Java EE 6, three new namespaces exist to allow names to refer to global, application, or module scope. By using the corresponding standard namespace prefixes of java:global, java:app, or java:module, a resource can be made available to other components in a wider scope than just the component, and the name would be portable across container implementations.

We will use the application namespace in our examples because we think of the application scope as being the most useful and reasonable scope in which to make a data source available.

As of Java EE 7, containers provide a default data source (available at the JNDI name java:comp/DefaultDataSource), and if the provider is a native implementation for the server, it may make use of this default. In other cases, the data source will need to be specified.

Some providers offer high-performance reading through database connections that are not associated with the current JTA transaction. The query results are then returned and made conformant with the contents of the persistence context. This improves the scalability of the application because the database connection does not get enlisted in the JTA transaction until later on when it absolutely needs to be, usually at commit time. To enable these types of scalable reads, the non-jta-data-source element value would be supplied in addition to the jta-data-source element. An example of specifying these two is in Listing 14-3.

Listing 14-3. Specifying JTA and Non-JTA Data Sources

```
<persistence-unit name="EmployeeService">
    <jta-data-source>java:app/jdbc/EmployeeDS</jta-data-source>
    <non-jta-data-source>java:app/jdbc/NonTxEmployeeDS</non-jta-data-source>
</persistence-unit>
```

Note that the "EmployeeDS" is a regularly configured data source that accesses the employee database, but "NonTxEmployeeDS" is a separate data source configured to access the same employee database but not be enlisted in JTA transactions.

Mapping Files

In Chapter 13, we used XML mapping files to supply mapping metadata. Part or all of the mapping metadata for the persistence unit may be specified in mapping files. The union of all the mapping files (and the annotations in the absence of xml-mapping-metadata-complete) will be the metadata that is applied to the persistence unit.

You might wonder why multiple mapping files might be useful. There are actually numerous cases for using more than one mapping file in a single persistence unit, but it really comes down to preference and process. For example, you might want to define all the persistence-unit-level artifacts in one file and all the entity metadata in another file. In another case, it may make sense for you to group all the queries together in a separate file to isolate them from the rest of the physical database mappings. Perhaps it suits the development process to even have a file for each entity, either to decouple them from each other or to reduce conflicts resulting from the version control and configuration management system. This can be a popular choice for a team that is working on different entities within the same persistence unit. Each may want to change the mappings for a particular entity without getting in the way of other team members who are modifying other entities. Of course, this must be negotiated carefully when there really are dependencies across the entities such as relationships or embedded objects. It makes sense to group entity metadata together when the relationships between them are not static or when the object model may change. As a general rule, if there is strong coupling in the object model, the coupling should be considered in the mapping configuration model.

Some might just prefer to have a single mapping file with all the metadata contained within it. This is certainly a simpler deployment model and makes for easier packaging. There is built-in support available to those who are happy limiting their metadata to a single file and willing to name it "orm.xml". If a mapping file named "orm.xml" exists in a META-INF directory on the classpath, for example beside the persistence.xml file, it does not need to be explicitly listed. The provider will automatically search for such a file and use it if one exists. Mapping files that are named differently or are in a different location must be listed in the mapping-file elements in the persistence.xml file.

Mapping files listed in the mapping-file elements are loaded as Java resources (using methods such as ClassLoader.getResource(), for example) from the classpath, so they should be specified in the same manner as any other Java resource that was intended to be loaded as such. The directory location component followed by the file name of the mapping file will cause it to be found, loaded, and processed at deployment time. For example, if we put all our persistence unit metadata in META-INF/orm.xml, all our queries in META-INF/employee_service_queries.xml, and all our entities in META-INF/employee_service_entities.xml, we should end up with the persistence-unit-level definition shown in Listing 14-4. Remember, we don't need to specify the META-INF/orm.xml file because it will be found and processed by default. The other mapping files could be in any directory, not necessarily just the META-INF directory. We put them in META-INF just to keep them together with the orm.xml file.

Listing 14-4. Specifying Mapping Files

```
<persistence-unit name="EmployeeService">
    <jta-data-source>java:app/jdbc/EmployeeDS</jta-data-source>
    <mapping-file>META-INF/employee_service_queries.xml</mapping-file>
    <mapping-file>META-INF/employee_service_entities.xml</mapping-file>
</persistence-unit>
```

Managed Classes

Managed classes are all the classes that must be processed and considered in a persistence unit, including entities, mapped superclasses, embeddables, and converter classes. Typical deployments will put all the entities and other managed classes in a single JAR, with the `persistence.xml` file in the `META-INF` directory and one or more mapping files also tossed in when XML mapping is used. The deployment process is optimized for these kinds of deployment scenarios to minimize the amount of metadata that a deployer has to specify.

The set of entities, mapped superclasses, embedded objects, and converter classes that will be managed in a particular persistence unit is determined by the provider when it processes the persistence unit. At deployment time it may obtain managed classes from any of four sources. A managed class will be included if it is among the following:

- *Local classes:* The annotated classes in the deployment unit in which its `persistence.xml` file was packaged.

- *Classes in mapping files:* The classes that have mapping entries in an XML mapping file.

- *Explicitly listed classes:* The classes that are listed as `class` elements in the `persistence.xml` file.

- *Additional JARs of managed classes:* The annotated classes in a named JAR listed in a `jar-file` element in the `persistence.xml` file.

As a deployer you may choose to use any one or a combination of these mechanisms to cause your managed classes to be included in the persistence unit. We will discuss each in turn.

Local Classes

The first category of classes that gets included is the one that is the easiest and will likely be used the most often. We call these classes local classes because they are local to the deployment unit. When a JAR is deployed with a `persistence.xml` file in the `META-INF` directory, that JAR will be searched for all the classes that are annotated with `@Entity`, `@MappedSuperclass`, `@Embeddable`, or `@Converter`. This will hold true for various types of deployment units that we will describe in more detail later in the chapter.

This method is clearly the simplest way to cause a class to be included because all that has to be done is to put the annotated classes into a JAR and add the `persistence.xml` file in the `META-INF` directory of the JAR. The provider will take care of going through the classes and finding the entities. Other classes may also be placed in the JAR with the entities and will have no effect on the finding process, other than perhaps potentially slowing down the finding process if there are many such classes.

Classes in Mapping Files

Any class that has an entry in a mapping file will also be considered a managed class in the persistence unit. It need only be named in an `entity`, `mapped-superclass`, `embeddable`, or `converter` element in one of the mapping files. The set of all the classes from all the listed mapping files (including the implicitly processed `orm.xml` file) will be added to the set of managed classes in the persistence unit. Nothing special has to be done apart from ensuring that the classes named in a mapping file are on the classpath of the unit being deployed. If they are in the deployed component archive, they will likely already be on the classpath. If they aren't, they must be explicitly included in the classpath just as the explicitly listed ones are (see the following "Explicitly Listed Classes" section).

Explicitly Listed Classes

When the persistence unit is small or when there is not a large number of entities, we may want to list classes explicitly in class elements in the persistence.xml file. This will cause the listed classes to be added to the persistence unit.

Since a class that is local to the deployment unit will already be included, we don't need to list it in a class element. Explicitly listing the classes is really useful in three main cases.

The first is when there are additional classes that are not local to the deployment unit JAR. For example, there is an embedded object class in a different JAR that we want to use in an entity in our persistence unit. We would list the fully qualified class in the class element in the persistence.xml file. We will also need to ensure that the JAR or directory that contains the class is on the classpath of the deployed component, for example, by adding it to the manifest classpath of the deployment JAR.

In the second case, we want to exclude one or more classes that may be annotated as an entity. Even though the class may be annotated with @Entity, we don't want it to be treated as an entity in this particular deployed context. For example, it may be used as a transfer object and need to be part of the deployment unit. In this case, we need to make use of a special element called exclude-unlisted-classes in the persistence.xml file, which disables local classes from being added to the persistence unit. When exclude-unlisted-classes is used, none of the classes in the local classes category described earlier will be included.

■ **Note**   There was a bug in the JPA 1.0 persistence_1_0.xsd schema that the default value of the exclude-unlisted-classes element was false. This meant that a value of true needed to be explicitly included as content, such as <exclude-unlisted-classes>true<exclude-unlisted-classes/>, instead of being able to simply include the empty element to signify that only the classes listed in the <class> elements need to be considered as entities. Some vendors actually worked around it by not validating the persistence.xml against the schema, but to be portable in JPA 1.0 you should explicitly set it to true when you want to exclude the unlisted classes. The bug was fixed in the JPA 2.0 persistence_2_0.xsd schema.

The third case is when we expect to be running the application in a Java SE environment and we list the classes explicitly because that is the only portable way to do so in Java SE. We will explain deployment to the Java SE non-server environment later in the chapter.

Additional JARs of Managed Classes

The last way to get managed classes included in the persistence unit is to add them to another JAR and specify the name of the JAR in a jar-file element in the persistence.xml. The jar-file element is used to indicate to the provider a JAR that may contain annotated classes. The provider will then treat the named JAR as if it were a deployment JAR, and it will look for any annotated classes and add them to the persistence unit. It will even search for an orm.xml file in the META-INF directory in the JAR and process it just as if it were an additionally listed mapping file.

Any JAR listed in a jar-file entry must be on the classpath of the deployment unit. We must do this manually, though, since the server will not automatically do it for us. Again, this may be done by either putting the JAR in the lib directory of the EAR (or WAR if we are deploying a WAR), adding the JAR to the manifest classpath of the deployment unit, or by some other vendor-specific means.

When listing a JAR in a `jar-file` element, it must be listed relative to the parent of the JAR file in which the `META-INF/persistence.xml` file is located. This matches what we would put in the classpath entry in the manifest. For example, assume the enterprise archive (EAR), that we will call `emp.ear`, is structured as shown in Listing 14-5.

Listing 14-5. Entities in an External JAR

```
emp.ear
    emp-ejb.jar
        META-INF/persistence.xml
    lib/emp-classes.jar
        examples/model/Employee.class
```

The contents of the `persistence.xml` file should be as shown in Listing 14-6, with the `jar-file` element containing "lib/emp-classes.jar" to reference the `emp-classes.jar` in the `lib` directory in the EAR file. This would cause the provider to add the annotated classes it found in `emp-classes.jar` (`Employee.class`) to the persistence unit, and because the jar is in the `lib` directory of the EAR, it would automatically be on the application classpath.

Listing 14-6. Contents of persistence.xml

```
<persistence-unit name="EmployeeService">
    <jta-data-source>java:app/jdbc/EmployeeDS</jta-data-source>
    <jar-file>lib/emp-classes.jar</jar-file>
</persistence-unit>
```

Shared Cache Mode

At the end of Chapter 12, we went into some detail about caching and the cache that is shared by all the entity managers obtained from the same entity manager factory. In the "Static Configuration of the Cache" section of that chapter, we described the options for setting the shared cache mode, but we will summarize here how the `shared-cache-mode` element works in the `persistence.xml` file.

The `shared-cache-mode` element is optional, but when specified it may be set to one of the five options listed in Table 14-1.

Table 14-1. *shared-cache-mode Options*

Value	Description
UNSPECIFIED	The provider chooses whatever option is most appropriate for that provider.
ALL	Cache all the entities in the persistence unit.
NONE	Do not cache any of the entities in the persistence unit.
DISABLE_SELECTED	Cache all entities except those annotated with @Cacheable(false).
ENABLE_SELECTED	Cache no entities except those annotated with @Cacheable(true).

It doesn't make much sense to explicitly designate UNSPECIFIED as the option because it is exactly equivalent to not specifying the value at all and offers no real information. When not set, the element will be defaulted by the provider to whichever of the other four options makes the most sense for that provider.

The next two options, ALL and NONE, are "sweeping" options, meaning that they affect all the entities in the persistence unit, without exception. Any @Cacheable annotations will be ignored when either of these options is set.

The DISABLE_SELECTED and ENABLE_SELECTED options are "discretionary" options, and are used in conjunction with the @Cacheable annotation to determine the entities that are cached and those that are not. If the default for your provider is one of the discretionary options and you end up using the @Cacheable annotation to affect which entities get cached, you might want to explicitly set this element to the desired/expected mode instead of relying upon the default provider behavior. This will avoid confusion that could result from switching providers and getting a different default that does not consider the @Cacheable annotations.

Validation Mode

The validation-mode element in the persistence.xml file determines whether validation is enabled or not (see the "Enabling Validation" section in Chapter 12). It may be set to AUTO, meaning that in the container environment, validation is enabled, but when not running in the container, validation will be enabled only if there is a validation provider available. Setting it to CALLBACK will enable validation and assume that a validation provider is on the classpath.

The default is AUTO, which enables validation, so if you do not intend to use validation, we recommend that you explicitly disable it by setting the validation-mode element to NONE. This will bypass the validation provider checks and prevent you from incurring any validation overhead if at some point later on a provider happens to show up on the classpath.

Adding Properties

The last section in the persistence.xml file is the properties section. The properties element gives a deployer the chance to supply standard and provider-specific settings for the persistence unit. To guarantee runtime compatibility, a provider must ignore properties it does not understand. While it is helpful to be able to use the same persistence.xml file across different providers, it also makes it easy to mistakenly type a property incorrectly and have it unintentionally and silently ignored. An example of adding some vendor properties is shown in Listing 14-7.

Listing 14-7. Using Provider Properties

```
<persistence-unit name="EmployeeService">
    ...
    <properties>
        <property name="eclipselink.logging.level"
                  value="FINE"/>
        <property name="eclipselink.cache.size.default"
                  value="500"/>
    </properties>
</persistence-unit>
```

Building and Deploying

One of the big wins that a standard persistence API brings is not only a portable runtime API but also a common way to compose, assemble, and configure an application that makes use of persistence. In this section, we will describe some of the popular and practical choices that are used to deploy persistence-enabled applications.

Deployment Classpath

In some of the previous sections we say that a class or a JAR must be on the deployment classpath. When we say this we mean that the JAR must be accessible to the EJB JAR, the web archive (WAR), or the enterprise application archive (EAR). This can be achieved in several ways.

The first is by putting the JAR in the manifest classpath of the EJB JAR or WAR. This is done by adding a classpath entry to the `META-INF/MANIFEST.MF` file in the JAR or WAR. One or more directories or JARs may be specified, as long as they are separated by spaces. For example, the following manifest file classpath entry will add the `employee/emp-classes.jar` and the `employee/classes` directory to the classpath of the JAR that contains the manifest file:

```
Class-Path: employee/emp-classes.jar employee/classes
```

A better way to get a JAR into the deployment unit classpath is to place the JAR in the library directory of the EAR. When a JAR is in the library directory, it will automatically be on the application classpath and accessible by all the modules deployed within the EAR. By default, the library directory is the `lib` directory in the EAR, although it may be configured to be any directory using the `library-directory` element in the `application.xml` deployment descriptor. The `application.xml` file would look something like the skeletal one shown in Listing 14-8.

Listing 14-8. Setting the Application Library Directory

```
<application ... >
    ...
    <library-directory>myDir/jars</library-directory>
</application>
```

When you are deploying a WAR and want to put an additional JAR of entities on the classpath, you can put the JAR in the `WEB-INF/lib` directory of the WAR. This causes the JAR to be on the classpath, and the classes in it are accessible to all the classes in the WAR.

Vendors usually provide their own vendor-specific way for deployers to add classes or JARs to the deployment classpath. This is usually offered at the application level and not at the level of a JAR or WAR; however, some may provide both.

Packaging Options

A primary focus of the Java Persistence API is its integration with the Java EE platform. Not only has it been integrated in fine-grained ways, such as allowing injection of entity managers into Java EE components, but it also has special status in Java EE application packaging. Java EE allows for persistence to be supported in a variety of packaging configurations that offer flexibility and choice. We will divide them up into the different module types that the application might be deployed into: EJB modules, web modules, and persistence archives.

EJB JAR

Modularized business logic has traditionally ended up in session bean components, which is why session beans were designed with JPA to be the primary Java EE component clients of persistence. Session beans have traditionally been deployed in an EJB JAR, although since Java EE 6 they may also be deployed in a WAR with web components. For a discussion on deploying in a WAR, see the next section.

We assume that the reader is familiar with packaging and deploying EJB components in an EJB JAR, but if not, there are many books and resources available to learn about it.

As of EJB 3.0, we no longer need to have an `ejb-jar.xml` deployment descriptor, but if we choose to use one, it must be in the `META-INF` directory. When defining a persistence unit in an EJB JAR, the `persistence.xml` file is not optional. It must be created and placed in the `META-INF` directory of the JAR alongside the `ejb-jar.xml` deployment descriptor, if it exists. Although the existence of `persistence.xml` is required, the contents may be very sparse indeed, in some cases including only the name of the persistence unit.

The only real work in defining a persistence unit is to decide where we want our entities and managed classes to reside. We have a number of options available to us. The simplest approach is to simply dump our managed classes into the EJB JAR along with the EJB components. As we described in the "Local Classes" section earlier in the chapter, as long as the managed classes are correctly annotated, they will be automatically discovered by the provider at deployment time and added to the persistence unit. Listing 14-9 shows a sample enterprise application archive file that does this.

Listing 14-9. Packaging Entities in an EJB JAR

```
emp.ear
    emp-ejb.jar
        META-INF/persistence.xml
        META-INF/orm.xml
        examples/ejb/EmployeeService.class
        examples/model/Employee.class
        examples/model/Phone.class
        examples/model/Address.class
        examples/model/Department.class
        examples/model/Project.class
```

In this case, the `orm.xml` file contains any mapping information that we might have at the persistence-unit level, such as setting the schema for the persistence unit. In the `persistence.xml` file, we would need to specify only the name of the persistence unit and the data source. Listing 14-10 shows the corresponding `persistence.xml` file (without the namespace header).

Listing 14-10. Persistence.xml File for Entities Packaged in an EJB JAR

```
<persistence ...>
    <persistence-unit name="EmployeeService">
        <jta-data-source>java:app/jdbc/EmployeeDS</jta-data-source>
    </persistence-unit>
</persistence>
```

If we wanted to separate the entities from the EJB components, we could put them in a different JAR and reference that JAR in a `jar-file` entry in the `persistence.xml` file. We showed a simple example of doing this in the "Additional JARs of Managed Classes" section, but we will show one again here with an additional `orm.xml` file and `emp-mappings.xml` mapping file. Listing 14-11 shows what the structure and contents of the EAR would look like.

Listing 14-11. Packaging Entities in a Separate JAR

```
emp.ear
    emp-ejb.jar
        META-INF/persistence.xml
        examples/ejb/EmployeeService.class
    lib/emp-classes.jar
        META-INF/orm.xml
        META-INF/emp-mappings.xml
        examples/model/Employee.class
        examples/model/Phone.class
        examples/model/Address.class
        examples/model/Department.class
        examples/model/Project.class
```

The emp-classes.jar file containing the entities would be on the classpath since it is in the library directory of the EAR, as described in the "Deployment Classpath" section. In addition to processing the entities found in the emp-classes.jar file, the orm.xml file in the META-INF directory will also be detected and processed automatically. We need to explicitly list the additional emp_mappings.xml mapping file in a mapping-file element, though, in order for the provider to find it as a resource. The persistence unit portion of the persistence.xml file is shown in Listing 14-12.

Listing 14-12. Persistence.xml File for Entities Packaged in a Separate JAR

```
<persistence-unit name="EmployeeService">
    <jta-data-source>java:app/jdbc/EmployeeDS</jta-data-source>
    <mapping-file>META-INF/emp-mappings.xml</mapping-file>
    <jar-file>lib/emp-classes.jar</jar-file>
</persistence-unit>
```

Web Archive

The web archive has become the most popular deployment vehicle for applications since almost everything a typical web application needs can be housed within it. Web artifacts and frameworks, business components like EJBs, CDI beans, and Spring beans, as well as persistent entities can all be deployed inside a web archive without the need for a separate deployment module. By using the WAR as the deployment vehicle for all three code tiers, the EJB JAR and EAR units become unnecessary, and the WAR becomes the new EAR equivalent.

The downside is that a WAR is a little more complex than the EJB JAR, and learning to package persistence units in web archives requires understanding the relevance of the persistence.xml file location. The location of the persistence.xml file determines the persistence unit root. The root of the persistence unit is defined as the JAR or directory that contains the META-INF directory where the persistence.xml file is located. For example, in an EJB JAR, the persistence.xml file is located in the META-INF directory of the root of the JAR, so the root of the persistence unit is always the root of the EJB JAR file itself. In a WAR, the persistence unit root depends upon where the persistence unit is located within the WAR. The obvious choice is to use the WEB-INF/classes directory as the root, which would lead us to place the persistence.xml file in the WEB-INF/classes/META-INF directory. Any annotated managed classes rooted in the WEB-INF/classes directory will be detected and added to the persistence unit. Similarly, if an orm.xml file is located in WEB-INF/classes/META-INF, it will be processed. The web components and bean components are also placed in the classes directory. An example of packaging a persistence unit in the WEB-INF/classes directory, with the accompanying other application classes, is shown in Listing 14-13. We have included the web.xml file, but it is no longer necessary if annotations on the servlet are used.

Listing 14-13. Packaging Entities in the WEB-INF/classes Directory

```
emp.war
    WEB-INF/web.xml
    WEB-INF/classes/META-INF/persistence.xml
    WEB-INF/classes/META-INF/orm.xml
    WEB-INF/classes/examples/web/EmployeeServlet.class
    WEB-INF/classes/examples/ejb/EmployeeService.class
    WEB-INF/classes/examples/model/Employee.class
    WEB-INF/classes/examples/model/Phone.class
    WEB-INF/classes/examples/model/Address.class
    WEB-INF/classes/examples/model/Department.class
    WEB-INF/classes/examples/model/Project.class
```

The `persistence.xml` file would be specified in exactly the same way as is shown in Listing 14-10. If we need to add another mapping file, we can put it anywhere on the deployment unit classpath. We just need to add a `mapping-file` element to the `persistence.xml` file. If, for example, we put `emp-mapping.xml` in the `WEB-INF/classes/mapping` directory, we would add the following element to the `persistence.xml` file:

```
<mapping-file>mapping/emp-mapping.xml</mapping-file>
```

Since the `WEB-INF/classes` directory is automatically on the classpath of the WAR, the mapping file is specified relative to that directory.

Persistence Archive

If we want to allow a persistence unit to be shared or accessible by multiple components, either in different Java EE modules or in a single WAR, we should use a persistence archive. It also promotes good design principles by keeping the persistence classes together. We saw a simple persistence archive back in Chapter 2 when we were first getting started and observed how it housed the `persistence.xml` file and the managed classes that were part of the persistence unit defined within it. By placing a persistence archive in the `lib` directory of an EAR, or in the `WEB-INF/lib` directory of a WAR, we can make it available to any enclosed component that needs to operate on the entities defined by its contained persistence unit.

The persistence archive is simple to create and easy to deploy. It is simply a JAR that contains a `persistence.xml` in its `META-INF` directory and the managed classes for the persistence unit defined by the `persistence.xml` file.

Listing 14-14 shows the contents of the WAR that we showed in Listing 14-13, but in this case it uses a simple persistence archive, `emp-persistence.jar`, to define the persistence unit that we have been using in the previous examples. This time, we need to only put the persistence archive in the `WEB-INF/lib` directory, and it will be both on the classpath and detected as a persistence unit.

Listing 14-14. Packaging Entities in a Persistence Archive

```
emp.war
    WEB-INF/web.xml
    WEB-INF/classes/examples/web/EmployeeServlet.class
    WEB-INF/classes/examples/ejb/EmployeeService.class
    WEB-INF/lib/emp-persistence.jar
        META-INF/persistence.xml
        META-INF/orm.xml
        examples/model/Employee.class
        examples/model/Phone.class
        examples/model/Address.class
        examples/model/Department.class
        examples/model/Project.class
```

If the `emp-persistence.jar` JAR part of Listing 14-14 looks familiar, that's because it is virtually the same as the EJB JAR structure that we showed in Listing 14-9 except that it is a persistence archive JAR instead of an EJB JAR. We just changed the name of the JAR and took out the session bean classes. The contents of the `persistence.xml` file can be exactly the same as what is shown in Listing 14-10. Just as with the other archive types, the `orm.xml` file in the `META-INF` directory will be automatically detected and processed, and other XML mapping files may be placed within the JAR and referenced by the `persistence.xml` file as a `mapping-file` entry.

Managed classes may also be stored in a separate JAR external to the persistence archive, just as they could be in other packaging archive configurations. The external JAR would be referenced by the `persistence.xml` file as a `jar-file` entry with the same rules for specification as described in the other cases. This is neither recommended nor useful, though, since the persistence archive itself is already separated from the other component classes. Seldom will there be a reason to create yet another JAR to store the managed classes, but there may be a case when the other JAR is pre-existing, and you need to reference it because you can't or don't want to put the `persistence.xml` file in the pre-existing JAR.

Persistence archives are actually a very tidy way of packaging a persistence unit. By keeping them self-contained (if they do not reference external JARs of classes using `jar-file` entries), they do not depend on any other components of the application but can sit as a layer underneath those components to be used by them.

Persistence Unit Scope

For simplicity, we have talked about a persistence unit in the singular. The truth is that any number of persistence units may be defined in the same `persistence.xml` file and used in the scope within which they were defined. You saw in the preceding sections, when we discussed how managed classes get included in the persistence unit, that local classes in the same archive will be processed by default. If multiple persistence units are defined in the same `persistence.xml` file, and `exclude-unlisted-classes` is not used on either one, the same classes will be added to all the defined persistence units. This may be a convenient way to import and transform data from one data source to another, simply by reading in entities through one persistence unit and performing the transformation on them before writing them out through another persistence unit.

Now that we have defined and packaged our persistence units, we should outline the rules and ways to use them. There are only a few, but they are important to know.

The first rule is that persistence units are accessible only within the scope of their definition. We have already mentioned this in passing a couple of times, and we hinted at it again in the "Persistence Archive" section. We said that the persistence unit defined within a persistence archive at the EAR level was accessible to all the components in the EAR, and that a persistence unit defined in a persistence archive in a WAR is accessible only to the components defined within that WAR. In fact, in general a persistence unit defined from an EJB JAR is seen by EJB components defined by that EJB JAR, and a persistence unit defined in a WAR will be seen only by the components defined within that WAR. Persistence units defined in a persistence archive that lives in the EAR will be seen by all the components in the application.

The next part is that the names of persistence units must be unique within their scope. For example, there may be only one persistence unit of a given name within the same EJB JAR. Likewise, there may be only one persistence unit of a given name in the same WAR, as well as only one persistence unit of the same name in all the persistence archives at the EAR level. There may be a named persistence unit name in one EJB JAR and another that shares its name in another EJB JAR, or there may even be a persistence unit with the same name in an EJB JAR as there is in a persistence archive. It just means that whenever a persistence unit is referenced either within a `@PersistenceContext`, a `@PersistenceUnit` annotation, or a `createEntityManagerFactory()` method, the most locally scoped one will get used.

A final comment about naming is that just because it's possible to have multiple persistence units with the same name in different component archive namespaces doesn't mean that it is a good idea. As a general rule, you should always give persistence units unique names within the application.

Outside the Server

There are some obvious differences between deploying in a Java EE server and deploying to a Java SE runtime environment. For example, some of the Java EE container services will not be present, and this spills out into the runtime configuration information for a persistence unit. In this section, we will outline the differences to consider when packaging and deploying to a Java SE environment.

Configuring the Persistence Unit

As before, the place to start is the configuration of the persistence unit, which is chiefly in the creation of the `persistence.xml` file. We will outline the differences between creating a `persistence.xml` file for a Java SE application and creating one for a Java EE application.

Transaction Type

When running in a server environment, the transaction-type attribute in the persistence unit defaults to being JTA. The JTA transaction layer was designed for use within the Java EE server and is intended to be fully integrated and coupled to the server components. Given this fact, JPA does not provide support for using JTA outside the server. Some providers may offer this support, but it cannot be portably relied upon, and of course it relies upon the JTA component being present.

The transaction type does not normally need to be specified when deploying to Java SE. It will just default to being RESOURCE_LOCAL, but may be specified explicitly to make the programming contract more clear.

Data Source

When we described configuration in the server, we illustrated how the jta-data-source element denotes the JNDI location of the data source that will be used to obtain connections. We also saw that some servers might even default the data source.

The non-jta-data-source element is used in the server to specify where resource-local connections can be obtained in JNDI. It may also be used by providers that do optimized reading through non-JTA connections.

When configuring for outside the server, not only can we not rely upon JTA, as we described in the transaction type section, but we cannot rely upon JNDI at all. We therefore cannot portably rely upon either of the data source elements in Java SE configurations.

When using resource-local transactions outside the server, the provider obtains database connections directly vended out by the JDBC driver. In order for it to get these connections, it must obtain the driver-specific information, which typically includes the name of the driver class, the URL that the driver uses to connect to the database, and the user and password authentication that the driver also passes to the database. This metadata may be specified in whichever way the provider prefers it to be specified, but all vendors must support the standard JDBC properties in the properties section. Listing 14-15 shows an example of using the standard properties to connect to the Derby database through the Derby driver.

Listing 14-15. Specifiying Resource-Level JDBC Properties

```
<persistence-unit name="EmployeeService">
    ...
    <properties>
        <property name="javax.persistence.jdbc.driver"
            value="org.apache.derby.jdbc.ClientDriver"/>
        <property name="javax.persistence.jdbc.url"
            value="jdbc:derby://localhost:1527/EmpServDB;create=true"/>
        <property name="javax.persistence.jdbc.user"
            value="APP"/>
        <property name="javax.persistence.jdbc.password"
            value="APP"/>
    </properties>
</persistence-unit>
```

Providers

Many servers will have a default or native provider that they will use when the provider is not specified. It will automatically call into that provider to create an EntityManagerFactory at deployment time.

When not in a server, the factory is created programmatically using the Persistence class. When the createEntityManagerFactory() method is invoked, the Persistence class will begin a built-in pluggability protocol that goes out and finds the provider that is specified in the persistence unit configuration. If none was specified, the first one that it finds will be used. Providers export themselves through a service that exists in the provider JAR that must be on the classpath. The net result is that the provider element is not required.

In the majority of cases when only one provider will be on the classpath, the provider will be detected and used by the `Persistence` class to create an `EntityManagerFactory` for a given persistence unit. If you are ever in a situation in which you have two providers on the classpath and you want a particular one to be used, you should specify the provider class in the `provider` element. To prevent runtime and deployment errors, the `provider` element should be used if the application has a code dependency on a specific provider.

Listing the Managed Classes

One of the benefits of deploying inside the server is that it is a highly controlled and structured environment. Because of this, the server can support the deployment process in ways that cannot be achieved by a simple Java SE runtime. The server already has to process all the deployment units in an application and can do things like detecting all the managed persistence classes in an EJB JAR or a persistence archive. This kind of class detection makes persistence archives a very convenient way to bundle a persistence unit.

The problem with this kind of detection outside the server is that the Java SE environment permits all kinds of different class resources to be added to the classpath, including network URLs or any other kind of resource that is acceptable to a classloader. There are no official deployment unit boundaries that the provider is aware of. This makes it difficult for JPA to require providers to support doing automatic detection of the managed classes inside a persistence archive. The official position of the API is that for an application to be portable across all vendors it must explicitly list all the managed classes in the persistence unit using `class` elements. When a persistence unit is large and includes a large number of classes, this task can become rather onerous.

In practice, however, some of the time the classes are sitting in a regular persistence archive JAR on the filesystem, and the provider runtime can do the detection that the server would do in Java EE if it can just determine the JAR to search in. For this reason, many of the major providers actually do support detecting the classes outside the server. This is really kind of an essential usability issue since the maintenance of a class list would be so cumbersome as to be a productivity bottleneck unless you had a tool manage the list for you.

A corollary to the official portability guideline to use `class` elements to enumerate the list of managed classes is that the `exclude-unlisted-classes` element is not guaranteed to have any impact in Java SE persistence units. Some providers may allow this element to be used outside the server, but it is not really very useful in the SE environment anyway given the flexibility of the classpath and packaging allowances in that environment.

Specifying Properties at Runtime

One of the benefits of running outside the server is the ability to specify provider properties at runtime. This is available because of the overloaded `createEntityManagerFactory()` method that accepts a `Map` of properties in addition to the name of the persistence unit. The properties passed to this method are combined with those already specified, normally in the `persistence.xml` file. They may be additional properties or they may override the value of a property that was already specified. This may not seem very useful to some applications, since putting runtime configuration information in code is not normally viewed as being better than isolating it in an XML file. However, one can imagine this being a convenient way to set properties obtained from a program input, such as the command line, as an even more dynamic configuration mechanism. In Listing 14-16 is an example of taking the user and password properties from the command line and passing them to the provider when creating the `EntityManagerFactory`.

Listing 14-16. Using Command-Line Persistence Properties

```
public class EmployeeService {
    public static void main(String[] args) {
        Map props = new HashMap();
        props.put("javax.persistence.jdbc.user", args[0]);
```

```
        props.put("javax.persistence.jdbc.password", args[1]);
        EntityManagerFactory emf = Persistence
            .createEntityManagerFactory("EmployeeService", props);
        // ...
        emf.close();
    }
}
```

System Classpath

In some ways, configuring a persistence unit in a Java SE application is actually easier than configuring in the server because the classpath is simply the system classpath. Adding classes or JARs on the system classpath is a trivial exercise. In the server, we may have to manipulate the manifest classpath or add some vendor-specific application classpath configuration.

Schema Generation

Schema generation used to just refer to the process of taking the mappings in the persistence unit and inferring a possible schema of database tables to support those mappings. However, it now also includes more than simple table generation. Schema generation properties and scripts can now be used to create and/or drop the existing tables, and even cause data to be preloaded into them before running an application.

▪ Note Except where noted, the term "schema generation" refers to the generation of tables for a pre-existing database schema, not necessarily issuing an actual "CREATE SCHEMA" database command.

One of the complaints around schema generation is that you can't specify everything that you need to be able to finely tune the table schemas. This was not accidental. There are too many differences between databases and too many different settings to try to put in options for every database type. If every database-tuning option were exposed through JPA, we would end up duplicating the features of Data Definition Language (DDL) in an API that was not meant to be a database schema generation facility. As we mentioned earlier, the majority of applications find themselves in a meet-in-the-middle mapping scenario in any case, and when they do have control over the schema, the final schema will typically be tuned by a database administrator or someone with the appropriate level of database experience.

▪ Tip Although many of the schema generation annotation elements have been present since JPA 1.0, the specification did not require that providers support generation of tables until JPA 2.1. It was also in JPA 2.1 that the schema generation properties and API methods were introduced.

The Generation Process

There are a number of different aspects of schema generation that can be specified independently or in combination with each other. Before we dive into them we'll go over some of the concepts of schema generation and the basic process so that you can get a feel for what is happening. Then in subsequent sections we will describe the properties and annotations that can be used to produce a desired result.

Schema generation is done by a part of the persistence provider that we'll call the generation processor. This processor is responsible for taking some inputs and generating one or more outputs. The inputs can be either the application domain objects with accompanying mapping metadata (in either annotation or XML form), or pre-existing DDL scripts accessible to the processor (either packaged within the application or referenceable from it). The outputs will be DDL that is either executed in the database by the processor or written out to script files. Figure 14-1 shows a simple view of the processor.

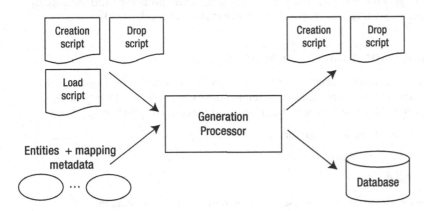

Figure 14-1. *The Generation Processor*

The schema generation process will typically happen either when the application is deployed (for example, when in a container), or when the entity manager factory gets created (on a `Persistence.createEntityManagerFactory()` invocation in Java SE).

There are three distinct operations supported by schema generation. You can create the schema objects, drop the schema (delete the schema objects), or preload data into a schema. Although the create and drop schema operations are specified within the same property, you can also mix and match which operations you want executed. The order in which they will be performed is going to be dictated by what is sensible, though. For example, if all three are specified, the old schema will first be dropped, the new one will be created, and then the data will be preloaded.

To control the inputs and outputs and what occurs during schema generation processing a number of standard properties can be specified either statically in the `persistence.xml` file or dynamically in a runtime call in Java SE to `Persistence.createEntityManagerFactory()` or `Persistence.generateSchema()`. Properties passed in at runtime will override properties defined in the `persistence.xml` file.

Deployment Properties

The standard properties that can be specified in `property` elements in the `persistence.xml` descriptor are listed in the sections below. Vendors may offer additional properties and options that overlap or subsume these, but the options listed here must be supported by all compliant vendors and should be used by applications wishing to remain portable. The properties all fall into one of two categories: generation output and generation input.

■ **Tip** Some of the properties described in this section specify that a URL be supplied as a value either for a script source or a script target location. While the specification does not prescribe any other format, in many cases providers do support the use of a simple file path.

Generation Output

The very presence of one of the first two properties in this category determines that a schema generation operation occurs, either in the database or to scripts. The property value dictates which schema operations are to occur in the targeted location. The properties are not exclusive, meaning that more than one property can be included, causing the schema generation process to generate to multiple targets.

The second two properties (create-target and drop-target) are script output specifier properties and are used in combination with the script action property (`javax.persistence.schema-generation.scripts.action`).

javax.persistence.schema-generation.database.action

This property will cause the schema generation actions specified in the property value to occur in the database. It is the most common and most useful property, and over three quarters of applications will likely be able to get away with specifying just this one property, with a value of `drop-and-create`, for schema generation. The possible values are:

- `none` (default): Do no schema generation in the database.

- `create`: Generate the schema in the database.

- `drop`: Drop the schema from the database.

- `drop-and-create`: Drop the schema from the database and then generate a new schema in the database.

Example:

```
<property name="javax.persistence.schema-generation.database.action"
    value="drop-and-create"/>
```

javax.persistence.schema-generation.scripts.action

This property is used to cause schema generation to generate output scripts. It may be used instead of, or in addition to, the `javax.persistence.schema-generation.database.action` property. The value of the property determines whether a creation script, or dropping script will be generated, or both. The possible values are:

- `none` (default): Generate no scripts.

- `create`: Generate a script to create the schema.

- `drop`: Generate a script to drop the schema.

- `drop-and-create`: Generate a script to drop the schema and a script to create the schema.

Note that there must be corresponding script targets for each value. If the `create` option is specified, then the `javax.persistence.schema-generation.scripts.create-target` property must also be supplied and have a value. If the drop option is specified, then the `javax.persistence.schema-generation.scripts.drop-target` property must be supplied and have a value. If `drop-and-create` is specified, then both properties must be supplied with values.

Example:

```
<property name="javax.persistence.schema-generation.scripts.action"
    value="create"/>
<property name="javax.persistence.schema-generation.scripts.create-target
    value="file:///c:/scripts/create.ddl"/>
```

javax.persistence.schema-generation.scripts.create-target

This property is used to specify the location at which to generate the creation script and is used in conjunction with the `javax.persistence.schema-generation.scripts.action`. The value is a file URL and must specify an absolute path rather than a relative one. Use of this property in a container may be somewhat limited, depending upon the degree of file system access the container allows.

Example:

```
<property name="javax.persistence.schema-generation.scripts.action"
    value="create"/>
<property name="javax.persistence.schema-generation.scripts.create-target"
    value="file:///c:/scripts/create.ddl"/>
```

javax.persistence.schema-generation.scripts.drop-target

This property is used to specify the location at which to generate the dropping script and is used in conjunction with the `javax.persistence.schema-generation.scripts.action`. Similar to the script create-target property, the value of this property is a file URL and must specify an absolute path rather than a relative one. Like the script create-target property, use of this property in a container may be somewhat limited.

Example:

```
<property name="javax.persistence.schema-generation.scripts.action"
    value="drop"/>
<property name="javax.persistence.schema-generation.scripts.drop-target"
    value="file:///c:/scripts/drop.ddl"/>
```

Generation Input

The first two properties in this category specify whether the schema creation and dropping should be generated based upon the mapping metadata, scripts, or both. They are really only useful for the special "both" case of mixing metadata with scripts, though[1].

If the sources are combined, there is the additional option of ordering which happens first, the schema creation from the mapping metadata or the scripts. The option to use both sources is not likely to be a common requirement but can be useful to make specific customizations to a schema mostly generated from the metadata.

The second pair of properties, create-script-source and drop-script-source, can be used to specify the exact scripts to use as the inputs, and the last one, sql-load-script-source, can be used to preload data into the schema. The value of each of these three properties can be a file path relative to the root of the persistence unit or a file URL that is accessible by the persistence provider in whatever environment it is running in.

If an output property is specified, but no input property, the mapping metadata will be used as input.

javax.persistence.schema-generation.create-source

This property determines what input should be considered when generating the DDL to create the schema. The possible values are:

- `metadata`: Generate schema from mapping metadata.
- `script`: Generate schema from existing script.

---

[1] Metadata is the default input, so if metadata is the desired input, it does not need to be specified. If scripts are the desired inputs, then the create-script-source or drop-script-source properties could be specified without the need to specify either the create-source or drop-source.

- `metadata-then-script`: Generate schema from mapping metadata then from an existing script.

- `script-then-metadata`: Generate schema from an existing script then from mapping metadata.

Example:

```
<property name="javax.persistence.schema-generation.create-source"
    value="metadata-then-script"/>
```

javax.persistence.schema-generation.drop-source

This property determines what input should be considered when generating the DDL to drop the schema. The possible values are:

- `metadata`: Generate DDL to drop schema from mapping metadata.

- `script`: Use existing script to get DDL to drop schema script.

- `metadata-then-script`: Generate DDL from mapping metadata, then use an existing script.

- `script-then-metadata`: Use an existing script, then generate DDL from mapping metadata.

Example:

```
<property name="javax.persistence.schema-generation.drop-source"
    value="metadata-then-script"/>
```

javax.persistence.schema-generation.create-script-source

This property specifies a script to use when creating a schema.
Example:

```
<property name="javax.persistence.schema-generation.scripts.create-script-source"
    value="META-INF/createSchema.ddl"/>
```

javax.persistence.schema-generation. drop-script-source

This property specifies a script to use when dropping a schema.
Example:

```
<property name="javax.persistence.schema-generation.scripts.drop-script-source"
    value="META-INF/dropSchema.ddl"/>
```

javax.persistence. sql-load-script-source

This property specifies a script to use when preloading a schema.
Example:

```
<property name="javax.persistence.sql-load-script-source"
    value="META-INF/loadData.ddl"/>
```

Runtime Properties

The deployment properties described in the above section may also be passed in at runtime, but in some cases the property values must be objects instead of the strings that were discussed in the "Deployment Properties" section. Table 14-2 outlines the differences with using the runtime properties instead of deployment properties.

Table 14-2. *Runtime Schema Generation Property Differences*

Property Name	Difference
javax.persistence.schema-generation.create-script-source	java.io.Reader instead of String file path
javax.persistence.schema-generation.drop-script-source	
javax.persistence.sql-load-script-source	
javax.persistence.schema-generation.scripts.create-target	java.io.Writer instead of String file path
javax.persistence.schema-generation.scripts.drop-target	

Mapping Annotations Used by Schema Generation

When we mentioned schema generation in Chapter 4, we promised to go over the mapping annotation elements that are considered when schema generation occurs. In this section, we will make good on that pledge and explain which elements get applied to the generated schema.

A couple of comments are in order before we start into them, though. First, the elements that contain the schema-dependent properties are, with few exceptions, in the physical annotations. This is to try to keep them separate from the logical non-schema-related metadata. Second, these annotations are ignored, for the most part[2], if the schema is not being generated. This is one reason why using them is a little out of place in the usual case, since schema information about the database is of little use once the schema has been created and is being used.

Unique Constraints

A unique constraint can be created on a generated column or join column by using the unique element in the @Column, @JoinColumn, @MapKeyColumn, or @MapKeyJoinColumn annotations. There are not actually very many cases where this will be necessary because most vendors will generate a unique constraint when it is appropriate, such as on the join column of one-to-one relationships. Otherwise, the value of the unique element defaults to false. Listing 14-17 shows an entity with a unique constraint defined for the EMPNAME column.

Listing 14-17. Including Unique Constraints

```
@Entity
public class Employee {
    @Id private int id;
    @Column(name="EMPNAME", unique=true)
    private String name;
    // ...
}
```

---

[2]The exception to this rule may be the optional element of the mapping annotations, which may result in a NON NULL constraint, but which may also be used in memory to indicate that the value is or isn't allowed to be set to null.

Note that the unique element is unnecessary on the identifier column because a primary key constraint will always be generated for the primary key.

A second way of adding a unique constraint is to embed one or more @UniqueConstraint annotations in a uniqueConstraints element in the @Table, @SecondaryTable, @JoinTable, @CollectionTable, or @TableGenerator annotations. Any number of unique constraints may be added to the table definition, including compound constraints. The value passed to the @UniqueConstraint annotation is an array of one or more strings listing the column names that make up the constraint. Listing 14-18 demonstrates how to define a unique constraint as part of a table.

Listing 14-18. Unique Constraints Specified in Table Definition

```
@Entity
@Table(name="EMP",
       uniqueConstraints=@UniqueConstraint(columnNames={"NAME"}))
public class Employee {
    @Id private int id;
    private String name;
    // ...
}
```

Null Constraints

Constraints on a column may also be in the form of null constraints. A null constraint just indicates that the column may or may not be null. It is defined when the column is declared as part of the table.

Null constraints are defined on a column by using the nullable element in the @Column, @JoinColumn, @MapKeyColumn, @MapKeyJoinColumn, or @OrderColumn annotations. A column allows null values by default, so this element really needs to be used only when a value for the field or property is required. Listing 14-19 demonstrates how to set the nullable element of basic and relationship mappings.

Listing 14-19. Null Constraints Specified in Column Definitions

```
@Entity
public class Employee {
    @Id private int id;
    @Column(nullable=false)
    private String name;
    @ManyToOne
    @JoinColumn(nullable=false)
    private Address address;
    // ...
}
```

Indexes

When a primary key is created during sequence generation it will automatically be indexed. However, additional indexes may be generated on a column or sequence of columns in a table by using the indexes element and specifying one or more @Index annotations, each of which specifies an index to add to the table. The indexes element can be specified on the @Table, @SecondaryTable, @JoinTable, @CollectionTable, and @TableGenerator annotations. Listing 14-20 shows an example of adding an index on the "EMPNAME" column during schema generation of the "EMP" table. We named the index, but the provider would name it for us if we did not specify a name.

Note that multiple comma-separated column names can be specified in the `columnNames` string in the case of a multi-column index. An optional ASC or DESC can also be added to the column using the same syntax as in the `@OrderBy` annotation (see Chapter 5). By default they will be assumed to be in ascending order. We can even put an additional uniqueness constraint on the index using the `unique` element.

Listing 14-20. Adding an Index

```
@Entity
@Table(name="EMP",
        indexes={@Index(name="NAME_IDX", columnNames="EMPNAME", unique=true)})
public class Employee {
    @Id private int id;
    @Column(name="EMPNAME")
    private String name;
    // ...
}
```

Foreign Key Constraints

When an entity includes one or more join columns then during schema generation persistence providers may choose to generate foreign key constraints based upon those entity relationships. It is neither prescribed nor advised that they either generate them or not generate them, so different providers may do different things. You can control whether a foreign key constraint gets generated for a join column by using the `foreignKey` element in the `@JoinColumn`, `@PrimaryKeyJoinColumn`, or `@MapKeyJoinColumn` annotations. The `@ForeignKey` annotation is specified in the `foreignKey` element to explicitly set whether the constraint is to be generated, optionally give the constraint a name, and possibly even specify the exact constraint definition to be used. Listing 14-21 shows a join column with a foreign key constraint that includes both the constraint mode of CONSTRAINT and an explicit constraint definition. Note that the constraint is self-referential.

Listing 14-21. Foreign Key Constraint Definition on a Join Column

```
@Entity @Table(name="EMP")
public class Employee {
    @Id private int id;
    private String name;
    @ManyToOne
    @JoinColumn(name="MGR",
            foreignKey=@ForeignKey(
                value=ConstraintMode.CONSTRAINT,
                foreignKeyDefinition="FOREIGN KEY (Mgr) REFERENCES Emp(Id)"))
    private Employee manager;
    // ...
}
```

The `foreignKey` element may also be used in an annotation that includes a group of join columns. For example, the `value` element of `@JoinColumns` is an array of `@JoinColumn`, but if the `foreignKey` element is specified in `@JoinColumns`, it will apply to all of the join columns together. It would be unspecified to include both a `foreignKey` element in `@JoinColumns` as well as a `foreignKey` element in one or more of the embedded `@JoinColumn` annotations. Similar behavior would apply for the `value` elements of the `@PrimaryKeyJoinColumns` and `@MapKeyJoinColumns` annotations, for the `joinColumns` elements of `@AssociationOverride`, `@CollectionTable`, and `@JoinTable`, and the `pkJoinColumns` element of `@SecondaryTable`. Listing 14-22 shows how to enforce that the provider not generate foreign key constraints for the secondary table primary key join columns (that in this case are using the default names).

Listing 14-22. Disabling Foreign Key Constraints Added on a Secondary Table

```
@Entity @Table(name="EMP")
@SecondaryTable(name="EMP_REC",
                foreignKey=@ForeignKey(ConstraintMode.NO_CONSTRAINT))
public class Employee {
    @Id private int id;
    private String name;
    //...
}
```

Note that the @JoinTable annotation has an additional inverseForeignKey element that applies a @ForeignKey annotation to the join columns in its inverseJoinColumns element.

String-Based Columns

When no length is specified for a column that is being generated to store string values, the length will be defaulted to 255. When a column is generated for a basic mapping of a field or property of type String, char[], or Character[], its length should be explicitly listed in the length element of the @Column annotation if 255 is not the desired maximum length. Listing 14-23 shows an entity with explicitly specified lengths for strings.

Listing 14-23. Specifying the Length of Character-Based Column Types

```
@Entity
public class Employee {
    @Id
    @Column(length=40)
    private String name;
    @ManyToOne
    @JoinColumn(name="MGR")
    private Employee manager;
    // ...
}
```

You can see from the previous example that there is no similar length element in the @JoinColumn annotation. When primary keys are string-based, the provider may set the join column length to the same length as the primary key column in the table that is being joined to. This is not required to be supported, however.

It is not defined for length to be used for large objects; some databases do not require or even allow the length of lobs to be specified.

Floating Point Columns

Columns containing floating point types have a precision and scale associated with them. The precision is just the number of digits that are used to represent the value, and the scale is the number of digits after the decimal point. These two values may be specified as precision and scale elements in the @Column annotation when mapping a floating point type. Like other schema generation elements, they have no effect on the entity at runtime. Listing 14-24 demonstrates how to set these values.

Listing 14-24. Specifying the Precision and Scale of Floating Point Column Types

```
@Entity
public class PartTimeEmployee {
    // ...
    @Column(precision=8, scale=2)
    private float hourlyRate;
    // ...
}
```

■ **Tip** Precision may be defined differently for different databases. In some databases and for some floating point types it is the number of binary digits, while for others it is the number of decimal digits.

Defining the Column

There may be a time when you are happy with all the generated columns except for one. The type of the column isn't what you want it to be, and you don't want to go through the trouble of manually generating the schema for the sake of one column. This is one instance when the columnDefinition element comes in handy. By hand-rolling the DDL for the column, we can include it as the column definition and let the provider use it to define the column.

The columnDefinition element is available in all the column-oriented annotation types, including @Column, @JoinColumn, @PrimaryKeyJoinColumn, @MapKeyColumn, @MapKeyJoinColumn, @OrderColumn, and @DiscriminatorColumn. Whenever a column is to be generated, the columnDefinition element may be used to indicate the DDL string that should be used to generate the type (not including the trailing comma). This gives the user complete control over what is generated in the table for the column being mapped. It also allows a database-specific type or format to be used that may supersede the generated type offered by the provider for the database being used.[3] Listing 14-25 shows some definitions specified for two columns and a join column.

Listing 14-25. Using a Column Definition to Control DDL Generation

```
@Entity
public class Employee {
    @Id
    @Column(columnDefinition="NVARCHAR2(40)")
    private String name;
    @Column(name="START_DATE",
            columnDefinition="DATE DEFAULT SYSDATE")
    private java.sql.Date startDate;
    @ManyToOne
    @JoinColumn(name="MGR", columnDefinition="NVARCHAR2(40)")
    private Employee manager;
    // ...
}
```

In this example, we are using a Unicode character field for the primary key and then also for the join column that refers to the primary key. We also define the date to be assigned the default current date at the time the record was inserted (in case it was not specified).

---

[3]The resulting column must be supported by the provider runtime to enable reading from and writing to the column.

Specifying the column definition is quite a powerful schema generation practice that allows overriding of the generated column to an application-defined custom column definition. But the power is accompanied by some risk as well. When a column definition is included, other accompanying column-specific generation metadata is ignored. Specifying the precision, scale, or length in the same annotation as a column definition would be both unnecessary and confusing.

Not only does using `columnDefinition` in your code bind you to a particular schema but it also binds you to a particular database since the DDL tends to be database-specific. This is just a flexibility/portability trade-off, and you have to decide whether it is appropriate for your application.

Summary

It is a simple exercise to package and deploy persistence applications using the Java Persistence API. In most cases, it is just a matter of adding a very short `persistence.xml` file to the JAR containing the entity classes.

In this chapter, we described how to configure the persistence unit in the Java EE server environment using the `persistence.xml` file and how in some cases the name may be the only setting required. We then explained when to apply and how to specify the transaction type, the persistence provider, and the data source. We showed how to use and specify the default `orm.xml` mapping file and then went on to use additional mapping files within the same persistence unit. We also discussed the various ways that classes may be included in the persistence unit and how to customize the persistence unit using standard and vendor-specific properties.

We looked at the ways that persistence units may be packaged and deployed to a Java EE application as part of an EJB archive, a web archive, or a persistence archive that is accessible to all the components in the application. We examined how persistence units may exist within different scopes of a deployed Java EE application and what the name-scoping rules were. We then compared the configuration and deployment practices of deploying an application to a Java SE environment.

Finally, we showed how a schema can be generated in the database to match the requirements of the persistence unit using either scripts or the domain model and the mapping metadata. We cautioned against using the generated schema for production systems, but showed how it can be used during development, prototyping, and testing to get up and running quickly and conveniently.

In the next chapter, we will consider the accepted and best practices for testing applications that use persistence.

CHAPTER 15

Testing

One of the major selling points of JPA has been the drive toward better testability. The use of plain Java classes and the ability to use persistence outside of the application server has made enterprise applications much easier to test. This chapter will cover unit testing and integration testing with entities, with a mix of modern and traditional test techniques.

Testing Enterprise Applications

Testing is generally accepted as being a good thing, but how exactly should we go about doing it? Almost all enterprise applications are hosted in some kind of server environment, whether it is a servlet container like Apache Tomcat or a full Java EE application server. Once deployed to such an environment, the developer is much more isolated from the application than if he was developing in a Java SE runtime environment. At this point, it can be tested only using the public interface of the application, such as a browser using HTTP, web service, RMI, or a messaging interface.

This presents an issue for developers because to do unit testing we want to be able to focus on the components of an application in isolation. An elaborate sequence of operations through a web site may be required to access a single method of a bean that implements a particular business service. For example, to view an Employee record, a test client might have to log in using a user name and password, traverse several menu options, execute a search, and then finally access the record. Afterward, the HTML output of the report must be verified to ensure that the operation completed as expected. In some applications, this procedure may be short-circuited by directly accessing the URL that retrieves a particular record. But with more and more information cached in HTTP session state, URLs are beginning to look like random sequences of letters and numbers. Getting direct access to a particular feature of an application may not be easy to achieve.

Java SE clients (so called "fat" clients) that communicate with databases and other resources suffer from the same problem despite their ability to execute the program without the need for an application server. The user interface of a Java SE client may well be a Swing application requiring special tools to drive it in order to do any kind of test automation. The application is still just a black box without any obvious way to get inside.

Numerous attempts have been made to expose the internals of an application to testing while deployed on a server. One of the first was the Cactus[1] framework, which allows developers to write tests using JUnit, which are then deployed to the server along with the application and executed via a web interface provided by Cactus. Other frameworks adopted a similar approach using RMI instead of a web interface to control the tests remotely. Currently, a framework called Arquillian[2] has started to gain some popularity and uses a related approach. We will briefly discuss Arquillian at the end of the chapter.

Although effective, the downside to these approaches is that the application server still has to be up and running before we can attempt any kind of testing. For developers who use test-driven development (TDD), in which tests are

---

[1]Visit http://jakarta.apache.org/cactus/ for more information.
[2]http://arquillian.org

written before code and the full unit test suite is executed after every development iteration (which can be as small as a change to a single method), any kind of interaction with the application server is a bit of a problem. Even for developers who practice a more traditional testing methodology, frequent test execution is hampered by the need to keep the application server running, with a packaging and deployment step before every test run.

Clearly, for developers who want to break a Java EE application into its component parts and test those components in isolation, there is a need for tools that will let us directly execute portions of the application outside of the server environment in which it is normally hosted.

Terminology

Not everyone agrees about exactly what constitutes a unit test or an integration test. In fact, it is quite likely that any survey of a group of developers will yield a wide variety of results, some similar in nature while others venture into completely different areas of testing. Therefore we feel it is important to define our terminology for testing so that you can translate it into whatever terms you are comfortable with.

We see tests falling into the following four categories:

- *Unit tests:* Unit tests are written by developers and focus on isolated components of an application. Depending on your approach, this may be a single class or a collection of classes. The only key defining elements in our opinion are that the unit test is not coupled to any server resources (these are typically stubbed out as part of the test process) and executes very quickly. It must be possible to execute an entire suite of unit tests from within an IDE and get the results in a matter of seconds. Unit test execution can be automated and is often configured to happen automatically as part of every merge to a configuration management system.

- *Integration tests:* Integration tests are also written by developers and focus on use cases within an application. They are still typically decoupled from the application server, but the difference between a unit test and an integration test is that the integration test makes full use of external resources such as a database. In effect, an integration test takes a component from an application and runs in isolation as if it were still inside the application server. Running the test locally makes it much faster than a test hosted in an application server, but still slower than a unit test. Integration tests are also automated and often run at least daily to ensure that there are no regressions introduced by developers.

- *Functional tests:* Functional tests are the black box tests written and automated by quality engineers instead of developers. Quality engineers look at the functional specification for a product and its user interface, and seek to automate tests that can verify product behavior without understanding (or caring) how it is implemented. Functional tests are a critical part of the application development process, but it is unrealistic to execute these tests as part of the day-to-day work done by a developer. Automated execution of these tests often takes place on a different schedule, independent of the regular development process.

- *Acceptance tests:* Acceptance tests are customer-driven. These tests, usually conducted manually, are carried out directly by customers or representatives who play the role of the customer. The goal of an acceptance test is to verify that the requirements set out by the customer are fulfilled in the user interface and behavior of the application.

In this chapter, we will focus only on unit tests and integration tests. These tests are written by developers for the benefit of developers and constitute what is called white box testing. These tests are written with the full understanding of how the application is implemented and what it will take not only to test the successful path through an application but also to trigger failure scenarios.

Testing Outside the Server

The common element between unit tests and integration tests is that they are executed without the need for an application server. Unfortunately for Java EE developers, this has traditionally been very difficult. Applications developed before the Java EE 5 release are tightly coupled to the application server, often making it difficult and counterproductive to attempt replicating the required container services in a stand-alone environment.

To put this in perspective, let's look at Enterprise JavaBeans as they existed in EJB 2.1. On paper, testing a session bean class should be little more than a case of instantiating the bean class and invoking the business method. For trivial business methods, this is indeed the case, but things start to go downhill quickly once dependencies get involved. For example, let's consider a business method that needs to invoke another business method from a different session bean.

Dependency lookup was the only option in EJB 2.1, so if the business method has to access JNDI to obtain a reference to the other session bean, either JNDI must be worked around or the bean class must be refactored so that the lookup code can be replaced with a test-specific version. If the code uses the Service Locator[3] pattern, we have a bigger problem because a singleton static method is used to obtain the bean reference. The only solution for testing beans that use Service Locators outside the container is to refactor the bean classes so that the locator logic can be overridden in a test case.

Next we have the problem of the dependent bean itself. The bean class does not implement the business interface, so it cannot simply be instantiated and made available to the bean we are trying to test. Instead, it will have to be subclassed to implement the business interface, and stubs for a number of low-level EJB methods will have to be provided because the business interface in EJB 2.1 actually extends an interface that is implemented internally by the application server.

Even if we get that to work, what happens if we encounter a container-managed entity bean? Not only do we have the same issues with respect to the interfaces involved but the bean class is also abstract, with all the persistent state properties unimplemented. We could implement them, but our test framework would rapidly start to outgrow the application code. We can't even just run them against the database as we can with JDBC code because so much of the entity bean logic, relationship maintenance, and other persistence operations are available only inside an EJB container.

The dirty secret of many applications written using older versions of Java EE is that there is little to no developer testing at all. Developers write, package, and deploy applications; test them manually through the user interface; and then hope that the quality assurance group can write a functional test that verifies each feature. It's just too much work to test individual components outside of the application server.

This is where EJB, CDI, and JPA come in. In later versions of EJB, a session bean class is a simple Java class for local beans. No special EJB interfaces need to be extended or implemented. Likewise with CDI beans. To unit test the logic in a session or CDI bean, we can often just instantiate it and execute it. If the bean depends on another bean, we can instantiate that bean and manually inject it into the bean being tested. If you are testing code that uses the entity manager and want to verify that it is interacting with the database the way you expect it to, just bootstrap the entity manager in Java SE and make full use of the entity manager outside of the application server.

In this chapter, we will demonstrate how to take a bean and JPA code from a Java EE application and run it outside the container using unit testing and integration testing approaches. It is much easier than it was in the past.

JUnit

The JUnit test framework is a de facto standard for testing Java applications. JUnit is a simple unit testing framework that allows tests to be written as Java classes. These Java classes are then bundled together and run in suites using a test runner that is itself a simple Java class. Out of this simple design a whole community has emerged to provide extensions to JUnit and integrate it into all major development environments.

---

[3] Alur, Deepak, John Crupi, and Dan Malks. *Core J2EE Patterns: Best Practices and Design Strategies, Second Edition*. Upper Saddle River, N.J.: Prentice Hall PTR, 2003, p. 315.

Despite its name, unit testing is only one of the many things that JUnit can be used for. It has been extended to support testing of web sites, automatic stubbing of interfaces for testing, concurrency testing, and performance testing. Many quality assurance groups now use JUnit as part of the automation mechanism to run whole suites of end-to-end functional tests.

For our purposes, we will look at JUnit in the context of its unit testing roots, and also at strategies that allow it to be used as an effective integration test framework. Collectively we look at these two approaches simply as developer tests because they are written by developers to assist with the overall quality and development of an application.

We will assume that you are familiar with JUnit 4 (which makes use of annotations) at this point. Introductory articles and tutorials can be found on the JUnit web site at www.junit.org. Many books and other online resources cover testing with JUnit in extensive detail.

Unit Testing

It might seem counterintuitive at first, but one of the most interesting things about entities is that they can participate in tests without requiring a running application server or live database. In the following sections, we will look at testing entity classes directly and using entities as part of tests for Java EE components. We will also discuss how to leverage dependency injection in unit tests and how to deal with the presence of JPA interfaces.

Testing Entities

Entities are unlikely to be extensively tested in isolation. Most methods on entities are simple getters or setters that relate to the persistent state of the entity or to its relationships. Business methods may also appear on entities, but are less common. In many applications, entities are little more than basic JavaBeans.

As a rule, property methods do not generally require explicit tests. Verifying that a setter assigns a value to a field and the corresponding getter retrieves the same value is not testing the application so much as the compiler. Unless there is a side effect in one or both of the methods, getters and setters are too simple to break and therefore too simple to warrant testing.

Key things to look for in determining whether or not an entity warrants individual testing are side effects from a getter or setter method (such as data transformation or validation rules) and the presence of business methods. The entity shown in Listing 15-1 contains nontrivial logic that warrants specific testing.

Listing 15-1. An Entity that Validates and Transforms Data

```
@Entity
public class Department {
    @Id private String id;
    private String name;
    @OneToMany(mappedBy="department")
    private Collection<Employee> employees;

    public String getId() { return id; }
    public void setId(String id) {
        if (id.length() != 4) {
            throw new IllegalArgumentException(
                "Department identifiers must be four characters in length");
        }
        this.id = id.toUpperCase();
    }

    // ...
}
```

The setId() method both validates the format of the department identifier and transforms the string to uppercase. This type of logic and the fact that setting the identifier can actually cause an exception to be thrown suggests that tests would be worthwhile. Testing this behavior is simply a matter of instantiating the entity and invoking the setter with different values. Listing 15-2 shows one possible set of tests.

Listing 15-2. Testing a Setter Method for Side Effects

```java
public class DepartmentTest {

    @Test
    public void testValidDepartmentId() throws Exception {
        Department dept = new Department();
        dept.setId("NA65");
        Assert.assertEquals("NA65", dept.getId());
    }

    @Test
    public void testDepartmentIdInvalidLength() throws Exception {
        Department dept = new Department();
        try {
            dept.setId("NA6");
            Assert.fail("Department identifiers must be four characters");
        } catch (IllegalArgumentException e) {
        }
    }

    @Test
    public void testDepartmentIdCase() throws Exception {
        Department dept = new Department();
        dept.setId("na65");
        Assert.assertEquals("NA65", dept.getId());
    }
}
```

Testing Entities in Components

The most likely test candidate for entities is not the entity but the application code that uses the entity as part of its business logic. For most applications this means testing session beans, managed beans, CDI beans, Spring beans, or whatever flavor of enterprise component you are using. If the entities are obtained or initialized outside the scope of the component, testing is made easy in the sense that the entity class can simply be instantiated, populated with entity data and set into the bean class for testing. When used as a domain object in application code, an entity is no different from any other Java class. You can effectively pretend that it's not an entity at all.

Of course, there is more to unit testing a bean than simply instantiating entities to be used with a business method. We also need to be concerned with the dependencies that the bean has in order to implement its business logic. These dependencies are usually manifested as fields on the bean class that are populated using a form of dependency injection (or in some cases dependency lookup).

When writing unit tests, the goal is to introduce the minimum set of dependencies required to implement a particular test. If you are testing a business method that needs to invoke a method on a separate interface, you should worry only about providing a stubbed version of the interface. If the bean uses a data source but is not relevant to your testing, then ideally you want to ignore it entirely.

Dependency injection is the key to effective unit testing. By removing such things as the JNDI API from bean code and eliminating the need for the Service Locator pattern, you can ensure that the bean class has few dependencies on the container. You need only instantiate the bean instance and manually inject the required resources, the majority of which will be either other beans from the application or test-specific implementations of a standard interface.

As we explained in Chapter 3, the setter injection form of dependency injection is the easiest to use in unit tests. Because the setter methods are almost always public, they can be invoked directly by the test case to assign a dependency to the bean class. Field injection is still easy to deal with, so long as the field uses package scope because the convention for unit tests is to use the same package name as the class that is being tested.

When the dependency is another bean, you must make a choice about whether all the dependencies of the required bean class must be met or whether a test-specific version of the bean should be used instead. If the business method from the dependent bean does not affect the outcome of the test, it may not be worth the effort to establish the full dependency. As an example, consider the bean shown in Listing 15-3. We have shown a single method for calculating years of service for an employee that retrieves an Employee instance using the EmployeeService session bean.

Listing 15-3. Using the EmployeeService Bean in a Different Business Method

```
@Stateless
public class VacationBean {
    public static final long MILLIS_PER_YEAR = 1000 * 60 * 60 * 24 * 365;
    @EJB EmployeeService empService;

    public int getYearsOfService(int empId) {
        Employee emp = empService.findEmployee(empId);
        long current = System.currentTimeMillis();
        long start = emp.getStartDate().getTime();
        return (int)((current - start) / MILLIS_PER_YEAR);
    }

    // ...
}
```

Because the only thing necessary to verify the getYearsOfService() method is a single Employee instance with a start date value, there might not be a need to use the real EmployeeService bean, particularly if it has external dependencies of its own that might make it hard to instantiate. A simple subclass of the EmployeeService class that returns an entity instance preconfigured for the test is more than sufficient. In fact, the ability to specify a well-known return value from the findEmployee() method makes the overall test much easier to implement. Listing 15-4 demonstrates using a test-specific subclass implementation of a bean. The implementation is defined as an anonymous inner class in the test class. Creating an implementation specifically for a test is called mocking the class, and the instantiated instance is referred to as a mock object.

Listing 15-4. Creating a Test-Specific Implementation of a Bean

```
public class VacationBeanTest {
    @Test
    public void testYearsOfService() throws Exception {
        VacationBean bean = new VacationBean();
        bean.empService = new EmployeeService() {
            public Employee findEmployee(int id) {
                Employee emp = new Employee();
```

```
            emp.setStartDate(new Time(System.currentTimeMillis() -
                                   VacationBean.MILLIS_PER_YEAR * 5));
            return emp;
        }

        // ...
    };
    int yearsOfService = bean.getYearsOfService(0);
    Assert.assertEquals(5, yearsOfService);
}

// ...
}
```

The Entity Manager in Unit Tests

The EntityManager and Query interfaces present a challenge to developers writing unit tests. Code that interacts with the entity manager can vary from the simple (persisting an object) to the complex (issuing a JP QL query and obtaining the results). There are two basic approaches to dealing with the presence of standard interfaces:

- Introduce a subclass that replaces methods containing entity manager or query operations with test-specific versions that do not interact with JPA.

- Provide custom implementations of standard interfaces that may be predictably used for testing.

Before covering these strategies in detail, consider the session bean implementation shown in Listing 15-5 that provides a simple authentication service. For such a simple class, it is surprisingly challenging to unit test. The entity manager operations are embedded directly within the authenticate() method, coupling the implementation to JPA.

Listing 15-5. Session Bean that Performs Basic Authentication

```
@Stateless
public class UserService {
    @PersistenceContext(unitName="EmployeeService")
    EntityManager em;

    public User authenticate(String userId, String password) {
        User user = em.find(User.class, userId);
        if (user != null) {
            if (password.equals(user.getPassword())) {
                return user;
            }
        }
        return null;
    }
}
```

The first technique we will demonstrate to make this class testable is to introduce a subclass that eliminates entity manager calls. For the UserService example shown in Listing 15-5, entity manager access must first be isolated to a separate method before it can be tested. Listing 15-6 demonstrates such a refactoring.

Listing 15-6. Isolating Entity Manager Operations for Testing

```
@Stateless
public class UserService {
    @PersistenceContext(unitName="EmployeeService")
    EntityManager em;

    public User authenticate(String userId, String password) {
        User user = findUser(userId);
        // ...
    }

    User findUser(String userId) {
        return em.find(User.class, userId);
    }
}
```

With this refactoring complete, the `authenticate()` method no longer has any direct dependency on the entity manager. The `UserService` class can now be subclassed for testing, replacing the `findUser()` method with a test-specific version that returns a well-known result. Listing 15-7 demonstrates a complete test case using this technique.

Listing 15-7. Using a Subclass to Eliminate Entity Manager Dependencies

```
public class UserServiceTest {
    static final String USER_ID = "test_id";
    static final String PASSWORD = "test_password";
    static final String INVALID_USER_ID = "test_user";

    @Test
    public void testAuthenticateValidUser() throws Exception {
        MockUserService service = new MockUserService();
        User user = service.authenticate(USER_ID, PASSWORD);
        Assert.assertNotNull(user);
        Assert.assertEquals(USER_ID, user.getName());
        Assert.assertEquals(PASSWORD, user.getPassword());
    }

    @Test
    public void testAuthenticateInvalidUser() throws Exception {
        MockUserService service = new MockUserService();
        User user = service.authenticate(INVALID_USER_ID, PASSWORD);
        Assert.assertNull(user);
    }

    class MockUserService extends UserService {
        private User user;

        public MockUserService() {
            user = new User();
            user.setName(USER_ID);
            user.setPassword(PASSWORD);
        }
```

```
        User findUser(String userId) {
            if (userId.equals(user.getName())) {
                return user;
            }
            return null;
        }
    }
}
```

This test case has the advantage of leaving the original authenticate() method implementation intact, only overriding the findUser() method for the test. This works well for classes that have been refactored to isolate persistence operations, but these changes cannot always be made. The alternative is to mock the EntityManager interface. Listing 15-8 demonstrates this approach.

Listing 15-8. Using a Mock Entity Manager in a Unit Test

```
public class UserServiceTest2 {
    static final String USER_ID = "test_id";
    static final String PASSWORD = "test_password";
    static final String INVALID_USER_ID = "test_user";

    @Test
    public void testAuthenticateValidUser() throws Exception {
        UserService service = new UserService();
        service.em = new TestEntityManager(USER_ID, PASSWORD);
        User user = service.authenticate(USER_ID, PASSWORD);
        Assert.assertNotNull(user);
        Assert.assertEquals(USER_ID, user.getName());
        Assert.assertEquals(PASSWORD, user.getPassword());
    }

    @Test
    public void testAuthenticateInvalidUser() throws Exception {
        UserService service = new UserService();
        service.em = new TestEntityManager(USER_ID, PASSWORD);
        User user = service.authenticate(INVALID_USER_ID, PASSWORD);
        Assert.assertNull(user);
    }

    class TestEntityManager extends MockEntityManager {
        private User user;

        public TestEntityManager(String user, String password) {
            this.user = new User();
            this.user.setName(user);
            this.user.setPassword(password);
        }
```

```
        public <T> T find(Class<T> entityClass, Object pk) {
            if (entityClass == User.class && ((String)pk).equals(user.getName())) {
                return (T) user;
            }
            return null;
        }
    }
}
```

The advantage of this approach over subclassing is that it leaves the original bean class unchanged while allowing it to be unit tested. The MockEntityManager class referenced in the test is a concrete implementation of the EntityManager interface with empty method definitions. All methods that return a value return null or an equivalent instead. By defining it separately, it can be reused for other test cases. Many unit test suites contain a small set of mocked interfaces that can be reused across multiple tests.

■ **TIP**   Check out www.mockobjects.com for further information on mock object techniques and open source tools to assist with mock object creation.

Integration Testing

Integration testing, for our purposes, is an extension of unit testing that takes components of a Java EE application and executes them outside of an application server. Unlike unit testing, in which we went to great lengths to avoid the entity manager, in integration testing we embrace it and leverage the fact that it can be used in Java SE.

The following sections explore using JPA outside of an application server in order to test application logic with a live database, but without starting the application server. To better approximate the runtime environment, the same provider should be used for testing as is used in production.

Using the Entity Manager

In Listing 15-5, we demonstrated a bean that performed basic authentication against a User object retrieved from the database. To unit test this class, a number of techniques were presented to replace or mock the entity manager operation. The downside to this approach is that the test code required to work around external dependencies in the application code can quickly reach a point where it is difficult to maintain and is a potential source of bugs.

Instead of mocking the entity manager, a resource-local, application-managed entity manager may be used to perform tests against a live database. Listing 15-9 demonstrates a functional test version of the UserService test cases.

Listing 15-9. Integration Test for UserService Bean

```
public class UserServiceTest3 {
    static final String USER_ID = "test_id";
    static final String PASSWORD = "test_password";
    static final String INVALID_USER_ID = "test_user";

    private EntityManagerFactory emf;
    private EntityManager em;

    @Before
    public void setUp() {
```

```
        emf = Persistence.createEntityManagerFactory("hr");
        em = emf.createEntityManager();
        createTestData();
    }

    @After
    public void tearDown() {
        if (em != null) {
            removeTestData();
            em.close();
        }
        if (emf != null) {
            emf.close();
        }
    }

    private void createTestData() {
        User user = new User();
        user.setName(USER_ID);
        user.setPassword(PASSWORD);
        em.getTransaction().begin();
        em.persist(user);
        em.getTransaction().commit();
    }

    private void removeTestData() {
        em.getTransaction().begin();
        User user = em.find(User.class, USER_ID);
        if (user != null) {
            em.remove(user);
        }
        em.getTransaction().commit();
    }

    @Test
    public void testAuthenticateValidUser() throws Exception {
        UserService service = new UserService();
        service.em = em;
        User user = service.authenticate(USER_ID, PASSWORD);
        Assert.assertNotNull(user);
        Assert.assertEquals(USER_ID, user.getName());
        Assert.assertEquals(PASSWORD, user.getPassword());
    }
    @Test
    public void testAuthenticateInvalidUser() throws Exception {
        UserService service = new UserService();
        service.em = em;
        User user = service.authenticate(INVALID_USER_ID, PASSWORD);
        Assert.assertNull(user);
    }
}
```

This test case uses the fixture methods `setUp()` and `tearDown()` to create `EntityManagerFactory` and `EntityManager` instances using the Java SE bootstrap API and then closes them when the test completes. The test case also uses these methods to seed the database with test data and remove it when the test completes. The `tearDown()` method is guaranteed to be called even if a test fails due to an exception. Like any JPA application in the Java SE environment, a `persistence.xml` file will need to be on the classpath in order for the `Persistence` class to bootstrap an entity manager factory. The file must contain the JDBC connection properties to connect to the database, and if the managed classes were not already listed, `class` elements would also need to be added for each managed class. If the transaction type was not specified, it will be defaulted to the correct transaction type according to the environment; otherwise, it should be set to `RESOURCE_LOCAL`. This example demonstrates the basic pattern for all integration tests that use an entity manager.

The advantage of this style of test versus a unit test is that no effort was required to mock up persistence interfaces. Emulating the entity manager and query engine in order to test code that interacts directly with these interfaces suffers from diminishing returns as more and more effort is put into preparing a test environment instead of writing tests. In the worst-case scenario, incorrect test results occur because of bugs in the test harness, not in the application code. Given the ease with which JPA can be used outside the application server, this type of effort may be better spent establishing a simple database test environment and writing automated functional tests.

However, despite the opportunity that testing outside the application server presents, care must be taken to ensure that such testing truly adds value. Quite often, developers fall into the trap of writing tests that do little more than test vendor functionality as opposed to true application logic. An example of this mistake is seeding a database, executing a query, and verifying that the desired results are returned. It sounds valid at first, but all that it tests is the developer's understanding of how to write a query. Unless there is a bug in the database or the persistence provider, the test will never fail. A more valid variation of this test would be to start the scenario farther up the application stack by executing a business method on a session façade that initiates a query and then validating that the resulting transfer objects are formed correctly for later presentation by a JSP page.

Test Setup and Teardown

Many tests involving persistence require some kind of test data in the database before the test can be executed. If the business operation does not create and verify the result of a persistence operation, the database must already contain data that can be read and used by the test. Because tests should ideally be able to set and reset their own test data before and after each test, we must have a way to seed the database appropriately.

This sounds pretty straightforward; use JDBC to seed the database during `setUp()` and again during `tearDown()` to reset it. But there is a danger here. Most persistence providers employ some kind of data or object caching. Any time data changes in the database without the persistence provider knowing about it, its cache will get out of sync with the database. In the worst-case scenario, this could cause entity manager operations to return entities that have since been removed or that have stale data.

It's worth reiterating that this is not a problem with the persistence provider. Caching is a good thing and the reason why JPA solutions often significantly outperform direct JDBC access in read-mostly applications. The Reference Implementation, for example, uses a sophisticated shared-cache mechanism that is scoped to the entire persistence unit. When operations are completed in a particular persistence context, the results are merged back into the shared cache so that they can be used by other persistence contexts. This happens whether the entity manager and persistence context are created in Java SE or Java EE. Therefore, you can't assume that closing an entity manager clears test data from the cache.

There are several approaches we can use to keep the cache consistent with our test database. The first, and easiest, is to create and remove test data using the entity manager. Any entity persisted or removed using the entity manager will always be kept consistent with the cache. For small data sets, this is very easy to accomplish. This is the approach we used in Listing 15-9.

For larger data sets, however, it can be cumbersome to create and manage test data using entities. JUnit extensions such as DbUnit[4] allow seed data to be defined in XML files and then loaded in bulk to the database before each test begins. So given that the persistence provider won't know about this data, how can we still make use of it? The first strategy is to establish a set of test data that is read-only. As long as the data is never changed, it doesn't matter whether the entity exists in the provider cache or not. The second strategy is to either use special data sets for operations that need to modify test data without creating it or to ensure that these changes are never permanently committed. If the transaction to update the database is rolled back, the database and cache state will both remain consistent.

Another option is to use the `javax.persistence.sql-load-script-source` property described in Chapter 14. Creating a script and letting the provider execute it on startup is a simple way to pre-load the database. However, because it is a persistence unit level property it will only occur once at persistence unit startup time, making it less practical to do on a test-by-test basis.

The last thing to consider is explicit cache invalidation. Prior to JPA 2.0, access to the second-level cache was vendor-specific. As discussed in Chapter 12, we can now use the `Cache` interface to explicitly clear the second-level cache between tests. The following method demonstrates how to invalidate the entire second-level cache given any `EntityManagerFactory` instance:

```
public static void clearCache(EntityManagerFactory emf) {
    emf.getCache().evictAll();
}
```

If there are any open entity managers, the `clear()` operation on each should be invoked as well. As we have discussed before, the persistence context is a localized set of transactional changes. It uses data from the shared cache but is actually a separate and distinct data structure.

Switching Configurations for Testing

One of the advantages of JPA is that metadata specified in annotation form may be overridden or replaced by metadata specified in XML form. This affords us a unique opportunity to develop an application targeting the production database platform and then provide an alternate set of mappings (even query definitions) targeted to a test environment. While this is a common practice and has its benefits, it's worth noting that if you are running on a test database with alternate mappings and query definitions, there will clearly be at least some differences between the test installation and running in production. Production testing is always going to be necessary, but testing earlier in the cycle on a test database can be done on a more convenient or more accessible database platform and can catch some bugs earlier in the cycle.

In the context of testing, the Java SE bootstrap mechanism will use the `persistence.xml` file located in the `META-INF` directory on the classpath. As long as the persistence unit definition inside this file has the same name as the one the application was written to, the test version can retarget it as necessary to suit the needs of the integration test.

There are two main uses for this approach. The first is to specify properties in the `persistence.xml` file that are specific to testing. For many developers, this will mean providing JDBC connection information to a local database so that tests do not collide with other developers on a shared database.

The second major use of a custom `persistence.xml` file is to customize the database mappings for deployment on a completely different database platform. For example, if Oracle is your production database and you don't want to run the full database on your local machine, you can adjust the mapping information to target an embedded database such as Apache Derby.

---

[4]Visit `http://dbunit.sourceforge.net/` for more information.

■ **Note** At the risk of sounding somewhat biased, might we humbly suggest Oracle XE. It represents the power of the Oracle database conveniently sized to an individual machine at no cost. Many of the examples in this book (including the advanced SQL query examples) were developed on Oracle XE.

As an example of when this would be necessary, consider an application that uses the native sequencing of the Oracle database. Derby does not have an equivalent, so table generators must be used instead. First, let's consider an example entity that uses a native sequence generator:

```
@Entity
public class Phone {
    @SequenceGenerator(name="Phone_Gen", sequenceName="PHONE_SEQ")
    @Id @GeneratedValue(generator="Phone_Gen")
    private int id;
    // ...
}
```

The first step to get this entity working on Derby is to create an XML mapping file that overrides the definition of the "Phone_Gen" generator to use a table generator. The following fragment of a mapping file demonstrates how to replace the sequence generator with a table generator:

```
<entity-mappings>
    ...
    <table-generator name="Phone_Gen", table="ID_GEN",
                     pk-column-value="PhoneId">
    ...
</entity-mappings>
```

This is the same technique we applied in Chapter 13 when we discussed overriding a sequence generator.

Finally, we need to create a new persistence.xml file that references this mapping file. If the overrides were placed in a mapping file called derby-overrides.xml, the following persistence unit configuration would apply the mapping overrides:

```
<persistence>
    <persistence-unit name="hr">
        ...
        <mapping-file>derby-overrides.xml</mapping-file>
        ...
    </persistence-unit>
</persistence>
```

Unlike the mapping file, which sparsely defines overrides, all the information that was present in the production persistence.xml file must be copied into the test-specific version. The only exception to this is the JDBC connection properties, which will now have to be customized for the embedded Derby instance.

Minimizing Database Connections

Integration tests execute slower than unit tests due to the nature of the database interaction, but what might not be obvious from the test case shown in Listing 15-9 is that two separate connections are made to the database, one each for the `testAuthenticateValidUser()` and `testAuthenticateInvalidUser()` tests. JUnit actually instantiates a new instance of the test case class each time it runs a test method, running `setUp()` and `tearDown()` each time as well. The reason for this behavior is to minimize the chance of data stored in fields from one test case interfering with the execution of another.

While this works well for unit tests, it may lead to unacceptable performance for integration tests. To work around this limitation, the `@BeforeClass` and `@AfterClass` features of JUnit 4 may be used to create fixtures that run only once for all of the tests in a class. Listing 15-10 demonstrates a test suite class that uses this feature at the level of the entire test suite.

Listing 15-10. One-Time Database Setup for Integration Tests

```
@RunWith(Suite.class)
@Suite.SuiteClasses({UserServiceTest3.class})
public class DatabaseTest {
    public static EntityManagerFactory emf;

    @BeforeClass
    public static void setUpBeforeClass() throws Exception {
        emf = Persistence.createEntityManagerFactory("hr");
    }

    @AfterClass
    public static void tearDownAfterClass() throws Exception {
        if (emf != null) { emf.close(); }
}}
```

Using this test suite as a starting point, all test cases added to the `@Suite.SuiteClasses` annotation can have access to the correctly populated `EntityManagerFactory` static field on the `DatabaseTest` class. The `setUp()` method of each test case now only needs to reference this class to obtain the factory instead of creating it each time. The following example demonstrates the change required for the `UnitServiceTest3` test case from Listing 15-9:

```
@Before
public void setUp() {
    emf = DatabaseTest.emf;
    em = emf.createEntityManager();
    createTestData();
}
```

This is a useful technique to minimize the cost of acquiring expensive resources, but care must be taken to ensure that side effects from one test do not accidentally interfere with the execution of other tests. Because all tests share the same entity manager factory, data may be cached or settings may be changed (supported by some entity manager factories) that have an unexpected impact later on. Just as it is necessary to keep the database tables clean between tests, any changes to the entity manager factory must be reverted when the test ends, regardless of whether the outcome is a success or a failure. It is usually a good idea to clear the cache, as we showed in the "Test Setup and Teardown" section.

Components and Persistence

More often than not, beans in an integration test are no different from beans in a unit test. You instantiate the bean, supply any necessary dependencies, and execute the test. Where we start to diverge is when we take into account issues such as transaction management and multiple bean instances collaborating together to implement a single use case. In the following sections, we will discuss techniques to handle more complex bean scenarios when testing outside of the container.

Transaction Management

Transactions lie at the heart of every enterprise application. We made this statement back in Chapter 3 and drove it home in Chapter 6, demonstrating all the different ways in which entity managers and persistence contexts can intersect with different transaction models. It might come as a surprise, then, to learn that when it comes to writing integration tests, we can often sidestep the stringent transactional requirements of the application to easily develop tests outside the container. The following sections will delve into when transactions are really required and how to translate the container-managed and bean-managed transaction models of the Java EE server into your test environment.

When to Use Transactions

Except for resource-local application-managed entity managers, which are less frequently used in the Java EE environment, transaction management is the purview of session beans and other components that use JPA. We will focus specifically on session beans, but the topics we cover apply equally to transactional persistence operations hosted by any other transaction-capable components.

The transaction demarcation for a session bean method needs to be considered carefully when writing tests. Despite the default assumption that transactions are used everywhere in the application server, only a select number of methods actually require transaction management for the purpose of testing. Because we are focused on testing persistence, the situation we are concerned with is when the entity manager is being used to persist, merge, or remove entity instances. We also need to determine whether these entities actually need to be persisted to the database.

In a test environment, we are using resource-local, application-managed entity managers. Recall from Chapter 6 that an application-managed entity manager can perform all its operations without an active transaction. In effect, invoking persist() queues up the entity to be persisted the next time a transaction starts and is committed. Furthermore, we know that once an entity is managed, it can typically be located using the find() operation without the need to go to the database. Given these facts, we generally need a transacted entity manager only if the business method creates or modifies entities, and executes a query that should include the results.

Although not required to satisfy business logic, a transaction may also be required if you want the results of the operation to be persisted so that they can be analyzed using something other than the active entity manager. For example, the results of the operation can be read from the database using JDBC and compared to a known value using a test tool.

The main thing we want to stress here before we look into how to implement transactions for session bean tests is that more often than not, you don't really need them at all. Look at the sequence of operations you are testing and consider whether the outcome will be affected one way or the other first if the data must be written to the database, and later if it truly must be committed as part of the test. Given the complexity that manual transaction management can sometimes require, use transactions only when they are necessary.

Container-Managed Transactions

One of the most important benefits of container-managed transactions is that they are configured for bean methods entirely using metadata. There is no programming interface invoked by the bean to control the transaction other than on contextual objects,[5] and even this occurs only in certain circumstances. Therefore, once we decide that a particular bean method requires a transaction to be active, we need only start a transaction at the start of the test and commit or roll back the results when the test ends.

---

[5]See the setRollbackOnly() method on the EJBContext interface

Listing 15-11 shows a bean method that will require an open transaction during a test. The `assignEmployeeToDepartment()` method assigns an employee to a given department and then returns the list of employees currently assigned to the department by executing a query. Because the data modification and query occur in the same transaction, our test case will also require a transaction.

Listing 15-11. Business Method Requiring a Transaction

```
@Stateless
public class DepartmentService {
    private static final String QUERY =
        "SELECT e " +
        "FROM Employee e " +
        "WHERE e.department = ?1 ORDER BY e.name";

    @PersistenceContext
    EntityManager em;

    public List<Employee> assignEmployeeToDepartment(int deptId, int empId) {
        Department dept = em.find(Department.class, deptId);
        Employee emp = em.find(Employee.class, empId);
        dept.getEmployees().add(emp);
        emp.setDepartment(dept);
        return em.createQuery(QUERY, Employee.class)
                .setParameter(1, dept)
                .getResultList();
    }

    // ...
}
```

Because we are using a resource-local entity manager, we will be simulating container-managed transactions with `EntityTransaction` transactions managed by the test case. Listing 15-12 shows the test case for the `assignEmployeeToDepartment()` method. We have followed the same template as in Listing 15-9, so the `setUp()` and `tearDown()` methods are not shown. Before the bean method is invoked, we create a new transaction. When the test is complete, we roll back the changes because it isn't necessary to persist them in the database.

Listing 15-12. Testing a Business Method that Requires a Transaction

```
public class DepartmentServiceTest {
    // ...

    private void createTestData() {
        Employee emp = new Employee(500, "Scott");
        em.persist(emp);
        emp = new Employee(600, "John");
        em.persist(emp);
        Department dept = new Department(700, "TEST");
        dept.getEmployees().add(emp);
        emp.setDepartment(dept);
        em.persist(dept);
    }
```

```
    @Test
    public void testAssignEmployeeToDepartment() throws Exception {
        DepartmentService bean = new DepartmentService();
        bean.em = em;
        em.getTransaction().begin();
        List result = bean.assignEmployeeToDepartment(700, 500);
        em.getTransaction().rollback();
        Assert.assertEquals(2, result.size());
        Assert.assertEquals("John", ((Employee)result.get(0)).getName());
        Assert.assertEquals("Scott", ((Employee)result.get(1)).getName());
    }

    // ...
}
```

Bean-Managed Transactions

For a bean that uses bean-managed transactions, the key issue we need to contend with is the UserTransaction interface. It may or may not be present in any given bean method and can be used for a number of purposes, from checking the transaction status to marking the current transaction for rollback, to committing and rolling back transactions. Fortunately, almost all the UserTransaction methods have a direct correlation to one of the EntityTransaction methods. Because our test strategy involves a single entity manager instance for a test, we need to adapt its EntityTransaction implementation to the UserTransaction interface.

Listing 15-13 shows an implementation of the UserTransaction interface that delegates to the EntityTransaction interface of an EntityManager instance. Exception handling has been added to convert the unchecked exceptions thrown by EntityTransaction operations into the checked exceptions that clients of the UserTransaction interface will be expecting.

Listing 15-13. Emulating UserTransaction Using EntityTransaction

```
public class EntityUserTransaction implements UserTransaction {
    private EntityManager em;

    public EntityUserTransaction(EntityManager em) {
        this.em = em;
    }

    public void begin() throws NotSupportedException {
        if (em.getTransaction().isActive()) {
            throw new NotSupportedException();
        }
        em.getTransaction().begin();
    }

    public void commit() throws RollbackException {
        try {
            em.getTransaction().commit();
        } catch (javax.persistence.RollbackException e) {
            throw new RollbackException(e.getMessage());
        }
    }
}
```

```
    public void rollback() throws SystemException {
        try {
            em.getTransaction().rollback();
        } catch (PersistenceException e) {
            throw new SystemException(e.getMessage());
        }
    }

    public void setRollbackOnly() {
        em.getTransaction().setRollbackOnly();
    }
    public int getStatus() {
        if (em.getTransaction().isActive()) {
            return Status.STATUS_ACTIVE;
        } else {
            return Status.STATUS_NO_TRANSACTION;
        }
    }

    public void setTransactionTimeout(int timeout) {
        throw new UnsupportedOperationException();
    }
}
```

Note that we have implemented setTransactionTimeout() to throw an exception, but this does not necessarily have to be the case. If the transaction timeout is set simply to prevent processes from taking too long to complete, it might be safe to ignore the setting in an integration test.

To demonstrate this wrapper, first consider Listing 15-14, which demonstrates a variation of the example from Listing 15-11 that uses bean-managed transactions instead of container-managed transactions.

Listing 15-14. Using Bean-Managed Transactions

```
@Stateless
@TransactionManagement(TransactionManagementType.BEAN)
public class DepartmentService {
    // ...
    @Resource UserTransaction tx;

    public List<Employee> assignEmployeeToDepartment(int deptId, int empId) {
        try {
            tx.begin();
            Department dept = em.find(Department.class, deptId);
            Employee emp = em.find(Employee.class, empId);
            dept.getEmployees().add(emp);
            emp.setDepartment(dept);
            tx.commit();
            return em.createQuery(QUERY, Employee.class)
                    .setParameter(1, dept)
                    .getResultList();
```

```
        } catch (Exception e) {
            // handle transaction exceptions
            // ...
        }
    }

    // ...
}
```

Using the UserTransaction wrapper is simply a matter of injecting it into a session bean that has declared a dependency on UserTransaction. Because the wrapper holds onto an entity manager instance, it can begin and end EntityTransaction transactions as required from within the application code being tested. Listing 15-15 shows the revised test case from Listing 15-12 using this wrapper to emulate bean-managed transactions.

Listing 15-15. Executing a Test with Emulated Bean-Managed Transactions

```
public class DepartmentServiceTest {
    // ...

    @Test
    public void testAssignEmployeeToDepartment() throws Exception {
        DepartmentService bean = new DepartmentService();
        bean.em = em;
        bean.tx = new EntityUserTransaction(em);
        List result = bean.assignEmployeeToDepartment(700, 500);
        Assert.assertEquals(2, result.size());
        Assert.assertEquals("John", ((Employee)result.get(0)).getName());
        Assert.assertEquals("Scott", ((Employee)result.get(1)).getName());
    }

    // ...
}
```

Note that although the UserTransaction interface is used, that doesn't mean it's actually necessary for any particular test. If the transaction state doesn't affect the outcome of the test, consider using an implementation of the UserTransaction interface that doesn't do anything. For example, the implementation of UserTransaction shown in Listing 15-16 is fine for any case where transaction demarcation is declared but unnecessary.

Listing 15-16. A Stubbed UserTransaction

```
public class NullUserTransaction implements UserTransaction {
    public void begin() {}
    public void commit() {}
    public void rollback() {}
    public void setRollbackOnly() {}
    public int getStatus() {
        return Status.STATUS_NO_TRANSACTION;
    }
    public void setTransactionTimeout(int timeout) {}
}
```

The test case shown in Listing 15-12 could also have tested the bean from Listing 15-14 if the empty
`UserTransaction` wrapper from Listing 15-16 was also injected into the bean instance. This would disable the
bean-managed transactions of the actual business method, allowing the transactions of the test case to be used instead.

Container-Managed Entity Managers

The default entity manager type for most beans is container-managed and transaction-scoped, but in the case of
stateful session beans they can also be extended. In either case, the goal of testing outside the container is to map the
application-managed entity manager used by the test to one of these container-managed entity manager types.

The good news for testing code that uses the extended entity manager is that the application-managed entity
manager offers almost exactly the same feature set. It can usually be injected into a stateful session bean instance in
place of an extended entity manager, and the business logic should function without change in most cases.

Likewise, most of the time the transaction-scoped entity manager works just fine when an application-managed
entity manager is used in its place. The main issue we need to deal with in the case of transaction-scoped entity
managers is detachment. When a transaction ends, any managed entities become detached. In terms of a test, that
just means that we need to ensure that `clear()` is invoked on the transaction boundary for our test entity manager.

We may also need to deal with the issue of propagation. In some respects, propagation is easy in a test
environment. If you inject the same application-managed entity manager instance into two bean instances, the
beans share the same persistence context as if the entity manager were propagated with the transaction. In fact, it is
far more likely that you will need to inject multiple entity managers to simulate the intentional lack of propagation
(such as a bean that invokes a `REQUIRES_NEW` method on another bean) than that you will have to do anything special
for propagation.

Let's look at a concrete example of transaction propagation using the examples we first introduced in Chapter 6.
Listing 15-17 shows the implementation of the `AuditService` bean that performs audit logging. We have used setter
injection in this example to contrast it against the version from Chapter 6.

Listing 15-17. AuditService Session Bean with Setter Injection

```
@Stateless
public class AuditService {
    private EntityManager em;

    @PersistenceContext(unitName="hr")
    public void setEntityManager(EntityManager em) {
        this.em = em;
    }

    public void logTransaction(int empNo, String action) {
        // verify employee number is valid
        if (em.find(Employee.class, empNo) == null) {
            throw new IllegalArgumentException("Unknown employee id");
        }
        LogRecord lr = new LogRecord(empNo, action);
        em.persist(lr);
    }
}
```

Likewise, Listing 15-18 shows a fragment from the `EmployeeService` session bean that uses the `AuditService`
session bean to record when a new `Employee` instance has been persisted. Because both the `createEmployee()`
and `logTransaction()` methods are invoked in the same transaction without a commit in between, the persistence
context must be propagated from one to the other. Again we have used setter injection instead of field injection to
make the bean easier to test.

Listing 15-18. EmployeeService Session Bean with Setter Injection

```
@Stateless
public class EmployeeService {
    EntityManager em;
    AuditService audit;

    @PersistenceContext
    public void setEntityManager(EntityManager em) {
        this.em = em;
    }

    @EJB
    public void setAuditService(AuditService audit) {
        this.audit = audit;
    }

    public void createEmployee(Employee emp) {
        em.persist(emp);
        audit.logTransaction(emp.getId(), "created employee");
    }

    // ...
}
```

Using the previous two session beans as an example, Listing 15-19 demonstrates how to emulate propagation between two transaction-scoped, container-managed entity managers. The first step to make this testable is to instantiate each session bean. The AuditService bean is then injected into the EmployeeService bean, and the test entity manager instance is injected into both session beans. The injection of the same EntityManager instance effectively propagates any changes from the EmployeeService bean to the AuditService bean. Note that we have also used the entity manager in the test to locate and verify the results of the business method.

Listing 15-19. Simulating Container-Managed Transaction Propagation

```
public class TestEmployeeService {
    // ...

    @Test
    public void testCreateEmployee() throws Exception {
        EmployeeService empService = new EmployeeService();
        AuditService auditService = new AuditService();
        empService.setEntityManager(em);
        empService.setAuditService(auditService);
        auditService.setEntityManager(em);
        Employee emp = new Employee();
        emp.setId(99);
        emp.setName("Wayne");
        empService.createEmployee(emp);
        emp = em.find(Employee.class, 99);
```

```
        Assert.assertNotNull(emp);
        Assert.assertEquals(99, emp.getId());
        Assert.assertEquals("Wayne", emp.getName());
    }

    // ...
}
```

Other Services

There is more to most beans than just dependency injection and transaction management. For example, as we saw in Chapter 3, beans can also take advantage of lifecycle methods. Other services that are beyond the scope of this book include security management and interceptors.

The general rule is that in a test environment, you need to manually perform the work that would have otherwise been done automatically by the container. In the case of lifecycle methods, for example, you will have to explicitly invoke these methods if they are required for a particular test. Given this requirement, it is a good idea to use package or protected scope methods so that they can be manually invoked by test cases.

That being said, be aggressive in determining the true number of things that have to occur in order for a test to succeed. Just because security roles have been declared for a session bean method doesn't mean that it actually has any effect on the test outcome. If it doesn't have to be invoked prior to the test, don't waste time setting up the test environment to make it happen.

Using an Embedded EJB Container for Integration Testing

When multiple session beans collaborate to implement a particular application use case, a lot of scaffolding code may be required to get things up and running. If multiple test cases share similar graphs of session beans, some or all of this code may have to be duplicated across multiple test cases. Ideally, we want a framework to assist with issues such as dependency injection in our test environment.

Fortunately, EJB supports just such a container. An embedded EJB container supports EJB Lite, a subset of the overall EJB feature set. EJB Lite includes support for local session beans, interceptors, container-managed transactions (assuming the availability of a stand-alone JTA transaction manager implementation) and security, and JPA, but does not include support for remote session beans, message-driven beans, web service endpoints, timers, or asynchronous session beans. It offers more than enough to handle the different dependency scenarios we have described so far.

To demonstrate how to use an embedded EJB container for integration testing with session beans and the entity manager, we will revisit the propagation test case from the preceding "Container-Managed Entity Managers" section and convert it to use an embedded container.

■ **Tip** Embedded EJB containers were introduced in EJB 3.1.

Unlike the other forms of integration techniques we have looked at so far, an embedded EJB container requires no mocking of standard interfaces or subclassing of beans to override behavior specific to the server. As long as an application fits within the subset of the EJB specification supported by embedded containers, it can be used as-is.

Bootstrapping the embedded container is straightforward. You compile and package the classes as normal into an EJB jar file and add that jar file to the test classpath in order for the embedded container bootstrap mechanism to locate it. The static `createEJBContainer()` method of the `javax.ejb.embeddable.EJBContainer` class can then be used to create an EJB container and load the module from the classpath. Listing 15-20 demonstrates the bootstrapping process. Additional options for the container may be specified by passing in a `Map` of properties, but for basic tests with a single module, no special configuration is required.

Listing 15-20. Bootstrapping an Embedded EJB Container Within a Test Case

```
public class TestEmployeeService {
    private EJBContainer container;

    @Before
    public void setUp() {
        container = EJBContainer.createEJBContainer();
    }

    @After
    public void tearDown() {
        container.close();
    }

    // ...
}
```

Once the container has initialized, we need to get access to session beans in order to test them. The embedded container exposes its internal JNDI directory of session beans via the getContext() method of the EJBContainer class. The test code must then make a global JNDI lookup in order to access a particular session bean. A global lookup does not require references or an environment naming context. Instead, the module name (derived from the jar name) and session bean names are composed to form a unique name under the JNDI root "global". Listing 15-21 demonstrates this technique assuming the beans have been packaged in an EJB jar file called hr.jar.

Listing 15-21. Acquiring a Session Bean Reference from an Embedded EJB Container

```
public class TestEmployeeService extends TestCase {
    private EJBContainer container;

    // ...

    private EmployeeService getServiceBean() throws Exception {
        return (EmployeeService) container.getContext().lookup("java:global/hr/EmployeeService");
    }

    private EntityManager getEntityManager() throws Exception {
        return (EntityManager) container.getContext().lookup("java:global/hr/HRService");
    }

    // ...
}
```

With access to a live session bean, we can now write test methods as if we were running code directly within the application server. Listing 15-22 completes this example with a new version of testCreateEmployee() that uses the bean reference from the embedded container.

Listing 15-22. Testing a Session Bean Acquired from an Embedded EJB Container

```java
public class TestEmployeeService {
    // ...

    @Test
    public void testCreateEmployee() throws Exception {
        EmployeeService bean = getServiceBean();
        Employee emp = new Employee();
        emp.setId(99);
        emp.setName("Wayne");
        bean.createEmployee(emp);
        EntityManager em = getEntityManager();
        emp = em.find(Employee.class, 99);
        Assert.assertNotNull(emp);
        Assert.assertEquals(99, emp.getId());
        Assert.assertEquals("Wayne", emp.getName());
    }

    // ...
}
```

As discussed earlier in the "Switching Configurations for Testing" section, a custom persistence.xml file appropriate to the test environment may be required and should be packaged in the EJB jar file used on the system classpath. Likewise, sharing the EJB container across test executions will likely improve overall test suite performance, but again care must be taken not to accidentally influence the outcome of other tests with state maintained by the EJB container.

For two session beans, this approach is arguably overkill compared with the same test case shown in Listing 15-19. But it should be easy to see even from this small example how complex bean relationships can be realized using an embedded EJB container.

Test Frameworks

As long as technologies continue to get created and evolve, test frameworks will be right behind, trying to make the testing of code that uses those technologies more manageable. Since the release of JPA a few frameworks have surfaced with varying levels of JPA support to enable integration testing. While the details of using these frameworks is beyond the scope of this book, we thought it might be beneficial to at least mention and provide a pointer to them. You can then go off and do some exploring on your own to see if any of them will meet your needs. If you hear of others that have specific support for JPA but that are not included in this section please let us know, and we can include them in subsequent editions of the book.

JPA-Unit

The JPA-Unit framework (https://code.google.com/p/jpa-unit) is a simple little test framework that primarily supports testing non-container JPA applications. It doesn't support JTA transactions so it's somewhat limited. It is integrated with JUnit, and tests are added by subclassing a JPA-Unit framework test case class. It provides injection of an entity manager and support for automatic pre-loading of entity data based upon a custom-formatted XML data file. This may be sufficient for an application with very simple requirements, but is not likely to offer enough for the majority of enterprise applications. It also doesn't seem to be very regularly maintained and hasn't had any updates or action on its web site for over 1.5 years as of this writing.

Spring TestContext

The TestContext framework in Spring is not a uniquely JPA framework, but it does include the Spring support for injection of JPA objects like the entity manager and entity manager factory (using the standard `@PersistenceContext` and `@PersistenceUnit` annotations). It can integrate with JUnit, TestNG, EasyMock, and other unit testing frameworks when it comes time for test definition and execution. Because so much of the framework is based on the testing of Spring components, though, adopting its test model won't make as much sense if your application is not Spring-based. For applications that do use Spring Data JPA this framework might be worth investigating.

Arquillian

For testing Java EE applications that make use of CDI beans or EJBs to manipulate JPA entities the Arquillian framework (`http://arquillian.org`) could be your best bet for an integration testing framework. It provides support for running tests in a non-server environment (making use of standalone CDI and EJB containers) as well as running tests within the container. It integrates with JUnit and TestNG, and fits in reasonably well with those testing models. Because it packages up the test classes and necessary framework infrastructure classes into an archive and even deploys it into the server, there is an additional method that must be supplied to define what bits and pieces need to be included in that application archive. The rest is fairly easy to do once the environment has been correctly configured.

Arquillian has a couple of dependencies that should be known beforehand, though. The first is on ShrinkWrap, a JBoss tool that packages artifacts up into an archive. The second is on the existence of a container adapter for the container being deployed to. Not all containers are supported, so if you are deploying to an unsupported target server you could be out of luck. Check the web site to see if your container is supported.

Best Practices

A full discussion of developer testing strategies is beyond the scope of this chapter, but to make testing of application code that uses entities easier, consider adopting the following best practices:

- Avoid using the entity manager from within entity classes. This creates a tight coupling between the domain object and the persistence API, making testing difficult. Queries that are related to an entity, but not part of its object-relational mapping, are better executed within a session façade or data access object.

- Prefer dependency injection to JNDI lookups in referencing beans. Dependency injection is a key technology for simplifying tests. Instead of mocking the JNDI interfaces to provide runtime support for unit testing, the required values can be directly assigned to the object using a setter method or field access. Note that accessing private fields from a test case is bad form. Either use package private fields as the target for injected objects or provide a setter method.

- Isolate persistence operations. Keeping `EntityManager` and `Query` operations separate in their own methods makes replacing them easier during unit testing.

- Refactor when necessary. Don't be afraid to refactor application code to make it more test-friendly so long as the refactoring benefits the application as a whole. Method extraction, parameter introduction, and other refactoring techniques can help break down complex application logic into testable chunks, improving the overall readability and maintainability of the application in the process.

- Use an existing framework when possible. If a framework already does most of what you need to do, clearly you can save time and resources by making use of it and possibly just adding the extra bits that you need. It may even be appropriate to propose those changes back to the framework committers for inclusion in a subsequent framework release.

These approaches can help support your testing style, regardless of the approach you choose to use.

Summary

In this chapter, we started with an exploration of testing enterprise applications and the challenges that have traditionally faced developers. We also looked at the different types of testing performed by developers, quality engineers, and customers; and we refined our focus to look specifically at developer tests for JPA applications.

In the section on unit testing, we looked at how to test entity classes and then pulled back to look at how to test beans in combination with entities in a unit test environment. We introduced the concept of mock objects and explored how to test code that depends on the entity manager without actually using a real entity manager.

In our discussion of integration testing, we discussed how to get the entity manager up and running in JUnit tests in the Java SE environment and the situations where it makes sense to use this technique. We covered a number of issues related to the entity manager, including how to safely seed a database for testing, how to use multiple mapping files for different database configurations, and how to minimize the number of database connections required for a test suite. We also looked at how to make use of an embedded EJB container for integration testing.

We looked at how to use session beans in integration tests and how to deal with dependency-injection and transaction-management issues. For transaction management, we looked at how to emulate container-managed and bean-managed transactions, as well as how to simulate persistence context propagation in a test environment. We concluded with a short survey of JPA test frameworks and a summary of some best practices to consider when building Java EE applications using JPA.

Index

■ J, K

■ L